# TABLE OF CONTENTS

KU-310-161

*Radi*

# Java™ Programming
## Advanced Topics

### Joe Wigglesworth
IBM Toronto Lab
### Paula Lumby
IBM Toronto Lab

COURSE TECHNOLOGY

Thomson Learning™

ONE MAIN STREET, CAMBRIDGE, MA 02142

Australia • Canada • Denmark • Japan • Mexico • New Zealand • Philippines
Puerto Rico • Singapore • South Africa • Spain • United Kingdom • United States

*Java Programming: Advanced Topics* is published by Course Technology.

| | |
|---|---|
| *Associate Publisher* | Kristen Duerr |
| *Product Manager* | Jennifer Muroff |
| *Associate Product Manager* | Tricia Coia |
| *Editorial Assistant* | Jennifer Adams |
| *Production Editor* | Megan Cap-Renzi |
| *Developmental Editor* | Jill Batistick |
| *Marketing Manager* | Susan Ogar |
| *Text Designer* | Kim Munsell |
| *Cover Designer* | Efrat Reis |

© 2000 Course Technology, a division of Thomson Learning.
Thomson Learning is a trademark used herein under license.

ALL RIGHTS RESERVED. No part of this work may be reproduced, transcribed, or used in any form or by any means—graphic, electronic, or mechanical, including photocopying, recording, taping, Web distribution, or information storage and retrieval systems—without prior written permission of the publisher.

Sun is a registered trademark of Sun Microsystems. Java and JavaBeans are trademarks of Sun Microsystems. JBuilder is a registered trademark of the Inprise Corporation.

## Disclaimer

Course Technology reserves the right to revise this publication and make changes from time to time in its content without notice.

The Web addresses in this book are subject to change from time to time as necessary without notice.

For more information, contact Course Technology, One Main Street, Cambridge, MA 02142; or you can find us on the World Wide Web at *www.course.com*.

For permission to use material from this text or product, contact us by
- Web: www.thomsonrights.com
- Phone: 1-800-730-2214
- Fax: 1-800-730-2215

IBM, Visual Age, and DB2 are registered trademarks of IBM Corporation.

ISBN 0-7600-1098-6

Printed in Canada

1 2 3 4 5 6 7 8 9 10 WC 04 03 02 01 00

# PREFACE

Welcome to *Java Programming: Advanced Topics*! This book was written for programmers who understand the basics of the Java programming language and now want to explore advanced Java programming topics so that they may unlock the full potential of the Java programming language. The Java programming language has made such a dramatic entrance into the world of software development that qualified Java programmers who understand the language's advanced topics are sure to be in great demand. This book will allow you to quickly develop advanced Java skills to the level of Certified Java Programmer, as defined by the Sun Certified Java Programmer Examination.

The early chapters of this book act as a refresher and describe the basics of the Java language in detail. The middle chapters move through the essential and powerful programming techniques supported by the Java language, including:

- extending existing classes
- implementing interfaces
- exception handling
- multithreading
- cloning objects
- run-time type information
- inner classes

Much of the latter half of this book gives overviews of the packages provided by the Java platform. These packages are analogous to C++ class libraries, but have the great advantage of being available and standard on all implementations of the Java platform. The classes in these packages support:

- stream I/O and random-access file I/O
- collection classes
- programming graphical user interfaces for applications using the AWT and Swing APIs
- creating applets
- creating JavaBean components
- networking, including RMI
- servlets and Java Server Pages (JSPs)
- Java database connectivity

This book includes two special sections that introduce Integrated Development Environments (IDEs). In Chapter 1, step-by-step instructions walk the reader through an introduction to IBM VisualAge for

Java and in Chapter 12 the reader learns to design a class visually with IBM VisualAge for Java. Each of these IDE sections can be skipped without missing any of the important Java programming concepts presented in the chapter.

# FEATURES

*Java Programming: Advanced Topics* is an exceptional book because it also includes the following features:

- **Code examples** In addition to code examples included with the syntax, source code for working programs is included to provide additional examples of a concept or to illustrate common and preferred usage. All the code examples that appear are provided on the CD-ROM in the examples.jar file so that you do not need to type any of the examples that appear in the book.

- **Moving from C++ Tips** Many programmers who are learning the Java programming language are already experts in the C++ programming language. Appendix C contains directions on how to access an extensive list of tips, organized by subject, that highlight differences between the C++ and Java programming languages, and subtleties that might create problems if you assume that the two languages work exactly alike.

- **Version Watch** This book was developed using the Java 2 platform. All example code was tested and all programming exercises can be completed with version 1.2 of the Java SDK, Standard Edition. The Java language is still evolving and has undergone changes since it was first announced. Version Watches provide information on important changes to the Java platform that have been made since the initial release of the version 1.0 JDK.

  Some features have been deprecated, that is, they are no longer recommended for use in the Java 2 platform, because the same functionality is provided by new and improved features. Generally, the Java 2 platform continues to accept and run programs that contain deprecated features. However, you should not use them when you create new code. If you look at programs written for early versions of Java and see constructs that do not agree with the current description of the language or standard classes, you may find that the old code is using a deprecated feature.

- **Mini Quiz** Mini quizzes appear throughout each chapter as a way for readers to check that they understand the concepts presented up to that point. Appendix E contains instructions on how to access the answers to the mini quizzes.

- **Code** All code appears as `int=3`.

- **Keywords** Keywords appear as **int**.

- **Program file names** Program file names appear as **examples.jar**.

- **New terms** New terms appear like **this**.

# CT TEACHING TOOLS

All the teaching tools for this text are found in the Instructor's Resource Kit, which is available from the Course Technology Web site (www.course.com) and on CD-ROM.

- **Instructor's Manual**  The Instructor's Manual has been quality assurance tested. It is available on CD-ROM and through the Course Technology Faculty Online Companion on the World Wide Web. The Instructor's Manual contains the following items:

  - Additional coverage of Visual Basic concepts such as Sorting and Binary Search.

  - Answers to all the questions and solutions to all the exercises.

  - Chapter Notes, which contain background information from the author about the Chapter Case and the instructional progression of the chapter.

  - Technical Notes, which include troubleshooting tips as well as information on how to customize the readers' screens to closely emulate the screen shots in the book.

- **Course Test Manager Version 1.2 Engine and Test Bank**  Course Test Manager (CTM) is a cutting-edge Windows-based testing software program, developed exclusively for Course Technology, that helps instructors design and administer examinations and practice tests. This full-featured program allows instructors to randomly generate practice tests that provide immediate on-screen feedback and detailed study guides for incorrectly answered questions. Instructors can also use CTM to create printed and online tests over the network. Tests on any or all chapters of this textbook can be created, previewed, and administered entirely over a local area network. CTM can grade the tests automatically at the computer and can generate statistical information on individual as well as group performance. A CTM test bank has been written to accompany this text and is included on the CD-ROM. The test bank includes multiple-choice, true/false, short answer, and essay questions.

- **Solution Files**  Solution files contain possible solutions to all the problems students are asked to create or modify in the chapters and cases. (Due to the nature of software development, student solutions might differ from these solutions and still be correct.)

- **Data Files**  Data files, containing all data that readers will use for the chapters and exercises in this textbook, are provided through Course Technology's Online Companion on the Instructor's Resource Kit CD-ROM and on the Student Resource Kit CD-ROM. A Help file includes technical tips for lab management. See the "Read This Before You Begin" page preceding Chapter 1 for more information on data files.

- **CD-ROM**  The *Java Programming: Advanced Topics* CD-ROM contains IBM VisualAge for Java Professional Edition 2.0, Borland JBuilder 3.0 University Edition, Borland JBuilder 3.0 Enterprise Edition 60 Day Trial Version, IBM DB2 UDB Personal Edition V5.2, and the source and compiled code for all the sample programs in this book. The code files are combined in a Java archive file, **examples.jar**. For further instructions on copying these files and applications to your computer, refer to the ReadMe file on the CD-ROM. You can view the ReadMe file using an html editor or a web browser. For more information on the CD-ROM, refer to the "Read This Before You Begin" page preceding Chapter 1.

# ACKNOWLEDGMENTS

Joe Wigglesworth thanks his parents for their support through the years and thanks his wonderful wife, Maria, and their bright-eyed baby boy, Darius, for their patience and understanding through the long process of creating and editing the manuscript. Without support from Maria and smiles from Darius, this book would not have been possible.

Paula Lumby expresses her gratitude to her children Joy, Alison, and Thomas, for surviving with a distracted and over-busy mother. These three wonderful young people made the book possible by supporting their mother and each other while this book was being written.

We extend a special thank you to Sheila Richardson of the IBM Toronto Lab, who provided the original vision for this book and whose support and know-how facilitated our completion of both this book and its predecessor: *Java Programming: Making the Move from C++.*

# READ THIS BEFORE YOU BEGIN

## To the Reader

### CD-ROM

The *Java Programming: Advanced Topics* CD-ROM contains:
- ➤ IBM VisualAge for Java Professional Edition 2.0
- ➤ DB2 UDB Personal Edition V5.2
- ➤ Borland JBuilder University Edition 3.0
- ➤ Borland JBuilder Enterprise Edition 3.0 60 Day Trial Version
- ➤ Source and compiled code for all the sample programs and programming questions in this book
- ➤ Instructions for installing the Beans Development Kit and JavaServer Web Development Kit from Sun Microsystems

The sample source files are combined in a Java archive file, **examples.jar**. The question source files are combined in a Java archive file, **question.jar**. For further instructions on copying these files to your computer, refer to the **ReadMe.html** file on the CD-ROM. You can view the **ReadMe.html** file using a web browser or HTML editor.

### Using Your Own Computer

If you are going to work through this book using your own computer, you need:
- ➤ **Computer System**  Microsoft Windows 95, Microsoft Windows 98, or Microsoft Windows NT 4.0 (or later), and the Java Software Development Kit (SDK), Standard Edition V1.2 must be installed on your computer. Installing the Borland JBuilder University Edition 3.0 will also install the Java SDK. Please refer to the **ReadMe.html** file for details.
- ➤ **Sample Programs**  The source and compiled code for all the sample programs in this book are provided on the CD-ROM supplied with this book.

  The programs are combined in the Java archive file, **examples.jar**. The file contains several Java packages, in a folder structure that follows Java naming conventions. Classes are distributed into the packages. The packages have the following names, each beginning with "examples.":

  ```
  applet   beans      collections  i18n         io        rtti      windows
  awt      classes    errors       inheritance  network   servlets
  basic    cloning    exceptions   inner        observe   threads
  ```

  The package **examples.errors** contains classes that appear in the book with deliberate errors in them, and therefore cannot be run. The other packages roughly correspond to the major topics covered in this book.

  The file **question.jar** contains the code that appears in end-of-chapter exercises. The code is organized into Java packages, with names beginning with "questions.c" followed by the chapter number (**questions.c1**, **questions.c2**, **questions.c3**, and so on.)

  You should copy the files **examples.jar** and **questions.jar** from the CD-ROM onto your hard disk. For your convenience, you can create one subfolder to hold these files. For further instructions on copying these files to your computer, refer to the **ReadMe.html** file on the CD-ROM.

### IBM VisualAge for Java Professional Edition V2.0

IBM VisualAge for Java is a true rapid application development (RAD) tool. A unique and popular feature of VisualAge for Java is the visual Composition Editor. With the Composition Editor, you can rapidly create GUIs for applets and applications, and integrate the GUI components of your program with other Java code. The product provides a fully integrated IDE, a true incremental build, and a good debugger. It generates 100% Pure Java code. VisualAge for Java can also create and consume JavaBean components. The Full Professional Version of VisualAge for Java for Windows is included in the VisualAge for Java folder on the CD-ROM. Please refer to the **ReadMe.html** file on the CD-ROM for installation instructions.

### IBM DB2 UDB Personal Edition V5.2

The DB2 Universal Database family of relational database products offers open, industrial-strength database management for decision support, transaction processing, and an extensive range of business applications. The DB2 family spans AS/400 systems, RISC System/6000 hardware, IBM mainframes, non-IBM machines from Hewlett-Packard and Sun Microsystems, and operating systems such as OS/2, Windows (95 & NT), AIX, HP-UX, SINIX, SCO OpenServer, and Solaris Operating Environment. Please refer to the **ReadMe.html** file on the CD-ROM for installation instructions.

### Borland JBuilder University Edition 3.0

JBuilder University Edition will help your students learn Java fast with a professional IDE that includes a fully integrated application browser, project manager, code editor, HTML viewer, graphical debugger and compiler. Please refer to the **ReadMe.html** file on the CD-ROM for installation instructions.

### Borland JBuilder Enterprise Edition 3.0 60 Day Trial Version

The Enterprise Edition of JBuilder 3 includes third-generation DataExpress components for simplified data access and management as well as an integrated suite of SQL tools. Please refer to the **ReadMe.html** file on the CD-ROM for installation instructions.

### Visit Our World Wide Web Site

Additional materials designed especially for users of *Java Programming: Advanced Topics* and other Course Technology products are available on the World Wide Web. Go to **http://www.course.com**.

## To the Instructor

The Java source and compiled code for all the example programs in this book are provided on the book's companion CD-ROM. You can also download these files over the Internet. See the inside front cover of this book for more details.

The example source files and programming question source files are in the Java archive files **examples.jar** and **question.jar**, respectively. Please refer to the "Using Your Own Computer" section for information on working with these files.

The solution files are combined in the file **answers.jar**. The file contains packages with names beginning with "answers.c" followed by the chapter number (answers.c1, answers.c2, answers.c3 and so on).

### Course Technology Data Files

You are granted a license to copy the data files to any computer or computer network used by readers who have purchased this book.

## CHAPTER 1

# INTRODUCTION TO JAVA PROGRAMMING

---

**In this chapter you will:**

➤ Gain some insight into nature and goals of the Java language.

➤ Review the historical context in which Java technology was developed.

➤ Learn how to use the basic tools the Java 2 Software Development Kit (SDK) provides.

➤ Explore IBM's VisualAge for Java integrated development environment.

➤ Enter, compile, and run your first program.

➤ Add comments of all kinds, including **doc comments**, to your code.

➤ Use the **javadoc** tool together with **doc comments** to document your classes.

➤ Use the **jar** tool to package Java applications, applets, components, or servlets for distribution.

---

## INTRODUCTION

Welcome to Java programming. This book discusses the Java programming language and how to create Java programs and components for use in a wide variety of environments. Whether you are a student using this book as the text for a programming course or a professional programmer teaching yourself the Java programming language to expand and update your skill set, this book is for you.

If you are an experienced programmer, you may be eager to start experimenting with Java technology. Therefore, a large part of this first chapter takes you through the development process for a small, but complete, Java program. The scenarios for entering, compiling, and running the sample program serve as an introduction to Java development environments and verification that you are set up to start programming.

The rest of the chapter explains the main elements of the Java platform. A brief history of Java technology shows how the Internet, object-oriented programming, and experiments in creating a portable operating system formed a matrix for this new technology as well as why Java technology is revolutionizing the computer industry.

## OVERVIEW OF THE JAVA PLATFORM

The appeal of the Java programming language is that it is more than just a programming language; it is also a platform. Most programming languages have no features for multithreading, GUI-building, or networking. They force you to use a hardware or operating system-dependent API that binds programs to a specific hardware or operating system. The Java platform is the first technology to fully integrate a programming language and API for threads, sockets, GUI components, and much more—in a way that lets you build programs that can run on a wide range of hardware architectures and host native operating systems.

When you install Java technology, you load the Java platform on your system. The Java platform includes the **Java Virtual Machine (JVM)** and a number of packages that support the compiler, interpreter, and run-time environment for the Java programming language. These **packages** are analogous to standard libraries of predefined functions or classes in other programming languages. Each package contains reusable classes that you can access in your programs. The classes that make up the API provided by the Java platform are called the **core classes**. All core classes are grouped into packages.

You can choose from several Java application-development tools. You can use the Java 2 SDK, which is available free for Windows and Solaris environments from Sun Microsystems. Other vendors offer ports of the Java 2 SDK on other platforms. The CD-ROM that accompanies this book contains the Java 2 SDK for Windows platforms.

Several software vendors market integrated development environments for Java programmers. Each proprietary tool provides a graphical user interface (GUI) that lets you enter, compile, debug, and run your programs. Many integrated development environments provide additional features, such as code generators or source-code version control. A popular product with professional programmers is **VisualAge for Java** from IBM. The CD-ROM that accompanies this book contains VisualAge for Java version 2.

Later in this chapter, you will enter and run a program using Java 2 SDK and VisualAge for Java. To install all the software, you need to follow the instructions and scenarios in this book, follow the instructions in the ReadMe html file on the accompanying CD-ROM, or refer to the "Read This before You Begin" section at the beginning of this book.

# WHERE IS THE JAVA PLATFORM USED?

The Java platform has made a huge impact on the computer industry in recent years. More and more companies are adopting the Java platform, and Java programmers are writing programs that are mission-critical or that profoundly change the ways in which the companies work. Java is helping companies web-enable their operations and enter the world of electronic commerce. The fact that microchip manufacturers can embed the Java platform in their chips and Java programmers can develop code that runs almost anywhere draws industry professionals to Java technology.

Consider the following ways in which you can use Java:

➤ To create standalone programs that can run on computers of any size and vary enormously in size and complexity. Anything from a personal assistant embedded in a piece of jewelry to an order-entry system running on a supercomputer can be written in Java.

➤ To write small programs that run in Web pages. Some programs are downloaded from a network along with HTML documents and run by a Web browser.

➤ To produce Java classes that can act as extensions to your Web server. Some programs prepare dynamic content in Web pages on the Web server before the pages are sent to the browser.

➤ To distribute programs over a network. Java classes on one machine can pass data to and from classes on other machines and call methods of classes that reside on other machines.

➤ To use Java-based technology to meet the demands of enterprise-wide distributed environments. Sun Microsystems, IBM, and other companies at the forefront of Java development participate in committees that establish standards that define how Java classes work with transaction processors, objects written in other languages, and many forms of heterogeneous environments. These standards continue to evolve.

Different environments require different kinds of Java programs. This book teaches you how to create three types of programs:

➤ **Applications** can run standalone on a computer of any size, and can be anything from large suites of software to simple utilities. They can run from the command line or have a GUI. Whether applications include interfaces to connect to networks, databases, or other applications, depends on the set of APIs that the application uses. You can use all the API and language features covered in this book, with the exception of the servlet API in Chapter 18, in Java applications.

Java applications run only in the JVM. They are compiled not for a particular processor instruction set or operating system, but for the Java platform itself. Recently, IBM and some other leading companies have produced compilers that compile Java source into native executable modules and dynamically loadable or shared libraries for their proprietary operating systems.

➤ **Applets** are programs that can be launched from HTML documents. **HTML** stands for HyperText Markup Language and is the markup (tagging language) used by Web pages. HTML has tags specifically designed for applets. Java-enabled Web browsers have a JVM to run applets when the browser displays the HTML document. Applets tend to be small programs and are often used to add visual or multimedia effects to Web pages. Chapter 14 of this book is devoted to applets.

➤ **Servlets**, like applets, are programs that generate content for Web pages. Unlike applets, servlets run on Java-enabled Web servers and generate HTML documents that are sent to the client browser for display. For example, you can use servlets to process an HTML form submitted by a Web client and then to generate a response page.

Use applets when the Web page is the same for all clients that request it, except that it contains some display that requires local processing, such as an animation. Use servlets when the HTML document provides a view of information that is specific to the client request and that is based on data that is available to the server. Servlets are usually small, but often call larger programs, such as database managers, to extract information to include in the Web page. A variation on servlets is **Java Server Pages ( JSPs)**. JSPs are written in HTML but contain embedded Java code that is compiled and run on the server. Chapter 18 discusses servlets and JSPs.

The Java platform supports software components. Components are reusable classes for assembling large programs by using classes as software building blocks. Although the concept is not new and is addressed by other technologies, the Java technology has made true code reusability attainable by introducing the following two standards:

➤ **JavaBeans** are Java classes or groups of Java classes that conform to a strict set of standards. You build beans to make your classes reusable, configurable software components. By using development tools, programmers can assemble programs by adding beans to a work surface and connecting them in a manner analogous to wiring a circuit board using standard microprocessor chips. Many of the core classes, especially those that are types of visual objects for GUIs, are beans. Chapter 15 describes the JavaBeans standard and how to create and use beans.

➤ **Enterprise Java Beans (EJBs)** are a promising, emerging technology. The EJB standard defines a software architecture for server-side components in distributed enterprise environments. The goal is to let programmers concentrate on the business logic that their Java classes perform. An **Enterprise Java Server (EJS)** looks after services such as transaction processing, security, and naming services to locate and identify EJBs. Generally, you need an EJB development tool to build and deploy EJBs. Because EJBs are an advanced topic, they are not covered in this book.

Programmers have used Java for applications and applets as long as the Java platform has been available. The Java platform provides everything you need to create applications and applets.

The development kits for servlets and JSPs are not part of the Java 2 Standard Edition. They are downloadable for free from Sun Microsystems and work with version 1.1.6 or higher of the Java 1.1 platform or the Java 2 SDK.

The Java platform has supported JavaBeans since version 1.1. The introduction of the JavaBeans standard effected many of the major changes made between the original 1.0 version and the 1.1 version of the standard development kits.

The EJB development tools, like the servlet kits, are not included in the Java 2 Standard Edition. The Java 2 Enterprise Edition supports EJBs.

## WHAT IS JAVA?

With the Java programming language, Sun developed a language and development paradigm that was platform–independent and, with the Internet in mind, secure. Sun has composed a comprehensive definition of Java in a white paper, *The Java Language, An Overview*:

> **Java: A simple, object-oriented, network-savvy, interpreted, robust, secure, architecture-neutral, portable, high-performance, multithreaded, dynamic language.**

Sun Microsystems, which is the authoritative source on the Java programming language, crams many adjectives into this one sentence, but it boldly presents the Java programming language and its definition for the world to evaluate. The following subsections discuss each adjective in turn.

**Java Is Simple** The designers of the Java programming language deliberately designed the Java language and APIs to be easy to learn and use, compared to other general purpose languages such as C and C++. As easy as it is, Java is still a full-fledged general purpose language designed for experienced programmers who generally find that they can leverage their programming skills to quickly move to Java.

The syntax of the Java programming language is based on the C programming language. Many of the object-oriented programming concepts are the same as in C++ and are implemented with similar constructs. With this starting point, the designers of the Java programming language did not bring forward into Java the aspects of C and C++ that are most error-prone or difficult to use. By including no constructs for performing arithmetic operations on pointers, they eliminated what is arguably the greatest source of complexity, memory leaks, and other errors in C and C++ programs. The JVM also handles memory allocation and deallocation automatically, thereby greatly reducing the load on the programmer. C++ programmers generally agree that Java is a simpler programming language because some of the more advanced constructs of C++, such as templates and overloaded operators, have no equivalent in Java.

On the other hand, the language is evolving, and new features tend to add complexity. The original API, or set of core classes, was much smaller in the original version of the Java platform than it is now. For example, the number of API increased from about 200 in the original Java platform to about 500 in version 1.1, and then to about 1600 in Java 2.

 The developers of the Java language introduced some language features between the original 1.0 version and the 1.1 version of the Java platform. Although the programming language changed little since version 1.1, the API has continued to develop, and several core classes were changed or added. The greatest single addition was the **Java Foundation Classes (JFC)**.

**Java Is Network-Savvy**  Part of the success of Java comes from its features for networking and distributing objects in an enterprise environment. The Java platform includes a package called **java.net** that supports network programming. In the sense that using the core classes in **java.net** makes network computing simple, the Java platform is network-savvy.

The Java platform provides API and tools to address major concerns related to networking, including authorized access, user identification, security, and integrity of transferred data. Other tools let your programs use objects that were written in Java and that reside on other computers on the network. Chapter 17 describes some of these tools and features.

When programming for networks and distributed environments, programmers sometimes must use specialized tools and API in addition to the Java platform. Industry-wide organizations, and not just the developers of the Java platform, set industry standards. For example, the Object Management Group (OMG), defines a language for interoperability between different object-oriented languages called the Interface Definition Language (IDL) for use with the Common Object Request Broker Architecture (CORBA). The Java platform does include tools that help you connect your Java programs to IDL, but you cannot always expect the Java platform to provide the complete solution.

**Java Is Interpreted**    The Java platform compiler translates Java source code into bytecode. **Bytecode** is an architecturally neutral representation of code written in the Java programming language. The Java interpreter processes bytecode, rather than Java source code, when you run a Java program. The compilation step is crucial. During this step, the compiler identifies and eliminates many errors, and it optimizes the bytecode.

Some computer manufacturers provide true Java compilers that translate Java source code into load modules in the native code of hardware platforms and that can be run outside the JVM. For example, the IBM High Performance Java compilers can create executable programs for Windows, OS/2, System 390, AS/400, and AIX from Java source. The resulting code can run faster than bytecode because it is not interpreted, but it is not portable.

**Java Is Robust**    The design of the Java platform ensures that programs run correctly and do not break when the unexpected happens. Although correctness can never be guaranteed, several Java features increase the robustness of running programs:

➤ Programs run within the JVM cannot access native system resources, except through the API provided by the JVM. Therefore, a Java program cannot access a region of memory that application programs are not allowed to use, call a system API improperly, or perform other low-level operations that can be the source of errors in programs written in other languages.

➤ The JVM performs automatic memory management. The Java language gives you far fewer opportunities to misuse memory than languages that expect the programmer to request and release memory explicitly. The programmer cannot access arbitrary memory addresses, and the JVM automatically checks array bounds at runtime. As a result, programs never intentionally access memory that they should not or mistakenly access memory addresses other than what they intended.

➤ The Java platform has a mechanism for handling errors or unexpected conditions. Programs written in most programming languages terminate prematurely and abruptly when they cannot complete an operation. The JVM creates objects called **exceptions** to contain information about error or unexpected conditions. The exception object records what type of exception occurred and from where it originated. You can write your program to handle many types of exceptions. For example, if your program tries to read a file that does not exist, your program can catch the exception and take appropriate action. This exception model is not unique to Java, but it is used more consistently here than in most other programming environments.

➤ The language is type safe, which means that you cannot use information in a way that is not intended, based on the type assigned to the information. You cannot play the sort of tricks that serve as shortcuts and that are often the sources of error in other languages. For example, you cannot overlay a data structure in the system with your own structure and then modify the data structure itself.

**Java Is Secure**   The JVM can run code that originates on the local machine (typically, an application) or that is downloaded from the network (typically, an applet). By default, local code is trusted, and remote code is untrusted. You can accept default security policies or establish more fine-grained access controls. For example, you can let only certain people run certain servlets.

Additional security policies control what code is allow to do:

➤ The JVM runs untrusted code in a sandbox. A **sandbox** is separate area for executing code that has limited privileges. Code from the sandbox has limited access to the file system and is not allowed to perform actions that might jeopardize the integrity of the JVM or local system. For example, untrusted code cannot write to local files, directly access native code, or read certain systems properties.

➤ Bytecode loaded from an untrusted source, such as an unknown server on the Internet, is verified before it is executed. The verifier is a safety mechanism. It ensures that bytecode files are structurally correct. For example, it checks that every instruction has a valid operation code.

➤ The JVM can trust applets if the applets have a recognized digital signature key.

 The developers of the Java platform have refined and extended the sandbox model and the security features of the Java platform over the years. The concept of signed applets was introduced by version 1.1 of the Java 2 SDK. The developers of the Java platform added tools and API to Java 2 to make setting up customized policies easier and more flexible than before.

**Java Is Architecture-Neutral and Portable**   The Java platform provides architectural neutrality in part by allowing no implementation-defined features. For example, the target processor and the compiler determine the storage allocated for primitive types in C and C++, but the storage mapping for primitive types is defined by the Java platform for all implementations on all target processors.

Portability is the major benefit of architectural neutrality. Bytecode is portable because it runs on all implementations of the JVM. Any JVM can run a valid Java program, regardless of what implementation of the Java platform the program was created on, and all JVMs produce exactly the same results for that program.

Portability has its price, however. Architecturally neutral code cannot exploit the latest and greatest features of any one platform. There is always a trade-off among features, performance, and portability.

**Java Is High-Performance**    The performance penalty for interpreting Java bytecode rather than running native compiled code can be surprisingly small. **Just-in-time (JIT)** compilers improve the performance of Java programs. A JIT compiler is a platform-specific program that plugs into the JVM and transforms architecturally neutral bytecode into platform-specific object code. When you run Java programs compiled by a JIT compiler, you bypass the bytecode interpreter, which provides a performance boost. In addition, programs that contain many loops can run faster if compiled with a JIT compiler than if bytecode must be reinterpreted on every pass through every loop.

**Java Is Multithreaded**    The Java platform includes classes that specifically support multithreaded programs. Chapter 11 covers the API and language keywords that you use in multithreaded programs. If you have programmed in other languages for multithreading, you may be pleasantly surprised to find that tasks that can be difficult to program in other languages—such as creating, launching, and synchronizing threads—are easy with the Java language and API.

**Java Programming Language Is Dynamic**    The word *dynamic* may have different meanings, depending on the context of its use:

➤ At runtime, the JVM loads classes dynamically as required and does not load a class until the first time a running program references the class. The JVM does not require that all classes used by a program be loaded or even exist before a program begins execution.

➤ The JVM uses dynamic binding to determine which method to call when more than one class in the same inheritance hierarchy provides an implementation of the called method. Chapter 5 describes dynamic binding, which is a technique used by many object-oriented languages.

➤ The software-development process itself has a dynamic quality. You can incrementally build the set of the classes that make up your program, test them, and combine them in different ways.

# BRIEF HISTORY OF JAVA TECHNOLOGY

The history of Java is not very long. The story starts at the beginning of the 1990s, when Sun Microsystems was working on consumer electronics. Software for consumer electronics was developed to run on the cheapest chips available. If prices changed so that a different chip set became cheaper, the developers had to switch to that chip. Sun pursued the goal of creating software that was portable so that it could be switched quickly to new or less expensive chips.

In pursuit of this goal, Sun created an experimental, hand-held computer called the *7, which was intended for controlling home appliances. James Gosling was the technical leader of the project. The *7 never became a retail product, but the developers at Sun began to see that the computer language they developed for the *7 could be useful in other ways. For instance, the team could apply it to the Web, where compactness and simplicity are important requirements. Others envisioned it for embedded systems in electronic appliances, enterprise-wide applications, and network computing.

At first, the language was called Oak, supposedly in honor of a tree that grew outside Gosling's window. When the development team learned that there was already a computer language called Oak, they had to change the name and eventually settled on Java, perhaps in recognition of the role caffeine plays in software development. A pleasing side-effect is that, when it comes to coining derivative names, such as "beans," Java may have more potential than Oak.

The announcement of the Java programming language generated an unprecedented amount of interest in the software-development world. The official history is very short:

➤ Sun Microsystems officially announced the Java programming language in May 1995. Before then, alpha and beta versions were available so that programmers could play with the language and start to apply and master it. The first official developers' tool set and API for the Java platform was called the **Java Development Kit (JDK)**.

➤ Since 1995, the number of programmers using Java has been growing at an ever-increasing rate. Most popular Web browsers provided a built-in 1.0 JVM to support applets shortly after the first Java platform became available.

➤ Sun Microsystems announced Version 1.1 of the JDK in 1997. This version added some features to the Java programming language and significant additions and modification to the set of classes that make up the Java API. The developers of Java introduced the JavaBeans standard with this version. After some months, most popular Web browsers upgraded their built-in JVMs to be compatible with version 1.1.

➤ During 1997, 1998, and 1999, Sun Microsystems updated the JDK several times. Sun also made the Java Foundation Classes ( JFC) available in 1998 as a separate download that could be used with JDK version 1.1.6 and later.

➤ Sun Microsystems released the servlet API in the Java Servlet Development Kit ( JSDK) early in 1998. Proprietary Web servers that support servlets started to appear about the same time, and some servers (such as IBM's WebSphere) included support for Java Server Pages based on early versions of the JSP specification.

➤ Before its release late in 1998, the Java 2 platform was eagerly anticipated and was commonly referred to as version 1.2 of the JDK. When the Java 2 platform was announced, the set of tools and API was renamed the Java 2 Software Development Kit, Standard Edition. The JFC was fully integrated into Java 2. The Java 2 platform also provides for improved support for database access and distributed computing, interoperability with CORBA, and a Java 2 plug-in JVM for Web browsers.

➤ A consortium of companies completed the first specification for Enterprise Java Beans (EJBs) near the end of 1998. Several companies started to market Enterprise Java Servers to support EJBs.

➤ In June 1999, Sun announced three editions of the Java 2 platform. The first is Java 2 Standard Edition (J2SE), which is the SDK described in the bulk of this book. The second is Java 2 Enterprise Edition (J2EE), which includes Enterprise Java Beans and formalizes the concept of web applications. **Web applications** are web-based solutions that consist of Java programs, HTML pages, and other assets deployed in an *n*-tier enterprise environment. The third edition, Java 2 Micro Edition, refers to Java platforms for devices such as Web phones, smart cards, and hand-held productivity tools.

➤ In August 1999, Sun released the JSP specification version 1.0 and the JavaServer Web Development Kit as a reference implementation of this specification.

It is interesting to note that Sun Microsystems continued some development of version 1.1 of the Java platform after announcing Java 2. Sun may support the 1.1 platform for some time or at least while the industry as a whole completes the transition to Java 2.

Many companies now market Java application-development tools and related products. You can, for example, purchase or download collections of JavaBeans from many sources. A number of companies have jointly set up certification programs based on Java technology. For more details on becoming a certified Java programmer or developer, see Appendix A.

# JAVA TOOLS

The Java platform includes a tool set for developing Java programs. The Java 2 SDK tools run only in a command-line window and provide basic functionality. Nevertheless, they are adequate for developing Java programs, and you can work through this book using them.

VisualAge for Java and other proprietary products give integrated development environments with features such as rapid application development, SmartGuides (Wizards to automate common tasks), productivity aids, and features that provide connectivity with other proprietary software.

It is a good idea to check the Web sites for your development environment for links to support, samples and demonstrations, technical articles, frequently asked questions (FAQ), and online tutorials, as well as for upgrades. For a list of sites from which you can get implementations of Java technology for a variety of platforms, and a wealth of information about Java-related products and technology, see the list of **Uniform Resource Locators (URLs)** in Appendix D, "Java Resources on the World Wide Web."

The following list contains the most frequently used tools provided by the Java platform. The example commands apply to the Windows implementation of Java platform. Most of the commands are cross-platform, but the options and syntax may vary according to the file system and command-line processor of the host operating system. Complete documentation of all tools for specific implementations of the Java platform is included in the documentation for Java 2 platform.

➤ **javac** is the Java compiler. Run **javac** to create the bytecode for applications, applets, and servlets. To use **javac**, you must supply as input a Java source file with the file extension .java. The output consists of one or more bytecode files with the file extension .class.

The Java platform has strict naming conventions for files and classes. If the class can be run as an application or used by other classes that are not in the same package, the file that contains the source must have the same name as the class. Names are case-sensitive in the Java platform, even on operating systems on which filenames are not case-sensitive, and filenames must match class names exactly, including uppercase and lowercase. You can include the absolute path to find the file; otherwise, the compiler assumes the filename is relative to the current folder. You must include the file extension .java. For example, to compile the file that contains the class `MyClass`, the command is:

```
javac MyClass.java
```

➤ **java** is the Java interpreter. To run an application, enter the **java** command followed by the name of the class you want to run and any command-line arguments you want to pass to the program. Do not include the file extension because you are supplying a class name, not a filename. The class name is case-sensitive. For example, to run the class `MyClass`, the command is:

```
java MyClass
```

Conforming to the file-naming conventions is important because the interpreter loads bytecode from the file with the extension .class and with the case-sensitive base filename that matches the class name. If the class is in a package, the package must be in a folder that has the same case-sensitive name as the package. You must specify the package name in the **java** command, but you separate the package name and class name with dots instead of the character your operating system uses to indicate subfolders. For example, if `TestClass` is a class in a package called `testing`, and testing is a subfolder of the current package, the commands to compile and run `TestClass` on Windows-based platforms are:

```
javac testing\TestClass.java
java testing.TestClass
```

➤ **appletviewer** is a utility that runs applets outside a Web browser. The command-line arguments for **appletviewer** are one or more URLs for HTML documents. For a file that resides on the local file system, the URL is the same as the filename. Specify the path relative to the current folder. The **appletviewer** tool discards all text in the HTML document except HTML tags that point to applets. The tool then runs each applet in the viewer window. For example, to view the applets used by Web page **mypage.htm**, which is in a folder called **myweb**, you can enter the following from the folder that contains **myweb**:

```
appletviewer myweb\mypage.htm
```

For the **appletviewer** command, whether filenames are case-sensitive depends on your browser and the native operating system. You still must be careful about filenames because the tags in the HTML document give the location of the .class file for the applet relative to the current folder when you issue the **appletviewer** command.

➤ **jdb** is the Java debugger. This debugger has limited functionality; the proprietary Java application-development products have more sophisticated debuggers.

➤ **javadoc** generates a web of HTML documents that make up online documentation for packages of classes. One popular, innovative feature of Java technology is the ability to generate online documentation for your classes automatically, by using **javadoc** and a unique format for comments in your code. The "Doc Comments" section of this chapter describes how to insert the tags that this tool recognizes into your Java source code, how to run the **javadoc** tool, and how to use the output.

➤ **native2ascii** is a useful tool if you are developing programs for the international market. In the Java platform, all characters are stored in the international character set called **Unicode**. This tool converts files from the character sets that are commonly used in North America and Western Europe into Unicode. For more information about Unicode and internationalizing a program, see Chapter 16.

➤ The **jar** utility combines several files into a single **Java archive (JAR)** file. In this book, and in industry, JAR files are also known as .jar files. A JAR file is like a zip file, except that the data is not always compressed. JAR files are a convenient for deploying and distributing programs. You can combine resources such as graphics or sound clips together with classes that use them in a JAR, as the section "Packaging a Program for Distribution" later this chapter explains. Downloading one JAR file is much more efficient than downloading related files separately.

The **JVM** can load .class files directly from JAR files, and most Java development environments can create and read JAR files.

All the example programs in this book are available in one JAR file on the CD-ROM that accompanies this book. See the instructions for using the JAR file in the "Read This Before You Begin" section of this book.

All the Java 2 SDK tools have options that you can specify on the command line. A full description of the tools is beyond the scope of this book but is provided by the Java 2 platform documentation.

## HOW THE JAVA 2 SDK TOOLS FIND FILES

Commands that take class names as arguments, such as **java** and **javac**, must find the file that contains the source or bytecode. You can specify the full path to the file or a path relative to the current folder. For example, if you are in the folder D:\myJava, the following commands compile and run public class `MyClass`:

```
javac D:\myJava\MyClass.java
javac MyClass.java
```

These commands also have a **–classpath** option so that you can tell the Java platform to look in certain folders or in .jar or .zip files for the code. You can use the abbreviation **–cp** with the **java** command. To search more than one location, specify several paths separated by semicolons. For example, if you are in any folder on any drive, the following command finds and runs the public class `MyClass`:

```
java –cp C:\jars\my.jar;D:\myJava MyClass
```

**1**

The locations are searched in the order that they appear in the **classpath** option, so the command above looks in the JAR file **my.jar** before finding **MyClass.class** in the myJava folder. On operating systems that have environment variables, you can set up an environment variable called CLASSPATH to hold the search list. From a command prompt, use a **SET** command such as the following:

```
SET CLASSPATH=C:\jars\my.jar;D:\myJava;%CLASSPATH%
```

In this **SET** command, the **%CLASSPATH%** represents the previous value of CLASSPATH, so the new locations are inserted at the beginning of the existing search path. If you set the CLASSPATH in a command-line window, the settings hold for the duration of the command-line session. Use features of your operating system to set the CLASSPATH permanently.

The **–classpath** command option overrides the CLASSPATH environment variable. You do not have to specify the location of the core classes in the classpath. The core classes are contained in .jar files that reside in the subfolder jre\lib, which is contained in the directory into which you installed the Java platform.

Usually, Java programs are built from many classes. What does the compiler do when the source it is processing uses another class? The **javac** compiler looks for the referenced class in the path specified by the **–classpath** option or CLASSPATH environment variable and by using the class name to identify the file. The **javac** command also has a **–sourcepath** option that you can use to specify the location of input source files stored in a folder that is different than the compiled classes folder. If you do not specify a sourcepath, the compiler searches the same locations for source and bytecode. Use the **–d** option to tell the compiler to output the bytecode files to a different folder from the location of the source.

What if there is no .class file, but there is a .java file? What if there is a .class file, but its modification timestamp is earlier than that of the .java file? In either case, the .java file is compiled to create an up-to-date .class file. If neither a .java file nor a .class file exists in the search path, the compiler reports an error.

By default, the **javac** compiler checks the validity of .class files automatically. A side-effect of this mechanism is that you can run **javac** against one class and the compiler can inform you of an error in another class in a different file. If you find these error messages annoying, try to make sure all referenced classes are compiled first.

Like the compiler, the **java** command locates bytecode files by class name. It can dynamically load classes that your class calls while your program is running. To find the referenced class, the command searches the folders listed in the CLASSPATH environment variable. If the JVM cannot find a .class file, it terminates your program with an error message.

# YOUR FIRST JAVA PROGRAM

Now that you know what Java is and have a background in the SDK tool set, it is time to start programming. You begin with the small but complete Java program supplied in this section. Read and try to understand the code. Later in this chapter, you enter and run this program using the tools provided by the Java platform and then by using the VisualAge for Java IDE. The program itself is short, but the listing shown here is lengthened by several comments.

The following program is an application designed to run from a command-line window. The input is supplied as command-line arguments, and the output is returned to console. When given a number followed by a word beginning with C, the program interprets the number as degrees on the Celsius scale, converts it to degrees Fahrenheit, and outputs the result. Additionally, when given a number followed by a word beginning with F, the program interprets the number as degrees on the Fahrenheit scale, converts it to degrees Celsius, and outputs the result.

```java
package examples.basic;
/** A simple Java starter program
    Converts temperatures between C and F
 */

public class TempConvert {
   private static double temp;
   private static String scale;

   /** internal method to convert Celsius to Fahrenheit
    */
   static double cToF( double degrees ) {
     return 9 * degrees / 5 + 32;
   }

   /** internal method to convert Fahrenheit to Celsius
    */
   static double fToC( double degrees ) {
     return 5 * ( degrees - 32 ) / 9;
   }

   /** main method of temperature conversion class
    * takes two input argument from command line
    * @param args[0] degrees as a real number
    * @param args[1] temperature scale C or F
```

```
    * @exception NumberFormatException occurs if the
    *     first argument cannot be parsed as a number
    */
   public static void main( String[ ] args ) {
   // print usage message and stop if
   //     less than two arguments supplied
     if ( args.length < 2 ) {
        System.out.println(
        "usage: TempConvert number C|F" );
        return;
     }  // end of if statement

   // translate the first argument to a double value
   //     using a technique that works for all
   //     versions of the Java platform
     temp = ( new Double( args[0] ) ).doubleValue();
   // The following simpler technique on Java 2 only
   //     temp = Double.parseDouble( args[0] );

   // From the second argument, select C-to-F or F-to-C
   // Base selection on first character of input string
     switch ( args[1].charAt( 0 ) ) {
   // store resulting scale and overwrite temperature
        case 'C': scale = "Fahrenheit";
   temp = cToF( temp );
   break;
        case 'F': scale = "Celsius";
   temp = fToC( temp );
   break;
   // if input scale not recognized, print message
        default:  System.out.println(
            "Specify scale as C or F only " );
            return;
     } // end of select statement

   // output the input arguments and the converted
   //     temperature and scale
     System.out.println( args[0] + " " + args[1]
        + " converted to " + temp + " " + scale );
     return;
   }  // end of main method

} // end of class
```

This program, like every Java program, is made up of classes. All executable code must belong to a class. Like many of the sample programs in the early chapters of this book, this temperature-conversion program is deliberately small so that it can be contained in a single class. Even though it is small, this short program uses many different language constructs.

Do not worry if this first program seems very complicated now. The next few chapters will explain each construct separately and in considerable detail. The following section gives a line-by-line breakdown of the code in the TempConvert class.

## Breakdown of the TempConvert Class

The temperature conversion program consists of one class called TempConvert. This class contains three executable units of code, or methods:

➤ cToF converts degrees from Celsius to Fahrenheit

➤ fToC converts degrees from Fahrenheit to Celsius

➤ **main** is where execution starts and where most of the logic resides

If you have programmed before—especially if you have used C or C++—many of the statements in the class may be easily readable. However, some constructs, such as the complex-looking declaration of **main**, may be puzzling. The following dissection of this class may dispel some of the mystery. As much as possible, given the limitations of the page width of this textbook, the layout of the code follows Java programming conventions.

The first line in the file is a package statement. The package statement tells the Java compiler where to put the class and the interpreter where to find it. The source code for this example is included in the JAR file on the CD-ROM that accompanies this book. This class is in the package **examples.basic**. The structure of packages mirrors the file system, so you can find this source code in the examples\basic subfolder of the folder in which you unpacked the JAR file **examples.jar**. The name of a source file always matches the name of the public class that it contains, so this source code is found in the file **TempConvert.java**.

```
package examples.basic;
```

Consider the next three lines in the file:

```
/** A simple Java starter program
    Converts temperatures between C and F
    */
```

These lines make up one comment. Comments in the Java programming language can be block comments enclosed in /* and */ characters or single-line comments that begin with // and run to the end of the line. This comment is a doc comment because it starts with the sequence /**. The Java compiler treats doc comments as block comments. **Doc comments** are used with the **javadoc** tool to generate user documentation and are discussed later in this chapter. The rest of the comments in this program are omitted from this discussion.

The definition of the `TempConvert` class starts on the next line:

```
public class TempConvert {
```

In the above line, the first keyword, **public**, indicates that this class can be used from anywhere. A class that is not public can only be used by the other classes that are in the same package. In the Java programming language, there are two choices for granting access to a class:

➤ Declare a class public to make it accessible from everywhere.

➤ Omit the keyword public to limit access to within the package that contains the class.

The `TempConvert` class stores two data items, or fields, outside of any methods. The first field is called `temp` and stores a floating-point number in double precision. The number represents a temperature in degrees. The second field is called `scale` is a string and contains "Celsius" or "Fahrenheit" to indicate in what scale `temp degrees` is measured.

At this point, these variables have no values; they are declared for future use. The following statements declare them as **static** so that any method of the class, including **main**, can use them. The keyword **static** has a number of very important uses and is described in Chapter 4. The same statements also declare them as **private** so that they are not accessible except within methods of the `TempConvert` class.

```
private static double temp;
private static String scale;
```

The next lines define the first method, `cToF`, which converts temperatures from the Celsius scale to Fahrenheit. The method is **static** and **public**, so any program can load this class and call this method.

```
public static double cToF( double degrees ) {
    return 9 * degrees / 5 + 32;
}
```

The keyword **double** before the method name specifies that the method produces a result that is a double precision number. The input to the method is enclosed in the parentheses, **( )**, that follow the method name. The value input is represented by a double precision variable that will be called **degrees** inside this method. The body of the method is enclosed in the braces { }. This method body has only one line of code. The keyword **return** states that the value of the following expression is the output from the method, and the expression calculates the Fahrenheit temperature based on the value of **degrees**.

The second method, **fToC**, converts temperatures from the Fahrenheit scale to Celsius and is shown below. Its structure is similar to the **cToF** method. Note that the expression here includes parentheses. These are required to ensure that the calculations are preformed in the correct order. By default, arithmetic operations progress from left to right, except that multiplication, **\***, and division, **/**, are performed before addition, **+**, and subtraction, **-**. With the parentheses in their current position, the JVM starts evaluating the expression by subtracting 32 from the value of **degrees**.

```
public static double fToC( double degrees ) {
    return 5 * ( degrees - 32 ) / 9;
}
```

The third and last method is the **main** method, which is the entry point of the program. When you run the **java** command and provide a class name, the JVM starts execution by calling the **main** method of that class.

```
public static void main( String[] args ) {
```

The Java programming language is very strict about the form of the method **main**:

➤ You must grant unrestricted access to the **main** method by declaring it **public**.

➤ The keyword **static** declares that the method applies to the whole class rather than to a particular object. The **main** method must be static.

➤ The return type must be **void** because **main** does not return a value to the JVM.

➤ The method **main** must have one argument, and it must be an array of **String** objects. The square brackets, **[ ]**, specify an array. Giving the **String** array the identifier **args** is a convention, not a rule. Command-line arguments are passed to **main** through this array.

As shown below, the first statement in the main method spans five lines. The keyword **if** starts a conditional statement. The expression enclosed in parenthesis tests whether two or more command-line arguments were passed to the program. All arrays have a field called **length** that gives the number of elements in the array. Here, **args.length** is an expression that evaluates to the number of command-line arguments supplied when the class was run.

```
if ( args.length < 2 ) {
    System.out.println(
        "usage: TempConvert number C|F" );
    return;
}
```

The rest of the conditional statement is enclosed in braces and is executed only if `args.length` is less than two. The **println** method is called to write the string "usage: TempConvert number C | F" to the console. The object called **out** is defined in the core class **System** and refers to console output. Notice how the name of the class, **System**, the name of a member of that class, **out**, and the method **println** called for **out** are joined by dots. This is how you call a method that belongs to another class. The argument to the **println** method is the string to print and is specified between parentheses following the method name.

Without a complete set of command-line arguments, the temperature conversion cannot continue, and the program stops when the **return** statement is executed. This return occurs only when the conditional statement is executed. If at least two command-line arguments are supplied, the **println** and **return** are skipped and execution continues after the brace that ends the conditional statement.

The next two lines, which are shown below, may look strange. The first line takes the string that holds the first command line argument, `args[0]`, extracts a double precision value from the string, and then stores that value in the class variable `temp`. The second line is a comment, but uncommented, it would do exactly the same thing. The difference is that the first version works in all versions of the Java platform, and the second uses a method that became available in the Java 2 platform. How the conversion works and the introduction of the **Double.parseDouble** method are left to the discussion of the standard wrapper class **Double** in Chapter 3.

```
      temp = ( new Double( args[0] ) ).doubleValue();
//    temp = Double.parseDouble( args[0] );
```

What happens if the first command-line argument cannot be read as a number? For example, 22, -10, and 45.7 are valid but 1a2b, twelve, and 5..6 are not valid numbers. If a user runs the program and supplies an input argument that is not a number, the program stops at this line and JVM outputs a message that reports a **NumberFormatException**.

What the program does with the input value depends on whether the second command-line argument is a string beginning with C, F, or some other character. The keyword **switch**, shown in the code below, begins a construct that is useful for multiway conditional execution. The brace at the end of this line indicates the start of a list of cases. Each case consists of a block of code, and the value of the expression enclosed in parentheses following the keyword **switch** determines which one is executed.

The expression ( `args[1].charAt( 0 )` ) looks at the string that is the second command line argument, `args[1]`, and then takes its first character, `charAt( 0 )`. For example, if the command-line arguments are "32" and "Fog", the value or the switch expression is the character F. This program does

not care how you spell Fahrenheit or Celsius, as long as the word begins with
an uppercase F or C.

```
switch (  args[1].charAt( 0 )  ) {
}
```

The statements following the label **Case 'C'** are executed if the switch expression matches the character C. In the Java programming language, statement labels
end with a colon. Three things happen when the following case runs.

1. The **String** variable **scale** is assigned the literal string "Fahrenheit". Note
   that a single character is enclosed in single quotation marks and that the
   value of a **String** object is enclosed in double quotation marks.

2. The value of the variable **temp**, which previously contained a temperature
   in degrees Celsius, is overwritten with the value converted into degrees
   Fahrenheit. Notice the call of the method **cToF** and that the calling statement passes the previous value of **temp** as an argument to the method.
   The JVM executes the method and then assigns the value returned from
   **cToF** to the variable **temp**.

3. The **break** keyword tells the JVM to skip all remaining statements in the
   switch statement so that only the statements for this case run.

```
case 'C': scale = "Fahrenheit";
     temp = cToF( temp );
     break;
```

The statements following the **Case 'F':** are executed if the switch expression
matches the character F. These three lines convert the degrees input by the user
from Fahrenheit to Celsius, much like the previous case converts from Celsius
to Fahrenheit.

```
case 'F': scale = "Celsius";
     temp = fToC( temp );
     break;
```

The final case in this switch statement is used only when none of the preceding cases matches the switch expression and is identified by the label **default**.
In other words, these lines are executed only when the temperature scale specified in the command-line argument does not begin with F or C. Characters
in the Java programming language is case-sensitive, so c and f do not match C
and F. The default action is to print a message to the console using the **println**
method and then to stop the program by issuing **return** from the **main**
method. The closing brace ends the switch statement, including all of its cases.

```
default:  System.out.println(
          "Specify scale as C or F only " );
     return;
}
```

The next line of code can be reached only after a temperature has been converted successfully. The **println** method is called now to output the result of the conversion. The argument of this method must be one **String** object, so the argument is built in the string expression:

```
args[0] + " " + args[1] + " converted to " +
temp + " " +     scale
```

In the above expression, the + operator performs string concatenation. The output consists of the first command-line argument, which is an element zero of a string array, followed by a string containing one space, the second command-line argument, and then the literal string " converted to ". The Java platform knows how to convert all numeric types to strings, so **temp** can be appended to the output using the + operator.

Finally, another space and the value of the string **scale** are added to the output.

```
System.out.println( args[0] + "   " + args[1]
    + " converted to " + temp + " " + scale );
```

As shown below, the **return** statement stops the program, and the final closing braces indicate the end of the body of the **main** method body and of the class definition.

```
        return;
    }
}
```

Three conditions can stop the program before it prints out the converted temperature and stops. The output that is sent to the console appears on the screen. If the program completes successfully, it displays the converted temperature. If one of the following conditions apply, a different message displays:

➤ If less than two command-line arguments are supplied, the **return** in the if statement is executed.

➤ If the first command-line argument cannot be parsed as a number, the JVM detects the problem and deals with it by **throwing an exception**. You can write programs that handle exceptions and continue running, but this program ignores exceptions and is terminated when one occurs.

➤ If the second command-line argument starts with any character other than F or C, the **return** in the default case of the switch statement is executed.

## ENTERING AND RUNNING A PROGRAM

As with most of the programs in this book, you can run the `TempConvert` class using the tools that come with the Java SDK, commercial application-development packages such as IBM's VisualAge for Java, or another development tool of your choice. The CD-ROM that accompanies this book includes three development packages:

➤ The Java 2 platform provides a suite of command-line tools. These tools provide basic functionality, require minimal system resources to run, and are widely used because they are free.

➤ IBM VisualAge for Java provides a fully integrated IDE. It operates on an internal code repository and has features to import from and export to the native file system. It is popular with professional programmers because it provides many time-saving features, including true incremental build, an excellent debugger, browsers that give quick and easy access to classes, and built-in version control.

A unique and popular feature of VisualAge for Java is the Visual Composition Editor. With the Composition Editor, you can build Graphical User Interfaces (GUIs) for applets and applications visually and integrate the GUI components of your program with other Java code.

➤ The third is JBuilder. The CD-ROM includes the University Edition and a trial copy of the Enterprise Edition.

The tools provided on the CD-ROM that accompanies this book and the instructions for running them apply to Windows platforms. The Java programming language is the same on all platforms, but you may notice some difference in the development tools on different native operating systems.

You can run all the sample programs in this book from the Java archive (JAR) file that is included on the CD-ROM that accompanies this book.

You should install the Java 2 platform and sample programs in the file **examples.jar**, as described in the **ReadMe.html** file on the CD-ROM that accompanies this book. Some sample programs require additional steps to run from the .jar file. In these cases, detailed instructions are provided with the listing of the class in this book.

The instructions in the following sections tell you how to extract the source for the `TempConvert` class from the file **examples.jar** and then how to compile and run it as though you had just entered the code manually.

## Running the First Program with the SDK

To prepare the source file:

1. Open a command-line window and create a working folder. For example, if you want to work on your D drive in a new folder called myJava, type:

```
D:
md myJava
cd myJava
```

You are now in your new myJava folder on the D drive. You can extract the source file directly from the CD-ROM.

2. Substitute the drive letter of your CD-ROM for G and enter the following commands:

```
jar -xf G:\examples.jar examples\basic\TempConvert.java
```

The **jar** command displays messages only when errors occur, so if it appears that nothing has happened, the command has most likely succeeded. The Java platform is case-sensitive. If your files did not extract, double-check your use of uppercase and lowercase letters and try again.

The JAR file mirrors the structure of packages and folders. The **jar** command with option **-xf** extracts files from a .jar file. Here, it creates a folder named examples and a folder basic within examples and then copies the file **TempConvert.java** into examples\basic\.

If the **jar** command was successful, you are ready to compile the program. You should then skip Steps 3, 4, and 5 and move to the next set of steps. If you cannot extract the source file from the JAR file, you can enter the source code manually by continuing with Step 3.

3. The `TempConvert` class is in package `examples.basic`. Java package names must match folder names, so you must create the examples folder and then the basic folder within examples. Set up the folders with the following commands:

```
md examples
cd examples
md basic
cd basic
```

4. Now, open a text editor and create a file named **TempConvert.java**. in the **examples\basic** folder. Be sure to use an editor that can handle long filenames. Type in the code for the class `TempConvert` exactly as listed here. The comments have been removed to reduce the amount of typing:

```
package examples.basic;
public class TempConvert {
    private static double temp;
    private static String scale;

    static double cToF( double degrees ) {
        return 9 * degrees / 5 + 32;
    }

    static double fToC( double degrees ) {
        return 5 * ( degrees - 32 ) / 9;
    }
```

```
public static void main(String args[]) {
    if ( args.length < 2 ) {
      System.out.println(
          "usage: TempConvert number C|F");
      return;
    }
    temp = ( new Double( args[0] ) ).doubleValue();

    switch ( args[1].charAt( 0 ) ) {
        case 'C': scale = "Fahrenheit";
          temp = cToF( temp );
          break;
        case 'F': scale = "Celsius";
            temp = fToC( temp );
            break;
        default:  System.out.println(
            "Specify scale as C or F only ");
              return;
    }
    System.out.println( args[0] + " " + args[1]
      + " converted to " + temp + " " + scale );
    return;
  }
}
```

5. Return to the myJava folder.

You are ready to compile the source file.

To compile the source file:

1. At the command-line prompt, type:

   `javac examples\basic\TempConvert.java`

   You see no messages unless the compiler finds an error. Because you copied a working program, there should be no errors.

If you had to enter the program manually and did get error messages, check for typing mistakes. The error messages should help you locate the error. Suppose, for example, that you deleted the semicolon from the end of the following line:

```
        temp = cToF( temp );
        break;
```

The error message gives the line number, states the error, and indicates the position of the problem. The message reported for this error is:

```
TempConvert.java:25; ';' expected
                temp = cToF( temp )
                                   ^
```

When the class compiles successfully, you can run it.

To run the class:

1. Enter the **java** command and supply the class name qualified by the package names. On the same line, enter a number followed by a space and "Celsius" or "Fahrenheit", as in:

```
java examples.basic.TempConvert 212 Fahrenheit
```

The output for this input is:

```
212 Fahrenheit converted to 100.0 Celsius
```

## IBM VisualAge for Java

VisualAge provides a powerful development tool for the Java platform and has many features that this exercise does not demonstrate. Nevertheless, you can use VisualAge to create a very simple class, as well as to build large applications or packages of classes. The hub of the VisualAge for Java development environment is a window called the Workbench. The **Workbench** is the main window that opens when you start VisualAge for Java.

You can import the entire **examples.jar** or selected classes from a JAR file or folder into VisualAge. To give you a more complete introduction to the Workbench, the following instructions take you through the process of entering the `TempConvert` class as though you were developing it from scratch. VisualAge provides a number of **SmartGuides** that automate common tasks. During this scenario, you will get a chance to use many of the SmartGuides.

Before you can use VisualAge for Java, you must install it or have access to a machine on which it is installed.

To start VisualAge for Java on Windows platforms:

1. Click **Start**, point to **Programs**, point to **IBM VisualAge for Java for Windows**, and then click **IBM VisualAge for Java.**

The VisualAge for Java banner window appears, followed by the Quick Start window.

You use the Quick Start window to select the SmartGuide for the task you want to complete. To make the selection, you must click one of the following five buttons:

➤ The **Create a new applet** button starts the SmartGuide that creates a new applet.

➤ The **Create a new class** button starts the SmartGuide that creates a new class.

➤ The **Create a new interface** button starts the SmartGuide that creates a new interface. **Interfaces** define the behaviors that some classes must provide.

➤ The **Continue working with a class/interface** button opens a dialog box in which you select an existing class or interface with which you can work. If you return later to the sample class you are about to create in this exercise, you can click this button to reopen the class.

➤ The **Go to the Workbench** button opens the Workbench window. This window may not appear if the box **Show this window at startup** has been deselected on a previous session using VisualAge—in which case, VisualAge opens directly to the Workbench.

To open the VisualAge for Java Workbench:

1. Select **Go to the Workbench,** and then click **OK**.

VisualAge stores all your work in its internal workspace and provides browsers to navigate to the items on which you want to work. When you first open the Workbench, you will see a window that looks like Figure 1-1. Your list of projects may differ slightly from the list in Figure 1-1. The preloaded projects shown in the figure contain the packages provided by the Java platform and some packages provided by IBM.

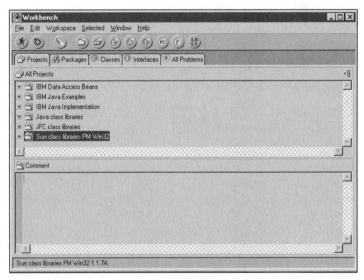

**Figure 1-1** VisualAge Workbench

The Workbench has a menu bar and a toolbar for quick access to the most common actions. For example, the toolbar has the **Run**, **Debug**, and **Search** buttons. The Workbench is designed to look like a notebook with a tab for

1

each of its main pages. You can click on a tab to open the associated page of the Workbench. The pages give you a variety of ways to access the code in your workspace:

➤ In the **Projects** page, you can select an existing project with which to work. The page features a list of the projects and the packages in each project. From this page, you can perform tasks such as creating new projects, deleting projects, and adding packages to projects.

➤ In the **Packages** page, you can locate packages and work with them. The page features a list of the packages that are available, and you can click a package to see the classes and methods it contains. You can perform tasks such as creating packages, adding classes to packages, and deleting packages.

➤ In the **Classes** page, you can get a more detailed look at classes and the methods that any one class contains. You can modify source code and perform add, search, compare, and delete operations on classes.

➤ In the **Interfaces** page, you can work on Java types that are interfaces rather than classes.

➤ In the **All Problems** page, you can investigate any classes that have unresolved problems. You can click any error message to bring the code in which the problem is detected into an editable panel.

Feel free to explore the Workbench before returning to the start position to enter the `TempConvert` program. If you get lost, you can return to the project browser by clicking on the **Projects** tab. If you have moved into another window, close that window or return to the Workbench by selecting **Workbench** from the **Window** menu.

In VisualAge for Java, you organize your work into **projects** in order to keep together the classes and packages that you created for a specific purpose. For example, the instructions for this exercise tell you to create a project called `learning` to hold the classes and packages that you work on while using this book. You may create a separate project for each chapter, topic, or exercise, if you prefer. When you export a project out of the IDE, all the classes and packages it contains are written to the file system following JVM conventions. But the project's name and the project, as a separate entity, do not exist outside the VisualAge IDE.

To create a new project:

1. Click the fourth toolbar button from the left. The icon on the button looks like a folder.

2. The **Add Project** SmartGuide window appears. Make sure the **Create a new project named:** button is selected, type the name **learning** into the text box so that the window looks like Figure 1-2, and click **Finish**.

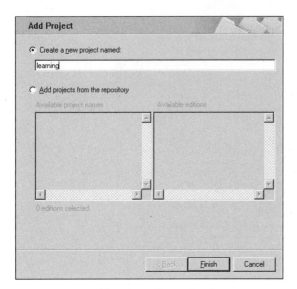

**Figure 1-2**   Add Project SmartGuide

Projects contain packages. Packages are recognized by the Java platform, so you should choose package names with care.

To create the `TempConvert` class in the `examples.basic` package:

1. Make sure the **learning** project is highlighted. Click it, if necessary, to select it.

2. Click the fifth toolbar button from the left. The icon on the button looks like a box wrapped in string. It is similar to the Add Project smartGuide in Figure 1-2.

3. The **Add Package** SmartGuide window appears. It is similar to the **Add Project** SmartGuide in Figure 1-2. Make sure **the Create a new package named:** button is selected, type the name **examples.basic** into the text box, and then click **Finish**.

Now that the `learning` package is not empty, a symbol appears to its right. The browsers display projects, packages, and classes in a dynamic tree view. When the symbol is a +, you can click to see the list of packages in `learning`. When the symbol is a −, you can click to compress the list of contents. Now, you can create the class.

To create the class:

1. Right-click on the **examples.basic** package.

2. When the popup menu appears select **Add >** and then **class...** You can use the popup menus, instead of the Workbench toolbar buttons.

3. The **Create Class** SmartGuide window appears. Check that the correct project and package name are entered in the top two boxes. You can click the **Browse** button to open a window in which you can find and select the project `learning` and the package `examples.basic`, if necessary.

4. Make sure the **Create a new class** button is selected, and then type the name **TempConvert** into the text box so that the window looks like Figure 1-3.

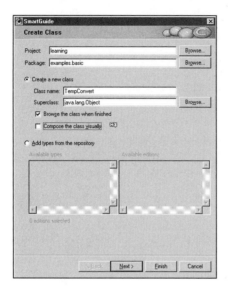

**Figure 1-3**    Create Class SmartGuide

5. Do not change superclass name **java.lang.Object**. Select **Browse the class when finished**, but not **Compose the class visually**, and then click **Finish**.

A new window, shown in Figure 1- 4, opens. This class window displays the new class **TempConvert**. The top half of the window lists methods in the class, and the bottom half is an editor pane, into which you can type the contents of the class. VisualAge has generated a skeleton outline of the class definition and given you one method that has the same name as the class. This method is a default constructor. You do not have to create a default constructor because the Java platform can provide one that is adequate for this class, but VisualAge generates one for you. In doing so, VisualAge is generating code that conforms to good programming practice.

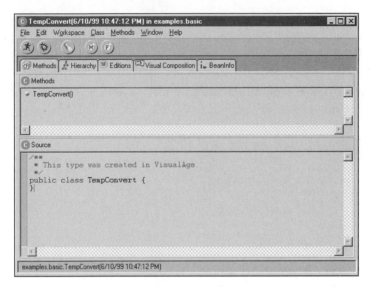

**Figure 1-4**   A Class Window view of the TempConvert class

To complete the definition of the **TempConvert** class:

1. In the editor pane, position the cursor after the open brace, {, and manually enter two lines of code shown in bold here. The contents of the editor pane should be:

```
/**
 * This type was created in VisualAge.
 */
public class TempConvert {
    private static double temp;
    private static String scale;
}
```

2. Right-click in the editor pane and select **Save** from the popup menu. This compiles the class definition and saves your work so far. If you made any mistakes entering the fields, an error message appears in an error window. Click **OK** to close the error window, correct the code, and repeat until a silent return from **Save** indicates a clean compile.

VisualAge has SmartGuides for adding fields and methods to classes. You do not have to use the SmartGuides and sometimes it is quicker to enter the code manually, just as you did for the two fields **temp** and **scale**. For the methods, use the SmartGuides.

3. Right-click in the upper pane of the class browser. Select **Add >** and then **Method...** from the popup menus.

4. The **Create Method** SmartGuide appears. Make sure the **Create a new method** button is selected, and enter `double cToF( double degrees )` into the text field so that the SmartGuide looks like Figure 1-5. Click **Next >**.

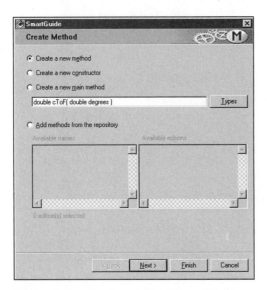

**Figure 1-5**   Create Method SmartGuide

5. The next window is the **Attributes** SmartGuide for methods. Note that the **public** radio button is selected by default. Select the **static** checkbox also. Click **Finish**.

6. You return to the class browser. Now, two methods are listed: `TempConvert( )` and `cToF( )`. The symbol **S** beside the `cToF` method indicates this is a static method. `cToF` is selected, and the editor pane displays the skeleton code. Replace the return statement:

`return 0;`

with:

`return 9 * degrees / 5 + 32;`

so that the window looks like Figure 1-6.

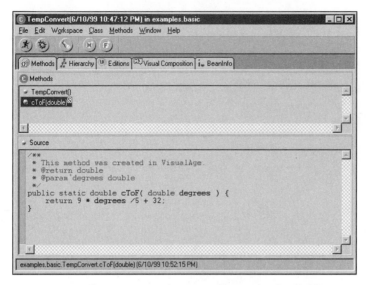

**Figure 1-6**  Class Browser showing the method TempConvert.cToF

7. Right-click in the editor pane and select **Save** from the popup menu. Correct typing errors or any other errors, if necessary.

A warning window pops up only if the method contains compile errors. The warning window gives you up to three options—**Save**, **Correct**, or **Cancel**. You can save a method with errors because sometimes you must temporarily leave problems unresolved. VisualAge marks a saved method that contains errors with a red **X** and lists it in the **All Problems** tab of the workbench. If VisualAge can fix the problem automatically, the **Correct** button is available on the warning window. Here, you should click **Cancel** and correct the error manually.

8. Repeat Steps 3 to 7 for the method **fToC**. The only differences between these methods is the name, **fToC** instead of **cToF**, and the return statement, which in **fToC** should be:

```
return 5 * ( degrees — 32 ) / 9;
```

9. Add the **main** method last. Right-click in the upper pane of the class browser. Select **Add >** and then **Method...** from the popup menus.

10. When the **Create Method** SmartGuide appears, select the **Create a new main method** button, note that the correct form for main appears in the text box, and click **Finish**. You can skip the method **Attributes** SmartGuide because the VisualAge automatically makes the **main** method static.

11. Back in the class browser, the editor panel lists the skeleton of the **main** method. Into the method, you can type the lines shown in bold in the following listing, or you can cut and paste the lines from another editor if

you have the source for this class stored in a file. When you are done, the editor window should contain the following lines:

```java
/**
 * This method was created in VisualAge.
 * @param args java.lang.String[]
 */
public static void main(String args[]) {
        if ( args.length < 2 ) {
          System.out.println(
              "usage: TempConvert number C|F" );
          return;
        }
        temp = ( new Double( args[0] ) ).doubleValue();

        switch ( args[1].charAt( 0 ) ) {
           case 'C': scale = "Fahrenheit";
                   temp = cToF( temp )
                   break;
           case 'F': scale = "Celsius";
                   temp = fToC( temp );
                   break;
           default:  System.out.println(
                   "Specify scale as C or F only" );
                   return;
        }
        System.out.println( args[0] + " " + args[1]
          + " converted to " + temp + " " + scale );
        return;

}
```

12. Right-click in the editor pane, and select **Save** from the popup menu. Correct errors, if necessary, just as you did with the **cToF** and **fToC** methods.

13. Make sure none of the methods have red **X**'s beside them, indicating errors. Then, close the class window to return to the Workbench.

It is time to test the **TempConvert** program inside the IDE.

To run the program:

1. In the Workbench, expand the tree view of the **learning** project and **examples.basic** package, if necessary, so you can see the class **TempConvert** listed. The symbol **C** in a green circle indicates a class. The running-man icon after a class name indicates a class that is ready for execution. If you expand the **TempConvert** class, the Workbench now looks like Figure 1-7.

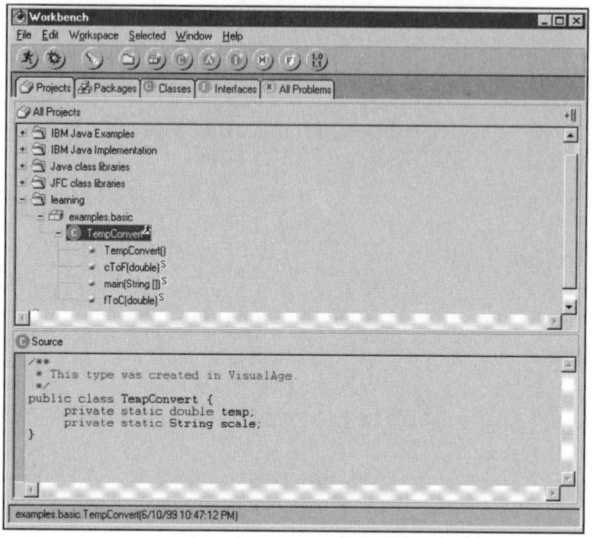

**Figure 1-7**   VisualAge Workbench

2. Right-click on `TempConvert` to select it and open the popup menu. You must use this menu to enter the arguments that you would type on the command line if you were using the **java** command.

3. Select **Properties**, the bottom item in the popup menu, to open the **Properties** window for the `TempConvert` class. This window has three tabs. The first tab, labeled **Program,** should be displayed so that the window looks like Figure 1-8. You use the second tab, **Class Path**, for programs that use classes from other projects, JAR files, or folders in the file system. The third tab, **Info**, gives information such as the time the class was last modified and its version number.

4. In the **Command-line arguments** text field, type a number, followed by a space and the word "Celsius" or "Fahrenheit". Click **OK**.

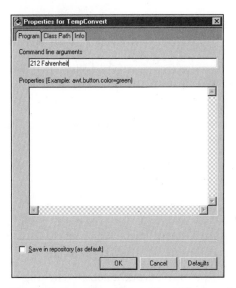

**Figure 1-8**    Class Properties Window for the TempConvert class

5. Back in the WorkBench, click the **Run** button on the toolbar. **Run** is the first button; it shows an icon of a running person. The program now runs.

6. If the program runs successfully, the **Console** window opens. The console window, shown in Figure 1-9, shows the output for input arguments "212" and "F". If the console window does not open automatically, click **Console** in the **Window** menu.

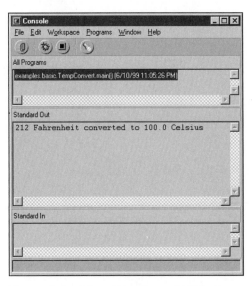

**Figure 1-9**    VisualAge Console Window

The Console window in Figure 1-9 has three panels:

➤ The top panel lists program threads that are running or have recently ended.

➤ The middle panel contains output sent the standard output stream. Here, you should see the expected output from running the class.

➤ For programs that take command-line input, you use the bottom panel for standard input. Type here what you would type on the command line. For this program, no further action is required.

If your program works, you can run it repeatedly.

To run a program again:

1. You can clear the contents of the **Console** window at any time by click-ing the first toolbar button from the left. The **Clear** icon looks like a blackboard eraser. Closing the Console window is optional.

2. To run the program again, return to the workbench by clicking on the **Workbench** window or selecting **Workbench** from the **Windows** menu. Right-click the `TempConvert` class, and open the **Properties** window from the popup menu exactly as you did for the test run.

3. Enter different **Command-line arguments**, click **OK** and, then click the **Run** button again.

If your program does not work, you can use the VisualAge debugger to find the source of the error. So that you can see an incorrectly executing program, you will introduce an error into this program.

To deliberately introduce an error:

1. Open the **Properties** window for the `TempConvert` class and change the **Command line arguments** to "**bad input**", omitting the quotation marks. Click **OK.**

2. Click **Run** again. This time, the debugger window opens automatically and looks like Figure 1-10.

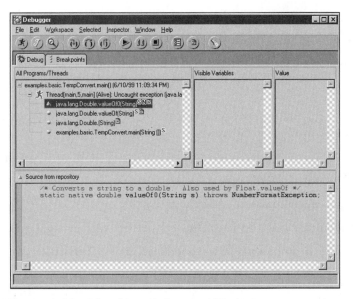

**Figure 1-10** VisualAge Debugger Window

VisualAge provides a full-function debugger. The debugger window opens when the program encounters an error condition, or exception, or when it reaches a line of code where you have set a breakpoint. In the previous steps, an exception has occurred because input string "bad" does not conform to a valid number format.

In any editor window, you can set **breakpoints** on an executable line of code by double-clicking in the margin to the right of the line. A blue circle in the margin indicates a breakpoint. If a class runs to a line where a breakpoint is set, execution is suspended and the debugger window opens. Then you can step through the code line by line, step over or into method calls, run to the end of the current method, run to the next breakpoint, and so on. When execution is suspended by a breakpoint, you can modify code, recompile, and continue to run using the modified code.

The debugger window has four panes, three across the top and one below:

➤ **All Programs/Threads:** The top-left pane lists the running threads or programs and the active methods. If you resize this pane to make it broader, you can see that the **main** method is alive but reporting an **uncaught exception**. The lines below **main** show that the exception is thrown in the highlighted method **java.lang.Double.valueOf( )**, which is called by the constructor **java.lang.Double( )**, which is called, in turn, by `TempConvert.main( )`.

➤ **Visible Variables:** The middle-top pane lists variables visible in the high-lighted method. If you highlight different methods, the contents of this pane change.

➤ **Value:** The top-right pane shows the values of variables selected in the middle-top pane.

➤ **Source:** The bottom pane is an editor window showing the source of the highlighted method, if the source is available.

Because this class has thrown with an exception, you must terminate the program and the debugging session.

To stop the program and close the debugger:

1. Select the line in the top-left pane with the running person symbol.

2. Right-click to bring up a popup menu, and select **Terminate**.

3. Close the debugger window to return to the workbench.

If you do not know what went wrong, you can now set breakpoints before the line that caused the problem and run the program again to monitor execution with the debugger. In this case, we know the problem is bad input.

At this point, it is a good idea to version the `TempConvert` class. Versioning makes a permanent copy of the current state of a project, package, or class in the code repository. You can continue to work with the class, make more versions, or even delete the class, and later reload saved versions from the repository. The versioning capability of VisualAge is a great productivity aid to professional programmers because it serves as a source code control system that is integrated into the IDE.

To version the class:

1. Right-click on the `TempConvert` class in the workbench to bring up the popup menu.

2. Select **Manage** and then **Version** from the popup menus.

3. The **Versioning Selected Items** window appears. Accept the default version number, 1.0 for the first version, and click **OK**.

4. If you want to see what version numbers are loaded into your workspace, click the rightmost button on the workbench toolbar. If projects, classes, or packages are not versioned, the date and time they were last changed is printed after their name. For versioned items, the version number appears.

5. Click the rightmost toolbar button again to hide version numbers.

Ultimately, you usually want to deploy your program by exporting the project, package, or class out of the VisualAge repository into the file system. You can

**1**

export source and compiled code to a JAR file or to a file folder, or copy VisualAge's internal representation of the code to a repository file.

To export the source and compiled bytecode for the `TempConvert` class to the file system:

1. Click on the `TempConvert` class in the workbench to select it. Make sure the class is highlighted.

2. Select **Export** from the **File** menu.

3. The **Export SmartGuide** starts. Select **Directory** in the first window and click **Next >**.

4. The **Export to a directory** window opens, as shown in Figure 1-11. Enter the name of a destination folder in the **Directory** text field, or click the **Browse** button to find and select a destination folder. In Figure 1-11 the destination is **D:\myJava.**

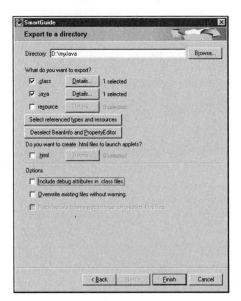

**Figure 1-11** VisualAge Export SmartGuide

5. Select **.class** and **.java** from the first three buttons.

6. Deselect **Include debug attributes in .class files** from the Options buttons.

7. Click **Finish**. If the destination folder does not exist, a message window pops up asking if you want to create it now. Click **Yes**. If the export is about to overwrite an existing file, a window pops up asking whether or not to proceed. Click **Yes** if you do not mind replacing an existing copy of the class or **No** to stop the export.

If you now look at the file system outside VisualAge, you should find the files **examples\basic\TempConvert.java** and **exmples\basic\TempConvert.class** in the folder you specified. The .java file is suitable for compiling with the **javac** command, and the .class file can be run with the **java** command.

The last step is to close VisualAge.

To close VisualAge:

1. Click **Exit VisualAge** from the **File** menu.

2. A window opens to tell you that your workspace will be saved. Click **OK** to exit or **Cancel** to return to the workbench.

You can run many of the sample programs in the following chapters in VisualAge using these steps as a guide. To save on input time, you can import the entire contents of the file **examples.jar** into the `learning` project you created here. To use the import SmartGuide, open the workbench and click **Import** on the **File** menu.

# COMMENTS IN THE JAVA PROGRAMMING LANGUAGE

The Java programming language recognizes three kinds of comments:

➤ Single-line comments start with a double slash, **//**, and continue to the end of the line of source code.

➤ Block comments start with a slash and an asterisk, **/\***, and terminate with an asterisk and a slash, **\*/**. They can start anywhere in a line, span several lines, and stop anywhere.

➤ Doc comments start with a slash and two asterisks, **/\*\***, and terminate with one asterisk and a slash, **\*/**. Because doc comments conform to the syntax of block comments, the compiler can treat both types of comments the same.

Use single-line comments whenever possible. The following lines demonstrate what can happen when you deliberately or inadvertently nest block comments:

```
/* start outer comment
/* inner comment */
end outer comment */
```

When it parses these lines, the compiler sees that the first **/\*** starts a comment and ignores everything up to the next **\*/,** including the second **/\***. Therefore, the characters **end outer comment \*/** are treated as code, and the result is a compile error. It is a good idea to reserve block comments for the sole purpose of commenting out large chunks of code. You can then nest single-line comments within a block comment. For example, the following lines compile correctly:

```
/* start outer comment
// inner comment
end outer comment */
```

## Doc Comments

Most Java development environments provide a utility for generating HTML documentation directly from Java source code. The resulting documentation is suitable for other programmers who use your classes and is not intended for end users. The documentation lists classes, methods, arguments, and other information that programmers need to know when they use your classes in their programs.

In the Java SDK, the **javadoc** tool generates HTML pages from the declarations in your classes. When run on a suite of packages, the **javadoc** tool creates a web of HTML pages. The web has a page for each class that lists all methods and fields in the class, and much more. The web includes pages that show all classes in a hierarchy diagram, list all packages, list all classes in each package, and provide an index of fields and methods in all classes.

You can insert descriptive text into your source code and have that text automatically included in the documentation produced by **javadoc**. Doc comments are the mechanism you use to add descriptions to **javadoc** output. Use doc comments to explain the purpose of a class, what methods do, what the arguments represent, and so forth. A good example of **javadoc** output based on extensive doc comments is the Core API component of the online documentation for the Java platform API.

Unlike the other kinds of comments, doc comments are meaningful only when placed before declarations. Misplaced doc comments are ignored. You can put doc comments before the declarations of classes and members, but not before executable statements within methods. Generally, you provide doc comments for the elements of Java code that are important to the programmers using the code. For example, you usually describe the arguments of a method and what the method returns. Doc comments can appear before the following kinds of declarations:

➤  Class
➤  Interface
➤  Method
➤  Field

The example programs in this book use doc comments, and all the constructs that doc comments can describe are covered in the early chapters of this book. For example, in the `TempConvert` class, doc comments precede the declaration of **main**:

```
/** main method of temperature conversion class
 * takes two input argument from command line
 * @param args[0] degrees as a real number
 * @param args[1] temperature scale C or F
 * @exception NumberFormatException occurs if the
 * first argument cannot be parsed as a number
 */
 public static void main(String [] args) {
```

Notice that the first line of the doc comment for this method is a short description of the method. As a rule, you should start the doc comments for classes and methods with a one-sentence summary of the class or method.

To parse a doc comment, **javadoc** looks at the characters that come after /** and before the matching */. It discards the * characters at the start of each line. For all but the first line, **javadoc** also ignores blanks and tabs preceding the initial * characters. The text, which remains after the * characters and the whitespace are trimmed off, is incorporated into the HTML documentation.

A doc comment should start with a one-sentence overview of the item being documented. Because the text is inserted into HTML documents, you can include HTML markup. Avoid using HTML tags for headings, because the tool generates its own headings. You may have to experiment to find out which tags are safe. As a rule of thumb, HTML tags that change the font or highlight characters work well, but HTML tags that alter the structure of an HTML document may conflict with **javadoc** presentation. The following code has a doc comment that uses HTML tags **<code>** and **</code>** to highlight a name:

```
/** Method to write X to <code>System.out</code>.
 */
```

## Using javadoc Tags

In addition to including HTML tags, you can include **javadoc** tags in your doc comments. Use them to generate subheadings such as "Parameters," "Returns," and "See Also" in the description of classes, interfaces, and members.

1

*Syntax*

*@tag*

---

*Dissection*

All **javadoc** tags start with an @ character. Each tag must start a new line. Whether the tag is appropriate or not depends on what it precedes. The **javadoc** tags and the headings that they produce are listed here, in the order that they usually appear in source code:

---

*Tags*

➤ To create a heading "Author," insert the following tag:

**@author** *author_name*

You can put this tag before a class or an interface. The name can be any string. This tag is ignored unless you include the **-author** option when you run **javadoc**.

➤ To create a heading "Version," insert the tag:

**@version**

You can put this tag before a class or an interface. Often, the version text follows a numerical pattern such as 1.1 or 3.0.2. This tag is ignored unless you include the **–version** option when you run **javadoc**.

➤ To create a heading "Parameters," insert the following tag:

**@param** *variable_name*

This tag goes before the definition of a method. It gives the name of one argument of a method followed by a description. If the method has more than one argument, provide a **@param** tag for each argument. Group these tags together.

➤ To create a heading "Returns," insert the following tag:

**@return** *description*

Put this tag before a method definition to describe the return value of a method.

➤ To create a heading "Throws," insert the either of two synonymous tags:

**@exception** *fully-qualified_class_name description*

**@throws** *fully-qualified_class_name description*

Put this tag before a method definition to list and describe an exception that the method can throw. The fully qualified class name is a hypertext link to the exception class. If the method can throw more than one type of exception, provide an **@exception** or **@throws** tag for each exception class. You should group these tags together.

➤ To create a heading "See Also," insert one of the following tags:

**@see** *package.class_name*

**@see** *package.class_name#field_name*

**@see** *package.class_name#method_name(argument_list)*

Use this tag in any doc comments to insert cross-references in the HTML documentation. This tag creates a hypertext link to another class or member. You can omit the package name for classes in the current package and the class name for other members of the same class. You can include any number of **@see** tags for one declaration.

➤ To generate an inline hypertext link, insert the following tag including the braces, { }, anywhere in a doc comment.

**{@link** *name label*}

You can use this tag in any doc comment. Unlike other **javadoc** tags, a {@link} often appears in the middle of a sentence in a doc comment. For example, if the following appears in a doc comment in a class called MyClass:

```
To do magic, use the {@link #myMethod(args) myMethod}
method.
```

The resulting HTML includes:

```
To do magic, use the <a
href="MyClass.html#myMethod(args)">
myMethod</a> method.
```

➤ To create a heading "Since," insert the following tag:

**@since** *text*

You can use this tag in any doc comment. The text explains when the package, class, or member became available. In the Java platform API documentation, the text is usually "JDK 1.0", "JDK 1.1", or "JDK 1.2", reflecting the fact that the Java 2 SKD was previously called the Java Development Kit (JDK).

➤ To create a heading "Deprecated," insert the following tag:

**@deprecated** *text*

Typically, you use the **@deprecated** tag for a package, class, or method that is legacy code from an earlier version. If you cannot delete old code because others still depend on it, this tag gives you an opportunity at least to inform users that the class or method may not be available in the future. The text should include either "Replaced by. . ." or "No replacement."

➤ To say that a class is serializable means that objects of the class can be saved, usually by writing the object to file, in a form suitable for restoring later. Object serialization is discussed in Chapter 8. You should indicate fields that are saved when the object is serialized using one of the following tags:

**@serial** *field_description*

**@serialField** *field_name field_type field_description*

**@serialData** *data_description*

---

The compiler looks at doc comments as it is compiling a class and sets an attribute on the .class file for any deprecated class, method, or interface that it finds. Whenever a class is compiled, the .class file attributes of the classes, methods, and interfaces that the class uses are checked to see if they are deprecated. The compiler prints a warning when asked to compile code that uses a deprecated class, interface, or method.

The Java 2 platform introduced a number of enhancements to doc comments. A new concept of **doclets** was introduced and is described briefly in the following section "Creating HTML from javadoc." Superficially, the **javadoc** tool appears to work much as it did in the original Java platform, but the architecture of the tool has been reworked so that the format and content of the resulting HTML is determined by doclets.

You can include package-level comments and systemwide comments. To do this, you provide separate HTML files containing package descriptions and summary statements. For meaningful summary comments, an earlier convention becomes a rule for doc comments in Java 2: The first sentences in each package and class description should be a summary statement.

The **javadoc** tags have changed since the original Java platform:

➤ The **@since** tag was introduced in version 1.1. of Java platform. There was no need to indicate new elements in the original version.

➤ The **{@link}** and **@throws** tags are new with Java 2. The **@throws** tag is added because you use it to describe exceptions listed in the throws clause of the method.

➤ Java 2 enhanced object serialization and added the **@serial**, **@serialData**, and **@serialField** tags.

## Creating HTML from javadoc

The only reason to include doc comments, rather than ordinary comments, in your code is to prepare to run the **javadoc** tool or the feature of your IDE that generates HTML documentation from source code. Usually, you run **javadoc** against the source for all classes in a package or suite of packages. The tool parses the doc comments in the input files. To get HTML output in the standard format, simply run the **javadoc** program.

You can customize the **javadoc** output by writing a doclet. A **doclet** is a plug-in program for the **javadoc** tool that formats and outputs the required documentation. By default, **javadoc** uses a standard doclet that comes with the Java platform. The **javadoc** tool preprocesses the doc comments into a data structure and delegates to a doclet the job of converting the data into output. A doclet could, for example, generate documentation that conforms to your company's style guidelines, generate XML or RTF files rather than HTML, recognize customized **javadoc** tags, or perform special tasks such as detecting methods that have no doc comments. The classes in the package **com.sun.javadoc** provide the API used by doclets.

Regardless of whether you use the standard doclet or another doclet for customized output, you run the **javadoc** command to create the documentation.

### Syntax

**javadoc** [*options*] *package_or_class_names*

### Dissection

The most commonly used options of the **javadoc** tool are listed below. After the options you can supply one or more class names or package names separated by spaces.

### Options

➤ **-author**

Specify the **author** option to tell **javadoc** to process @**author** tags, which are ignored by default.

➤ **-classpath** *path;path;*

The **-classpath** option tells **javadoc** where to look for classes that are referenced in the definition of classes being documented. For example, the return type of a method may be a referenced class. Classes mentioned in doc comments are not referenced classes. The **javadoc** tool loads referenced classes while it is running and prints a message if it cannot find them.

➤ **-d** *folder_name*

If you want to place the HTML output files in any other folder than the current folder, specify a destination with the **-d** option. The folder must already exist.

**1**

➤ -doclet *class*

The **–doclet** option gives the name of the class that starts the doclet to be used by this run of **javadoc.** Omit this tag to use the standard doclet.

➤ -nodeprecated

Specify **nodeprecrated** to exclude sections marked with the @deprecated tag.

➤ -noindex

Specify **noindex** to tell **javadoc** not to output the index page that **javadoc** creates by default.

➤ -notree

Specify **notree** to tell **javadoc** not to output the class hierarchy page that **javadoc** creates by default.

➤ -overview *path\filename*

If you want overview documentation, you must prepare a source file for the overview. The **overview** option gives the name of this file. Typically, you use a file named overview.html that resides in the same folder as the top-level package.

➤ -package

Specify **package** to include all classes and members except those with private access. The default is **protected**.

➤ -private

Specify **private** to include all classes and members. The default is **protected**.

➤ -protected

Specify **protected** to include protected and public classes and members. This is the default.

➤ **–public**

Specify **public** to include only public classes, interfaces, and members. The default is **protected**.

➤ -sourcepath *path;path;...*

When **javadoc** is operating on packages, you can specify search paths for the packages in the **–sourcepath** option

➤ **–version**

Specify **version** to tell **javadoc** to process @version tags, which are ignored by default.

*Code Example*

```
javadoc —d docs monit.gain monit.loss
Loading source files for monit.gain
Loading source files for monit.loss
Constructing Javadoc information...
Building tree for all the packages and classes...
Building index for all the packages and classes...
Generating docs\overview-tree.html...
Generating docs\index-all.html...
Generating docs\deprecate-list.html...
Building index for all classes...
Generating docs\allclasses-s\packages.html...
Generating docs\overview-summary.html...
Generating docs\overview-frame.html...
Generating docs\monit\gain/package-summary.html...
Generating docs\monit/gain/package-tree.html...
Generating docs\monit\gain/package-frame.html...
Generating docs\monit\loss/package-summary.html...
Generating docs\monit\loss/package-tree.html...
Generating docs\monit\loss/package-frame.html...
Generating docs\monit\gain/Storm.html...
. . . lines omitted for other classes
Generating docs\serialized-form.html...
Generating docs\package-list...
Generating docs\help-doc.html...
Generating docs\stylesheet.css...
```

*Code Dissection*

This **javadoc** command generates documentation on two packages—
monit.gain and monit.loss—that reside in the current folder. One of the
classes in the monit.gain package is called Storm. The resulting documentation
is added to an existing subfolder of the current folder called docs. The output listed
here appears on the console when you run **javadoc**. Of course, the output of
interest is the set of HTML files that the console output says it is generating.

When documenting packages, the **javadoc** tool locates input files much like
the **javac** compiler:

1. You can specify another input location than the current folder by including
   the **—sourcepath** option.

2. If you omit **—sourcepath**, **javadoc** uses the paths specified with the
   **—classpath** option for both source and referenced classes.

3. If you specify neither option, **javadoc** uses the paths set in the
   CLASSPATH environment variable.

4. If the CLASSPATH is not set, **javadoc** looks in the current folder.

To run **javadoc** on one or more classes, you must either go to the folder that contains the classes or give the full path to the source files. The **–sourcepath** option applies only at the package level. For example, to generate documentation just for the `monit.gain.Storm` class when monit is a subfolder of folder myJava on the D drive, issue the command:

```
javadoc D:\myJava\monit\gain\Storm.java
```

If you followed the instructions in *"Read This Before You Begin"* to extract the files from the JAR file named **examples.jar**, the set of packages containing the example programs from this book reside on your hard drive. If you have not created the HTML documentation yet, you can do so now. Go to the folder containing **examples.jar**. Enter the following command:

```
examples\buildHTML
```

This batch file contains the following two commands:

```
mkdir docs
javadoc –d docs examples.basic examples.classes ...
```

The documentation is now complete, and you can look at the documentation you just created. Because the files are HTML files, use your Web browser. Open the Web browser, and load one of the files created by **javadoc**: **docs/index.html**. Your display should look similar to the page partially shown in Figure 1-12. To maximize the amount of the page displayed, all Netscape toolbars are hidden in the Netscape session that is displayed in Figure 1-12.

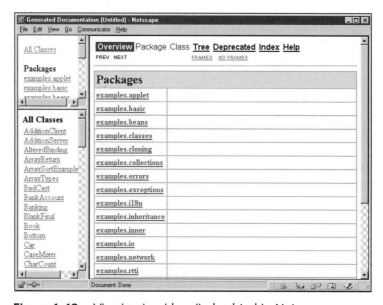

**Figure 1-12**   Viewing jars/docs/index.html in Netscape

The file **index.html** lists all the packages documented in this HTML web. Each package name is a hypertext link to a page containing a list of classes in that package. Look up `TempConvert` class to see the effects of the doc comments in the **TempConvert.java** file.

To see the effects of the doc comments in the `TempConvert` class:

Click package **examples.basic** to bring up a list of the classes in the `basic` package. Click **TempConvert** in that list to display the page that is partially shown in Figure 1-13 and Figure 1-14.

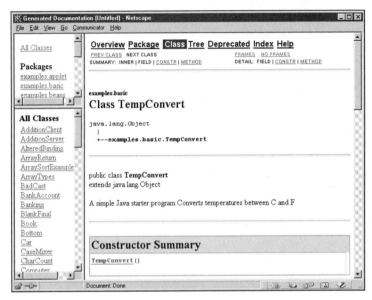

**Figure 1-13**   The top of the generated HTML page for a class

In Figures 1-13 and 1-14, notice that the description of the class and the description of method **main** use the text from the doc comments in the source file. The **javadoc** output includes additional useful information, such as the class-relationship diagram near the top of the page. Use the links at the top of the page to navigate the documentation web. For example, click **index** to see a page that lists fields and methods in alphabetic order and provides links to each one. Note that fields and methods in referenced classes are included. Click **Help** for an explanation of how the documentation web is organized.

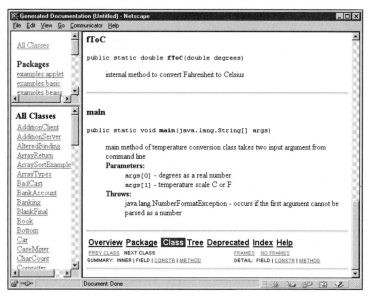

**Figure 1-14**    The bottom of the generated HTML page for a class

# PACKAGING A PROGRAM FOR DISTRIBUTION

A very important step in software development is packaging your code for distribution and ensuring that your users can install or deploy your classes. When you work in Java, you often end up with a large number of relatively small files containing classes, multimedia resources, data, and possibly your source and **javadoc** output. The standard way to distribute these files is to combine them into a Java archive file using the **jar** tool.

Before you run the **jar** tool, make sure your files reside in the proper folders on your file system. The resulting JAR file contains a folder structure that mirrors the folders and subfolders you input to the **jar** command. You can list input files individually, but an easy and common practice is to specify folder names and let the tool automatically process all files and subfolders in the folders you specify.

*Syntax*

**jar** [*options*] [*manifest*] *destination input-files*

*Dissection*

The most commonly used forms of the **jar** command for building and extracting files from a JAR file are listed here.

### Options

To specify an option, include its letter to the option token. For example, to specify options **c**, **f**, and **v**, specify option **cvf**. Note that option letters are case-sensitive. Some options are:

➤ **c** Create a new or empty JAR.

➤ **t** Type a list of the contents of an existing JAR.

➤ **x** Extract files from an existing JAR.

➤ **f** The JAR file is named in a jar command. If you do not supply this argument and a name for the JAR file, the tool reads from or writes to the console.

➤ **m** Include manifest information from the named manifest file.

➤ **0** (digit 0) Do not compress the contents of the JAR. If you omit this option, the JAR file is compressed using the same compression format as a .zip file.

➤ **M** Do not create a manifest file.

➤ **u** Update an existing file by adding files or changing the manifest.

➤ **v** Send verbose status output to the console.

### Manifest

An optional manifest within the JAR lists the files in the jar and information about the elements stored in those files. You do not need a manifest for ordinary classes. However, you must specify that a class is a JavaBean in the manifest. Chapter 15 describes how to package JavaBeans. If you prepare or have a manifest in a separate file, specify the manifest filename after the options on the command line.

### Destination

Specify the JAR filename after the options and optional manifest file.

### Input Files

List the input files, which may include the JAR itself if you are working with an existing JAR. You can use wildcards in file names. For example, specify * to include all files in the current folder.

### Code Example

```
jar 0cf myProg.jar myApp media
```

1

### Code Dissection

The current folder has two subfolders: myApp contains the classes in a package called **myApp**, and media contains audio and image files used by the classes. With this command, you can package them all into one JAR called myProg. The resulting JAR is not compressed and has a default manifest.

### Code Example

```
jar tf examples.jar
```

### Code Dissection

The **jar** command lists the contents of **examples.jar**.

You can distribute packages of classes that are used by applications, applets, and servlets in JAR files.

➤ To deploy an application distributed in a JAR file, make sure the JAR file is listed on your CLASSPATH.

➤ Applets are invoked from HTML files. The HTML **<APPLET>** tag has attributes for naming the applet class and required JAR files and is described in Chapter 14. When a Web server downloads an HTML file that contains APPLET tags, it also downloads all .class and .jar files named in the APPLET tag.

➤ As described in Chapter 18, you must put servlet classes in a folder reserved by the web server to deploy servlets. If the classes used by the servlets are in one or more JARs, set the CLASSPATH for the Web server to include the JARs.

## SUMMARY

The Java programming language is one component of the **Java platform**. Sun Microsystems officially announced the Java programming language in 1995 and gave the world a new programming paradigm with the potential that programs can be written only once and then run anywhere. The language is designed to work with networks, the World Wide Web, and can be used in anything from the smallest embedded systems to the largest enterprise-wide applications.

To set up your workstation for Java programming, you install the Java platform, which contains the language, a number of packages that contain the core classes, and the **Java Virtual Machine (JVM).** The JVM gives the Java platform its architecture-neutral development and run-time environment. The JVM translates Java source code into a platform-independent form called **bytecode**.

With the Java programming language, you can write standalone **applications** that run in the JVM, **applets** that are embedded in Web pages and run by Java-enabled Web browsers or **servlets** that run in Java-enabled Web servers. JVM provides security by controlling what that program can do. By default, down-loaded applets are considered untrusted and cannot access certain local resources or perform actions that potentially compromise the security of the JVM.

A variety of application development tools are available. The Java platform is available free of charge from Sun Microsystems for Windows and Solaris oper-ating systems and from other vendors for a wide range of other platforms. The Java platform provides a suite of command-line tools. For an IDE with a GUI, you can acquire products such as VisualAge for Java from IBM.

Filenames are important in the Java platform. Here are some rules to follow for naming classes, packages, and files:

➤ If you use the basic Java platform tools, you compile Java source code into bytecode with the following command:

**javac** *filename*

➤ You load and run classes with the following command:

**java** *classname*

➤ To run applets, you must load the **HTML** document that contains the applet into a Web browser or run an **appletviewer** utility.

➤ To generate HTML documentation from the source code, use the follow-ing command:

**javadoc** [*options*] *class_or_package_names*

➤ There are strict rules for naming files and folders. The JVM depends on these rules to locate classes, so that they can be dynamically loaded as required at run-time.

➤ A source file can contain only one public class and must have the same name as the class. The extension for a source file is .java.

➤ The compiler creates files that also have the same name as the class, but the extension is .class.

➤ If classes are collected into a package, they must reside in the one folder, and the folder name must be the same as the package name.

➤ You can organize packages using root names, such as mywork in mywork.a, mywork.b, and mywork.c. Packages that share a root name must reside in a subfolder of a folder with the same name as the root. For example, a class in mywork.a must reside in subfolder **a** of folder **mywork**.

➤ The JVM searches the paths stored in the CLASSPATH environment vari-able for packages and classes to load.

The Java programming language itself is object-oriented. The syntax bears a strong resemblance to C and has many of the object-oriented features of C++. In the Java programming language, every program element belongs to a class, and a program is a collection of classes.

The executable code in classes makes up the methods of the class. A class also can store data in fields. Methods and fields are the members of a class. To be usable as an application, a class must have a **main** method.

Many of the features of the Java programming language are provided not just by the language, but also by the core classes. The core classes in the package **java.lang** support the language. Java programs make extensive use of the core classes.

One of the innovative features of the Java programming language is doc comments. The **javadoc** tool can parse Java source code and generate an HTML documentation web. You use doc comments to provide the text in the HTML pages. Doc comments begin with **/\*\*** and end with **\*/**. You can include HTML tags to format the text in doc comments and **javadoc** tags to add subtitles for specific information.

The SDK provides a mechanism for packaging Java classes with resources, such as HTML, GIF, and data files, for distribution and deployment. You can combine all the files your classes need in **Java Archive (JAR)** files using the **jar** tool. Source, bytecode, and other files used by all the example programs in this book are in a JAR file **examples.jar** on the CD-ROM that accompanies this book.

## QUESTIONS

1. True or False:

   The Java platform contains only the class libraries needed for developing Java programs, and you must purchase development tools separately.

2. True or False:

   The **appletviewer** program is an extremely simple Web browser that only knows how to display Java applets.

3. If you issue the command `javac MyClass.java` and `MyClass` uses the public class `HerClass`, which, in turn, uses the public class `HisClass`, which of the following statements accurately describe what source files are compiled? Select the best answer.

   a. The files **MyClass.java**, **HerClass.java**, and **HisClass.java** are compiled immediately.

b. The files **MyClass.java**, **HerClass.java**, and **HisClass.java** are compiled only if the modification timestamp is more recent than the .class byte-code file with the same base filename.

c. The file **MyClass.java** is compiled immediately, but **HerClass.java** and **HisClass.java** are compiled only when a statement that uses them is executed, and only if the modification timestamp is more recent than the .class bytecode file with the same base filename.

d. The files **MyClass.java** and **HerClass.java** are compiled if the modification timestamp is more recent than the .class bytecode file with the same base filename. File **HisClass.java** is not compiled because **MyClass.java** does not have any direct dependency on it.

e. File **MyClass.java** is compiled immediately. **HerClass.java** is compiled if the modification timestamp is more recent than the .class bytecode file with the same base filename. The file **HisClass.java** is compiled if **HerClass.java** is compiled *and* if the **HisClass.java** modification time-stamp is more recent than its .class bytecode file.

4. True or False:

   You can put only one class definition in a single .java source file.

5. On an operating system that treats filenames as case-sensitive, which of the following declarations are valid for a class for which the source is stored in the file Fred.java? Select as many as apply:

   a.
   ```
   package myPackage;
   public class Fred {
   static void main( String[] args ) {
      /* body of Fred.main */
      }
   }
   class Joe {
      //     body of class Joe
   ```

   b.
   ```
   package myPackage;
   public class FRED {
      // body of class FRED
   }
   ```

   c.
   ```
   public class Fred {
   int month = 1;
   int day = 21;
   }
   ```

d. `static void Fred.main( String[] args )  {`

`// body of Fred.main}`

`}`

6. What is allowed as a return type of the **main** method that is the entry point of a Java application? Select all that apply.

a. **int**

b. No return type may be specified

c. **void**

d. Any integral type, including **char**

e. **int** or **void**

f. Any defined type

7. How do you distinguish a doc comment from other comment styles?

8. Which of the following are special tags recognized by the **javadoc** tool? Select all that apply.

a. **@param**

b. **@exception**

c. **@obsolete**

d. **@returns**

e. **@author**

9. True or False:

Doc comments are recognized wherever they are placed within a source file.

10. What kinds of HTML tags should not be used within doc comments?

11. What **javadoc** tag is used to create a hypertext link to another class or method?

---

# EXERCISES

## Debugging

1. Correct the error in the following program:

```
package questions.c1;
public class Debug1_1
    public static void main( String[] args )
        int a = 6;
```

```
            // now output the result of doubling the
            variable a //
            System.out.println( "The answer is " +  a*2 );
      }
   }
```

2. Correct the error in the following program:

```
package questions.c1;
   public class Debug1_2
   public static void main( String[] args )
      /* declare a variable
      int a = 6;
      /* output its square root
      System.out.println( Math.sqrt( a ) );
   }
}
```

3. Correct the following program:

```
package questions.c1;
int a = 0;
int z = 20;
public class Debug1_3
   public static void main( String[] args )
      for ( int b = a; b < z; b += 2; )
      System.out.println( b );
   }
}
```

## Complete the Solution

1. Use the **jar** tool to extract the file **questions.c1.Complete1_1.java** from the **question.jar** file on the CD-ROM that accompanies this book. Complete the class `Complete1_1` by adding a statement that outputs the result of dividing the variable **z** by the variable **y**.

2. Use the **jar** tool to extract the file **questions.c1.Complete1_2.java** from the **question.jar** file on the CD-ROM that accompanies this book. Add doc comments to the program `Complete1_2`.

## Discovery

1. Modify the **main** method of the **TempConvert** class to accept uppercase or lowercase letters to indicate the input temperature scale.

2. Add additional doc comments to the **TempConvert** class, and then run the **javadoc** utility against the source to create HTML documentation.

3. Write an application to calculate a person's body mass index (BMI) by applying the following formula:

*BMI = weight_in_kilograms / height_in_meters$^2$*

Use the TempConvert class as a model for your class. The user must input his or her height in meters and weight in kilograms as command-line arguments. The program calculates and prints the BMI. To test the program, use the fact that a large person who is 2 meters tall and weighs 100 kg has a BMI of 25.

4. If you found Question 3 easy, enhance the program to accept height in inches or meters and weight in kilograms or pounds. Add command-line arguments to specify the scales. You can use the following conversion formula:

*1 kilogram = 2.2 pounds*
*1 meter = 39.36 inches*

5. BMI values in the range 20 to 27 are considered compatible with good health, with 22 to 25 being the ideal range for average body types. If your program is correctly outputting BMI values, enhance it to print a message for the five possibilities:

➤ BMI is too low for optimum health.

➤ BMI is low but not a health risk.

➤ Congratulations for an ideal BMI.

➤ BMI high but not a health risk.

➤ BMI is too high for optimum health.

## CHAPTER TWO

# ELEMENTARY PROGRAMMING CONCEPTS

## In this chapter you will:

➤ Learn the introductory syntax and semantics of the Java programming language.

➤ Write simple programs that perform console input and output.

☕ Recognize correctly constructed variable declarations and identifiers.

☕ Write code using if and switch statements and identify legal argument types for these statements.

☕ Write code using all forms of loops, including labeled and unlabeled use of break and continue; state the values taken by loop counter variables during and after loop execution.

☕ Identify all Java programming language keywords.

☕ State the effect of using a variable of any kind when no explicit assignment has been made to it.

☕ Determine the result of applying any operator, including assignment operators, to operands of any type.

☕ In an expression involving the operators & | && || and variables of known values, state which operands are evaluated and the value of the expression.

☕ Write code using the following methods of the **java.lang.Math** class: **abs, ceil, floor, max, min, random, round, sin, cos, tan,** and **sqrt.**

☕ State the correspondence between index values in the argument array passed to a main method and the respective command line arguments.

## INTRODUCTION

All programs in all languages contain a repertory of statements with which you build your code. Procedures or subprograms combine statements into functional units. Expressions within statements are evaluated while the program is running. This chapter covers these common elements in the Java programming language, and some features that are specific to this new language.

## VARIABLES AND IDENTIFIERS

All variables have both a type and an identifier. The type determines the nature of a variable, and the identifier is the variable's name in the Java code. Variables can be categorized by type:

➤ **Primitive types** are predefined types for single data items such as numbers, characters, or boolean values.

➤ **Reference types** are aggregates, including classes and arrays. Many predefined core classes exist, and you can also define your own classes.

A declaration associates a name with a type and defines a new variable for the Java code to use. The simplest form of declaration is that of a variable inside a method.

*Syntax*

*type identifier* **[** = *initializer* **]**;

*Dissection*

➤ The *type* is any type or class name recognized in the Java programming language. If the type is a class, the variable is an object that instantiates that class.

➤ The *identifier* can be any legal name except keywords and the reserved literals **true**, **false**, and **null**. The Java keywords are listed in Table 2-1.

➤ Including an *initializer* is optional, but the Java compiler flags as an error any attempt to access the value of an uninitialized variable.

*Code Example*

```
int AOK;
float blossom;
char c = 'c', d2;
boolean flag = true;
String greeting = "Hello";
Dog phydoux = new Dog( "poodle" );
```

*Code Dissection*

The first four declarations create variables of primitive types.

Strings are not primitive types. They are provided by the core class **String**.

The last of the declarations creates an object called **phydoux** for which the type is a user-defined class, **Dog**.

A variable that is declared inside a method is local to the method. You can define local variables anywhere within a method body. You can add them as you need them or follow the convention of declaring them only at the start of blocks.

Variables have scope that determines when the identifier is visible and usable by the code. The scope of a local variable extends from its declaration to the end of the immediately enclosing block, with the one exception that the scope of variables defined in the initialization of **for** loops is the body of the **for** loop.

Variables that are declared outside methods are called **fields**. Fields, like methods, are members of the class in which they are declared. Their scope is the class in which they are declared. Chapter 4 explains how the fields and methods declared in a class make up the behavior and attributes of the class. The declaration of a field is slightly more complicated than the declaration of a method.

## Syntax

[*access_specifier*] [*qualifier*] *type identifier* [ = *initializer*];

## Dissection

➤ Variables that are fields of a class have an access specifier that determines whether other classes can use them. You can specify **public**, **private**, or **protected**. As with a class, if you omit the access specifier, the field has default access and is accessible only from classes in the same package. Specify **public** to make the field accessible from anywhere. Specify **private** to restrict access to the class in which the field is declared. Use the specifier **protected** with inheritance. Local variables cannot have access specifiers.

➤ The Java programming language recognizes a number of qualifiers. The qualifier **static** declares a field to be common to the whole class. A static field, also known as a class variable, can be used regardless of whether any variables that instantiate the class have been created. In contrast, every instance of a class has its own copy of the nonstatic variables defined in the class. If you omit the qualifier **static**, the field can be used only with an object of the class. Local variables cannot be static.

➤ The *type* is any valid type in the Java programming language.

➤ The *identifier* is any identifier recognized by the Java programming language.

➤ The *initializer* is optional. If you omit it, the Java programming language automatically assigns a default initial value determined by the type of the field.

## Code Example

```
public boolean inStock;
private static int counter = 60;
private String[] message;
Dog chester = new Dog ( "Great Dane" );
```

---

*Code Dissection*

The first two fields are of primitive type. The **boolean** **inStock** is implicitly initialized to **false**. Because it is a nonstatic field, **inStock** can be later set to **true** for some instances of the class and to **false** for others. All instances of the class share the same **counter**. If you decrease **counter** for one instance, it decreases for all instances. Indeed, you do not need to have any instances to use **counter**. The field **message** is an array of **String** variables and initially contains no strings. The initial value of every element in **message** is **null**. The declaration of **chester** may be the declaration of a local variable, or it may declare a nonstatic field with default access if it is not inside a method. This declaration creates a new **Dog** object.

---

You can declare fields before, after, or between method declarations in your class. A common convention is to group the fields by access specifier and put them before the first method in the class definition.

You cannot declare variables or methods outside a class.

Names in the Java platform are case-sensitive. For variable names, the convention is to use lowercase for letters, except when the name is more than one word. Then, the first letter in all but the first word is often capitalized for readability.

The first character in an identifier must be a letter, an underscore, or a dollar sign. Subsequent characters can be letters, digits, underscores, or dollar signs. You should avoid starting identifiers with a dollar sign because that usage is reserved for code that is generated automatically rather than manually.

Internally, the Java Virtual Machine (JVM) uses the Unicode character set. This character set supports all alphanumeric characters in the major modern languages and is far less restrictive than the ASCII character set. For more information about Unicode, see "Internationalization" on the CD-ROM. Any Unicode letter or digit is allowed in an identifier. For example, your identifiers can contain accented characters, symbols, or digits that do not belong to the ASCII set of digits: 0, 1, 2, 3, 4, 5, 6, 7, 8, and 9. The Java programming language follows Unicode rules specifying which character codes are numeric characters and which are alphabetic.

You can enter any Unicode character directly or use a Unicode escape sequence. One reason for using the escape sequence is that you may have no other way of entering or displaying the character. You can use Unicode characters anywhere, not just in strings.

---

*Syntax*

**\u***XXXX*

---

*Dissection*

➤ *XXXX* is the four-digit, hexadecimal code for the desired Unicode character.

---

*Code Example*

```
String delta\u0394 = "deltaδ";
```

2

*Code Dissection*

This declaration creates a string for which the identifier and value are both **delta**δ. You can also put the character δ in the identifier name and the Unicode escape sequence in the literal string.

## JAVA PROGRAMMING LANGUAGE KEYWORDS

Table 2-1 lists the Java programming language keywords. These words are reserved for use in constructs of the language, and you cannot use them as identifiers.

| | | |
|---|---|---|
| abstract | float | return |
| boolean | for | short |
| break | goto | static |
| byte | if | super |
| case | implements | strictfp |
| catch | import | switch |
| char | instanceof | synchronized |
| class | int | this |
| const | interface | throw |
| continue | long | throws |
| default | native | transient |
| do | new | try |
| double | operator | void |
| else | package | volatile |
| extends | private | while |
| final | protected | widefp |
| finally | public | |

**Table 2-1**   Java programming language keywords

The words **const**, **goto**, **operator**, **byvalue**, **cast**, **future**, **generic**, **inner**, **outer**, **test**, and **var** are reserved, so you cannot use them as identifiers. The Java programming language does not use them now, but may add them in the future. The literals **true**, **false**, and **null** are literals, not keywords. Therefore, they do not appear in Table 2-1.

In addition to including these reserved words, the Java programming language is rich in the names of packages, classes, and methods that make up the core Java classes. In this book, you can spot keywords and the names of the core classes and their methods because they are highlighted with a special font (as in **class** or **void**) when they appear in a sentence, unless the word is used in its ordinary English meaning.

# EXPRESSIONS

Expressions can contain a single variable or constant, or they can consist of operators and operands. You use parentheses to group elements, to override operator precedence during evaluation, and to make the expression more readable. An assignment operator in an expression gives values to variables, and an assignment expression is often a complete statement. Following are some expressions that are valid if the variables they use have been defined, have values, and are of appropriate types:

```
a = 2 + 2
( b - 3.3 ) * ( d + 4.175 ) /  sqrt( 5.0 )
t < 32 || t > 212
"carte " + "blanche"
allbits & tflag
5 / 9.0 * ( F - 32 )
```

The operators and operands that make up an expression determine the expression's type. The expressions can have types such as **char**, **int**, **float**, **double**, **boolean**, and **String**. Boolean expressions are logical expressions that can have either one of two values: **true** or **false**. The value of a string expression is an object of the **String** class.

One type of expression that you never use in the Java programming language is the pointer expression. You use the term **object reference** for a Java programming language concept that is similar, but not identical, to pointers and references in C and other programming languages. Apart from being an operand of an assignment, object references cannot be used in expressions. In other words, the Java programming language allows no pointer arithmetic. You can still use object references to access the actual objects, but you cannot manipulate the object references themselves.

## Operators

Table 2-2 lists the Java operators, grouped by precedence. The number in the first column indicates precedence; the value has no significance other than to show the order of evaluation when more than one operator appears in an expression. The operators in precedence group 1 are executed before those in group 2, and so on. When precedence does not determine the order of evaluation, expressions are processed from left to right, except that for the right-associative operators, the operand on the right is evaluated first. For example, the assignment operators are right-associative because the operand on the right must be evaluated before its value is assigned to the operand on the left. The first column of Table 2-2 indicates right-associative operators with a letter *R* following the precedence value.

**Table 2-2**  Operators in the Java programming language

| Precedence | Operator | Description |
|---|---|---|
| 1 | [ ] | Array index |
| 1 | . | Member |
| 1 | ( argument_list ) | Method call |
| 1 | expression++ | Postfix increment |
| 1 | expression-- | Postfix decrement |
| 2R | ++expression | Prefix increment |
| 2R | --expression | Prefix decrement |
| 2R | + | Unary plus |
| 2R | - | Unary minus |
| 2R | ~ | Bitwise negate |
| 2R | ! | Logical NOT |
| 3R | new | Creation |
| 3R | (type) expression | Cast |
| 4 | * | Multiplication |
| 4 | / | Division |
| 4 | % | Modulus |
| 5 | + | Addition string concatenation |
| 5 | - | Subtraction |
| 6 | << | Left shift |
| 6 | >> | Right shift with sign propagation |
| 6 | >>> | Right shift with zero fill |
| 7 | < | Less than |
| 7 | > | Greater than |
| 7 | >= | Greater than or equal to |
| 7 | <= | Less than or equal to |
| 7 | instanceof | Is an instance of |
| 8 | == | Equal to |
| 8 | != | Not equal to |
| 9 | & | Bitwise AND<br>Logical AND without short-circuiting |
| 10 | ^ | Bitwise XOR |

*continued*

**Table 2-2**  Operators in the Java programming language (continued)

| Precedence | Operator | Description |
|---|---|---|
| 11 | \| | Bitwise OR |
|  |  | Logical OR without short-circuiting |
| 12 | && | Logical AND with short-circuiting |
| 13 | \|\| | Logical OR with short-circuiting |
| 14 | ? : | If ? then : else |
| 15R | = | Assignment |
|  | += |  |
|  | -= *= /= %= |  |
|  | >>= <<= |  |
|  | >>>= |  |
|  | ^= |  |
|  | &= \|= |  |

There are several points worth noting regarding the use of operators:

➤ The Java programming language allows you to apply **&** and **|**, as well as **&&** and **||**, to values of **boolean** type.

➤ When the operands evaluate to **true** or **false**, the difference between **&** and **&&** and between **|** and **||** is whether the evaluation of the expression uses short-circuiting. **Short-circuiting** means to not evaluate the second operand when the first operand fully determines the result of the operation. For example, (**true || ** *expression*) is **true** and (**false && ** *expression*) is **false**, regardless of the value of the second operand. Short-circuiting saves execution time, but can cause errors if your code depends on side effects of evaluating the second operand. The Java programming language does not use short-circuiting when **&** and **|** are applied to **boolean** operands, which gives the program a chance to decide whether to use the short-circuiting versions of these operators.

➤ The operators >>> and >>>= perform a logical right shift. Because the Java programming language has no unsigned types, you would have no way to do an unsigned shift without this operator. The >> operator repeatedly shifts in a new sign bit. The >>> operator brings in a zero bit whether the variable has a positive or negative value. This is a logical shift.
The operators << and >> perform arithmetic shifts. For example, the result of 0xFFFFFF0A >> 4 is 0xFFFFFFF0, and the result of 0xFFFFFF0A >>> 4 is 0x0FFFFFF0.

➤ The **instanceof** operator provides run-time type information. You can use it to determine whether a variable is an instance of a particular class or a superclass of that class. In this context, a superclass is a wider type than the particular class, similar to a C++ base class.

➤ The + and += operators perform string concatenation when used with operands of type **String**. These operators actually create a third string, formed by appending the characters of the second string to the first string. The new string is stored separately from the two input strings, which remain unchanged.

The Java programming language supports the comma operator, but only in a **for** loop to separate subexpressions in the initialization, control, and iteration expressions. Not many programmers use the comma operator in the Java programming language. It only gives you a way to separate statements to get side effects. For example:

```
for ( int i = 0, j = 5; i  < j; i++, j-- ) {
    System.out.println( "counting: " + i + "-" + j );
}
```

This line produces the following output:

```
counting 0-5
counting 1-4
counting 2-3
```

---

**Mini Quiz 2-1**

Do you know why a logical left shift is not required?

---

**Mini Quiz 2-2**

Explain why the output of the following lines of code is **x+y** = 12:

```
int x = 1, y = 2;
System.out.println( "x+y = " + x + y );
```

---

## Floating-point Support in the Math Class

The Java platform includes a class called **Math**. You can use this class as a library of built-in floating-point methods and constants that you can use in arithmetic expressions. For example, the **Math** class defines the constants **Math.PI** and **Math.E** to represent the standard mathematical constants $\pi$ and $e$. In these constants, the dot means that the constants **PI** and **E** are members of the class named **Math**. Table 2-3 lists some commonly used methods of the **Math** class, along with a brief description of what they do.

**Table 2-3**   Methods in the Math class

| Method | Description |
|---|---|
| int abs( int )<br>long abs( long )<br>float abs( float )<br>double abs( double ) | Returns the absolute value of the argument. |
| double ceil( double ) | Returns the smallest double whole number greater than or equal to the argument. |
| double cos( double ) | Returns the cosine of the argument, which specifies radians. |
| double exp( double ) | Returns $e^a$, where a is the value of the argument. |
| double floor( double ) | Returns the largest double whole number that is smaller than the argument. |
| double log( double ) | Returns $\log_e$ (a), where a is the value of the argument. |
| int max( int, int )<br>long max( long, long )<br>float max( float, float )<br>double max( double, double ) | Returns the larger of the two arguments. |
| int min( int, int )<br>long min( long, long )<br>float min( float, float )<br>double min( double, double ) | Returns the smaller of the two arguments. |
| double pow( double, double ) | Returns $a^b$, where a is the first argument and b is the second. |
| double rint( double ) | Returns the closest whole number to the argument. In the case of a tie, it returns the even number. |
| double random() | Returns a pseudo random number in the range 0.0 to 1.0. |
| int round( double ) | Returns the closest integer to argument |
| long round( float ) | Returns the closest long integer to the argument. |
| double sin( double ) | Returns the sine of the argument, which specifies radians. |
| double sqrt( double ) | Returns the square root of the argument. |
| double tan( double ) | Returns the tangent of the argument, which specifies radians. |

All of these methods are static methods of the **Math** class. You do not have to create an object of a class to use a static method defined in that class.

*Syntax*

**Math.method(** *argument_list* **)**

*Dissection*

➤ To call *method*, give the class name, **Math**, followed by the dot operator and the method name.

➤ If the returned value is assigned to a variable, the variable must have the same type or a type that has a greater range of values. For example, you can assign the return value of type **int** to a variable of type **int, long, float**, or **double**. Assignment to a variable that has a type with a smaller range of values is an error, unless you explicitly cast the return value to the type of the variable.

*Code Example*

```
package examples.basic;
/** a class to demonstrate the Math class
  * and working with primitive types */
public class DoMath {
    public static void main( String[] args ) {
        double y = 5.678;
        double x = Math.sqrt( y );
        float a = -4.56F;
        float b = Math.abs( a );
        int r = 56;
        float s = -67.5F;
        int t = (int) Math.max( r, s );
        System.out.println( x );
        System.out.println( b );
        System.out.println( t );
    }
}
```

*Code Output*

```
2.382855429941145
4.56
56
```

*Code Dissection*

This program assigns to the variable **y** the value of the square root of the variable **x**. The single argument of **Math.sqrt** has type **double**. If you supply an argument with a numeric type that has a smaller range, such as **float** or **int**, the value is implicitly cast to a **double** when the method is called.

Next, this program assigns to the variable **b** the value of the absolute value of the variable **a**. Different versions of the **Math.abs** method exist; this example uses the version that takes an argument of type **float**.

Finally, the program assigns to the variable **t** the value either of **r** or **s**, depending on which is greater. In this case, the method **Math.max(float, float)** is called, and the value of **r** is cast to a **float**. The return value has type **float** and must be explicitly cast to **int** to be assigned to **t**.

# CONSTANTS

In the Java programming language, you create a constant by specifying the qualifier **final** in the declaration of a variable. **final** prevents the value of that variable from changing. You can create constants of any type.

*Syntax*

[*access_specifier*] [**static**] **final** *type identifier* [ = *value*];

*Dissection*

➤ The *access_specifier* is optional for fields and not allowed for local variables.

➤ The qualifier **static** is optional for fields and not allowed for local variables.

➤ The **final** keyword specifies that the value of the variable is constant.

➤ The *type* is any valid type.

➤ The *identifier* is any identifier. Following the common convention of using all uppercase letters in the names of constants makes your code more readable.

➤ Usually you assign a value when you declare a constant, even if it is a static field. If you omit the initial value, the constant is called a blank final until it is initialized. After it is initialized, it becomes a constant. A constant cannot be changed after it is initialized.

*Code Example*

```
package examples.basic;
public class ConstantThings {
    private static final int ARRAY_SIZE = 57;
    public static void main( String[] args ) {
        String[] stringThings;
        stringThings = new String[ARRAY_SIZE];
        stringThings[0] = "Howdy pardner";
        System.out.println( stringThings[0] );
    }
}
```

2

*Code Output*

```
Howdy pardner
```

*Code Dissection*

The constant `ARRAY_SIZE` in this class is a **private static** field. Because the field is private, this constant can be used only inside this class. Because the field is static, the main method does not have to create a **ConstantThings** object to use the `ARRAY_SIZE` field. The constant represents the integer value 57.

The **main** method creates an array of strings, using the constant `ARRAY_SIZE` to set the number of elements in the array. The rest of **main** puts a string in the first element of the array and then prints that element.

You can also apply **final** to methods and classes. A **final** method cannot be overridden. You cannot derive a class from a **final** class. These applications of the keyword **final**, as well as the full implications of access specifiers, are explained in Chapter 5. The more general meaning of **final** is that the behavior of the construct it qualifies cannot be changed. When applied to a field or a variable, **final** creates a constant.

Usually, constants are **static final** fields. For example, the **Math** class contains two constants that are static and final. These constants are also public, so you can use them anywhere:

➤ **Math.E** is the closest possible **double** value to the base of natural logarithms.

➤ **Math.PI** is the closest possible **double** value to the ratio of the circumference of a circle to the diameter.

For example, the following method could be in any class:

```
double area( double radius ) {
    return Math.PI * radius * radius;
}
```

Version 1.1 of the Java programming language was the first version to let programmers use **final** without **static**. Earlier versions required that final variables be static fields. Previously, you could not declare nonstatic constants or constants that were local to methods. As well as removing the restricted use of constants, version 1.1 made it optional to initialize a constant in the same statement that declares it.

## Blank Final Constants

If you do not assign a value to a constant when you declare it, the constant is known as a blank final. A **blank final** is simply a constant that is given its value separately from its declaration. It takes the first value assigned to it, and then cannot be changed. A statement that initializes blank finals is the only context in which a final variable may appear on the left of an assignment operator.

The following example is a class in which **main** has a constant local variable z, which is created as a blank final.

The structure of packages mirrors the file system, so you will find the source code for this sample in the examples\errors subfolder of the folder in which you unpacked the JAR file **examples.jar**. The name of a source file always matches the name of the public class that it contains, so this source code is found in the file **BlankFinal.java**.

```
package examples.errors;
/** A class defined to create
  * intentionally an error with blank finals
  */
public class BlankFinal {
    public static void main( String[] args ) {
        final int y = 6;
        final int z;
        y = 0;             // Error! Value already fixed
        if ( y < 0 ) {
            z = 12;        // Okay. No previous value
        } else {
            z = -12;       // Okay. No previous value
        }
        z = 13;            // Error! Value already fixed
        System.out.println( "The answer is " + z/y );
    }
}
```

In the preceding example, the variables y and z are local constants because they are declared inside the method **main**, but only z is created as a blank final constant. A useful feature of blank finals is that their value can be computed and fixed at run time.

Following is a simple case in which a value is set based on the value of y. If you attempt to compile the preceding example exactly as shown, two compiler errors result:

```
BlankFinal.java:9: Can't assign a value to a final
variable: y
        y = 0;         // Error! Value already fixed
        ^

BlankFinal.java:15: Can't assign a second value to
a blank final variable: z
        z = 13;        // Error! Value already fixed
        ^

2 errors
```

The errors reflect the fact that the value of a constant cannot be changed after it has been set.

Fields can also be blank finals. For example, the `ConstantThings2` class can be coded as follows:

```
package examples.basic;
public class ConstantThings2 {
    private static final int ARRAY_SIZE;
    public static void main( String[] args ) {
        String[] stringThings;
        stringThings = new String[ARRAY_SIZE];
        stringThings[0] = "Howdy pardner";
        System.out.println( stringThings[0] ) );
    }
    static {
        ARRAY_SIZE = 57;
    }
}
```

A static blank final field must be given an initial value in a static initializer block. The following lines are the static initializer block for the `ConstantThings2` class:

```
static {
    ARRAY_SIZE = 57;
}
```

Chapter 4 includes a full discussion of static fields, also known as class variables. What happens when nonstatic fields are blank finals? You can initialize them in either of two ways:

➤ Assign an initial value in every constructor of the class.

➤ Provide an instance initializer block. Such blocks are often used in inner classes, and are described in Chapter 9.

## STATEMENTS

Statements are terminated by a semicolon. You form a block statement by enclosing one or more statements within braces, { and }.

Table 2-4 lists the keywords that can affect the flow of control within methods.

**Table 2-4**  Conditional and iterative statements

| Keyword | Description |
|---------|-------------|
| break | Exits an enclosing **do**, **case**, **for**, or **while** block |
| case | Labels a selection in a **switch** statement |
| continue | Ends the current iteration of the enclosing **do**, **for**, or **while** block |
| default | Begins the default selection in the **switch** statement |
| do | Begins a block that must be executed at least once, and then repeats until the **while** condition evaluates to **false** |
| else | Begins a statement or block to execute when the condition of the matching **if** evaluates to **false** |
| for | Begins a counted loop |
| if | Controls the conditional execution of a block or statement and of the optional matching **else** clause |
| switch | Begins a block in which the statements following **case** or **default** labels are selectively executed |
| while | Begins a conditional loop |

# if Statements

Using **if** statements is the most common way to program conditional execution.

---
*Syntax*

**if (** *boolean_expression* **)**
  *statement_or_block*
**[** *else*
    *statement_or_block*
**]**

---
*Dissection*

➤ The else clause is optional.

➤ The statement following the condition or the keyword **else** can be a simple statement ending with a semicolon, or a block enclosed in braces.

➤ **if** statements can be nested, in which case each **else** is matched with the immediately preceding **if**. The Java programming language follows the same rules of nesting as does C++.

---
*Code Example*

```
if ( i > j ) {
    i = j;
} else {
    i = 0;
}
```

2

This code example sets the variable **i** equal to **j** if **i** has a value greater than **j**; otherwise, it sets **i** equal to 0.

## switch Statements

You use the **switch** keyword to select one or more alternate statements or blocks of code to execute.

*Syntax*

```
switch ( integral_expression ) {
  case selector1:
    statements or blocks
    [break;]
  [case selector2:
    statements or blocks]
  [. . .]
  [default:
  statements or blocks]
}
```

*Dissection*

➤ The expression following the keyword **switch** must have type **byte**, **short**, **int**, **long**, or **char**.

➤ Any number of **case** labels are allowed. The selector value for each case must be a compile-time integral expression.

➤ The label **default** is optional. It can be anywhere within the switch statement, but is typically at the end.

➤ The *integral_expression* is evaluated. Then, control goes to the first **case** label for which the value of the selector equals the value of the switch expression. No further matching will be done.

➤ If none of the **case** labels match the *integral_expression* and a **default** label is present, control passes to the statements following the **default** label.

➤ Using **break** to exit the switch statement is optional, but very common. Control passes from each case label to the next, including **default**, until a **break** or the end of the switch is encountered.

*Code Example*

```
char c;
// ...
switch ( c ) {
```

```
      case 'a':
      case 'A':
         System.out.println( "You chose a" );
         break;
      case 'b':
      case 'B':
         System.out.println( "You chose b" );
         break;
      default:
         System.out.println( "Default case" );
}
```

## while Statements

Use **while** to program conditional loops. A while loop is most appropriate when you want to repeat some action until a condition occurs. For example, use a **while** loop to read from a file until you reach the end of the file. You can also set up a **while** loop to loop indefinitely, if you are sure that some external event will terminate the loop.

### Syntax

**while (** *boolean_expression* **)**
   *statement_or_block*

### Dissection

➤ The expression is evaluated before the start of each pass through the loop. It must evaluate to **true** or **false**.

➤ The statement or block following the expression is executed repeatedly as long as the while expression is **true**. It is never executed if the condition is **false** the first time the boolean expression is evaluated.

➤ The loop ends when the expression is evaluated and the result is **false**, or when a break statement is encountered in the loop. A continue statement ends the current pass though the loop.

### Code Example

```
int i = 0;
while ( i <= 5 ) {
    i++;
    System.out.println( "i = " + i );
}
```

## do Statements

Use **do** statements to program conditional loops when you want to force the body of the loop to execute at least once.

*Syntax*

**do**
   *statement_or_block*
**while** ( *boolean_expression* );

*Dissection*

➤ The expression following **while** is evaluated at the end of each pass through the loop. It must evaluate to **true** or **false**.

➤ The statement or block following the **do** is executed one time, and then repeatedly, as long as the while expression is **true**. One pass is guaranteed; the while expression is not evaluated until the end of the first pass through the loop.

➤ The loop ends when the expression is evaluated and the result is **false**, or when a break statement is encountered in the loop. A continue statement ends the current pass though the loop.

*Code Example*

```
char c;
do {
  // read a single character into c
} while ( c != 'q' );
```

## for Statements

Use **for** statements for counted loops. A **for** loop is appropriate when you know in advance how many times to repeat the loop or when you want a counter to be automatically updated on each pass.

*Syntax*

**for** ( *initialization*; *termination_expression*; *step* )
   *statement_or_block*

*Dissection*

➤ If you declare variables in the initialization clause, their scope is the body of the **for** loop. Usually you set the initial value of a counter in this clause.

➤ The termination expression is evaluated before the start of each pass through the loop. It must evaluate to **true** or **false**. Usually the value of the counter is a term in this expression.

➤ The *step* statement is executed when each pass through the loop ends and before the termination expression is evaluated for the next pass. Usually the *step* modifies the value of the counter in a predictable way.

➤ The statement or block is executed repeatedly, as long as the termination expression is **true**.

➤ The loop ends when the expression is evaluated and the result is **false**, or when a break statement is encountered in the loop. A continue statement ends the current pass through the loop.

*Code Example*

```
for ( int k = 0; k <= 10; k++ ) {
    a[k] = k;
}
```

*Code Dissection*

This code sets the values of 11 elements in an array of integers. In each pass, the integer k is used as the index of one element in the array, and the value of k is assigned to that element. For example, on the third pass, the element at index 2 in a is given the value 2.

For this code to work, the **int** array a must be declared before the loop and must have at least 11 elements.

## Getting Out of Loops

You can leave loops prematurely with the keywords **break** and **continue**. You can put **break** and **continue** statements anywhere inside a loop. You can also use **break** in any enclosing statement, but **continue** is allowed only in **for**, **while**, or **do** loops.

The simple form of the **break** statement performs almost the same function in **do**, **for**, and **while** loops that it performs in **switch** statements. It terminates the loop and gives control to the next statement outside the loop.

```
for ( int k = 0; k <= 5; k++ ) {
    if ( k == 3 ) {
        break;
    }
    System.out.println( "loop count " + k );
}
```

The output is

```
loop count 0
loop count 1
loop count 2
```

A **continue** statement terminates the current iteration only, and control passes to the point where the JVM evaluates the **boolean** expression to determine whether to pass through the loop again.

```
for ( int k = 0; k <= 5; k++ ) {
    if ( k == 3 ) {
        continue;
    }
    System.out.println( "loop count " + k);
}
```

The output is

```
loop count 0
loop count 1
loop count 2
loop count 4
loop count 5
```

Both the **break** and **continue** statements can transfer control to locations other than the first statement after the loop. They can transfer control to a labeled **do**, **while**, or **for** statement. Use this construct to get out of nested loops.

---

*Syntax*

*label***:**
*outer_do_while_or_ for* **{**
        *// ...*
        *inner_do_while_or_ for* **{**
                *// ...*
                **break** *label***;**
                *// ...*
                **continue** *label***;**
                *// ...*
        **} // end inner loop**
        *// ...*
**} // end outer loop**

---

*Dissection*

➤ A label looks like an identifier, but is followed by a colon that sets it apart from the statement that it labels.

➤ Inside the loop, you can follow a **continue** or **break** keyword with the name of the label of any enclosing loop. This construct is called a labeled **break** or labeled **continue**.

➤ A labeled **break** transfers control to the statement following the labeled enclosing block.

➤ A labeled **continue** transfers control to the point where the decision whether to make another pass through the labeled loop is made.

*Code Example*

```
package examples.basic;
public class Findit {
    public static void main( String[] args ) {
        int row = 0, col = 0;
        int[][] a = { { 7,4,0 },{ 0,5,0 },{ 2,0,6 } };
        search:
        for ( row = 0; row < 3; row++ ) {
            for ( col = 0; col < 3; col++ ) {
                if ( a[row][col] == 0 ) {
                    break search;
                }
                System.out.println( a[row][col]
                    + " at (" + row + "," + col + ")" );
            }
        }
        System.out.println( "zero at (" + row + ","
            + col + ")" );
    }
}
```

*Code Output*

```
7 at (0,0)
4 at (0,1)
zero at (0,2)
```

*Code Dissection*

The `Findit` class demonstrates a labeled **break**. The **main** method creates a three-by-three array a of type **int** and initializes it. Then, **main** searches in a until it finds an element that has the value zero. Two nested **for** loops are used to access each element in turn. When one element satisfies the condition of being equal to zero, the labeled **break** is executed. Here, the third element that was tested matches zero. At that point, the **break** statement transfers control out of both the inner loop and the labeled outer loop.

*Code Example*

```
package examples.basic;
public class Findit2 {
    public static void main( String[] args ) {
```

```
        int row = 0, col = 0;
        int[][] a = { { 7,4,0 },{ 0,5,0 },{ 2,0,6 } };
        search:
        for ( row = 0; row < 3; row++ ) {
            for ( col = 0; col < 3; col++ ) {
                if ( a[row][col] == 0 ) {
                    continue search;
                }
                System.out.println( a[row][col]
                    + " at (" + row + "," + col + ")" );
            }
        }
    }
}
```

---

*Code Output*

```
7 at (0,0)
4 at (0,1)
2 at (2,0)
```

---

*Code Dissection*

`Findit2` is a variation on the `Findit` class. Two lines have changed: The
**print** statement outside the loop is gone, and the labeled **break** has been
changed to a labeled **continue**. These changes affect the logic considerably.
When an element that matches zero is found, the labeled **continue** passes
control out of the inner loop to the start of the next iteration of the outer
loop. Here, the effect is that the value of every element in a row is printed
until a zero is found in that row. Then, the search skips over the rest of the row
and starts on the next row.

---

The labeled **break** and labeled **continue** provide an elegant and robust way of
getting out of nested loops.

> **Mini Quiz 2-3**
> How would you modify the `Findit2` class to print all nonzero elements of the array?

---

# METHODS

Every Java method is a member of a class. There are no exceptions, not even
with the **main** method. All method declarations include the return type,
method name, argument list, and body of the method.

---

*Syntax*

[*access_specifiers*] [*qualifiers*] *return_type method_name* ( *argument_list* )
[**throws** *exception_list*]
   *block*

---

*Dissection*

➤ Like every field, every method has its own access specifier. You can specify **public**, **private**, or **protected**, or omit the specifier to accept the default of package access.

➤ Qualifiers are optional. Include the keyword **static** to make the method usable by any code that has access to the method and the class, regardless of whether any objects of the class have been created. If you omit **static**, the method can be used only with objects of the class. The qualifier **final** determines how the method can be used with inheritance.

➤ The return type is not optional. Specify **void** if the method does not return a value. A Java method can return any type, including primitive types, class types, and arrays.

➤ The method name must be a valid identifier. A common convention is to use lowercase letters in method names, except when the name is the con-catenation of recognizable words. In such cases, the first letter of all but the first word is capitalized. For example, `myMethod, catch22, and getMarketShare` are potential method names.

➤ The parentheses must always be present. They enclose arguments of the method. If the method takes no arguments, just include the empty pair of parentheses. If the argument takes more than one argument, separate the arguments with a comma. In the argument list, you must specify the type of each argument followed by the identifier by which it is known in the method. For example, a method that takes three arguments, two integers, and an array of strings might have an argument list that looks like the following:

`(int first, int last, String[] s )`

➤ Whether the throws clause is required depends upon what the method does. This clause lists any exceptions that can occur while the method is running and that may prevent the method from returning as expected. Chapter 6 explains that exceptions are a mechanism for handling errors or unexpected situations. For example, a method that performs file I/O may not be able to complete its task because of a problem reading from or writing to the file. The declarations of methods that work with files may include the clause **throws IOException**.

➤ The body of the method is any number of statements enclosed in braces, { and }.

---

*Code Example*

```
long setflag( int position, long flag ) {
    long mask = 1;
    return flag | ( mask << ( position-1 ) );
}
```

> **Mini Quiz 2-4**
>
> If you delete all parentheses from the following expression, does the value change?
>
> ```
> flag | ( mask << ( position-1 ) )
> ```

A method that takes no arguments and returns no value can take the following form:

**[**access_specifiers**]** **[**qualifiers**]** *void method_name* **()**
**[throws** *exception_list***]**
 *block*

When you call a method that is in another class, use the dot operator. For example, the following line calls a method in the **Math** class:

```
double d = Math.sqrt( 150.0 );
```

Use the dot notation to call a method with an object of the class, as in the following example:

```
System.out.println( "out is an object declared in class"
                    + " System" );
```

## Arguments

All arguments are passed by value in the Java programming language. Some arguments are actual values for primitive types, such as integers and characters, and others are object references for reference types, such as **String**, the other core classes, or any class that you might define.

The method always receives a copy of the argument. It cannot alter the original value in the calling routine. For example, you cannot write a method, such as the following, to swap the value of integers:

```
public class NoGoodSwap {
    public void swap( int a, int b ) {
        int temp x = a;
        a = b;
        b = temp;
    }
}
```

To be more accurate, you can compile and run such a method, but the altered values are lost when the method returns.

When the argument is an object reference, the fact that the method has a copy of the actual argument is not a problem. A copy of an object reference is just as useful for modifying an object as the original. The reference gives the method access to the actual object so that the method can perform all actions that are valid for that object. Unless the object is immutable, as are some of the objects in the core classes, a method can use the object reference to modify the object. **Immutable objects** are objects that cannot be changed because the class does not give direct access to any fields and provides no methods that can alter the values of fields.

You can qualify the argument with the keyword **final**, just as you can make variables **final**. A **final** argument cannot be changed during the execution of the method. The compiler flags any attempt to assign a value as an error. Use **final** arguments to ensure that the value of an argument remains constant for the duration of the method:

```
public static void f( final int a, final int b ) {
    while ( a < b ) {
        // ...
        a++; // error! can't change a final argument
        System.out.println( "a = " + a );
    }
}
```

If an argument that is an object reference is declared **final**, the method cannot alter the object reference. The method can still work with the object, but its **final** object reference cannot be changed to refer to a different object:

```
public static void g( final Dog d ) {
    d.setName("Rover"); // changing the Dog object d is OK
    d = new Dog( "Retriever" ); //error, cannot change d
}
```

Version 1.1 of the Java platform introduced the ability to qualify an argument as final.
When you call a method in the Java programming language, you must provide a value for every argument in the argument list.

## Return Values and return Statements

A method can return at most one object. A method that is declared with return type **void** returns nothing. It can have a **return** statement but cannot return a value.

A method that has any other return type than **void** must have at least one **return** statement.

*Syntax*

**return** [*expression*]**;**

*Dissection*

➤ The *expression* can be as complicated or simple as you want, but it must evaluate a value that can be assigned to a variable with the return type of the method. It can be a single number or character, **true** or **false**, an object reference, or an instance of a class or an array, but it must always be a single entity.

➤ The return statement terminates execution of a method. A method can have multiple return statements. Only one return statement is executed for each invocation of the method.

## Local Variables

Variables declared within a method are local variables, and the only place local variables can occur is inside a method.

## The main Method

The method called **main** is a very special one. Most sample classes in this book have a **main** method. That is because these sample programs are small applications that you can run from the command line, or from an icon on your desktop if you take the trouble to create an icon for them. The use of a **main** method distinguishes applications that run on their own from applets that are embedded in HTML documents and that are started by a web browser. Applications must have at least one class with a **main** method.

Any class can have a **main** method, and more than one class that is used in the same application can have a method named **main**. You may find it handy to declare a **main** method for almost every class so that you can test the class in isolation from the larger application.

When you start the JVM by issuing the **java** command and providing the name of a class, or do the equivalent with an integrated development environment (IDE), the JVM looks for the public class inside the .**class** file with the same base name as the class. Next, the JVM looks in that class for the method named **main**. If no such method exists, the virtual machine outputs an error message. If **main** is found, the JVM passes control to it. In other words, the **main** method is an entry point into your class.

> **Mini Quiz 2-5**
>
> Can there be ambiguity when more than one class contains a method named **main**?

*Syntax*

**public static void main( String[ ]** *args* **) [throws** *exception_list***]**
   *block*

*Dissection*

➤ The virtual machine does not recognize **main** as the entry point for a class unless it is **static**, **public**, has return type **void**, and has a single argument that is an array of strings.

➤ The **main** method must be declared both **static** and **public**. It is **static** because it applies to the whole class, and **public** so that it can be called from outside the class.

➤ The single argument of **main** is an array of strings, for which the notation is **String[]**. This array contains the arguments supplied when the program is run.

➤ Any exceptions that may occur in main but that are not handled must be listed after the keyword **throws**. Chapter 6 provides more details about exceptions.

The **main** method never returns a value, and therefore cannot supply a return code to the JVM. A **return code** is a mechanism by which an application can pass back to the operating system or parent process some indication of whether the run completed successfully or terminated with an error code. Because the handling of application return codes is platform-specific, the Java platform isolates the ability to terminate with a return code to the method **exit** in the standard class **System**. To terminate with a return code, call **System.exit** and pass an integer return code as an argument.

# CONSOLE I/O

Console I/O means input from the keyboard and output to a command-line window on the screen. The Java platform provides basic support for console I/O. The features for developing graphical user interfaces (GUIs) are extensive, and are provided by classes that come with the Java platform. Chapters 12 and 13 give an overview of these classes. Other input- and output-related topics, such as manipulating files, are the subject of Chapter 8.

For simplicity, all sample programs in the early chapters of this book run in command-line mode. Although this section describes only the simplest—and arguably most useful—features of console I/O, it should be enough to get you started.

You may find console input and output useful in GUI-based programs for inserting debugging output or creating program logs. For most applications, the console is unlikely to be your main source for input and your destination for output. Most modern applications have a GUI, and few programs—except simple utilities—run in command-line mode.

## Simple Stream Input and Output

The Java platform implements the concept of stream I/0. Streams are sequential sources and destinations for characters and bytes. They can be associated with the keyboard for input and the screen in character mode for output. Files, and even connections to other computers on a network, can be associated with streams. Any number of bytes can be written to output streams or read from output streams at a time. But output is always added to the end of the stream and input is always taken from the front of the stream, so that characters flow through like an orderly queue. Three standard streams are defined for input, output, and error output, as shown in Table 2-5. These stream objects are **public**, **static**, **final** fields of the core class **System**.

**Table 2-5**   Standard Stream objects

| Full name | Type |
| --- | --- |
| java.lang.System.in | java.io.InputStream |
| java.lang.System.out | java.io.PrintStream |
| java.lang.System.err | java.io.PrintStream |

In the sample programs, you have already seen a number of statements similar to the following:

```
// prints one line: hello number 2
int id = 2;
System.out.println( "hello number " + id );
```

The **PrintStream** class provides several methods, including **print** and **println**. These two methods have one argument, which can be an object of any primitive or reference type. The difference between them is that **print** outputs just the argument you pass to it, and **println** adds a newline character. Use **print** if you are building up the output line a bit at a time, and use **println** when each call is to produce a separate line of output.

The most common way to build up the argument to print is to give an argument of type **String** and to use the string concatenation operator, +, to concatenate elements in a string expression. If an item is a number, as `id` is in the preceding line of code, it is converted to a string during the evaluation of the string expression. When you are concatenating numbers, be careful that at least one operand of each + is a **String**. Otherwise, the + performs arithmetic addition, which may not be what you intended.

```
System.out.println( 1 + 2 + 3 );        // output is 6
System.out.println( "1" + 2 + 3 );       // output is 123
System.out.println( "1" + ( 2 + 3 ) );    // output is 15
```

Programming console input is more complicated than programming console output. The reason is that you usually want to read a full line at a time, so you wait for the user to press Enter and let the operating system handle the pressing of Backspace and other inline edits.

Code that reads one line from the console is usually similar to the following lines:

```
java.io.BufferedReader br;
br = new java.io.BufferedReader(
    new java.io.InputStreamReader( System.in ) );
String line = br.readLine();
```

To understand these lines, you must be comfortable with the concept of wrapping an object of one class around an object of another class. Many of the classes in the I/O package **java.io** are wrapper classes. A **wrapper class** is essentially a class that provides different behavior for an object than the behavior established by the class of the object. In other words, a wrapper class gives you another way of using the object it wraps. The preceding lines of code provide a good example of wrapper classes.

For console input, you start with the standard stream object **System.in**. The first layer of wrapping creates an **InputStreamReader** object for **System.in**. The core class **InputStreamReader** is in the package **java.io**. This class implements a character-input stream that reads bytes from a byte-oriented input stream and converts the bytes to characters. For **System.in**, **InputStreamReader** converts the input from the character encoding of the native operating system to Unicode. In the following expression, the **new** keyword creates an **InputStreamReader** object:

```
new java.io.InputStreamReader( System.in )
```

The next step is to instantiate a **BufferedReader** object. In other words, the second layer of wrapping creates a **BufferedReader** object for the **InputStreamReader** object.

```
java.io.BufferedReader br;
br = new java.io.BufferedReader(
    new java.io.InputStreamReader( System.in ) );
```

The reason for using a **BufferedReader** object is that the **BufferedReader** class provides the **readLine** method, which is the easiest way to read a complete line into a **String** object. This **BufferedReader** object is called br, and the **readLine** method returns an object reference for a **String**, so the following line actually reads the input:

```
String line = br.readLine();
```

All this wrapping of one object inside another may seem like a lot of trouble to go through just to read in a line of text. In Chapter 8, you will take advantage of flexibility that classes such as **InputStreamReader** and **BufferedReader** bring to the Java platform. These two classes are considered **filter classes** because the bytes from the input stream pass through them and are converted into the format in which the program chooses to receive them.

## Parsing an Input String

Often, the next step after reading a line of input is to parse it, or break it into separate tokens. A **token** usually consists of a sequence of characters that does not include a space, newline, tab, or other nonprinting characters. These characters are often called whitespace. The following lines show how to extract numbers and words from a string. For demonstration, the first token in this line is interpreted as an integer, the second as a floating-point number, and all remaining tokens as one string:

```
java.util.StringTokenizer st
    = new java.util.StringTokenizer( line );
int k = Integer.parseInt( st.nextToken() );
float f = Float.parseFloat( st.nextToken() );
String s = st.nextToken();
while ( st.hasMoreTokens() ) {
    s += " " + st.nextToken();
}
```

 The methods **Float.parseFloat** and **Double.parseDouble** were added as part of the Java 2 platform. Previously, parsing a **String** to extract a floating-point value required a temporary object of type **Float** or **Double**, as in the following line:

```
float f = Float.valueOf( st.nextToken() ).floatValue();
```

To tokenize a string, you can use the **StringTokenizer** class provided by the **java.util** package. Use a **StringTokenizer** object as a wrapper for a **String** object. The first of these statements creates a **StringTokenizer** object called st to manipulate an existing **String** called **line**:

```
java.util.StringTokenizer st
    = new java.util.StringTokenizer( line );
```

By default, a **StringTokenizer** object interprets whitespace characters as delimiters between tokens. You can call methods of **StringTokenizer** to customize this behavior. For example, you can specify that the delimiter be a comma.

*Class*

**java.util.StringTokenizer**

*Purpose*

This utility class extracts tokens from a string, one by one.

*Constructors*

➤ StringTokenizer( String *s* )

StringTokenizer( String *s*, String *delimiter* )

StringTokenizer( String *s*, String *delimiter*, Boolean *returnDelimiters* )

The constructor builds a **StringTokenizer** for the **String** specified in the first argument. By default, whitespace separates tokens, but you can specify one or more alternative delimiter characters in a second argument of type **String**. If you want each delimiter to be returned as a **String** of length one, set the **boolean** argument to **true**. If this argument is **false** or omitted, delimiters are skipped.

*Methods*

➤ **String nextToken()**

This method returns the next token in the **StringTokenizer** object, or throws an exception if no more tokens are available.

➤ **boolean hasMoreTokens()**

This method returns **true** if another token can be extracted from the **StringTokenizer** object, or **false** otherwise. You should call **hasMoreTokens** before **nextToken**, and call **nextToken** only if **hasMoreTokens** returns **true**.

The next three lines perform equivalent tasks for an integer, a floating-point number, and a string. In all three cases, the code extracts the next token from **line** by applying the method **nextToken** to **st**, and converts it to the required type.

➤ The method **parseInt** of the **Integer** class returns the **int** value represented by a string. The argument is the object returned by **nextToken**. The **Integer** class is a wrapper class for the primitive type **int**, and is described in Chapter 3.

```
int k = Integer.parseInt( st.nextToken() );
```

➤ The method **parseFloat** of the **Float** class returns the float value represented by a string. The argument is the object returned by **nextToken**. The **Float** class is a wrapper class of the primitive type **float**, and is described in Chapter 3.

```
float f = Float.parseFloat( st.nextToken() );
```

➤ To get the third token as a string, simply call **nextToken**. However, building up s to contain all the tokens that remain on the input line involves repeatedly calling **nextToken** until the method **hasMoreTokens** returns **false**.

```
String s = st.nextToken();
while( st.hasMoreTokens() ) {
    s += " " + st.nextToken();
}
```

One potential disadvantage of a **StringTokenizer** is that it folds multiple, adjacent whitespace characters into one delimiter. You cannot use the default delimiter if you want to preserve multiple spaces between words.

## Exploring a Console I/O Sample Program

The following program listing does a bit of everything, in terms of simple console input and output. As usual, the program is contained in a public class, this time called **ConsoleTest**.

The **main** method of this class does all the work. Notice that the declaration of **ConsoleTest.main** contains a throws clause because the **java.io** package can throw exceptions for certain input and output error conditions.

```
package examples.basic;
/** A class to demonstrate how simple console I/O is used
  */
public class ConsoleTest {
   /** The test method for the class
     * @param args Not used
     * @exception java.io.IOException
     *                Unspecified I/O exception
     */
   public static void main( String[] args )
        throws java.io.IOException {
      int i = 10;
      int j = 20;
      double d = 99.101;

      System.out.print( "Here are some values: " );
      System.out.println( i + " " + j + " " + d );
      System.out.println(
```

```
                    "Enter an integer, a float, and a string:" );

          java.io.BufferedReader br;
          br = new java.io.BufferedReader( new
               java.io.InputStreamReader( System.in ) );
          String line = br.readLine();

          java.util.StringTokenizer st = new
               java.util.StringTokenizer( line );
          int k = Integer.parseInt( st.nextToken() );
          float f = Float.parseFloat( st.nextToken() );
          String s = st.nextToken();
          while( st.hasMoreTokens() ) {
              s += " " + st.nextToken();
          }

          System.out.println( "Here's your data: " );
          System.out.println( k );
          System.out.println( f );
          System.out.println( s );
     }
}
```

The output is

```
Here are some values: 10 20 99.101
Enter an integer, a float, and a string:
13 34.6 Quick brown fox
Here's your data:
13
34.6
Quick brown fox
```

---

# SUMMARY

Most of the programming concepts covered in this chapter are common to many programming languages, but the syntax may be different. If you have used C or C++, the Java programming language should look very familiar because its designers made a conscious effort to leverage the syntax of C++. However, most popular programming languages, regardless of whether they are procedural or object–oriented in nature, have variables with identifiers, and declaration and initialization statements. They also have a set of arithmetic and other operators for use in expressions and in keywords that appear in the flow of control statements. These operators are also a way of receiving input from the keyboard and of sending output to the screen. Some of the key points to remember are:

➤ Valid identifiers for the Java programming language begin with a letter, an underscore, or a dollar sign. After the first character, subsequent characters may be letters, numbers, underscores, or dollar signs. You can include Unicode characters.

➤ A full range of arithmetic, boolean, relational, bit manipulation, and assignment operators are supported.

➤ The core class **Math** provides many useful mathematical methods, such as **abs**, **sqrt**, **random**, and many more, and the two constants **PI** and **E**. These methods and constants are all public and static, so you can use them from anywhere and need not create an object of the **Math** class.

➤ Use the keyword **final** to declare constants. You can initialize constants in their declarations, or create blank finals, which cannot be changed after they are assigned a value.

➤ The statements that can alter the flow of control in a method contain the following keywords:

| | | | |
|---|---|---|---|
| **break** | **case** | **continue** | **default** |
| **do** | **else** | **for** | **if** |
| **switch** | **while** | | |

➤ The condition in an **if** statement, and the expression that determines whether to terminate a loop, must be **true** or **false** and cannot be numeric.

➤ The scope of variables declared in the initializer of a **for** statement is restricted to the **for** statement itself. The **continue** and **break** statements can use labels to jump out of more than one level of nested loops.

➤ Method declarations take the following form:

[*access_specifiers*] [*qualifiers*] *return_type* method_name ( *argument_list* )
    **[throws** *exception_list*]
    *block*

➤ All methods must be members of a class. Every method is declared with an explicit access specifier or is given the default access. All arguments are passed by value.

➤ The form of the **main** method is

**public static void main( String[ ]** *args* **) [throws** *exception_list*]
    *block*

➤ More than one class can have a method called **main**, but only the **main** method in the **public** class that is used to tell the JVM to run is the entry point for an application. It is a good idea to provide a **main** method as a test method for classes. Applets written in the Java programming language do not have a **main** method. **main** never returns a value. The JVM passes command-line arguments to the class and does not include the name of the program.

➤ The Java platform supports streams for console I/O. The simplest way to output to the console is to call the methods **System.out.print** and

**System.out.println.** The best way to perform console input is to use the wrapper classes **BufferedReader** and **InputStreamReader** to read a line at a time. Use the **StringTokenizer** class to break the line or any string into individual tokens.

## QUESTIONS

1. Which of the following are legal Java identifier names? Select all that apply.

   a. `counter1`

   b. `$index`

   c. `name-7`

   d. `Iterator.Class`

   e. `array`

2. Examine the following code:

```
public class Quiz2_1 {
    public static void main( String[] args ) {
        int a = 8;
        int b = -8;
        System.out.print( a << 2 );
        System.out.println( ", " + ( b >> 1 ) );
    }
}
```

   Which one of the following statements correctly describes the behavior when this program is compiled and run?

   a. Compilation is successful and the output is `32, -4`

   b. Compilation is successful and the output is `16, 4`

   c. Compilation is successful and the output is `32, 2147483644`

   d. Compilation is successful and the output is `16, 2147483644`

   e. The compiler rejects the expression `(b >> 1)` because you cannot use the `>>` operator with a negative value as the left operand.

3. How is a Unicode escape sequence distinguished?

4. Examine the following set of tokens:

   | | | |
   |---|---|---|
   | **goto** | **unsigned** | **class** |
   | **switch** | **null** | **double** |
   | **label** | **transient** | **template** |

   Which of the following statements are true? Select all that apply.

   a. **template** and **unsigned** are not reserved words.

b. All of the words in the list are reserved words.

c. **label** is not a reserved word.

d. **goto** is a reserved word, but its use is not allowed.

e. **null** is a keyword.

5. What qualifier do you include in the declaration of a variable to prevent its value from being changed after an initial value has been assigned?

6. True or false: The Java programming language defines operators for string concatenation.

7. Examine the following code:

```
public class Quiz2_2 {
    public static double foo ( double a, double b ) {
        return( a > b ? a : b );
    }
    public static void main( String[] args ) {
        System.out.println( foo( 3.4, 6.3 ) );
    }
}
```

Which one of the following statements correctly describes the behavior when this program is compiled?

a. Compilation is successful and the output is **6.3**

b. Compilation is successful and the output is **3.4**

c. The compiler rejects the expression ( **a > b ? a : b** ) because the Java programming language does not support the ? : ternary operator.

d. The compiler rejects the expression **foo( 3.4, 6.3 )** because it does not evaluate to a string value.

8. If the variable **t** of type **short** contains the bit pattern 1111 0000 0000 1010, which of the following statements are true? Select all that apply.

a. The result of **t >> 4** is 0000 1111 0000 0000.

b. The result of **t >>> 4** is 0000 1111 0000 0000.

c. The result of **t >> 4** is 1111 1111 0000 0000.

d. The result of **t >>> 4** is 1111 1111 0000 0000.

e. The result of **t >>> 4** is 1010 1111 0000 0000.

9. True or false: The input stream object **System.in** directly supports the function of reading a **String** object from the input stream.

10. Examine the following set of operators:

**&& || & |**

Which of the following statements are true? Select all that apply.

a. All of the operators are logical operators.

b. These operators can be applied only to **boolean** values.

c. The operator || evaluates its right argument only if the left argument evaluates to **false**.

d. The operators || and | perform an exclusive OR operation.

e. The operator & evaluates its right argument if the left argument evaluates to **true**.

11. If st is a **StringTokenizer** object that contains no tokens, which of the following lines fail because they attempt to access an element that does not exist?

a.
```
if ( st.hasMoreTokens() &
    Integer.parseInt( st.nextToken( ) ) != 0 ) { /*
    ... */ }
```

b.
```
if ( st.hasMoreTokens() &&
    Integer.parseInt( st.nextToken( ) ) != 0 ) { /*
    ... */ }
```

c.
```
if ( st.hasMoreTokens() |
    Integer.parseInt( st.nextToken( ) ) != 0 ) { /*
    ... */ }
```

d.
```
if ( st.hasMoreTokens() ||
    Integer.parseInt( st.nextToken( ) ) != 0 ) { /*
    ... */ }
```

12. Examine the following lines of code:

```
for ( a = 0; a < 3;  a++ ) {
   if ( a == 1 ) continue;
   for ( b = 0; b < 3; b++ ) {
      if ( b == 1 ) break;
      System.out.println( a + ",  " + b );
   }
}
```

Which of the following lines are included in the output when the method that contains these lines is run? Select all that apply.

a. 0, 0

b. 0, 1

c. 0, 2

d. 1, 0

e. 1, 1

f. 1, 2

g. 2, 0

h. 2, 1

i. 2, 2

13. Examine the following code:

```
public class Quiz2_3 {
    public static void main( String[] args ) {
        int x = 010;
        int y = 0x10;
        int z = 10;
        System.out.println( x + y + z );
    }
}
```

Which one of the following correctly describes the behavior when this program is compiled?

a. Compilation is successful and the output is 30.

b. Compilation is successful and the output is 36.

c. Compilation is successful and the output is 34.

d. The compiler rejects the expression y = 0x10 because letters of the alphabet are not allowed in numeric constants.

e. The compiler rejects the expression y = 0x10 because a hexadecimal value cannot be assigned to an int variable.

## EXERCISES

### Debugging

1. Correct all errors in the following code:

```
package questions.c2;
public class Debug2_1 {
    public static void main( String[] args ) {
        int x = 8;
        if ( x = 0 ) {
            System.out.println( x );
        } else {
            System.out.println( x*2 );
        }
    }
}
```

2. Correct all errors in the following code:

```
package questions.c2;
public class Debug2_2 {
```

```
       private final int MIN;
       private final int MAX;
       public Debug2_2() {
           MAX = 10;
       }
       public Debug2_2( int input ) {
           MIN = input;
       }
       public static void main( String[] args ) {
           Debug2_2 a = new Debug2_2();
           Debug2_2 b = new Debug2_2( 15 );
       }
   }
```

3. Correct all errors in the following code:

```
package questions.c2;
public class Debug2_3 {
    public static void main( String[] args ) {
        char c = 'x';
        int x = 17;
        double y = 21.4;
        if ( x * y > 400 )
            switch ( c ) {
              case 'a':
                System.out.println( c );
              default
                 System.out.println( "Not 'a'" );
            }
            x = 24;
        else {
            x = 25;
        }
    }
}
```

4. Correct all errors in the following code:

```
package questions.c2;
public class Debug2_4 {
    private int x = 11;
    public void main( String args ) {
        Debug2_4 a = new Debug2_4();
    }
    public int getX() {
        return x;
    }
    public void setX( int newValue ) {
        x = newValue;
    }
}
```

5. Correct all errors in the following code. There are semantic errors as well as syntax errors. The purpose of this class is to determine whether the first

of the two integer values passed as command-line arguments to the program is a multiple of the second integer value passed as a command-line argument. The class must also print the ratio created by dividing the first value by the second.

```
package questions.c2;
public class Debug2_5 {
   public static int main( String[] args ){
   int num1 = Integer.parseInt( args[1] );
   int num2 = Integer.parseInt( args[2] );
   float x = num1/num2;
   if ( num1 = x * num2 )
      System.out.println( num1, "is a multiple of",
num2 );
   else
      System.out.println( "num1/num2 = ", x );
   }
}
```

## Complete the Solution

1. Extract the file **questions\c2\Complete2_1.java** from the file **question.jar** on the CD-ROM. Complete the Complete2_1 class definition by adding statements to the nested loops so that when the variable j reaches the value of 7, it will leave the inner loop and go to the next value of the variable i in the outer loop.

2. Extract the file **questions\c2\Complete2_2.java** from the file **question.jar** on the CD-ROM. Complete the Complete2_2 class definition by adding code to the call of the method **println** in this question's class so that the output is a list of the command-line arguments passed to **main**.

3. Extract the file **questions\c2\Complete2_3.java** from the file **question.jar** on the CD-ROM. Complete the Complete2_3 class definition by adding code to the **main** method so that the **main** method will convert the first argument passed on the command line to a floating point number, calculate the absolute value of the number, and then write the absolute value to **System.out**.

4. Extract the file **questions\c2\Complete2_4.java** from the file **question.jar** on the CD-ROM. Complete the Complete2_4 class definition by adding an FtoC method. The method receives an integer number of degrees Fahrenheit to return the equivalent temperature in whole degrees Celsius, using the formula $C = ( 5 / 9 ) ( F - 32 )$.

5. Extract the file **questions\c2\Complete2_5.java** from the file **question.jar** on the CD-ROM. Complete the Complete2_5 class definition by adding code to the **main** method to print a message saying whether each integer value in the range −2 to 2 is odd or even. (An efficient way to tell if an integer is odd or even is to AND it with the value 1.)

## Discovery

1. Create a class called `SquaresAndRoots` in which a **main** method reads a floating-point number from the console and then outputs the square and square root of the number to the console. Code the **main** method to prompt for input repeatedly until the user enters the end-of-file character used by the native operating system. The program quits in response to end-of-file.

2. Assume your monetary system has only quarters worth 25 cents, dimes worth 10 cents, nickels worth five cents, and pennies worth one cent. A dollar is 100 cents. Write a class called `Coins`. The **main** method receives as a command-line argument an integer that represents an amount of money, in cents, and prints the number and type of coins required to make up that amount of money using the smallest possible number of coins. If the input value is greater than one dollar, consider only the portion less than one dollar. The output lists types of coins only if at least one coin of that type is required.

   If the input is 70, the output is

   ```
   4 coins required:
   2 quarters
   2 dimes
   ```

   If the input is a multiple of 100 or less than 1, the output is

   ```
   No coins required.
   ```

3. Create a **public static** method called `gcd` in a class called `Euclid`. This method takes two integers as arguments and returns an integer that is the greatest common denominator of the arguments. The algorithm is based on the following Euclidean principles:

   ➤ The greatest common denominator (gcd) of any two integers equals the gcd of the absolute value of those integers.

   ➤ The gcd of any integer and zero is the value of the integer.

   ➤ The gcd of any two integers x and y is equal to the gcd of y and the value of x modulo y.

   ➤ For example, gcd (-20, -8) = gcd (20, 8) = gcd(8, 4) = gcd(4, 0) = 4.

   The `gcd` method must be recursive. Write a main method that tests `gcd` with five different pairs of values.

# TYPES

## In this chapter you will:

➤ Select the most appropriate type when declaring variables.

☕ State the range of primitive data types, and declare literal values for **String** and all primitive types using all permitted format bases and representations.

☕ Write code that declares, constructs, and initializes arrays of any base type using any of the permitted forms for declaration and for initialization.

☕ State the effect of using a variable or array element of any kind when no explicit assignment has been made to it.

☕ Describe the significance of the immutability of **String** objects.

➤ Create, manipulate, and convert between **String** and **StringBuffer** objects.

☕ Determine the effect of passing variables of reference and primitive types into methods that perform modifying operations on the variables.

➤ Identify the earliest point in a method when variables of reference types may be garbage collected, in the absence of compiler optimization.

☕ Determine the result of applying the **boolean equals(object)** method to any combination of the classes **java.lang.String**, **java.lang.Boolean**, and **java.lang.Object**.

➤ Describe the methods that **Object** class provides for all variables of reference types.

➤ Use wrapper classes to enclose variables of primitive types in objects.

## INTRODUCTION

This chapter covers the types provided by the Java programming language and the types you can define yourself. Classes, the cornerstone of object-oriented programming, fall into the latter group. The Java platform provides many classes, known as the **core classes**, and uses many of the core classes to support the Java programming language itself. This chapter discusses a number of core classes that provide specific support for types.

The basics of Java types[1] are covered in this chapter. Chapters 4 and 5 look in detail at classes and interfaces, a new feature introduced by the Java programming language, and how classes and interfaces can be related in an inheritance hierarchy. Inheritance is the key to powerful object-oriented techniques such as polymorphism.

The Java programming language does not have a primitive type for strings. However, two core classes, **String** and **StringBuffer**, support strings. Because string manipulation is a very important programming technique and many programmers consider strings to be, at least conceptually, a fundamental kind of data, this chapter tells you how to use these two classes.

# STRONG TYPES

The Java programming language is a strongly typed language. A **strongly typed** language is one that enforces a comprehensive set of rules about how you use objects of different types. Of course, the traditional purpose of types, which is to determine how the bits that make up data items should be mapped onto storage, is retained. However, objects in object-oriented languages have behavior as well as data. Strong typing adds restrictions to ensure that objects remain true to their intended behavior. For example, there are limitations about casting or using an object as though it has a different type.

An example of a language that is not strongly typed is JavaScript. JavaScript allows variables that have no type attached to them. You can use an identifier and assign a string, integer, floating point, or other type of data to it. One identifier can represent different types of data at different times.

# PRIMITIVE AND REFERENCE TYPES

When you program in the Java programming language, every variable that you declare belongs to one of two categories: primitive types or reference types. In your code, literals, such as numbers and literal strings, are all of primitive type. The types in each category are listed in Table 3-1.

You refer to a variable of a primitive type by its name. The syntax looks similar for a variable of a reference type, but the identifier is really the name of an object reference through which the object can be accessed. The object itself has no name. The JVM implements object references as pointers to the storage occupied by objects. Object references are entities separate from the objects to which they refer, but the Java programming language does not consider object references to be a separate type.

---

[1] Throughout this text, we use the term *Java type* rather than *type for the Java programming language.*

**Table 3-1** Java types

| Type | Category | Description |
|---|---|---|
| boolean | primitive | Logical value **true** or **false** |
| char | primitive | Integral type that holds the representation of a single character |
| byte | primitive | 8-bit signed integral value |
| short | primitive | 16-bit signed integral value |
| int | primitive | 32-bit signed integral value |
| long | primitive | 64-bit signed integral value |
| float | primitive | Floating-point value |
| double | primitive | Double-precision, floating-point value |
| array | reference | Indexed set of elements of the same primitive or reference type |
| class | reference | Object that can contain data and behavior |
| interface | reference | Specification of behaviors that a class may implement |

If you are accustomed to using a programming language that has pointers, one of the greatest adjustments you must make is to work without a primitive type for pointers. However, it is not true to say that the Java programming language has no pointers. Object references are pointers behind the scenes, but you can use them only in specific ways. You cannot use the values of object references as integral values. You cannot perform arithmetic or bit manipulations on such values.

The Java programming language does provide a limited ability to access object references separately from the objects to which they refer. You can create a **reference object** for an existing variable of reference type by using one of classes in the package **java.lang.ref**. Later in this chapter, you learn that the Java platform has a **garbage collector** that can automatically delete objects that your program no longer uses. The classes **SoftReference**, **WeakReference**, and **PhantomReference** let you interact with the garbage collector. For example, if you are storing objects in a local cache that you manage yourself, you may want to let an object be garbage collected. You do this because the only reference to the object is in the cache. This an advanced technique, and the circumstances that require reference objects are beyond the scope of this book.

The **java.lang.ref** package was introduced in the Java 2 platform in response to developer demand. As the Java platform is increasingly used in enterprise applications, which often are connected to databases and run in distributed environments, developers are finding that they need more control over the garbage collector, or at least notification when the reachability status of objects in the local JVM changes. Previous versions of the JDK had no reference objects. Interaction with the garbage collector may be an area with scope for more enhancements in the future.

When you pass variables as arguments to methods, you always pass primitive types by value and reference types by reference. If an argument has a primitive type, a copy of its value is made and the called method works with the copy. As a result, if the value is modified inside the method, the new value is not passed back to the calling routine. When you pass a variable of a reference type, no copy of the object is made and the object reference is passed to the method. The object reference gives the method access to the storage reserved for the object. If the class of the passed object provides the necessary methods, the method can modify the contents of the object permanently.

## The boolean Type

A **boolean** variable can have one of two values: **true** or **false**. The boolean literals **true** and **false** are part of the Java programming language and are spelled in all lowercase letters.

The most interesting thing about the **boolean** type is that it is not numeric. You cannot cast **true** to be an integer, and you cannot cast an integer to be a boolean. The type **boolean** is a distinct type.

## The char Type

A **char** variable represents one character, encoded in a platform–independent definition of characters called Unicode. Unicode defines a 16-bit representation of characters. The Unicode character set includes the characters required for most major modern languages and is not limited to the North American or Western European alphabets. The seven-bit industry-standard ASCII character set is a subset of Unicode.

Character literals are enclosed within single quotation marks. Double quotation marks enclose literal strings.

You can use a **char** wherever an **int** is valid without explicitly casting. You can also explicitly cast a character to any size integer and cast an integer to a character. Such casts can lose precision because representation of a character is a 16-bit unsigned value. An **int** is 32 bits in the Java programming language and can always hold a 16-bit **char**. However, when you are casting from the **int** to the **char**, only the low-order 16 bits are used. Many of the methods of the core classes that operate on characters take an argument of type **int**. For example, the following line returns the position of the dot character in a **String** object called `fileName`. The argument of **indexOf** has type **int**, so the actual parameter `'.'` is implicitly cast to an **int**:

```
int suffix = fileName.indexOf('.');
```

## Escape Sequences

You can use escape sequences in your code to represent characters that do not display or that cannot be easily entered on the keyboard. The term **escape sequences** may be a misnomer because the sequences begin with a backslash rather than the escape control character. Table 3-2 shows escape sequences used in the Java programming language.

**Table 3-2** Escape sequences

| Escape Sequence | Represents | Escape Sequence | Represents |
|---|---|---|---|
| \b | Backspace | \' | Single quote ( ' ) |
| \f | Form feed (new page) | \" | Double quote ( " ) |
| \n | New line | \d, \dd, or \ddd | Octal value in the range 0 to 377 |
| \r | Carriage return | \xdd | Hexadecimal value in the range 00 to FF |
| \t | Tab | \udddd | Unicode character value |
| \\ | Backslash ( \ ) | | |

You can use Unicode escape sequences for the value of a single character or values of sets of characters in string constants. The representation of a Unicode character starts with **\u**, followed by four hexadecimal digits. You can put Unicode escape sequences anywhere within a program, even in class names and variable names. For example, you can create a constant called π, instead of **PI** to represent the value 3.14159. Doing this may not be advisable, however, because the character may not be visible when you display the source. Nevertheless, it is important to note that the Java programming language does not require that identifiers contain only ASCII characters.

Unicode escape sequences are processed before the code is compiled. For example, the compiler rejects a literal string that contains the sequence \u000a, which becomes a Unicode line-feed character because you cannot include line feed in a string literal.

## Integer Types

The Java programming language has four integer types: **byte**, **short**, **int**, and **long**. All of the integer types are signed. The range of integers is never from zero to some large, positive number. Instead the range is always from a negative number to a positive number. The integer types have fixed sizes on all platforms. Table 3-3 gives the size and range of the integer types.

**Table 3-3** Integer types

| Type | Size in Bits | Range |
| --- | --- | --- |
| byte | 8 | -128 to 127 |
| short | 16 | -32768 to 32767 |
| int | 32 | -2,147,483,648 to 2,147,483,647 |
| long | 64 | -9,223,372,036,854,775,808 to 9,223,372,036,854,775,807 |

Types **byte** and **short** are intended mostly for saving space when storing information. When you perform calculations on variables of type **byte** or **short**, they are promoted to type **int**.

 Most hardware currently used is not designed to handle integers that are 64 bits long. If you do not need the extra range, use **int** instead of **long** for better performance.

When you supply a numeric literal, the Java programming language assigns type **int** if the value will fit into 32 bits, or type **long** if it requires more than 32 bits of storage. You can append the letter **L** or **l** to force explicitly the type of the literal to **long**.

Numeric literals can be decimal, octal, or hexadecimal. The first character in a decimal literal must be one of the digits 1 to 9, and a decimal integer can contain only the digits 0, 1, 2, 3, 4, 5, 6, 7, 8, and 9. Do not start a decimal number with a zero, because a leading 0 means octal and a leading 0x or 0X indicates hexadecimal. Table 3-4 presents some example literals.

**Table 3-4** Example literals

| Type: | int | int | int | long | int |
| --- | --- | --- | --- | --- | --- |
| Base: | Decimal | Decimal | Hexadecimal | Decimal | Octal |
| | 6 | −1873 | 0xABF8 | 30000000000L | 0777 |

# Floating-point Types

The Java programming language has two floating-point types: **float** and **double**. The floating-point types have fixed sizes on all platforms, as shown in Table 3-5.

**Table 3-5** Floating-point types

| Type | Number of Bits | Approximate Significant Decimal Digits |
|------|----------------|----------------------------------------|
| float | 32 | 6 — 7 with a range of ±3.40282347E+38 |
| double | 64 | 15 with a range of ±1.79769313486231570E+308 |

**3**

Floating-point storage conforms to the IEEE 754 standard. It provides distinct values for positive and negative zeros, positive and negative infinities, and a special value called **NaN. POSITIVE_INFINITY** represents a number that is too large to hold, even as a **double**, and can be the result of dividing a very large number by a very small number with the same sign. Similarly, **NEGATIVE_INFINITY** represents a negative number that exceeds the range of a **double**.

The **NaN** value is a very interesting constant because its value is "not a number." It can represent the result of a floating-point operation that would otherwise cause an error, such as dividing by zero or calculating the square root of a negative number.

Floating-point literals can contain a decimal point, an exponent, or both. The suffix letters **f** and **F** indicate type **float**, and the suffix letters **d** and **D** indicate type **double**. By default, numbers that contain a decimal point have type **double**. Table 3-6 presents some floating-point literals.

**Table 3-6** Example floating-point literals

| float | double | float | double | double | float |
|-------|--------|-------|--------|--------|-------|
| 67.925f | 0.45 | 5.2e5F | 6.73E-6 | 2.345d | -8.4126f |

The Java platform provides two reference types to augment the primitive floating-point types. The classes **BigInteger** and **BigDecimal** make up the package **java.math**.

**BigInteger** objects are similar to primitive integer variables except that their value can grow without limit. The **BigInteger** class provides methods analogous to methods of the **Math** class that operate primitive integer types and additional methods, such as testing for prime numbers, performing modular arithmetic, and manipulating bits. **BigInteger** objects play an important role in the cryptography that is the basis for many of Java's security features.

**BigDecimal** objects hold signed decimal numbers accurate to an arbitrary level of precision and may be useful for currency operations. This class gives you control over rounding and scaling behavior and provides methods to perform basic arithmetic operations.

The **java.lang.math** package and classes **BigInteger** and **BigDecimal** were introduced in version 1.1 of the Java platform.

## Casting Primitive Types

The rules for casting are simple for the primitive types. You can cast from any type to a type that allows a greater range of values without specifying a cast operator. If you want to cast to a type that has a smaller range of values, you have to use a cast operator explicitly to indicate that you intended the cast to happen. Otherwise, the Java compiler flags a cast that might lose information as an error.

Implicit conversions from integer type to floating–point type are allowed, but the reverse requires an explicit cast. The Java programming language casts a **byte** to a **short**, a **short** to an **int**, an **int** to a **long**, and a **float** to a **double** automatically, as required. Any integral type can be cast to **float** or **double** without requiring a cast operator.

---

**Mini Quiz 3-1**

The statement short **x** = 123; compiles successfully. Why does the compiler reject the following statements?

```
int i = 123;
short x = i;
```

---

# OBJECT REFERENCES

Variables of reference types reside in a very different part of storage from variables of primitive types. Variables of primitive types are local variables. They reside in the stack space for the method to which they belong. Storage for objects of reference types is allocated from the program heap. The **program heap** is that area of memory, also called dynamic memory, from which storage is allocated and freed, independently of the stack, as required during program execution. However, the object references, as distinct from the objects to which they refer, are added to the stack along with the objects of primitive types. In this sense, object references themselves are primitive values. The content of the object reference is the location of an object on the heap.

## Creating Objects of a Reference Type

To create an object of a reference type and to obtain a reference for the object, use the **new** keyword.

**3**

---

*Syntax*

*ClassName ObjectReference* = **new** *ClassName*( *constructor_arguments* );

---

*Dissection*

➤ The *ClassName* specifies which class the object instantiates. On the left side of the assignment operator, it specifies the type of the object being created, as in any declaration.

➤ The *ObjectReference* is the identifier for the new variable.

➤ The expression new *ClassName*( ) acquires space on the heap for the new object and calls the constructor of the class that the object instantiates. The constructor is a method that prepares the object for use, and it can take arguments. The arguments are enclosed in the parentheses. The parentheses are always required, even if the constructor has no arguments.

---

*Syntax*

*ClassName ObjectReference;*

*ObjectReference* = **new** *ClassName*( *constructor_arguments* );

---

*Dissection*

➤ You can create an object separately from declaring the object reference, by defining each in separate statements. After you declare an object reference, it has the value null until it is assigned an object reference returned by **new**.

---

*Code Example*

```
SomeType x = new SomeType();
```

---

*Code Dissection*

This statement creates an object of the **SomeType** class. No input arguments are required to build the object. The object reference for the object has the identifier **x**.

---

Chapter 9 gives another form for the **new** keyword that allows an inner class to be defined at the same time that an object of the inner class is created. Inner classes are an advanced programming technique.

Inner classes did not exist when the first version of the Java platform was released. Inner classes and the enhanced syntax of the **new** keyword were introduced in version 1.1 of the Java platform.

## Assigning Values to Object References

You can use the assignment operator with object references. Be careful when you assign values to object references. Consider the following lines of code:

```
SomeType a = new SomeType();
SomeType b = new SomeType();
// omitted lines give a and b different contents
a = b;
```

The statement a = b; is valid, but is deceptive in its simplicity. This statement does not assign the contents of object b to object a. This statement assigns the value of the object reference b to the object reference a, creating a second reference for the object called b. Both a and b now refer to the object created in the second line of the example, and the object created in the first line has one less reference. The Java programming language provides a way to solve the problem of copying object references instead of objects, by introducing a method called **clone**. In the Java programming language, you clone an object to create an identical copy. Cloning is covered in Chapter 7.

## Passing Object References as Arguments

When you pass objects of reference types as arguments to a method, you are really passing an object reference, not a copy of the object. Because object references themselves are primitive types, they are always passed by value. The method gets a copy of the object reference and can modify the copy without changing the original. At the same time, the called method can use the object reference to the object and can make changes to the storage allocated for the object. These changes are not undone when the method returns.

If an argument is qualified with the keyword **final**, the method cannot change the argument, which is effectively a constant for the duration of the method. What does this mean for reference types? Consider the following method taken from a class that provides some sort of address book objects:

```
public void addEntry( final NameNumber person ) {
    if ( numEntries < MAXENTRIES ) {
        phoneBook[numEntries++] = person;
        person.setIndex( numEntries );
    }
}
```

When an object reference is a **final** argument, the qualifier **final** applies to the object reference but not to the actual object. Therefore, you cannot change the object reference in the method. For example, this method cannot change the object reference **person** to refer to a different **NameNumber** object. But the method can modify the object **person** by calling a mutator method of the **NameNumber** class. A **mutator** method is one whose purpose is to set, or change, the contents of fields of a class. Here, the method

`NameNumber.setIndex` may record the value of field `numEntries` in a private field of the `person` object. Note that the elements in the array `phoneBook` are object references, and there is no problem assigning the value of the object reference `person` to one of them.

## Deleting Objects of Reference Types

The JVM keeps track of how many object references refer to a particular object. When an object has no object references, your program can no longer access the object. This is correct behavior in a Java program; you are not expected, or even able, to delete objects of reference types explicitly. Instead, you rely on the system to clean up the heap occasionally and to remove all objects you are no longer using.

You can tell the JVM you are finished with an object, but you do not have to do even that. The way to sever the association between an object and an object reference is to assign another value to the object reference. To make an object reference refer to no object, assign the constant **null**.

*Syntax*

*objectReference* **= null;**

*Dissection*

➤ A statement of this form says, "I am finished using the object to which this object reference refers, so I do not mind if the JVM discards the object."

You can also test any object reference to see if its value equals **null**. You usually do this to determine whether an object has been created, with a statement similar to the following:

```
if ( x == null ) {
    // x does not refer to an object
    // the statement: x.doit(); causes an exception
}
else {
    // x refers to an object that can be used
    // the statement: x.doit(); can run successfully
}
```

## Collecting Garbage Automatically

A most welcome feature of the Java platform is that the JVM automatically cleans up the heap from time to time. Programmers using the Java platform do not have to keep track of all memory they allocate from the heap and explicitly deallocate it. A garbage collector sweeps through the list of objects periodically and reclaims the resources held by unreferenced objects.

What does garbage collection destroy? All objects that have no object references are eligible for garbage collection. These may be objects for which the references have gone out of scope and no longer exist on the stack, or objects for which you have assigned **null**. When the count of references for an object drops to zero, the object is eligible for garbage collection.

When does garbage collection occur? This question is hard to answer because the JVM decides when to start the garbage collector. Typically the garbage collector runs only when available memory is becoming low. It may never run at all if your program makes modest demands on memory. The best approach is not to build into your code any dependence on the timing of garbage collection.

You cannot prevent the garbage collector from running, but you can request it to run.

---

*Class*

**java.lang.System**

---

*Purpose*

The **System** class provides a number of useful methods. Some are API for the Java platform.

---

*Methods*

➤ **void gc()**
   Call the **gc** method to request that the JVM schedule the garbage collector to run soon.

---

Deliberately starting garbage collection may be appropriate if you can anticipate that the garbage collector is likely to run soon and that your program is at a point where the impact of running the garbage collector is minimal. The use of this method does not force the garbage collector to run; it is only a request.

# THE OBJECT CLASS

The **Object** class is the common ancestor class of all classes you can have in a Java program. The name of the class might not be very creative, but it reflects the fact that **Object** is a superclass of all classes. All variables of reference type are instances of **Object**, including arrays. Every method of **Object** is inherited, directly or indirectly, by all other classes. This means that the **Object** class provides a set of methods that all objects have. Because it is the root of the entire class hierarchy, **Object** is a common denominator for all objects.

The methods in the **Object** class provide a convenient and standard interface that helps clients of a class work with objects of that class. When you create a new class, you often provide customized definitions of some of these methods so that your class supports a standard set of behaviors in a way that is meaningful for objects of the class.

## Class
**java.lang.Object**

## Purpose
The **Object** class is the direct or indirect superclass of all Java classes. All classes can inherit the methods of this class or provide their own implementations. This book refers to the implementations provided by **Object** as default implementations.

## Methods

➤ **Object clone()**
The **clone** method returns a copy of the object for which the method is called. The value of every field is duplicated, regardless of whether the field has a primitive type or is an object reference. The object referred to by a contained object reference is not duplicated.

➤ **boolean equals( Object )**
The **equals** method returns **true** if two objects are considered equal, and **false** otherwise. The default implementation compares just the object references, and is equivalent to a conditional expression such as ( a == b ), where a and b are references for the objects in question. In other words, the base **equals** method returns **true** only when you compare two references for the same object.

➤ **void finalize()**
The garbage collector calls the **finalize** method before destroying the object. By default, the method does nothing, but you can provide implementations to perform specialized cleanup.

➤ **Class getClass()**
**getClass** returns an object that can be used to obtain run-time type information about an object.

➤ **int hashCode()**
The **hashCode** method returns an integer suitable for determining the hash code for an object. Hash codes are used to locate the entries for objects in hash tables. The JVM uses hash tables extensively as a data structure for random access to objects.

➤ **void notify()**
**void notifyAll()**
**void wait()**
You can use **notify**, **notifyAll**, and **wait** in a multithreaded program to perform interthread communication. Signaling and synchronization between threads are essential to ensure that there are no timing or other conflicts when different threads share objects.

➤ **String toString()**
The **toString** method returns a printable representation of the object. The **System.out.println** method can output strings and the primitive types. When **println** encounters an object that it does not understand, it calls **toString** and outputs the returned value. The default implementation of this method does not do much; it returns a character string that is the hexadecimal representation of the reference for the object.

# WRAPPER CLASSES FOR PRIMITIVE TYPES

In the object-oriented sense, all variables of the primitive types and reference types are objects, with a lowercase *o*. Reference types are also **Objects**, with a capital *O*, because they belong to a class that inherits from **Object**. Being an **Object** has many advantages. Is there a way to extend the advantages of being an **Object** to the primitive types? To fill this obvious need, the Java platform includes wrapper classes for all of the primitive types. A **wrapper class** is essentially a class that provides different behavior for a type than the behavior established by the definition of that type. In other words, a wrapper class gives you another way of using the object it wraps. For example, a wrapper for an integer can contain an integer and define methods that are useful for working on integral values.

Wrapper classes encapsulate the primitive types in a class, so that reference semantics apply. Table 3-7 lists the wrapper classes and their primitive types.

**Table 3-7**   Wrapper classes

| Wrapper Class | Primitive Type |
|---------------|----------------|
| Boolean | boolean |
| Byte | byte |
| Character | char |
| Double | double |
| Float | float |
| Integer | int |
| Long | long |
| Short | short |

The names of the wrapper classes start with an uppercase letter. Except for **Integer** and **Character**, the capitalization is all that distinguishes the wrapper class names from the primitive types.

The original version of the Java platform did not include wrapper classes for the primitive types **byte** and **short**. Version 1.1 of the Java platform introduced the classes **Byte** and **Short**.

The classes **Byte**, **Double**, **Float**, **Integer**, **Long**, and **Short** derive from a common class called **Number**, so you can manipulate objects of these types at a more general level. For example, you can call the method **byteValue** to get the value of the number converted to a single byte. In some cases, the value must be rounded or truncated to fit in one byte, but this method is available for all **Number** objects.

The Java platform includes constants and utility methods related to the primitive types in the appropriate wrapper class. For example, the **Integer** class contains the constants **Integer.MAX_VALUE** and **Integer.MIN_VALUE**. The **Character** class defines the methods **Character.isDigit** and **Character.isSpace**. By placing these handy constants and methods in the most appropriate wrapper class, the Java platform makes them much easier to locate than they would be if they were all members of some generic utility class. Like the methods in the **Math** class, these constants and methods are always available, regardless of whether any wrapper class objects have been created. For example, the following code makes sure no information is lost before casting a **long** to an **int**:

```
long l;
int i = 0;
// assign value to l
if ( l <= Integer.MAX_VALUE &&  l >= Integer.MIN_VALUE ) {
   i = (int) l;
}
```

All these wrapper classes directly or indirectly inherit from **Object**. Therefore, standard methods such as **toString**, **clone**, and **equals** are available. This inheritance is particularly useful when you want to create generic collections of objects. The wrapper classes can participate in such collections, but the primitive types cannot. Chapter 10 describes the collection classes that the Java platform provides.

Unfortunately, the wrapper classes are all immutable. They do not provide mutator methods that allow the programmer to change their values. For example, passing variables of type **Integer** rather than **int** does not result in integer input–output method arguments.

---

**Mini Quiz 3-2**

What happens when you write and run a swap method such as the following?

```
void swap( Integer a, Integer b ) {
   Integer temp = new Integer ( a.intValue() );
   a = b;
   b = temp;
}
```

You cannot define any classes that inherit from the wrapper classes, because the wrapper classes are declared to be **final**. In the Java programming language, you can mark a class with the keyword **final** so that no one can use it as the equivalent of a base class. The creators of the Java programming language clearly thought it best to prevent you, for example, from creating your own kind of number that inherits all the attributes of class **Integer** and has some special qualities. They imposed this restriction not to create awkwardness, but to enhance security and performance.

# ARRAYS

Arrays are objects of reference type. They can contain a fixed number of elements of any one type. An individual element is identified by the object reference for the array followed by an integral index value enclosed in square brackets, [ and ]. The individual elements can be used like individual variables. For example, the following statement assigns the value 5 to the third element in an array named **a**:

```
a[2] = 5;
```

An array variable is really an object reference for the array object. Therefore, only the object reference is on the program stack; the array itself is placed on the heap. This scheme has a slight disadvantage because you lose a little bit of performance compared to storing array elements on the stack.

Object references for array objects are defined quite similarly to other reference types.

*Syntax*

*type*[ ] *identifier*;
*type identifier*[ ];

*Dissection*

➤  The two forms are equivalent, but the first is preferable because it gives the full type information first.

➤  Use the square bracket syntax to declare the object reference, but do not specify a size because size is not part of the array type.

*Code Example*

```
int[] a;
int a[];
```

*Code Dissection*

The variable **a** is an object reference to an array of **int**.

An object reference is not useful on its own, so you must also create the actual array. As with all reference types, you use the **new** keyword to create an array.

---

*Syntax*

*type* **[ ]** *identifier* **= new** *type* **[** *size* **]**;

---

*Dissection*

➤  As with all reference types, you can declare the reference and create the object in one statement or two.

---

*Code Example*

```
a = new int[5];
int[] x = new int[5];
```

---

*Code Dissection*

In the first statement the existing object reference **a** is assigned the new array object. In the second statement the variable **x** is defined to be an object reference for the new array of integers.

---

You cannot specify a negative size. If you do, a run-time exception of the type **java.lang.NegativeArraySizeException** is raised. You can create an array with size zero. However, you can use a zero-length array only as a placeholder because you cannot put anything into it!

After the array has been created, you cannot extend it. For example, an array of five integers is always going to be five integers, and you cannot make it hold six or more integers. However, you can use an integer expression for the size of the array, and calculate how many elements to allow at run time. You can also change the object reference to point to a different array. The following two lines of code create two arrays. The first has five elements and the second 10. But the net effect is to replace the five-element array with a 10-element array and to continue to use the object reference **a**.

```
int[] a = new int[5];
a = new int[10];
```

> **Mini Quiz 3-3**
> If no other object references refer to the array of five elements in the two previous lines, can you use the array again in your program? If yes, how? If no, what can happen to it?

You can initialize an array when you declare it.

---

*Syntax*

*type*[] *identifier* = { *initializer_list* };

---

*Dissection*

➤ If you create arrays with objects that already exist, you do not have to use the **new** keyword. Just put the objects in an *initializer_list*. Elements in the list are separated by commas, and the list is enclosed in braces.

---

*Code Example*

```
double[] x = { 5.67, 4.59, 0.0005, -23455.6 };
String[] light = { "sun", "moon" };
long[] places = { 10, 10*10, (long)Math.pow( 10.0,3.0 )};
```

*Code Dissection*

The syntax works for numeric and string literals and arbitrary expressions.

---

An **anonymous array** is an array object that has no name. This form can be useful when you want to give a new value to an existing object reference. Anonymous arrays are also a handy way to pass an array of known values into a method without creating the array and giving it a name, when you have no other use for the array.

The second of the following lines creates an anonymous array; the right side of the second statement initializes the array:

```
double[] x = { 1.1, 1.2, 1.3, 1.4 }; // initial value
x =  new double[] { 0.1, 0.2, 0.3, 0.4 }; // assign a
                                        // different value
```

 When the Java platform was first released, programmers could initialize an array only in the statement that defined it. The ability to use a list of values enclosed in braces to change an object reference became available in version 1.1 at the same time that the platform introduced the anonymous array.

## Array Indexes and Lengths

The indexing for arrays is zero-based. **Zero-based indexing** means the first element is at zero. Index values go up in steps of one so that the index of the last element equals the size of the array minus one. In the Java platform, every time you use an array index, it is checked against the array bounds at run time. This safety and security feature prevents you from using the array to access memory outside the storage reserved for the array.

You can easily find out the size of the array. Every array stores its size as read-only data in a field called **length.**

---

*Syntax*

*arrayName.***length**

---

*Dissection*

➤ You can get size of an array at any time. The field **length** is public and has type **int**. Because **length** is a field rather than a method, do not follow it with parentheses.

---

*Code Example*

```
int[] myArray = { 5, 6, 99, -45, 0 };
for( int j = 0; j < myArray.length; j++ ) {
    System.out.println( myArray[j] );
}
```

---

*Code Output*

```
5
6
99
-45
0
```

---

*Code Dissection*

In these lines, the value of the expression **myArray.length** is 5.

---

The following class is called **ArrayTypes.** It is a public class, and therefore must be in a file called ArrayTypes.java. The structure of packages mirrors the file system, so you will call this source code in the examples\basic subfolder of the folder in which you unpacked the JAR file examples.jar. The class has only one method, the **main** method, in which it creates, and then works with, two arrays.

```
package examples.basic;
/** A class demonstrating the use of arrays
   */
public class ArrayTypes {
    /** A method that creates and manipulates two integer
      * arrays
      * @param args Not used
      */
    public static void main( String[] args ) {
        int[] a, b;
        a = new int[3];
```

```
        b = new int[3];
        for ( int i = 0; i < a.length; i++ ) {
            a[i] = i * i;
            System.out.println( i + " squared is "
                                    + a[i] );
        }
        for ( int i = 0; i < b.length; i++ ) {
            b[i] = i * i * i;
            System.out.println( i + " cubed is " + b[i] );
        }
    }
}
```

The output is

```
0 squared is 0
1 squared is 1
2 squared is 4
0 cubed is 0
1 cubed is 1
2 cubed is 8
```

**Mini Quiz 3-4**

Why is there no problem declaring i twice in this example?

## Returning an Array from a Method

The return type of a method can have array type.

*Syntax*

*type* [ ] *methodName( arguments ) { }*

---

*Dissection*

➤ The square brackets following the return type indicate that the method returns an object reference for an array.

➤ No size is specified for the array. Size is not part of the type. It does not matter whether the array contains five elements or a thousand. However, it is important to give the type for the elements in the array.

## Code Example

```java
package examples.basic;
/** A method demonstrating how arrays can be a
  * return type
  */
public class ArrayReturn {
    /** A method that returns an array object
      * @param flag A boolean value for which
      *             array to return
      * @returns An integer array object
      */
    public int[] returnsArray( boolean flag ) {
        int[] array1 = { 1, 2, 3, 4, 5, 6, 7, 8, 9, 10 };
        int[] array2 = { 10, 20, 30, 40, 50 };
        if ( flag ) {
            return array1;
        } else {
            return array2;
        }
    }
    /** The test method for the class
      * @param args Not used
      */
    public static void main( String[] args ) {
        ArrayReturn x = new ArrayReturn();
        System.out.println( x.returnsArray( true ).length );
        System.out.println( x.returnsArray( false ).length );
    }
}
```

## Code Output

```
10
5
```

---

**Mini Quiz 3-5**

This `ArrayReturn` program demonstrates a number of Java programming
language features. Use it to test your understanding of several topics covered so far:

- Where is the storage for `array1` and `array2` allocated in `returnsArray`?
- Are the **boolean** expressions **true** and **false** passed to `returnsArray` by value or by reference?
- What is the type of x?
- What is the type of `x.returnsArray`?
- What does the notation `/**`, `@param`, `@returns` mean?

## Copying Arrays

Because arrays are reference types, you cannot copy the contents of one array into another with the assignment operator. Use the utility method **arraycopy**, which is provided by the **System** class in the package **java.lang**.

---

*Class*

**java.lang.System**

---

*Purpose*

The **System** class provides a number of useful methods and objects.

---

*Methods*

➤ **void arraycopy( Object** *source,* **int** *SourcePos,* **Object** *destination,*
**int** *destinationPos,* **int** *number***)**

The **arraycopy** method copies the specified number of elements from the source array to the destination array. Specify the first position in the source array from which to take an element, the position in the destination array in which to put that element, and the number of elements.

---

The following class uses the **arraycopy** method:

```
package examples.basic
/** class to demonstrate method arraycopy
  */
public class MergeArrays {
   public static void main( String[] args ) {
      int[] x = { 5, 4, 0, -2, 53, -3 };
      int[] y = { 100, 101 };
      for( int i = 0; i < x.length; i++ ) {
         System.out.print( " " + x[i] );
      }
      System.out.println();
      System.arraycopy( y, 0, x, 3, y.length );
      for( int i = 0; i < x.length; i++ ) {
         System.out.print( " " + x[i] );
      }
      System.out.println();
   }
}
```

The output is

```
5 4 0 -2 53 -3
5 4 0 100 101 -3
```

The **arraycopy** method has some useful features. You can use it to copy a whole array or just a part of an array. You can even specify source and destination areas that overlap in the same array. Therefore, you can use this method to shift contents within an array. However, you cannot use **arraycopy** to create a new array. It does not allocate memory. The method fails if the source and destination arrays do not already exist or do not have enough space to perform the copy.

If the elements in the array are object references, the object references, and not the referenced objects, are copied.

## Using Multidimensional Arrays

Arrays can be multidimensional. If an array is two-dimensional, it is an array of arrays. Two-dimensional arrays do not have to be rectangular; in other words, the individual inner arrays can have different lengths. When using the **length** field of a multidimensional array, it is important to note that it refers to the length of the first dimension and is not a product of all the dimensions. The Java programming language puts no limit to the number of dimensions that an array must have. The only limit is your ability to visualize the complex data structures that you are creating!

---

*Syntax*

**type[][] identifier;**

---

*Dissection*

➤ The index for each array dimension has its own set of square brackets.

---

You may find it helpful to visualize the first index as rows and the second as columns in a two-dimensional table. If there is a third index, you can visualize it as depth in a three-dimensional table, and so on. Regardless of how you visualize them, arrays of all dimensions occupy linear areas of storage, and you should not be concerned with the placement of individual elements relative to each other.

The example in Figure 3-1 demonstrates a variety of two-dimensional arrays. The array named c is rectangular, two by four, but arrays b and d are jagged in the sense that if you drew a diagram of them, they would look uneven, as Figure 3-1 indicates.

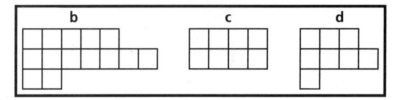

**Figure 3-1** Two-dimensional arrays

 **Performance Tip** Because two-dimensional arrays are really just arrays of arrays, accessing an element of a two-dimensional array is twice as expensive as accessing an element of a one-dimensional array. The cost increases proportionally as you add more dimensions. Think twice before using a two-dimensional array. If you can visualize the data structure in some other way than as rows and columns of data, you may be able to use one of the collection classes that are described in Chapter 10 or simplify the data structure enough to use a one-dimensional array.

In the following example, array d contains some integers and is set up by the initializer list. The array d is an array of three arrays. The braces in the declaration of d group the numbers into the three arrays that make up d, and open and close the initializer lists for the three arrays.

Here is an example showing different ways of creating multidimensional arrays:

```java
package examples.basic;
/** A class to demonstrate the initialization and
  * use of multidimensional arrays
  */
public class MultDimArrayTypes {
    /** The test method of the class
      * @param args Not used
      */
    public static void main( String[] args ) {
        int[][] b;
        b = new int[3][];
        b[0] = new int[5];
        b[1] = new int[7];
        b[2] = new int[2];
        b[0][4] = 1256;
        int[][] c = new int [2][4];
        c[0][1] = -6754;
        int[][] d = { { -5,-6,8 }, { -2,11,3456,5 }, { 7 } };
        System.out.println( "b[0][4]=" + b[0][4] +
            " c[0][1]=" + c[0][1] + " d[1][3]=" + d[1][3] );
    }
}
```

The output is

```
b[0][4]=1256 c[0][1]=-6754 d[1][3]=5
```

Note that this example creates **d** without using the **new** keyword.

The example uses only integers, but all types work equally well. When you create arrays of reference types, the elements of the arrays are actually references for objects, and each one is initialized to the value **null**. Because **int** is a primitive type, the arrays in the example actually contain integer values. If the elements are object references, you must give them values before using them. If you use a **null** object reference, an exception occurs.

# STRINGS

The Java platform provides two classes for strings in the standard language package, **java.lang**. The two classes are **String** and **StringBuffer**. Therefore, strings are objects of predefined reference types. The **String** class is the main class for strings. You can use a **StringBuffer** when you are working within a string. For example, when you are modifying the contents of a string, the **StringBuffer** class may provide more flexibility than the **String** class.

**String** objects are immutable. You cannot change the contents of a string or change its size after storage has been allocated. However, you can concatenate **String**s. The JVM implements the string concatenation operators, **+** and **+=**, by using **StringBuffer** objects behind the scenes, so that there is no performance or size penalty in using these operators on **String** objects.

## Working with String Objects

The Java programming language provides a convenient way to create **String** objects.

---

*Syntax*

**String** *identifier* = "*literal string*";
**String** *identifier* = **new String** ( *arguments_ of _constructor* );

---

*Dissection*

➤ The object reference for the string is defined and refers to the **String** object constructed to represent the string literal. String literals are enclosed in double quotation marks. Two consecutive double quote characters, "", is a valid string and represents an empty string.

➤ You can also create **String** objects using the **new** operator and any of the constructors of the **String** class.

---

---

*Code Example*

```
String name = "Joe";
String name = new String( "Joe" );
```

---

*Code Dissection*

These two statements are equivalent. The first form is more common because it is simpler.

---

Many classes provide a method **toString** that returns a string representation of the information in the class. A very common way to obtain a **String** object is to call **toString** or another method that returns an object reference for a **String**.

> **Mini Quiz 3-6**
>
> How many objects and object references does the following declaration create? Where are they stored?
>
> ```
> String[] seasons = { "winter",
>                      "spring",
>                      "summer",
>                      "fall" };
> ```

To access the character at a particular position, use the **charAt** method of the **String** class:

```
String jabberwock = "Jabberwock";
char c = jabberwock.charAt(6);      // assigns 'w' to c
```

Use the **+** or **+=** operators to concatenate strings, as you have already been doing to build up the output line in many code examples. How can these operators work when **String** objects are immutable? The effect of these operators can be deceptive. Consider the following line:

```
jabberwock += "y";
System.out.println( jabberwock );   // the output is:
                                    // Jabberwocky
```

No **String** objects are changed when the first statement is executed. Instead, a new string is built, the contents of which are the result of concatenating two string objects. The reference **jabberwock** is associated with the new string. The string previously referenced by **jabberwock** has one less object reference, and may have just become a candidate for garbage collection.

If you want to know the length of a string, call the method **length**. For strings, **length** is a method. For arrays, **length** is a field. Therefore, the syntax for determining the number of characters in a string is not consistent with the syntax for determining the number of elements in an array. Notice the difference in these two statements:

```
if ( monthName.length() > 12 )
    { /* the string has more than 12 characters */ }
if ( days.length > 31 )
    { /* the array has more than 31 elements */ }
```

To compare **String** objects, use the **equals** method, not the == operator. The == operator just tells you whether the object references are the same.

```
if ( monthName.equals( "January" ) )
    { /* the contents of monthName is "January" */ }
```

If your **String** objects contain characters other than those used in U.S. English, you may find that **equalsIgnoreCase** does not work as expected. Different languages and character sets can have different rules for mapping between uppercase and lowercase characters. **Locale** objects capture national characteristics, and **Collator** objects apply the rules for comparing strings. The **Locale** and **Collator** classes are described in "Internationalization" on the CD-ROM, as part of the discussion of programming for different cultural environments.

The following example demonstrates the difference between the **equals** method and the **==,** or equality, operator:

```
package examples.basic;
/** A class to demonstrate how to define and
  * use String objects
  */
public class StringCompare {
   /** The test method for the class
     * @param args Not used
     */
   public static void main( String[] args ) {
      String s1 = new String( "Hello" );
      String s2 = new String( "Hello" );
      System.out.println( "Comparing references yields "
                         + ( s1 == s2 ) );
      System.out.println( "Comparing using equals() yields "
                         + s1.equals( s2 ) );
   }
}
```

The output is

```
Comparing references yields false
Comparing using equals() yields true
```

If the declarations read String s1="Hello" and String s2="Hello", comparing object references would have also yielded **true**. The JVM stores literal strings in a separate pool and does not make duplicates. Therefore, both references **s1** and **s2** refer to the same object: the string literal object "Hello".

---

*Class*

**java.lang.String**

---

*Purpose*

The **String** class provides many methods for string manipulation. Only the most frequently used are listed here.

---

*Constructors*

➤ **String()**
   **String( String** *s* **)**
   **String( StringBuffer** *sb* **)**
   **String( byte[]** *b* **)**
   **String( char[]** *c* **)**

   The constructors create **String** objects. You can supply many types of input, not all of which are listed here. The constructor with no arguments creates an empty string. The **String** class is unique in that the JVM creates **String** objects also from statements of the following form:
   **String** *identifierf=fliteral_string*;

---

*Methods*

➤ **char charAt( int** *position* **)**
   The **charAt** method returns the character located at the specified position in the string.

➤ **int compareTo( String** *s* **)**
   Use **compareTo** to compare **String** objects. It returns a negative number if the string for which you called the method comes before the contents of the argument in alphabetic order. Zero is returned if both strings are the same, and a positive number is returned if the argument string comes first. This method mimics the behavior of the C function **strcmp**.

➤ **String concat( String** *s* **)**
   Use **concat** to concatenate the specified **String** object *s* to the string for which you called the method. The method returns the resulting string.

➤ **boolean equals( Object** *o* **)**
   The **equals** method tests for equality. It returns **true** if the object is a string that has the same length and contains the same characters as the string for which the method is called, and **false** otherwise.

➤ **boolean equalsIgnoreCase( Object** *o* **)**
This method is like **equals**, except that the comparison of characters treats uppercase and lowercase versions of the same character as matching.

➤ **int indexOf( int** *character* **)**
**int indexOf( int** *character*, **int** *position* **)**
**int indexOf( String** *s* **)**
**int indexOf( String** *s*, **int** *position* **)**
Call **indexOf** to locate the first occurrence of the specified character or **String** in the string for which you are calling the method. The method returns negative one if no match is found. Note that the argument for a character has type **int**. If you supply a second argument of type **int**, it specifies the start position of the search.

➤ **int lastIndexOf( int** *character* **)**
**int lastIndexOf( int** *character*, **int** *position* **)**
**int lastIndexOf( String** *s* **)**
**int lastIndexOf( String** *s*, **int** *position* **)**
This method is like **indexOf**, except that it returns the position of the last occurrence of a character or **String**.

➤ **int length()**
The **length** method returns the number of characters in the string.

➤ **String substring( int** *start* **)**
**String substring( int** *start*, **int** *end* **)**
Use **substring** to extract a **String** from a larger string. The first **int** argument is the position of the first character to extract. The optional second **int** argument is not the position of the last character to extract, but the position following the last character to extract. The next sample program uses this method.

➤ **String toLowerCase()**
This method returns a **String** identical to the string for which the method is called, except that all alphabetic characters are forced to lowercase.

➤ **String toString()**
This method returns a **String** identical to the string for which the method is called.

➤ **String toUpperCase()**
This method returns a **String** identical to the string for which the method is called, except that all alphabetic characters are forced to uppercase.

➤ **String trim()**
This method returns a **String** identical to the string for which the method is called, except that it removes all leading and trailing whitespace characters.

Here is an example that uses the **substring** method:

```
package examples.basic;
/** A class to demonstrate how to use String.substring
  * method
  */
public class SubstringExample {
   /** The test method for the class
     * @param args Not used
     */
   public static void main( String[] args ) {
      String s1 = new String( "The quick brown fox" );
      String s2 = s1.substring( 4, 8 );
      String s3 = s1.substring( 4, 9 );
      System.out.println( "The second word is " + s2 );
      System.out.println( "The second word is " + s3 );
   }
}
```

The output is

```
The second word is quic
The second word is quick
```

## Working with StringBuffer Objects

**String** and **StringBuffer** are independent classes and are unrelated by inheritance, except that both directly extend the **Object** class. It is interesting to note that neither of these classes derives from the other and that they have no common methods or fields except the methods that every class inherits from **Object**. Use the **StringBuffer** class if you have a string that must change dynamically, and use **String** in most other circumstances. You can think of the **StringBuffer** class as the working space for manipulating the characters, and the **String** class as the place where the final result is put and used.

The methods defined by **String** and **StringBuffer** classes give a good indication of how you should use each class. For example, the **equals** method of the **String** class is very useful because it overrides the default **equals** method to compare the contents of **Strings**. However, **StringBuffer** uses the default **equals** method, so **equals** tests the references rather than the contents of **StringBuffer** objects.

*Class*

**java.lang.StringBuffer**

## Purpose

The **StringBuffer** class has methods for modifying strings. Only the most frequently used methods are listed here.

## Constructors

➤ **StringBuffer()**
**StringBuffer( int** *size* **)**
**StringBuffer( String** *s* **)**
If you do not supply an argument to the **StringBuffer** constructor, it creates an empty **StringBuffer** with the capacity for 16 characters. Alternatively, you can specify an initial capacity or string.

## Methods

➤ **StringBuffer append( String** *s* **)**
**StringBuffer append( Object** *o* **)**
The **append** method appends a **String** or string representation of an object to the **StringBuffer**, and returns a reference to the modified **StringBuffer**.

➤ **StringBuffer insert( int** *position*, **char[]** *characters* **)**
**StringBuffer insert( int** *position*, **Object** *o* **)**
The **insert** method inserts characters or the string representation of an object into a **StringBuffer** at the specified position. It returns a reference to the modified **StringBuffer**.

➤ **void setCharAt( int** *position*, **char** *character* **)**
You can replace the character in a **StringBuffer** at the specified position with the character that you specify.

➤ **void deleteCharAt( int** *position* **)**
You can delete a character at the specified position. All following characters move up and the **StringBuffer** is shortened by one character.

➤ **int capacity()**
The **capacity** method specifies the number of characters the **StringBuffer** can hold. The returned value may be more than the number of characters currently stored in the **StringBuffer** object.

➤ **void setLength( int** *size* **)**
Call this method to truncate or pad the contents of the **StringBuffer** to the number of characters specified in the argument.

➤ **int length()**
The **length** method returns the number of characters in the **StringBuffer**.

➤ **StringBuffer delete( int** *start*, **int** *end* **)**
The delete method removes all characters from the index specified by the

start position up to the character before the specified end position. All following characters move up, shortening the **StringBuffer**. No changes are made if the start and end positions are the same.

➤ **StringBuffer replace( int** *start*, **int** *end*, **String** *s* **)**
Call the **replace** to delete the substring of characters starting at the index given by start position up to the character before the end position and insert in their place the contents of the specified **String**. The **StringBuffer** may be lengthened or shortened depending on the relative lengths of the old and replacement strings.

➤ **StringBuffer reverse()**
The **reverse** method reverses the order of the characters in a **StringBuffer** and returns a reference to the modified object.

➤ **String substring( int** *start* **)**
**String substring( int** *start*, **int** *end* **)**
The **substring** method creates and returns a **String** that contains a substring of the **StringBuffer**. You can specify just the index for the first character in the **StringBuffer** to copy it and all following characters, or optionally also specify the index+1 of the last character to be included in the substring.

The version 1.1 of the Java platform and the Java 2 platform have added methods to the **String** and **StringBuffer** classes. In particular, the methods to delete characters and extract or replace a substring of a **StringBuffer** object were introduced by the Java 2 platform.

The **String** class has a constructor that creates a **String** from a **StringBuffer**. A **StringBuffer** constructor creates a **StringBuffer** with the same contents as a **String**. In short, it is easy to convert between **String** and **StringBuffer** classes.

If you are going to append frequently to build up a string in a **StringBuffer** object, you can increase efficiency by setting an initial size large enough to hold the maximum number of characters expected in the string.

## SUMMARY

- The Java programming language has primitive types and reference types.
- The primitive types are **boolean, char, byte, short, int, long, float**, and **double**. The Java platform defines the way that the JVM stores these types, which is independent of the target architecture. This architecture neutrality is a portability feature.

- A **boolean** can have the value **true** or **false** only. The Java programming language does not treat zero or nonzero integral expressions as boolean values, and a **boolean** is not a numeric type.

- Characters are stored in two-byte Unicode. Character arrays are not strings. Use **byte,** not **char**, for single-byte integers.

- The values of variables of types **byte** and **short** are cast to int for arithmetic calculations. The advantage of **byte** and **short** variables is that they require less memory than **int** variables. All integer types always hold signed values.

- Casting from one numeric type to another numeric type with a greater range of values is automatic, as required. If the cast converts to a numeric type with a narrower range of values, you must code the cast explicitly.

- Arrays, classes, and interfaces are reference types.

- Every object of a reference type has one or more object references. The Java platform allocates storage for the actual object on the heap and maintains a separate local entity, the object reference, to access the object. In your code, you must use the object reference to access the object.

- Use the **new** keyword to create a variable of a reference type. Always include parentheses, as in the following example:

```
ClassName objectName = new ClassName();
```

- You do not have to deallocate storage when you are finished with a variable for a reference type. The Java platform automatically keeps track of object references and knows when an object cannot be used because it has no more object references. Periodically, the JVM automatically performs garbage collection. Garbage collection destroys unreferenced objects so that the storage allocated to them can be reused.

The Java platform defines a class **Object** to be the common ancestor for all the reference types. The methods of **Object** are available to all classes and provide a standard way to work with objects. These methods include **clone**, **equals**, and **toString**.

The Java platform defines wrapper classes for the primitive types. The wrappers are reference-type equivalents of the primitive types. They also provide a number of useful methods and fields, such as **Character.isDigit** and **Integer.MAX_VALUE**.

Arrays are variables of reference type. You can use the **new** keyword when you create an array, or when you let an initializer determine the size of the array, as in the following example:

```
int[] x = new int[5];
int[] y = { 3, 5, 8, 13, 21 };
```

A method can return an object reference for an array. You can copy an array as one object by calling the method **System.arraycopy**, and you can use the **length** field of an array to determine its size. The Java programming language allows multidimensional arrays.

**String** is a class for strings. It provides a number of useful methods, such as **charAt**, **equals**, **substring**, **indexOf**, and **compare**. The built-in operators **+** and **+=** perform string concatenation. **String** objects are immutable; any operation on a **String** object that seems to be changing the object's value actually creates another **String** object, which becomes the result of the operation.

If you are composing a string from several other strings, or need to change a string dynamically, you can also use the **StringBuffer** class.

# QUESTIONS

1. Which of the following types does the Java programming language support? Select all that apply.

    a. integer

    b. Integer

    c. Object

    d. object

2. What is the range of values that a **short** can represent?

    a. 0 to 256

    b. −127 to 128

    c. $-2^{15}$ to $(2^{15}-1)$

    d. 0 to $2^{16}$

3. Examine the following code:

```
public class Quiz3_1 {
    public static void main( String[] args ) {
        float x = 2.345;
        double y = 3.14;
        short a = 2;
        short b = 3;
```

```
        short c = a * b;
        System.out.println( x );
        System.out.println( a + b + c );
    }
}
```

Which of the following statements are true? Select all that apply.

a. Compilation is successful and the output from running the code is

```
2.345
11
```

b. Compilation is successful and the output from running the code is

```
2.345
236
```

c. The compiler rejects the expression `float x = 2.345;` because of incompatible types.

d. The compiler rejects the expression `short c = a * b;` because of incompatible types.

4. Examine the following code:

```
public class Quiz3_2 {
    public static void main( String[] args ) {
        String a = "Hello ";
        String b = "World!";
        f( a, b );
        System.out.println( a );
    }
    public static void f( String x, String y ) {
        x += y;
    }
}
```

Which one of the following statements correctly describes the behavior when this program is compiled and run?

a. Compilation is successful and the output is `Hello`.

b. Compilation is successful and the output is `World!`

c. Compilation is successful and the output is `Hello World!`

d. The compiler rejects the expression `x += y` because it is not possible to increment the value of a **String** object.

5. Examine the following code:

```
public class Quiz3_3 {
```

```
        public static void main( String[] args ) {
            String a = new String( "Hello" );
            String b = new String( "Hello" );
            System.out.println( a == b ? "true" : "false" );
        }
    }
```

Which one of the following statements correctly describes the behavior when this program is compiled and run?

a. Compilation is successful and the output is

   true

b. Compilation is successful and there is no output.

c. Compilation is successful and the output is

   false

d. The compiler rejects the expression ( a == b ? "true" : "false" ) because the == operator cannot be used with reference type objects.

e. Compilation is successful and the output is

   a == b ?

6. Examine the following code:

```
    public class Quiz3_4 {
        public static void main( String[] args ) {
            StringBuffer sb1 = new StringBuffer( "Hello" );
            StringBuffer sb2 = new StringBuffer( "Hello" );
            boolean result = sb1.equals( sb2 );
            System.out.println( result );
        }
    }
```

Which one of the following statements correctly describes the behavior when this program is compiled and run?

a. Compilation is successful and the output is

   true

b. Compilation is successful and the output is

   1

c. Compilation is successful and the output is

   false

d. The compiler rejects the expression System.out.println( result ) because a boolean value can't be directly written to the console.

e. Compilation is successful and the output is

   0

7. Examine the following code:

```java
public class Quiz3_5 {
    public static void main( String[] args ) {
        int[] a = { 0, 1, 2, 3, 4 };
        int b[] = { 10, 11, 12, 13, 14 };
        a = b;
        b = new int[] { 20, 21, 22, 23, 24 };
        for ( int i=0; i<a.length && i<b.length; i++ )
        {
            System.out.println( a[i] + " " + b[i] );
        }
    }
}
```

**3**

Which one of the following statements correctly describes the behavior when this program is compiled and run?

a. Compilation is successful and the output is as follows:

```
10 20
11 21
12 22
13 23
14 24
```

b. The compiler rejects the expression `i < a.length && i < b.length` because the parentheses are missing from the calls to the **length** method.

c. The compiler rejects the expression `int b[] = { 10, 11, 12, 13, 14 }` because the square brackets must follow the array type, not the array name.

d. Compilation is successful and the output is as follows:

```
30
32
34
36
38
```

8. Which of the following is legal syntax for declaring arrays? Select all that apply.

a. `int[] x = { 5 };`

b. `int y[];`

c. `String s[] = "bread", "milk", "chocolate";`

d. `Object[][] theList;`

e. `Object anotherList[][];`

9. Examine the following code:

```
public class Quiz3_6 {                         // 1
    public static void main( String[] args ) {  // 2
        Integer x = null;                        // 3
        if ( args.length >= 1 ) {                // 4
            x = new Integer( args[0] );          // 5
        }                                        // 6
        if ( args.length >= 2 ) {                // 7
            x = new Integer( args[1] );          // 8
        }                                        // 9
        System.out.println( x );                 // 10
        x = null;                                // 11
    }                                            // 12
}                                                // 13
```

What is the first line after which the object created on line 5 can be garbage collected?

   a. line 6

   b. line 8

   c. line 9

   d. line 11

   e. line 13

10. Examine the following variable declarations:

```
String s = "";
float f = 0F;
int i = 0;
```

Which of the following statements are valid? Select all that apply.

   a. s += f;

   b. f += s;

   c. i += f;

   d. i = f;

   e. f = i;

# EXERCISES

## Debugging

1. Correct the following program so that the output prints two lines: "A wild dog is wild" and "A pet cat is tame".

```
package questions.c3;
public class Debug3_1 {
   public static void main( String[] args ) {
      StringBuffer wild = "fox";
      StringBuffer tame = "dog";
      wild = tame;
      tame.setCharAt( 0, 'c' );
      tame.setCharAt( 1, 'a' );
      tame.setCharAt( 2, 't' );
      wild.insert( 1, "wild " );
      tame.insert( 1, "pet " );
      System.out.println( "A " + wild + " is wild" );
      System.out.println( "A " + tame + " is tame" );
   }
}
```

2. Correct all the errors in the following program:

```
package questions.c3;
public class Debug3_2 {
   public static void main( String[] args ) {
      if ( args.length >= 2 ) {
         short x, y;
         x = Short.parseShort( args[0] );
         y = Short.parseShort( args[1] );
         short z = x + y;
         System.out.println( z );
      }
   }
}
```

3. Correct all the errors in the following program:

```
package questions.c3;
public class Debug3_3 {
   public static void main( String[] args ) {
      if ( args.length >= 1 ) {
         String arg1 = args[0];
         if ( arg1[0] == 'A' ) {
            arg1[0] = 'a';
         }
      }
   }
}
```

4. Correct all the errors in the following program:

```
package questions.c3;
public class Debug3_4 {
   public static void main( String[] args ) {
```

```
            String[12] months;
            months = { "Jan",  "Feb",  "Mar",
                       "Apr",  "May",  "Jun",
                       "Jul",  "Aug",  "Sep",
                       "Oct",  "Nov",  "Dec" };
        if ( args.length >= 1 ) {
            int index = Integer.parseInt( args[0] );
            if ( index > 0 && index < 12 ) {
                System.out.println( months[index] );
            }
        }
    }
}
```

5. Correct all the errors in the following program:

```
package questions.c3;
public class Debug3_5 {
    public static void main( String[] args ) {
        Object[] stuff = new Object[5];
        stuff[0] = "eggs";
        stuff[1] = new StringBuffer( "flour" );
        stuff[2] = 3.56;
        stuff[3] = 'c';
        stuff[4] = 123;
        for( int i = 0; i < stuff.length; i++ ) {
            System.out.println( stuff[i] );
        }
    }
}
```

## Complete the Solution

1. Extract the file **questions\c3\Complete3_1.java** from the file **question.jar** on the CD-ROM. Complete the `Complete3_1` class definition by by providing implementations for the methods `getCharAt` and `shiftChars`. The method `shiftChars` moves each element in the array the specified number of positions to the right if the argument is greater than zero or to the left is the argument is less than zero. The leftmost element has index value zero. Give empty elements the value '0'.

2. Extract the file **questions\c3\Complete3_2.java** from the file **question.jar** on the CD-ROM. Complete the `Complete3_2` class definition by providing an implementation of the `prettyMoney` method. This method receives as input an object of type **Float** and returns a string that represents the value in U.S. or Canadian dollars and cents. For example, if the input is 12345.6789, the output is $12,345.68. For any value less than one penny, return $0.00.

3. Extract the file **questions\c3\Complete3_3.java** from the file **question.jar** on the CD-ROM. Complete the `Complete3_3` class definition by adding an `asString` method to the class. The `asString` method returns value fields **x** and **y** in the following format: ( x, y ).

4. Extract the file **questions\c3\Complete3_4.java** from the file **question.jar** on the CD-ROM. Complete the `Complete3_4` class definition by adding code to print out the title of the HTML source file whose name is passed as an argument to the **main** method. An HTML file should have only one title that is enclosed in the tags **<title>** and **</title>**. HTML tags are not case-sensitive, and it is possible for an HTML file not to have a title. There are no spaces in **<title>** and **</title>**. The title itself can be several words and span lines.

5. Extract the file **questions\c3\Complete3_5.java** from the file **question.jar** on the CD-ROM. Complete the `Complete3_5` class definition by completing the **main** method so that it determines the type of the command-line argument. Use the wrapper classes for the primitive types **boolean**, **double**, and **long** to print as many of the following statements as apply:

```
The input is true
The input is false
As a real number, the input is ...
As an integer, the input is ...
```

With the wrapper classes, you cannot test whether the input is a valid number, and will have to accept that the try and catch constructions supplied in the code cover that situation.

6. Complete the method **main** in this question's class so that it determines the type of the command-line argument. Use the wrapper classes for the primitive types **boolean**, **double**, and **long** to print as many of the following statements as apply:

```
The input is true
The input is false
As a real number, the input is ...
As an integer, the input is ...
```

When you run your code, some input strings make the program terminate with a message that refers to a **NumberFormatException**. The **Double** and **Long** wrapper classes deal with requests to create an object from a string that is not a valid number and does so by using a standard Java technique called **throwing an exception**. In Chapter 6, you learn how to handle this and other exceptions so that your program can recover, print a more user-friendly message, and continue. For this exercise, it is sufficient to write a method that runs as long as possible for any particular input string.

## Discovery

1. Create a class called HTMLTitle, starting with your working version of the class Complete3_4. This new class adds enhancements to handle the following situations:

   a. Truncate titles to 80 characters if they are longer.

   b. Print a message if the HTML file has a **\<title\>** tag, but no following **\</title\>**.

   c. Print a message if the HTML file has a **\</title\>** tag, but no preceding **\<title\>** tag.

   d. Print a message if the HTML file has more than one title.

   e. Allow for the absence of a space between the first word of the title and the **\<title\>** tag, and between the last word of the title and the **\</title\>** tag.

   f. Allow the absence of a space between the **\<title\>** tag and the preceding word, and the **\</title\>** tag and the following word.

2. Create a class called BitField that holds an array of 16 boolean flags in a static field. Write methods that perform the following operations on the array:

   a. Set a flag to **true**.

   b. Set a flag to **false**.

   c. Change the setting of a flag to the opposite of its current setting.

   d. Return the value of a flag.

   e. Return the number of flags set to **true**.

3. Create a class called Letters that contains a two-dimensional array of two-by-five integers. One dimension represents the letters A, E, I, O, and U, and the other dimension represents uppercase or lowercase. Read a file line by line into a **String**. Count and record the number of occurrences of each vowel in uppercase or lowercase. When you have finished reading the file, print the following lines, inserting the number of appearances of the vowel in lowercase and uppercase, and the total appearances:

```
A: ... lowercase, ... uppercase, ... Total
E: ... lowercase, ... uppercase, ... Total
I: ... lowercase, ... uppercase, ... Total
O: ... lowercase, ... uppercase, ... Total
U: ... lowercase, ... uppercase, ... Total
```

## CHAPTER FOUR

# CLASSES AND PACKAGES

**In this chapter you will:**

☕ State the benefits of encapsulation in object oriented design and write code that implements tightly encapsulated classes.

☕ Declare class classes, methods, and variables making appropriate use of all permitted modifiers, including **static**, **public**, and **final**. State the significance of the modifiers when used alone and in combination.

☕ For a given class, determine whether the JVM provides a default constructor and state the prototype of that constructor.

☕ State the effect of using a variable of any kind when no explicit assignment has been made to it.

☕ Write code to call overloaded constructors and other methods.

➤ Use the keyword **this** to chain constructor calls and to act as an object reference

☕ State the behavior that is guaranteed by the garbage collector and write code that explicitly makes objects eligible for collection.

☕ Identify correctly constructed package declarations, import statements, and class declarations in a source file.

➤ Recognize the names of packages included in the Java platform and briefly describe the purpose of each package.

## INTRODUCTION

You cannot even begin to program in the Java programming language without using at least one class. This chapter explains how to define and use classes and the members of classes. You will define your own classes and create instances of the classes.

In the Java programming language, the usual practice is to collect classes that form logical groupings into a package. **Packages** are collections of classes that the language recognizes. You have already used some packages, including **java.lang**, to support the basic constructs of the Java programming language, and **java.io**, for stream input and output. In this chapter, you learn how to store and access packages, and how to create your own packages.

# CLASSES AND OBJECT ORIENTED PROGRAMMING

If you have programmed in an object-oriented (OO) language such as C++ or Smalltalk, you should appreciate that it is not just a syntactic quirk of the Java programming language that forces you to put all your code into classes. If your background is in C, non-object-oriented versions of **BASIC**, or other procedural languages, get ready for the paradigm shift into OO. Boiled down to its essence, implementing object-oriented programs means defining classes and reusing existing classes in such a way that the program is driven entirely by methods calls between the classes.

In OO, you no longer design a program based on the flow of control. Flowcharts are of little use. Instead you start by analyzing the real-life entities, relationships, and scenarios that your program is to model. Object-oriented analysis (OOA) focuses on the **problem domain**. The analysis leads to an object-oriented design (OOD) process in which you determine what classes or **types** of objects you need. What information or **attributes** must objects of each type hold? What is their behavior or, in OO terms, what **messages** from other objects can they process? Then, at implementation stage, you program classes in Java or another object-oriented programming language. In the Java programming language, attributes become fields of classes, and messages become methods of classes.

As an illustration, consider that a banking model is likely to include a type for bank accounts, with attributes such as account number and balance. Bank accounts objects should accept messages from account owners to perform deposits, withdrawals, and other transactions. The account owners are another type of object, with attributes such as owner name and address.

The bank or branch office is also a type. Unlike accounts and owners, you may impose a restriction that there can be only one bank object in your program, but the bank is still an object that has its own type. You may want to add a transaction log attribute to bank accounts for use when the bank sends monthly statements to account owners. Objects of type transaction log typically contain a collection of objects of type transaction. They accept messages from accounts to add transactions to the log—for example, to record a deposit—and from the bank to print or clear the log.

When designing classes, you should concentrate on the interface between classes before coding their internal workings. For example, determine which class provides the deposit method, and then determine which classes may call the deposit method. Do the same for all methods. Make sure all the scenarios you can think of are covered. In the process, draw up a list of attributes that each class must maintain. Eventually, you will arrive at a fairly accurate specification for the classes you need.

At this point you may be wondering, "What sets the various scenarios in motion and what controls the sequence of method calls?" In modern applications, control is often given to the user who drives the program through its graphical user interface (GUI). Chapters 12 and 13 explain how to write a GUI-driven program. It turns out that OO techniques are well suited for programming GUIs. Similarly, distributed environments, where messages may come from remote computers and where there is no central control, lend themselves to OOP. One of the greatest challenges for programmers converting to OO is not to think sequentially of program flow. Instead, they must trust that classes will interact correctly if the design is good and the coding is faithful to the design.

Another phenomenon occurs in object-oriented development: the analysis, design, implementation, test, and deployment stages tend to overlap and become cyclic as you iterate toward a solution. For example, testing can reveal a weakness that was overlooked during analysis and implementation and that should be addressed by a design change. Far from being a problem, this non-linear process provides strength. You can build and deploy part of the solution to prove that key classes interact properly. Then, you can refine and expand the solution as you add classes. In addition, you can create a quick, simple implementation of classes for speedy deployment and then improve performance or robustness during subsequent iterations.

If the internal implementation and public interface of a class are clearly separated, you can completely rewrite one or more methods and no other class may need to be changed. The concept of **encapsulation** refers to the fact that fields and methods can be hidden from the outside world. Declare selected methods in a way that makes them visible to other classes and those methods that make up the interface of that class. It is a good practice to hide all attributes, or in Java terms, declare all fields private, and provide methods that other classes can call to get and set values. This approach enforces encapsulation of attributes and gives your class a chance to validate or filter requests to set values.

Object-oriented analysis and design is a science and art in its own right. Careers can be made designing object models and the models can be independent of the programming language in which they are to be implemented. As a programmer, your starting point may be an object model that was created by an architect or object modeler. You may work on just a few of the classes in a project that requires dozens or hundreds of types of objects. The rest of this chapter focuses on the features of the Java programming language that you use to implement an object-oriented program.

# JAVA CLASSES

A class is a distinct type. A class type is as usable as **char**, **Int**, and all the other primitive types and core classes provided by the Java platform. The online SDK documentation provides a complete list of the core classes.

For a clear understanding of the underlying concepts, it is important to know the correct terms to describe Java classes and members. A **class** is a type of object, and the objects of a class have both the data and behaviors that the class encapsulates. The data elements and behaviors of a class are the **members** of the class. Members can belong to a class as a whole or to individual objects of the class. The **methods** of a class establish behaviors, and the data is stored in the **fields**.

When created, an object of the class instantiates the class and can therefore be called an **instance** of the class. Instances are most often called **objects** and form the basis of object-oriented programming. However, in some contexts, the term "instance" is more suggestive of the fact that each instance is built according to its blueprint: the class definition. As you have seen, when an identifier is associated with a reference type, the identifier actually names a Java **object reference**, which is a separate entity from the actual object being referenced. Objects are always accessed through object references and have no identifiers apart from their object references.

The term **variable** is often used loosely. A variable can have primitive type or reference type. A variable can be any entity that has an identifier, regardless of whether the value is indeed variable. The Java programming language has different kinds of variables:

➤ **Local variables** are declared inside a block, and therefore inside a method.

➤ **Instance variables** are fields specific to one instance of the class.

➤ **Class variables** are fields shared by all objects of the class. These are the static fields of a class.

> **Mini Quiz 4-1**
>
> To create a bank account class for the banking example described in "Classes and Object Oriented Programming", you must define variables to represent a bank balance and an account number. Should these two variables be instance, class, or local variables?

Classes can be independent of each other or related by **inheritance**. Inheritance is described in Chapter 5. If two classes are in a parent-child relationship, in the Java programming language the parent is called the **superclass**, and the child is called the **subclass**.

All classes in this chapter are top-level classes. A **top-level class** may be contained in a package, but not in another class. If a class definition is nested inside another class definition, the contained class is called a **nested class** and may not be a top-level class. In the Java programming language, a class can not only be nested inside another class, but can also be a member of the outer class. Classes that are members are called **inner classes**. Using inner classes is an advanced topic and is covered in Chapter 9.

 Both inner classes and nested classes are features added to the Java programming language in version 1.1. In the original version of the language, all classes were top-level classes, and the term "top-level class" was not used.

# DEFINING A CLASS

Java source files contain one or more class definitions. The only statements that can appear outside a class definition are comments, package statements, and import statements.

*Syntax*

**[public] class** *class_name* **{**
    *// body of class*
**}**

*Dissection*

➤ Starting a class definition with the keyword **public** is optional. This keyword is an access specifier that gives all other classes access to the class. If you omit **public**, the class is assigned the default of package access, which means that other classes in the same package can use the class, but that the class is not accessible from outside the package.

➤ The **class** keyword indicates that the statement is a class definition.

➤ The *class_name* can be any valid identifier.

➤ Additional forms that a class definition can take for inheritance are described in Chapter 5, and for inner or nested classes, in Chapter 9.

➤ The body consists of the definitions of the members of the class. It is enclosed in braces, **{** and **}**.

*Code Example*

```
package examples.classes;
/** An introductory class definition
  */
public class FirstClass {
   private int id;
```

```
        public void setId( int newId ) {
            id = newId;
        }
        public int getId() {
            return id;
        }
    }
```

The example contains a class called **FirstClass**. It is a public class, and therefore is found in a file called FirstClass.java. The structure of packages mirrors the file system, so you will find this source code in the examples\classes subfolder of the folder in which you unpacked the JAR file examples.jar.

This example also demonstrates some conventions that are not rules of the Java programming language.

Most Java programmers use both uppercase and lowercase letters in class names, using uppercase for the first letter and the first letter of recognizable words in the class name.

In this example, the programmer declares the field id at the top of the class, before methods. This is a convention used in this book, not a rule of the Java programming language. You can declare fields anywhere in the class. Many programmers group fields by their access specifier.

# Defining Members

A class definition consists of the definitions of the members of that class. The members can be methods, fields, or inner classes.

# Defining Methods

You must define the members of your class completely within the class definitions. Only native and abstract methods can have declarations but not definitions inside the class.

*Syntax*

[*access_specifier*] [*qualifiers*] *return_type method_name( argument_list )*
        [**throws** *exception_list*]
   *block*

*Dissection*

> ➤ Every member has its own access specifier. You can begin the declaration of each method with one of the access specifiers **public, private**, or **protected**, or you can accept the default of package access. You must not use **package** as an access specifier. You get the package access by omitting the access specifier.

**public** access lets all classes use the member.

**protected** access is generally used with inheritance.

Default or package access means that all classes in the same package can use the member, but the member is not available outside the package.

**private** access means that the member is available only within the class.

➤ There are five qualifiers that you can apply to methods:

The **abstract** keyword creates a method that has no body or implementation. You declare methods to be **abstract** to force all subclasses of your class to override, rather than inherit, the method.

The **final** keyword creates a method that cannot be overridden by a subclass. The subclass inherits the method.

The **native** keyword indicates a method that is implemented in a language other than the Java programming language. Many of the core classes use native methods to provide platform independence. All specific implementations of the Java platform include classes that are written for the native platform on which it is installed. The native methods in the core classes are the interface between the Java platform and the native operating system. You can write your own native methods for your classes. Appendix C gives a brief description and example of implementing a native method in the C language on Intel platforms.

The **static** keyword ensures that the method applies to the class. A static method is a class method, and can be used regardless of whether any objects of the class have been created. The core classes provide many class methods. For example, the **java.lang.Math** class provides **sqrt, max, random**, and many more methods that you can use without instantiating the **Math** class.

The **synchronized** keyword prevents different threads in a multithreaded program from interfering with each other in cases when the method can run on more than one thread. If a method is synchronized, only one thread can use it at a time.

➤ The **throws** clause in a method declaration lists exceptions that may occur while the method is running and that are not handled inside the methods. You can examine this clause to see what possible abnormal conditions may prevent the method from completing as expected.

➤ The block is the body of the method and consists of one or more statements enclosed in braces, { and }.

*Code Example*

```
public static long factorial( int n ) {
    if ( n < 3 ) return n;
    else return n * factorial( n-1 );
}
```

*Code Dissection*

This `factorial` method recursively calculates the factorial of the integer value supplied in the argument list.

# Defining Fields

As with methods, fields can have declarations but not definitions inside the class.

*Syntax*

[*access_specifier*] [*qualifiers*] *type identifier* [= *initializer*];

*Dissection*

➤ As with methods, every field has its own access specifier. You can begin the declaration of a field with one of the access specifiers **public**, **private**, or **protected**, or you can accept the default of package access.

➤ There are four qualifiers that you can apply to fields:

After a field that is declared **final** has been assigned an initial value, that value cannot be changed. Use this qualifier to create constants. If the field is an object reference, declaring it **final** means that the reference cannot be changed to refer to a different object, but the object itself does not become constant.

As with methods, a field that is declared **static** belongs to the class, and all instances of the class share it. In contrast, every instance of the class has its own copy of instance variables.

You can declare some fields to be **transient** when you are defining a class with object serialization in mind. Object serialization involves writing a whole object to an output stream and reading it back later. If a field contains temporary information that you do not need to save or has a type that cannot be serialized, you should declare the field to be **transient** to exclude it when the object is serialized.

If your class may be used in multithreaded programs, consider declaring fields to be **volatile** to prevent situations in which values assigned in one thread may not be picked up in other threads. The keyword **volatile** suppresses optimizations that might effectively discard changes made to the value of a field by a different thread.

➤ Assigning an initial value to a field in the declaration is optional.

*Code Example*

```
private String message = "Greetings";
```

*Code Dissection*

The field **message** has type **String** and can be directly accessed only by the class in which it is defined. The message is initialized to contain the word **"Greetings"**.

---

The ability to serialize an object was added to the **java.io** package in version 1.1 of the Java platform. Originally, **transient** was a reserved word, but not a meaningful keyword.

## Initializing Fields

You can assign initial values to fields when you declare them. You can initialize a class variable either in its declarations or in a construction called an initializer block. **Initializer blocks** are described with static members in this chapter and inner classes in Chapter 9.

All fields are implicitly initialized if you do not explicitly assign an initial value. Table 4–1 lists the default initial values for different types.

**Table 4-1**  Default initial value of fields

| Field Type | Default Initial Value | Field Type | Default Initial Value |
|---|---|---|---|
| boolean | false | float | +0.0f |
| char | '\u0000' | double | +0.0d |
| byte, short, int | 0 | reference variables | null |
| long | 0L | | |

The Java programming language does not initialize local variables automatically. You must explicitly assign initial values when you declare variables inside a method. For example, the method `convertKilo2Pounds` in the following class `Metric` contains the local variable `ratio`. The variable is declared and immediately given a value.

```
public class Metric {
    public static float convertKilo2Pounds( float k ) {
        float ratio = 2.2;
        return k * ratio;
    }
}
```

The Java compiler lets you declare a local variable without an initializer, but flags an error if you use a variable before it has been given a value. Unlike fields, local variables do not have default values, and the Java programming language forces you to initialize them.

# USING A DEFINED CLASS

Because classes are reference types, you use object references to refer to instances of classes. To create references for objects, use the usual syntax to declare fields of any known type.

## Syntax

*[access_specifier]* *[qualifiers]* *class_name identifier;*

## Dissection

➤ As with variables of primitive types, you can declare more than one instance of a class by listing identifiers separated by commas. The following statements create two object references for the **FirstClass** class.

## Code Example

```
FirstClass f1, f2;
```

## Code Dissection

This declaration is a complete statement. It declares two object references, but does not create the objects.

To create objects of a class, use the **new** keyword.

## Syntax

*object_reference* = **new** *class_name( arguments_of_constructor );*

## Dissection

➤ The **new** keyword calls a constructor, which is a special method that has the same name as the class. Constructors initialize the object. You can pass arguments to the constructor. You must include the parentheses after the constructor name, even if you are using a constructor that has no arguments.

## Code Example

```
f1 = new FirstClass();   // parentheses are always required
f2 = new FirstClass();
```

## Code Dissection

These two statements create two objects and assign the object references to **f1** and **f2**.

You can create the object reference and the instance in one statement.

## Syntax

[*access_specifier*] [*qualifiers*] *classname identifer* = new
*class_name*( *arguments_of_constructor* );

## Dissection

➤ To pass arguments to the constructor that creates the object, include the
arguments between the parentheses following the class name.

**4**

## Code Example

```
FirstClass f3 = new FirstClass();
```

## Code Dissection

This statement declares an object reference, creates an instance of
**FirstClass**, and sets the value of the object reference.

There are situations where you can use the **new** keyword without an object
reference. For example, you can create an object in the argument list when you
call a method. The called method receives a reference from its argument list.
The calling method has no object reference and therefore cannot use the
object. This is useful when you have no need to refer to an object by name.

## Syntax

*method_name* ( **new** *class_name*( *arguments_of_constructor* ) );

## Dissection

➤ This statement creates an object inside the expression passed as an argument to use as a term within the expression.

## Code Example

```
saw( new Lumber( "hardwood" ) );
```

## Code Dissection

This statement creates an instance of the class **Lumber**, but does not give the
instance a name because the **Lumber** object is used only as an argument of the
method **saw**.

To call a member method, use the dot operator with the reference for an object.
Use object references as though they are the actual objects they represent.

---

*Syntax*

class_name.method( arguments_of_method )
object_reference.method( arguments_of_method )

---

*Dissection*

➤ The dot operator is used to call a method, regardless of whether it is a class method or an instance method.

➤ You can omit the class name and dot operator when a class method calls another class method of the same class.

➤ You can omit the class name and dot operator when an instance method calls a class method of the same class.

➤ You can omit the object reference and dot operator when an instance method calls another instance method of the same class for the same object.

---

*Code Example*

```
package examples.classes;
/** Another introductory class definition
   */
public class SecondClass {
    private int id;
    /** Test method for the class
     * @param args not used
     */
    public static void main( String[] args ) {
        SecondClass f1, f2;
        f1 = new SecondClass();
        f2 = new SecondClass();
        f1.setId( 502 );
        f2.setId( 496 );
        int idHolder = f1.getId();
        System.out.println( idHolder );
        System.out.println( f2.getId() );
    }
    public void setId( int newId ) {
        id = newId;
    }
    public int getId() {
        return id;
    }
}
```

---

*Code Output*

502
496

---

**4**

---

### Code Dissection

The `SecondClass` class has a **main** method, so you can test the class with the **java** command. This **main** method creates two instances of `SecondClass`, sets the `id` field for each instance, and then prints out the value of the fields. Note that `idHolder` is a local variable defined in **main** to hold the value returned from `getid` for `f1`.

---

The `SecondClass` program is also an example of using a **main** method as a test program for your class. You can write all your class methods without considering whether the class will be the entry point of an application. When you add a **main** method, your class becomes executable. You can give every class its own entry point, by giving each one a **main** method with the standard declaration:

```
public static void main( String[] args ) {
    /* . . . */
}
```

---

**Mini Quiz 4-2**

How does the Java platform know where to start when more than one class in an application has a **main** method?

---

## USING CONSTRUCTORS AND FINALIZERS

**Constructors** are methods that prepare newly created objects for use. **Finalizers** are methods that perform whatever actions should be completed before the objects are discarded.

In the Java programming language, the most common way to invoke a constructor is through the **new** keyword, as shown in the preceding section. The **java.lang.Class.newInstance** method and the new **java.lang.reflect.Constructor.newInstance** method also invoke the constructor, but they are not commonly used.

 Version 1.1 of the Java platform introduced the method **java.lang.reflect.Constructor.newInstance** along with the entire package **java.lang.reflect**. This package supports run-time type information and is known as the reflection API. **java.lang.reflect** defines the Constructor class.

All objects of reference types are stored on the program heap. When you are finished with an object, you are not responsible for freeing memory on the heap. Instead, the Java platform automatically performs garbage collection from time to time. Not having to explicitly destroy an object leaves a gap when it comes to performing specialized cleanup before throwing away an object. For example, how do you flush the contents of a buffer to an output file before you destroy the object that contains the buffer? Finalizers perform this function.

## Constructors

You have already seen that when you create an object with the **new** keyword, you essentially call the constructor. You can include the arguments for the constructor. You must always include the parentheses, even if you are using a constructor that takes no arguments. Here are some statements that construct objects:

```
File outputFile = new File( args[1] );
Fraction third = new Fraction( 1, 3 );
Whatever thing = new Whatever();
```

When you define your Java class, you define constructors much like you define other methods. The rules are as follows:

➤ Give the constructor the same name as the class name.

➤ Do not specify a return type, not even **void**. A constructor cannot return a value.

➤ You can specify as many arguments as you like. The arguments can have any defined type, including the class of the constructor.

The Java programming language provides default constructors if you do not define any constructors for a class. The compiler-generated constructor takes no arguments. All the example programs in this book so far rely on default constructors. If you define your own constructor, the compiler no longer provides a default constructor. Therefore, if you define one constructor, you must define all the forms of constructors that your class needs.

For example, if you define one constructor that has at least one argument, your class does not have a constructor with no arguments unless you also explicitly define one.

Here is an example of a class that has an explicit constructor:

```
package examples.classes;
/** A Java class for text labels of arbitrary
  * length limit
  */
public class LabelText {
    private static final int MAX_TEXT = 20;
    private String label;
    /** Class constructor
      * @param inputText The text to be assigned
      *                  to the label
      */
```

```
      public LabelText( String inputText ) {
         System.out.println(
            "Creating a LabelText object" );
         if ( inputText.length() <= MAX_TEXT ) {
            label = inputText;
         } else {
            System.err.println(
               "Input label text is too long!" );
            //NOTE: next line extracts 20 chars at
            //        index 0 to 19
            label = inputText.substring( 0, MAX_TEXT );
         }
      }
      /** Provide the string representation of the object
        * @return The label text
        */
      public String toString() {
         return label;
      }
      /** Method to output the contents of the object
        * to <code>System.out</code>
        */
      public void print() {
         System.out.println( label );
      }
      /** Test method for the class
        * @param args Not used
        */
      public static void main( String[] args ) {
         LabelText a = new LabelText( "Capital Losses" );
         LabelText b
            = new LabelText( "Really Big Capital Gains" );
         a.print();
         System.out.println( a );
         b.print();
         System.out.println( b );
      }
   }
```

The output is

```
Creating a LabelText object
Creating a LabelText object
Input label text is too long!
Capital Losses
Capital Losses
Really Big Capital G
Really Big Capital G
```

**4**

**Mini Quiz 4-3**

Trace through the code and output to see when the constructors are called.

## Finalizers

Because the Java platform frees memory for you when objects are destroyed, you often do not need finalizers. Generally, you should use finalizers only for necessary cleanup tasks other than deallocating memory and even then you should use them sparingly. A commonly used alternative to providing finalizers is to define a method called **close** or **dispose** that can be called explicitly as needed. You should not build into your code dependency on the timing of activities of finalizers. Otherwise, you are forced to run the finalizers explicitly before executing the dependent code.

*Syntax*

**protected void finalize() [throws Throwable]**
    *block*

*Dissection*

➤ You should declare **finalize** with the access specifier **protected**. A finalizer cannot have private or package access because it overrides a protected method of **Object**. Public access is valid, but giving users of your class access to this method is very dangerous and not recommended.

➤ The **finalize** method cannot take arguments or return a value. You can include whatever valid code you want.

➤ Although it is not strictly necessary, you should include the clause **throws Throwable** to allow for a subclass to include a finalizer that does throw an exception.

➤ The block is the body of the finalizer method.

*Code Example*

```
protected void finalize() throws Throwable {
    MyOutputStream.flush();
}
```

*Code Dissection*

This finalizer flushes any output that remains in a field that is the object reference for an output stream object.

The output of the finalizer consists of whatever data is left in the output stream when the finalizer is run, and the output stream determines the destination of the output.

---

In inheritance hierarchies, there are additional considerations for finalizers in classes that have superclasses other than **Object**.

If the class of an object that is destroyed during garbage collection has a **finalize** method, the finalizer is run before the storage for the object is freed. Therefore, the automatic running of finalizers is tied to garbage collection. Do not rely on garbage collection to run finalizers, because you cannot control when, or even whether, garbage collection occurs. The Java Virtual Machine (JVM) may never perform garbage collection if it does not run low on memory.

You should never call the **finalize** method directly. Let the JVM decide when the method needs to be run.

---

*Class*

**java.lang.System**

---

*Methods*

➤ **void runFinalizersOnExit( boolean** *b* **)**
If you call **runFinalizersOnExit** and supply an argument that evaluates to **true**, the JVM guarantees to run the finalizers for all objects some time before program termination. When the argument is **false** or the **runFinalizersOnExit** method is not called, finalizers may run, but there is no guarantee that they will run. This method has been deprecated in the Java 2 platform and is no longer recommended because it is inherently unsafe.

➤ **void runFinalization()**
Call **runFinalization** to request that the JVM run finalizers for all objects that have been discarded but for which finalizers have not yet run. There is no guarantee that finalizers will be run as a result of calling **runFinalization**.

---

You can call **runFinalization** anytime. You should do so only when performing this cleanup is imperative for your application to perform properly. This method is most effective when used after calling the method **System.gc** to request that garbage collection take place.

Version 1.1 of the Java platform introduced the method **runFinalizersOnExit**. Previously you had no way to force finalizers to run at the end of a program. Unfortunately, the method has proved to be inherently unsafe in the multithreaded environment of the JVM and has been deprecated in the Java 2 platform.

To make your programs more efficient and easier to maintain, let the virtual machine decide when to finalize objects. The technique of forcing finalization is inefficient.

Here is an example class that has a finalizer:

```java
package examples.classes;
/** A Java class to demonstrate how a finalizer
 * method is defined and used
 */
public class FinalizerClass {
   private int a, b;
   /** Class default constructor method */
   public FinalizerClass() {
      a = 1;
      b = 2;
      System.out.println( "Constructing an object!" );
   }
   /** Class finalizer method
     * @exception Throwable Any exception at all
     */
   protected void finalize() throws Throwable {
      System.out.println( "Doing object cleanup!" );
   }
   /** Test method for the class
     * @param args Not used
     */
   public static void main( String[] args ) {
      FinalizerClass x = new FinalizerClass();
      FinalizerClass y = new FinalizerClass();
      x = null;
      y = null;
      System.gc();
      System.runFinalization();
   }
}
```

Possible output is

```
Constructing an object!
Constructing an object!
Doing object cleanup!
Doing object cleanup!
```

The declaration of `FinalizerClass.finalize` includes a **throws** clause that allows any exception to be thrown. The throws clause is not required for this class, but including it gives subclasses the opportunity to throw exceptions in their finalizer methods.

## REFERENCE OBJECTS AND THE GARBAGE COLLECTION

Developers using sophisticated techniques, such as object caches and flexible data–mapping schemes, may require finer control over the finalization process than finalize methods provide. The set of classes in the package **java.lang.ref** provides a measure of interaction with the garbage collector. You can create a **reference object** by instantiating the classes **SoftReference**, **WeakReference**, or **PhantomReference** and passing an object reference to an object used by your program as an argument of the constructor. When the garbage collector operates on objects, it changes the **reachability** level of the object. You can use the reference classes to determine the status of an object and then perhaps perform specialized finalization actions. Reachability levels are described in Table 4–2.

**Table 4-2**  Reachability levels of objects

| Level | Description |
|---|---|
| Strong | An object is strongly reachable while your program is using object references for it. |
| Soft | When there are no more strong references, an object may still be reachable by a reference object of type **SoftReference**. If memory is low, garbage collector may clear soft references. |
| Weak | The garbage collector can finalize objects that have only weak references. |
| Phantom | After an object has been finalized, it can have a reference object that is a **PhantomReference**. |
| Unreachable | The memory occupied by unreachable objects can be reclaimed by the JVM. These objects are not reachable by any sort of reference object. |

The Java platform has matured since it was originally released and has proven itself to be flexible, reliable, and fast enough for use in mission critical, largescale projects. The package **java.lang.ref** was introduced in the Java 2 platform to meet the demands of developers whose Java programs test the size and other constraints of the computer or network upon which their programs run.

## OVERLOADING METHODS

You can define two or more different methods in the same class and give them the same name. This is called method overloading. Typically, you overload methods because you want different versions of a method to have the same name because they have similar functionality, but to take different inputs. The method name is common, but the argument lists are different. For example, you may want methods to calculate the area of a square given the coordinates of the two corners, the length of one side, or the reference for a square object. You can overload any method, including constructors and **main**.

The **signature** of the method consists of the following:

➤ The name of a method

➤ The number of arguments

➤ The types of the arguments

If two methods have different signatures, they are different methods. Two methods are not ambiguous if their argument lists have different numbers of elements or if at least one argument of one method has a different type than the argument in the same position in the argument list of the other method.

The signature does not extend to the return type. You cannot overload a method by defining two versions that differ only in the return type.

To overload a method name, simply define all the versions of that method that you want. Make sure the argument lists are different. The compiler uses a process called name mangling to generate distinct internal names for the method. The **name mangling** process involves adding characters to the function name that represent the encoded argument types. You call an overloaded method exactly as you call any method. Let the compiler determine which argument list is the best match, and then run the correct method.

Consider the following method:

```
void myWay( int ival, float fval ) { /* …*/ }
```

You can call **myWay** with two-argument combinations such as an **int** and an **int**, a **short** and a **float**, or a **char** and a **long**. When you do so, the process you are using is implicit casting, not overloading.

Use overloading when you need more than type promotions to provide all required variations on argument lists. Use overloading also if you do not want the type to be cast. For example, if you want the method to do something different when an argument has character type than when the argument has another integral type, overload the method to provide both **char** and **int** versions. For example, you can provide, instead of a single method **myWay**, the following overloaded versions:

```
void myWay( char ival, float fval ) { /* …*/ }
void myWay( long lval, double dval ) { /* …*/ }
void myWay( String[] sval ) { /* …*/ }
```

When you call an overloaded method, the Java compiler first checks whether the types of the arguments in the call exactly match the types of the arguments in the declaration of one of the overloaded methods. If there is a match, that method is called. If not, the Java compiler casts the arguments in the calling statement, following the usual rules that prevent loss of information through implicit casting. The called method casts arguments to types with the closest, but not smaller, ranges compared to the types of the calling arguments.

Here is a simple example of method overloading:

```java
package examples.classes;
/** A class definition to show how a method name
  * can be overloaded
  */
public class TelNumber {
   /** Print a telephone number
     * @param s the telephone number as a string
     */
   public static void printTelNumber( String s ) {
      // check for digits only
      for ( int i = 0; i < s.length(); i++ ) {
         if ( ! Character.isDigit( s.charAt( i ) ) ) {
            System.out.println( "Not valid: " + s );
            return;
         }
      }
      // format string into (ddd) ddd-dddd
      StringBuffer sb = new StringBuffer( s );
      while ( sb.length() < 10 ) {
         sb.insert( 0, '0' );
      }
      sb.insert( 6, '-' );
      sb.insert( 3, ") " );
      sb.insert( 0, '(' );
      System.out.println( sb );
   }
   /** Print a telephone number if it falls within
     * the valid range. This method will convert
     * the long to a string and then call the
     * printTelNumber method that takes String
     * input
     * @param l the telephone number as a long
     */
   public static void printTelNumber( long l ) {
      if ( l >= 0 && l < 10000000000L ) {
         // convert the number to a string
         printTelNumber( Long.toString( l ) );
      } else {
         System.out.println( "Not valid: " + l );
      }
```

4

```
    }
    /** Test method for the class
      * @param args not used
      */
    public static void main( String[] args ) {
        printTelNumber( "abcdefghij" );
        printTelNumber( "4166448300" );
        printTelNumber( 1234567890 );
        printTelNumber( -5 );
        printTelNumber( 5439432 );
        printTelNumber( "" );
    }
}
```

The output is

```
Not valid: abcdefghij
(416) 644-8300
(123) 456-7890
Not valid: -5
(000) 543-9432
(000) 000-0000
```

In this case, there are two versions of the method `printTelNumber`. One takes a `String` as an argument, and the other takes a **long**. The **main** method tests both overloaded `printTelNumber` methods.

## Overloading Constructors

Very often, the method you want to overload is the class constructor. This is because you want to provide alternative ways of creating an object. You may want a default constructor, a constructor that sets initial values, a constructor that copies another object of the same class, or a constructor that converts from another type.

None of these objectives poses any problem. You can overload the constructor just like you overload any other method.

The case of providing a default constructor and a constructor that accepts input values is interesting. For the call, you use the method **this**.

In the Java programming language, the **this** method is a synonym for a constructor. In other words, one constructor can call another constructor.

*Syntax*

**this(** *arguments_of_called_constructor* **);**

## Dissection

➤ Calling **this** is allowed only once in each constructor definition, and the call must be the first line in the constructor. You can chain together any number of constructors in this way. You can use this technique to achieve an effect similar to default arguments for constructors.

## Code Example

```java
package examples.classes;
/** A class representing a fraction
  */
public class Fraction {
   private int num, den;
   public Fraction() {
      this( 0, 1 );
   }
   public Fraction( int initNum ) {
      this( initNum, 1 );
   }
   public Fraction( int initNum, int initDen ) {
      num = initNum;
      if ( 0 == initDen ) {
         initDen = 1;        // don't allow a zero
                             // denominator!
      }
      den = initDen;
   }
   /** Convert the object to a string
     */
   public String toString() {
      return num + "/" + den;
   }
   /** Test method for the class
     * @param args not used
     */
   public static void main( String[] args ) {
      Fraction a = new Fraction();
      Fraction b = new Fraction( 2 );
      Fraction c = new Fraction( 3, 4 );
      System.out.println( a );
      System.out.println( b );
      System.out.println( c );
   }
}
```

---

*Code Output*

```
0/1
2/1
3/4
```

---

*Code Dissection*

The constructors are linked in this **Fraction** class so that you can create a **Fraction** in three ways. One constructor with two arguments initializes the numerator and the denominator. The constructor with one integer argument assumes the desired denominator is one. The constructor with no arguments sets a default initial value of 0/1.

---

When one constructor calls another, the calling constructor is essentially calling another method to operate on the object being created. In this sense, the keyword **this** is a reference to the current object.

# USING THIS AS AN OBJECT REFERENCE

In the Java programming language, **this** can also be a reference for the object for which a method is called. You can use it in any instance method. Class methods apply to the whole class, and instance methods apply to a specific object. The **this** keyword has no meaning in class methods.

To return a reference to the current object from a method, return **this**. The return type of the method must be the name of the class, as in the method **setStockNumber** from the next sample program. Returning **this** facilitates a programming technique that many programmers find advantageous. You can chain together method calls for the same instance using the dot operator, as in the following line:

```
x.setStockNumber( 1235693 ).setPrice( 123.34F );
```

This line of code first calls **setStockNumber**, which can modify the object for reference **x** and returns **this**. Next, the statement calls **setPrice**, with the **x** returned from **setStockNumber**. Constructs such as this are common in the Java programming language and in other object-oriented languages. Execution moves from left to right. The effect compounds operations on the same object.

Three methods in the **MyStock** class also use **this** to access data files in constructs such as **this.price**. Using **this** in this way is not required because the fields belong to the current object by default. However, **this** does emphasize the fact that **price** is a member of the object and is not a class variable, argument, or local variable.

It is also common to use **this** to select a field that is hidden by a local variable of the same name, as in the following method:

```
public MyStock setPrice( float price ) {
   this.price = price;
   return this;
}
```

Here is a class that demonstrates using **this** as an object reference:

4

```
package examples.classes;
/** A class definition to demonstrate the use
  * of the this reference
  */
public class MyStock {
   private int stockNumber;
   private float price;
   public MyStock setStockNumber( int stockNumber ) {
      this.stockNumber = stockNumber;
      return this;
   }
   public MyStock setPrice( float price ) {
      this.price = price;
      return this;
   }
   public int getStockNumber() {
      return this.stockNumber;
   }
   public float getPrice() {
      return this.price;
   }
   /** The test method for the class
     * @param args Not used
     */
   public static void main( String[] args ) {
      MyStock x = new MyStock(), y = new MyStock();
      x.setStockNumber( 1235693 ).setPrice( 123.34F );
      y.setStockNumber( 1234833 ).setPrice( 11.57f );
      System.out.println( x.getStockNumber() + " "
                        + x.getPrice() );
      System.out.println( y.getStockNumber() + " "
                        + y.getPrice() );
   }
}
```

The output is

```
1235693 123.34
1234833 11.57
```

# USING STATIC MEMBERS

Static members are class variables and class methods, because they are associated with the class, and not with any particular object or instance of the class. Non-static members are instance variables and instance methods.

Class variables are static fields. One use of class variables is to share information among objects of the class. If two or more instances use the same class variable, they are accessing the same location in storage. Each instance has its own storage location for instance variables. In the next sample program, the class variable `count` records the number of objects created for the class `Counted`. Any method of a class, static or nonstatic, can use a class variable.

Defining constants by using the qualifiers **final** and **static** is another common use for class variables. The qualifier **final** ensures that a constant cannot be changed. **static** ensures that a constant is available regardless of whether any instances of that class have been created. For example, the core class **Math** defines some useful constants, such as **Math.PI. Math.PI** is static, final, and also public, so it can always be accessed.

Class methods are static methods. Declare a method to be **static** if you want it to be available even when no objects of the class exist. You use class methods in many of this book's example programs. All methods of the **System** class are static. For example, the following statements call class methods of the **System** class:

```
System.exit( -1 );
System.gc();
```

You can supply either the name of the class or any instance of that class to reach a static member. Use the dot notation with the name of the class just as you do with an instance variable.

## Syntax

*class_name.static_member_name*
*object_name.static_member_name*

## Dissection

➤ When you use the latter form, you use the object name just as an indicator of type. The object name can even have the value **null**. A class method does not have access to the reference **this** because the method does not apply to an object, regardless of whether an object is named in the method call.

Here is a program that uses a static member to count the number of instances of a class that have been created but not yet destroyed:

```
package examples.classes;
/** A Java class to demonstrate how static members
 *  are defined, initialized, and used.
 */
public class Counted {
   private int value;
   private static int count = 0;   // simple init clause
   /** Default constructor method */
   public Counted() {
      ++count;
      System.out.println( "Creating a "
                            + "Counted object" );
      value = -1;
   }
   /** Class finalizer */
   public void finalize() {
      --count;
      System.out.println( "Destroying a "
                            + "Counted object" );
   }
   /** Method to return the number of objects
    *  @return The number of existing objects of
    *     the class
    */
   public static int getCount() {
      return count;
   }
   /** Mutator method to set the value of the object
    *  @param newValue The new value for the object
    *  @return The updated object
    */
   public Counted setValue( int newValue ) {
      value = newValue;
      return this;
   }
   /** Accessor function to obtain the value of
    *  the object
    *  @return The value of the object
    */
   public int getValue() {
      return value;
   }
   /** The test method for the class
    *  @param args Not used
    */
   public static void main( String[] args )
   {
```

4

```
       Counted a = new Counted();
       Counted b = new Counted();
       Counted c = new Counted();
       System.out.println( "There are "
                            + Counted.getCount()
                            + " Counted objects" );
       Counted d = new Counted();
       System.out.println( "There are "
                            + Counted.getCount()
                            + " Counted objects" );
       a = null;
       System.gc();           // start garbage collection
       System.runFinalization();
       System.out.println( "There are "
                            + a.getCount()
                            + " Counted objects" );
       /* without the next three method calls, the
        * objects b, c, and d would be picked up in
        * the preceding garbage collection
        */
       b.setValue( 1 );
       c.setValue( 2 );
       d.setValue( 3 );
    }
}
```

The output is

```
Creating a Counted object
Creating a Counted object
Creating a Counted object
There are 3 Counted objects
Creating a Counted object
There are 4 Counted objects
Destroying a Counted object
There are 3 Counted objects
```

This example class called Counted has a class variable, count, and a class method, getCount. The initialization of count shows the simplest way to initialize class variables. In this case, the initialization is not necessary because it sets the default value, but it is worth including for clarity. The constructor and finalizer apply to instances of the class. In this case, the constructor increments count, and the finalizer decrements it. Thus count becomes a record of the number of instances created but not yet finalized.

Do you notice that the three calls to setValue in **main** assign values that are never used? In this simple program, these statements do have a purpose other than being representative of a larger application. The Java compiler optimizes code, usually with beneficial effects. In this example, the optimization actually throws away the objects you are counting if the compiler determines that the objects are not used. The three calls of `setValue` access a, b, and c just to prevent the compiler from making them available for garbage collection before the call of **println**.

 Be careful with any logic that depends on garbage collection. Optimization can dramatically affect when garbage collection happens and what objects it destroys.

## Initializing Static Members

You can initialize a class variable in the same way that you can initialize a local variable or instance variable. The Java programming language lets you assign the initial value in the definition of a class variable.

The Java programming language has another form of initializer for class variables: the static initialization block. A **static initialization block** looks rather like a class method with no return type, arguments, or name.

---

*Syntax*

**static {**
   *identifier* = *value*; **// repeat for as many fields as desired**
**}**

---

*Dissection*

➤ You must declare variables before they are initalized in a static intialization block. Typically, you use a static initialization block when a simple initialization clause is not sufficient to give a field its initial value. In the initialization block, you can create objects, call methods, or include any valid Java code you want. A class can have no static initialization blocks, one such block, or more than one. Initialization occurs when the class is loaded, and proceeds from left to right and top to bottom, through the initialization blocks. Any exceptions that may be generated by statements in a static initialization block must be handled within the block.

---

*Code Example*

```
static final int FREEZING;
static {
    FREEZING = 32;
}
```

---

---

*Code Dissection*

The static initialization block declares and then initializes the constant
FREEZING.

---

Here is a program that uses a static initialization block:

```java
package examples.classes;
/** A Java class to demonstrate how static members
  * are defined, initialized, and used.
  */
public class StaticNames {
   private static String[] names;
   /** Method to write the list of names to a
     * specified <code>PrintStream</code> object
     * @param s The printstream to which the names
     *           are written
     */
   public static void printNames(
      java.io.PrintStream s ) {
      for ( int i = 0; i < names.length; i++ ) {
         s.println( names[i] );
      }
   }
   /** The test method for the class
     * @param args Not used
     */
   public static void main( String[] args ) {
      printNames( System.out );
   }
   /** Static initializer */
   static {
      names = new String[4];
      names[0] = "Billy"
      names[1] = "Alyssa";
      names[2] = "Amanda";
      names[3] = "Henry";
   }
}
```

The output is

```
Billy
Alyssa
Amanda
Henry
```

The **StaticNames** class contains a static array of **String** objects. The four strings in the array **names** are created and initialized at load time so that the **main** method has only to print elements of **names**.

A static initialization block cannot throw an exception, or call any other method that may throw an exception, unless it handles the exception inside the block.

## Class Methods and Inheritance

The Java programming language has rules about class methods in classes that are related by inheritance:

➤ Class methods must be defined in the class nearest the root of the class hierarchy that uses them. A class can call all the static members that are defined in its superclass as though they were defined in the class itself, but cannot redefine them. To express this concept in the correct terminology of inheritance, class methods are inherited, but cannot be overridden. Class methods are implicitly final.

➤ Similarly, class methods cannot be abstract. An abstract method is one that has an argument list and return type but no implementation in the class. Usually you define an abstract method to force subclasses to override the method with a full definition.

# USING PACKAGES

Java classes are grouped into packages. All classes, regardless of whether they are included in the core classes or you write them yourself, belong to a package.

There are several ways programmers decide what classes to put into the same package. The following are three common schemes:

➤ Categorize classes into logical groupings and make a package for each group

➤ Build packages that contain sets of classes designed to be used together

➤ Collect classes together for convenient distribution

You can create packages that serve all of these purposes. Often the best time to decide what packages to create is early in the development cycle, when you are designing your classes and before you create the individual classes. This top-down approach helps you organize your files and is particularly helpful when your classes depend on each other.

The Java programming language starts with the premise that you are designing classes to work together. Packages embody this premise for top-level classes. Indeed, all classes and members have package access by default. Unless you explicitly set more restricted access on individual members, classes in the same package can call methods and use fields defined in all classes in the same package. Packages can have classes and interfaces that are available only within the package. Package access is more restrictive than public access and less restrictive than private access.

So far, all your classes have been top-level classes, and the only way to group top-level classes is into packages. The Java programming language also supports nested classes and inner classes. Using nested and inner classes is not an alternative to grouping classes into packages. It is a refinement that is appropriate in specific situations.

You can reuse the same names in different packages without causing conflicts. The full name of a class is the concatenation of the package name, with the class name, using the dot operator.

*Syntax*

*package_name.class_name*

*Dissection*

➤ When you access a class that is in a different package, chain together the name of the package and the name of the class with dots.

*Code Example*

```
trees.Maple
```

*Code Dissection*

If the class `Maple` is in the package `trees`, the full class name is `trees.Maple`.

To avoid name clashes, you only need to make sure your identifiers are unique within your package. The full name of a class includes the name of its packages. You never include files or use a class from another package without also specifying the package name, so it does not matter if another package contains a class with the same name as one of your classes.

Membership in a package is established at the file level. All classes in one file must belong to the same package. To include a file in a package, insert a **package** statement as the first noncomment source line in the file.

*Syntax*

**package** *package_name*;

*Dissection*

➤ If you omit the package declaration, the contents of a file are added to a default, unnamed package.

➤ Only comments may appear before a package statement in your source. The compiler outputs an error message if it finds a package statement anywhere else.

**4**

*Code Example*

```
package trees;
```

*Code Dissection*

All files that make up a package named **trees** must begin with this statement.

# Package Names, File Names, and Folders

You must store a public class in a source file with the same name as the class. As a consequence, a .java file can contain only one public class. Similarly, you must store a package in a subfolder with the same name as the package. A package can contain any number of classes, just as a subfolder can contain more files than you should ever want to put there. You can use the following general guidelines to put a class into a package using the JDK:

1. Insert a package declaration at the start of the file containing the Java source code for the class. For example, if your class is called **Maple** and you want to put it in the package called **trees**, use a text editor to insert the following line before the first line of code in your file Maple.java:

```
package trees;
```

2. Store the source file in a folder with the same name as the package. For example, put the file **Maple.java** in a subfolder called trees.

3. Compile the class as usual. If **Maple.java** is in the current folder, enter the command

```
javac Maple.java
```

4. Make sure the parent folder of the package folder is included in the **CLASSPATH** environment variable so that the **java** command can find your class. For example, if the trees folder is in the woodwork folder on the D drive, and the woodwork folder is not on your **CLASSPATH**, you can add D:\woodwork to your **CLASSPATH** environment variable on Intel-based platforms by typing the following DOS command in a command-line window:

```
SET CLASSPATH=D:\woodwork;%CLASSPATH%
```

5. If the class compiles successfully, you can run it from the command line by entering the following command:

```
java trees.Maple
```

## Subpackages

You can combine packages into other packages. Looking at the same feature from the top down, a package can have subpackages. For example, the **java** package has many subpackages, one of which is **java.lang**. To create subpackages, reflect the package hierarchy in your folder structure. Make the top-level, or most inclusive, package at the root of a subfolder tree. For subpackages, create properly named subfolders. You can further divide the subpackages into more levels, by putting the files into more levels of subfolders.

To access a class in such a hierarchic structure, chain together the subfolder and filenames, using the dot notation. Start with the highest-level, or most inclusive, package.

Here are some facts about a hypothetical public class named **Pine** in a package named `conifers`, where `conifers` is a subpackage of a package named `trees`. The parent folder of trees is included in the **CLASSPATH** environment variable. On Intel-based platforms, this example would become:

| | |
|---|---|
| Filename for the source. | trees\conifers\Pine.java |
| First line in the source. | `package trees.conifers;` |
| Command to compile the source when Pine.java is in the current folder. If Pine.java is not in the current folder, you can include an absolute or relative path. | **javac Pine.java** |
| Command to run `Pine.main`, if such a method exists and trees is the subfolder of the current folder. | **java trees.conifers.Pine** |

For example, if the absolute path name and filename are: D:\forest\trees\conifers\Pine.java, then the **CLASSPATH** would have to include D:\forest for the class `trees.conifers.Pine` to be found.

### Mini Quiz 4-4

If there is a boolean instance variable in class `Pine` named `alpine`, what is the code to set `alpine` to **true** from within `Pine.main`, from another class in `conifers`, and from another class in the `trees`?

## Import Statements

You import packages to simplify your code. An import statement merely sets up a shorthand for package and class names. The code for the imported package is not treated as though it appears in the current file.

You do not have to import a package to use it. You can always use and access any public class or interface that is in another package. You can use them simply by supplying the fully qualified name. For example, to use the **StringTokenizer** class of the **java.util** package, it is sufficient to declare a **StringTokenizer** object as follows:

```
java.util.StringTokenizer a;
```

Using these long, fully qualified names can quickly become tedious. If you frequently access a particular class or use several classes from certain packages, you can include import statements in the source file for the class.

---

*Syntax*

**import** *package_name.class_name*;
**import** *package_name.\**;

---

*Dissection*

➤ To import one class from a package, use **import** *package_name.class_name*;. To import all classes in a package, use **import** *package_name.\**;. Place your import statements after your package declaration and before all class or interface definitions in your source file. Include as many import statements as you want. It is considered better style to import individual classes rather than entire packages at once. As a result, your code is more understandable because it lists the origin of each class used. But use common sense. No one wants to wade through dozens of import statements!

➤ Every Java source file implicitly imports the package **java.lang**. The effect is similar to starting every file with **import java.lang.\*;**.

➤ The package **java.lang** supports the actual Java programming language. All the classes that the example programs in this book use, but which you do not import or specify with fully qualified names, are in the **java.lang** package. Explicitly importing **java.lang.\*** does no harm, but is not necessary.

---

*Code Example*

```
import java.util.StringTokenizer;
import java.util.*;
StringTokenizer st = new String Tokenizer( s );
```

---

---

*Code Dissection*

If you include one of the two import statements, you can declare a
**StringTokenizer** object st for a **String** object s with this declaration:
`StringTokenizer st = new StringTokenizer( s );`.

---

*Code Example*

```
java.util.StringTokenizer st =
   new java.util.StringTokenizer( s );
```

---

*Code Dissection*

This statement is equivalent to the version you must use if your class does not
have either of the two import statements.

---

## Core Java Packages

Table 4–3 lists the core Java packages and states, very briefly, the features each
package supports.

**Table 4-3**   Standard Java packages

| Package Name | Supports |
|---|---|
| java.applet | Applet programming |
| java.awt<br>■ java.awt.color<br>■ java.awt.datatransfer<br><br>■ java.awt.dnd<br>■ java.awt.event<br>■ java.awt.font<br>■ java.awt.geom<br>■ java.awt.im<br><br>■ java.awt.image<br>■ java.awt.image.renderable<br><br>■ java.awt.print | GUI programming<br>■ Classes for color spaces<br>■ Inter-application data transfer and cut-and-paste<br>■ Drag and drop support<br>■ Event-handling classes<br>■ Character fonts<br>■ Two-dimensional geometry<br>■ Framework for Japanese, Chinese, and Korean text input<br>■ Manipulating images<br>■ Producing rendering-independent images<br>■ General printing API |
| java.beans<br><br>■ java.beans.beancontext | The Java component model known as JavaBeans<br>■ Runtime context for JavaBeans |
| java.io | Input and output through data streams, serialization and the file system |
| java.lang<br>■ java.lang.ref<br>■ java.lang.reflect | The Java programming language<br>■ Reference object classes<br>■ Information describing classes and interfaces |

**Table 4-3**  Standard Java packages (continued)

| Package Name | Supports |
|---|---|
| java.math | Arbitrary precision arithmetic |
| java.net | Network programming |
| java.rmi<br>■ java.rmi.activation<br>■ java.rmi.dgc<br>■ java.rmi.registry<br><br>■ java.rmi.server | Invocation of methods on remote objects<br>■ Remote object activation<br>■ Distributed garbage collection<br>■ Registry for objects accessible through RMI<br>■ Server-side RMI support |
| java.security<br>■ java.security.acl<br><br>■ java.security.cert<br>■ java.security.interfaces<br>■ java.security.spec | The security framework<br>■ An obsolete package, superseded by the content of java.security<br>■ Parsing and managing certificates<br>■ RSA algorithm for generating keys<br>■ Key specification and algorithm parameters |
| java.sql | The JDBC package for relational (SQL) databases |
| java.text | Internationalized text, dates, numbers and messages |
| java.util<br><br>■ java.util.jar<br>■ java.util.zip | Collections, event model, date and time, utility classes<br>■ Reading and writing JAR files<br>■ Reading and writing ZIP files |
| javax.accessiblity | Assistive technology to access GUIs |
| javax.swing<br><br>■ javax.swing.border<br><br>■ javax.swing.colorchooser<br>■ javax.swing.event<br>■ javax.swing.filechooser<br>■ javax.swing.plaf<br>■ javax.swing.plaf.basic<br>■ javax.swing.plaf.metal<br>■ javax.swing.plaf.multi<br><br>■ javax.swing.table<br>■ javax.swing.text<br><br>■ javax.swing.text.html<br>■ javax.swing.tree<br>■ javax.swing.undo | Operating system-independent components for building GUIs<br>■ Drawing specialized borders around components<br>■ Used by JColorChooser component<br>■ Events fired by Swing components<br>■ Used by JFileChooser component<br>■ Pluggable look and feel<br>■ Basic look and feel<br>■ Metal look and feel<br>■ Combining auxiliary and basic look and feel<br>■ Table components<br>■ Editable and non-editable text components<br>■ Creating HTML editors<br>■ Tree components<br>■ Undo/redo capabilities in a text editor |

4

**Table 4-3** Standard Java packages (continued)

| Package Name | Supports |
|---|---|
| org.omg.CORBA | Mapping between OMG CORBA API and Java API |
| ■ org.omg.CORBA.DynAnyPackage | ■ Provides the exceptions used with the DynAny interface |
| ■ org.omg.CORBA.ORBPackage | ■ Provides the exception InvalidName and the exception InconsistentTypeCode |
| ■ org.omg.CORBA.portable | ■ Provides a portability layer that makes it possible for code generated by one vendor to run on another vendor's ORB |
| ■ org.omg.CORBA.TypeCodePackage | ■ Provides the user-defined exceptions BadKind and Bounds |
| ■ org.omg.CosNaming | ■ Provides the naming service for Java IDL |
| ■ org.omg.CosNamingContextPackage | ■ Provides the exceptions used in the package org.omg.CosNaming and also the Helper and Holder classes for those exceptions |

The set of standard classes expanded enormously between version 1.0 of the Java platform and the Java 2 platform. The classes in the **javax.swing** packages were available for download before Java 2, and early versions could be used with JDK 1.1. The following packages were added to the standard Java platform in Java 2:

| | | |
|---|---|---|
| java.awt.color | java.beans.beancontext | javax.accessibility |
| java.awt.dnd | java.lang.ref | javax.swing.* |
| java.awt.font | java.rmi.activation | org.omg.* |
| java.awt.geom | java.security.cert | |
| java.awt.im | java.security.spec | |
| java.awt.image.renderable | java.util.jar | |

Many of the new packages reflect the growing use of Java technology in enterprise wide and distributed environments. For example, Java 2 provides enhanced support for remote method invocation and security, and a way to link to the Common Object Request Broker Architecture (CORBA) that is a industry standard used in heterogeneous environments.

The other main direction of development of the Java platform has been in classes used for creating graphical user interfaces. Mostly, these classes fall into the **java.awt** and **javax.swing** packages. Chapter 12 and 13 cover the Abstract Windowing Toolkit, which has been available since the original Java platform but has undergone changes, and the Java Foundation Classes, which include the set of GUI-building classes that is familiarly called Swing.

The core classes that the Java platform provides are organized into packages. These classes compose the API that supports the Java language and the features described in this book.

A full description of the packages, the classes they contain, and all the members that you can use is beyond the scope of this book. Later chapters of this book do discuss many of the packages in more detail. You can find comprehensive and frequently updated documentation for the Sun SDK. To download this documentation from the Web, use the URLs listed in Appendix D.

**4**

---

## SUMMARY

In this chapter you explored classes, which are the heart of object-oriented programming in the Java programming language.

Classes should be the implementation of a design, or object model, that reflects the types of real world objects, relationships between objects, and scenarios that your programs are representing. In the Java programming language, simple class definitions take this form:

```
[public] class class_name {
  // body of class
}
```

Include the access specifier **public** if the class is to be usable from anywhere. By default, classes have package access, which means only other classes in the same package can use it.

Classes have members that must be defined in the body of the class. Data members are fields, and methods are executable code. You should use access specifiers to enforce encapsulation. Carefully determine which members make up the interface between the class and the outside world, and declare only those to be public. A field declaration looks like this:

```
[access_specifier] [qualifiers] type identifier
[= initializer];
```

You can include initializations inside the class, even for static fields. Use static initializer blocks to initialize class variables when your initializations involve more complicated logic than assignment statements. By default, fields are initialized to zero, **null**, or **false**, depending on the type of the field. The compiler does not initialize local variables, and considers it an error if you access a local variable that has not been assigned a value.

The full form of a method declaration is:

```
[access_specifier] [qualifiers] return_type method_name(
argument_list )
        [throws exception_list]
block
```

Access specifers are:

**public**    default or package, indicated by blank    **protected**    **private**

Optional qualifiers for both methods and fields are:

**final**    **static**

A method or field that is declared **static** applies to the class methods and class variables. You can use a class method without an object. Class variables are shared by all objects of the class. Declare a field **final** to make it a constant. A **static** field, even if it is **final**, can be initialized in a static initializer block. Here is an example.

```
public class MyClass {
    static int myField;
    {  myField = 12; }
}
```

To access a member of a class from methods that are not members of the class, use the dot notation to connect the class name to a field or method name. If the class is in a package, connect the package name to the front of the class with another dot operator. The syntax can look like the following:

*package.subpackage.class.object.method*()

You usually create an object, or instance, of a class by using the **new** keyword and assigning the result to a reference for the object, as in:

```
object_reference = new class_name( arguments_of_
constructor );
```

The **new** keyword calls the constructor of the class. Java classes have constructors, but no destructors. Automatic garbage collection is used to free memory when required. You can write finalizers, which are methods that perform other cleanup when an instance is destroyed. You can call **System.runFinalizersOnExit** or **System.runFinalization** to ensure that finalizers run, rather than depending on automatic garbage collection.

You can overload methods by creating more than one method with the same name but with differing argument lists. Overloading constructors is very common. One constructor can call another by using the keyword **this** as a method call in the first line of the constructor. This is a handy way to consolidate the logic for creating objects, and at the same time give the impression that constructors have default arguments.

Here is an example:

```
public class MyClass {
   MyClass( ) {
      this(0);
   }
   MyClass( int value) {
      myField = value;
   }
}
```

**4**

Instance methods can refer to the object for which the method is called, by using the reference **this**. Return **this** if you want to return the object. You can also refer to another member of the class as **this.**_member_name_ in the method, for clarity.

It is common to group classes into packages. Classes in the same package have special access privileges to each other. Also, you can reuse the same names in different packages without conflict because the package name is part of the full class name.

The Java programming language has strict rules for your file structure and file-names. Only one public class is allowed in a single source file. If a .java file contains a public class, the file must have the same name as the class. The compiler creates a separate .class file for every public and nonpublic class.

Classes in the same package must be stored in the same folder, and the folder name must match the package name.

The first line in source files should be a **package** statement naming the package to which the class or classes in the file belong. Import statements follow the package statement. You can use the classes or packages of classes that are named in import statements without having to enter their fully qualified names.

The Java platform provides many packages. The packages include the core classes that make up a standard API for all programmers on all implementations of the Java platforms.

# QUESTIONS

1. Examine the following code:

```
public class Quiz4_1 {
   int x;
   public int increment() {
      return ++x;
   }
   public static void main( String[] args ) {
```

```
    Quiz4_1 a = new Quiz4_1();
    System.out.println( a.increment() );
  }
}
```

Which of the following statements are true? Select all that apply.

a. The compiler rejects the expression **++x** because **x** is being used before it is initialized.

b. Compilation is successful and the output from running the code is 1.

c. The compiler rejects the expression **a.increment()** because it does not evaluate to a **String**.

d. The compiler rejects the expression **new Quiz4_1( )** because parentheses are not allowed when there are no constructor arguments.

2. Examine the following code:

```
public class Quiz4_2 {
    private static final double A = 5.6;
    private double b;
    Quiz4_2( double z1, double  z2 ) {
        b = z1 * z2;
    }
    Quiz4_2( double z ) {
        if ( z > 0.0 ) {
            this( z, 2.0 );
        } else {
            this( z, 1.0 );
        }
    }
    public static void main( String[] args ) {
        System.out.println( new Quiz4_2 ( 4.0, 3.0 ) );
    }
    public String toString() {
        return( "b = " + b );
    }
}
```

Which one of the following statements correctly describes the behavior when this program is compiled and run?

a. The compiler rejects the expression **new Quiz4_2( 4.0, 3.0 )** because it is not possible to create an object without a name.

b. Compilation is successful and the output is **b = 12.0**.

c. The compiler rejects the expression **this( z, 2.0 )** because it is not the first statement in the method.

d. The compiler rejects the second definition of the method **Quiz4_2** because the name has already been defined.

3. Which of the following qualifiers can be used with members of a class? Select all that apply.

    a. **static**

    b. **const**

    c. **public**

    d. **private**

    e. **package**

4. True or False: Assuming `value` is a **float** instance variable of a class, a class method of the class can output its value with the following statement:

```
System.out.println( this.value );
```

5. Examine the following code:

```
public class Quiz4_4 {
    private static int a;
    private static int b;
    public static void main( String[] args ) {
        System.out.println( a + " " + b );
    }
    static {
        a = 100;
    }
    static {
        b = 200;
    }
}
```

Which of the following statements correctly describes the behavior when this program is compiled and run? Select all that apply.

    a. The compiler rejects the attempt to define a method called `static`.

    b. The compiler rejects the attempt to define two static initialization blocks.

    c. Compilation is successful and the output is 0  0.

    d. Compilation is successful and the output is 100  200.

    e. Compilation is not successful because the argument of **main** must be `(String[] args)`.

6. Examine the following code:

```
import java.lang.*;
import java.util.StringTokenizer;
package mypackage;
public class Quiz4_5 {
    public static void main( String[] args ) {
        String a = "Hello World!";
```

```
        StringTokenizer st
          = new StringTokenizer( a );
        String token1 = st.nextToken();
        System.out.println( token1 );
    }
  }
```

Which of the following statements are true? Select all that apply.

a. The compiler rejects the statement import java.lang.*; because that package is already implicitly imported.

b. The compiler rejects the statement package mypackage; because it is not the first statement of the file that is not a comment.

c. Compilation is successful and the output is Hello World!

d. Compilation is successful and the output is Hello.

e. The compiler rejects the statement

StringTokenizer st = new StringTokenizer( a );

because the class name **StringTokenizer** is not fully qualified with the name of its package.

7. Examine the following code:

```
public class Quiz4_6 {
    Boolean condition;
    public void testCondition() {
        if ( condition ) {
            System.out.println( "TRUE!" );
        } else {
            System.out.println( "FALSE!" );
        }
    }
    public static void main( String[] args ) {
        Quiz4_6 a = new Quiz4_6();
        a.testCondition();
    }
}
```

Which of the following statements are true? Select all that apply.

a. The compiler rejects the expression if ( condition ) because condition is being used before it is initialized.

b. The value of the variable condition is **null** when it is tested in the first statement of testCondition.

c. Compilation is successful and the output from running the code is TRUE!

d. Compilation is successful and the output from running the code is FALSE!

e. The compiler rejects the expression if ( condition ) because it does not evaluate to a boolean value.

8. Which of the following are valid statements for declaring local variables within a method body? Select all that apply.

a. `final int a;`

b. `static int b;`

c. `transient int c;`

d. `volatile int d;`

e. `static final int e;`

9. Which of the following are valid statements for declaring fields of a class? Select all that apply.

a. `final int a;`

b. `static int b;`

c. `transient int c;`

d. `volatile int d;`

e. `static final int e;`

10. Examine the following code:

```java
public class Quiz4_7 {
    private int value;
    public Quiz4_7( int input ) {
        value = input;
    }
    public String toString() {
        return String.valueOf( value );
    }
    public static void main( String[] args ) {
        Quiz4_7 a = new Quiz4_7();
        Quiz4_7 b = new Quiz4_7( 42 );
        System.out.println( a );
        System.out.println( b );
    }
}
```

Which of the following statements are true? Choose as many as are appropriate.

a. Compilation is successful and the output from running the code is 42.

b. The compiler rejects the statement new Quiz4_7() because the definition of a no-argument constructor is missing.

c. Compilation is successful and the output from running the code is as follows:

```
null
42
```

d. Compilation is successful and the output from running the code is as follows:

```
a
b
```

11. Examine the following code:

```
import java.util.Date;
// -X-
public class Quiz4_8 {
    // class definition
}
```

Which of the following statements are valid if inserted at the line marked -X-? Select all that apply.

a. `import java.util.StringTokenizer;`

b. `package java4cpp.questions.c4;`

c. `class AnotherClass { }`

d. `public class AThirdClass { }`

---

# EXERCISES

## Debugging

1. Correct all errors in the following program:

```
package questions.c4;
public class Debug4_1 {
    public static void main( String[] args ) {
        int x;
        if ( args.length > 0 )
        x = args.length;
        report();
    }
        public static report( x ) {
        System.out.println( x );
    }
}
```

2. Correct all errors in the following program:

```
package questions.c4;
public class Debug4_2 {
    private double x;
    public void Debug4_2( double input ) {
        x = input;
```

```
    }
    public String toString() {
        return String.valueOf( x );
    }
    public static void main( String[] args ) {
        Debug4_2 a = new Debug4_2( -7.3 );
        System.out.println( a );
    }
}
```

**4**

3. Correct all errors in the following program:

```
package questions.c4;
public class Debug4_3 {
    private double x;
    public Debug4_3( double input ) {
        x = input;
    }
    public String toString() {
        return String.valueOf( x );
    }
    void finalize() throws Throwable {
        System.out.println( "Goodbye!" );
    }
    public static void main( String[] args ) {
        Debug4_3 a = new Debug4_3( -7.3 );
        System.out.println( a );
        System.gc();
        System.runFinalize();
    }
}
```

4. Correct all errors in the following program so that the list displayed contains the numbers 0.1 to 1.0 in steps of 0.1. Do not make any changes to the **main** method.

```
package questions.c4;
public class Debug4_4 {
    private static double[] a;
    public static void displayList() {
        for( int i = 0; i < a.length; i++ ) {
            System.out.print( a[i] + " " );
        }
        System.out.println();
    }
    public static void main( String[] args ) {
        displayList();
    }
    {
        a = new double[10];
        for( int i = 0; i < a.length; i++ ) {
            a[i] = (i+1)/10;
```

```
        }
      }
    }
```

5. Correct all errors in the following program:

```
package questions.c4;
public class Debug4_5 {
   private double x;
   private double y;
   public Debug4_5( double d1, double d2 ) {
      X = d1;
      y = d2;
   }
   public Debug4_5( double d1 ) {
      this( d1, 0.0D );
   }
   public Debug4_5() {}
   public ~Debug4_5() {}
   public static void displayValues() {
      System.out.println( "Value x = " + x );
      System.out.println( "Value y = " + y );
   }
   public static void main( String[] args ) {
      Debug4_5 a = new Debug4_5( 5.6, 9.345 );
      a.displayValues();
   }
}
```

6. Correct all errors in the following program:

```
package questions.c4;
public class Debug4_6 {
   Debug4_6( int n) {
      String data = new String[n];
      for ( int = 0; i < n; i++ )
      data[i] = args[i];
      int count = n;
   }
   public static void main( String[] args ) {
      int n = args.length;
      if ( n ) {
         Debug4_6 D46 = new Debug 4_6( n );
      }
      System.out.println( n );
      if ( !n ) return;
         for ( int i = 0; i < D46.count; i++ )
            System.out.println( data[i] );
   }
}
```

## Complete the Program

1. Extract the file **questions\c4\Pair.java** from the file **question.jar** on the CD-ROM. Complete the `Pair` class definition by providing a **main** method that constructs an instance of the `Pair` class with a **Double** object and an **Integer** object as input and then writes the object to **System.out**.

2. Extract the file **questions\c4\Student.java** from the file **question.jar** on the CD-ROM. Complete the `Student` class definition by providing all the missing methods that are needed for the given main method to compile and execute successfully.

3. Extract the file **questions\c4\Point3D.java** from the file **question.jar** on the CD-ROM. Complete the `Point3D` class definition by adding a **finalize** method that prints the final contents of the `Point3D` object to **System.out** just before the object is destroyed.

4. Extract the file **questions\c4\Fibonacci.java** from the file **question.jar** on the CD-ROM. The main method of the Fibonacci class calculates the first 25 numbers in the `Fibonacci` sequence and provides a method to return the value of any particular value in the sequence. Complete the `Fibonacci` class definition by providing a static initialization block that calculates the first **MAXFIB** numbers in the sequence. The first two numbers in the sequence are 0 and 1. Every other number in the sequence is the sum of the two numbers that precede it in the sequence. For example, the Fibonacci sequence starts 0, 1, 1, 2, 3, 5, 8, 13....

5. Extract the file **questions\c4\Constructors.java** from the file **question.jar** on the CD-ROM. Complete the `Constructors` class definition by adding two more constructors to simulate the use of default values. The **int** default for the first parameter is 0, and the **double** default for the second parameter is 1.0. Both of the constructors you add should call the constructor provided.

## Discovery

1. Create a public class called `SentenceFormatter` that takes a **String** object as the single argument of the constructor. The class should have at least one private field, an array of strings in which each element is a token extracted from the **String** passed to the constructor. For simplicity, assume the input consists of a set of words without punctuation. Provide the following instance methods in addition to the constructor:

   - `public int getWordCount()`
     returns the number of words in the string.

- **`public String getWordAt( int position )`**
  returns the word in the position indicated by the argument, or null if the index is greater than the number of words in the string or less than 0. The first word is in position 1.

- **`public String sentence()`**
  returns the string formatted as a sentence. The letter of the first word is capitalized and a period is added to the end.

- **`public String heading()`**
  returns the string with the first letter of every word capitalized.

- **`public String justify( int size, int justification )`**
  returns the string truncated or expanded to the number of characters specified in the first argument. If the second argument equals the public field `SentenceFormatter.RIGHT`, the method appends trailing spaces if necessary. If the second argument equals the public field `SentenceFormatter.LEFT`, the method inserts leading spaces if necessary. If the second argument is `SentenceFormatter.CENTER`, the method might add both leading and trailing spaces.

- **`public static void main( String[] args )`**
  is a test method to exercise every other method.

2. Create a public class called `StringReverser` that takes a **String** object as a constructor parameter. The class should have one private field of type `SentenceFormatter`, the class you created to answer the previous exercise. Make sure that `StringReverser` and `SentenceFormatter` are in the same package. Provide the following methods:

- A constructor that takes a **String** object as an argument.

- **`String wordsReversed()`**
  returns the string with the words in the reverse order.

- **`boolean reversible()`**
  returns **true** if the string is the same with the words in the original order and in reverse order, and **false** otherwise. For example, "all for one and one for all" is reversible but "every man for himself" is not. Consider any one-word string to be reversible.

- **`public static void main( String[] args )`**
  is a test method to exercise every other method.

3. Create a class called `Inventory` that contains three arrays with elements of type **String**, **int**, and **float**. An element in the **String** array holds an identifying code for an item that a store might sell. The element at the corresponding index position in the integer array is the number of that

item in stock, and the corresponding element in the **float** array is the retail price. The constructor takes one argument, which is the size of the arrays. The class must have at least the following additional public methods:

- `public int update( String ID, int quantity,`
  `float price )`
  adds or updates a stock item. If an item with the specified ID already exists, the method prints a warning and updates the int and **float** arrays. Otherwise, the method writes new values into all three arrays. The return value is the number of items recorded in the arrays when the update is complete.

- `public void setQuantity( String ID, int quantity )`
  changes the recorded number in stock for the item that matches the specified ID. If no items match the specified ID, the method prints a warning.

- `public int getQuantity( String ID )`
  returns the number in stock for the item that matches the specified ID. If no items match the specified ID, a warning is printed and the return value is zero.

- `public void setPrice( String ID, float price )`
  changes the recorded price for the item that matches the specified ID to the specified price. If no items match the specified ID, the method prints a warning.

- `public float getPrice( String ID )`
  returns the price for the item that matches the specified ID to the specified price. If no items match the specified ID, the method prints a warning, and the return value is zero.

- `public void update( String ID, int number )`
  changes the number in stock for the item whose identifier matches the specified ID to the specified quantity, and adds the specified number to the number in stock. A negative number represents a sale or loss of stock. If no items match the specified ID, the method prints a warning.

- `public void update( String ID, float percent )`
  increases the price for the item that matches the specified ID by the specified percent. The percentage can be negative to reduce the price. If no items match the specified ID, the method prints a warning.

- `public void stockReport()`
  prints an inventory report in the following format, where a *c* represents a character and a *d* represents a digit:
  ```
  Item cccc: in stock: d price: ddddd.ddd
  Item ccc: in stock: ddd price: dddd.ddddd
  Item cccccc: in stock: dd price: dddd.dd
  ...
  Total value of inventory: dddddddd.ddddd
  ```

- `static public void main( String[] args )`
  is a test method that exercises all the other methods.

Provide as many private methods and fields as you want to simplify coding this class. For this exercise, you can assume the user always supplies sensible arguments. For example, you do not have to check for a negative price or allow for an attempt to create more items than there is room for in the array. However, you may find it interesting to test such situations and see what happens.

## CHAPTER FIVE

# INHERITANCE

## In this chapter you will:

➤ Determine when it is appropriate to use inheritance to model real-world relationships between types.

☕ Write code that implements tightly encapsulated classes that have *is a* and *has a* relationships.

☕ Write code to construct instances of a concrete (non-abstract) class.

☕ Identify correctly constructed interface declarations and implementations.

☕ State the significance of access specifiers **public**, **protected**, and **private** and other modifiers including **final** and **abstract**.

☕ Write code to call overridden methods and parental constructors, and describe the effect of these calls.

☕ State the legal return types for any method given the declaration of all related methods in the method's class or parent classes.

➤ Use the keyword **super** as an object reference.

➤ Correctly chain finalizer methods so that they call the finalizer methods of parent classes.

## INHERITANCE AND OBJECT ORIENTED PROGRAMMING

Classes are the building blocks of object-oriented programs. In the previous chapter, you learned how to design an application by determining the classes you needed, how the classes used each other, and how you could implement a program in terms of the messages, or method calls, between the classes. That is a good start. Your next building block on your way to modeling relationships between classes is to understand how to relate classes by inheritance. Much of the power of OO programming stems from the ability to model types related by inheritance.

Often, the real-world objects that you model with your program fall into natural classifications. For example savings accounts and checking accounts are both bank accounts. The best way to model relationships like this is with inheritance. To know when to use inheritance in object-oriented analysis, you look for generalization of types and the for specialization of types. You gain design flexibility by defining a separate type for the more general category, in this case a bank account, and then by defining more specialized types, such as saving and checking accounts, that inherit from the general type. In Java, you define **supertypes**, or **superclasses**, for the more general type and **subtypes**, or **subclasses**, for the more specialized types. As a result, you only have to implement the common behavior once. Inheritance also makes your design more robust. For example, it ensures that the various kinds of bank accounts share the essential characteristics of all bank accounts.

Sometimes, you will find opportunities for inheritance to be less obvious than with the bank account example. Considerable analysis is often required to identify opportunities for using inheritance. Consider these guidelines when implementing inheritance relationships:

➤ Make the supertype the more general, or wider type, and the subclass the more specific, or narrow, type.

➤ Always make a subtype capable of doing everything a supertype can do.

➤ Ensure that a subtype holds all information that the supertype holds.

➤ Add attributes and behavior to a subclass to define behavior that is more specialized than what is found in the superclass.

➤ Remember that you can create hierarchies of sub- and supertypes. You can use a tree diagram, with the supertype at the top, to illustrate a hierarchy, as shown in Figure 5.1.

➤ For optimal design, move common characteristics toward the root of the hierarchy tree.

➤ Remember that undesirable inherited behavior or attributes duplicated in different classes usually indicate poor design.

➤ Allow different subclasses of the same superclass to do the same thing, but differently. Each subclass can provide its own implementation of behavior defined in the superclass, or inherit the superclass behavior by default.

➤ Force subclasses to provide a behavior by creating an abstract version of the behavior in the superclass for cases where in which it makes no sense for the superclass to provide a default behavior. For example, the bank account superclass can have an abstract withdraw method because each type of account must allow withdrawals but implement them differently.

➤ Consider defining the supertype, or ultimate supertype of a hierarchy, as an abstract type. An abstract type cannot be instantiated, but can establish the characteristics of all subtypes. For example, the banking model may not let account owners open a generic bank account, but does let them open savings or checking accounts.

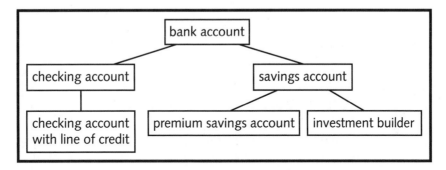

**Figure 5-1** A hierarchy of bank account classes

It is difficult to choose from among inheritance, *is a* relationships, or *has a* relationships when creating your banking application. Some types of objects must contain references to other objects. For example, whenever a bank account object lets owners perform a transaction such as deposit and withdrawal, it creates a transaction record and stores that record in a transaction log. You can model this behavior by defining types for individual transactions and the transaction log. Does the log inherit from the supertype of transaction? No, it uses the *has a* containment relationship. The set of transactions held by the log is implemented as a field that could be an array or one of the collection classes you will learn about in Chapter 10. On the other hand, an inheritance hierarchy relating the different types of transactions might exist in an extensive banking model.

# JAVA PROGRAMMING LANGUAGE SUPPORT FOR INHERITANCE

The Java programming language fully supports inheritance. Many of the core classes of the Java platform are related by inheritance. For example several kinds of input and output streams inherit, directly or indirectly, from classes **java.io.Reader** and **java.io.Writer**, respectively. A **StringReader** and a **BufferedReader** are both **Reader** objects. Therefore, they have all characteristics of the Reader class plus additional methods, such as the method **BufferedReader.readLine** that you used in previous chapters, to provide more specialized functionality.

Every Java class belongs to an inheritance hierarchy. Unless you explicitly specify otherwise, your classes are direct subclasses of the core class **Object**.

The **Object** class is the common ancestor of all Java classes and is the root of the Java class hierarchy. This is why all Java classes, including those you define yourself, inherit a default set of behaviors from the **Object** class. You can create your own hierarchies within this all-embracing Java hierarchy.

The process of defining a new class that inherits from an existing class is called **extending** a class. You add fields or methods to your new subclass to give it additional capabilities, or override methods inherited from the superclass to customize or complete their implementation. Unlike other programming languages, Java requires that a class have only one direct superclass. Compare this to C++, which lets a class inherit explicitly from several other classes, using what is called multiple inheritance. The Java programming language has a rather elegant alternative to multiple inheritance: you can define *interfaces*, and classes can implement any number of interfaces. An interface, like a class, is a type and defining an interface is similar to defining a class, except that an interface can contain only constants and abstract methods. In addition, an interface cannot be instantiated. Just as a class can extend a superclass, it can **implement** an interface. The is-a relationship applies equally to the superclass that a class extends and to all interfaces that a class implements.

You can define classes to be abstract. Like interfaces, **abstract classes** cannot be instantiated, but they can be extended. Like interfaces, abstract classes can contain methods without implementations. But, unlike interfaces, abstract classes can also define methods with complete implementations. Use abstract classes when you want to provide some default method implementations or instance variables in the superclass. The standard class **java.io.Reader** is an example of abstract class.

The rest of this chapter looks in detail at the features of the Java programming language that support inheritance.

# EXTENDING CLASSES

In the Java programming language, you achieve inheritance by extending a class. Every Java class implicitly extends **Object**. To inherit from another class explicitly, use the keyword **extends**. You can explicitly extend **Object** using the following form, but it is never necessary.

*Syntax*

```
[public] [qualifiers] class class_name extends superclass_name {
    /* member definitions */
}
```

## Dissection

➤ The optional class access specifier must be either **public** or omitted to assign package access by default. You can apply the access specifiers **private** and **protected** to a class that is defined inside another class. Nesting class definitions is described in Chapter 9.

➤ You can qualify the new class with any of the following optional qualifiers: **final**, **abstract**, or **static**. Declare a class with **final** or **abstract** to determine whether it can or must be used as a superclass. You can apply the qualifier static only to a class that is defined inside another class.

➤ The keyword **extends** introduces the name of the superclass. You can name only one superclass. If you omit the keyword **extends** from a class definition, the class implicitly extends **java.lang.Object**.

## Code Example

```
public class SavingsAccount extends BankAccount {
    // the members of SavingsAccount are defined here
}
```

## Code Dissection

The class **SavingsAccount** is a subclass of **BankAccount**. It inherits all methods and fields defined in superclass **BankAccount** and has, in addition, the members and fields defined in the **SavingsAccount** class definition.

---

Here is a class that can be used as a superclass. This example contains a class called **HasX**. It is a public class, and is therefore found in a file called **HasX.java**. The structure of packages mirrors the file system, so you will find this source code in the examples\inheritance subfolder of the folder in which you unpacked the JAR file examples.jar.

```
package examples.inheritance;
/** A Java superclass to demonstrate inheritance
  * concepts
  */
public class HasX {
    private int x;
    /** Method to set the value of the object
      * @param inputX The field's new value
      */
    public void setX( int inputX ) {
        x = inputX;
    }
    /** Method to get the value of the object
      * @return The value of the field
```

```
      */
   public int getX() {
      return x;
   }
   /** Method to write X to <code>System.out</code>
      */
   public void showX() {
      System.out.println( x );
   }
}
```

The class `HasX` has a private field `x`, public methods to set and get the value of `x`, and a public method to output the value of `x`. The next class, `HasXY`, extends `HasX`:

```
package examples.inheritance;
/** An example Java subclass used to demonstrate
  * inheritance concepts
  */
public class HasXY extends HasX {
   private int y;
   /** Method to set the object's value
     * @param inputY The field's new value
     */
   public void setY( int inputY ) {
      y = inputY;
   }
   /** Method to get the object's value
     * @return The value of the field
     */
   public int getY() {
      return y;
   }
   /** Method to write Y to <code>System.out</code>
      */
   public void showY() {
      System.out.println( y );
   }
   /** The test method for the class
     * @param args not used
     */
   public static void main( String[] args ) {
      HasXY obj = new HasXY();
      obj.setY( 20 );
      obj.setX( 10 );
      obj.showY();
      obj.showX();
   }
}
```

The output is

```
20
10
```

The class `HasXY` is a subclass of `HasX`. It has an additional field `y`, methods to get, set, and output `y`, and a **main** method for testing. The **main** method creates a `HasXY` object, `obj`. The `obj` object is also a `HasX` object and has all the members of both `HasX` and `HasXY`.

## Final Classes

Declare a class with **final** to prevent it from ever being used as a superclass. This ensures that your class is never extended and that its methods are never overridden. Some of the core Java classes are final, including the wrapper classes for the primitive types and **String**. As a result, you cannot extend **Integer** to create subclasses such as `EvenInteger` or `PositiveInteger`.

Making a class final improves performance. The method-call mechanism is quicker because method overriding is not possible. The **String** class is probably final for this reason alone. Security is another reason for making a class final. You can disallow subclasses to prevent anyone from creating classes that change the implementations of methods you rely upon. You can also declare individual methods to be final, to prevent them from being overridden when you choose not to make the whole class final.

## Abstract Classes

Declare a class with **abstract** if the intention is never to instantiate the class. Do this to design a class for use only as a superclass. You can then extend the class and create objects of the subclasses. The only way to use an abstract class is to extend it.

You can also declare methods to be abstract, but only within abstract classes. Abstract methods have no body, or implementation, and must be overridden in any extending class that is not also abstract.

An abstract class can contain a mixture of abstract methods and fully implemented methods. This is useful in situations where some of the characteristics of objects can be inherited from the superclass and others depend on the particular subclass the objects instantiate. You must make methods abstract to force the subclasses to provide an implementation.

Here is a variation on the `HasX` and `HasXY` classes in which the superclass is an abstract class:

```
package examples.inheritance;
/** A Java superclass to demonstrate inheritance
  * concepts
```

```
   */
public abstract class HasX2 {
   private int x;
   /** Method to set the value of the object
     * @param inputX The field's new value
     */
   public void setX( int inputX ) {
      x = inputX;
   }
   /** Method to get the value of the object
     * @return The value of the field
     */
   public int getX() {
      return x;
   }
   /** Method to somehow display the X value
     */
   public abstract void showX();
}
```

The class `HasX2` is explicitly declared to be an abstract class. If you remove the keyword **abstract** before the keyword class, `HasX2` is still implicitly abstract, because it contains the abstract method `showX`. You make the method abstract by explicitly qualifying it with **abstract** and removing the method body. As a result, each subclass must provide its own implementation of `showX`. You cannot create a `HasX2` object because the class definition is incomplete. The following class definition, `HasXY2`, extends `HasX2` and implements the abstract `showX` method.

```
package examples.inheritance;
/** An example Java subclass used to demonstrate
  * inheritance concepts
  */
public class HasXY2 extends HasX2 {
   private int y;
   /** Method to set the object's value
     * @param inputY The field's new value
     */
   public void setY( int inputY ) {
      y = inputY;
   }
   /** Method to get the object's value
     * @return The value of the field
     */
   public int getY() {
      return y;
   }
   /** Method to write the value of Y to
     * <code>System.out</code>.
     */
   public void showY() {
      System.out.println( y );
```

```
      }
      /** Method to write the value of X to
       * <code>System.out</code>. This is required
       * because this method is an abstract
       * method in the superclass.
       */
      public void showX() {
         System.out.println( getX() );
      }
      /** The test method for the class
       * @param args Not used
       */
      public static void main( String[] args ) {
         HasXY2 obj = new HasXY2();
         obj.setY( 20 );
         obj.setX( 10 );
         obj.showY();
         obj.showX();
      }
}
```

The output does not change as a result of the modifications to the code, and remains the following:

```
20
10
```

**Mini Quiz 5-1**

Suppose you want to represent birds in an inheritance hierarchy for which the superclass is called `Birds`. You can have subclasses for `SongBirds`, `BirdsOfPrey`, `FlightLessBirds`, `WaterFowl`, and the like. Design a simple class hierarchy. Where do you define the method `fly`?

## The Problem of Multiple Inheritance

Consider the bank account example introduced in the opening section of Chapter 4 and used again in this chapter. What if the bank wants to create a new kind of account that provides checking privileges and that pays interest? The new account has the characteristics of both a checking account and a savings account. If Java allowed multiple inheritance, the new class could extend both the savings account class and the checking account class. Figure 5-2 shows the resulting pattern, which is sometimes called diamond inheritance.

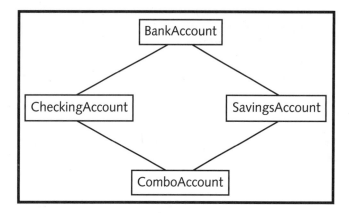

**Figure 5-2** A hierarchy of bank account classes

Diamond inheritance can cause problems. In Figure 5-2 `ComboAccount` inherits attributes (such the `balance` field) of `BankAccount` through both `CheckingAccount` and `SavingsAccount`. The person programming `ComboAccount` may not even know that the `BankAccount` class is a common superclass. What happens when `ComboAccount` updates `balance`? Does it update the copy inherited from `SavingAccount` or `CheckingAccount`? Depending on the implementation of inheritance, `ComboAccount` may have two `balance` fields or the update to `balance` may not be reflected properly in one of its superclasses.

The Java programming language does not provide for multiple inheritance. In its place, the language provides interfaces to encapsulate methods so that they can be implemented in other classes.

## IMPLEMENTING INTERFACES

An interface is like a design document for the external features of a class. Defining an interface establishes the public methods that must be provided by classes that implement the interface. An interface defines public methods that are abstract and that have no implementations. It can have fields, but they must be static and final.

Interfaces provide a mechanism for a subclass to define the behaviors from sources other than the direct and indirect subclass's superclasses.

The Java platform provides a number of interfaces that are covered in later chapters of this book. One of these is **Runnable** from the package **java.lang**. The **Runnable** interface defines the behavior required to execute as a separate thread in a multithreaded program. Threads are separate paths through one program that can be executing at the same time. All threads must have a method **run**, which acts like the **main** method for the thread. One way to define a class that can run as a thread is to define it to implement **Runnable**. This interface includes the method **run**.

You can design your own interfaces, much like you can define your own classes. Use the keyword **interface** rather than the keyword **class** in the definition.

*Syntax*

[public] **interface** *interface_name* [extends *interface_name*] {
    /* *declaration of members* */
}

*Dissection*

➤ Like a class, an interface can have public access or the default package access.

➤ An interface can extend another interface. In this way, you can accumulate the behaviors from layers of interfaces into one powerful or specialized interface.

➤ An interface can contain methods, but the following restrictions apply:

All methods are abstract.

You cannot define the implementation of methods in an interface.

You can explicitly include the qualifier abstract in the method declaration, but you do not have to, because it is implied.

You cannot include methods that are qualified with the keywords **native**, **static**, **synchronized**, or **final**.

All methods are public.

You can explicitly include the access specifier **public**, but you do not have to, because the default access for methods in an interface is public rather than package.

➤ An interface can contain fields, but they are all static and final. In other words, the only data items allowed in interfaces are constants. If you omit the qualifiers **static** and **final**, the Java programming language silently provides them for you!

*Code Example*

```
public interface Artistic {
    public void sketch();
}
```

---

*Code Dissection*

The interface `Artistic` contains just one method. The method is implicitly abstract. Any class that implements `Artistic` must provide an implementation of `sketch`.

---

> **Mini Quiz 5-2**
>
> Why can you not use `final` and `static` as qualifiers for methods in an interface?

Any class can implement one or more interfaces by including the **implements** keyword in its class definition.

*Syntax*

---

[public] [*qualifiers*] **class** *class_name* **implements** *interface_name*
[*, interface_name*] {
   / * *declaration of members* * /
}

---

*Dissection*

➤ As always, a class can have explicit public access or the default package access.

➤ A class that implements an interface can be **final** or **abstract**, just like any other class.

➤ The keyword **interface** introduces the name of the interface that the class implements. A class can implement more than one interface. List all the interfaces' names, separated by commas.

---

*Code Example*

```
public class Painter implements Artistic {
    public void sketch() {
        System.out.println( "pen and ink drawing" );
    }
}
public class Sculptor implements Artistic, Runnable {
    public void sketch() {
        System.out.println( "Charcoal drawing" );
    }
    public void run() {
        sketch();
    }
}
```

## Code Dissection

Because the `Sculptor` class implements two interfaces—`Artistic` and the core interface **Runnable**—it must implement methods defined in both interfaces: `sketch` and `run`. When the Java Virtual Machine (JVM) starts this class as a thread, it executes the `Sculptor.run` method.

All classes that implement `Artistic` must have a fully implemented `sketch` method. This class can be instantiated. The class can also define new methods.

**5**

A class can implement an interface as well as extend another class. Indeed, one of the reasons for implementing the interface **Runnable**—rather than the core class **Thread**, which provides a more complete framework for threads—is that your class may already be extending some class other than **Object**.

## Syntax

[public] [*qualifiers*] **class** *class_name* **extends** *superclass_name*
**implements** *interface_name* **[**, *interface_name* **]** {
  /* *declaration of members* */
}

## Dissection

➤ A class can simultaneously extend a superclass and implement one or more interfaces.

## Code Example

```java
public class Designer extends Thread implements Artistic {
   public void sketch() {
       System.out.println( "conceptual drawing" );
   }
   public void run() {
      sketch();
   }
 }
```

## Code Dissection

This class extends **Thread**, so that it can inherit the full support for threads that the **Thread** class provides. The `Designer` class can do so because it has no other superclass than **Object**. After extending **Thread**, `Designer` still has **Object** as a superclass, but now **Object** is an indirect superclass. The specialized behavior of a `Designer` is specified in the interface `Artistic`.

Like the `Sculptor` class, the `Designer` class implements **run**, but this class is overriding the **run** method of the **Thread** class.

Like the `Painter` and the `Sculptor` classes, the `Designer` class would be rejected by the compiler if the class did not provide an implementation for `sketch`.

---

When a class implements an interface, objects of that class are also considered to be instantiations of the interface. Using the example classes in this section, a `Designer` is an `Artistic` object as well as a **Thread** and a **Runnable** object, a `Sculptor` is both a **Runnable** object and an `Artistic` object, and a `Painter` is an `Artistic` object.

**Mini Quiz 5-3**

Why is an interface not allowed to implement another interface or to extend or implement a class?

Here is a file that contains two interfaces and two classes:

```
package examples.inheritance;
interface Inflatable {
   public void inflate();
}
interface Kickable {
   public void kick();
}
class SportsBall {
   public void manufacture() {
      System.out.println( "Making a sports ball." );
   }
}
public class SoccerBall extends SportsBall
         implements Inflatable, Kickable {
   public void inflate() {
      System.out.println( "Inflating a soccer ball." );
   }
   public void kick() {
      System.out.println( "Kicking a soccer ball." );
   }
   public static void g1( Inflatable x ) {
      x.inflate();
   }
   public static void g2( Kickable y ) {
      y.kick();
   }
   public static void g3( SportsBall z ) {
      z.manufacture();
   }
   public static void main( String[] args ) {
      SoccerBall ball = new SoccerBall();
```

```
        ball.inflate();
        ball.kick();
        ball.manufacture();

        g1( ball );
        g2( ball );
        g3( ball );
    }
}
```

The output is

```
Inflating a soccer ball.
Kicking a soccer ball.
Making a sports ball.
Inflating a soccer ball.
Kicking a soccer ball.
Making a sports ball.
```

The class `SoccerBall` acquires the method `inflate` from `Inflatable`, `kick` from `Kickable`, and `manufacture` from `SportsBall`. `SoccerBall` must provide implementations for `inflate` and `kick`, but can simply inherit `manufacture`.

`SoccerBall` also defines methods `g1`, `g2`, and `g3`. These functions give you a sneak preview of dynamic binding in the Java programming language. The **main** method declares the object `ball` to be an instance of the class `SoccerBall`. Because `SoccerBall` extends `SportsBall`, `ball` is also an object reference for the class `SportsBall`, and can be passed into the argument `z` of `g3`. Similarly, `ball` is an `Inflatable` object reference and also a `Kickable` object reference, because `SoccerBall` implements both interfaces. The same mechanism of dynamic binding that lets you pass a `SoccerBall` object to a `SportsBall` argument of `g3` lets you pass a `SoccerBall` object to the `Inflatable` argument `x` of `g1` and to the `Kickable` argument `y` of `g2`. This mechanism is called **polymorphism**.

## APPLYING ACCESS SPECIFIERS TO MEMBERS

The full implications of access specifiers become clear only in terms of inheritance. Every member of every Java class, as well as the class itself, has an access specifier. For simplicity, most members of classes declared so far in this book have been public.

The Java programming language uses three access specifier keywords: **private**, **protected**, and **public**. The fourth access type, package, is a default that you cannot specify explicitly.

Table 5-1 describes the access methods of the Java programming language. Summary statements follow in order to reiterate the meanings of each access type in more general terms. The more restrictive accesses are in columns on the right side of the table and less restrictive accesses are in columns on the left.

| Situation | Public | Protected | Default or package | Private |
|---|---|---|---|---|
| Accessible to a non-subclass from the same package? | yes | yes | yes | no |
| Accessible to a subclass from the same package? | yes | yes | yes | no |
| Accessible to a non-subclass from a different package? | yes | no | no | no |
| Accessible to a subclass from a different package? | yes | no (fields) yes (methods) | no | no |
| Inherited by a subclass in the same package? | yes | yes | yes | no |
| Inherited by a subclass in a different package? | yes | yes | no | no |

**Table 5-1** Java access specifiers

Access specifiers establish whether members of a class can be inherited by subclasses or accessed by other classes. The access can depend upon whether the classes are in the same package or related by inheritance.

> **public** grants unlimited access to all classes.

> **protected** gives unlimited access to classes in the same package. It also allows all subclasses to access methods, regardless of whether the subclasses are in the same package. A subclass from a different package can inherit fields but not access them directly. A class that is in a different package and is not a subclass has no access to **protected** members.

> No keyword for default access exists. This access is called **package** access, and applies when the access specifier is omitted. Package access grants unlimited access to classes in the same package, but no access to classes outside the package.

> **private** allows no access to the member from outside the class.

## An Example of Cross-Package Protected Access

The following program demonstrates how protected access works for a subclass in a different package. The classes `Location2D` and `Location3D` are in `examples.inheritance` and `examples.errors`, respectively.

Here is the definition of the class `Location2D`. It contains protected fields
`x` and `y`.

```
package examples.inheritance;
/** An example point in 2D space
  */
public class Location2D {
    protected int x = 0, y = 0;
    public Location2D( int initX, int initY ) {
        x = initX;
        y = initY;
    }
    public Location2D() {
        this( 0, 0 );
    }
}
```

The class `Location2D` also uses the **this** method in the constructor with no
arguments, to initialize `x` and `y` to zero by default.

Here is the definition of class `Location3D`. This class extends `Location2D`.
The class `Location3D` contains a deliberate error.

```
package examples.errors;
import examples.inheritance.Location2D;
/** A class intended to create an error
  */
public class Location3D extends Location2D {
    protected int z;
    public Location3D( int initX, int initY,
                       int initZ ) {
        x = initX;
        y = initY;
        z = initZ;
    }
    public static void show2D( Location2D p2 ) {
        // The line below results in a compiler error
        // because the data members are not accessible
        System.out.println( "( " + p2.x + ", " + p2.y
                          + " )" );
    }
    public static void show3D( Location3D p3 ) {
        System.out.println( "( " + p3.x + ", " + p3.y
                          + ", " + p3.z + " )" );
    }
    static public void main( String[] args ) {
        Location3D a = new Location3D( 1, 2, 3 );
        Location3D.show3D( a );
    }
}
```

This file begins by importing class `examples.inheritance.Location2D` so that the file can refer to the class simply as `Location2D`. The constructor and the method `Show3D` use `x` and `y` correctly. A class can use public and protected members it inherits from the superclass just like members it defines for itself. The error is that method `Print2D` uses `x` and `y` as members of `Location2D`. In other words, the class `Location3D` is trying to access protected fields of its superclass through an object of the superclass instead of through one of its own objects. Because that superclass is in another package, the compiler flags an error.

# THE OBJECT REFERENCE SUPER

Can instance methods call instance methods from other classes in the same hierarchy? The only way to call instance methods is with an object reference, and dynamic binding ensures that the method called for an object is the one implemented or inherited by the class that the object instantiates.

Sometimes it is useful to call the method of the superclass, bypassing any overriding method in the subclass. Therefore, the Java programming language provides an object reference **super** that refers to the superclass for the current object.

## Syntax

**super**.*method_name*( *argument_list* )

## Dissection

➤ Any method of a subclass can use **super** to call a method of the superclass, unless prohibited by the access specified for the method.

➤ You can use **super** as an object reference to chain upward only one level in the class hierarchy. An expression such as the following is not valid:
super.super.*method_name*( *argument_list* )

## Code Example

```
public String toString() {
    return( super.toString() + "Passengers: " + passengers );
}
```

## Code Dissection

Here, **toString** in a subclass calls the very method that it overrides. The return type of **toString** in the superclass is also **String**, so the value returned by this method is the concatenation of strings.

What if the superclass does not override the called method, but inherits the implementation of its superclass? The expression uses the implementation of the method that the superclass uses, and searches the inheritance hierarchy if necessary to find it. If the superclass does not implement or inherit the method, the compiler rejects the method call, even if the calling subclass does implement the method. In the case of the method **toString**, an implementation of it is always found even if it is the default inherited from **Object**. Calling **super.toString()** in an instance method is never an error.

## CONSTRUCTORS AND INHERITANCE

The superclass object is created before the subclass object at every level in the class hierarchy. Here is an example based on three related classes: Bottom , Middle, and Top.

```
package examples.inheritance;
/** A class used to demonstrate inheritance
  * concepts
  */
public class Bottom extends Middle {
   public Bottom() {
      System.out.println( "Constructing a Bottom "
                            + "class object" );
   }
   /** Test method for the class
     * @param args not used
     */
   public static void main( String[] args ) {
      Bottom x = new Bottom();
   }
}
/** Example top class in a hierarchy
  */
class Top {
   public Top() {
      System.out.println( "Constructing a Top "
                            + "class object" );
   }
}
/** Example middle class in a hierarchy
  */
class Middle extends Top {
   public Middle() {
      System.out.println( "Constructing a Middle "
                            + "class object" );
   }
}
```

The output is

```
Constructing a Top class object
Constructing a Middle class object
Constructing a Bottom class object
```

The `Bottom` class extends `Middle`, which in turn extends `Top`. When the **main** method of `Bottom` creates a `Bottom` object, the messages printed by the constructors confirm the order in which the constructors are called.

By default, the JVM calls the constructor of the superclass and passes no arguments. Therefore, the superclass should have a constructor that takes no arguments. Also, the superclass is constructed automatically before the subclass. What if the superclass requires some initialization? The Java programming language addresses the question of initializing the superclass with a special method called **super**. It works for superclass constructors much like the method **this** works for constructors of the same class.

---

*Syntax*

**super(** *arguments_of_superclass_constructor* **);**

---

*Dissection*

➤ A subclass constructor can explicitly invoke a superclass constructor with the **super** method. You must insert the call to **super** only when you want to pass arguments to the constructor of the superclass.

➤ If you do not explicitly call **super**, the Java compiler calls it for you, with no arguments. This is the mechanism by which superclasses are automatically built first. An error results if the superclass does not have a constructor without parameters.

➤ The **super** method can appear only in constructors and must be the first line in the constructor.

➤ The one exception to the rule that execution of a constructor starts with a call to **super** is when the first statement in your constructor is a call to **this**. The default **super** defers to **this**. You are not allowed to call both **this** and **super** from one constructor. But you can chain your constructors together through calls to **this**, until one of the constructors explicitly or implicitly calls **super**.

---

*Code Example*

```
package examples.inheritance;
class ReadingMatter {
    boolean available_online;  // false by default
    String title;
```

```
    public ReadingMatter() {
       this.title = "TBA";
    }
    public ReadingMatter( String title ) {
       this.title = title;
    }
}
public class Book extends ReadingMatter {
    String author;
    int numPages;
    public Book( String title, String author,
                 int numPages ) {
       super( title );
       this.numPages = numPages;
       this.author = author;
    }
}
```

---

*Code Dissection*

A `Book` object has four fields: `available_online`, `title`, `author`, and
`numPages`, the first two of which are inherited from `ReadingMatter`. The
superclass constructor initializes the field `title` and accepts the default value
for the field `available_online`. The constructor for `Book` must explicitly
call **super** to pass the title of the book on to the superclass constructor before
initializing the fields `author` and `numPages`.

---

## An Example of Constructing Related Objects

Here is a set of three classes that demonstrate constructing related objects:

```
package examples.inheritance;
/** A class used to demonstrate inheritance concepts
  */
public class Vehicle {
    private int wheels, range;
    /** Class constructor
      * @param w number of wheels
      * @param r range in kilometers
      */
    public Vehicle( int w, int r ) {
       wheels = w;
       range = r;
    }
    /** Represent the object as a string
      * @return The object as a String
      */
```

```
    public String toString() {
       return ( "Wheels: " + wheels
                  + " Range: " + range );
    }
}
```

The class `Vehicle` has one constructor with two arguments. Those arguments initialize the fields `wheels` and `range`. The class also provides an implementation of the method **toString**.

```
package examples.inheritance;
/** A class used to demonstrate inheritance concepts
   */
public class Car extends Vehicle {
   private static final int NUMBER_OF_WHEELS = 4;
   private int passengers;
   /** Class constructor
      * @param p number of passengers
      * @param r range in kilometers
      */
   public Car( int p, int r ) {
      super( NUMBER_OF_WHEELS, r );
      passengers = p;
   }
   /** Represent the object as a string
      * @return The object as a String
      */
   public String toString() {
      return( super.toString() + " Passengers: "
               + passengers );
   }
}
```

The class `Car` is a subclass of `Vehicle`. Because `Car` extends `Vehicle` and the only constructor of `Vehicle` takes two arguments, `Car` must call **super**. The `Car` class adds a third field, **passengers**, which the constructor initializes after it calls **super**. Assume that all cars have four wheels, so that a constant fills the parameter of the superclass constructor. Notice that the **toString** method of the `Car` class calls the **super.toString** method to build the line to output.

The third class is a test class for `Vehicle` and `Car`:

```
package examples.inheritance;
/** A class used to demonstrate inheritance concepts
   */
public class VehicleTest {
   /** Test method for the class
      * @param args Not used
      */
   public static void main( String[] args )
```

```
   {
      Car c = new Car( 5, 500 );
      System.out.println( "Car: " + c );
   }
}
```

The output is

`Car: Wheels: 4 Range: 500 Passengers: 5`

These classes demonstrate the uses of the keyword **super**:

➤ The constructor of the class `Car` calls the constructor of the superclass `Vehicle` by using the method **super**.

➤ Both `Vehicle` and `Car` override **toString**. The **toString** method of `Car` uses the object reference **super** to call the **toString** method of `Vehicle`.

# FINALIZER METHODS AND INHERITANCE

An inconsistency exists between object construction and destruction. A constructor for a superclass always runs before the constructor of the subclass. The pattern repeats as often as required to make sure that an object is built in the proper order. Moreover, the Java platform calls the **super** constructor implicitly if a call is not explicitly coded.

Finalizer methods of subclasses do not call the finalizers of their superclasses automatically. This may seem to be an omission, but in fact, the finalizer of a subclass overrides, and therefore replaces, the finalizer of its superclass. Only one finalizer is called implicitly for an object. Explicitly calling the finalizer method for a superclass is never an error, because all objects can inherit a default **finalize** from **Object**. You may define many classes without a finalizer, but all classes have at least the finalizer method inherited from the **Object** class.

If you want to chain together the finalizer methods of your subclasses and superclasses, you must do it manually. Fortunately, the Java programming language gives you a simple construct for calling the finalizer of the superclass: Simply add the following statement to the end of your finalizer method.

*Syntax*

**super.finalize();**

*Dissection*

➤ This statement should be the last statement in your finalizer method so that the superclass is available throughout the execution of the subclass finalizer.

➤ The only method that should explicitly call a finalizer is the finalizer of a direct subclass.

➤ Finalizers can take no arguments and have return type **void**.

➤ You should specify protected access when you define a finalizer method for a class. Include the clause **throws Throwable** in case the method, or a method invoked by the method, can throw an exception.

---

*Code Example*

```
protected void finalize() throws Throwable {
   // perform cleanup
   super.finalize();
}
```

---

**Mini Quiz 5-4**

Why is `protected` the most appropriate access specifier for a finalizer method?

When does the first finalizer in the chain of subclass and superclass finalizers run? Can you ensure that it runs?

---

Here are two classes that demonstrate chaining finalizer methods. They are stored in the same file.

```
package examples.inheritance;
/** A class used to demonstrate how inheritance
  * influences finalization
  */
public class FinalizerClass extends FinalizerSuper {
   /** Class default constructor method
     */
   public FinalizerClass() {
      System.out.println( "Constructing the "
                              + "subclass" );
   }
   /** Class finalizer method
     * @exception Throwable any exception at all
     */
   protected void finalize () throws Throwable {
      System.out.println( "Finalizing the "
                              + "subclass" );
      super.finalize();
   }
   /** Test method for the class
     * @param args Not used
     */
   public static void main( String[] args ) {
      FinalizerClass fc = new FinalizerClass();
   }
}
```

```
class FinalizerSuper {
   /** Class default constructor method */
   public FinalizerSuper() {
      System.out.println( "Constructing the "
                             + "superclass" );
   }
   /** Class finalizer method
     * @exception Throwable Any exception at all
     */
   protected void finalize() throws Throwable {
      System.out.println( "Finalizing the "
                             + "superclass" );
      super.finalize();    // calls Object.finalize()
   }
}
```

The output includes the first two and possibly all of the following lines:

```
Constructing the superclass
Constructing the subclass
Finalizing the subclass
Finalizing the superclass
```

The public class `FinalizerClass` extends the class `FinalizerSuper`. Both classes have finalizer methods that end with the statement **super.finalize();**. In the class `FinalizerSuper`, the statement runs the finalizer of the **Object** class, which does nothing.

## OVERRIDING METHODS

When you create a subclass, that class inherits all the methods of the superclass by default. The subclass can redefine the inherited methods, as well as define new methods. In this way, subclasses can augment and customize the behavior inherited from their superclasses. The process of redefining methods that a subclass would otherwise inherit is called **overriding** methods.

All classes directly or indirectly extend **Object**, and therefore inherit a common set of methods by default. It is common practice to override methods in the following situations:

➤ Override **toString** to provide a string representation of instances suitable for printing.

➤ If objects may be compared for equality, override **equals**.

➤ When you override **equals**, you should also override **hashCode**. The JVM uses hash tables to access objects, and the value returned by **hashCode** locates the entry for an object in a table. If two or more objects are equal, in the sense that the **equals** method returns **true**, they should have the same hash code. Hash tables are discussed in Chapter 10.

➤ If any of the fields are object references, override **clone** so that the instances can be copied properly. Cloning is discussed in Chapter 7.

When you call an overridden method, the version of the method that is used is determined by the class of the object rather than by the type of the object reference in the calling statement. The following program demonstrates this:

```
package examples.inheritance;
class SuperOverload {
    public String toString() {
        return "superclass";
    }
}
class SubOverload extends SuperOverload {
    public String toString() {
        return "subclass";
    }
}
public class TestOverload {
    public static void main( String[] args ) {
        SuperOverload a = new SuperOverload();
        SubOverload b = new SubOverload();
        // SubOverload.toString
        System.out.println( a.toString() );
        // SuperOverload.toString
        System.out.println( b.toString() );
        // a is a SuperOverload ref to SubOverload object
        a = b;
        // SubOverload.toString
        System.out.println( a.toString() );
    }
}
```

The output is

```
superclass
subclass
subclass
```

The overloading of methods must conform to the following rules:

➤ The signature and the return type of the method must be identical in the superclass and the subclass. The signature includes the name of the method, the number of arguments, and the type of each argument. For example, the compiler rejects the following files because the method **f** is overloaded with different return types:

```
package examples.errors;
/** A class used to demonstrate how overloaded methods
must have the exact same return type
*/
public class MisMatch extends SuperClass {
    public MisMatch f() {
        return this;
    }
}
class SuperClass {
    public SuperClass f() {
        return this;
    }
}
```

**5**

The output from the **javac** command is

```
examples\errors\MisMatch.java:7:
The method examples.errors.MisMatch f( ) declared in
class examples.errors.MisMatch cannot override the
method of the same signature declared in class
examples.errors.SuperClass. They must have the same
return type.
    Public MisMatch f() {
                     ^

1 error
```

➤ A throws clause lists the types of exceptions that can occur during execution of the method, or the methods that the method calls. You cannot add types to the list of exceptions in the overridden method, but you can remove types and make the throws clause more restrictive.

➤ The access specifier of the overriding method must be the same as, or less restrictive than, the access specifier in the superclass. You may, for example, inherit a protected method and override it with a public method. In a subclass, you can make overriding methods more accessible, but never less accessible, than the methods in the superclass.

➤ You can override a method with an abstract method, even if the overridden method is not abstract. Do this if you do not want to implement the method, but want to force all classes that extend your class to implement the method.

➤ You can also override an abstract method with a method that is not abstract.

These rules have implications that you should consider when you define a class that may be extended. When your class becomes a superclass, it imposes limitations on how its methods may be overridden:

➤ You cannot do much to get around the fact that return types in overriding methods and overridden methods must match. In some cases, returning the type **Object** is appropriate and can accommodate all the reference types.

➤ Consider that the overriding methods cannot throw exceptions that you do not allow in your throws clause. The easiest way to let overriding methods throw any exceptions is to specify **throws Throwable**, which allows all exceptions.

➤ If you declare a method to be public, you force all overriding methods also to be public.

What happens when the signatures in the superclass and subclass do not match? Of course, if the names are different, the methods are different. If the names are the same but the argument lists differ, a different mechanism comes into play: overloading. In the Java programming language, methods in a subclass can both overload and override a method from the superclass. For example, suppose that a superclass defines the following method:

```
void myWay( int ival, float fval ) { /* ... */ }
```

The method definitions in the subclass shown in Table 5-2 have different effects.

| Method | Effect |
|---|---|
| `void myWay( int ival, float fval ) {`<br>`    // . . .`<br>`}` | overriding |
| `void myWay( long ival, double fval ) {`<br>`    // . . .`<br>`}` | overloading |
| `void myWay( String[] sval ) {`<br>`    // . . .`<br>`}` | overloading |
| `private void myWay( int ival, float fval ) {`<br>`    // . . .`<br>`}` | error:<br>more restrictive access |
| `int myWay( int ival, float fval ) {`<br>`    // . . .`<br>`}` | error:<br>return type mismatch |

**Table 5-2** Methods in a subclass

## An Example of Overriding and Overloading a Method

The following program shows how a subclass can overload and override a superclass method:

```
package examples.inheritance;
/** A class used to demonstrate the interaction
  * among methods that are both overridden and
  * overloaded
  */
public class OverloadOverride {
    /** Test method for the class
      * @param args not used
```

```
                */
          public static void main( String[] args ) {
             SubClass1 x = new SubClass1();
             x.chewGum( 2.4 );   //overriding subclass method
             x.walk( 100.345 );  //overloaded superclass method
             x.walk( 89 );       //overloaded subclass method
          }
      }
      /** An example superclass */
      class SuperClass1 {
          public void chewGum( double x ) {
             System.out.println( "SuperClass1.chewGum( double )"
                                 + " called" );
          }
          public void walk( double x ) {
             System.out.println( "SuperClass1.walk( double )"
                                 + " called" );
          }
      }
      /** An example subclass */
      class SubClass1 extends SuperClass1 {
          public void chewGum( double x ) {
             // override superclass function chewGum
             System.out.println( "SubClass1.chewGum( double )"
                                 + " called" );
          }
          public void walk( int x ) {
             // overload superclass function walk
             System.out.println( "SubClass1.walk( int )"
                                 + " called" );
          }
      }
```

The output is

```
SubClass1.chewGum( double ) called
SuperClass1.walk( double ) called
SubClass1.walk( int ) called
```

Class SubClass1 extends class SuperClass1. The superclass has two methods, chewGum and walk. This subclass overrides chewGum and overloads walk. The class OverloadOverride calls three different methods—the chewGum of SubClass1, the walk of SuperClass1, and the walk of SubClass1— for an object of class SubClass1.

# DYNAMIC BINDING

Dynamic binding is a manifestation of polymorphism in the Java programming language. Unfortunately, the word polymorphism means different things to different people and is often misunderstood. Very loosely, polymorphism allows the same code to have different effects at run time, depending on the context in which the code is used. Sometimes polymorphism is defined broadly to include features supported by programming languages other than Java. Most experts agree that dynamic binding is the only form of polymorphism supported by the JVM.

Dynamic binding resolves what method to call at run time when the method has been implemented by more than one class in an inheritance hierarchy. The JVM looks at the type of the object for which the call is made, not at the type of the object reference in the calling statement. The JVM then binds the call to the method implemented or inherited by the type of the object. For example, if `ba` is a variable of type `BankAccount`, the statement `ba.withdraw( 100.00 );` may result in a call to method `SavingsAccount.withdraw` or `CheckingAccount.withdraw`, depending on whether `ba` is referring to a savings or checking account object at the time the call is made. As a result, you can write a very general method that operates on any kind of bank account and trust JVM to determine at run time which version of the method to call.

In general, dynamic binding gives you tremendous flexibility in your programs. You can exploit *is a* relationships by writing code for the superclass that will work for all subclasses. You do not have to do any special coding to take advantage of dynamic binding, because it is automatic. However, you can exert some control over whether dynamic binding occurs with the keywords **abstract** and **final**.

---

### Syntax

[ *access_specifier* ] **abstract** *return_type method*_name( *argument_list* )
         [throws *exception_list*];

---

### Dissection

➤ Use the keyword **abstract** to indicate that the method has no implementation in the current class.

➤ An abstract method has no body. Therefore, there is no block of code or { } in the declaration.

---

### Code Example

```
public abstract double profit( Revenue r, Costs c );
```

---

### Code Dissection

The method **profit** is abstract. The declaration specifies that it has two arguments—an object reference to a **Revenue** object, and an object reference to a **Costs** object—and that it returns a value of type **double**. But this declaration gives no indication of how the return value is calculated.

---

When you declare a method to be abstract, you are forcing all subclasses to override the method with a full implementation. Any class that contains an abstract method must also be declared abstract. Including the keyword **abstract** in the declarations of both the class and the method is repetitious, because a class with at least one abstract method is itself abstract. Nevertheless, the repetition is required.

*Syntax*

[ *access_specifier* ] **final** *return_type method_name* ( *argument_list* )
          [throws *exception_list*]

*Dissection*

➤ Use the keyword **final** to prevent the method from being overridden in subclasses.

*Code Example*

```
public final String greeting( String name ) {
    return ( "Hello " + name + "!" );
}
```

*Code Dissection*

The method `greeting` cannot be overridden by a subclass of the class in which this method is defined.

You can also apply the qualifier **final** to a class definition. The effect of **final** is to prohibit the overriding of the method or the extending of the class. The effect is to turn off dynamic binding for methods. Two reasons exist for doing this:

➤ *Security.* When a class is extended, the subclass has an opportunity to change or add behavior. To prevent a subclass from overriding your implementation with something potentially malevolent, declare your class or method final.

➤ *Performance.* The lookup and dispatch algorithm of dynamic binding imposes some overhead at run time. If you turn off dynamic binding, the method call can be executed a little quicker, and you may have additional opportunities for code optimization.

When should you use an interface rather than an abstract superclass? One reason is to let classes that have other superclasses implement the interface. But what if other superclasses are not a factor? As a rule of thumb, abstract classes are more appropriate when some of the behaviors can be implemented in the superclass because they are common to all subclasses. If none of the behaviors can be specified in a way that is useful to all the subclasses, use an interface.

> **Mini Quiz 5-5**
>
> Can you include a **main** method to test an abstract class?

When you use the object reference **super** to call a method in a superclass, you are altering how the JVM resolves method calls through dynamic binding. You are explicitly specifying which class in the hierarchy to search first for the method. This is the only exception to the rule that the type of the object alone determines what version of an overridden method is called.

The following program demonstrates the effect of using **super** to call an overridden method:

```
package examples.inheritance;
/** A class used to demonstrate how dynamic
  * binding can be altered by using the
  * <b>super</b> reference.
  */
public class AlteredBinding {
   /** Test method for the class
     * @param args not used
     */
   public static void main( String[] args ) {
      D x = new D();
      x.g1();
      x.g2();
   }
}
/** An example superclass */
class B {
   public void f( String caller ) {
      System.out.println( "B.f() called by "
                              + caller );
   }
}
/** An example subclass */
class D extends B {
   public void f( String caller ) {
      System.out.println( "D.f() called by "
                              + caller );
   }
   public void g1() {
      f( "subclass" );         // this will call D.f( )
   }
   public void g2() {
      super.f( "subclass" ); // cannot use B.f() here
   }
}
```

The output is

```
D.f() called by subclass
B.f() called by subclass
```

This example program contains a class B, a class D that extends B, and a class AlteredBinding that creates and exercises a D object. The method g2 in D calls the method f from the superclass. The call takes the form super.f() because the syntax B.f() is an error in this context.

## Dynamic Binding and Superclass Constructors

Dynamic binding always calls the implementation of a method in the class that matches the type of the object for which the method is called. The only exception is that if a subclass does not implement the method, the version inherited from its superclass is used. The Java programming language applies this rule even during the construction of the superclass, even before the constructor for the subclass has been run!

A superclass constructor can call a method of a subclass while it is building the superclass portion of a subclass object, if the subclass overrides a super-class method. Therefore, you must be careful when you call methods from constructors. For example, consider the ReadingMaterial and Book classes from earlier in this chapter. The ReadingMaterial constructor may call a Book method while it is setting up the fields that a Book inherits from ReadingMaterial. If that method depends on subclass fields that have not yet been initialized, it uses the default initial value of zero, **false**, or **null**, depending on the type of the field. As a result, the method may not work as expected, and the object may not be built properly.

The safest strategy is to declare any methods used by constructors to be final or private. However, this strategy is not always acceptable, because it prevents the methods from ever being overridden. Rewriting the constructor may be a solution. However, the problem remains, because a class that is not final can never know how future subclasses may extend it.

Here is a sample program that demonstrates a superclass constructor calling a subclass method:

```
package examples.inheritance;
/** A class used to demonstrate how dynamic binding
  * works when superclass objects are constructed.
  */
public class Construction {
   /** Test method for the class
     * @param args not used
     */
   public static void main( String[] args ) {
      SuperClass y = new SuperClass();
```

```
            SubClass x = new SubClass();
            x.g();
        }
    }
    /** An example superclass */
    class SuperClass {
        public SuperClass() {
            f();        // which f() will be called?
        }               // SuperClass.f() or SubClass.f()?
        public void f() {
            System.out.println( "SuperClass.f() called" );
        }
        public void g() {
            f();        // which f() will be called?
        }               // SuperClass.f() or SubClass.f()?
    }
    /** An example subclass */
    class SubClass extends SuperClass {
        public void f() {
            System.out.println( "SubClass.f() called" );
        }
    }
```

The output is

```
SuperClass.f() called
SubClass.f() called
SubClass.f() called
```

Class `SubClass` extends class `SuperClass`. Both `SubClass` and
`SuperClass` implement method `f`. The constructor of `SuperClass` calls `f`.
When the `SuperClass` object `y` is created, the `SuperClass` constructor
calls `SuperClass.f`. When the `SubClass` object `x` is created, the
`SuperClass` constructor calls `SubClass.f`.

# SUMMARY

Support for inheritance is essential in any object–oriented language.

A class that is based on an existing class is a **subclass**, and the existing class is the
**superclass**. Subclassing is a technique for defining classes that have additional or
more specialized behavior and attributes compared to those of the more general
superclass. The subclass extends the superclass with the keyword **extends**, as in the
following syntax:

[*access*] [*qualifiers*] **class** *subclass_name* **extends** *superclass_name* { /*...*/ }

Interfaces are similar to classes except that they are declared with the
keyword **interface**. All methods in an interface are implicitly abstract and public. The only fields allowed in interfaces are constants. Interfaces can extend

other interfaces. Use interfaces to design but not to implement behavior for future classes.

Classes do not extend interfaces, but you can implement interfaces by using the following syntax:

[*access*] [*qualifiers*] **class** *class_name* **implements** *interface_name* { /* ... */ }

A class that implements an interface must provide implementations for all the methods in the interface. Otherwise, it is an abstract class. Classes can implement one or more interfaces, and can also extend a superclass.

A class can implement any number of interfaces as well as extend one class.

The access specifiers for members are **public**, **private**, and **protected**. The default access, package, does not have a keyword and applies if you omit the access specifier from a member declaration. The specifier **private** restricts access to within the class. The default gives access to all classes in the same package. Protected access is less restrictive than the default in that it lets subclasses access methods and inherit members regardless of whether the subclasses are in the same package. Public access is wholly unrestricted.

Subclasses can overload methods from their superclass, override them, or inherit them. If the argument lists are different, the method is overloaded. If the signatures are the same, the method is overridden and must comply with a number of restrictions, including the requirement that the return types must match. Methods that are not implemented in the subclass are inherited. Overriding and inheriting methods comprise a very powerful technique that lets subclasses customize and augment behaviors established by the superclass.

You cannot extend a class declared with **final** or override a method declared with **final**.

A class declared with **abstract** or that contains an abstract method cannot be instantiated. A method declared with **abstract** has no implementation, and must be overridden by a subclass. Declare a class or method to be abstract to force subclasses to implement methods.

Superclass objects are always created before subclass objects. To pass arguments to a superclass constructor, you must explicitly call the superclass constructor with the **super** method, using the following syntax:

**super(** *arguments_of_superclass_constructor* **);**

By using the keyword **super**, you can ensure that a subclass can call any superclass implementation of a method. Because the Java programming language does not automatically chain superclass and subclass finalizers, you should do so explicitly, using **super.finalize()**.

The Java programming language dynamically binds all nonprivate instance methods by default. Dynamic binding applies even while constructing the superclass portion of subclass objects. The keyword **final** turns off dynamic binding for the class or method to which it is applied.

# QUESTIONS

1. List all access specifiers that are less restrictive than **protected**.

2. Examine the following code from a single source file:

```java
interface Calculator {
   public void calculate();
}
interface Microwave {
   public void cook();
}
public class Quiz5_2 implements Calculator,
                                Microwave {
   public void calculate() {
      System.out.println( "calculating" );
   }
   public void cook() {
      System.out.println( "cooking" );
   }
   public static void main( String[] args ) {
      Quiz5_2 x = new Quiz5_2();
      x.calculate();
      x.cook();
   }
}
```

Which of the following statements are true when the code is compiled and run? Select all that apply.

a. The compiler rejects the attempt to implement two interfaces at once.

b. The compiler rejects the definition of the class `Quiz5_2` because it implements two interfaces but does not extend anything.

c. Compilation is successful and the output is
```
calculating
cooking
```

d. The compiler indicates an error because the interfaces and the class are not in separate source files.

e. It is optional for the class `Quiz5_2` to implement the methods `calculate` and `cook`.

3. Examine the following code taken from a single source file:

```java
class Vehicle {
    protected void goSomewhere() {
        System.out.println( "travelling..." );
    }
}
public class Bicycle extends Vehicle {
    public void goSomewhere() {
        System.out.println( "pedalling..." );
    }
    public static void main( String[] args ) {
        Bicycle x = new Bicycle();
        x.goSomewhere();
    }
}
```

**5**

Which of the following statements are true when the code is compiled and run? Select all that apply.

a. The compiler rejects the definition of the class **Bicycle** because the keyword **extends** is not appropriate for a superclass and should be replaced by the keyword **implements**.

b. The compiler rejects the definition of **Bicycle.goSomewhere** because its access specifier does not match the access specifier of **Vehicle.goSomewhere**.

c. Compilation is successful and the output is **travelling**...

d. Compilation is successful and the output is **pedalling**...

e. It is optional for the class **Bicycle** to implement the method **goSomewhere**.

4. Examine the following code taken from a single source file:

```java
abstract class Barbeque {
    public abstract void ignite();
    public void cook() {
        System.out.println( "put food on the "
                          +"grill and wait" );
    }
}
class GasBarbeque extends Barbeque {
    public void ignite() {
        System.out.println( "turn on gas and "
                          +"light match" );
    }
}
class CharcoalBarbeque extends Barbeque {
    public void ignite() {
        System.out.println( "pour on lighter "
                          +"fluid and light match" );
    }
}
```

```
public class Cookout {
    public static void makeDinner( Barbeque b ) {
        b.ignite();
        b.cook();
    }
    public static void main( String[] args ) {
        GasBarbeque gb = new GasBarbeque();
        CharcoalBarbeque cb = new CharcoalBarbeque();
        makeDinner( gb );
        makeDinner( cb );
    }
}
```

Which of the following statements are true when the code is compiled and run? Select all that apply.

a. The compiler rejects the definition of `Cookout.makeDinner` because it is not possible to instantiate the argument **b** of the abstract class `Barbeque`.

b. The compiler rejects the definition of the classes `GasBarbeque` and `CharcoalBarbeque` because they do not implement the method `Barbeque.cook`.

c. Compilation is successful and the output is

```
turn on gas and light match
put food on the grill and wait
pour on lighter fluid and light match
put food on the grill and wait
```

d. The compiler rejects the statements `makeDinner( gb );` and `makeDinner( cb );` because the type of **gb** or **cb** does not match the input type of `Barbeque`.

5. Which of the following are valid class definitions? Select all that apply.

a. `final class A { }`

b. `class B { }`

c. `public final class C { }`

d. `public abstract class D { }`

e. `abstract final class E { }`

6. Examine the following code taken from a single source file:

```
class A {
    protected Integer doSomething() {
        return new Integer( 2 );
    }
}
public class B extends A { }
```

Which of the following methods are valid for class B? Select all that apply.

a.
```
protected Integer doSomething(){
    return new Integer( 3 );
}
```

b.
```
public Integer doSomething() {
    return new Integer( 3 );
}
```

c.
```
Integer doSomething() {
    return new Integer( 3 );
}
```

d.
```
protected Object doSomething() {
    return new Integer( 3 );
}
```

e.
```
protected Number doSomething() {
    return new Integer( 3 );
}
```

7. Examine the following code taken from a single source file:

```
class A {
    protected double d = 3.14;
    public static void f() {}
    public void g() {}
}
class B {
    public void m() {}
}
class C extends A {
    protected static void s() {}
    void t() {}
}
```

Which of the following methods have direct access to the field A.d? Select all that apply.

a. A.f()

b. A.g()

c. B.m()

d. C.s()

e. C.t()

8. List the Java keyword or keywords that are used to indicate an is *a* relationship between two classes.

9. Examine the following code taken from a single source file:

```
class X {
   public X() {
      System.out.println( "Constructing X" );
      f();
   }
   protected void f() {
      System.out.println( "X.f()" );
   }
   protected void g() {
      System.out.println( "X.g()" );
   }
}
public class Y extends X {
   public Y() {
      System.out.println( "Constructing Y" );
      f();
   }
   protected void f() {
      System.out.println( "Y.f()" );
   }
   public static void main( String[] args ) {
      new Y();
   }
}
```

Which of the following lines appear in the output when the code is compiled and run? Select all that apply.

a. `Constructing Y`

b. `X.f()`

c. `Constructing X`

d. `Y.f()`

e. `X.g()`

10. Which of the following statements correctly declare an abstract method `f`? Select all that apply.

a. `void abstract f();`

b. `private abstract void f();`

c. `protected abstract void f();`

d. `public abstract void f() {};`

e. `public void f() = 0;`

11. Examine the following class definitions for one file:

```
class B {
   protected long l;
   B( long l ) {
      this.l = l;
   }
```

```
      B() {
         l = 99;
      }
}
class C extends B {
   public float f;
   public String s = "hello";
   C ( String s, float f ) {
      this.s += " " +  s;
      this.f = f;
   }
   C ( String s ) {
      // -x-
      l = Math.abs( l );
   }
}
```

5

Which of the following statements are allowed at the line marked **-x-**?
Select all that apply.

a. `super( 27L );`

b. `f = 2.75F;`

c. `super( 3L ); this ( s, 0.5F );`

d. `B( 0L );`

e. `this( s, 10 );`

12. Examine the following class definitions:

```
class B {
   int f( int i ) {
      return i + i;
   }
   int f( int i, int j ) {
      return i + j;
   }
   int f( char c ) {
      return c;
   }
}
public class C extends B {
   int f( int i, int j ) {
      return super.f( i, j );
   }
   int f( int i ) {
      return -i ;
   }
   double f( double d ) {
      return Math.sqrt( d );
   }
   public static void main( String args[]) {
      C c = new C();
      B b = new B();
```

```
System.out.println( c.f( 5, 10 ) + " " +
                    ( ( B )c ).f( 4 ) + " " +
                    c.f( 9D ) + " " +
                    c.f( 'A' ) );
      }
}
```

Which of the following statements are true when the code is compiled and run? Select all that apply.

a. The compiler rejects the method `C.f` because only a constructor can call another constructor.

b. The compiler rejects the method `B.f` because a **char** cannot be returned as an **int**.

c. Compilation is successful. Because the Unicode representation of A is the same as the integral value 65, the output is `15 -4 3.0 65`.

d. Compilation is successful. Because the Unicode representation of A is the same as the integral value 65, the output is `15 8 3 65`.

e. The compiler rejects the call `c.f( 'A' )` as ambiguous between `C.f( int )` and `B.f( char )`.

13. You have acquired some code that you are modifying. The code uses random numbers and calls the method **nextGaussian** with an object of type **java.security.SecureRandom**. Because it is a core class, you can look up **SecureRandom** in the JDK documentation. The method **nextGaussian** is not described there. Where should you look next?

a. At the comments in the code you are modifying.

b. In the javadoc output for the code you are modifying.

c. In the superclass of the class in which the call to **nextGaussian** occurs, and then in its superclass, and so on, until you reach the class **Object**.

d. In the class **java.util.Random**, which the JDK says is the superclass of **java.security.SecureRandom**.

e. In any subclasses of **java.security.SecureRandom** defined in the JDK or in the code you are modifying.

# EXERCISES

## Debugging

1. Correct the error(s) in the following program:

```
package questions.c5;
class DebugShape {
    public abstract double getPerimeter() {};
    public abstract double getArea() {};
```

```
   }
   public class DebugSquare extends DebugShape {
      private double length;
      public DebugSquare( double l ) {
         length = l;
      }
      public abstract double getPerimeter() {
         return 4 * length;
      }
      public abstract double getArea() {
         return length * length;
      }
   }
```

2. Correct the following program so that the `calculate` method in class `Debug5_2` overrides the `calculate` method in the superclass of `Debug5_2`:

```
package questions.c5;
class A {
   double baseValue = 3.14;
   public void setBaseValue( double d ) {
      baseValue = d;
   }
   public double calculate( double x, double y ) {
      return x * y / baseValue;
   }
}
public class Debug5_2 extends A {
   private static final float ALT_BASE = 2.5F;
   float calculate( float x, float y ) {
      return x * y / ALT_BASE;
   }
}
```

3. Correct the errors in the following program:

```
package questions.c5;
class Identifiable {
   private int idNum =  -1;
   public Identifiable( int id ) {
      idNum = id;
   }
   public void setID( int id ) {
      idNum = id;
   }
}
public class StockItem extends Identifiable {
   private double price = 0.00;
   public void setPrice( double p ) {
      price = p;
   }
```

```
        public static void main( String[] args ) {
            StockItem s = new StockItem();
            s.setID( 12343567 );
            s.setPrice( 34.67 );
        }
    }
```

4. Correct the errors in the following program:

```
package questions.c5;
class Tool {
    private String name = "";
    public void setName( String n ) {
        name = n;
    }
    public String getName() {
        return name;
    }
    String toString() {
        return name;
    }
}
public class Hammer extends Tool {
    private int weight;
    public void setWeight( int w ) {
        weight = w;
    }
    public int getWeight() {
        return weight;
    }
    String toString() {
        return Tool.toString() + " "
                + String.valueOf( weight );
    }
    public static void main( String[] args ) {
        Hammer sledge = new Hammer();
        sledge.setName( "sledgehammer" );
        sledge.setWeight( 10 );
        System.out.println( sledge );
    }
}
```

5. Correct the errors in the following program:

```
package questions.c5;
interface RiceCereal {
    protected void snap();
    protected void crackle();
    protected void pop();
}
public class Krispies implements RiceCereal {
    protected void snap() {
        System.out.println( "Snap!" );
```

```
        }
        protected void crackle() {
            System.out.println( "Crackle!" );
        }
        public static void main( String[] args ) {
            Krispies k = new Krispies();
            k.snap();
        }
    }
```

## Complete the Solution

5

1. Extract the file **questions\c5\TabbyCat.java** from the file **question.jar** on the CD-ROM. Add the `Cat` interface definition with the methods `eat`, `sleep`, and `play` so that the class `TabbyCat` will compile successfully.

2. Extract the file **questions\c5\Customer.java** from the file **question.jar** on the CD-ROM. Add a `Customer` class definition that extends the `Person` class and adds a field of the type `Purchase`. Add a **main** method to the Customer class that creates a Customer object.

3. Extract the file **questions\c5\Book.java** from the file **question.jar** on the CD-ROM. Add a `Book` class definition that extends the abstract class `ReadingMaterial`. Since reading material comes in many forms, the content is the generic type **Object**. The `Book` class can use the String class as its content type.

4. Extract the file **questions\c5\Stackable.java** from the file **question.jar** on the CD-ROM. Complete the `Stackable` interface definition by adding methods that should be part of the implementation of any stack. A `Stackable` object can have any reference type but must store and retrieve elements on a last-in-first-out basis.

5. Extract the file **questions\c5\Deal.java** from the file **question.jar** on the CD-ROM. Add a `Hand` class definition that implements the interface `Stackable` from the previous question and that stores a stack of objects. Use the classes `Deal` and `Card` provided in the file Deal.java. The class `Deal` is the public class to test `Hand`, and `Card` is the type of object that `Deal` stores in `Hand` objects.

   The class `Deal` does not deal cards in the usual manner. From an unshuffled deck, it gives one card at a time to a player chosen at random. Dealing stops as soon as one player has a full hand. Then the contents of all hands are printed, listing the cards in the opposite order to that in which each player received them.

## Discovery

1. Create a set of classes to implement the banking model described in the "Classes and Object-Oriented Programming" section of Chapter 4 and the "Inheritance and Object-Oriented Programming" section of this chapter. To recap:

   - A bank has account owners, each of whom may have one or more bank accounts.

   - This bank provides two kinds of bank accounts: savings accounts and checking accounts.

   - All accounts accept deposits, and provide a method to print the current balance in the same way.

   - All accounts allow withdrawals, provided that the balance never falls below zero. If a withdrawal from a checking account is greater than the current balance, the bank attempts to transfer the shortfall from the account owner's savings account. If there are sufficient funds in the savings account to cover the shortfall, the withdrawal proceeds. Otherwise, the bank cancels the withdrawal transaction.

   - At the end of every month, the bank adds interest to the savings accounts. The interest equals 1% of the minimum balance for the account for that month.

   - The bank records every deposit (cancelled or successful), withdrawal, transfer, and interest payment as a transaction.

   - At the end of every month, the bank issues a statement for each bank account. The statement lists the transactions completed during the month.

   Write classes to implement the banking model and a test class to simulate one month of activity.

2. Create a hierarchy of classes for the geometric shapes square, rectangle, circle, right-angled triangle, line, and point. All shapes have an origin, or position. All shapes have a name, such as "line" or "square." All shapes have a method for calculating the area, which is simply to return zero for lines or points. Define an interface with the common methods and fields for shapes. Define classes for at least the six types of shapes mentioned here and any more you can think of. Use inheritance to express relationships such as the fact that a square is a rectangle. Provide a variety of constructors for the different ways of representing shapes. For example, you can construct a square from lower-left and upper-right corners or from origin (lower-left) and length of a side. In the test method, create an array that contains at least two shapes of each type. Then calculate and print the area of each shape in the array.

## CHAPTER SIX

# EXCEPTIONS

---

**In this chapter you will:**

➤ Write code to create exceptions when errors or unexpected conditions arise.

➤ Write code to handle exceptions.

☕ Write code that makes proper use of exceptions and exception handling clauses (**try, catch,** and **finally**) and declares methods and overriding methods that throw exceptions.

➤ Understand the difference between checked and unchecked exceptions and know which kind to use.

➤ Deal with exceptions that are not completely handled when they are first caught.

➤ Use the finally clause to alter the usual order of execution in the code.

---

## INTRODUCTION TO EXCEPTIONS

An **exception** is a representation of an error condition or any situation that is not the expected result of a method. Exceptions can be divided into two categories:

➤ Some exceptional conditions are directly related to the functionality of a method. For example, an exception is raised when you try to open a file in read mode, if no file with the specified name is available. Exception handling can provide a recovery mechanism for these sorts of situations.

➤ You can never predict when some exceptions can occur. Some unpredictable exceptions are the result of logic errors in the code. For example, one of the most common causes is misuse of a **null** object reference. These exceptions often are unrecoverable errors or conditions that only the Java Virtual Machine (JVM) or operating system can detect. By default, these exceptions terminate the program.

Exceptions isolate the code that deals with unusual or error situations from the regular program logic. The act of detecting an abnormal condition and generating an exception is called **throwing** an exception. An object that encapsulates the unexpected condition represents the exception. The act of throwing an exception alters the normal flow of control and starts the search for a **handler,** which is code written specifically to recover from the exception. When the handler takes control, it **catches** the exception. When the handler is done, control passes back to the program, but not in the same place where the exception interrupted the program. The whole process is called **handling** the exception.

Exception handling is a very elegant and object-oriented methodology that is packaged with the Java programming language. You should code all your methods to throw exceptions whenever they cannot complete their operation. If you can detect an error or condition for which the only sensible action is to abandon whatever your method is trying to do, throw an exception that encapsulates the problem.

Any programming language supports exception handling in order to shift the performance penalty of error handling out of the usual path of execution. Code that deals with exceptional conditions is consolidated and removed to a separate error path. As a result, programmers cannot ignore exceptions; the program terminates if exceptions are not handled when they occur.

## ENCAPSULATING EXCEPTIONS IN TRY BLOCKS

To program exception handling, you must use try blocks. A **try block** is a Java programming language construct that encloses one or more Java statements. Exceptions are thrown by **throw statements**. You enable exception handling by placing throw statements inside try blocks. Exception handlers take the form of **catch clauses** that follow the body of the try block. If an exception is thrown, the JVM immediately stops executing the Java code, including all methods started but not completed when the exception is thrown, and looks for a handler in the catch clauses in the enclosing try blocks. If no exception is thrown, the compiler runs the statements in the try block as usual and ignores the catch clauses.

*Syntax*

```
try {
    // statements that are monitored for exceptions
    [ throw exception;          // statements that throw exceptions ]
    // statements that are monitored for exceptions
}
[catch ( exception_class  object_reference ) {
    // blocks that handle exceptions
}]
[finally {
    // statements always executed at the end of the try block
}]
```

*Dissection*

---

➤ The try block includes any catch clauses that follow the block of statements, and an optional **finally clause**.

➤ Usually at least one throw statement exists in a try block. The throw statement may not be visible if it is inside a method that is called by a statement in the try block.

➤ You can have zero, one, or more catch clauses. Each catch clause catches a different kind of exception object, and is never executed unless it catches an exception. The compiler can execute at most one catch clause each time the try block is run.

➤ You do not have to match every type of exception that is thrown in the try block with a catch clause. Include a catch clause for the exceptions you want to handle for this try block.

➤ The finally clause is optional if you have at least one catch clause. If you have no catch clauses, you must provide a finally clause. The compiler always executes the statements inside a finally clause at the end of the try block, regardless of whether an exception is thrown and caught or the entire try block runs without an exception.

---

You can nest try blocks. When you do so, catch and finally clauses are associated with the closest preceding try block.

When the try block is complete and either no exception is thrown or an exception is thrown and caught, the compiler executes the statements following the block in the usual manner. In this way, exception handling interrupts the regular flow of control when an exception occurs, but does not otherwise affect the flow of control.

If an exception is thrown in the try block and not caught by one of the catch clauses, the exception is an **uncaught exception**. The search for a handler continues to the next enclosing try block, if there is one.

## Exception Handling and the Call Stack

What happens if a method that is called inside a try block throws the exception? The Java programming language keeps a record of the methods that are active at any one time, arranged so that the last method called is always the last method in the list, in what is called the **call stack**. When an exception occurs, the JVM unwinds the call stack until a handler for that exception is found. Stack entries for each method are cleared in turn, just as though the methods are returning normally. Therefore, control can jump back several levels of method calls without corrupting the program stack. If the call stack is completely unwound, the program terminates, which is what happens when an exception is thrown but never caught.

The Java platform ensures that an uncaught exception is the most likely reason for terminating your Java program prematurely. The Java interpreter outputs a stack trace before terminating the program because of an uncaught exception. The stack trace lists all the methods in the call stack when the exception occurred, and makes it easy to determine the origin of the error.

## Declaring Uncaught Exceptions

If you throw an exception in a method, you must either catch and handle that exception in the method or list it in the **throws clause** in the method declaration. The throws clause lists the types of exceptions a method is allowed to transfer, uncaught, to the calling method.

---

*Syntax*

[*access_specifiers*] [*qualifiers*] *return_type method_name*( *argument_list*)
[**throws** *exception_list*]
   *block*

---

*Dissection*

➤ A method definition must include a throws clause if any uncaught exceptions can occur while the method is running.

➤ The throws clause need not list exceptions that are thrown and caught inside a method because they have no impact outside the method.

➤ You can omit the throws clause if the method does not throw any uncaught exceptions and does not call any method that throws uncaught exceptions.

---

*Code Example*

```
void myMethod() throws IOException {
    // body of method
}
```

---

*Code Dissection*

The method **myMethod** or a method that it calls can throw an exception of type **IOException**. This method performs input or output but does not catch exceptions of type **IOException**.

---

When you are programming using the Java programming language, you can rely on the throws clause to determine, short of bugs and run-time errors such as out-of-memory conditions, all possible outcomes of a method: it completes successfully or throws one of the listed types of exceptions. Even the **main** method must have a throws clause if exceptions occur and not be caught during the method's execution. In the case of **main**, the throws clause provides a list of reasons that the program may terminate prematurely.

The Java compiler verifies the correctness and completeness of the throws clause for every method. Because the compiler is very demanding when it checks the throws clause, coding the exception list requires attention to detail.

You can also use the throws clause to put some restraints on the behavior of the subclasses of your class, because the throws clause limits the types of uncaught exceptions allowed in overriding methods.

An overriding method cannot list more exception types in the throws clause than the overridden method does. However, it can list fewer exceptions. In other words, the method closest to the base of the inheritance hierarchy limits the types of uncaught exceptions that can be thrown by all methods that will ever override that method.

You can list exception classes in the throws clause even if they are not actually thrown from within the method, to allow an overriding method in a subclass to throw objects of the additional exception classes.

## THROWING EXCEPTIONS

The core classes throw many of the exceptions that occur in a Java program. For example, many of the methods in the classes that support input and output can throw an **IOException**. Much like methods in the core classes, your methods can throw exceptions to respond to requests that they cannot complete.

Use a throw statement to throw an exception. You can place a throw statement directly inside a try block. Alternatively, you can wrap a try block around the call to the method that contains the throw statement. If you see a throw statement in the code of a method but no try block, the usual reason is that the handling of the exception is left to a calling method.

*Syntax*

**throw [new]** *exception*[( *arguments_of_constructor* )]**;**

*Dissection*

➤ The **throw** keyword starts the exception mechanism.

➤ The object reference for an exception object is thrown. The object can instantiate one of the exception classes provided by the Java platform or an exception class of your own.

➤ The most common coding practice is to create an exception object in the throw statement. As always, use the **new** keyword to create the object and include the argument list for the constructor. You can also throw an exception object that already exists.

*Code Example*

```
throw new WrongPasswordException( "Access denied" );
```

*Code Dissection*

A login or user validation method can throw an exception if the user does not enter the correct password. The `WrongPasswordException` class must be defined and accessible to the class that contains this throw statement.

All exceptions are objects. The most important concept in mastering the throwing of exceptions is knowing what types of objects a method should throw. The Java programming language does not let you throw primitive values or arbitrary objects. You can throw only objects that directly or indirectly extend the class **java.lang.Throwable**.

The thrown object carries information about the error condition. Sometimes the type of the object is all that a handler needs. Other handlers can use the fields and methods of the exception object.

A handler can call some very useful methods that are provided by the **Throwable** class.

*Class*

**Throwable**

*Methods*

➤ **String getMessage( )**
Returns a printable message stored in the exception object.

➤ **void printStackTrace( )**
**void printStackTrace( PrintStream** *s* **)**
**void printStackTrace( PrintWriter** *s* **)**
Prints a representation of the call stack at the time the exception object is created. These methods print to the specified stream or, if no stream argument is specified, to the standard stream **System.err**.

## Checked and Unchecked Exceptions

The Java programming language has two types of exceptions, checked and unchecked. Only checked exceptions must be listed in the throws clause, so you usually use only checked exceptions for exception handling. Unchecked exceptions are intended only for severe, unpredictable errors that could happen in any method. Let your code ignore unchecked exceptions, because you gain little by identifying them as potential problems. Examples of unchecked exception situations are **NullPointerException** and **ArrayIndexOutOfBoundsException**.

The Java package **java.lang** contains the core classes **Exception**, **RuntimeException**, and **Error**, all of which extend **Throwable**. If you want to create your own classes specifically for use as exceptions, the preferred method is to define the classes to extend **Exception** but not **RuntimeException** or **Error**, because objects of type **RuntimeException** and **Error** are unchecked exceptions. Objects of classes that extend **RuntimeException** or **Error** are also unchecked exceptions.

Figure 6-1 shows the inheritance relationships among all these classes, and how the type of exception you create depends on the choice of superclass. The method's throws clause must list only exceptions that are **Exception** objects.

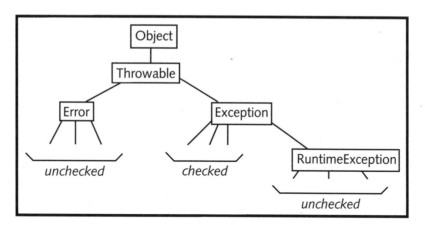

**Figure 6-1**   Classes of throwable objects

**Mini Quiz 6-1**

What is the simplest correct and complete throws clause that you can use with all the methods to let them throw any valid object?

## Throwing Exceptions in Finalizers

Finalizers are methods that perform cleanup when you have finished using objects. The JVM ignores uncaught exceptions thrown by finalizers. Therefore, if you throw an exception in a finalizer, you should also catch it. On the other hand, if the application is not affected by uncaught exceptions that leak out of finalizers, simply ignoring them does no harm.

# CATCHING EXCEPTIONS

Throwing an exception is one side of the story. So far you know how to stop the forward momentum of the program when the unexpected occurs. The other side of the story is catching the exception and providing a handler.

If an exception is to be handled, as well as thrown, the path through the code must enter a try block before it reaches the throw statement. Catch clauses are exception handlers in the Java programming language. You code the recovery for an exception in a catch clause. The catch clause can belong to the try block in which the exception is thrown; if you have nested try blocks, the catch clause can belong to an outer try block.

*Syntax*

**catch ( [final]** *exception_type object_reference* **) {**
    *// handle the exception*
**}**

*Dissection*

➤ A catch clause begins with the keyword **catch**. It looks like the definition of a method named `catch` except that there is no return type or access specifier, and no other qualifier.

➤ A catch clause has one argument, which is enclosed in parentheses. The argument must be an object reference for the class **Throwable** or a subclass of **Throwable**.

➤ Just like the arguments of methods, the argument of a catch clause can optionally be declared **final**. If the argument is final, the catch clause cannot assign another value to the object reference for the exception. However, the contents of the exception may be changed if the exception class provides mutator methods.

*Code Example*

```
catch ( WrongPasswordException e ) {
    System.out.println( e.getMessage () );
}
```

## Code Dissection

This catch clause can catch an exception of type `WrongPasswordException` or a subclass of `WrongPasswordException` that is thrown in the same try block or an inner, nested try block. This handler outputs to the standard output stream whatever message is stored inside the exception object.

---

**Mini Quiz 6-2**

When arguments of methods are declared with final, the value of arguments of primitive type remains constant throughout the execution of the method. Does this rule also apply to final arguments of catch clauses? Why or why not?

**6**

When an exception occurs, the catch clauses are checked in the following order:

1. The search for a handler starts with the catch clauses for the try block in which the exception is thrown. The type of each catch argument is tested in the order in which the catch clauses appear in the try block. If a catch type matches the exception type, that catch clause runs. Then, control passes to the finally clause, if one is present. If no finally clause exists, control passes to the statement following the last catch clause.

2. If no catch clauses for the try block can catch the exception, the finally clause runs, if there is one. Then the search moves on to the next enclosing try block. The call stack is unwound as required.

3. Ultimately, there may be no more try blocks and no handler for the exception. The program ends when the call stack is fully unwound. In other words, the default behavior of an exception is to terminate the program.

The Java programming language gives you no command to resume execution at the point where the exception was thrown. The end of a catch clause does not work like a return from a method. The call stack has been unwound and execution must carry on from the end of the try block.

In the next sample program, you see an exception handler that calls one of the methods of **Throwable** to print the stack trace without stopping the program. The sample contains a public class called **Fraction**. Because it is a public class, it is found in a file called **Fraction.java**. The structure of packages mirrors the file system, so you will find this source code in the examples\exceptions subfolder of the folder in which you unpacked the JAR file **examples.jar**. The first files define the exception classes used by the program.

```
package examples.exceptions;
/** Class of objects thrown when a mathematical
  * exception is detected
  */
```

```
class MathException extends Exception {}
/** Class of objects thrown when division by
  * zero is detected
  */
class DivideByZeroException extends MathException {}
/** Class of errors thrown when a zero
  * denominator is detected in a fraction
  */
class ZeroDenominatorException extends MathException {}
```

The first three classes define specialized types of exceptions. Classes ZeroDenominatorException and DivideByZeroException both extend **MathException**, which in turn extends the core class **Exception**.

The class Fraction uses exceptions to deal with denominators of zero:

```
/** A class to represent mathematical fractions
  */
public class Fraction {
   private int num;    // fraction numerator
   private int den;    // fraction denominator
   /** Constructor without arguments
     */
   public Fraction() {
      num = 0;
      den = 1;
   }
   /** Class constructor for whole numbers.
     * The denominator is set to 1.
     * @param initNum numerator value
     */
   public Fraction( int initNum ) {
      num = initNum;
      den = 1;
   }
   /** Class constructor
     * @param initNum numerator value
     * @param initDen denominator value
     * @exception ZeroDenominatorException
     *               if a zero denominator is
     *               specified
     */
   public Fraction( int initNum, int initDen )
         throws ZeroDenominatorException {
      if ( 0 == initDen ) {
         throw new ZeroDenominatorException();
      }
      num = initNum;
      den = initDen;
   }
   /** Divide one fraction by another
```

```
         * @param divisor The divisor fraction
         * @exception ZeroDenominatorException
         *              if a fraction with a zero
         *              denominator is created
         * @exception DivideByZeroException
         *              if the divisor is zero
         */
        Fraction divideBy( Fraction divisor )
                    throws DivideByZeroException,
                        ZeroDenominatorException {
           if ( 0 == divisor.num ) {
              throw new DivideByZeroException();
           }
           return new Fraction( num * divisor.den,
                             den * divisor.num );
        }
        /** The test method for the class
         * @param args not used
         */
        public static void main( String[] args ) {
           try {
              Fraction a = new Fraction( 1, 0 );
           }
           catch( MathException x ) {
              System.err.println( "A math error occurred" );
           }
           try {
              Fraction a = new Fraction( 37, 0 );
           }
           catch( ZeroDenominatorException x ) {
              System.err.println( "A zero denominator " +
                        "was detected" );
           }
           catch( MathException x ) {
              System.err.println( "A math error occurred" );
           }
           try {
              Fraction a = new Fraction( -7, 0 );
           }
           catch( MathException x ) {
              System.err.println( x );
           }
           try {
              Fraction a = new Fraction( -102, 6 ),
                    b = new Fraction( 0 );
              Fraction c = a.divideBy( b );
           }
           catch( MathException x ) {
              x.printStackTrace( System.err );
           }
        }
    }
```

6

The annotated output is

➤ `A math error occurred`
The first line is output by the handler for `MathException` as the result of the attempt to create the fraction 1/0.

➤ `A zero denominator was detected`
The second line is output by the handler for the `ZeroDenominatorException` as the result of the attempt to create the fraction 37/0.

➤ `examples.exceptions.ZeroDenominatorException`
The third try block attempts to create the fraction -7/0. This time, a `MathException` is caught, but the handler outputs the contents of the exception object rather than a simple message.

➤ `examples.exceptions.DivideByZeroException`
　　`at examples.exceptions.Fraction.divideBy`
　　`( Fraction.java:69 )`
　　`at examples.exceptions.Fraction.main`
　　`( Fraction.java:107 )`
The remaining lines of output are a stack trace produced by the handler for the `MathException` which was thrown as a result of the attempt to divide a by b. The trace first prints the contents of the exception, then gives the locations in the call stack where the exception occurred.

The constructor that has two input parameters throws a `ZeroDenominatorException` if the given denominator value is zero. The method `divideBy` can throw either a `DivideByZeroException` directly or a `ZeroDenominatorException` when it creates a new fraction. In this case, the programmer has chosen to place all the try blocks and handlers in the **main** method, so that each declaration of each `Fraction` in **main** can demonstrate a different handler for a `MathException`. The **main** method handles all the exceptions that may occur within it, so **main** does not require a throws clause of its own.

## Incompletely Handled Exceptions

The Java programming language gives you three options for dealing with exceptions in catch clauses:

➤ You can use a catch clause to catch an exception and handle it.

➤ You can omit a catch clause for an exception and let the call stack unwind further looking for a handler in an outer try block.

➤ You can catch the exception and then **rethrow** it. In the catch clause, you can throw the exception that has just been caught without completely handling it. For example, you can catch an exception, inspect it, and then determine that this handler cannot completely deal with the situation. The handler can take some actions first, or simply decide to pass the exception further up the call stack immediately. You may also decide to substitute the caught exception with another that is more applicable or understandable.

To rethrow an exception, throw the same object you caught using an ordinary throw statement. Use the argument of the catch clause as the argument of the throw statement.

Here is a simple program that throws and rethrows an exception:

```
package examples.exceptions;
/** A user-defined checked exception class to be
  * used when an illegal integer value is detected
  */
class IllegalValueException extends Exception {
    private int value;
    /** Class constructor
      * @param iv the illegal value that was
      *              detected
      */
    public IllegalValueException( int iv ) {
        value = iv;
    }
    /** Method to get the illegal value
      * @return the illegal value
      */
    public int getValue() {
        return value;
    }
    /** Method to set the illegal value
      * @param iv the illegal value
      * @return the updated IllegalValueException
      *              object
      */
    public IllegalValueException setValue( int iv ) {
        value = iv;
        return this;
    }
}
```

The class `IllegalValueException` defines a throwable type that is a checked exception. An `IllegalValueException` has a field, `value`, to hold an integer, and methods to set and get the value of the integer.

The class `ReThrow` contains some utility methods to demonstrate the kinds of things you can do with exceptions:

```
package examples.exceptions;
/** A class to demonstrate rethrowing an exception
  */
```

```java
public class ReThrow {
    /** A utility class method that always throws
     * an exception
     * @exception IllegalValueException For
     *              demonstration purposes
     */
    public static void methodThrowsException()
        throws IllegalValueException {
            throw new IllegalValueException( 150 );
    }
    /** A utility class method that catches, alters,
     * and rethrows IllegalValueException exceptions
     * @exception IllegalValueException An uncaught
     *              exception from a called method
     */
    public static void methodReThrowsException()
            throws IllegalValueException {
        try {
            methodThrowsException();
        }
        catch( IllegalValueException ive ) {
            System.out.println( "Caught illegal value "
                                + ive.getValue() );
            if ( ive.getValue() > 100 ) {
                ive.setValue( ive.getValue() - 100 );
                throw ive;
            }
        }
    }
    /** Test method for the class
     * @param args Not used
     */
    public static void main( String[] args ) {
        try {
            methodReThrowsException();
        }
        catch( IllegalValueException ive ) {
            System.out.println( "Caught illegal value "
                                + ive.getValue() );
        }
    }
}
```

The output is

```
Caught illegal value 150
Caught illegal value 50
```

The method `methodThrowsException` simply creates an `IllegalValueException`, sets `value` to 150, and throws the exception. The method `methodReThrowsException` calls the method `ThrowsException2` and catches the exception. This handler prints a message, subtracts 100 from `value`, and rethrows the exception. The **main** method contains an outer try block. The catch clause of this outer try block catches the exception when it is rethrown. You can see from the output that the `value` in the rethrown exception has been modified to 50.

## COMPLETING A TRY BLOCK WITH A FINALLY CLAUSE

**6**

Often you want to make sure that some code runs at the end of a try block, no matter how the block ends. If you find yourself duplicating the same statements that follow the throw statements in a try block in every catch clause, move those statements into a finally clause. The finally clause runs also if control leaves the try block as a result of a **return**, **continue**, or **break**. In all cases, you have a chance to perform cleanup, or do whatever processing you feel should be completed at the end of the try block.

*Syntax*

**try** {
         // *statements that are monitored for exceptions*
}
**[catch(** *exception_class object_reference* **)** {
         // *0, 1, or more catch blocks*
}]
**[finally** {
         // *statements always executed at the end of the try block*
}]

*Dissection*

➤ If a finally block is present, the statements it contains are always executed when control leaves the try block.

➤ If a finally block is present, the catch clauses are optional.

➤ The finally block is optional if the try block has at least one catch clause. A try block that has no catch clauses must have a finally clause.

*Code Example*

```
MyClass temp;
try {
   temp = new MyClass();
   // work with temp
}
```

```
finally {
    temp = null;
}
```

*Code Dissection*

The object `temp` is required only inside this try block, so the finally clause sets its object reference to **null**. The object can then be removed from memory the next time the JVM runs garbage collection.

The finally clause records the reason it was entered so that, when it ends, it reinstates the flow of control that it interrupted. Here are some examples that show how the finally clause fits in the flow of control:

➤ If the try block ends normally, the finally clause runs, followed by the first statement after the finally clause.

➤ If a statement within the try block throws an exception, and a catch clause in the try block catches the exception, the finally clause runs immediately after the catch clause, followed by the first statement after the finally clause.

➤ If a statement within the try block throws an exception, and no catch clause in the try block catches the exception, the finally clause runs before the call stack unwinds further in search of a handler.

➤ When a break or continue statement transfers control outside the try block, the statements in the finally clause run first.

➤ If the method ends with a return statement inside a try block, the finally clause runs before the method returns.

What if the finally clause itself changes the flow of control? For example, if a finally clause contains a throw statement, the handling of that exception takes precedence over whatever control flow was in progress when the finally clause was entered. Interrupting exception handling by throwing another exception in a finally clause is possible. However, doing so is not advisable because it creates opportunities for problems in the unwinding of the stack for exception handling. You should either avoid throwing exceptions in a finally clause, or at least arrange to catch them locally. In any event, take care when altering the flow of control in a finally clause.

This sample program uses methods from the input and output package **java.io**. The program throws and catches **IOException** objects and demonstrates several features of exception handling.

```
package examples.exceptions;
import java.io.*;
/** A class to help demonstrate how the finally
```

```
      * clause can be used with a try block
      */
public class CharCount {
   /** Method to count characters in a file
     * @param args[0] The name of the file to be
     *                 opened for character counting
     */
   public static void main( String[] args ) {
      if ( args.length == 0 ) {
         System.err.println( "Please provide "
                           + "a file name." );
      } else try {
         FileReader input
            = new FileReader( args[0] );
         int charCount = 0;
         try {
            while ( input.read() != -1 ) {
               charCount++;
            }
            System.out.println( "There were "
                              + charCount
                              + " characters" );
         } catch( IOException iox ) {
            System.err.println( "Exception occurred "
                              + "at character "
                              + charCount );
            System.err.println( iox );
         } finally {
            input.close();
         }
      } catch( IOException iox ) {
         System.err.println( "Error opening or "
                           + "closing the file "
                           + args[0] );
      }
   }
}
```

This program counts the number of characters in the file specified as its command line argument. To run it from the directory in which you unpacked **examples.jar**, enter this command on one line:

```
java examples.exceptions.CharCount
examples\exceptions\CharCount.java
```

The output is

```
There were 1373 characters
```

You can specify the relative or absolute path to any file to count the characters it contains. If the program cannot find the file, as may happen with the following command:

```
Java examples.exceptions.CharCount D:\aFolder\notHere.txt
```

The output is

```
Error opening or closing the file D:\aFolder\notHere.txt
```

The purpose of this program is to count and output the number of characters in a file. The local variable `charCount` in **main** is the counter.

The **main** method contains nested try blocks. The outer block opens a file for reading. Opening a file can cause an **IOException**, and the outer try block has a handler to catch that exception. The inner try block reads characters from the file, an operation that can throw a different **IOException**. The catch clause for the inner try block handles an exception caused by reading the file.

The finally clause for the inner try block closes the file, regardless of whether the program is read successfully to the end of the file. The method **read**, which **FileReader** inherits from **InputStreamReader**, returns the value –1 to indicate that the end of the file has been reached. The inner try block reads until either the end of the file or a read error throws an **IOException**.

# SUMMARY

The Java programming language provides a number of constructs that you can use when the unexpected happens during execution of your code. Exceptions are objects that encapsulate errors or exceptional conditions. In the Java programming language, all run-time errors are exceptions. Unhandled exceptions terminate your program. Use exception handling to recover and to continue running your program, or at least to end your program more gracefully than with an abnormal termination.

Generally, you leave severe errors to the JVM, because your code usually cannot detect them and can take no reasonable steps to recover from them. Use exception handling for conditions that relate to the tasks that your methods are designed to perform and that prevent your methods from completing successfully.

In the Java programming language, you use the following keywords to handle exceptions:

**catch    finally    throw    throws    try**

Here is the form of the statements that relate to exception handling:

[*access_specifiers*] [*qualifiers*] *return_type method_name*( *argument_list* )

```
    [throws exception_list]
{
    // statements that are not monitored for exceptions
    try {                                           // start of try block
        // statements that are monitored for exceptions
        [throw exception_object;                    // throw statement]
        // statements that are monitored for exceptions
    }
[catch( exception_class object_reference ) {   // start of catch clause
        // statements                              // exception handler
        [throw exception_object;                   // throw statement]
    }]
    [finally {                                      // start of finally clause
        // statements always executed at the end of the try block
    }]
    // statements that are not monitored for exceptions
}
```

Usually, all exceptions for which you use exception handling are checked exceptions. Checked exceptions are instances of the core class **java.lang.Exception** or a subclass of **Exception**. The core classes define and use many exceptions. For example, methods in the core classes that perform I/O throw **IOException** objects if they encounter a problem reading or writing files. You can also define your own exception classes. To ensure that instances of your exception classes are checked exceptions, extend the **Exception** class or a subclass of **Exception** other than **RunTimeException**.

Instances of the core classes **java.lang.RuntimeException** and **java.lang.Error**, and all classes that extend these two classes, are unchecked exceptions.

For each type of checked exception that can occur during the execution of your method, you must do one of the following:

- List the exception class in the throws clause of the method declaration. The throws clause informs calling methods what exceptions may leak out of your method.

- Catch and handle the exception in your method.

Try blocks enclose the statements that are monitored for exceptions or that are involved in exception handling. You can nest try blocks.

A throw statement raises an exception. You can throw only objects that instantiate the core class **java.lang.Throwable** or a subclass of **Throwable**. The classes **Exception**, **RuntimeException**, and **Error** all extend **Throwable**.

When an exception is thrown, the flow of control through the program stops and the search for a handler begins. The JVM looks first at the catch clauses of the immediately enclosing try block, and then works outward, unwinding the call stack as it goes.

A catch clause is an exception handler. It has a single argument, which must be an object reference for an exception class. Each catch clause handles a different type of exception that can be thrown in the try block. A throw statement inside a catch clause can rethrow the exception instead of completely handling it.

If there is no catch clause for an exception that occurs, the exception is uncaught. An uncaught exception can be caught by an outer try block. If the exception is never caught, the JVM terminates your program and prints a trace of the call stack at the time the exception was thrown.

A try block must have at least one catch clause if no finally clause exists. A finally clause is optional if at least one catch clause exists.

The statements in a finally clause are always executed at the end of a try block. Regardless of whether an exception has been thrown, all the statements in the try block have completed successfully, or a return, break, or continue statement transfers control out of the try block. The finally clause gives you an opportunity to perform cleanup in one place for all possible routes out of a try block.

When a try block completes, control passes to the statement following the try block. Control never returns to the point where the exception occurred.

## QUESTIONS

1. Which of the following types of objects can be thrown as an exception? Select all that apply.

   a. **String**

   b. **Integer**

   c. **int**

   d. **Error**

   e. **Exception**

2. How is a checked exception distinguished from an unchecked exception?

3. Examine the following code:

```
class BinEmpty extends Exception { }
class StockBin {
```

```
    private int itemsInBin = 0;
    public StockBin( int initialCount ) {
        itemsInBin = initialCount;
    }
    public void removeFromBin() throws BinEmpty {
        if ( itemsInBin == 0 ) {
            throw new BinEmpty();
        } else {
            --itemsInBin;
        }
    }
}
public class Warehouse {
    public static void main( String[] args ) {
        try {
            StockBin b = new StockBin( 1 );
            b.removeFromBin();
            b.removeFromBin();
        }
        catch( BinEmpty be ) {
            System.out.println( "Oops, no more!" );
        }
        finally {
            System.out.println( "Cleaning up" );
        }
    }
}
```

Which of the following statements are true when the code is compiled and run? Select all that apply.

a. The compiler rejects the definition of the method `Warehouse.main` because it does not have a throws clause declaring the exception class **BinEmpty**.

b. The class **BinEmpty** defines a class of checked exceptions.

c. Compilation is successful and the output is
```
Oops, no more!
Cleaning up
```

d. Compilation is successful and the output is
```
Oops, no more!
```

4. Examine the following code:

```
class E1 extends Exception { }
class E2 extends E1 { }
public class Quiz6_1 {
    public static void f( boolean flag ) throws E1, E2 {
        if ( flag ) {
            throw new E1();
```

```
      } else {
          throw new E2();
      }
  }
  public static void main( String[] args ) {
      try {
          f( true );
      }
      catch( E1 e1 ) {
          System.out.println( "Caught E1" );
      }
      catch( E2 e2 ) {
          System.out.println( "Caught E2" );
      }
  }
}
```

Which of the following statements are true when the code is compiled and run? Select all that apply.

a. The compiler rejects the definition of the method `Quiz6_1.`**main** because it does not have a throws clause declaring the exception classes `E1` and `E2`.

b. The compiler rejects the catch clause for `E2` because it is unreachable.

c. Compilation is successful and the output is
```
Caught E1
Caught E2
```

d. Compilation is successful and the output is
```
Caught E1
```

5. Examine the following code:

```
class E1 extends Exception { }
class E2 extends E1 { }
class SuperQuiz6_2 {
    public void f( boolean flag ) throws E1 {
    }
}
public class Quiz6_2 extends SuperQuiz6_2 {
    // -- X --
}
```

Which of the following function definitions are valid when placed at the line marked -- X --? Select all that apply.

a. `public void f( boolean flag ) throws E1 { }`

b. `public void f( boolean flag ) { }`

c. `public void f( boolean flag ) throws E2 { }`

d. `public void f( boolean flag ) throws E1, E2 { }`

e. `public void f( boolean flag ) throws Exception { }`

6. Which class is the superclass of all classes of objects that may be thrown as exceptions?

7. Examine the following code:

```
class E1 extends Exception { }
class E2 extends E1 { }
public class Quiz6_3 extends SuperQuiz6_2 {
    public void f( boolean flag ) throws E1 {
        // -- X --
    }
}
```

Which of the following statements are valid when placed at the line marked -- X --? Select all that apply.

  a. `throw new Exception( );`

  b. `throw new E1( );`

  c. `throw new E2( );`

  d. `throw new Object( );`

  e. `throw new Error( );`

8. Examine the following code:

```
public class Quiz6_4 {
    public static void main( String[] args ) {
        f( false );
        f( true );
    }
    public static void f( boolean flag ) {
        try {
            if( flag ) {
                return;
            } else {
                System.out.println( flag );
            }
        } finally {
            System.out.println( "Cleaning up" );
        }
    }
}
```

Which of the following statements are true when the code is compiled and run? Select all that apply.

  a. The compiler rejects the definition of the method `Quiz6_4.f` because the try block it contains does not have a catch block.

  b. The compiler rejects the definition of the method `Quiz6_4.f` because the try block does not contain any statements that may throw an exception.

c. Compilation is successful and the output is `false`.

d. Compilation is successful and the output is

```
false
Cleaning up
```

e. Compilation is successful and the output is

```
false
Cleaning up
```

9. Examine the following code:

```
class E1 extends Exception { }
class E2 extends E1 { }
public class Quiz6_5 {
    public static void main( String[] args ) {
        try {
            throw new E1();
        }
        // -- X --
    }
}
```

Which of the following statements are valid when placed at the line marked `-- X --`? Select all that apply.

a. `catch ( Exception x ) { }`

b. `catch ( final Exception x ) { }`

c. `catch ( final E1 x ) { }`

d. `catch ( E2 x ) { }`

e. `catch ( ... ) { }`

10. What method of any exception object can be used to display the contents of the program stack at the time the exception occurred?

# EXERCISES

## Debugging

1. Correct all the errors in the following program.

```
package questions.c6;
class D61_OutOfRangeException extends Exception {
}
public class Debug6_1 {
    public static final int MAX_X = 1000;
    public static final int MIN_X = 10;
    private int x;
    public int getX() {
        return x;
```

```
        }
        public void setX( int value ) {
            if ( value >= MIN_X && value <= MAX_X ) {
                x = value;
            } else {
                throw new D61_OutOfRangeException();
            }
        }
        public static void main( String[] args ) {
            Debug6_1 a = new Debug6_1();
            a.setX( 275 );
            System.out.println( a.getX() );
        }
    }
```

**6**

2. Correct all the errors in the following program without changing the definition of the interface:

```
    package questions.c6;
    interface IfaceDebug6_2 {
        public void f( int input );
    }
    class D62_OutOfRangeException extends Exception {
    }
    public class Debug6_2 implements IfaceDebug6_2 {
        public static final int MAX_X = 1000;
        public static final int MIN_X = 10;
        private int x;
        public void f( int input ) {
            setX( input );
        }
        public int getX() {
            return x;
        }
        public void setX( int value ) {
            if ( value >= MIN_X && value <= MAX_X ) {
                x = value;
            } else {
                throw new D62_OutOfRangeException();
            }
        }
        public static void main( String[] args ) {
            Debug6_2 a = new Debug6_2();
            a.f( 275 );
            System.out.println( a.getX() );
        }
    }
```

3. Correct all the errors in the following program:

```
    package questions.c6;
    class D63_E1 extends Exception {
```

```
        }
        class D63_E2 extends D63_E1 {
        }
        public class Debug6_3 {
            private int x;
            public String toString() {
                return String.valueOf( x );
            }
            public void f( int input ) throws Exception {
                x = input;
                throw D63_E1;
            }
            public static void main( String[] args ) {
                Debug6_3 a = new Debug6_3();
                try {
                    a.f( 275 );
                } catch ( Exception e ) {
                    System.out.println( e );
                } catch ( D63_E1 e ) {
                    System.out.println( e );
                }
                System.out.println( a );
            }
        }
```

4. Correct the programming style error in the following program:

```
        package questions.c6;
        class D64_E1 extends Exception {
        }
        class D64_E2 extends D64_E1 {
        }
        public class Debug6_4 {
            public static void g() throws D64_E2 {
                System.out.println( "Processing here" );
                throw new D64_E2();
            }
            public static void cleanUp() {
                System.out.println( "Clean up processing here" );
            }
            public static void main( String[] args ) {
                try {
                    g();
                } catch ( D64_E2 e ) {
                    System.out.println( e );
                    cleanUp();
                } catch ( D64_E1 e ) {
                    System.out.println( e );
                    cleanUp();
                }
                cleanUp();
            }
        }
```

5. Correct all the errors in the following program:

```
package questions.c6;
class TooBigException {
   private double value;
   public TooBigException( double errorValue ) {
      value = errorValue;
   }
   public double getErrorValue() {
      return value;
   }
}
public class Debug6_5 {
   private double pressure = 10.0;
   public void setPressure( double newPressure )
                           throws TooBigException {
      if ( newPressure > 2*pressure ) {
         // pressure must be increased slowly
         throw TooBigException();
      } else {
         pressure = newPressure;
      }
   }
   public double getPressure() {
      return pressure;
   }
   public static void main( String[] args ) {
      try {
         Debug6_5 x = new Debug6_5();
         x.setPressure( 15.0 );
         x.setPressure( 25.0 );
         x.setPressure( 60.0 );
      } catch ( TooBigException tbe ) {
         System.out.println( tbe.value );
      }
   }
}
```

6

## Complete the Solution

1. Extract the file **questions\c6\Complete6_1.java** from the **question.jar** file on the CD-ROM. This file contains the class questions.c6.Complete6_1. Add the exception classes needed for this program to compile and run.

2. Extract the file **questions\c6\Complete6_2.java** from the **question.jar** file on the CD-ROM. This file contains the classes questions.c6.Complete6_2 and IndexTooBigException. Complete the questions.c6.Complete6_1 program by using the IndexTooBigException class for cases in which the required character count is larger than the string.

3. Expand upon your answer to the previous question by adding a second exception type, `NegativeIndexException`, that is thrown if a negative count is specified in the method `getBeginChars`.

4. Expand upon your answer to the previous question by adding a common superclass exception type, `IndexException`, for both `NegativeIndexException` and `IndexTooBigException`. Move the `getErrorValue` method and the `value` field, used by both subclasses for handling the invalid index value, into the superclass. The subclass constructors should use the method **super** to set the illegal value. Put three catch blocks in the **main** method: one for the superclass and one for each subclass.

5. Extract the file **questions\c6\SetOfCharacters.java** from the **question.jar** file on the CD-ROM. This file contains the class `questions.c6.SetOfCharacters`. Complete the `SetOfCharacters` class so that it throws an `AlreadyInSetException` if an attempt is made to add a character to a set for the second time. Add the exception class `AlreadyInSetException`. Take advantage of the exception class's superclass constructor to set a message that indicates which character is in error.

## Discovery

1. Create a class called `Stack` that encapsulates an array of integers and provides methods for pushing a value onto the stack, popping a value off the stack, and for peeking at the value on the top of the stack. There should also be a method, `isEmpty`, that returns a boolean value to indicate whether the stack is empty. Since the stack is being built around an array which will have a fixed size, you should add another method, `isFull`, to return a value indicating whether room exists for another item on the stack.

   Add exception classes with a common superclass called `StackException`. The subclasses should be `EmptyStackException`, which is thrown when an attempt is made to pop or peek at an empty stack, and `FullStackException`, which is thrown when an attempt is made to push an item onto a full stack. Don't forget to write a **main** method that tests all of your methods.

2. Add exception handling to the `Inventory` class described in the exercises at the end of Chapter 4. Wherever the program prints a warning, replace that action with a statement that throws an exception.

   Add exception classes with a common superclass called `InventoryException`. Example subclasses that you may choose to create include `ItemNotFoundException`, `NegativePriceException`, and `ArrayOverflowException`. The **main** method should catch all these exceptions and print error messages.

# CLONING AND RTTI

---

**In this chapter you will:**

➤ Clone objects so that the result is a deep, rather than shallow, copy.

➤ Use the interface **Cloneable** to control whether instances of a class you define can be cloned.

➤ Use the interface **Cloneable** to control whether instances of subclasses of your class must be, can optionally be, or cannot be cloned.

☕ Determine the result of applying assignment and *instanceof* operators to operands of any type.

➤ Investigate the class named **Class**, with which you can get information about a class at run time.

➤ Understand why some casts between class types are safe, whereas others throw an exception, and learn how to handle this exception.

➤ Use the Reflection API to get run-time information about fields, methods, and primitive types.

➤ Call a method or a constructor for a class with the Reflection API.

---

## INTRODUCTION

You have used objects of primitive and reference types, including user-defined classes. This chapter elaborates on two specific facets of classes: cloning, or duplicating objects, and obtaining run-time type information (RTTI) about objects and classes. The package **java.lang** includes the classes and interfaces that support these two activities. Otherwise, they are quite separate topics. This chapter combines them because both are programming techniques that operate on classes, rather than simply calls to methods of classes to achieve other ends. Learning about these topics can greatly increase your understanding of the nature of classes.

To successfully complete this chapter, you must fully understand the material in the previous chapters of this book. To understand how cloning and RTTI work, you must have a solid understanding of Java types, classes, inheritance, and even exception handling.

# CLONING OBJECTS

Before long, you are bound to run into the deceptively simple-sounding problem of copying objects. For the primitive types, there is no problem: just use the assignment operator. However, using the assignment operator with object references changes only the references, not the objects referenced.

To copy objects of reference types, you must clone the objects. Cloning involves calling the method **clone**, which is available for all objects of reference types, including instances of classes and arrays.

---

*Class*

```
java.lang.Object
```

---

*Purpose*

The **Object** class defines methods that are available in all objects of reference types.

---

*Methods*

➤ **Object clone()**
The method **clone** creates a duplicate of the object for which the method is called and returns an object reference to the new object. The returned value must be cast for the actual type of the object.

---

The following lines show why using the assignment operator to copy objects may not have the desired effect.

```
Pair x = new Pair( 5, 6 );
Pair y = new Pair( 54, 40 );
x = y;
```

As shown in Figure 7-1, these lines produce two object references, **x** and **y**, for the same object, instead of two object references for separate but identical objects. Also, the object that **x** originally referred to may not be accessible through any object reference and thus becomes available for garbage collection.

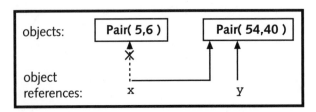

**Figure 7-1** Assigning object references

Figure 7-2 shows what happens when this code fragment is rewritten to call **clone**, as follows:

```
Pair x = new Pair( 5, 6 );
Pair y = new Pair( 54, 40 );
x = ( Pair ) y.clone();
```

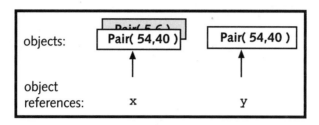

**Figure 7-2** Calling Object.clone

Now **x** and **y** are object references for two different objects that are identical to each other.

You must cast the value returned from **clone** to an object reference for the correct type of object. If you feel this casting is unsafe, rest assured that the Java Virtual Machine (JVM) throws an exception of the type **ClassCastException** if the cast is inappropriate.

> **Mini Quiz 7-1**
>
> Why must the clone method of all classes return an object reference for an **Object**?

For the reference types, you usually want to make a deep copy rather than a shallow copy of an object. When you create a **shallow copy**, you duplicate the data members of an object regardless of whether some members are object references. A shallow copy makes no attempt to make duplicates of the referenced objects. As a result, the copy and the original can contain object references for the same object. A **deep copy** duplicates the objects referred to by object references, and inserts a new object reference for the duplicate object into the copy. Figure 7-3 illustrates a shallow and deep copy of an object **z** that contains an object reference for object x.

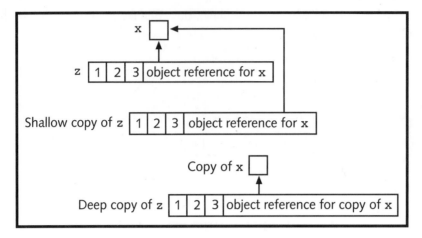

**Figure 7-3** Shallow and deep copies

The method **Object.clone** performs a shallow copy. It copies all fields of the original object to the new object, regardless of whether the fields are primitive types or object references. This works for many, but not all, classes. If a class is mutable and has any fields that are object references to mutable objects of reference type, the class should provide an implementation of **clone** that returns a deep copy. Alternatively, you may want to prevent an object from being cloned. For example, if instances of a class cannot be duplicated in some safe and meaningful way, the class should not be cloneable.

Next comes the question of how to tell whether the classes of object references that are fields in the class also override the **clone** method. Often, whether your class is cloneable depends on whether all fields in the class are cloneable. The Java platform includes a core interface called **Cloneable** for the specific purpose of indicating whether objects are cloneable.

## Making Objects Cloneable

One of the cornerstones of the philosophy of the Java programming language is that subclasses inherit no surprising behavior from superclasses. In the case of copying objects, whether cloning works depends upon whether the class is defined to implement the core interface **Cloneable**. If a class is declared to implement **Cloneable**, you can assume it is safe to call clone for instances of that class and use the objects produced by the **clone** method. If you call **clone** for a class that does not implement **Cloneable**, the exception **CloneNotSupportedException** is thrown. This may not be the behavior you want, but it is safer than and preferable to a default clone that gives no outward sign of error and creates a corrupt copy.

If you call **clone** for an instance of a class that uses the default method **Object.clone**, you must take one of the following actions:

➤ Wrap a try block around the call of **clone** and catch the possible **CloneNotSupportedException**.

➤ Add the **CloneNotSupportedException** exception to the throws clause for the method that calls **clone**.

The definition of **clone** in the **Object** class lists **CloneNotSupportedException** in its **throws** clause. When you override **Object.clone** in your class, you have the option of removing **CloneNotSupportedException** from the throws clause of your **clone** method.

The **Cloneable** interface is an example of a marker interface. **Marker interfaces** have no methods. Note, for example, that the interface **Cloneable** does not define the method **clone**. The sole purpose of a marker interface is to attach a piece of type information to a class. In this case, declaring a class with **implements Cloneable** means that the class supports cloning of its objects. When you define a class, you can use **Cloneable** like an on-off switch. If you implement **Cloneable**, the class supports cloning. That is all you have to do to enable the inherited **clone** method. If you do not implement **Cloneable**, the clone method throws an exception. Pseudocode for **Object.clone** is essentially as follows:

```
if the object is an instance of Cloneable
   then make a shallow copy of the entire object
   else throw a CloneNotSupportedException
end if
```

Here is an example class called `Pair`. Because `Pair` is a public class, it is found in a file called Pair.java. The structure of packages mirrors the file system, so you will find this source code in the examples\cloning subfolder of the folder in which you unpacked the JAR file examples.jar. It has only two fields and they are integers. Therefore, the default **clone** method is adequate.

```java
package examples.cloning;
/** An example class used to demonstrate how to
  * enable cloning for a class without fields that
  * contain object references.
  */
public class Pair implements Cloneable {
   private int a, b;
   /** Class constructor method
     * @param a Initial value for the first field
     * @param b Initial value for the second field
     */
```

```
public Pair( int initA, int initB ) {
   a = initA;
   b = initB;
}
/** Convert object to String representation
  * @return The value of the array as a String
  */
public String toString() {
   return "( " + a + ", " + b + " )";
}
/** The test method for the class
  * @param args Not used
  * @exception CloneNotSupportedException
  *                 If clone not supported by
  *                 inherited clone method
  */
public static void ( String[] args )
      throws CloneNotSupportedException {
   Pair x = new Pair( 5, 6 );
   System.out.println( x );
   Pair y = ( Pair ) x.clone();
   System.out.println( y );
}
}
```

The output is

```
( 5, 6 )
( 5, 6 )
```

The method **main** contains a throws clause because the class inherits
**Object.clone**, which can throw the exception **CloneNotSupportedException**.

## Overriding the Default Clone Method

For objects related by an inheritance hierarchy to be cloned correctly, each
class in the hierarchy that has object reference fields must override **clone**. The
reason is that the class at each level of the hierarchy is responsible for cloning
the fields it defines, and relies on the **clone** method of its superclass to copy
the fields it inherits. Here are some guidelines for implementing **clone**:

➤ If classes outside the package, other than subclasses, are to be allowed to
use your implementation of the **clone** method, declare your method with
access specifier **public**. The **Object.clone** method is a protected method.

➤ When you implement **clone**, it is not necessary to program it to deal with
fields of the primitive types. You can leave them for the default **clone**
method to handle.

➤ Define the **clone** method to copy objects for all fields that are reference objects. The only exceptions to this rule are object references for immutable objects. For example, objects of classes like **String** and the wrapper classes for the primitive types such as **Integer**, **Character**, and **Double** cannot be changed. Because the objects are immutable, clones that have references to the same object cannot cause problems. A different complication occurs when one or more fields are object references for classes that do not support cloning. When this happens, you must fall back on the "brute force" method of creating a new object of the class and then calling public methods to copy the fields one by one.

➤ To make sure every superclass in the hierarchy has a chance to copy the fields it defines, start your definition of **clone** with the following statement:

```
super.clone();
```

This statement calls the **clone** method of the superclass. You should repeat the statement in every superclass until **Object.clone** initiates the cloning process by making a shallow copy of the entire object. Then, as the call stack retreats, each class should call the **clone** methods for its object references to mutable objects. In the end, everything is cloned correctly.

Here is an example of a class that inappropriately uses the default **clone** method:

```
package examples.cloning;
/** An example class used to demonstrate what
  * happens when the default Object.clone method
  * is not overridden in a class with object
  * reference fields.
  */
public class IntArrayShared implements Cloneable {
   private int[] a;
   /** Class constructor method
     * @param size The maximum number of elements
     * @param initValue The initial value given
     */
   public IntArrayShared( int size, int initValue ) {
      a = new int[size];
      for( int i = 0; i < a.length; i++ ) {
         a[i] = initValue;
      }
   }
   /** Obtain the value of an array element
     * @param index the array index of interest
     * @return the value at the specified index
     */
   public int elementAt( int index ) {
      return a[index];
   }
```

```
    /** Set the value of an array element
      * @param index the array index to be updated
      * @param newValue the new value given
      */
    public void setValue( int index, int newValue ) {
       a[index] = newValue;
    }
    /** Converts the object into a String
      * @return The value of the array as a String
      */
    public String toString() {
       StringBuffer sb = new StringBuffer( "[ " );
       for( int i = 0; i < a.length; i++ ) {
          sb.append( a[i] + " " );
       }
       return sb.append( "]" ).toString();
    }
    /** The test method for the class
      * @param args Not used
      * @exception CloneNotSupportedException
      *                 The inherited clone method may
      *                 throw this exception
      */
    public static void ( String[] args )
          throws CloneNotSupportedException {
       IntArrayShared x = new IntArrayShared( 5, 0 );
       IntArrayShared y = ( IntArrayShared ) x.clone();
       System.out.println( x );
       System.out.println( y );
       x.setValue( 2, 9999 );
       System.out.println( x );
       System.out.println( y );
    }
}
```

The output is

```
[ 0 0 0 0 0 ]
[ 0 0 0 0 0 ]
[ 0 0 9999 0 0 ]
[ 0 0 9999 0 0 ]
```

The reference field a, which is an array of integers, is not immutable.
Therefore, the inherited **Object.clone** method does not properly clone the
field. Notice from the output that the clones are not independent.

Here is how the **clone** method should be written. This method is taken from
the example class **examples.cloning.IntArray**. The class **IntArray** is

identical to the previous example, `IntArrayShared`, except that `IntArray` overrides the **clone** method with the following method:

```
/** Provide a clone method specifically for the
    * intArray class
    * @exception CloneNotSupportedException
    *               Superclass may throw this
    * @return A clone of the object
    */
  public Object clone()
        throws CloneNotSupportedException {
    IntArray newObject = ( IntArray ) super.clone();
    newObject.a = ( int[]) a.clone();
    return newObject;
  }
```

When you use this proper **clone** method, the output is as follows:

```
[ 0  0  0  0  0 ]
[ 0  0  0  0  0 ]
[ 0  0  9999  0  0 ]
[ 0  0  0  0  0 ]
```

The proper **clone** method has a number of notable features:

➤ The return type is **Object**, because it overrides **Object.clone**. Therefore, the returned object must be cast to type **IntArray**.

➤ It calls **super.clone** to clone the fields in the superclass. This statement could be omitted in this case, because **Object** is the direct superclass of **IntArray**. However, including this statement is never an error and is always the safest approach.

➤ Next, **IntArray.clone** calls the **clone** method for the field **a**, which is an array. Like any reference object, this array has a **clone** method. The **clone** method used by arrays makes a shallow copy, which is adequate in this case. If the elements of the array are themselves reference objects, as in an array of arrays, you have no choice but to clone each element explicitly. Unfortunately, a way to override the **clone** method of an array does not exist.

## Defining Cloneable Classes

The **Cloneable** interface gives the creator of the class the responsibility of deciding whether instances of the class are cloneable. Moreover, the decision affects not only the class being defined, but all subclasses that may extend the class in the future.

When you are deciding whether to implement the **Cloneable** interface, consider the impact on subclasses for which the class is the superclass, as well as on unrelated classes that use the class. Here are five possible approaches you can provide:

1. All objects of the class can be cloned. The simplest option is to support cloning fully, by:

   ➤ Defining the class with `implements Cloneable`.

   ➤ Inheriting or overriding the default **clone** method. If you override the method, do not throw any exceptions in your implementation, but do include **CloneNotSupportedException** in the throws clause.

   This approach provides the most flexibility for any subclasses. A subclass that extends the class has the same options for implementing cloning as the class had.

   Example:

   ```
   class SubClass extends SuperClass
                           implements Cloneable {
       // optionally implement clone
       public Object clone()
               throws CloneNotSupportedException {
         // do not throw CloneNotSupportedException
       }
   }
   ```

2. Objects of the class are cloneable only if all contained objects are also cloneable. This is an attractive option for classes that do not have control over what they contain. Collection classes usually use this technique. To support cloning conditionally:

   ➤ Define the class with `implements Cloneable`.

   ➤ Implement **clone**. For the fields of reference types, call the **clone** method of those classes. To give these contained objects an opportunity to throw an exception, include **CloneNotSupportedException** in the throws clause of the **clone** method.

   A subclass that extends this class has the same options for implementing cloning as the class.

   Example:

   ```
   class SubClass extends SuperClass
                           implements Cloneable {
       OtherClass fieldName;
       // Implement clone if fields are object
       // references
       public Object clone()
               throws CloneNotSupportedException {
         fieldName = (OtherClass) fieldName.clone();
   ```

```
            // do not throw CloneNotSupportedException
        }
    }
```

3. Objects of the class are not cloneable, but a subclass can extend the class in such a way that its objects are cloneable. To let subclasses support cloning, but not publicly support cloning in the class:

   ➤ Omit `implements Cloneable` from the class definition. Leave implementing the interface up to the subclass.

   ➤ Override or inherit the **clone** method. Even though the class is not cloneable, you should provide a **clone** method that correctly duplicates the fields defined in the class, for the sake of cloneable subclasses.

   Although this class does not allow cloning, a subclass can implement **Cloneable**, inherit or override the **clone** method, and become fully cloneable.

   Example:

```
class SubClass extends SuperClass {
    OtherClass fieldName;
    // implement clone if fields are object
    // references
    public Object clone()
            throws CloneNotSupportedException {
        fieldName = (OtherClass) fieldName.clone();
        // do not throw CloneNotSupportedException
    }
}
```

4. No object of the class or any class that extends the class can be cloned. Do not support cloning if you are designing a class of objects in which the subclass objects must be unique. For example, it may be a design criterion of the application that only one copy of an object is allowed. To prohibit cloning:

   ➤ Omit `implements Cloneable` from the class definition.

   ➤ Implement a **clone** method that always throws a **CloneNotSupportedException** object.

   Even if a subclass implements **Cloneable** and overrides **clone**, the exception is thrown when the subclass calls **super.clone** for the fields it inherits from your class. Therefore, you guarantee that no subclass can clone an object.

Example:

```
class SubClass extends SuperClass {
    // implement clone to throw an exception
    public Object clone()
                throws CloneNotSupportedException {
        throw new CloneNotSupportedException();
    }
}
```

5. The class is an abstract class and all subclasses are required to provide a **clone** method that does not throw **CloneNotSupportedException**. To force a subclass to support cloning:

➤ Optionally add `implements Cloneable` for clarity.

➤ Define a **clone** method and declare it to be **abstract**.

➤ Omit **CloneNotSupportedException** from the throws clause of **clone**.

Example:

```
abstract class SubClass extends SuperClass {
    public abstract Object clone();
}
```

---

**Mini Quiz 7-2**

a. Why must a superclass that forces subclasses to implement **Cloneable** be an abstract class?

b. Why must the class that extends a superclass with an abstract **clone** method override **clone**?

c. Why can the overriding method **clone** not throw the exception **CloneNotSupportedException**?

---

# RUN-TIME TYPE INFORMATION

Some programming challenges arise from the environments supported by the Java platform and the very nature of programs that you write in the Java programming language. For example, many programs are driven by a graphical user interface (GUI) or run in a distributed environment. As a result, you may find that your class has to deal with objects for which the type is not known. These objects may be instances of classes created by different programmers, and may even be instances of classes that did not exist when you wrote and tested your class. An important use of RTTI is to access members of classes that you cannot know about when you develop your class. For example, your method may extract information from a database and need the flexibility to display records for which the structure is unknown at development time.

RTTI can also be helpful in debugging the code. For example, one effect of dynamic binding may be that a method can receive a different type of object than it expects. The object received as an argument to a method can instantiate a subclass of the argument type. A good debugger can show you what is happening at run time, or you can use RTTI to determine whether you are operating on the type of object for which the method was designed.

RTTI also helps to make up for the lack of parameterized types in the Java programming language. For example, in an argument list, you must specify the type of every argument of every method, and the only flexibility is that dynamic binding lets you specify a superclass when a subclass object may actually be passed. You can pass the most general type, **Object**, to a method and let the method use RTTI to determine how to use the object.

**7**

## Determining the Type of Objects

Built into the Java programming language is an operator, **instanceof**, that you can use to ask if an object is an instance of a particular class or any of its subclasses. This operator is useful in situations such as the following: You are writing a method that receives an object reference, of a type such as **BankAccount**. The superclass **BankAccount** may be extended by the classes **CheckingAccount** and **SavingsAccount**. If the method must handle the different kinds of **BankAccount** subclasses differently, you can use the **instanceof** operator.

*Syntax*

*object_reference* **instanceof** *class_name*
*object_reference* **instanceof** *interface_name*

*Dissection*

➤ The operator **instanceof** returns a boolean value. The result is **true** if the object on the left of the operator is an instance of the class or a subclass of the class on the right of the operator. The result is **false** otherwise.

➤ You can also use **instanceof** to ask whether the class of the object implements a particular interface. For example, you may want to know if an object is **Cloneable**.

➤ The **instanceof** operator does not work for the primitive types. The leftmost argument must be an object reference. If the value of the object reference is **null**, **instanceof** returns **false**, regardless of the type of the object reference.

> ➤ If the object is an instance of a class that extends the class or implements the interfaces specified by the rightmost argument, the value returned by **instanceof** is **true**.

---

*Code Example*

```
if ( account instanceof CheckingAccount ) {
    // process a checking account
}
else {
    // process all other account types
}
```

---

*Code Dissection*

If the account object is a `CheckingAccount`, it must also be a `BankAccount`. The operator is most useful when you know the supertype, or superclass, of an object but you want to determine which subclass the object instantiates.

---

## Accessing Information about Classes at Run Time

For every class and every instance of a class that a program uses, the JVM creates an object with the type **Class**. This object contains information about the class, and is itself an instance of a class called **Class**. The Java platform creates the **Class** object automatically and stores in it several facts about the class, so that you can access the information at run time.

You can call a method to get the **Class** object for a class or an instance of a class.

---

*Class*

```
java.lang.Object
```

---

*Purpose*

The Object **Class** defines the methods that are available in all objects of reference types.

---

*Methods*

> ➤ **Class getClass()**
> The **getClass** method returns an object reference for a **Class** object.

You do not create **Class** objects, and no constructor for the class **Class** is available. Instead, use one of the following methods to access the **Class** object for a class or an object:

➤ Use the **Object.getClass** method for any object. All objects of reference type inherit this method. It is **public**, so you can always use it. Also the method is final so that you cannot override it. For example, the following statement gets the class for an object called `account`:

```
Class classAcc = account.getClass();
```

➤ If you know the name of a class or interface, you can use a class variable that the Java programming language adds to every class automatically. The name of the class variable is **class**, and it contains a reference to the corresponding **Class** object. For example, the following statement assigns an object reference for the **Class** object of the `BankAccount` class to `classBankAcc`:

```
Class classBankAcc = BankAccount.class;
```

➤ If you know the full name of the class or interface, call the **class** method **Class.forName**, passing the fully qualified name of the class as a **String** argument. For example, the following statement assigns an object reference for the **Class** object of the `BankAccount` class to `classBankAcc`, if the `BankAccount` class is in the subpackage `Banking` of the package `Financial`:

```
Class classBankAcc =
    Class.forName( "Financial.Banking.BankAccount" );
```

If the named class is not loaded into the JVM, calling this method forces the JVM to load the class. The next sample program uses this method.

 The field **class** was added after the original version of the Java platform, to simplify the process of accessing the **Class** object when the class name is known. This addition is one of many changes to enhance RTTI support in version 1.1 of the Java platform.
Support for RTTI changed very little between version 1.1 of the JDK and the Java 2 platform. One change of note in Java 2 is the introduction of an overloaded **Class.forName** method with three arguments.

---

**Mini Quiz 7-3**

This definition of the **class** field is

```
public static final Class class;
```

Why is it public, static, and final?

After you have a reference to a **Class** object, you can send messages to it to ask questions about the class that the object describes.

---

*Class*

`java.lang.Class`

---

*Purpose*

The **Class** class provides run-time information about Java classes.

---

*Methods*

➤ **Class forName( String** *classname***)**
  **Class forName( String** *classname***, boolean** *initialize***, ClassLoader** *loader***)**
  The **forName** method returns the **Class** object for the given class name. If you use the form with three arguments and set the boolean argument to **false**, the class is not initialized. Otherwise the JVM performs initialization. You can also specify which loader to use by providing an object of type **java.lang.ClassLoader** as the third argument. By default the JVM uses the bootstrap loader but you can provide a non-standard class loader to extend the way the JVM locates classes or to add security checks. You can specify a different **null** or **this.getClass().getClassLoader()** to use the default loader.

➤ **ClassLoader getClassLoader()**
  All **Class** objects contain a reference to their loader. The returned object is of type **java.lang.ClassLoader** and represents the loader that loaded the class or interface into the JVM.

➤ **String getName()**
  The **getName** method returns the fully qualified name of the class, interface, array, or primitive type.

➤ **Class getSuperclass()**
  The **getSuperclass** method returns a reference to the **Class** object for the superclass of the class. If called for an instance of **Object** or a type that is not a direct or indirect subclass of **Object**, the method returns **null**.

➤ **boolean isArray()**
  The **isArray** method returns **true** if the **Class** object represents an array type, and **false** otherwise.

➤ **boolean isInstance( Object** *object* **)**
  The **isInstance** method returns **true** if the specified object can cast to the type described by the **Class** object, and **false** otherwise. If the argument has the value **null**, this method returns **false**, regardless of the type of the argument.

➤ **boolean isInterface()**

The **isInterface** method returns **true** if the **Class** object represents an interface, and **false** otherwise.

➤ **Object newInstance()**

The **newInstance** method creates a new instance of the class and returns an object reference to the new object. You should cast the reference from type **Object** to the actual class of the object. If this method is used with the **Class** object of an interface or an abstract class, an **InstantiationException** is thrown. The noargument constructor of the class is called to create the new instance. If such a constructor does not exist, the program terminates with a **NoSuchMethod** run-time error.

7

---

**Mini Quiz 7-4**

- Under what circumstances can a class not have a no-argument constructor?
- Of the methods listed in the description of the **Class** class, only **forName** is a class method. Why is **forName** not an instance method like the others?

---

Here is a sample program that exercises the **instanceof** operator and the **Class** class:

```
package examples.rtti;
/** A class used to demonstrate RTTI concepts
  */
public class CreateByName {
  /** Test method for the class
    * @param args names of classes to be
    *            instantiated
    */
  public static void ( String[] args ) {
      for ( int i = 0; i < args.length; i++ ) {
          try {
              Class x = Class.forName( args[i] );
              Object y;
              try {
                  if ( x.isInterface() ) {
                      System.out.println( "The class " +
                          x.getName() + " is an interface "
                          + "and can't be instantiated." );
                  } else {
                      y = x.newInstance();
                      if ( y instanceof java.awt.Component ) {
                          System.out.println( "The GUI "
                              + "component class "
                              + x.getName() + " was specified." );
```

```
                    } else {
                        System.out.println( "The non-GUI "
                            + "component class "
                            + x.getName() + " was specified." );
                    }
                }
                } catch( InstantiationException ix ) {
                    ix.printStackTrace();
                } catch( IllegalAccessException iax ) {
                    iax.printStackTrace();
                } // end inner try
                } catch( ClassNotFoundException cnfx ) {
                System.err.println( "Sorry, the class "
                + args[i] + " could not be found." );
            } // end outer try
        } // end for
    } // end
} // end CreateByName
```

Suppose that you run this program with the following command on one line:

```
java examples.rtti.CreateByName java.lang.String
    java.awt.Button java.lang.Gazoom
    java.lang.Cloneable
```

The output is

```
The non-GUI component class java.lang.String was specified.
The GUI component class java.awt.Button was specified.
Sorry, the class java.lang.Gazoom could not be found.
The class java.lang.Cloneable is an interface and can't
be instantiated.
```

The **main** method receives the names as arguments. It obtains the **Class** object for each name supplied. The **main** method then tests whether the name represents an interface or a class. If it is an interface, **main** prints a message. Otherwise, **main** instantiates the class and then determines whether the object is a **Component**. The class **Component** is defined in the **java.awt** package, and **Button** is a subclass of **Component**. In all cases, **main** prints appropriate messages.

The use of **java.awt.Component** here is incidental. Any class would have served this purpose. The relevant part of this code is the nested try blocks and the catch clauses. When run with the input suggested above, the only exception thrown and caught is a **ClassNotFoundException**.

> ### Mini Quiz 7-5
>
> Which of the methods called by `examples.rtti.CreateByName.main` can throw the exceptions of the following types?
>
> - **InstantiationException**
> - **IllegalAccessException**
> - **ClassNotFoundException**

# CASTING BETWEEN TYPES

Whenever you cast between types, the operation may not be safe. In this context, **safe** means that no information can be lost or corrupted as a result of the cast. The JVM ensures that only safe casts are performed. For example, casting from a type with a narrower range of values to a type with a wider range of values, such as from a **float** to a **double** or from a subclass to its superclass class, is always safe. An unsafe cast can be from a wider type to a narrower type or between classes that are not a direct or indirect subclass and superclass of each other. For example, casting from **long** to **short** or from **String** to **Exception** is unsafe.

In the case of primitive types, the compiler allows explicit casting as a way for you to indicate that you know a particular cast may not be safe and are aware of the potential problems. For example, you can convert from **double** to a **float** if you cast explicitly. Even explicit casting has limits. For example, you cannot cast a **boolean** to an **int**.

For the reference types, deciding what is safe is not so easy. The compiler can detect casts between types that are not a subclass and superclass of each other, and some unsafe casts from superclass to subclass. When the compiler detects a cast that is definitely unsafe, it outputs an error message. When the compiler cannot tell whether a cast between classes is safe, it assumes the code is correct and leaves the JVM with the job of checking the cast at run time.

Therefore, some unsafe casts can be attempted at run time. When this happens, the JVM throws a **ClassCastException**. This exception can occur only in casts between subtypes and supertypes, because the compiler always detects other casts as errors.

The class **ClassCastException** extends **RunTimeException**. The reason is that casting exceptions are unpredictable. They can happen anywhere. If it were an **Exception**, you would have to list **ClassCastException** in the throws clause of every method that casts classes. You can still catch this exception, as the next sample program does.

> **Mini Quiz 7-6**
>
> A **RunTimeException** object is an **Exception** object. Why is it not necessary to list **ClassCastException** in the **throws** clause of a method that can throw it but that does not catch it?

In this sample program, the abstract class `Animal` is superclass to the classes `Reptile` and `Mammal`:

```
package examples.rtti;
/** Classes to demonstrate a run-time cast error
  */
public class BadCast {
   /** Test method for the class
    * @param args not used
    */
   public static void ( String[] args ) {
      Mammal horse = new Mammal( "horse" );
      Reptile snake = new Reptile( "snake" );
      Mammal mouse = new Mammal( "mouse" );
      horse.categorize();
      snake.categorize();
      mouse.categorize();
   }
}
/** A generic animal class
  */
class Animal {
   protected String name;

   public Animal( String name ) {
      this.name = name;
   }
   public void categorize() {
      try {
         if ( ( (Mammal) this ).isRodent() ) {
            System.out.println( "A " + name
                              + " is a rodent." );
         } else {
            System.out.println( "A " + name
                              + " is not a rodent." );

         }
      }
      catch ( ClassCastException ccx )  {
         ccx.printStackTrace();
      }
      try {
         int legs = ( (Reptile) this ).numLegs();
         System.out.println( "A " + name + " has "
                           + legs + " legs." );
```

```
            } catch ( ClassCastException ccx )  {
                ccx.printStackTrace();
            }
        }
    }
    /** The class representing all mammals
     */
    class Mammal extends Animal {
        private static String[] rodents
            = { "rat", "rabbit", "mouse", "beaver" };
        public Mammal( String name ) {
            super( name );
        }
        public boolean isRodent() {
            for ( int i = 0; i < rodents.length; i++ ) {
                if ( name.equals( rodents[i] ) ) {
                    return true;
                }
            }
            return false;
        }
    }
    /** The class representing all reptiles
     */
    class Reptile extends Animal {
        public Reptile( String name ) {
            super( name );
        }
        public int numLegs() {
            if ( name.equals( "snake" ) ) {
                return 0;
            } else {
                return 4;
            }
        }
    }
}
```

The output is

```
A horse is not a rodent.
java.lang.ClassCastException: examples.rtti.Mammal
        at examples.rtti.Animal.categorize
        ( BadCast.java:42 )
        at examples.rtti.BadCast.main
        ( BadCast.java:13 )
java.lang.ClassCastException: examples.rtti.Reptile
        at examples.rtti.Animal.categorize
        (BadCast.java:30)
        at examples.rtti.BadCast.main
        ( BadCast.java:14 )
A snake has 0 legs.
```

7

```
A mouse is a rodent.
java.lang.ClassCastException: examples.rtti.Mammal
        at examples.rtti.Animal.categorize
        ( BadCast.java:42 )
        at examples.rtti.BadCast.main
        ( BadCast.java:15 )
```

This program creates objects to represent different animals, each of which can be a `Mammal` or a `Reptile`. Both `Mammal` and `Reptile` classes extend the class `Animal`. The method `Animal.categorize` can receive any kind of animal as an argument. It casts the argument to a `Mammal` to call the `Mammal.isRodent` method and to a `Reptile` to call the `Reptile.numLegs` method. However, at run time, the `Mammal` objects `horse` and `mouse` cannot be safely cast to `Reptile` objects, and the `Reptile` object `snake` cannot be safely cast to a `Mammal`. When these casts are attempted, the JVM throws the exception **ClassCastException**.

# USING THE REFLECTION API

Sometimes you need to know much more about a type than the information provided by the **Class** class. For this purpose, you can use the classes in the package **java.lang.reflect**, otherwise known as the **Reflection API**. This set of classes increases the power and usefulness of the **Class** class.

The Reflection API supports an activity called **introspection**, which essentially asks a class to describe itself. JavaBeans technology depends on introspection. In Chapter 15, you learn that JavaBeans are classes that conform to a rigid coding standard, so that they can be used as input for JavaBeans-based development tools. The tools use introspection to analyze the JavaBeans, and then give the developers ways, often through graphical interfaces, of building programs quickly from the JavaBeans.

The Reflection API became available in version 1.1 of the Java platform. The **Class** class, as defined in the original Java platform, proved to be very useful. Nevertheless, the **java.lang.reflect** package was added to satisfy requests that the **Class** class be extended.

One of the most important advances in Java technology since the first release of the Java platform is the formulation of a standard for JavaBeans. Many of the changes introduced in version 1.1 converted the core classes into JavaBeans. One very important use of the Reflection API is to support JavaBeans-based tools.

The Reflection API gives an object the ability to reflect upon itself and discover its contents. The package **java.lang.reflect** defines a number of classes that together give a complete description of an object. Three classes represent the building blocks of classes: **Constructor**, **Method**, and **Field**. The most commonly used methods of these classes are listed.

*Class*

**java.lang.reflect.Constructor**

*Purpose*

Each instance of the **Constructor** class provides information about one constructor of a class, and provides a way for the calling program to create an object using the constructor.

*Methods*

➤ **Class[] getParameterTypes()**
The **getParameterTypes** method returns an array of **Class** objects for the arguments of the constructor. Each element of the array is an object reference for the **Class** object of one argument. The order of the elements reflects the order that the arguments are listed in the definition of the constructor.

➤ **Object newInstance( Object[]** *args* **)**
The **newInstance** method creates an instance of the class and returns an object reference for the new object. The elements in the array of type object **Object** are passed as arguments to the constructor.

*Class*

**java.lang.reflect.Method**

*Purpose*

Each instance of the **Method** class provides information about one method of a class, and provides a way for the calling program to call the method. The method may be a class method or an instance method, and may be abstract.

*Methods*

➤ **Class[] getParameterTypes()**
The **getParameterTypes** method returns an array of **Class** objects for the arguments of the method. Each element of the array is an object reference for the **Class** object of one argument. The order of the elements reflects the order that the arguments are listed in the definition of the method.

➤ **Class getReturnType()**
The **getReturnType** method returns an object reference for the **Class** object of the return type of the method.

➤ **Object invoke( Object** *object*, **Object[]** *args* **)**
The **invoke** method invokes the method with the object specified in the first argument. For a class method, the first argument has the value **null**. The elements in the array of type **Object** are passed as arguments to the method.

---

*Class*

**java.lang.reflect.Field**

---

*Purpose*

Each instance of the **Field** class provides information about one field of a class, and provides the calling program a way to get and set the value of the field. The field may be a class variable or an instance variable.

---

*Methods*

➤ **Class getType()**

➤ The **getType** method returns an object reference for the **Class** object of the field.

➤ **Object get( Object** *object* **)**
The **get** method returns the value of the field for the specified object. This class has methods to return the value of a field as values of the primitive types.

➤ **void set( Object** *object*, **Object** *value* **)**
The **set** method sets the value of the field for the specified object to the specified value.

---

The type of most arguments and of many return values of the methods in the Reflection API classes is **Object**. Therefore, you can actually pass any type of object, and any type may be returned. But what about the primitive types? The Reflection API classes use the wrapper classes for the primitive types. Some of the methods in these classes, such as **Field.getType** and **Method.getReturnType**, return an object reference for a **Class** object. Use the methods in the **Class** class with these object references to get more information about the returned objects.

The classes **Constructor**, **Method**, and **Field** implement an interface called **Member**. Therefore, all three classes provide the methods defined in **Member**.

---

*Interface*

**java.lang.reflect.Member**

---

*Purpose*

The class that implements this interface provides identifying information about a member of a class.

---

*Methods*

➤ **Class getDeclaringClass()**

➤ The **getDeclaringClass** method returns an object reference for the **Class** object of the class in which the member is defined.

➤ **String getName()**
The **getName** method returns the name of the member as a **String**.

➤ **int getModifiers()**
The **getModifiers** method returns the Java programming language's access specifiers and qualifiers that apply to the member. The return value is encoded in an **int**. Use the **Modifier** class to decode the **int** value.

Two additional classes complete the suite of Reflection API classes: **Array** and **Modifier**.

**7**

*Class*

**java.lang.reflect.Array**

*Purpose*

The **Array** class provides methods to manipulate a **Field** object as an array. The **Field** class only has methods for getting and setting individual values. Use this class with the **Field** class when the field is an array. To determine whether a **Field** object is an array, call the **Class.isArray** method and pass the value returned by **Field.getType**.

*Methods*

➤ **Object get( Object** *object*, **int** *position* **)**
The **get** method returns an object reference for the element at the specified position in the array. The **Array** class has methods that return the value of individual elements as values of the primitive types.

➤ **void set( Object** *object*, **int** *position* **)**
The **set** method sets the value of the element at the specified position to the value of the first argument.

➤ **int getLength()**
The **getLength** method returns the number of elements in the array.

➤ **Object newInstance( Class** *type*, **int** *length* **)**
The **newInstance** method creates a new array to hold the specified number of elements of the specified type, and returns an object reference for the new array.

➤ **Object newInstance( Class** *type*, **int[]** *dimensions* **)**
The **newInstance** method creates a new multidimensional array to hold the specified number of elements of the specified type, and returns an object reference for the new array.

---

*Class*

**java.lang.reflect.Modifier**

---

*Purpose*

The **Modifier** class contains a number of constants that represent the access specifiers and qualifiers that can be applied to members. It also provides class methods that return **true** if a member has a certain qualifier and **false** otherwise. For example, the method **isStatic( int** *value* **)** returns true only when called for a static member. The constant **STATIC** is an **int** representing the modifier **static**. Call the method **Member.getModifiers** to get the value to pass to the methods in this class.

---

> **Mini Quiz 7-7**
>
> There are 11 constants and 13 methods in the class **Modifier**, including **STATIC** and **isStatic**. The two extra methods are the constructor and **toString**. Can you guess the names of the other 10 fields and methods?

How can you access the **Class** object for a primitive type when you cannot invoke a method such as **getClass** for a primitive type? Each wrapper class for a primitive type has a field called **TYPE** that is a reference to the **Class** object for its corresponding primitive type. Just like the field **class** of all reference types, the field **TYPE** of wrapper classes is a public, static, and final field. For example, **Integer.TYPE** is a reference to the **Class** object for **int**. Be careful not to confuse **Integer.TYPE** with **Integer.class**. The first refers to the **Class** object for primitive type **int**, and the second refers to the **Class** object for the wrapper class **Integer**.

> **Mini Quiz 7-8**
>
> Why is the name of the field **TYPE**, as in **Integer.TYPE**, in uppercase, but the name of the field **class**, as in **Integer.class**, in lowercase?

What about methods that do not return a value, and have return type **void**? The package **java.lang** contains a wrapper class named **Void** for the primitive type **void**.

To provide run-time type information about **void**, the class **java.lang.Void** was added to the core classes at the same time as the Reflection API. The purpose of **Void** was to contain the **Void.TYPE** field.

Here is sample program that uses the Reflection API to make a list of the methods in the **String** class:

```
package examples.rtti;
import java.lang.reflect.*;
/** A class used to demonstrate the use of the
  * Reflection API
  */
public class ListStringMethods {
   /** Test method for the class
     * @param args not used
     * @exception ClassNotFoundException
     *                Thrown if the class being
     *                investigated isn't found
     */
   public static void ( String[] args )
       throws ClassNotFoundException {
      Method[] ma
         = String.class.getMethods();
      for ( int i = 0; i < ma.length; i++ ) {
         System.out.println( ma[i] );
      }
   }
}
```

The output is a complete list of the methods in the **String** class, and too long to include here. The first three lines are as follows:

```
public static java lang.String
     java.lang.String.copyValueOf(char[])
public static java.lang.String
     java.lang.String.copyValueOf(char[],int,int)
public static java.lang.String
     java.lang.String.valueOf(char)
```

In the class `ListStringMethods`, the **main** method declares an array of **Method** objects, ma, which is assigned the object reference obtained by calling the method **String.class.getMethods**. This one method call acquires a lot of information: Every method in the **String** class is described in an element of the returned array. The **Method** class overrides the **Object.toString** method so you can easily print out all the information about the method, including its access specifier.

# Calling Methods with the Reflection API

You can do more with the Reflection API than receive a great deal of useful information about a class. Now you have two ways to execute a method or a constructor:

➤ Call the method by name or create an object with the **new** keyword in the usual way. This is the obvious approach to take when you know the name of the method or type of the object when you are entering source code.

➤ Use a **Method** object or a **Constructor** object. This approach works when you must use the Reflection API to discover what methods are available or to determine the type of an object.

To call a method with the Reflection API, use the following instance method of the **Method** class:

**Object invoke( Object object, Object[] args )**

In the first argument of **invoke**, pass an object reference for the object on which the called method is to run, or specify **null** for class methods. Create an array of type **Object** for the arguments of the method and insert an object reference for the first argument of the method into the first element of the array, for the second argument into the second element, and so on. If an argument has a primitive type, wrap it with the appropriate wrapper class and insert the object reference for the wrapper instance in the array. Specify the array as the second argument of **invoke**.

If the called method returns a value, you retrieve the value through the object reference returned by **invoke**. If the return type is a primitive type, **invoke** returns an instance of the appropriate wrapper class.

If the called method does not return a value, **invoke** returns an object reference of type **Void**.

To create an instance of a class with the Reflection API, use the following instance method of the **Constructor** class:

**Object newInstance( Object[] args )**

The only argument of **newInstance** is an array that contains the arguments for the constructor. Build up this array in exactly the same way as you build up the array argument of **Method.invoke**. The **newInstance** method returns a reference to the newly created object, which you can cast to the appropriate class type.

The method **Constructor.newInstance** has one great advantage over the method **Class.newInstance:** You can pass arguments to the constructor.

In the original Java platform, the only way to call a constructor explicitly was to use the method **Class.newInstance**. The Reflection API introduced the method **Constructor.newInstance** with version 1.1. The method **Class.newInstance** still works, but only if the class has a constructor with no arguments.

Here is an example program that creates instances of classes using **Constructor.newInstance**:

```java
package examples.rtti;
import java.lang.reflect.*;
/** A class defined to demonstrate the Reflection API
   */
class FirstType {
   private String name;
   public FirstType( String name ) {
      this.name = name;
   }
   public FirstType() {
      this.name = "DefaultFirst";
   }
   public String toString() {
      return ( "A FirstType object named " + name );
   }
}
/** A class defined to demonstrate the Reflection API
   */
class SecondType {
   // explicit constructor needed for Reflection API
   public SecondType() {
      // intentionally left empty
   }
   public String toString() {
      return ( "A SecondType object" );
   }
}
/** A class used to show how the Reflection API can
   * be used to construct objects
   */
public class Construct {
   /** Test method for the class
      * @param args the class name to be constructed
      *       followed by any constructor arguments
      */
   public static void main( String [] args ) {
      if ( args.length == 0 ) {
         System.out.println( " usage: Construct"
                                 + " classname"
                                 + " [ctor_arg]" );
         return;
      }
      // get the class object for the specified class
```

```java
Class classObj = null;
try {
   classObj = Class.forName( args[0] );
} catch ( ClassNotFoundException ex ) {
   System.err.println( " Unknown class "
                           + args[0] );
   return;
}
// get constructor for class
Constructor ctor = null;
Class[] ctorTypes = new Class[args.length -1];
for ( int i = 0; i < args.length-1; i ++ ) {
   ctorTypes[i] = java.lang.String.class;
}
try {
   ctor = classObj.getConstructor( ctorTypes );
} catch ( NoSuchMethodException ex ) {
   String msg = "No constructor: ";
   msg += classObj.getName() + "(";
   for ( int i = 0; i < ctorTypes.length; i++ ) {
      msg += ctorTypes[i].getName();
      if ( i < ctorTypes.length-1 ) {
         msg += ", ";
      }
   }
   msg += " )";
   System.err.println( msg );
   return;
}
// build up the array of arguments
// for the constructor from the
// commmand-line arguments
String[] ctorArgs
   = new String[ctorTypes.length];
System.arraycopy( args, 1, ctorArgs, 0,
                  ctorTypes.length );
// call the constructor
Object obj = null;
try {
   obj = ctor.newInstance( ctorArgs );
} catch ( Exception ex ) {
   ex.printStackTrace();
   return;
}
// print the object created
System.out.println( obj );
   }
}
```

This program tried to create instances of either `FirstType` and `SecondType`, depending on which class name is specified in the argument list `Construct.main`. It may be useful to look at the code in more detail.

```
class FirstType {
   private String name;
   public FirstType( String name ) {
      this.name = name;
   }
   public FirstType() {
      this.name = "DefaultFirst";
   }
   public String toString() {
      return ( "A FirstType object named " + name );
   }
}
```

The class `FirstType` has two constructors: one with no arguments, and one that takes a single **String** as an argument. This simple class does no more than store either the **String** supplied to the constructor or a default **String** in the private field, `name`, and provide a **toString** method so that the contents of the class can be printed.

```
class SecondType {
   public SecondType() {}
   public String toString() {
      return ( "A SecondType object" );
   }
}
```

The class `SecondType` has only a no-argument constructor and a **toString** method. If a constructor is not explicitly supplied, the compiler can supply one and this program compiles successfully. However, the Reflection API does not recognize the compiler-supplied constructor and one must be supplied here.

```
public class Construct {
   public static void main( String [] args ) {
      if ( args.length == 0 ) {
         System.out.println( " usage: Construct"
                           + " classname"
                           + "[ctor_arg]" );
         return;
      }
```

The work happens in the **main** method of the test class `Construct`. This program expects the name of a class and the arguments of a constructor for that class to be supplied as command-line arguments. For simplicity, the program assumes the type of all arguments for the constructor is **String**. If no arguments are supplied, the program stops with a message.

```
Class classObj = null;
try {
    classObj = Class.forName( args[0] );
}
catch ( ClassNotFoundException ex ) {
    System.err.println( " Unknown class "
                              + args[0] );
    return;
}
```

The first step is to determine what kind of class the user wants to instantiate. The **Class.forName** method loads the specified class into the JVM, and returns the **class** object for that class. If no such class can be found, the JVM throws a **ClassNotFoundException**. Because **forName** expects the full class name, the exception is thrown if the user enters just **FirstType**, **SecondType**, or any other unknown class name. For the program to work with the example classes supplied in this file, the user must enter **examples.rtti.FirstType** or **examples.rti.SecondType**.

The exception handler provided by this catch clause for the **ClassNotFoundException** prints an appropriate message and then terminates the program.

```
Constructor ctor = null;
Class[] ctorTypes = new Class[args.length-1];
for ( int i = 0; i < args.length-1; i++ ) {
    ctorTypes[i] = java.lang.String.class;
}
```

Having determined that the class exists, the program prepares to call a constructor to instantiate the class. It declares a **Constructor** object, ctor, but needs to look at the argument list before identifying a specific constructor. Therefore, the next step is to build an array of type **Class**, ctorTypes, in which each element encapsulates the type of one argument for the constructor. Here, all arguments have type **String** and the number of arguments is determined by the command-line arguments entered by the user.

```
try {
    ctor = classObj.getConstructor( ctorTypes );
}
catch ( NoSuchMethodException ex ) {
    String msg = "No constructor: ";
    msg += classObj.getName() + "(";
    for ( int i = 0; i < ctorTypes.length; i++ ) {
        msg += ctorTypes[i].getName();
        if ( i < ctorTypes.length-1 ) {
            msg += ", ";
        }
```

```
      }
      msg += " )";
      System.err.println( msg );
      return;
   }
```

The purpose of this try block is to get a **Constructor** object for the required constructor. If such a constructor is available, the **getConstructor** method returns the **Constructor** object to `ctor`. Otherwise, the **getConstructor** method throws a **NoSuchMethodException**. The catch clause handles this exception by printing a message and terminating the program. In this case, the catch clause builds the message to contain the name of the constructor and the argument list. Notice that the method **getName** is used to return a printable representation of the type of each argument.

```
      String[] ctorArgs = new String[ctorTypes.length];
      System.arraycopy( args, 1, ctorArgs, 0,
                        ctorTypes.length );
```

Having determined that the required constructor is available, the program sets up the array of objects to pass to the constructor, `ctorArgs`. In this case, every element in the array is a **String**.

```
      Object obj = null;
      try {
         obj = ctor.newInstance( ctorArgs );
      }
      catch ( Exception ex ) {
         ex.printStackTrace();
         return;
      }
```

The variable `obj` is an object reference that will be assigned to the new object after it is created. The call of **newInstance** that creates the object is enclosed in another try block in case something unanticipated goes wrong while the program instantiates the object. This catch clause catches any checked exception, prints the call stack at the point where the exception occurs, and terminates the program.

```
   System.out.println( obj );
   }
}
```

Ultimately, the program may create a new object. The program announces this success by printing the object.

The output for this program depends on the command-line input. Here are some trial runs. (Some of the messages are split because they are too long to fit on one line in this book.)

➤ Command-line arguments:

```
examples.rtti.FirstType Hello
```

➤ Output:

```
A FirstType object named Hello
```

➤ Command-line arguments:

```
examples.rtti.FirstType one two three
```

➤ Output:

```
No constructor: examples.rtti.FirstType(
                         java.lang.String,
                         java.lang.String,
                         java.lang.String )
```

➤ Command-line arguments:

```
examples.rtti.SecondType
```

➤ Output:

```
A SecondType object
```

➤ Command-line arguments:

```
SecondType
```

➤ Output:

```
Unknown class SecondType
```

➤ Command-line arguments:

```
java.lang.String "Hello World"
```

➤ Output:

```
Hello World
```

## SUMMARY

Copying objects is not as simple as it sounds. For the primitive types, you can copy with the assignment operator. For the reference types, the assignment operator alters the value of the object reference so that it points to a different object, but does not make a copy.

The **Object** class defines a method that you should use to copy objects:

**Object clone()**

All objects of reference type, including arrays, can use this method. By default it performs a **shallow copy**. In other words, it copies the values of all fields that are contained in the object being cloned, regardless of whether the fields are primitive types or object references. Usually a **deep copy** is preferable. A deep copy duplicates contained objects, creates new object references for the duplicates, and inserts the new object references into the copy of the containing object.

If your classes contain fields that have reference types, you should override the **clone** method to perform a deep copy, with the proviso that a shallow copy is adequate for immutable, contained objects. You should start the implementation of **clone** with the statement **super.clone()** so that every class in the hierarchy can correctly copy the fields it defines.

To be cloneable, an object must be an instance of a class that implements the interface **Cloneable**. This is a marker interface that indicates whether a class allows cloning. The **clone** method throws an exception when called for an instance of a class that is not cloneable.

You can define classes that are cloneable or not cloneable. You can force subclasses of your classes to be cloneable, or prevent them from being cloneable. You have great flexibility because you can do the following in different combinations:

- Override or inherit **clone**

- Optionally define your class to implement **Cloneable**

- Optionally throw the exception **CloneNotSupportedException**

- Optionally catch the exception **CloneNotSupportedException**

- List or omit the exception in the throws clause of the **clone** method

Run-time type information (RTTI) is particularly important in the Java platform. Your class may be using classes from other sources, such as networks, and you sometimes cannot know the type of objects at development time. RTTI is also useful with dynamic binding.

The simplest form of RTTI involves using the **instanceof** operator:

*object_reference* **instanceof** *class_or_ interface_name*

This operator returns **true** if the first operand is an instance of the class, a subclass of the class, or a class that implements the interface specified in the second operand. It returns **false** otherwise.

For every class known to the JVM, an object of type **Class** exists. Every instance of a class has a field named **class** that is an object reference to a **Class** object. The **Class** class provides several methods that are described in this chapter. You can call these methods to find out, for example, whether a class is an interface, what its name is, and what the name of its superclass is. Three ways to access the **Class** object exist:

- Use the field **class**

- Call the following method of the **Class** class and supply the fully qualified class name as the argument:

  **Class forName( String** *class_name* **)**

- Call the following method of the **Object** class for an object:

  **Class getClass()**

Even the primitive types have **Class** objects; you access them by using the object reference **TYPE** that is a field of each wrapper class for the primitive types.

You also receive run-time type information when you are warned that you are trying to cast class types in an unsafe manner. The compiler rejects casts between classes that are not a direct or indirect superclass and subclass of each other. But some casts from superclass to subclass must be checked at run time, especially when dynamic binding is involved. The JVM throws a **ClassCastException** if you try performing an unsafe cast at run time.

For more extensive run-time type information, the Java platform provides the **Reflection API**. This API consists of five classes in the package **java.lang.reflect** (**Field**, **Method**, **Constructor**, **Array**, and **Modifier**) along with some other features such as the **Class** objects for the primitive types. The classes **Field**, **Method**, and **Constuctor** provide many methods that describe the building blocks of classes.

To find out what methods are available for an object at run time, call the following method of the **Class** class:

**Method[]getMethods()**

To call a method for which you do not know the name at compile time, use the following method of the **Method** class:

**Object invoke( Object** *object*, **Object[]** *args* **)**

You can create instances of classes three ways:

- Use the **new** operator in the usual fashion

- If you can use the no-argument constructor, call the following method of the **Class** class:

  **Object newInstance()**

■ To use any constructor, first get the **Constructor** object for the constructor by calling

**Constructor getConstructor( Class[]** *argtypes* **)**

of the **Class** class and then call the following method of the **Constructor** class:

**Object newInstance( Object[]** *args* **)**

---

## QUESTIONS

1. Which of the following methods are defined in the **Cloneable** interface? Select all that apply.

   a. **toString**

   b. **clone**

   c. **equals**

   d. **hashCode**

   e. **finalize**

2. Which of the following are references to objects of the class **Class**? Select all that apply.

   a. **Object.TYPE**

   b. **StringBuffer.class**

   c. **Long.TYPE**

   d. **Class.class**

   e. **Class.TYPE**

3. True or False: The **instanceof** operator returns **true** when the class of an object exactly matches the class specified.

4. Examine the following code:

```
public class Quiz7_4 {
   String s = "Good morning!";
   public Object clone()
           throws CloneNotSupportedException {
      Quiz7_4 result = ( Quiz7_4 ) super.clone();
      return result;
   }
   public static void main( String[] args )
         throws CloneNotSupportedException {
      Quiz7_4 x = new Quiz7_4();
      Quiz7_4 y = ( Quiz7_4 ) x.clone();
      System.out.println( y.s );
   }
}
```

7

Which of the following statements are true when the code is compiled and run? Select all that apply.

a. The compiler rejects the definition of the method `Quiz7_4.clone` because it returns a reference of type **Object**, not `Quiz7_4`.

b. Compilation is successful, but a **CloneNotSupportedException** is thrown when `Quiz7_4.main` executes.

c. Compilation is successful and the output is `Good morning!`

d. Compilation is successful, but the `Quiz7_4.clone` method does not give a correct result because the field `s` is not cloned.

5. Examine the following code:

```java
public class Quiz7_5 implements Cloneable {
    StringBuffer sb
        = new StringBuffer( "Good morning!" );
    public Object clone()
            throws CloneNotSupportedException {
        Quiz7_5 result = ( Quiz7_5 ) super.clone();
        result.sb = this.sb;
        return result;
    }
    public static void main( String[] args )
        throws CloneNotSupportedException {
        Quiz7_5 x = new Quiz7_5();
        Quiz7_5 y = ( Quiz7_5 ) x.clone();
        x.sb.append( " How are you today?" );
        System.out.println( y.sb );
    }
}
```

Which of the following statements are true when the code is compiled and run? Select all that apply.

a. The compiler rejects the definition of the method `Quiz7_5.clone` because it returns a reference of type **Object**, not `Quiz7_5`.

b. Compilation is successful, but a **CloneNotSupportedException** is thrown when `Quiz7_5.main` executes.

c. Compilation is successful and the output is `Good morning!`

d. Compilation is successful and the output is

   `Good morning! How are you today?`

e. The two `Quiz7_5` objects share the same **StringBuffer** object.

6. Examine the following code:

```
public class Quiz7_6 {
    public static void main( String[] args ) {
      Class c = Integer.TYPE;
      System.out.println( c.getName() );
   }
}
```

Which of the following statements are true when the code is compiled and run? Select all that apply.

  a. The compiler rejects **Class** as an unknown type because the following statement is missing: import java.lang.reflect.*;

  b. Compilation is successful and the output is Integer.

  c. Compilation is successful and the output is int.

  d. The compiler rejects the expression Integer.TYPE because it is missing parentheses.

7. Examine the following code:

```
class A { }
class B extends A { }
public class Quiz7_7 {
    public static void main( String[] args ) {
      A a = new A();
      System.out.println( a instanceof B );
   }
}
```

Which of the following statements are true when the code is compiled and run? Select all that apply.

  a. The compiler rejects the definitions of classes **A** and **B** because they are empty.

  b. Compilation is successful and the output is true.

  c. Compilation is successful and the output is false.

  d. The compiler rejects the following expression because the result of the **instanceof** operator cannot be printed:

  System.out.println( a instanceof B )

8. Whether you should implement the **Clone** method for a class that implements **Cloneable** depends on the types of the fields in the class. For which of the following types of instance variables should you consider implementing **clone**? Select all that apply.

   a. **Integer**

   b. **StringBuffer**

   c. **int**

   d. **String**

   e. **double[ ]**

9. Examine the following code:

```
public class Quiz7_9 {
    public static void main( String[] args ) {
        Integer i = new Integer( 6 );
        Long l = new Long( 10000000067L );
        Double d = new Double( 4.567 );
        Number n;
        n = d;
        d = i;
        l = (Long) i;
        System.out.println( l );
    }
}
```

   Which of the following statements are true when the code is compiled and run? Select all that apply.

   a. Compilation is successful and the output is 6

   b. The compiler rejects the expression: n = d

   c. The compiler rejects the expression: d = i

   d. The compiler rejects the expression: l = (Long) i

   e. Compilation is successful, but a **ClassCastException** is thrown when the program is run.

10. Which interface is implemented by all of the classes in the **java.lang.reflect** package that represent the contents of a class definition?

# EXERCISES

## Debugging

1. Correct all the errors in the following program.

```
package questions.c7;
public class Debug7_1 implements Cloneable {
   StringBuffer sb
      = new StringBuffer( "Sales Report for " );
   public Debug7_1 clone()
              throws CloneNotSupportedException {
      Debug7_1 result = super.clone();
      result.sb
         = new StringBuffer( this.sb.toString() );
      return result;
   }
   public static void main( String[] args )
              throws CloneNotSupportedException {
      Debug7_1 x = new Debug7_1();
      Debug7_1 y = x.clone();
      x.sb.append( "October" );
      System.out.println( y.sb );
   }
}
```

2. The output in the following program should be

```
Inventory count 300
```

Correct all the errors in the program:

```
package questions.c7;
class Debug7_2_Base {
   private int x;
   int getX() {
      return x;
   }
   public void setX( int newX ) {
      x = newX;
   }
}
public class Debug7_2 extends Debug7_2_Base
         implements Cloneable {
   StringBuffer sb
      = new StringBuffer( "Inventory count" );
   public Object clone()
              throws CloneNotSupportedException {
      Debug7_2 result = new Debug7_2();
      result.sb
         = new StringBuffer( this.sb.toString() );
      return result;
```

**7**

```
        }
        public static void main( String[] args )
              throws CloneNotSupportedException {
            Debug7_2 a = new Debug7_2();
            a.setX( 300 );
            Debug7_2 b = ( Debug7_2 ) a.clone();
            System.out.println( b.sb + " " + b.getX() );
        }
    }
```

3. Correct all the errors in the following program without making any changes to the **main** method:

```
    package questions.c7;
    class Debug7_3_Base {
        private StringBuffer name;
        public String getName() {
            return name.toString();
        }
        public void setName( String newName ) {
            name = new StringBuffer( newName );
        }
    }
    public class Debug7_3 extends Debug7_3_Base
                implements Cloneable {
        private double weight;
        double getWeight() {
            return weight;
        }
        public void setWeight( double newWeight ) {
            weight = newWeight;
        }
        public static void main( String[] args ) {
            Debug7_3 a = new Debug7_3();
            a.setWeight( 11.567 );
            a.setName( "Steel girders" );
            Debug7_3 b = ( Debug7_3 ) a.clone();
            System.out.println( b.getName() + " "
                                  + b.getWeight() );
        }
    }
```

4. Correct all the errors in the following program so that it takes a string from the command line, creates an instance of the class named in the string, and then outputs the class name without directly using the input string:

```
package questions.c7;
public class Debug7_4 {
    public static void main( String[] args ) {
        if ( args.length >= 1 ) {
            Object x = Class.newInstance( args[0] );
            System.out.println( x.getName );
        }
    }
}
```

5. The output for the following program is

```
Name: int is a primitive type.
```

Correct all the errors in the program:

```
package questions.c7;
public class Debug7_5 {
    public static void printClassInfo( Class c ) {
        System.out.print( "Name: " + c.getName() );
        if ( c.isPrimitive() ) {
            System.out.println( " is a primitive "
                                + "type." );
        } else {
            System.out.println( " is not a primitive
                                + "type." );
        }
    }
    public static void main( String[] args ) {
        int x = 1;
        printClassInfo( x.class );
    }
}
```

## Complete the Solution

1. Extract the file **questions\c7\Complete7_1.java** from the **question.jar** file on the CD-ROM. Complete the definition of the class `questions.c7.Complete7_1` by adding a **clone** method.

2. Extract the file **questions\c7\Complete7_2.java** from the **question.jar** file on the CD-ROM. Complete the definition of the class `questions.c7.Complete7_2` by adding a **clone** method.

3. Extract the file **questions\c7\Complete7_3.java** from the **question.jar** file on the CD-ROM. Complete the definition of the class `questions.c7.Complete7_3` by adding statements to the method `f` that use the **instanceof** operater to handle two specific subclasses of **Number**. If the parameter of `f` is an **Integer**, output the integer value divided by 2. If the parameter of `f` is a **Double**, output the double value divided by 2.5. Otherwise, do nothing.

4. Extract the file **questions\c7\Complete7_4.java** from the **question.jar** file on the CD-ROM. Complete the definition of the class `questions.c7.Complete7_4` by adding a try block and a catch clause for **ClassCastException** to method `f`. Write the exception handler to treat one specific subclass of **Number** differently from other **Number** subclasses. If the parameter of `f` is a **Long**, output the long value multiplied by 2. If the parameter of `f` is any other subclass of **Number**, output its value as a double multiplied by 3.

5. Extract the file **questions\c7\Complete7_5.java** from the **question.jar** file on the CD-ROM. Complete the program so that it takes a **string** as command line argument and prints a message if the class named in the string has a constructor without parameters.

## Discovery

1. Enhance the `Stack` class from the end of the previous chapter's exercises so that it is an array of **Object** objects, not integers. Then add a **clone** method to the new `ObjectStack` class that delegates the cloning of individual stack elements by calling the **clone** method of each element.

2. Create a class called `PropertyFinder` that has a method that analyzes the method input parameter of type **Object**. Using the Reflection API, the class will look for method pairs of the form void `setX( T )` and `T getX( )`, where `X` is some arbitrary string and `T` is a type. For every such pair that it finds, the class will write a message saying that the object has a property `X` of type `T`.

# INPUT AND OUTPUT

---

**In this chapter you will:**

➤ Perform stream input/output (I/O) with the core classes in the package **java.io**.

➤ Use the standard streams **System.in**, **System.out**, and **System.err**.

☕ Distinguish between byte-oriented and character-oriented streams.

☕ Write code that uses objects of the **File** class to navigate a file system.

☕ Select valid constructor arguments for **FilterInputStream** and **FilterOutputStream** subclasses from a list of classes in the **java.io** package.

☕ Write appropriate code to read, write, and update files using **FileInputStream**, **FileOutputStream**, and **RandomAccessFile** objects.

☕ Describe the permanent effects on the file system of constructing and using **FileInputStream**, **FileOutputStream**, and **RandomAccessFile** objects.

➤ Use object serialization.

---

## HOW THE JAVA PLATFORM SUPPORTS I/O

It is time to return to the matter of input and output, which is generally referred to as I/O. The first part of this chapter is about the package **java.io**, which supports console I/O, file I/O, I/O streams that are designed for bytes, and I/O streams that are designed for characters. The latter part of this chapter looks beyond the local workstation and expands the concept of input and output to making connections and transferring data between workstations on a network.

You can use all the features described in this chapter in applications, but applets are prohibited from some activities, as explained in Chapter 14. For example, an applet can perform file I/O on or establish connections with only the server system from which the applet originates. Default security mechanisms prevent applets from accessing files on the client workstation or connecting to other workstations on the network.

Not all forms of user interaction are considered I/O. For example, a very different mechanism manages graphical user interfaces (GUIs). Chapters 12 and 13 describe how to program a GUI. The **java.io** package supports data transfer between the program and the console, files, or network. The package does not provide facilities for drawing or displaying graphical components on the screen. Also, the I/O package does not support the mouse.

The first program in Chapter 2 gave a sneak preview of stream I/O, and most of the sample programs in this book use the stream I/O classes in **java.io**.

The importance of supporting I/O for characters that occupy more than one byte is increasing with the demand for software that is internationalized. Multibyte characters enable not only the North American and Western European character sets, but also the Middle Eastern, Asian, and other character sets. This chapter describes both byte-oriented and character-oriented I/O streams. Internally, the Java platform has only one type of character set, the 16-bit Unicode character set. The character streams support Unicode characters and other recognized character-encoding schemes. Byte-oriented streams are intended for handling noncharacter, or binary, information.

# Programming I/O

Most I/O in the Java platform operates through streams. In **stream** I/O, characters or bytes are read or written sequentially. For example, when a file is opened as a stream, all input or output starts at the beginning of the file and proceeds character by character or byte by byte to the end of the file. There is no inherent blocking into records or lines, and no direct access to any locations in the file other than the next byte or character position.

The core classes do not offer much formatting control for the output streams. If you are writing applets or applications for a graphical environment, you use a very different output mechanism, which is described in Chapters 12 and 13, to send your output on the screen. Therefore this limitation of the stream classes affects far fewer programs that it may at first seem. Console I/O is often used only for debugging or for quick and simple utilities. Console I/O on the Java platform is not very flexible. You may be disappointed if you want to set the width of fields or precision floating-point numbers when you write to the console or a formatted file.

When you program for the international market, you should format numbers, dates, times, and similar items according to the local customs of the users. The Java platform includes classes that help you internationalize your program. The package **java.text** gathers many of the classes and interfaces for handling local customs. "Internationalization" on the CD-ROM describes the programming techniques and core classes you can use to make your program international.

You can use the core class **DecimalFormat** in the package **java.text** to set patterns for formatting and parsing numbers. For example, you can specify grouping by thousands with commas as separators, set the minimum or maximum number of digits on either side of the decimal point, provide a different pattern for negative numbers, and specify how to represent percentages. Even if internationalization is not your goal, you may find that the classes in **java.text** can meet your number-formatting requirements.

Not all I/O in the Java platform is stream I/O. The package **java.io** includes the core class **RandomAccessFile,** which you can use to read and write arbitrary locations within a file without first having to read or write all the bytes or characters that precede that location. However, most I/O, including sequential file reading and writing, operates through streams.

The Java platform includes two dual hierarchies of classes that support streams: byte-oriented input and output, and character-oriented input and output. The byte-oriented streams are widely used, partly because they have been available since the original version of the Java platform and partly because they are adequate for the ASCII seven-bit character set used by English-language North American personal computers. The structure of the hierarchy of character-oriented stream classes mirrors that of the stream-oriented classes.

Object streams support object serialization and are the last set of streams described in this chapter.

The character-oriented streams and object streams became available in version 1.1 of the Java platform. The original version of the Java platform lacked support for I/O to character sets other than ASCII, and had no object serialization.

Version 1.1 of the Java platform also introduced the package **java.text** and full support for internationalization.

# BYTE-ORIENTED STREAM CLASSES

The hierarchies of the byte-oriented stream classes have a superclass for output and another superclass for input. All the classes in these hierarchies extend the input and output superclass directly or indirectly, and ultimately extend **Object**. Figure 8-1 shows the classes that support byte-oriented streams and how they are related. The shaded boxes represent abstract classes.

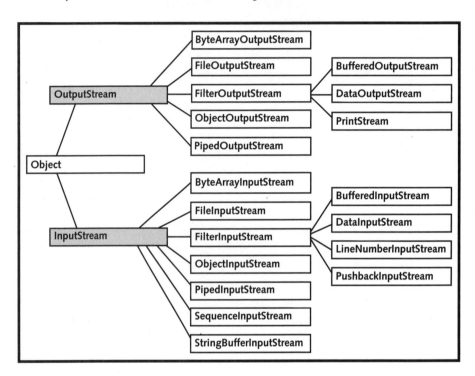

**Figure 8-1** Byte-oriented stream classes

The classes **java.io.InputStream** and **java.io.OutputStream** are the roots of a dual hierarchy that encapsulates most of byte-oriented I/O. The next sections of this chapter present highlights of the subclasses of **InputStream** and **OutputStream**.

## Predefined Stream Objects

All Java programs can use three stream objects that are defined in the **System** class of the **java.lang** package. These objects are **System.in**, **System.out**, and **System.err**.

---

*Class*

**java.lang.System**

---

*Purpose*

The **System** class provides the standard stream objects.

---

*Fields*

➤ **System.in**

The field **System.in** is a **java.io.BufferedInputStream** object. The field is often called the standard input stream. By default, this object encapsulates keyboard input. You can wrap a character-oriented stream around **System.in** to get buffered, character-oriented input from the console. This is desirable, because it gives the user the opportunity to backspace over errors, and relieves you of responsibility for processing every keystroke individually.

➤ **System.out**

The field **System.out** is a **java.io.PrintStream** object. The field is often called the standard output stream. By default, this object encapsulates output to a command-line window and is used for most command-line mode output. When you run a program with the **java** command, you can use features of your operating system to redirect the output to a file.

➤ **System.err**

The field **System.err** is a **java.io.PrintStream** object. It is often called the standard error stream. Output sent to **System.err** goes to a command line and can be mixed with output to **System.out**. The difference between **System.err** and **System.out** is that **System.err** is usually reserved for error messages, or log or trace information. Therefore, by directing **System.out** or **System.err** to a file, you can separate the desired program output from other messages.

---

**Mini Quiz 8-1**

**System.in**, **System.err**, and **System.out** are declared to be static, final, and public. What does this tell you about their use?

---

**print** and **println**, which are sets of overloaded methods of the **PrintStream** class, are particularly useful for console output. Most of the example programs in early chapters of this book use these methods. The difference between them is simply that **println** appends a line separator to its argument to produce a complete line of output. The **print** method does not add the line separator, so you can build up one line of output with several calls of **print**.

For example, examine the following lines:

```
for ( int i = 0; i < 10; i++ ) {
   System.out.print( '*' );
}
for ( int i = 0; i < 2; i++ ) {
   System.out.println( "one line" );
}
```

These lines produce the following output:

```
**********one line
one line
```

The methods **print** and **println** are overloaded to create versions specifically for the primitive types, for **char[]**, and for **String**. All other reference types use the version of **print** or **println** that takes an **Object** as input. This catch-all version essentially calls the **toString** method for the object and then outputs the resulting **String** object in the normal way. As a result, you can easily print textual representations of objects of any class that implements **toString**. Usually, when you anticipate that you will need to display a class in textual format, you implement **toString**. This conversion of data to text is a form of filtering. **PrintStream** is one of the filtered stream classes.

## Input and Output Methods

You perform most byte-oriented I/O operations by calling methods that are defined in the **InputStream** and **OutputStream** classes. The subclasses of **InputStream** and **OutputStream** add value by overriding and overloading these methods for specific circumstances.

---

*Class*

**java.io.InputStream**

---

*Purpose*

The **InputStream** class is the superclass of all byte-oriented input streams.

---

*Constructors*

➤ The constructor of this class, **InputStream()**, takes no arguments.

---

*Methods*

➤ **int available()**
The **available** method returns the number of bytes that can be read without blocking.

➤ **void close()**
The **close** method closes the input stream and frees the resources it was using.

➤ **void mark( int** *readlimit* **)**
The **mark** method is used to set a bookmark in the stream. You can return to the marked spot until the number of bytes specified in the argument have been read.

➤ **boolean markSupported()**
The **markSupported** method indicates whether the stream supports the setting of bookmarks.

➤ **int read()**
  **int read( byte[]** *buffer* **)**
  **int read( byte[]** *buffer*, **int** *offset*, **int** *length* **)**
The **read** method reads bytes from the input stream. To read one byte, supply no arguments and receive the data in the return value. To read bytes into an array, pass the array as a parameter. No more bytes are read than can be stored in the array, and the return value is the actual number of bytes read. You can also specify as an integer argument the first position in the array to fill, and, as a second integer argument, the maximum number of bytes to read.

➤ **void reset()**
The **reset** method repositions the stream to the bookmark.

➤ **long skip( long** *bytecount* **)**
The **skip** method reads but discards up to the number of bytes specified in the argument, and returns the actual number of bytes skipped.

*Class*

**java.io.OutputStream**

*Purpose*

The **OutputStream** class is the superclass of all byte-oriented output streams.

*Constructors*

➤ The constructor of this class, **OutputStream()**, takes no arguments.

---

*Methods*

➤ **void close()**
The **close** method closes the stream and frees the resources it was using.

➤ **void flush()**
The **flush** method forces any buffered bytes to be written.

➤ **void write( int** *b* **)**
**void write( byte[]** *bytebuffer* **)**
**void write( byte[]** *bytebuffer*, **int** *offset*, **int** *count* **)**
The **write** methods write either a single byte or an array of bytes. If you specify an array of bytes, you can optionally specify the first element in the array to write, and the number of bytes to write.

---

**Mini Quiz 8-2**

If you call the **write** method to output a single byte of data, why is the argument of type **int** instead of type **byte**?

## Filter Streams

A number of classes provide extra functionality in the sense that they add or override methods to preprocess output before actually writing the data, or post-process input after the data has been read. These are called filter streams. A set of classes that extend **FilterInputStream** or **FilterOutputStream** provides them.

The class **FilterInputStream** extends **InputStream**, and the class **FilterOutputStream** extends **OutputStream**. These abstract classes are designed to act as wrappers for the **InputStream** and **OutputStream** classes. To use a filter stream, you must already have an **InputStream** or an **OutputStream** object. When you create the filter stream object, specify an **InputStream** object or an **OutputStream** object as the argument of the constructor, as shown in Table 8-1.

**Table 8-1**   Byte-oriented filter streams

| Filter Streams | Description |
| --- | --- |
| **BufferedInputStream** and **BufferedOutputStream** | These classes provide buffering for input and output operations. Use these classes to increase efficiency. **System.in** is a **BufferedInputStream** object. |
| **DataInputStream** and **DataOutputStream** | These classes transmit data of specific types across a stream instead of treating a stream as a sequence of independent bytes. You can also call methods of these classes to read and write the binary representations of the primitive types. |
| **PushbackInputStream** | This class maintains a one-byte push-back buffer. With a push-back buffer, you can peek at the next byte in the input stream, and then either treat it as read or push it back into the input stream to be read later. |
| **PrintStream** | **PrintStream** implements methods for displaying data types textually. Two familiar methods in this class are **print** and **println**, and two familiar objects are **System.out** and **System.err**.<br>To convert the output into the representation of the characters native to the operating system, use the class **PrintWriter** instead of this class. |

## Other Byte I/O Classes

The **java.io** package defines many classes. Extensions of **InputStream** include the following:

► The class **ByteArrayInputStream** lets you read an array of bytes as though it is an **InputStream** object. To create a **ByteArrayInputStream** object, supply a parameter of type **byte[]** to the constructor.

► The class **SequenceInputStream** provides a mechanism for concatenating the data from two or more **InputStream** objects into a single, seamless stream.

► The class **PipedInputStream** implements half of a pipe and is especially useful for communication between threads. Chapter 11 tells you how to develop multithreaded programs and shows how you can create a pipe that is an input stream for one thread and an output stream for another.

Extensions of **OutputStream** include the following:

► The class **ByteArrayOutputStream** sends its output into an object of type **byte[]**. You can use this class to perform your own buffering, or to build an object that another piece of code reads as a **ByteArrayInputStream**.

➤ The class **PipedOutputStream** is the complementary class to **PipedInputStream**. Together, these two classes comprise a pipe that you can use for communication between threads.

# FILE I/O BASICS

Programming stream I/O to and from files is much like programming stream I/O to and from the console. After a stream is established, its usage is the same regardless of whether the ultimate destination is a file or the console.

Major differences exist between files and the standard console I/O objects **System.in**, **System.out**, and **System.err:**

➤ Before you can use a file, you must associate the file with a **FileInputStream or FileOutputStream object.**

➤ If you want to access the data in a file in random-access order, you must open it as a **RandomAccessFile**, not as a **FileInputStream**.

➤ In a network environment, the default security restrictions do not let applets do any file I/O on the client workstation. Applets can perform I/O only on files that reside on the server from which the applet originated.

When you perform stream I/O on a file, you are actually manipulating either a **FileInputStream** object or a **FileOutputStream** object. First you must set up the association between the object and the actual file. You can do this in either of two ways:

➤ You can pass the name of the file, as a **String**, to the constructor of the **FileInputStream** or **FileOutputStream** class.

➤ You can create a **File** object, passing the name of the file to the constructor of the **File** class. Then, create the stream object and pass the **File** object as a parameter of the constructor.

The second method has two steps, which are a little more work. Creating a **File** object has advantages:

➤ When you create the **File** object, you can perform checks, such as whether an input file exists and is read-only or has read-write capabilities. Use this approach if you want to check the status of the file before you open it. If you check the **File** object, as in the following sample code, you may be able to avoid throwing **IOException** objects for reasons such as writing to a read-only file.

➤ The **File** class provides a level of insulation from platform-dependent conventions such as whether a separator between subfolder names is a forward slash, /, or backslash, \.

Here is a sample program that checks whether a file can be written to. This program defines the class `FileChecking`. Because it is a public class, it is found in a file called **FileChecking.java**. The structure of packages mirrors the file system, so you will find this source code in the examples\io subfolder of the folder in which you unpacked the JAR file **examples.jar**.

```java
package examples.io;
import java.io.*;
/** Class used to demonstrate how to find out
  * information about a file
  */
public class FileChecking {
    /** Test method for the class
      * @param args[0] the filename to be used
      */
    public static void main( String[] args ) {
        if ( args.length < 1 ) {
            System.out.println( "Please supply a "
                                 + "filename" );
        } else {
            File f = new File( args[0] );
            if ( f.exists() ) {
                System.out.println( f.getName()
                                    + " exists:" );
                if ( f.canRead() ) {
                    System.out.println( "\tand can be "
                                        + "read" );
                }
                if ( f.canWrite() ) {
                    System.out.println( "\tand can be "
                                        + "written" );
                }
            } else {
                System.out.println( "Sorry, " + args[0]
                                    + " doesn't exist" );
            }
        }
    }
}
```

The two-step method does not give you the ability to reuse a **File** object for different **FileInputStream** or **FileOutputStream** objects unless it is for the same folder and filename. **File** objects are immutable and cannot be altered to reference another file.

Creating stream objects for file input does not in itself change the status of the files on the native file system. For example, creating and using a **FileInputStream** object makes no physical change to any data stored on disk. However, creating a **FileOutputStream** object or writing to a **RandomAccessFile** object does

8

modify physical storage. You create a new file when you use an output file that did not previously exist. What you write to files is permanently stored on disk, with the exception that if your program ends prematurely, some buffered output may be lost if it is still in a buffer when termination occurs.

Here is a sample program that demonstrates file I/O:

```
package examples.io;
import java.io.*;
import java.util.Random;
/** A class used to demonstrate file input and output
  */
public class CaseMixer {
    /** Method randomly sets case of characters in a
      * stream
      * @param args[0] The name of the input file
      *          ( defaults to standard in )
      * @param args[1] The name of the output file
      *          ( defaults to standard out )
      * @exception IOException
      *             if an error is detected opening or
      *             closing the files
      */
    public static void main( String[] args )
                            throws IOException {
        InputStream  istream;
        OutputStream ostream;
        if ( args.length >= 1 ) {
            File inputFile = new File( args[0] );
            istream = new FileInputStream( inputFile );
        } else {
            istream = System.in;
        }
        if ( args.length >= 2 ) {
            File outputFile = new File( args[1] );
            ostream = new FileOutputStream( outputFile );
        } else {
            ostream = System.out;
        }
        int c;
        Random mixer = new Random();
        try {
            while ( ( c = istream.read() ) != -1 ) {
                if ( mixer.nextFloat() < 0.5f ) {
                    c = Character.toLowerCase( (char) c );
                } else {
                    c = Character.toUpperCase( (char) c );
                }
                ostream.write( c );
            }
```

```
        }
        catch( IOException iox ) {
            System.out.println( iox );
        }
        finally {
            istream.close();
            ostream.close();
        }
    }
}
```

Suppose the input is as follows:

`The quick brown fox jumps over the lazy dog.`

The output may be the following:

`thE qUiCk BRown FOx JUmPs OVEr tHe lAZY DOg.`

This code reads characters from an input file, randomly forces each character into either uppercase or lowercase, and prints the result to an output file. The filenames are passed as parameters to **main**. If the parameters are missing, the program substitutes **System.in** and **System.out** for files. The actual input is performed with the method **read** of the **InputStream** class, and the output is performed with the method **write** of the **OutputStream** class. Notice that **read** takes no parameters but returns an **int**, which is stored in the local variable **c. The write** method has one parameter, which is also of type **int**. Both **read** and **write** can throw an **IOException**.

---

**Mini Quiz 8-3**

Why does the **main** function in the preceding example list **IOException** in its throws clause, as well as contain a catch block for **IOException**?

---

## File Navigation Methods

The **File** class gives you more than a way of checking the status of a file before you perform I/O on it. This class provides a number of methods that you can use to navigate the file system on your workstation, or on the server of an applet or application, in a platform-independent manner. It is worth noting that the Java platform does not define a separate class for folders. The **File** class does double duty as a representative of both kinds of file system objects.

If you have had the experience of programming with the API for different operating systems to perform simple file manipulations or to move around the file system on a variety of platforms, you will appreciate the **File** class.

---

*Syntax*

**java.io.File**

---

*Purpose*

The **File** class encapsulates most of the platform-dependent complexities of files and path names in a portable manner.

---

*Constructors*

➤ **File( String** *filename* **)**
**File( File** *folder*, **String** *filename* **)**
**File( String** *folder*, **String** *filename* **)**
You can create a **File** object by specifying only the filename or the file-name and the folder in which it resides. You can specify the folder by path name or with an existing **File** object.

---

*Methods*

➤ **boolean canRead()**
The **canRead** method returns **true** if the file is readable, and **false** otherwise.

➤ **boolean canWrite()**
The **canWrite** method returns **true** if you can write to the file, and **false** otherwise.

➤ **File createTempFile( String** *prefix*, **String** *suffix* **)**
**File createTempFile( String** *prefix*, **String** *suffix*, **File** *folder* **)**
The **createTempFile** method creates a temporary file with a name gener-ated using the given prefix and suffix. The prefix must be at least three characters long. The suffix may be **null**, in which case it defaults to ".tmp". If a folder is specified, the file is created in that folder. Otherwise it is created in the default temporary file directory.

➤ **boolean delete()**
The **delete** method deletes the file. The return value indicates success or failure.

➤ **void deleteOnExit( )**
The **deleteOnExit** method marks a **File** to be deleted on normal termi-nation of the JVM. It is particularly useful for cleaning up temporary files created by an application. The result of this method is irreversible, so you should use it with care.

➤ **boolean exists()**
The **exists** method returns **true** if the file already exists on disk, and **false** otherwise.

➤ **String getAbsolutePath()**
The **getAbsolutePath** method returns the platform-specific absolute path to the **File** object for which the method is called.

➤ **String getName()**
The **getName** method returns the name of the file. The value returned is the portion of the path that follows the last file separator character.

➤ **String getParent()**
The **getParent** method returns the name of the folder in which the file resides, or **null** if the file is in the root folder.

➤ **File getParentFile()**
The **getParentFile** method is similar to **getParent**, but returns a **File** object instead of a **String**. Using **getParentFile** may be more convenient for navigating through the file system because you do not have to create a **File** object from a returned **String**.

➤ **boolean isDirectory()**
The **isDirectory** method returns **true** if the file is a folder, and **false** otherwise.

➤ **boolean isFile()**
The **isFile** method returns **true** if the file is an ordinary file and **false** if it is a folder.

➤ **long lastModified()**
The **lastModified** method returns the system-specific time when the file was last modified.

➤ **String[] list()**
**String[] list( FilenameFilter** *filter* **)**
If the file is a folder, the **list** method returns an array that contains a list of the names of files that reside in the folder. You can specify an object of a class that implements the interface **java.io.FilenameFilter** to get only filenames accepted by a filter object.

➤ **File[] listFiles()**
**File[] listFiles( FileFilter filter )**
**File[] listFiles( FilenameFilter** *filter* **)**
The **listFiles** method is similar to **list**, but returns a **File[]** object instead of a **String[]**. Using **listFiles** may be more convenient for navigating through the file system because it saves the step of having to create **File** objects from a returned **String** array.

➤ **File[] listRoots()**
This method returns all file-system roots. Some file systems have more than one root. For example, Windows platforms have a file root associated with each drive letter whereas UNIX file systems have only a single file-system root called "/".

**8**

➤ **boolean mkdir()**
The **mkdir** method creates a folder with the name of this **File**. The return value indicates success or failure.

➤ **boolean setReadOnly()**
The **setReadOnly** method sets the file-system attributes of the file so that only read operations are allowed.

➤ **URL toURL()**
This method returns the file pathname into a **URL** object of the form **file://**_pathname_. If the pathname is a folder, the URL ends with a slash character. The **URL** class is discussed later in this chapter.

## Random-Access File I/O

The class **RandomAccessFile** supports byte-oriented I/O to and from random-access files. Use it to read and write data from or to any specified location within a file. **RandomAccessFile** objects are not streams. The class **RandomAccessFile** extends **Object**, not **InputStream** or **OutputStream**.

**RandomAccessFile** combines input and output operations in one class. It has the same **close**, **read**, and **write** methods as **InputStream** and **OutputStream**. In addition, it has the same methods for reading and writing primitive types as the **DataInputStream** and **DataOutputStream** classes. The **seek** method distinguishes this class from the stream I/O classes. The **seek** method selects the position within the file where the next I/O operation will begin. Another important difference is that you can both read and write a **RandomAccessFile** unlike any stream which must be either input or output but not both.

# CHARACTER STREAMS

The **java.io** package has classes that are specifically designed to support character streams. You can use them to work with characters, character arrays, and strings. The character streams differ from the byte streams mainly in that they operate on buffered input and output and properly convert each character from the encoding scheme of the native operating system to the Unicode character set used by the Java platform. In contrast, **InputStream** and **OutputStream**, and the classes that extend them, operate on bytes and arrays of bytes. The byte-oriented streams correctly handle only seven-bit ASCII characters, which have the same value as the first 128 Unicode characters. Character streams are sensitive to different character-encoding schemes and fully support international applications. Character conversions are described in more detail in "Internationalization" on the CD-ROM.

The hierarchy of classes that support character streams mirrors the structure of the hierarchy of classes that support byte-oriented streams. The superclass of character–oriented input stream I/O is **java.io.Reader**. The corresponding output stream is **java.io.Writer**. Like **java.io.InputStream** and **java.io.OutputStream**, the **Reader** and **Writer** classes are also direct subclasses of **Object**. Most byte stream classes have a corresponding character stream class. For example, **FileReader** is the character-oriented counterpart to **FileInputStream**, and **FileWriter** is the counterpart to **FileOutputStream**. Figure 8-2 shows character stream classes and how they are related.

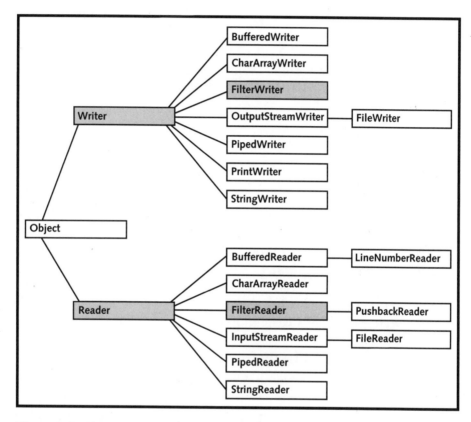

**Figure 8-2** Character stream classes

 The Java platform did not always support character I/O. The original release had only the byte-oriented streams. Therefore, the release was of limited use outside North America, even though it represented characters internally in Unicode. Version 1.1 of the Java platform added the character streams. The inherent overhead of encoding conversion for character streams is offset by buffering and improved implementation. The character streams can be more efficient than byte-oriented streams.

At the same time, the method **DataInputStream.readLine()** was deprecated because it does not properly convert the input characters. You may see this method used in old programs; this method still works, but you should use **BufferedReader.readLine()** instead.

There are filter-stream classes for the byte streams and separate filter-stream classes for the character streams. The base classes for character filter streams are **FilterReader** and **FilterWriter**. Both are abstract classes. Only **FilterReader** has a subclass that is part of the **java.io** package. The **PushbackReader** wraps a **Reader** object and adds the ability to push characters back into the stream. The size of the pushback buffer is an argument of the constructor parameter and has the default value of one character.

## Connecting Byte and Character I/O Classes

The Java platform includes adapter classes that bridge between character I/O classes and the byte I/O classes. These adapter classes are very useful because programs written for old versions of the Java platform sometimes use the **InputStream** and **OutputStream** classes for stream I/O.

The **InputStreamReader** and **OutputStreamWriter** classes perform the adaptation. For example, you can convert an existing **InputStream** object, such as **System.in,** by constructing an **InputStreamReader** object and passing the object reference for the **InputStream** object as the argument of the constructor. The resulting object can be used anywhere that a **Reader** object is required. "Internationalization" on the CD-ROM contains an example of using an **OutputStreamWriter** to take advantage of different character encodings when programming for the international market. Similarly, you can adapt the **System.err OutputStream** object for use as a **PrintWriter** object by creating an **OutputStreamWriter** object and passing a reference to the **System.err** object as an input argument. However, it is worth noting that this adaptation works in only one direction. You cannot create a stream object from a **Writer** object or a **Reader** object.

## Using Other Character I/O Classes

Many other classes besides **FileReader** and **FileWriter** extend **Reader** and **Writer**. Extensions of the **Reader** object include the following:

➤ The class **CharArrayReader** lets you read an array of characters as though it were a **Reader** object. To create a **CharArrayReader** object, supply a parameter of type **char[]** to the constructor of the object.

➤ The class **StringReader** lets you read a **String** as though it were a **Reader** object. To create a **StringReader** object, supply a parameter of type **String** to the constructor of the object.

➤ The class **PipedReader** implements half of a pipe and is especially useful for communication between threads. Chapter 11 describes developing multithreaded programs, and shows you how to create a pipe that is a reader stream for one thread and a writer stream for another.

Extensions of the **Writer** object include the following:

➤ The class **CharArrayWriter** sends its output into an object of type **char[]**. You can use this class to perform your own buffering, or to build an object that another piece of code reads as a **CharArrayReader**.

➤ The class **StringWriter** lets you write to a **StringBuffer** as though it were a **Writer** object. No input is necessary to create the **StringBuffer** object explicitly. Just construct the **StringWriter** object. You can accept the default initial size for the buffer, or specify an optional initial size as an argument of the **StringWriter** constructor. Use the method **getBuffer** to get the object reference for the **StringBuffer** object that contains the information that is written.

➤ The class **PipedWriter** is the complementary class to **PipedReader**. Together, these classes comprise a pipe that you can use for communication of character information between threads.

➤ The class **PrintWriter** is the character I/O equivalent of the **PrintStream** class. It has all the same methods as **PrintStream**, but has the internationalization support that **PrintStream** lacks. You can easily convert a **PrintStream** object to a **PrintWriter** object by constructing a **PrintWriter** and passing a reference to the **PrintStream** as the input parameter.

## Reading One Token at a Time

The class **StreamTokenizer** is a utility class in **java.io** that is not related to any of the other classes by inheritance. It lets you read a file as a sequence of tokens by encapsulating a **Reader** object and grouping the stream of input bytes into tokens. By default, tokens are delimited by whitespace, but you can call many methods to customize a tokenizing algorithm. **Whitespace** is any combination of space, newline, or tab characters. You can also call a method to find out on what line in the file a token appeared.

To use the **StreamTokenizer** class, first create a **Reader** object, and then pass the **Reader** object as a parameter to the constructor of the **StreamTokenizer** object.

### Mini Quiz 8-4

The current version of the Java platform lets you create a **StreamTokenizer** object for an **InputStream** object, but such use of **StreamTokenizer** is a deprecated feature. Why?

# OBJECT SERIALIZATION

During the discussion about reading and writing numbers, strings, and the like to and from files, have you been wondering if you can write entire objects to a file so that you can read them back later with their state intact? If so, you have anticipated the requirement to serialize objects. You may want to serialize an object to do the following:

➤ Transmit objects over a network

➤ Save objects to files between runs of your program, or perhaps write and then read objects later in the same application

For the primitive types, the byte-oriented filter classes **DataOutputStream** and **DataInputStream** provide methods to write and read binary representations of variables of all the primitive types or **String** objects to and from a file. But what about objects of other types? The simplistic approach of saving to a file on a field-by-field basis requires discipline and constant maintenance. Every time a field is added to the class, the methods for saving and restoring the objects must be updated. What happens when a field that is an object reference field is added? Should just the reference or the whole contained object be saved and restored?

**Object serialization** is a general solution that lets you write objects to I/O streams and then read them, without defining any additional methods. Object serialization properly handles not only the fields defined in the class, but also inherited fields and any subfields that these fields may have.

The object serialization feature is an important component of the Java Remote Method Invocation (RMI) enterprise API. RMI is discussed in Chapter 16. For now you should know that RMI allows an object in the Java programming language on one system to invoke a method of an object in the Java programming language across a network on a different system. You need object serialization to write objects that are arguments to methods to a stream on one system and to read from the stream at the other system. Typically, the data is transferred over a TCP/IP socket.

The original version of the Java platform had no facility for object serialization. Version 1.1 added this much-needed feature. That version also added the RMI API, which depends upon object serialization.
The Java 2 platform enhanced object serialization in a number of ways. Most of the changes affect the internal workings of serialization or are too specialized for inclusion in this description. Improvements include the addition of the **javadoc** serialization tags **@serial**, **@serialField**, and **@serialData**.

## Serializing Objects

Just as not all classes of objects can be cloned, not all classes of objects support serialization. By default, classes are not serializable. To let instances of a class be serialized, define the class with **implements Serializable**. The **Serializable** interface, like **Cloneable,** is a marker interface and contains no methods. Most of the classes in the **java.lang** package implement the **Serializable** interface. Commonly used classes in the **java.lang** package that do not implement **Serializable** are **Math**, **Process**, **Runtime**, **SecurityManager**, **System**, **Thread**, **ThreadGroup**, and **Void.** These omissions make sense for the following reasons:

➤ **Math** and **System** contain only class methods and variables.

➤ **Void** is just a placeholder and is essentially empty.

➤ The nature of the other classes is incompatible with the rationale for object serialization. The **Process**, **Runtime**, **SecurityManager**, **Thread**, and **ThreadGroup** objects are used as a program runs.

## Using Object Streams

Two stream classes support object serialization: **ObjectOutputStream** and **ObjectInputStream**. The next example program shows how to use them.

**ObjectOutputStream** is a subclass of **OutputStream**. To create an **ObjectOutputStream,** provide an existing **OutputStream** object as the argument of the constructor. In the upcoming example, the output object is an instance of **FileOutputStream** that was created in the usual way, but you can use an object of any subclass of **OutputStream**. For example, if you have established a pipe between two threads, you can use a **PipedOutputStream** object to send an object from one thread to the other.

**ObjectInputStream** is a subclass of **InputStream**. To create an **ObjectInputStream**, provide an existing **InputStream** object as the argument of the constructor. In the upcoming example program, the input object has type **FileInputStream**, but any subtype of **InputStream** is acceptable.

## Suppressing Serialization of Fields

The Java programming language does not require that every field in a class be serialized. Some fields may contain sensitive information that should not be transmitted over a network. Others may be references to objects of classes that do not implement **Serializable**. Also, classes can contain fields for temporary information that never needs to be serialized.

You can include the qualifier **transient** when you declare fields to indicate that they should not be serialized with instances of the class. Fields that have the **transient** qualifier are not output when the object is serialized. When the object is deserialized later, **transient** fields are given the default value normally used for fields of their type.

You can use the **transient** qualifier to indicate that certain fields of a class should never be serialized, but it is not very flexible. You cannot change the declaration of a field at run time to include it or to exclude it from serialization.

The Java platform provides an alternate approach for runtime control: You can add a private static final field with the name **serialPersistentFields** and type **ObjectStreamField[]** to the class. Set up each **ObjectStreamField** element in the **serialPersistentFields** array to represent a field to be serialized. Construct the element by specifying the name of the field as a **String**, and the **Class** object for the field.

 The qualifier **transient** has been a reserved word in the Java programming language since the original release, but had no use until the Java platform started to support object serialization in version 1.1.

The support for serialization that is automatically generated for a class is usually totally adequate. However, the designers of the Java platform know that programmers are sure to want some ability to customize serialization for a particular class. Therefore, the designers have given you two additional methods for this purpose: **readObject** and **writeObject**. These methods have two unusual characteristics:

➤ The **readObject** and **writeObject** methods are not part of any interface to be implemented or class to be extended.

➤ Even though the serialization support calls **readObject** and **writeObject**, they must be private methods.

You must define **readObject** and **writeObject** as in the following lines, which are taken from the next example program. If they are defined properly, the serialization support finds them and can use them.

```
private void readObject( ObjectInputStream ois )
   throws ClassNotFoundException, IOException {
   /* whatever you want */
   ois.defaultReadObject();
   /* whatever you want */
}
private void writeObject( ObjectOutputStream oos )
   throws IOException {
   /* whatever you want */
   oos.defaultWriteObject();
   /* whatever you want */
}
```

Make sure you call the **defaultReadObject** and **defaultWriteObject** methods in your customized methods. The **defaultReadObject** and **defaultWriteObject** methods do the actual serialization work. If you leave them out, not much happens.

Here is an example that uses object serialization. The class `ObjectToSave` is defined and implements **Serializable**.

```java
package examples.io;
import java.io.*;
/** A class defined to be used in
  * serialization operations.
  */
class ObjectToSave implements Serializable {
    static final long serialVersionUID
        = 7482918152381158178L;
    private int i;
    private String s;
    private transient double d;
    public ObjectToSave( int i, String s, double d ) {
        this.i = i;
        this.s = s;
        this.d = d;
    }
    public String toString() {
        return "i = " + i + ", s = " + s + ", d = " + d;
    }
    private void readObject( ObjectInputStream ois )
        throws ClassNotFoundException, IOException {
        System.out.println( "deserializing..." );
        ois.defaultReadObject();
        System.out.println( "deserialized" );
    }
    private void writeObject( ObjectOutputStream oos ) {
        throws IOException {
        System.out.println( "serializing..." );
        oos.defaultWriteObject();
        System.out.println( "serialized" );
    }
}
```
`} import java.io.*; // if saved in a separate file`
```java
/** A class used to demonstrate serializing objects
  * to and from a file.
  */
public class ObjectSaver {
    private static final String FILE_NAME
        = "objects.ser";
    /** Test method for the class
      * @param args not used
      */
    public static void main( String[] args ) {
        try {
            // create the object to be serialized
```

```
              ObjectToSave ots
                 = new ObjectToSave( 57, "pizza", 3.14 );
              // create the target File object and erase
              // any already existing file
              File objectFile = new File( FILE_NAME );
              if ( objectFile.exists() ) {
                 objectFile.delete();
              }
              // open the file, create the output stream,
              // and write the object
              FileOutputStream fos
                 = new FileOutputStream( objectFile );
              ObjectOutputStream oos
                 = new ObjectOutputStream( fos );
              oos.writeObject( ots );
              oos.close();
              // reopen the file and retrieve the object
              FileInputStream fis
                 = new FileInputStream( objectFile );
              ObjectInputStream ois
                 = new ObjectInputStream( fis );
              ObjectToSave retrieved
                 = (ObjectToSave) ois.readObject();
              ois.close();
              System.out.println( retrieved );
           }
        catch ( OptionalDataException x ) {
              System.out.println( x );
              x.printStackTrace();
           }
        catch ( ClassNotFoundException x ) {
              System.out.println( x );
              x.printStackTrace();
           }
        catch ( IOException x ) {
              System.out.println( x );
              x.printStackTrace();
           }
        }
     }
}
```

The output is:

```
serializing...
serialized
deserializing...
deserialized
i = 57, s = pizza, d = 0.0
```

This code includes its own customized serialization routines that do nothing more than print messages to the console when a serialization operation starts or finishes.

The class `ObjectSaver` does the actual work of creating an `ObjectToSave` object, opening the file, and writing the object into the file. After closing the file, `ObjectSaver` reopens the file and retrieves the object to verify that everything worked correctly.

Notice that when the transient field `d` is restored, it receives the default value for a double, which is zero.

## Specifying the Version Number

In the serialization sample program, did you notice the following unusual field in the `examples.io.ObjectToSave` class?

```
static final long serialVersionUID
   = 7482918152381158178L;
```

Just from looking at the code, you may suspect that this field serves no purpose. However, this field is a unique identifier that specifies the version of the class that was serialized. The version number is saved with the serialized object. When the object is restored, this field serves as a check that the object is being restored by a class definition that matches the version that created it.

You do not make up a version number. The value is calculated using a formula that takes the name of the class and its interfaces, fields, and methods. You can determine the value with the **serialver** tool supplied with the SDK, by entering the following command:

```
serialver class_name
```

For the class `examples.io.ObjectToSave`, the output is:

```
examples.io.ObjectToSave:
static final long serialVersionUID
   = 7482918152381158178L;
```

You can use cut and paste techniques to edit this number into your class definition. Alternatively, you may prefer not to define a **serialVersionUID** field and let the JVM generate one for you. The only drawback when the JVM generates the number automatically is that minor changes in the class definition, such as renaming a method or adding a method that does not require any new fields, result in a new version value. Objects serialized before such a change appear to be out of date when really they are not. If the needed version of the class cannot be found, the compiler throws a **ClassNotFoundException** object.

## Compatibility of Serialization Formats

The object serialization classes of the Java 2 platform write objects to object streams using a different format from earlier versions of the Java platform. As a result, objects serialized by the Java 2 API cannot be deserialized by classes compiled with versions of the Java platform before version 1.1.7. To identify the serialization stream format used, Java 2 defines two new constants, **PROTOCOL_VERSION_1** and **PROTOCOL_VERSION_2**, in the **java.io.ObjectStreamConstants** interface. Versions of the Java platform beginning with 1.1.7 can read both serialization stream versions, but earlier Java platform versions can read only the original stream version.

For those cases where compatibility requires that objects be serialized using the original version, the method **useProtocolVersion** has been added to the **ObjectOutputStream**. This method takes a protocol version constant as input and updates the **ObjectOutputStream** object to use the corresponding serialization stream version.

---

# SUMMARY

Most input to and output from the JVM is stream-based, regardless of whether your program is communicating with the console, files, or another program running on your network. The notable exception is that random-access file I/O does not use streams.

Support for I/O is provided by the core classes in the package **java.io**.

The Java platform supports byte-oriented streams that are usually adequate for working the 7-bit ASCII character set used by most English-language North American PCs and the character-oriented streams that convert characters from the native character encoding of the native operating system to Unicode.

For byte-oriented I/O, the two classes **InputStream** and **OutputStream** are the abstract classes that are the roots of the input and output class hierarchies, respectively.

The predefined console input stream object, **System.in**, and the console output stream objects, **System.out** and **System.err**, are **InputStream** and **OutputStream** objects. You should wrap a character-oriented stream class around **System.in** to ensure the data is converted correctly to Unicode.

The stream I/O model means that console I/O and file I/O are very similar. **FileInputStream** and **FileOutputStream** are the classes used for reading and writing files. Their constructors take either a string containing the filename or an object of the class **File**.

**File** objects are constructed by providing a string containing a filename in a platform-independent manner. **File** objects offer the capability to query the physical file it represents and find out whether it exists, whether it can be read or written, and so on. You can also use a **File** object to navigate the file system on your host in a platform-independent manner.

Filter stream classes are designed to wrap either an **InputStream** or an **OutputStream** class. They build on the base I/O functions and add features such as buffering and data pushback.

Several other classes extend the **InputStream** and **OutputStream** classes to provide capabilities such as reading and writing byte arrays, sequencing multiple streams as a single stream, and reading and writing pipes.

Use the class **RandomAccessFile** to read and write information at arbitrary locations within a file without first having to read or write information at the preceding locations.

The design of the character-stream class hierarchy is very similar to the byte-stream class hierarchy.

To enable programmers to read and write objects as a whole, the Java programming language provides **object serialization**. Objects are written to and read from **ObjectOutputStream** and **ObjectInputStream** objects. Only classes that implement the marker interface **Serializable** can be serialized. You can exclude individual fields within a class from the serialization operation by applying the **transient** qualifier. Customizing the serialization methods is supported but not usually necessary.

## QUESTIONS

1. Which of the following classes are subclasses of **InputStream**? Select all that apply.

   a. **SequenceInputStream**

   b. **File**

   c. **ObjectInputStream**

   d. **StringReader**

   e. **RandomAccessFile**

2. Which of the following classes can be passed as a parameter to the constructor of **FilterOutputStream**? Select all that apply.

    a. **PipedOutputStream**

    b. **BufferedWriter**

    c. **String**

    d. **File**

    e. **ByteArrayOutputStream**

3. True or False: The **RandomAccessFile** class extends neither **InputStream** nor **OutputStream**.

4. Examine the following code:

```java
import java.io.*;
public class Quiz8_4 {
    public static void main( String[] args )
                            throws IOException {
        PrintWriter pr = new PrintWriter( System.out );
        pr.println( "What a lovely day." );
        pr.flush();
    }
}
```

Which of the following statements are true when the code is compiled and run? Select all that apply.

    a. The compiler rejects the expression new `PrintWriter( System.out )` because it is not possible to construct a **PrintWriter** object from a **PrintStream** object.

    b. The **flush** method ensures that the information in the **PrintWriter** stream is written to the console.

    c. Compilation is successful and the output is `What a lovely day`.

    d. The throws clause in **main** is unnecessary since none of the methods in **main** throw an **IOException**.

5. Which class is used to represent a file system folder?

6. Which of the following statements will create a physical file in the file system, assuming that the file data1 does not already exist? Select all that apply.

    a. new `RandomAccessFile( "data1", "rw" );`

    b. new `File( "data1" );`

    c. new `FileOutputStream( "data1" );`

    d. new `FileOutputStream( new File( "data1" ) );`

    e. new `FileWriter( "data1" )`

7. Examine the following code:

```java
import java.io.*;
class SaveMe implements Serializable {
    boolean b = true;
    transient String s
        = "Something from the meat case, Linda?";
}
public class Quiz8_7 {
    private static final String FILE_NAME
        = "objects.ser";
    public static void main( String[] args ) {
        try {
            SaveMe sm = new SaveMe();
            File objectFile = new File( FILE_NAME );
            FileOutputStream fos =
            new FileOutputStream( objectFile );
            ObjectOutputStream oos =
                new ObjectOutputStream( fos );
            oos.writeObject( sm );
            oos.close();
            FileInputStream fis =
                new FileInputStream( objectFile );
            ObjectInputStream ois
                = new ObjectInputStream( fis );
            SaveMe retrieved = (SaveMe) ois.readObject();
            ois.close();
            System.out.println( retrieved.b );
            System.out.println( retrieved.s );
        }
        catch ( Exception x ) {
            System.out.println( x );
        }
    }
}
```

Which of the following statements are true when the code is compiled and run? Select all that apply.

a. The compiler rejects the method **Example.main** because all possible exceptions have not been handled by a catch clause or been identified in a throws clause.

b. The class **SaveMe** accepts the default value of the field **serialVersionUID**.

c. Compilation is successful and the output is

```
true
null
```

8

d. Compilation is successful and the output is

```
true
Something from the meat case, Linda?
```

e. The compiler rejects the definition of the class `Quiz8_7` because it does not implement the **Serializable** interface.

8. Which of the following classes do not implement the **Serializable** interface? Select all that apply.

a. **Integer**

b. **Process**

c. **String**

d. **Object**

e. **Thread**

9. Which of the following methods are defined in the **Serializable** interface? Select all that apply.

a. **serialize**

b. **readObject**

c. **writeObject**

d. **getSerialVersionUID**

e. **setSerialVersionUID**

---

# EXERCISES

## Debugging

1. Correct the following program so that it uses **Reader** and **Writer** subclasses for reading and writing characters.

```
package questions.c8;
import java.io.*;
public class Debug8_1 {
    public static void main( String[] args )
          throws IOException {
      InputStream  input;
      OutputStream output;
      if ( args.length >= 2 ) {
          input = new FileInputStream( args[0] );
          output = new FileOutputStream( args[1] );
      } else {
          input = System.in;
          output = System.out;
      }
      int c;
```

```
            try {
               while ( ( c = input.read() ) != -1 ) {
                  // change blanks to underscores
                  if ( c == ' ' ) {
                     c = '_';
                  }
                  output.write( c );
               }
            }
            catch( IOException iox ) {
               System.out.println( iox );
            }
            finally {
               input.close();
               output.close();
            }
         }
      }
```

**8**

2. Correct all the errors in the following program so that it outputs a message specifying the length of the line read for each line in the input file:

```
package questions.c8;
import java.io.*;
public class Debug8_2 {
   public static void main( String[] args )
            throws IOException {
      if ( args.length >= 2 ) {
         Reader   input;
         Writer output;
         String inputLine;
         input = new FileReader( args[0] );
         output = new FileWriter( args[1] );
         inputLine = input.readLine();
         try {
            while ( inputLine != null ) {
               output.println( "Line length = "
                                 + inputLine.length() );
               inputLine = input.readLine();
            }
         }
         catch( IOException iox ) {
            System.out.println( iox );
         }
         finally {
            input.close();
            output.close();
         }
```

```
        } else {
            System.err.println( "Usage is <input_file> "
                                  + "<output_file>" );
        }
    }
}
```

3. Correct all the errors in the following program so that the **StreamTokenizer** is used to output each of the tokens in the input file:

```
package questions.c8;
import java.io.*;
public class Debug8_3 {
    public static void main( String[] args )
            throws IOException {
        if ( args.length >= 1 ) {
            Reader   input;
            StreamTokenizer st;
            input = new FileReader( args[0] );
            st = new StreamTokenizer( input );
            try {
                while ( st.moreTokens() ) {
                    System.out.println( "token = "
                                         + st.getNext() );
                }
            }
            catch( IOException iox ) {
                System.out.println( iox );
            }
            finally {
                input.close();
            }
        } else {
            System.err.println( "Usage is "
                                  + "<input_file>" );
        }
    }
}
```

4. Correct all the errors in the following program:

```
package questions.c8;
import java.io.*;
public class Debug8_4 {
    private static final String FILE_NAME
        = "debug8_4.ser";
    int count = 11;
    Thread t = new Thread();
    String title = "Placeholder";
    public static void main( String[] args ) {
        try {
            File objectFile = new File( FILE_NAME );
```

```
            Debug8_4 x = new Debug8_4();
            x.count = 57;
            x.title = "Varieties";
            FileOutputStream fos =
               new FileOutputStream( objectFile );
            ObjectOutputStream oos =
               new ObjectOutputStream( fos );
            oos.writeObject( x );
            oos.close();
            FileInputStream fis =
               new FileInputStream( objectFile );
            ObjectInputStream ois
               = new ObjectInputStream( fis );
            Debug8_4 retrieved
               = (Debug8_4) ois.readObject();
            ois.close();
            System.out.println( retrieved.count );
            System.out.println( retrieved.title );
        }
        catch ( Exception x ) {
            System.out.println( x );
        }
    }
}
```

8

## Complete the Solution

1. Extract the file **questions\c8\Complete8_1.java** from the file **question.jar** on the CD-ROM. Complete the definition of the class `questions.c8.Complete8_1` by finishing the `initialize` method so that it fills the character array with characters read from the specified file.

2. Extract the file **questions\c8\Complete8_2.java** from the file **question.jar** on the CD-ROM. Complete the definition of the class `questions.c8.Complete8_2` by finishing the `getInt` method so that it reads an integer from the specified starting position in the specified file.

3. Extract the file **questions\c8\Complete8_3.java** from the file **question.jar** on the CD-ROM. Complete the definition of the class `questions.c8.Complete8_3` by adding methods `readObject` and `writeObject` to have them print messages indicating status of the serialization store and retrieve operations.

4. Add to the definition of class `question.c8.Complete8_3` by calculating and defining the appropriate **serialVersionUID** for the class.

## Discovery

1. Using the classes from the **java.io** package, create a simple copy utility in a class called `FileCopyUtility` that can copy the contents of an entire folder into a different folder. For an additional challenge, add support to your utility that allows the user to specify an option that will also recursively copy any subfolders of the specified folder.

2. Create a class called `HasAProfile` that maintains name, address, and phone number information in serialized form on disk so that it can be retrieved whenever a new `HasAProfile` object is constructed. If an error occurs when retrieving the information during object construction, the object will prompt the user for name, address, and phone number information and use the information to create a new serialized profile on disk.

## CHAPTER NINE

# NESTED AND INNER CLASSES

**In this chapter you will:**

➤ Know how and when to make your code more elegant by using inner classes.

☕ Declare inner classes, making correct use and stating the significance of all permitted modifiers, such as public, protected, private and static.

☕ Identify the correctly constructed inner classes of all forms.

☕ Write code to construct instances of inner classes, static inner classes, and anonymous inner classes.

➤ For a given inner class, describe the contents and lifetime of its state data.

➤ State which variables and methods in enclosing scopes are accessible form methods of inner classes.

## INTRODUCTION

This chapter will complete the discussion of classes. A **nested class** is a class that is defined inside the definition of another class. A nested class may also be an **inner class**, depending upon how it is defined. Inner classes are a new kind of class that is explained in this chapter. A nested class that is not an inner class is almost identical to the kind of class you have been using so far in this book. The differences relate mainly to scope and accessibility, and not to the nature of the class. Inner classes are very different in nature from other classes. An inner class can be a member of the class that encloses it or local to a block of code.

This chapter covers both nested classes and inner classes, and adopts the terms introduced in this paragraph to differentiate between these two very different ways of enclosing classes inside other classes. This book uses the term **enclosed class** for a nested class that is an inner class as well as for a nested class that is not an inner class. A class in which a definition of the enclosed class appears is an **enclosing class**. For simplicity, this book applies the term **nested class** to an enclosed class that is not a member or local inner class. It uses the term **inner class** otherwise. Java programmers also use the terms top-level inner classes or static inner classes (for reasons that you will soon see) for nested classes. The larger portion of the chapter is devoted to inner classes.

You could not define nested and inner classes in the original version of the Java programming language. At that time, only packages could enclose classes, and the only way to group classes was into packages. Nested and inner classes became available in version 1.1 of the Java platform.

You can certainly use the Java programming language without using inner classes. You do not even sacrifice program functionality by not using them. On the other hand, you can make your code more elegant and greatly improve the structure of your classes by using inner classes.

Nesting classes is an excellent way to collect a group of cooperating classes or interfaces. In Chapter 4, you learned how to organize classes into packages. Packages are a rather coarse-grained way to collect classes. Often you combine classes into packages when really the classes have no logical grouping except convenience or the fact that the files reside in the same folder. You can take advantage of inner classes and nested classes to indicate more clearly how classes interact with each other. The enclosing class and all that it encloses must still, however, belong to one package.

With enclosed classes, you can group classes with a finer granularity than you can with packages. In addition, the enclosed classes can share full access to private members of other enclosed classes in the same enclosing class.

The relationship between an enclosed class and enclosing class does not involve inheritance. A completely different set of rules determines the scope and accessibility of members between the enclosed and enclosing class. In fact, you can combine inner and nested classes with inheritance, by defining inner or nested classes that are subclasses and superclasses.

# NESTED CLASSES AND INTERFACES

A class or interface may be nested inside another class or interface. The simplest way to enclose a class inside another class is to nest their definitions one inside the other. You can even nest classes within interfaces, and interfaces within classes.

To define a nested class or interface, you must qualify the enclosed class with the keyword **static**. Do not omit this qualifier because, syntactically, the keyword **static** is all that distinguishes a nested class from an inner class.

*Syntax*

```
[public] [qualifiers] class enclosing _name {
    // . . .
    [access_specifier] [qualifiers] static class enclosed _name {
        // . . .
    }
}
```

*Dissection*

➤ The syntax of the enclosing class or interface definition is like any class or interface definition.

➤ You can declare nested classes to be public, protected, or private. If you omit an access specifier, the class has the default package access.

➤ Classes nested within interfaces are implicitly static, like fields defined in interfaces.

➤ The qualifiers **abstract** and **final** have their usual meaning when applied to nested classes.

*Code Example*

```
public interface outer {
    //. . .
    public static class inner {
        // . . .
    }
}
```

*Code Dissection*

Here, the class `inner` is nested inside the interface `outer`.

The keyword **static** is very appropriate for nested classes. They are not associated with instances of the enclosing class. It is the classes or interfaces, not objects, that are nested. The term **top-level class** refers to a class that is contained only in packages. Nested classes are top-level classes, just like all the classes you have seen so far in this book. They are enclosed in other classes but are not members of the enclosing classes.

What do access specifiers mean when applied to nested classes? The rules for accessing a nested class resemble the rules for accessing members of the enclosing class. Only the enclosing class can instantiate a private nested class. All classes in the same package can access a nested class with the default package. Protected nested classes can be accessed by classes in the same package and by classes that inherit from the enclosing class. You can always access public nested classes.

A nested class has no special privileges for accessing members of the enclosing class or other enclosed classes in the same enclosed class. It has the same access privileges as any other class in the same package. Nested classes can extend other classes, and can be extended by other classes.

The names of nested classes consist of package name, enclosing class names, and the simple name of the nested class, separated by dots. For example, in the next sample program, the class Node belongs to the package **examples** and subpackage **inner**, and is enclosed in the class Graph1. The name of the class is **examples.inner.Graph1.Node**.

To import all the classes nested within a class, use the asterisk, *, just as you do to import all the classes in a package. For example, you can import all the classes in the Graph1 class with the following statement:

```
import examples.inner.Graph1.*;
```

**Mini Quiz 9-1**

Can you tell just from the name **examples.inner.Graph1.Node** whether Node is a class or a package?

Here is a small application in which a class called Node is nested inside a class called Graph1. Because Graph1 is a public class, it is found in a file called Graph1.java. The structure of packages mirrors the file system, so you will find this source code in the examples\inner subfolder of the folder in which you unpacked the .jar file examples.jar.

```
package examples.inner;
import java.util.Hashtable;
import java.util.Enumeration;
/** Class representing an undirected graph composed
  * of nodes.  The node class is a top-level class
  * nested within the Graph1 class.
  */
public class Graph1 {
   private Hashtable nodeList = new Hashtable();
   /** Add a node to the graph
     * @param x the x coordinate of the node
     * @param y the y coordinate of the node
     */
   public void addNode( int x, int y ) {
      Node n = new Node( x, y );
      if ( ! nodeList.containsKey( n.key() ) ) ) {
         nodeList.put( n.key(), n );
      }
   }
   /** Get the object as a string
     * @return the object as a string
     */
   public String toString() {
```

```
        StringBuffer sb = new StringBuffer( "[ " );
        Enumeration e = nodeList.elements();
        while ( e.hasMoreElements() ) {
           sb.append( e.nextElement().toString()
                      + " " );
        }
        sb.append( "]" );
        return sb.toString();
    }
    /** Test method
      * @param args not used
      */
    public static void main( String[] args ) {
        System.out.println( "creating the graph" );
        Graph1 g = new Graph1();
        System.out.println( "adding nodes" );
        g.addNode( 4, 5 );
        g.addNode( -6, 11 );
        System.out.println( g );
    }
    /** The class representing nodes within the graph
      */
    private static class Node {
        private int x, y;
        public Node( int x, int y ) {
           this.x = x;
           this.y = y;
        }
        /** Determine the key value for a node
          * @return the key as a String
          */
        public Object key() {
           return x + "," + y;
        }
        /** Get the object as a string
          * @return the object as a string
          */
        public String toString() {
           return "(" + x + "," + y + ")";
        }
    }   // end of Node class
}   // end of Graph1 class
```

9

You can run this program from the .class files provided in the examples.jar file on the CD-ROM that accompanies this book. You can also compile and run the **Graph1** class using the SDK by entering the following commands:

```
javac examples\inner\Graph1.java
java examples.inner.Graph1
```

If you look at the files produced by the compiler, you notice that the compiler creates a .class file for each class even though Node is nested inside Graph1. The character $ in a filename separates an enclosing and an enclosed class. The two .class files for this example are the following:

➤ examples\inner\Graph1.class

➤ examples\inner\Graph1$Node.class

The output from running the program is:

```
creating the graph
adding nodes
[ ( 4,5 ) ( -6,11 ) ]
```

The order in which the nodes in the graph are listed may be reversed because the hash table data structure used to hold the nodes has no specified ordering.

A Graph1 object contains a collection of nodes stored in a hash table. The field nodeList is of type **Hashtable**. The core class **Hashtable** is defined in the package **java.util** and provides hash table objects. In the next chapter, you learn more about using **Hashtable** and the other collection classes. The first statement in the definition of the Graph1 class declares the nodeList field:

```
public class Graph1 {
    private Hashtable nodeList = new Hashtable();
```

The method addNode uses two methods from the **Hashtable** class:

➤ **containsKey** determines whether an object with a particular key is already stored in the hash.

➤ **put** adds a node object to the hash table.

```
public void addNode( int x, int y ) {
    Node n = new Node( x, y );
    if ( ! nodeList.containsKey( n.key() ) ) {
        nodeList.put( n.key(), n );
    }
}
```

The method **key** in the nested class **Node** generates identifying keys for the node objects. Note that Graph1 has exclusive use of Node because Node is private, and that Graph1 can access the members of Node. The methods addNode and **main** of Graph1 use Node exactly as they would use any class to which they have access.

```
    private static class Node {
        private int x, y;
        public Node( int x, int y ) {
            this.x = x;
            this.y = y;
         }
        public Object key() {
            return x + "," + y;
        }
        public String toString() {
            return "( " + x + "," + y + " )";
        }
    }
}
```

## INNER CLASSES

Inner classes are very different in nature from top-level classes. The term **top-level** applies to classes that are the top level of containment, excluding packages, and inner classes are always contained in other classes.

To understand why top-level classes and inner classes are so different in nature, you must consider the **state data** of objects. All instances of classes have **state data**. For objects of top-level classes, the state data is equivalent to the current instance of the class. The state data for an instance includes all the fields that it contains. The object reference **this** refers to the state data of one instance. The complicating factor for inner classes is that the object reference **this** relates not only to the current instance of the inner class, but also to the enclosing instances of all enclosing classes.

Compare what happens with subclasses to what happens with inner classes. An instance of a subclass has an independent copy of all the fields declared in the subclass and of all the fields inherited from its superclass. With inheritance you cannot create two objects that share the same copies of instance variables. If you instantiate a subclass and its superclass, you create two objects that can have some of the same fields, but they have different copies, or instances, of those fields. The superclass and subclass objects are completely separate objects.

In contrast, when you instantiate an inner class and the class that encloses it, the two objects are created with access to the same copies of the fields defined in the enclosing class. In fact, you must have an instance of the enclosing class with which to create the inner class. The inner class state data contains the inner class fields. The enclosing class state data contains the enclosing class fields. The object reference **this** for the inner class instance refers to both the inner and enclosing state data. In Figure 9-1, the gray boxes are included in the state data of both the enclosing and inner class objects.

This situation is analogous to the way in which all instances of the same class share class variables. Just as all instances of a class have access to the class variables and share a single copy of these fields, all inner class instances that share an enclosing instance have access to the fields of the enclosing instance and share a single copy of them.

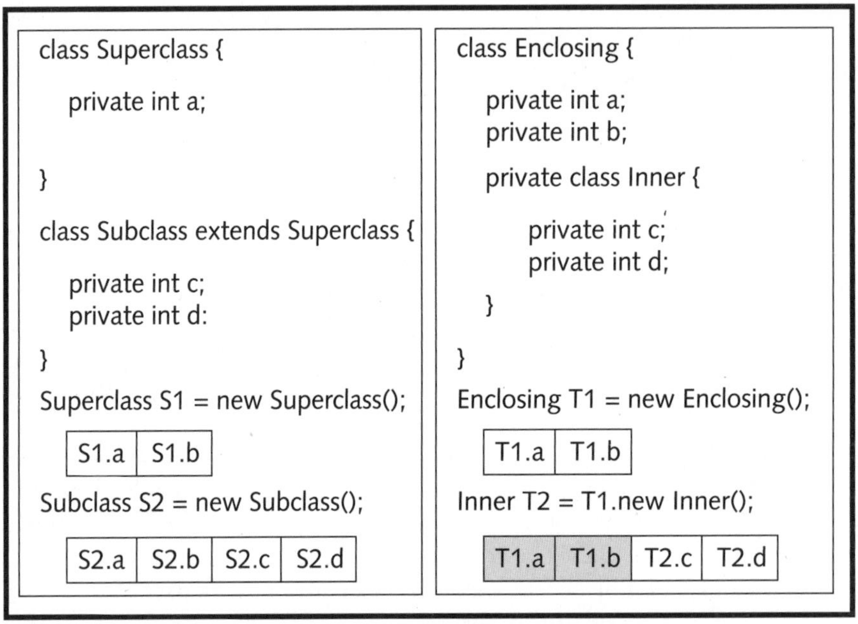

```
class Superclass {

    private int a;


}

class Subclass extends Superclass {

    private int c;
    private int d:

}

Superclass S1 = new Superclass();
```

| S1.a | S1.b |
|------|------|

```
Subclass S2 = new Subclass();
```

| S2.a | S2.b | S2.c | S2.d |
|------|------|------|------|

```
class Enclosing {

    private int a;
    private int b;

    private class Inner {

        private int c;
        private int d;

    }

}

Enclosing T1 = new Enclosing();
```

| T1.a | T1.b |
|------|------|

```
Inner T2 = T1.new Inner();
```

| T1.a | T1.b | T2.c | T2.d |
|------|------|------|------|

**Figure 9-1**    The inner class examples.inner.Computer.HardDrive listed in the VisualAge for Java class browser

Three kinds of inner classes are possible:

➤ **Member inner classes** are defined inside another class, at the same level as fields and methods. They are members of the enclosing class.

➤ **Local inner classes** are defined inside blocks of code. They are local to the enclosing method or block.

➤ **Anonymous inner classes** are local inner classes that have no name.

## Understanding the Reasons for Using Inner Classes

Programming inner classes is an advanced technique, and you may be wondering whether inner classes are worth the complications that they bring to the Java programming language. For example, you must use an expanded form of the **new** keyword to instantiate anonymous inner classes, and you must learn a new way to use the **super** method when inner classes have subclasses.

One benefit is the elegant way in which you can use them to create adapter classes within an existing class. **Adapter classes** are a programming design pattern intended to convert the interface of a class into a different interface that the class does not implement, but that the clients of the class expect. You can define adapter classes that are implemented as inner classes, in the places where they are used. The resulting classes also have access to the internal variables and methods of the enclosing class or block. The example class `Equation1` later in this chapter demonstrates using inner classes in this way.

An inner class is an elegant way to implement an interface when the interface defines only one method. This situation is common when you program graphical user interfaces. The Java platform provides many interfaces that react to user actions, and several of these interfaces contain only one method for a single user action. You write tidier source code if you define an anonymous inner class to implement the interface than if you define and create an instance of another top-level class. Using inner classes to implement one-method interfaces packages a block of statements so that it can be passed as an argument. The method that receives the instance of the inner class can then use the instance by calling the method as defined in the interface.

**9**

The impact of inner classes on your code depends very much on how you use them. They are not as critical as inheritance, without which object-oriented programming is severely limited. On the other hand, some awkward techniques become elegant when implemented with inner classes. You may even be tempted to take advantage of all the nuances of inner classes. If you are, take care not to create programs that are difficult to understand and maintain. If you use inner classes in a straightforward manner and for the purposes for which they were designed, you can reap considerable benefits from minimal effort.

## Defining Member Inner Classes

Inner classes are instance members of their enclosing classes. Define a member inner class like you define a nested top-level class, but do not qualify the inner class with the keyword **static**.

*Syntax*

```
[public] [qualifiers] class enclosing_class_name {
    // . . .
    [access_specifiers] [qualifiers] class enclosed_class_name {
    // . . .
    }
}
```

*Dissection*

➤ The syntax of the enclosing class definition is like any class definition.

➤ You can declare inner classes to be public, protected, or private, because they are members of the enclosing class. If you omit an access specifier, the class has the default package access.

➤ The qualifiers **abstract** and **final** have their usual meaning when applied to inner classes, but you cannot use the qualifier **static**. If you declare the enclosed class to be static, it becomes a nested class but not an inner class.

*Code Example*

```
public class Outer {
    //. . .
    private class Inner {
        // . . .
    }
}
```

*Code Dissection*

Here the class **Inner** is an inner class enclosed in the class **Outer**. Only **Outer** and other classes enclosed in **Outer** can access **Inner**, because **Inner** is private.

Every instance of the inner class must exist within an instance of the enclosing class. An inner class cannot be instantiated without an instance of the outer class. Therefore, you must associate the keyword **new** with an instance of the enclosing class to create an instance of an inner class.

*Syntax*

*enclosing _instance.***new** *inner_class***(** *arguments* **)**

*Dissection*

➤ The enclosing class instance must be an object reference for an existing object. If you are creating the inner class object in an instance method of the enclosing class, the object reference **this** is implied.

*Code Example*

```
public static void main( String[] args ) {
    Outer O = new Outer();
    Inner I = O.new Inner();
        // . . .
}
```

The next program is a reworking of the undirected graph classes Graph1 from the previous example program. This new class is called Graph2. The class Node is now a member inner class instead of a nested class. The lines that have changed since Graph1 appear in boldface.

```java
package examples.inner;
import java.util.Hashtable;
import java.util.Enumeration;
/** Class representing an undirected graph composed
 * of nodes.  The node class is a top-level class
 * nested within the Graph2 class.
 */
public class Graph2 {
   private Hashtable nodeList = new Hashtable();
   /** Add a node to the graph
    * @param x the x coordinate of the node
    * @param y the y coordinate of the node
    */
   public void addNode( int x, int y ) {
      // the use of "this." is not required here
      this.new Node( x, y );
   }
   /** Get the object as a string
    * @return the object as a string
    */
   public String toString() {
      StringBuffer sb = new StringBuffer( "[ " );
      Enumeration e = nodeList.elements();
      while ( e.hasMoreElements() ) {
         sb.append( e.nextElement().toString()
                     + " " );
      }
      sb.append( "]" );
      return sb.toString();
   }
   /** Test method
    * @param args not used
    */
   public static void main( String[] args ) {
      System.out.println( "creating the graph" );
      Graph2 g = new Graph2();
      System.out.println( "adding nodes" );
      g.addNode( 4, 5 );
      g.addNode( -6, 11 );
      System.out.println( g );
   }
   /** The class representing nodes within the graph
    */
   private class Node {
      private int x, y;
```

9

```
        public Node( int x, int y ) {
           this.x = x;
           this.y = y;
           // the use of "Graph2.this." is not
           // required here
           if ( ! Graph2.this.nodeList
                       .containsKey( key() ) ) {
              nodeList.put( key(), this );
           }
        }
        /** Determine the key value for a node
         * @return the key as a String
         */
        public Object key() {
           return x + "," + y;
        }
        /** Get the object as a string
         * @return the object as a string
         */
        public String toString() {
           return "( " + x + "," + y + " )";
        }
   }    // end of Node class
}    // end of Graph2 class
```

In this program, the single line that starts the definition of the enclosed class
Node determines its nature. This definition omits the keyword **static**. Because
Node does not have the **static** qualifier, it is an inner class.

```
private class Node {
```

The method addNode of the enclosing class Graph2 method has changed.
Where the method in Graph1 created an object of the nested class Node and
then conditionally called method addNode for the nodeList field, the
method in Graph2 has just one line:

```
this.new Node( x, y );
```

Because Node is a member of Graph2, its constructor can call addNode for the
nodeList field. To create the Node object, you must specify an enclosing
instance of the Graph2 class. Here, the object reference **this** indicates the current
Graph2 object. Because addNode is an instance method, the implicit **this** object
reference would have sufficed, but the expression **this.new** emphasizes the fact
that an enclosing instance is being associated with the object being created. The
next sample program demonstrates a situation where you cannot omit the object
reference **this**.

Now consider the constructor of the **Node** class, and consider in particular the use of the **this** object reference:

```
public Node( int x, int y ) {
   this.x = x;
   this.y = y;
   if ( ! Graph2.this.nodeList
               .containsKey( key() ) ){
     nodeList.put( key(), this );
   }
```

The state data of an inner class object includes current instances of the enclosing class as well as the immediate current instance of the inner class. These lines use two current instances: **this** and **graph2.this**.

For the inner class object, **this** refers to the enclosed instance containing the fields defined in the inner class. Thus, **this** for a **Node** object relates to the **Node**'s **x** and **y** fields. This constructor passes the current **Node** object, **this**, to the **put** method of the **Hashtable** class because **put** must receive the object reference for the object to add to the hash table in its first argument.

You can always access the current instance of an enclosing class with a qualified **this** object reference. In this constructor, the object reference, called **Graph2.this**, explicitly qualifies the **nodeList** field. In this case, the explicit qualification is not necessary because ambiguity exists and the conditional expression could read as follows:

```
( ! nodeList.containsKey( key() ) )
```

The only time you must explicitly qualify a member name is when a name conflict exists between a member in an enclosing class and a name inherited from a superclass.

## Avoiding Name Conflicts in Inner Classes

The potential for name conflicts is one of the complications inner classes add to the Java programming language. An inner class belongs to two hierarchies: its containment hierarchy and its inheritance hierarchy.

➤ The containment hierarchy for an inner class is the sequence of classes that enclose it, up to and including the top-level class at package scope.

➤ The inheritance hierarchy is the sequence of superclasses from which it inherits, up to and including the class **Object**.

If your inner class inherits a member with the same name as a member of the enclosing object, the unqualified name of the member is ambiguous. If a method of the inner class uses the member name without qualifying it, a compiler error results. Figure 9-2 demonstrates how name conflicts can arise.

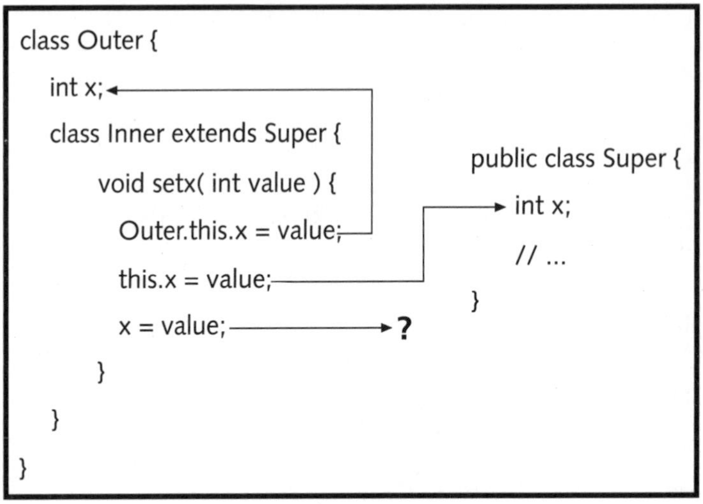

```
class Outer {
    int x;
    class Inner extends Super {
        void setx( int value ) {
            Outer.this.x = value;
            this.x = value;
            x = value;          ?
        }
    }
}
```

```
                    public class Super {
                        int x;
                        // ...
                    }
```

**Figure 9-2**  Name conflicts in inner classes

## Enclosing Objects of Inner Classes

You have seen what happens when you create a member inner class within an instance method of an enclosing class: the enclosing object defaults to the instance of the enclosing class for which the instance method is run. What happens when you create an instance of an inner class in a class method of the enclosing class? In this case, you must qualify the **new** keyword with an object reference for the enclosing object. When you create an instance of an inner class in a class method of the enclosing class, the enclosing object can be any instance of the enclosing class.

The state data of an inner class object includes the instance of the inner class and one instance of the enclosing class for every enclosing level. The fact that inner class objects have more than one instance has the following implications:

➤ More than one instance of inner classes can share the same enclosing object.

➤ Inner class objects have access to private members of enclosing classes. The members of the enclosing objects are extensions of the states of the inner class objects.

➤ If an enclosing class has more than one member inner class definition, each of the inner classes has access to the private members of the others.

➤ Every instance of an inner class is permanently associated with its enclosing instance. You cannot move an inner class object from one enclosing instance to another. The references to enclosing objects are immutable, just as the **this** reference is immutable. For example, a statement such as the following is not allowed:

```
outer_class.this
    = new outer_class( argument );    // not valid
```

➤ Inner classes may not contain class methods or class variables. The Java programming language specifies that the keyword **static** can qualify only the definition of a top-level construct. Because the entire body of an inner class is within the scope of one or more enclosing instances, an inner class cannot contain a top-level construct.

The following is a sample program in which an inner class, `HardDrive`, is instantiated in the **main** method of a class called `Computer`. Indeed, the `Computer` object `atWork` has two instances of `HardDrive`: `IDE1` and `IDE2`. Therefore, the two instances of `HardDrive` share the same enclosing object, `atWork`. Notice that the `HardDrive` class can use the private members of `Computer`. Further notes about the code follow the example program.

```
package examples.inner;
/** Class to represent the memory and hard drive
  * information of a computer
  */
public class Computer {
   /** Maximum number of hard drives in a computer */
   public static final int MAX_DRIVES = 4;
   private int installedDrives = 0;
   private HardDrive[] drives
      = new HardDrive[MAX_DRIVES];
   private int memMegs;
   /** Test method
     * @param args not used
     */
   public static void main( String[] args )
                              throws Exception {
      Computer atWork = new Computer( 64 );
      System.out.println( atWork );
      // must specify the enclosing object here
      HardDrive IDE1 = atWork.new HardDrive( 1024 );
      HardDrive IDE2 = atWork.new HardDrive( 2048 );
      System.out.println( atWork );
   }
   /** Construct a Computer object
     * @param memSize the amount of memory in MB
     */
   public Computer( int memSize ) {
      memMegs = memSize;
   }
   /** Provide a string representing the computer
     * @return string representation of the object
     */
```

**9**

```
        public String toString() {
           StringBuffer sb
              = new StringBuffer( "Memory: " + memMegs
                                  + "MB" );
           for ( int i=0; i<installedDrives; i++ ) {
              sb.append( ", Drive" + i + ": " );
              sb.append( drives[i].size + "MB" );
           }
           return sb.toString();
        }
        /** Class representing a hard drive within
         * a computer
         */
        public class HardDrive {
           private int size;
           /** Construct a hard drive object and add it
            * to the list of installed drives
            * if there is room
            * @param size Size of the drive in MB
            * @exception Exception thrown
            *     if there isn't room for
            *     the hard drive being added
            */
           public HardDrive( int size ) throws Exception {
              this.size = size;
              // add this drive to the enclosing computer
              if ( installedDrives < MAX_DRIVES ) {
                 drives[installedDrives++] = this;
              } else {
                 throw new Exception( "Sorry, no "
                                      + "more room." );
              }
           }
        }
     }
}
```

The output is

```
Memory: 64MB
Memory: 64MB, Drive0: 1024MB, Drive1: 2048MB
```

Because the code that creates the `HardDrive` objects is in the class method **main**, the **new** keyword that constructs Hard Drive objects must be qualified with the enclosing object, `atWork` as in the following lines:

```
HardDrive IDE1 = atWork.new HardDrive( 1024 );
HardDrive IDE2 = atWork.new HardDrive( 2048 );
```

Notice that the constructor of `HardDrive` adds each new `HardDrive` object to an array called `drives`, which is a private field of `Computer`. The array `drives` is an array of object references for the inner `HardDrive` objects that share the enclosing instance. The `HardDrive` constructor freely uses the private members of `Computer`, regardless of whether they are class variables, like `MAX_DRIVES`, or instance variables, like `installedDrives` and `drives`, as in the following lines:

```
if ( installedDrives < MAX_DRIVES ) {
   drives[installedDrives++] = this;
}
```

If you were to add another member inner class, `HardDriveController`, to the `Computer` class, objects of the `HardDrive` class would have access not only to all the members of the `Computer` class, but also to all the members of the `HardDriveController` class. Likewise, objects of the `HardDriveController` class would have access to all the members of the `Computer` and `HardDrive` classes.

Similarly, the enclosing class has access to private members of the inner class. The **toString** method, which overrides the default **toString** of the **Object** class so that you can print a report on the hard drives, can use the instance variable `size`.

9

---

**Mini Quiz 9-2**

If the enclosing class has full access to all fields in an inner class, why must you qualify the name of the field `size` in the following statement?

```
sb.append( drives[i].size + "MB" );
```

---

## Working with Subclasses of Member Inner Classes

You can extend a member inner class. Inheritance works in the same way for inner classes as it does for top-level classes, except that some new syntax is required to deal with inner classes. Here is the declaration of a subclass of the `Computer.HardDrive` class, defined in the previous example:

```
package examples.inner;
/** A class definition to show how it is possible
  * to use an inner class as a superclass
  */
public class SCSIHardDrive extends Computer.HardDrive {
   private static final int DRIVE_CAPACITY = 512;
   /** Construct a SCSI hard drive object within an
     * enclosing Computer instance
     * @param c the enclosing computer instance
     * @exception Exception is thrown if there is no
     *     room to put the hard drive into the computer
     */
   public SCSIHardDrive( Computer c ) throws Exception {
      c.super( DRIVE_CAPACITY );
   }
}
```

A subclass constructor can explicitly call the constructor of the superclass. If **super** is not called explicitly, the default constructor of the superclass is called implicitly. Inner classes add a complication: If the superclass is an inner class, an object of the superclass cannot be constructed without an enclosing object. Where should the enclosing object be specified? The most obvious place is within the call to the superclass constructor. The Java programming language puts the onus on you to call **super** explicitly when the constructor must be qualified or take arguments. The constructor of the `SCSIHardDrive` class calls the constructor of its superclass, the `Computer.HardDrive` class. You qualify the call with the `Computer` object passed as an argument to the constructor of `SCSIHardDrive`, so that the superclass object can be successfully constructed.

---

**Mini Quiz 9-3**

Can you instantiate a subclass of a member inner class with a default constructor?

---

# LOCAL INNER CLASSES

Classes declared inside methods are called **local inner classes**, to distinguish them from **member inner classes**. The only kind of class you can define inside a method is an inner class, and you define it by simply including the definition within a block of code.

Local inner classes differ from member inner classes in the following ways:

➤ They are private to the blocks in which they are defined, and cannot be declared with the keywords **public**, **private**, or **protected**. For this reason, the names of the classes cannot be used anywhere except the method in which they are defined.

➤ The methods of a local inner class have access to much more than just the fields defined within them. The state of a local inner class object includes:

- Its own fields, which cannot be qualified with **static**

- All local variables marked **final** within any enclosing method or local block

- All arguments of enclosing methods that are marked **final**

- One enclosing instance of each enclosing class up to and including the top-level class at package scope

➤ Objects of a local inner class and all the objects within their extended states live beyond the scopes in which they are created.

The extended lifetime of local inner classes arises because of the way the Java Virtual Machine (JVM) instantiates local inner classes. The JVM builds all objects of reference types, including instances of local inner classes, not on the stack but in a separate area of memory from which only the garbage collector can remove them. When creating objects of a local inner class, the JVM copies local variables and the method arguments into the object. If the arguments or local variables have reference types, objects of the local inner class hold object references for the arguments or variables and prevent the garbage collector from sweeping the referenced objects away. Therefore, the lifetime of method arguments and local variables continues after the method execution ends.

The compiler for the Java programming language must impose one condition so that instances of local class objects can have this extended lifetime: All arguments and local variables of the enclosing methods that are referenced by a local inner class must be qualified with **final**. The compiler rejects an inner class that breaks this rule because the inner class object has only copies of the arguments and local variables. If the inner classes could change these copies, the JVM would not  properly propagate the changes to the enclosing objects.

**9**

> ### Mini Quiz 9-4
>
> Do arguments and local variables of a method have to be constants if the method has an inner class that refers to them? In your answer consider objects of both primitive and reference types.

Local inner classes can be defined within both class and instance methods. When defined in an instance method, the local class can use all members of the enclosing class. When defined in a class method, the local class can use only class variables and class methods of the enclosing class. In all other ways, it does not matter whether the enclosing method is a class method.

The next sample program demonstrates many of the characteristics of local inner classes. Each instance of the class `Equation1` has a method `getResult` to solve an equation. The actual equation solved in this example has no particular meaning and is not based on any known mathematical formula. The interesting aspect of this class is that the method that returns the solution to the equation has an inner class that implements an interface. Because it implements the interface, the inner class must implement the method defined in that interface, which in this case is the method that solves the equation. Therefore, this example shows how an inner class can be an adapter class by implementing an interface that the enclosing class does not implement.

The following listing is the definition of the class `Equation1`. A top-level interface, `Equation1.Result`, is nested inside `Equation1`. The interface contains one method, `getAnswer`. The method `Equation1.getResult` has an inner class, `MyResult`, that implements `Equation1.Result` and therefore implements `getAnswer`. You look in more detail at some of the interesting constructs in the class after you see the code for entire program.

```java
package examples.inner;
/** A class definition to explore the use of local
  * inner classes
  */
public class Equation1 {
   private int equationInput;
   /** An interface defining the result from an
     * equation
     */
   public interface Result {
      public double getAnswer();
   }
   /** Constructor method
     * @param ei the equation input
     */
   public Equation1( int ei ) {
      equationInput = ei;
   }
   /** Create the result of the equation for the given
     * input values
     * @param input1 the first equation input
     * @param input2 the second equation input
     * @return the result object
     */
   public Result getResult(final int input1,
                           final int input2 ) {
      final int[] localVar={ 2,6,10,14};
      class MyResult implements Result {
         private int normalField;
         public MyResult() {
            normalField = 2;
         }
         public double getAnswer() {
            return (double) input1 / input2
                            - equationInput + localVar[2]
                            - normalField;
         }
      }
      return new MyResult();
   }
   /** The test method for the class
     * @param args not used
     */
```

```
    public static void main( String[] args ) {
        Equation1 e = new Equation1( 10 );
        Result r = e.getResult( 33, 5 );
        System.out.println( r.getAnswer() );
    }
}
```

The definition of the interface `Result` is nested inside the class `Equation1`, so this example is a complete solution. If you move the definition of `Result` out of the class and provide it elsewhere in the same package, there would be no impact on the rest of the `Example1` class. The interface `Result` contains one method, `getAnswer`, and all classes that implement this interface must implement this method. `getAnswer` returns a value of type **double**.

```
public class Equation1 {
    public interface Result {
        public double getAnswer();
    }
```

The class `Equation1` has a method, `getResult`, to solve the equation. The actual calculation is performed by the method `getAnswer` of the class `MyResult`, which is a local class defined in `getResult`. Because `MyResult` implements `Result`, the class must provide an implementation of the method `getAnswer`. This particular implementation is interesting because it uses data stored in different places to demonstrate the different kinds of extended state that a local inner class may have.

```
public Result getResult( final int input1,
                         final int input2 ) {
    final int[] localVar= {2,6,10,14};
    class MyResult implements Result {
        private int normalField;
        public MyResult() {
            normalField = 2;
        }
        public double getAnswer() {
            return ( double ) input1/input2
                            - equationInput
                            + localVar[2]
                            - normalField;
        }
    }
}
```

Notice that the five terms in the equation from which the answer is calculated are stored in different ways:

➤ `equationInput` is a private instance variable of the enclosing class.

➤ `input1` and `input2` are arguments of the instance method in which the local class is defined.

➤ `localVar[2]` is an element of an array that is a local variable of the instance method in which the local class is defined.

➤ `normalField` is a private instance variable of the local inner class.

Notice that the `getResult` method returns an object that it creates. There would be nothing special about such a construct if the type of `MyResult` were defined outside the method:

```
return new MyResult();
```

You must look in the **main** method to see where the object of the class `MyResult` is actually used. The **main** method calls `getAnswer` and writes the value to the standard output stream. Thus, a `MyResult` object is actually used long after the end of the scope in which the object is created. The arguments and the local variables of the method are available even though the method has finished.

```
public static void main( String[] args ) {
    Equation1 e = new Equation1( 10 );
    Result r = e.getResult( 33, 5 );
    System.out.println( r.getAnswer() );
}
```

> **Mini Quiz 9-5**
>
> What is the output of this program?
>
> Could you insert assignment statements into the method `getAnswer` to change the value of the elements of the array `localVar`, even though the array is a local variable in the method `getResult` and is declared to be final?

## ANONYMOUS LOCAL INNER CLASSES

The name given to the local inner class in the previous example may seem somewhat pointless. The name of a local inner class cannot be used outside the block in which the local class is defined. As in the `Equation1` example, all references to the type of an object of a local class use the name of the interface that the local class implements or the class that the local class extends. If you do not need to refer to a local class by its name inside the method, you can make it an anonymous inner class. Anonymous inner classes are always local to a code block.

# Creating Anonymous Inner Classes

Here is another example of inner classes adding complexity to the Java programming language. The **new** keyword has an enhanced form so that a class definition can follow it. Use the enhanced **new** keyword to declare anonymous inner classes.

*Syntax*

**new** [*class_or_interface_name*()] { *body_of_class* }

*Dissection*

➤ As always, the **new** keyword creates an object and returns the object reference for the new object. An anonymous inner class cannot have a constructor; if you supply arguments with the **new** keyword, they are passed to the constructor of the superclass.

➤ The optional *class_or_interface_name* is the name of either a class that is extended or an interface that is implemented by the anonymous class being defined. If you omit a class or interface name, the anonymous class extends the **Object** class.

➤ The members of the class are defined in the body of the class and enclosed in braces in the usual manner.

*Code Example*

```
new {
    String msg() {
        return "anonymous inner class";
    }
}
```

*Code Dissection*

This anonymous inner class contains one method that returns a **String**. You can call this method with the object for which the inner class is instantiated.

# Using Instance Initializers

Anonymous inner classes have neither names nor constructors. To initial an object, use an instance initializer. The syntax of instance initializers is very simple.

*Syntax*

```
{
    initialization_statements
}
```

*Dissection*

➤ An instance initializer is a nameless block of code surrounded by braces and placed anywhere inside the definition of a class.

➤ An instance initializer has the same syntax as a static initializer, but without the keyword **static**.

The use of instance initializer blocks is not limited to anonymous inner classes. You can include an instance initializer block in any class definition, even if you also define one or more constructors. Instance initializer blocks are executed before the constructor, but after the superclass constructor. They provide a very handy way to collect common initialization statements into one place when a class has more than one constructor.

The **Equation1** example program has been reworked to use an anonymous inner class, and the resulting class is called **Equation2**. All the changes required to convert the local inner class from the **Equation1** example to the anonymous inner class of the **Equation2** example are confined to the **getResult** method that follows and are shown in boldface:

```
/** Create the result of the equation for the given
  * input values
  * @param input1 the first equation input
  * @param input2 the second equation input
  * @return the result object
  */
  public Result getResult( final int input1,
                           final int input2 ) {
     final int[] localVar = { 2,6,10,14 };
     return new Result() {
        private int normalField;
        public double getAnswer() {
           return ( double ) input1 / input2
                             - equationInput
                             + localVar[2]
                             - normalField;
        }
        // this is an instance initializer block
        {
           normalField = 2;
        }
     };
  }
```

The definition of the local class is moved into the return statement and combined with the enhanced form of the **new** keyword.

The structure of `Equation1.getResult` is as follows:

```
public Result getResult( final int input1,
                         final int input2 ) {
   final int[] localVar = {2,6,10,14};
   class MyResult implements Result { /*. . . */ }
   return new MyResult();
}
```

The structure of `Equation2.getResult` is as follows:

```
public Result getResult( final int input1,
                         final int input2 ) {
   final int localVar[] = new int[10];
   return new Result() { /* . . . */ };
}
```

The constructor in the local class definition has been dropped:

```
public MyResult (){
   normalField = 2;
}
```

An instance initializer has been added to the body of the anonymous class:

```
{
   normalField = 2;
}
```

## EFFECTS ON GENERATED CLASS FILES

How does the file-naming scheme required by the JVM cope with inner and nested classes? A few extra naming rules and conventions apply:

➤ For the purpose of gaining access from other packages, all classes have either public or package access. If you declare a member class to be **protected**, its .class file defines it as a public class. If you declare a member class to be **private**, its .class file defines it as having package scope.

➤ Each nested top-level class or inner class is stored in its own .class file.

➤ The filename generated for .class files consists of the enclosing class name, followed by a dollar sign character ($), and then by the enclosed class name, for every level of nesting.

➤ An anonymous class is identified by a number.

For example, the Java compiler creates three .class files when it compiles the Equation2.java file:

➤ `Equation2.class`
As you probably expect, this file contains the public class `Equation2`.

➤ `Equation2$Result.class`
This file contains the nested interface `Result`.

➤ `Equation2$1.class`
This file is for the anonymous inner class.

The VisualAge for Java class browsers also uses the $ format to display or locate names of inner classes. For example, if you import the sample classes from this chapter into the VisualAge IDE, you can find the `examples.inner.Computer.HardDrive` inner class by searching for it by name:

1. Click the **Classes** tab of the workbench window to bring up the class browser.

2. Right-click in the list of classes to bring up a popup menu and then select **GoTo Class**.

3. When the **GoTo Class** SmartGuide appears, type `Compu`. Notice that the list of class names below the entry area shows all the classes beginning with the letters you type. As you add letters, the list gets shorter. You can type fewer or more letters until the class name you want appears in the list.

4. Select **Computer$HardDrive** from the displayed list of class names, making sure that the package **examples.inner** is also selected from the list of package names. Then, click **OK**.

The IDE returns you to the Class browser. Now `Computer$HardDrive` is highlighted in the list of classes and its source is displayed in the area at the bottom of the class browser window, as shown in Figure 9-3.

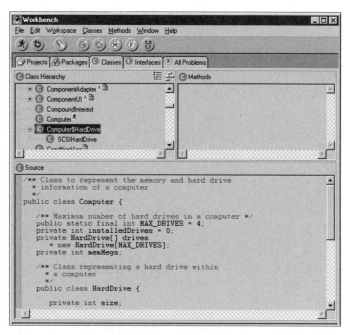

**Figure 9-3**    The inner class examples.inner.Computer.HardDrive listed in the
VisualAge for Java class browser

# Summary

A top-level class is a class that is contained only in packages and not in other classes. In the Java programming language, classes can also be contained in other classes.

You can define a class inside the definition of another class. The enclosed class is a nested class. Depending on how you define it, the enclosed class falls into one of the following categories:

➤ Nested top-level classes

➤ Member inner classes

➤ Local inner classes

➤ Anonymous local inner classes

Nested top-level classes are declared with the keyword **static**. Except for the fact that they are defined within another class, they have the same behavior and characteristics of top-level classes defined at package scope.

Member inner classes are defined inside another class. Their definitions are syntactically identical to those of nested classes except that they are not declared static.

Member inner classes must be instantiated as part of an instance of their enclosing class. Therefore, you can qualify the **new** keyword with an object reference to specify the enclosing object. You must qualify **new** if the object of an inner class is created in a class method.

The state data of an inner class object includes the current instance of the inner class and every enclosing object, up to and including the enclosing object of the top-level class at package scope. Thus, inner class objects have an extended state compared to top-level class objects. More than one inner class object can share enclosing objects.

Local inner classes are defined within a method, and their definitions are private to that method. Like member inner classes, local inner classes have state data that extends to include the enclosing object. In addition, the state data includes all method parameters and method local variables that are declared **final**.

After an object of a local inner class has been created, its lifetime continues even after the scope in which the class is declared ends.

Anonymous inner classes are local inner classes that do not have a name. Objects of such classes are created using an enhanced syntax for the **new** keyword:

**new** [*class_or_interface_name*()] { *body_of_class* }

Anonymous inner classes do not have constructors, but you can initialize their fields with instance initializer blocks. You can also use instance initializer blocks within top-level classes.

## QUESTIONS

1. Examine the following code:

```
public class Quiz9_1 {
    private int a = 200;
    public static void main( String[] args ) {
        Quiz9_1 x = new Quiz9_1();
        B y = new B();
    }
}
public class B {
    private int b = 100;
    }
}
```

Which of the following statements are true? Select all that apply.

a. The compiler rejects the definition of the B class because it is not declared with the **static** keyword.

b. Compilation is successful.

c. Class B is a member inner class.

    d. The compiler rejects the expression **new B( )** because it does not provide an enclosing instance for the object being created.

2. Examine the following code:

```
public class Quiz9_2 {
    // = X =
}
```

Which of the following class definitions are valid when placed at the line marked **-X-**? Select all that apply.

    a. `public class A { }`

    b. `protected class B { }`

    c. `public static class C { }`

    d. `private static class D { }`

    e. `static class E { }`

3. Examine the following code taken from a single source file:

```
public class Quiz9_3 {
    private int x;
    static public void main( String[] args ) {
        class A { };
    }
    protected class B { }
    public int getX() {
        class C { }
        return x;
    }
    private static class D { }
}
class E { }
```

Which of the classes are inner classes? Select all valid answers.

    a. A

    b. B

    c. C

    d. D

    e. E

4. Examine the following code taken from a single source file:

```
interface Y {
    public void f();
}
abstract class Z {
    public abstract void g();
```

```
              public void h() {
                  System.out.println( "Hello!" );
              }
      }
      public class Quiz9_4 {
              public static void main( String[] args ) {
                  // = X =
              }
      }
```

Which of the statements include valid definitions of anonymous inner classes when placed at position **–X–**? Select all that apply.

```
  a. Object y = new Y() {
          public void f() {
              System.out.println( "Choice a)" );
          }
     };
  b. Z z = new Z() {
          public void g() {
              System.out.println( "Choice b)" );
          }
     };
  c. Object y = new Y, Z() {
          public void f() {
              System.out.println( "Choice c)" );
          }
          public void g() {
              System.out.println( "Choice c)" );
          }
     };
  d. Z z = new Z() {
          public void h() {
              System.out.println( "Choice d)" );
          }
     };
  e. Object z = new Z() {
          public void g() {
              System.out.println( "Choice e)" );
          }
          public void h() {
              System.out.println( "Choice e)" );
          }
     };
```

5. Examine the following code taken from a single source file:

```
public class Quiz9_5 {
    public int calculate() {
        return a + b + c + d + e;
    }
```

```
    static public void main( String[] args ) {
        class A {
            private int a;
        };
    }
    protected class B {
        private int b;
    }
    class C {
        private int c;
    }
    private static class D {
        private int d;
    }
}
class E {
    private int e;
}
```

Which of the following statements are true? Select all that apply.

a. The compiler rejects the expression a + b + c + d + e because the variable a is undefined at that place in the file.

b. The compiler rejects the expression a + b + c + d + e because the variable b is undefined at that place in the file.

c. The compiler rejects the expression a + b + c + d + e because the variable c is undefined at that place in the file.

d. The compiler rejects the expression a + b + c + d + e because the variable d is undefined at that place in the file.

e. The compiler rejects the expression a + b + c + d + e because the variable e is undefined at that place in the file.

6. Examine the following code:

```
public class Quiz9_6 {
    public class C {
    }
}
```

Which of the following statements best describes the type of the class called C? Select the best answer.

a. local inner class

b. member inner class

c. member inner class at package scope

d. static member class

e. anonymous inner class

7. Examine the following code taken from a single source file:

```java
public class Quiz9_7 {
    static public void main( String[] args ) {
        class A {
            private int a;
        };
    }
    protected class B {
        private int b;
        public int calculate() {
            return a + b + cObj.c + dObj.d + e;
        }
    }
    class C {
        private int c;
    }
    private static class D {
        private int d;
    }
    private D dObj = new D();
    private C cObj = new C();
    private int e;
}
```

Which of the following statements are true? Select all that apply.

a. The compiler rejects the expression
   a + b + cObj.c + dObj.d + e because the variable a is undefined at that place in the file.

b. The compiler rejects the expression
   a + b + cObj.c + dObj.d + e because the variable b is undefined at that place in the file.

c. The compiler rejects the expression
   a + b + cObj.c + dObj.d + e because the variable cObj.c is
   undefined at that place in the file.

d. The compiler rejects the expression
   a + b + cObj.c + dObj.d + e because the variable dObj.d is
   undefined at that place in the file.

e. The compiler rejects the expression
   a + b + cObj.c + dObj.d + e because the variable e is undefined at that place in the file.

8. True or False: When you are creating an instance of any inner class, specifying an enclosing instance is optional.

9. Examine the following code:

```java
public class Quiz9_8 {
```

```
    public void calculate() {
        // - X -
    }
}
```

Which of the following class definitions are valid when placed at the line marked **-X-**? Select all that apply.

a. `public class A { };`

b. `protected class B { };`

c. `class C { };`

d. `private class D { };`

e. `static class E { };`

10. Examine the following code:

```
public class Quiz9_9 {
    class A {
        // - X -
    }
}
```

Which of the following definitions are valid when placed at the line marked **-X-**? Select all that apply.

a. `static int v;`

b. `private int w;`

c. `static final int x = 10;`

d. `transient int y;`

e. `final int z = 20;`

# EXERCISES

## Debugging

1. Correct all the errors in the following program.

```
package questions.c9;
public class Debug9_1 {
    public Debug9_1() {
        class A {
            int a = 6;
        }
        Debug9_1.A x = new Debug9_1.A();
        System.out.println( x.a );
    }
    public static void main( String[] args ) {
        new Debug9_1();
    }
}
```

2. Correct all the errors in the following program:

```
package questions.c9;
public class Debug9_2 {
    A x;
    public static void main( String[] args ) {
        Debug9_2 a = new Debug9_2();
        a.x = new A();
        System.out.println( a.x.getValue() );
    }
    class A {
        private String s = "pork chops and applesauce";
        public String getValue() {
            return s;
        }
    }
}
```

3. Correct the errors in the following program so that the output of the program is as follows:

```
Shopping List:
eggs & cheese
```

Here's the program listing:

```
package questions.c9;
interface ShoppingList {
    public void f();
    public void g();
}
public class Debug9_3 {
    public static void main( String[] args ) {
        ShoppingList y = new ShoppingList() {
            public void f() {
                System.out.println( "Shopping List:" );
            }
        }
        y.f();
        y.g();
    }
}
```

4. Correct the errors in the following program without adding initializers to the definitions of the strings **ON_MSG** and **OFF_MSG**:

```
package questions.c9;
interface Switch {
    public void on();
```

```
        public void off();
    }
    public class Debug9_4 {
        public static void main( String[] args ) {
            Switch s = new Switch() {
                public Switch() {
                    ON_MSG = "Switch on";
                    OFF_MSG = "Switch off";
                }
                public void on() {
                    System.out.println( ON_MSG );
                }
                public void off() {
                    System.out.println( OFF_MSG );
                }
                final String ON_MSG;
                final String OFF_MSG;
            };
            s.on();
            s.off();
        }
    }
```

5. Correct the errors in the following program so that the output, correct to two decimal places, is **148.41**:

```
package questions.c9;
public class Debug9_5 {
    public static double calculate( double x,
                                     double y ) {
        class Helper {
            double doSomething() {
                return Math.sqrt( x ) + Math.sqrt( y );
            }
        }
        Helper h = new Helper();
        return Math.exp( h.doSomething() );
    }
    public static void main( String[] args ) {
        System.out.println( calculate( 4.0, 9.0 ) );
    }
}
```

## Complete the Solution

1. Extract the file **questions\c9\Complete9_1.java** from the file **question.jar** on the CD-ROM. Complete **main** method of the **Complete9_1** class by adding a definition of an anonymous class that implements the **TapeRecorder** interface. Test your **TapeRecorder** object by calling all four of its methods.

2. Extract the file **questions\c9\Automobile.java** from the file **question.jar** on the CD-ROM. Complete the `Automobile` program by creating four instances of the `Tire` class that all share the `Automobile` object `a` as their enclosing instance.

3. Extract the file **questions\c9\Complete9_3.java** from the file **question.jar** on the CD-ROM. Complete the definition of the class `Complete9_3` by adding a top-level nested class called `StockItem`. Add a statement to the **main** method of the `Complete9_3` class to create the `StockItem` object `x`. Your `StockItem` class must implement the methods required by the **main**.

4. Extract the file **questions\c9\Complete9_4.java** from the file **question.jar** on the CD-ROM. Complete the definition of the class `Complete9_4` by defining a local class inside the **main** method. Your class definition should implement both the `Nameable` and `Identifiable` interfaces defined inside `Complete9_4`.

5. Extract the file **questions\c9\Complete9_5.java** from the file **question.jar** on the CD-ROM. Complete the definition of the class `Complete9_5` by completing `concatenate` method. Your method should define a class that implements the `Concatenates` interface. The method should then create a `Concatenates` object and use the object to create a string that is equivalent to the result of the expression `s1 + s2`.

## Discovery

1. Expand the `Graph2` example class in this chapter to include edges as well as nodes, and call the new class `EdgeNodeGraph`. You can start with the code in the file **examples\inner\Graph2.java** from the unpacked **examples.jar** file. In a graph, a start node and an end node define an edge. Create another member inner class called `Edge` that is nested in `EdgeNodeGraph` and is a peer of `Node`. You will need to expand the methods and fields of `EdgeNodeGraph` to allow the user to create edges and to query edges already in the graph. Add a **main** method to `EdgeNodeGraph` that tests the class by adding several nodes and edges.

2. Create a class called `MusicCollection`. This class must have member inner classes called `Artist` and `Recording`. The `Recording` class must have an inner class called `Track` that represents a single piece of music within a `Recording` object. A `MusicCollection` object must have an array of `Artist` objects and an array of `Recording` objects. `Recording` objects must have a single `Artist` object, for simplicity, and an array of `Track` objects. Add a **main** method to `MusicCollection` that tests the creation of all of these objects.

## CHAPTER TEN

# UTILITY AND COLLECTION CLASSES

## In this chapter you will:

➤ Look in the package **java.util** for a variety of useful utility classes.

➤ Set up an event-notification mechanism using **Observer** and **Observable** objects.

☕ Make appropriate selections of collection classes and interfaces to suit specified behavior requirements.

➤ Use iterators to traverse collections.

➤ Define your own collection classes.

## INTRODUCTION

In previous chapters, you learned most of the Java programming language and looked at a wide variety of sample programs. Now, you are ready to move on to programming topics such as abstract data structures and specialized techniques. Typically, at this stage, a programmer looks to leverage existing technology. In an object-oriented environment, this leverage comes from using existing code that is proven to be robust and efficient and is designed for reuse in new programs.

The Java platform provides a core set of classes to support the kinds of applications that programmers are likely to be developing with the Java programming language. You have already seen one of these packages, **java.io**, which supports I/O programming, in Chapter 8. This current chapter covers the package **java.util**, which provides a framework for collections and many other useful classes. The Java programming language allows you to take advantage of the specialized services that are provided by the core classes and ensures that your program is portable across all platforms that support the JVM. Moreover, the core classes are relatively easy to learn.

You can use this chapter as a guide to the classes of the collections framework that you can use to encapsulate the data structures in your programs. The framework contains many kinds of collections. Selecting appropriate and efficient implementations of data structures in the form of collection classes can improve the performance and robustness of your program.

# THE JAVA.UTIL PACKAGE

Many of the classes in **java.util** are part of the collections framework, but it would be misleading to present **java.util** as the collection-class package. Figure 10-1 shows the structures of the classes and interfaces in **java.util** that are not part of the collections framework. The shaded boxes represent abstract classes, and the rounded boxes represent interfaces.

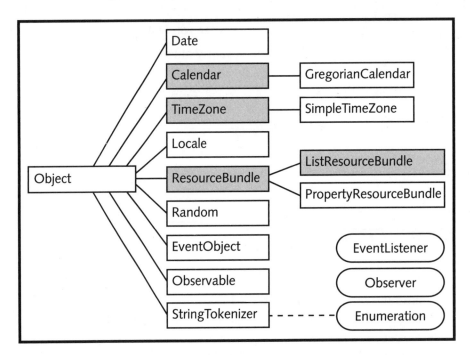

**Figure 10-1**  Some classes and interfaces in **java.util**

Several types defined in **java.util** are not related to collections. Some of the classes in **java.util**, such as the random-number generator, provide the exact Application Programming Interface (API) you need to meet specialized programming requirements. Classes in other packages use classes and interfaces in this package. For example, the **EventObject** class and **EventListener** interface form the basis for the classes and interfaces that support user interaction with a graphical user interface (GUI). You can use these classes directly, but you are more likely to use the classes in other packages that extend them. Table 10-1 summarizes the miscellaneous classes and interfaces in **java.util**.

**Table 10-1** General utility classes and interfaces in java.util

| Classes and Interfaces | Description |
| --- | --- |
| Date<br>Calendar<br>GregorianCalendar<br>TimeZone<br>SimpleTimeZone | These classes support dates and times, formatted for different cultural environments. You can call methods to convert between different date and time representations. If you have not set up a cultural environment, dates and times are formatted according to the default for your installation of the Java platform. These classes are described in more detail in the CD-ROM. |
| Locale<br>ResourceBundle<br>ListResourceBundle<br>PropertyResourceBundle | You use the locales and resource bundles when you are creating an applet or application for use in the international market. These four classes are described in the CD-ROM. |
| Observable<br>Observer | Use the Observable class and Observer interface in combination to set up a notification mechanism between classes. |
| Random | You can use or extend the Random class to generate sequences of pseudorandom numbers if the random method of the Math class does not meet your requirements. You can call methods to set the seed, which is an initial value from which following numbers are generated. Also you can obtain uniformly distributed pseudorandom numbers of type int, long, float or double, and Gaussian (normally) distributed numbers of type double.<br>The CaseMixer example class in Chapter 8 uses the Random class. |
| StringTokenizer | The StringTokenizer class is analogous to the StreamTokenizer class discussed in Chapter 8. Programmers frequently use this class to parse a String object or to read a line of data one token at a time, as described in Chapter 2. |
| EventObject<br>EventListener | The superclass for all event object classes is EventObject. Classes that act as handlers for these events implement the interface EventListener. Programming for events is an essential part of creating GUIs and is described in Chapters 12 and 13. |

Version Watch

The original release of the Java platform contained the Date class, but none of the other APIs for internationalization. From the beginning, the Java platform supported manipulation of date and time data. The original Date class was popular because working with raw date and time data tends to be a very messy programming exercise. The Date class still encapsulates date objects, but changes introduced in version 1.1 of the Java platform make the Calendar class the focal point of date and time operations.

# OBSERVERS AND OBSERVABLE OBJECTS

You can set up an event-notification mechanism using the **Observer** interface and the **Observable** class. An event is any change in the state of an object. For example, an event occurs when a field changes value. Many events receive no special treatment by a running program and have no impact on the flow of control. Often, however, you want objects to react to external events. How can you create objects that respond to changes in instances of other classes? The Java platform provides the **Observable** class and **Observer** interface for that purpose.

A different and more comprehensive event-handling mechanism drives GUI-based programs. In Chapters 12 and 13, you learn how to create programs that are driven by user-initiated events. The classes upon which user-interface events are based extend **EventObject.** Objects that handle the user-interface events are instances of classes that implement listener interfaces that extend **EventListener.**

The **Observable** class and **Observer** interface provide a simpler event-notification mechanism than the events and listeners that drive GUIs. In this mechanism, the events are changes in the state data of **Observable** objects, and instances of classes that implement the **Observer** interface can react to these events.

The **Observable** class drives the event-notification mechanism. If you define a class upon which other classes depend, you can define the class to extend **Observable.** Then, your program can notify all the **Observer** objects that are registered for an **Observable** object whenever that **Observable** object changes. You write code to call **notifyObservers** to alert the observers of possible changes. The **notifyObservers** method calls the **hasChanged** method to check if the object has changed. If it has changed, the JVM notifies the observers. The JVM considers the object changed if the **setChanged** method has been called since the last call of the **clearChanged** method and has not changed otherwise.

Most professional programmers follow a design pattern known as the model-view paradigm, in which the presentation of data is separated from the data itself. In the model-view programming paradigm, **Observable** objects represent data. This paradigm is also known as model-view separation or the Model-View-Controller (MVC) design pattern. It is discussed in Chapter 12 because the recommended approach to designing GUI-driven programs is to separate the model (the data and business logic) from the GUI (the display of data and user interface). The controller is the code that connects the view to the model.

*Class*

**java.util.Observable**

*Purpose*

Instances of classes that extend **Observable** are observable objects.

*Constructors*

➤ **Observable()**
The no-argument constructor is the only constructor available for this class.

*Methods*

➤ **void addObserver( Observer** *object* **)**
Call **addObserver** to register an object as an observer for this object.

➤ **void deleteObserver( Observer** *object* **)**
Call **deleteObserver** to remove the object from the list of observers.

➤ **void notifyObservers()**
**void notifyObservers( Object** *object* **)**
Calling **notifyObservers** calls the **hasChanged** method and, if the return value is **true**, the **update** method of all **Observers**. If you specify an object to be passed as an argument to the **update** method, the JVM calls **clearChanged** method for the current object.

➤ **void setChanged()**
Call **setChanged** to set the changed condition for the current object.

➤ **boolean hasChanged()**
The **hasChanged** method returns **true** if the current object has changed and **false** otherwise.

➤ **void clearChanged()**
Call **clearChanged** to clear the changed condition for the current object.

**10**

To create an observer, define a class that implements the interface **Observer**. To register the observer, call **addObserver** for the **Observable** object and pass the **Observer** object as the argument of the method. Because **Observer** is an interface rather than a class, you can easily adapt existing classes to be **Observers**. The **Observer** interface contains one method, **update**, which the JVM calls automatically whenever the **Observable** object for the **Observer** calls **notifyObservers**.

*Interface*

**java.util.Observer**

*Purpose*

Instances of classes that implement **Observer** can be notified of changes in **Observable** objects.

*Methods*

➤ **void update( Observable** *object*, **Object** *argument* **)**
**notifyObservers** for the **Observable** object calls the **update** method of
registered observers. If you provide an argument to the **notifyObservers**
method, the JVM passes the argument on to the second argument of
**update**. Otherwise, the second argument is **null**.

In the following sample program, the class `Pump` encapsulates an application in
which `Valve` is an **Observable** object and `Buzzer` is an **Observer** object.
Because `Pump` is a public class, it resides in a file called **Pump.java**. The structure of packages mirrors the file system, so you can find this source code in the
examples\observe subfolder of the folder in which you unpacked the JAR file
**examples.jar**.

```java
package examples.observe;
import java.util.Observable;
import java.util.Observer;
/** Class to demonstrate the use of the Observer
  * interface and the Observable class
  */
public class Pump {
   /** Method for creating a Pump, a Valve and
     * a Buzzer object and connecting the Valve
     * and Buzzer objects together
     * @param args not used
     */
   public static void main( String[] args ) {
      Pump p = new Pump();
      Valve v = p.new Valve();
      Buzzer b = p.new Buzzer();
      v.addObserver( b );
      v.setPressure( 150 );
      v.setPressure( 200 );
      v.setPressure( 75 );
   }
   /** A class representing a valve in a pump
     * that can be observed by other objects
     */
   private class Valve extends Observable {
      private int pressure;
      /** Method used to set the pressure at
        * the valve. It notifies its
        * observers of the change
        * @param p Updated pressure value
        */
      public void setPressure( int p ) {
         pressure = p;
         setChanged();
         notifyObservers();
      }
   }
```

```
        public int getPressure() {
           return pressure;
        }
    }
    /** Class representing the warning buzzer on a
     * pump. The buzzer sounds when the pressure
     * of the valve it is observing exceeds the
     * threshold and goes silent when the pressure
     * drops back below the threshold.
     */
    private class Buzzer implements Observer {
        private int threshold = 100;
        private boolean buzzerOn;
        /** This method is called whenever the valve
         * being observed changes
         * @param o the object under observation
         * @param arg optional argument, not used
         */
        public void update( Observable o, Object arg ) {
            Valve v = (Valve) o;
            if ( v.getPressure() > threshold
                 && buzzerOn == false ) {
               buzzerOn = true;
               System.out.println( "Buzzer on" );
            } else if ( v.getPressure() < threshold
                        && buzzerOn == true ) {
               buzzerOn = false;
               System.out.println( "Buzzer off" );
            }
        }
    }
}
```

The **main** method of the Pump class creates an enclosing Pump object. It also creates the Buzzer and Valve objects that are enclosed in the Pump object. Next, the **main** method registers Buzzer as an observer for the Valve. During execution, the **main** method sets the valve pressure to three different levels.

> **Mini Quiz 10-1**
>
> Are classes Buzzer and Value top-level nested classes or member classes?

The setPressure method of the Valve class sets the pressure and then calls two methods that Valve inherits from **Observable: setChanged** comes first, followed by **notifyObservers**. The Buzzer class implements the **update** method of the **Observer** interface to print the message "Buzzer on" or "Buzzer off", depending on the pressure in a Valve object and whether the buzzer is currently on or off.

Notice that the first argument of **update** has type **Observable** and must be cast to the type of the **Observable** object. The value of the second argument is **null** because the `setPressure` method does not pass an explicit object in the call of **notifyObservers**.

---

**Mini Quiz 10-2**

What mechanism calls the **Buzzer.update** method?

What is the output of this application?

---

# THE COLLECTIONS FRAMEWORK

Classes that comprise the collections framework make up a large part of the **java.util** package. Collections are objects created for the sole purpose of holding and organizing other objects. Usually, the contained objects are the same type or related types. Many application programs require some type of collection object for collecting and organizing data. Because this need is so common, the Java platform provides a collections framework. The collections framework supports abstract structures such as sets, lists, trees, maps, and hash tables. Arrays are collections. You can use methods defined in the interfaces of the collections framework to manipulate arrays in addition to the other data structures.

The Java platform has always provided collection classes. However, the framework is new with Java 2. Earlier versions of the Java platform provided these collection classes: **BitSet, Dictionary, Enumeration, Hashtable, Properties, Stack,** and **Vector**. These classes are still available, but the designers of the Java platform have reworked their implementations to use the collections framework.

The goals of the collections framework are to:

➤ Reduce the programming effort of developers by providing the most common data structures.

➤ Increase interoperability by defining a standard set of interfaces for collections to implement and for programmers to learn.

➤ Improve program quality through the reuse of tested software components.

The designers of the Java platform also built the framework to be easy to use and understand. Programmers can choose from several high-performance implementations collections: many collections are interchangeable because they implement common interfaces.

In addition to the collections themselves, many support classes and methods enhance the collection framework and make it more powerful. For instance, the APIs provide commonly required algorithms for sorting and searching. In addition, you can use methods for creating wrapper objects that make a collection read-only or synchronized for use in multithreaded applications. Of course, iterators for traversing the collections element by element also exist.

---

**Mini Quiz 10-3**

Can you create a collection of **int, float,** or other primitive types?

---

## Interfaces in the Collections Framework

Interfaces are the key to the flexibility and uniformity of the collections framework. Figure 10-2 shows the interfaces and classes that make up the framework.

**10**

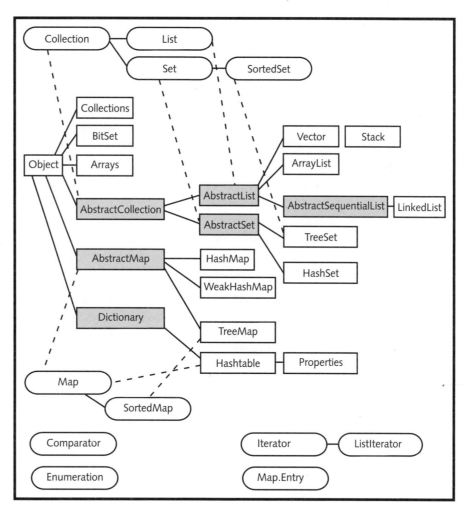

**Figure 10-2** The interfaces and classes

This diagram shows that nearly all the classes in the framework implement at least one of these interfaces: **Collection**, **List**, **Set**, **SortedSet**, **Map**, or **SortedMap**. The only exceptions are the following classes:

➤ **Collections** and **Arrays** consist entirely of static methods.

➤ **BitSet** and **Dictionary** are legacy classes inherited from earlier versions of the Java platform.

## The Collection Interface

The root interface of the framework is **Collection.** This interface defines the behavior common to all classes in the framework. The methods of this interface that add and remove elements of the collection accept objects of type **Object**. Because all classes either directly or indirectly extend the class **Object**, a **Collection** can hold any type of object. The **Collection** interface is defined to be general enough to be implemented by any class that defines a collection of individual objects. No assumption is made about whether the collection has unique values, whether the elements are ordered in a sequence, or whether the elements are sorted.

Some of the methods defined in the **Collection** interface are optional. Optional methods modify a collection object. Of course, any class that implements an interface must implement all its methods. But an immutable class that implements the interface will provide implementations of the optional methods that throw an **UnsupportedOperationException** when the method is called.

The collections framework does not include a class that directly implements the **Collection** interface. However, a data structure known as a **bag** is an example of such a class because it allows duplicate values, and its elements are unordered. No core bag class exists because the creators of the framework decided that programmer requirements for bags are not strong enough to merit adding such a collection.

Except for **WeakHashMap,** all the general purpose implementation classes in the framework implement the interfaces **Cloneable** and **Serializable**. However, neither **Collection** nor any of the other interfaces extend **Cloneable** or **Serializable**. This is by design and means that  programmers who implement the collections framework interfaces are not forced to implement **Cloneable** and **Serializable**. If you create a class that implements one of the collections interfaces, you must explicitly implement **Cloneable** and **Serializable** to let users of your collection clone or serialize instances of your collection class.

---

*Interface*

**java.util.Collection**

---

## Purpose

Instances of classes that implement **Collection** are objects that contain a collection of other objects.

## Methods

➤ **boolean add( Object** *element* **)**
The **add** method ensures that this collection contains the specified element. This is an optional operation.

➤ **boolean addAll( Collection** *c* **)**
Call **addAll** to add all the elements in the specified collection to this collection. This is an optional operation.

➤ **void clear()**
The **clear** method removes all the elements from the collection. This is an optional operation.

➤ **boolean contains( Object** *element* **)**
This method returns **true** if the collection contains the specified element.

➤ **boolean containsAll( Collection** *c* **)**
The **containsAll** method returns **true** if the collection contains all the elements in the specified collection.

➤ **boolean equals( Object** *o***)**
This method is patterned after the **equals** method of the **Object** class. For this interface, it compares for equality the specified object with this collection.

➤ **int hashCode()**
This method is patterned after the **hashCode** method of the **Object** class. Here, it returns the hash code value for the collection.

➤ **boolean isEmpty()**
The **isEmpty** method returns **true** if this collection contains no elements.

➤ **Iterator iterator()**
Use the **iterator** method to obtain an iterator for traversing the elements in the collection.

➤ **boolean remove( Object** *element* **)**
The **remove** method removes a single instance of the specified element from this collection, if it is present. This is an optional operation.

➤ **boolean removeAll( Collection** *c* **)**
The **removeAll** method removes all of this collection's elements that are also contained in the specified collection. This is an optional operation.

➤ **boolean retainAll( Collection** *c* **)**
Use the **retainAll** method to retain only the elements in the collection that are contained in the specified collection. This is an optional operation.

**10**

➤ **int size()**
The number of elements in the collection is returned by the **size** method.

➤ **Object[ ] toArray()**
**Object[ ] toArray( Object[]** *a* **)**
Use the **toArray** method to create an array containing all of the elements in the collection. The resultant array has type **Object[]** if no input array is specified. If an input array is specified, the returned array has the same type as the argument. The size of the input array does not matter and may be zero.

## The List Interface

The **List** interface extends the **Collection** interface to define the standard behavior for ordered collections, which are often referred to as sequences. Typically, a **List** implementation allows duplicate elements. Elements in a list have a position within the collection that is specified by an integer index value. As with arrays, these index values begin at zero and have a maximum value equal to the size of the list, minus one.

*Interface*

**java.util.List**

*Purpose*

Instances of classes that implement **List** are objects that contain an ordered collection of other objects.

*Methods*

➤ **boolean add( Object** *element* **)**
**void add( int** *index*, **Object** *element* **)**
The **add** method ensures that this collection contains the specified element. If you supply an index, this method inserts the element at the specified position. Otherwise, this method appends the element to the end of the list. Existing elements are not overwritten by this method. This is an optional operation.

➤ **boolean addAll( Collection** *c* **)**
**boolean addAll( int** *index*, **Collection** *c* **)**
Call **addAll** to insert all the elements in the specified collection into this collection. If you supply an index, this method inserts the contents of the collection at the specified position. Otherwise, the elements are appended to the end of the list. Existing elements are not overwritten. This is an optional operation.

➤ **void clear()**
The **clear** method removes all of the elements from the collection. This is an optional operation.

➤ **boolean contains( Object** *element* **)**
This method returns **true** if the collection contains the specified element.

➤ **boolean containsAll( Collection** *c* **)**
The **containsAll** method returns **true** if the collection contains all of the elements in the specified collection.

➤ **boolean equals( Object** *element* **)**
This method is patterned after the **equals** method of the **Object** class. For this interface, it compares the specified object with this collection for equality.

➤ **Object get( int** *index* **)**
This method returns the element of the list at the specified index.

➤ **int hashCode()**
This method is patterned after the **hashCode** method of the **Object** class. Here, it returns the hash code value for the collection.

➤ **int indexOf( Object** *element* **)**
Use this method to find the position of the first occurrence of the specified element in the list. If the element is not found, this method returns minus one.

➤ **boolean isEmpty()**
The **isEmpty** method returns **true** if this collection contains no elements.

➤ **Iterator iterator()**
Use the **iterator** method to obtain an iterator for traversing the elements in the collection in proper sequence.

➤ **int lastIndexOf( Object** *element* **)**
Use this method to find the position of the last occurrence of the specified element in the list. If the element is not found, the value minus one is returned.

➤ **ListIterator listIterator()**
**ListIterator listIterator( int** *index* **)**
Use the **listiterator** method to obtain an iterator for traversing the elements in the collection in proper sequence. If an index is supplied, the traversal begins at the specified position in the list.

➤ **boolean remove( Object** *element* **)**
**Object remove( int** *index* **)**
The **remove** method removes an element from the collection. If you specify an element, this method locates and then removes the first occurrence of that element. The **boolean** return value indicates whether an element was removed. If you specify an index, this method removes the element at that position and returns the removed element. This is an optional operation.

**10**

➤ **boolean removeAll( Collection** *c* **)**
The **removeAll** method removes this collection's elements that are contained in the specified collection. This is an optional operation.

➤ **boolean retainAll( Collection** *c* **)**
Use the **retainAll** method to retain only those elements in the collection that are contained in the specified collection. This is an optional operation.

➤ **Object set( int** *index*, **Object** *element* **)**
The **set** method puts the specified object into the collection at the specified position, overwriting the existing element at that position. The method returns the element that is overwritten. This is an optional operation.

➤ **int size()**
The number of elements in the collection is returned by the **size** method.

➤ **List subList( int** *beginIndex*, **int** *endIndex* **)**
The **subList** method returns a view of the portion of the list between the specified *beginIndex*, inclusive, and *endIndex*, exclusive.

➤ **Object[ ] toArray()**
**Object[ ] toArray( Object[ ]** *a* **)**
Use the **toArray** method to create an array containing all the elements in the collection. The resultant array has type **Object[ ]** if no input array is specified. If an input array is specified, the returned array is of the same type. The size of the input array does not matter and may be zero.

## The Set Interface

The **Set** interface extends the **Collection** interface to define the standard behavior for a collection that does not allow duplicate elements. The **Set** interface does not introduce any additional methods beyond what is defined in the **Collection** interface. The interface does, however, add restrictions to prevent duplicate elements.

*Interface*

**java.util.Set**

*Purpose*

Instances of classes that implement **Set** are objects that contain a collection of unique objects. Duplicate elements are prohibited.

*Methods*

➤ **boolean add( Object** *element* **)**
The **add** method ensures that this collection contains the specified element. If the element is already part of the set, **false** is returned. This is an optional operation.

➤ **boolean addAll( Collection** *c* **)**
Call **addAll** to add all the elements in the specified collection to this collection. If all the elements in the specified collection are already part of the set, **false** is returned. This is an optional operation.

➤ **void clear()**
The **clear** method removes all the elements from the collection. This is an optional operation.

➤ **boolean contains( Object** *element* **)**
This method returns **true** if the collection contains the specified element.

➤ **boolean containsAll( Collection** *c* **)**
The **containsAll** method returns **true** if the collection contains all of the elements in the specified collection.

➤ **boolean equals( Object** *o***)**
This method is patterned after the **equals** method of the **Object** class. For this interface, the method compares the specified object with this collection for equality.

➤ **int hashCode()**
This method is patterned after the **hashCode** method of the **Object** class. Here, the method returns the hash code value for the collection.

**10**

➤ **boolean isEmpty()**
The **isEmpty** method returns **true** if this collection contains no elements.

➤ **Iterator iterator()**
Use the **iterator** method to obtain an iterator for traversing the elements in the collection.

➤ **boolean remove( Object** *element* **)**
The **remove** method locates the specified element in the collection and, if the element is present, removes it. This is an optional operation.

➤ **boolean removeAll( Collection** *c* **)**
The **removeAll** method removes all the collection's elements that are contained in the specified collection. This is an optional operation.

➤ **boolean retainAll( Collection** *c* **)**
Use the **retainAll** method to retain only the elements in the collection that are contained in the specified collection. This is an optional operation.

➤ **int size()**
The **size** method returns the number of elements in the collection.

➤ **Object[] toArray()**
**Object[] toArray( Object[]** *a* **)**
Use the **toArray** method to create an array containing all of the elements in the collection. The array has type **Object[]**, if no input array is specified. If an input array is specified, the returned array has the same type. The size of the input array does not matter and may be zero.

### The SortedSet, Comparable, and Comparator Interfaces

**Date** objects sort in chronological order, **String** and **Character** objects sort in alphabetic order, and **Double**, **Float**, **Long**, **Integer**, **Short**, and **Byte** objects sort in numerical order. The sort order is the **natural ordering** of the class.

The **SortedSet** interface extends the **Set** interface to define the standard behavior for a set in which iterators always traverse the elements in order. The traversal follows either the ordering defined when the **SortedSet** is created or the natural order of the elements. Classes of elements that have a natural ordering implement the **java.lang.Comparable** interface. This interface has a single method, **compareTo**, that takes an **Object** as input and returns a negative integer, a zero, or a positive integer to indicate whether the input object is less than, equal to, or greater than the current object.

If a class does not have a natural ordering, you can use a **Comparator** object to define the ordering. The **Comparator** interface defines two methods. One is an **equals** method that acts like the **equals** method of the **Object** class. The second method, **compare,** takes two objects as input and returns a negative integer, a zero, or a positive integer to indicate whether the first object parameter is less than, equal to, or greater than the second object parameter.

---

*Interface*

**java.lang.Comparable**

---

*Purpose*

You can compare instances of classes that implement **Comparable** in order to determine their relative ordering.

---

*Methods*

➤ **int compareTo( Object *o* )**
This method compares the current object with the specified object and returns a negative integer, a zero, or a positive integer to indicate whether the current object is less than, equal to, or greater than the specified object, respectively.

---

*Interface*

**java.util.Comparator**

---

*Purpose*

Classes that implement **Comparable** use classes that implement **Comparator** to compare pairs of objects and to determine their relative ordering.

---

## Methods

➤ **int compare( Object** *first***, Object** *second* **)**
This method takes two objects as input and returns a negative integer, a
zero, or a positive integer to indicate whether the first **Object** argument is
less than, equal to, or greater than the second **Object** argument, respectively.

➤ **boolean equals( Object** *o***)**
This method is patterned after the **equals** method of the **Object** class. For
this interface, it compares for equality the specified object with this collection.

## Interface

**java.util.SortedSet**

## Purpose

Instances of classes that implement **SortedSet** are objects that contain a collection of unique objects that are maintained in sorted order. Duplicate elements are
prohibited. All the methods of the **Set** interface operate in the same fashion on
instances of classes that implement and **Set** and **SortedSet**, with two exceptions:

➤ The **Iterator** object returned by the **iterator** method traverses the set in
sorted order.

➤ The array returned by the **toArray** method has its elements in sorted order.

**SortedSet** provides the methods listed here in addition to the methods
defined by the **Set** interface.

## Methods

➤ **Comparator comparator()**
Use the **comparator** method to obtain a reference to the **Comparator**
object currently in use by the set. If the set uses natural ordering of its elements, the value **null** is returned.

➤ **Object first()**
The **first** method returns the first element in the set.

➤ **SortedSet headSet( Object** *element* **)**
Use the **headSet** method to obtain a **SortedSet** containing all the elements of the set that are less than the specified element.

➤ **Object last()**
The **last** method returns the last element in the set.

➤ **SortedSet subSet( int** *beginElement***, int** *endElement* **)**
The **subSet** method returns a view of the portion of the set between the
specified *beginElement*, inclusive, and *endElement*, exclusive.

**10**

➤ **SortedSet tailSet( Object** *element* **)**
Use the **tailSet** method to obtain a **SortedSet** containing all the elements
of the set that are greater than or equal to the specified element.

## The Map and Map.Entry Interfaces

The **Map** interface does not extend the **Collection** interface. Instead, it is the
fundamental interface for data structures that contain pairs of keys and values
in which key values must be unique. Both the keys and the values can be of
any reference type because the **Map** interface defines methods that work on
instances of **Object**. The **Map** interface provides methods to view a **Map** as a
**collection**:

➤ The method **keySet** returns all the keys in the map as a **Set** object.

➤ The method **values** returns a **Collection** containing all the values in
the map.

➤ The method **entrySet** returns the entire contents of the map as a **Set** of
**Map.Entry** objects.

The **Map.Entry** interface is defined within the **Map** class and defines the
behavior of the entries in these views.

*Interface*

**java.util.Map**

*Purpose*

Instances of classes that implement **Map** are objects that contain key-value
pairs with unique keys.

*Methods*

➤ **void clear()**
The **clear** method removes all of the key-value pairs from the map. This is
an optional operation.

➤ **boolean containsKey( Object** *key* **)**
This method returns **true** if the map contains the specified key.

➤ **boolean containsValue( Object** *value* **)**
This method returns **true** if the map contains the specified value.

➤ **Set entrySet()**
To obtain a view of the key-value pairs as a set of **Map.Entry** objects, use
this method. The object returned is a **Set** because keys guarantee unique
**Map.Entry** objects. The set returned does not support the **add** or **addAll**
methods.

➤ **boolean equals( Object** *o***)**
This method is patterned after the **equals** method of the **Object** class. For this interface, it compares the specified object with this **Map** for equality.

➤ **Object get( Object** *key* **)**
Use this method to obtain the value that maps to the specified key.

➤ **int hashCode()**
This method is patterned after the **hashCode** method of the **Object** class. Here, it returns the hash code value for this **Map**.

➤ **boolean isEmpty()**
The **isEmpty** method returns **true** if this **Map** contains no key-value pairs.

➤ **Set keySet()**
To obtain a view of the keys contained in this **Map**, use this method. The object returned is a **Set** because keys in a **Map** must be unique. The **Set** object returned does not support the **add** or **addAll** methods.

➤ **Object put( Object** *key***, Object** *value* **)**
The **put** method adds a key-value pair to this **Map** and returns the previous value associated with the given key. It returns **null** if the key did not previously exist in the **Map**. This is an optional operation.

➤ **void putAll( Map** *map* **)**
Use the **putAll** method to add all the key-value pairs from the specified **Map**. This is an optional operation.

➤ **Object remove( Object** *key* **)**
The **remove** method removes the key-value pair associated with the given key and returns the value associated with the key. If the key does not exist in this **Map**, **null** is returned. This is an optional operation.

➤ **int size()**
The number of key-value pairs in this **Map** is returned by the **size** method.

➤ **Collection values()**
Use the **values** method to obtain a view of the values in this **Map** as a **Collection** object. Because values are not guaranteed to be unique, a **Collection** object and not a **Set** object is returned. The **Collection** object returned does not support the **add** or **addAll** methods.

---

*Interface*

**java.util.Map.Entry**

---

*Purpose*

Instances of classes that implement **Map.Entry** represent key-value pairs when a **Map** object is viewed as a **Set**.

---

➤ **boolean equals( Object** *o***)**
This method is patterned after the **equals** method of the **Object** class. For this interface, **equals** compares the specified object with this map entry for equality.

➤ **Object getKey()**
Use this method to obtain the key for the map entry.

➤ **Object getValue()**
Use this method to obtain the value for the map entry.

➤ **int hashCode()**
This method is patterned after the **hashCode** method of the **Object** class. Here, it returns the hash code value for the map entry.

➤ **Object setValue( Object** *value* **)**
The **setValue** method changes the value for the key-value pair and returns the previous value. This is an optional operation.

## The SortedMap *Interface*

The **SortedMap** interface extends the **Map** interface to define the standard behavior for a map in which the key-value pairs are always sorted. The sort order is the natural ordering of the keys or some other ordering defined when the **SortedMap** is created. Classes of keys that have a natural ordering implement the **java.lang.Comparable** interface. If the key class does not have a natural ordering, you can use a **Comparator** object to define the ordering.

*Interface*

**java.util.SortedMap**

*Purpose*

Instances of classes that implement **SortedMap** are objects that contain key-value pairs that are maintained in sorted order by key. All the methods of the **Map** interface operate in the same fashion for objects of class that implement **SortedMap.** The methods that the **SortedMap** interface defines and the methods that the **Map** interface defines are listed here:

*Methods*

➤ **Comparator comparator()**
Use the **comparator** method to obtain a reference to the **Comparator** object currently in use by this **Map** for ordering its keys. If this **Map** uses the natural ordering of its keys, the value **null** is returned.

▶ **Object firstKey()**

The **first** method returns the key of the first key-value pair for this **Map**.

▶ **SortedMap headMap( Object** *key* **)**

Use the **headMap** method to obtain a **SortedMap** containing all the key-value pairs of this **Map** for which the key is less than the specified key.

▶ **Object lastKey()**

The **last** method returns the key of the last key-value pair in this **Map**.

▶ **SortedMap subMap( int** *beginKey*, **int** *endKey* **)**

The **subMap** method returns a view of the portion of this **Map** with key-value pairs having a key value between the specified *beginKey*, inclusive, and *endKey*, exclusive.

▶ **SortedMap tailMap( Object** *key* **)**

Use the **tailMap** method to obtain a **SortedMap** containing all the key-value pairs of this **Map** with a key value that is greater than or equal to the specified key.

## Traversing Collections with Iterators

With a collection, you use a separate **iterator** object to traverse the collection and to visit individual items in the proper order. Iterators, also known as **cursors**, are separate objects from the collections, rather than methods of the collection classes. Indeed, a single collection may have several different iterators associated with it.

In the Java platform, an iterator implements the **Iterator** interface. You do not directly create the iterators for collections. Instead, you call the **iterator** method of the collection to obtain one. In addition to methods for traversing a collection, **Iterator** objects provide a **remove** method for removing elements from a collection as the collection is being traversed.

**Iterator** objects returned by the general purpose implementations in the collections framework are **fail-fast** iterators. Methods of these objects throw a **ConcurrentModificationException** if the collection is modified structurally using methods other than those of the **Iterator** interface after the **Iterator** object is created. The rationale for throwing the exception is that it is better to trap the potential source of a problem than to suffer the undefined behavior to which such a modification could lead. The most common situation that causes this problem occurs when more than one thread in a program has access to a collection and threads are accessing the collection at the same time. Chapter 11 discusses multithreading and issues of concurrent execution.

Collections that implement the **List** interface also support **Iterator** objects that implement the **ListIterator** interface, which is an extension of the **Iterator** interface. Objects that implement **ListIterator** allow for backward and forward traversal

**10**

through a list. They also provide additional methods for modifying a list while it is being traversed.

---

*Interface*

**java.util.Iterator**

---

*Purpose*

You can use instances of classes that implement **Iterator** to traverse a collection and to remove elements from the collection during traversal.

---

*Methods*

➤ **boolean hasNext()**
This method returns **true** if there are more elements in the traversal.

➤ **Object next()**
This method returns the next element in the traversal.

➤ **void remove()**
This method removes the most recently returned element from the collection associated with the iterator. This is an optional operation.

---

*Interface*

**java.util.ListIterator**

---

*Purpose*

You can use instances of classes that implement **ListIterator** to traverse a list forward and backward. They also can be used to insert, replace, and remove elements from the list during traversal.

---

*Methods*

➤ **void add( Object** *element* **)**
This method inserts the specified element into the list. This is an optional operation.

➤ **boolean hasNext()**
This method returns **true** if there are more elements in forward traversing.

➤ **boolean hasPrevious()**
This method returns **true** if there are more elements in backward traversing.

➤ **Object next()**
This method returns the next element in forward traversing.

➤ **int nextIndex()**
This method returns the index of the element that would be returned by the subsequent call of the **next** method.

➤ **Object previous()**
This method returns the next element in backward traversing.

➤ **int previousIndex()**
This method returns the index of the element that would be returned by a subsequent call of the **previous** method.

➤ **void remove()**
This method removes the most recently returned element from the collection associated with the iterator. This is an optional operation.

➤ **void set( Object** *element* **)**
This method replaces the element returned by the most recent call to **next** or **previous** with the specified element. This is an optional operation.

## General Purpose Implementations

The interfaces that are part of the collections framework define, but do not implement, behavior. To instantiate a collection object, you must use classes that implement the interfaces. The collections framework contains many classes that are general purpose implementations because they are suitable for most programmers' requirements. For special cases, you may have to define new implementation classes.

When using these implementations, manipulate them using references of the interface types, not of the implementation types. This technique hides the implementation class and forces you to code the program using the interface type. As a result, you gain the ability to change the implementation at any time without affecting the code that uses the collection.

### List Implementations

Four classes in the framework are implementations of the **List** interface: **ArrayList**, **LinkedList**, **Vector**, and **Stack**. Of these, only the classes **ArrayList** and **LinkedList** were designed specifically to be part of the collections framework. Both **Vector** and **Stack** are legacy classes from the original version of the Java platform that have been retrofitted to become part of the framework. They will be discussed later in this chapter, along with the other legacy classes.

The **ArrayList** class implements a list using arrays. This makes an **ArrayList** object very quick when it comes to accessing elements of the list, but operations that insert elements in the middle of the list or that delete elements from the list are not as fast. The **LinkedList** implementation of a list may be a better choice if there will be many insertions and deletions. However, the **LinkedList** implementation is slower at accessing elements and must suffer the overhead of creating an object to hold each element of the list that the **ArrayList** does not have. For most cases, the **ArrayList** is the implementation of choice for the **List** interface.

---

*Class*

**java.util.ArrayList**

---

*Purpose*

Instances of the **ArrayList** class implement the **List** interface using arrays. Objects of this class should be manipulated using methods from the **List** interface.

---

*Constructors*

➤ **ArrayList()**
The no-argument constructor creates an empty list.

➤ **ArrayList( Collection** *c* **)**
The list is constructed and initialized with the elements from the specified collection in the order returned by the collection's iterator.

➤ **ArrayList( int** *initialCapacity* **)**
An empty list is created with the specified initial capacity. Setting a large initial capacity will improve performance for cases in which you know that the list will grow very large.

---

*Class*

**java.util.LinkedList**

---

*Purpose*

Instances of the **LinkedList** class implement the **List** interface using a linked list data structure. Objects of this class should be manipulated using methods from the **List** interface.

---

*Constructors*

➤ **LinkedList()**
The no-argument constructor creates an empty list.

➤ **LinkedList( Collection** *c* **)**
The list is constructed and initialized with the elements from the specified collection in the order returned by the collection's iterator.

---

The following program demonstrates the use of the **ArrayList** class and the **ListIterator** interface. The class `Line` manipulates an **ArrayList** of **java.awt.Point** objects. The class **Point** stores the x and y coordinates of a two-dimensional point, and implements the **toString** method to return a textual representation of a point.

Here is a class `Line`, which stores a line as a **Vector** of **Point** objects:

```java
package examples.collections;
import java.util.List;
import java.util.ArrayList;
import java.util.ListIterator;
import java.io.PrintStream;
import java.awt.Point;
/** A class to demonstrate the use of the ArrayList
  * and Iterator classes in the java.util package
  */
public class Line {
   private List points = new ArrayList();
   /** Set the starting point for a line
     * @param p the starting point
     */
   public void setStart( Point p ) {
      points.clear();
      points.add( p );
   }
   /** Set the next point in a line
     * @param p the next point
     */
   public void addPoint( Point p ) {
      points.add( p );
   }
   /** Print all the points in a line
     * @param ps the stream where the points
     *             will be printed
     */
   public void listPoints( PrintStream ps ) {
      ListIterator li = points.listIterator();
      while ( li.hasNext() ) {
         ps.println( li.next() );
      }
   }
   /** Test method for the class
     * @param args not used
     */
   public static void main( String[] args ) {
      Line x = new Line();
      x.setStart( new Point( 4, 11 ) );
      x.addPoint( new Point( -6, 1 ) );
      x.addPoint( new Point( 2, 3 ) );
      x.listPoints( System.out );
   }
}
```

The output is:

```
java.awt.Point[x=4,y=11]
java.awt.Point[x=-6,y=1]
java.awt.Point[x=2,y=3]
```

The **main** method of the **Line** class creates the **ArrayList**. Notice that the type of the object reference is **List**, not **ArrayList**. Using the **List** interface gives you the option of substituting a different **List** implementation without requiring any change to the rest of the program. The class provides these methods:

➤ `setStart` starts a new line with one point.

➤ `addPoint` adds a point to the line.

➤ `listPoints` outputs a textual representation of the points in the line.

The last of these methods uses a **PrintStream** object, `ps`, to output each point and an iterator, `e`, to visit each point in turn.

Do not be fooled into assuming that the declaration of `li` instantiates **ListIterator**. Instead, it declares an object reference for an object of unknown type that implements the **ListIterator** interface. The method **List.listIterator** for the object `points` creates the object. The actual class of the object returned by **List.listIterator** is unimportant. All that matters is that it implements **ListIterator**.

## Set and SortedSet Implementations

Two framework classes implement the **Set** interface: **HashSet** and **TreeSet**. In addition, the **TreeSet** also implements the **SortedSet** interface. The **HashSet** class uses a **HashMap** as its underlying data structure for organizing the set elements. The HashMap Class is described in the section "Map and SortedMap Implementations." No guarantee is made as to the ordering of the elements in a **HashSet**, and the ordering may even change as elements are added and removed. This implementation allows the **null** element.

The **TreeSet** class uses a **TreeMap** as its underlying data structure for organizing the set elements. If the elements' natural ordering is used, a **TreeSet** guarantees that the elements are kept in ascending order.

Choosing between these two implementations is simply a matter of deciding whether the set implementation must be sorted. If sorting is not required, use **HashSet** because it is much faster than **TreeSet**. If sorting is required, **TreeSet** is the right choice.

---

*Class*

**java.util.HashSet**

---

*Purpose*

Instances of the **HashSet** class implement the **Set** interface using a **HashMap** object. Objects of this class should be manipulated using methods from the **Set** interface.

---

*Constructors*

➤ **HashSet()**
The no-argument constructor creates an empty set.

➤ **HashSet( Collection** *c* **)**
The set is constructed and initialized with the elements from the specified collection in the order returned by the collection's iterator. Any duplicate elements in the specified collection are ignored.

➤ **HashSet( int** *initialCapacity* **)**
This constructor creates an empty set with the specified initial capacity. Setting a large initial capacity improves performance for cases in which you know that the set will grow to be very large.

➤ **HashSet( int** *initialCapacity*, **float** *loadFactor* **)**
This constructor creates an empty set with the specified initial capacity and load factor. Setting a large initial capacity improves performance for cases in which you know that the set will become very large. The load factor is a number between 0.0 and 1.0 and a measure of how full the set can become. A larger load factor uses memory more efficiently but can increase the time required to find elements.

**10**

*Class*

**java.util.TreeSet**

*Purpose*

Instances of the **TreeSet** class implement the **Set** and **SortedSet** interfaces using a **TreeMap** object to maintain a sorted set. Objects of this class should be manipulated using methods from either the **Set** or **SortedSet** interfaces.

*Constructors*

➤ **TreeSet()**
The no-argument constructor creates an empty set.

➤ **TreeSet( Collection** *c* **)**
The set is constructed and initialized with the elements from the specified collection according to the elements' natural order. Duplicate elements in the collection are ignored.

➤ **TreeSet( Comparator** *c* **)**
This constructor creates an empty set that will keep its elements sorted according to the ordering defined by the supplied **Comparator** object.

➤ **TreeSet( SortedSet** *s* **)**
This constructor constructs and initializes the set with the elements from the specified collection according to the same order as the specified sorted set. Duplicate elements in the collection are ignored.

The `SetsExample` class below demonstrates how to create and initialize a **Set** object as well as how to create a **SortedSet** object using a **Set** object as input:

```
package examples.collections;
import java.util.*;
/** A class to demonstrate the use of the Set
  * and SortedSet interfaces in the java.util package
  */
public class SetsExample {
    /** Test method for the class
      * @param args not used
      */
    public static void main( String[] args ) {
        // create a set and initialize it
        Set s1 = new HashSet();
        s1.add( new Integer( 6 ) );
        s1.add( new Integer( 100 ) );
        s1.add( new Integer( -89 ) );
        s1.add( new Integer( 2 ) );
        s1.add( new Integer( 57 ) );
        // iterate to display the set values
        Iterator i1 = s1.iterator();
        while ( i1.hasNext() ) {
            System.out.print( i1.next() + " " );
        }
        System.out.println();
        // create a SortedSet from a Set
        SortedSet s2 = new TreeSet( s1 );
        // iterate to display the set values
        Iterator i2 = s2.iterator();
        while ( i2.hasNext() ) {
            System.out.print( i2.next() + " " );
        }
        System.out.println();
    }
}
```

The output will look something like:

```
100 57 -89 6 2
-89 2 6 57 100
```

The actual output of the first line of output may vary because the sequence of the unsorted set is undefined. However, the sequence of elements in a sorted set is defined, so the second line of output cannot vary.

## Map and SortedMap Implementations

Five framework classes implement the **Map** interface: **HashMap**, **TreeMap**, **WeakHashMap**, **Hashtable**, and **Properties**. In addition, the **TreeMap** class also implements the **SortedMap** interface. Both **Hashtable** and **Properties** are legacy classes from the original version of the Java platform and have been retrofitted to become part of the framework. They are discussed later in this chapter in the section "Legacy Collections Framework Classes."

The **HashMap** class uses a hash table as its underlying data structure for organizing the key-value pairs. No guarantee is made as to the ordering of the keys in a **HashMap**, and the ordering may change as key-value pairs are added and removed. This implementation allows both **null** values and the **null** key.

The **TreeMap** class uses a red-black tree as its underlying data structure for organizing the key-value pairs. **Red-black trees** are balanced binary trees whose external nodes are sorted by a key and connected in a linked list. If the elements' natural ordering is used, a **TreeMap** guarantees that the elements will be kept in ascending order.

Choosing between these two implementations is simply a matter of deciding whether the map implementation must be sorted. If sorting is not required, use **HashMap** because it is much faster than **TreeMap**. If sorting is required, **TreeMap** is the right choice.

## Class

**java.util.HashMap**

**10**

### Purpose

Instances of the **HashMap** class implement the **Map** interface using a hash table data structure. Objects of this class should be manipulated using methods from the **Map** interface.

### Constructors

➤ **HashMap()**
The no-argument constructor creates an empty map.

➤ **HashMap( Map** *m* **)**
This constructor creates and initializes the map with the elements from the specified map in the order returned by the map's iterator.

➤ **HashMap( int** *initialCapacity* **)**
This constructor creates an empty map with the specified initial capacity. Setting a large initial capacity improves performance when you know that the map will become very large.

➤ **HashMap( int** *initialCapacity*, **float** *loadFactor* **)**
This constructor creates an empty map with the specified initial capacity and load factor. Setting a large initial capacity improves performance when you know that the map will become very large. The load factor is a number between 0.0 and 1.0 and a measure of how full the map is allowed to become. A larger load factor uses memory more efficiently but can increase the time required to find keys.

---

*Class*

### java.util. TreeMap

---

*Purpose*

Instances of the **TreeMap** class implement the **Map** and **SortedMap** interfaces using a red-black tree data structure to maintain a sorted map. Objects of this class should be manipulated using methods from either the **Map** or **SortedMap** interfaces.

---

*Constructors*

➤ **TreeMap()**
The no-argument constructor creates an empty map.

➤ **TreeMap( Map** *m* **)**
This constructor creates and initializes the map with the elements from the specified map according to the elements' natural order.

➤ **TreeMap( Comparator** *c* **)**
This constructor creates an empty map that will keep its keys sorted according to the ordering defined by the supplied **Comparator** object.

➤ **TreeMap( SortedMap** *s* **)**
This constructor creates and initializes the map with the elements from the specified map according to the same order as the specified sorted map.

---

The **WeakHashMap** implementation takes advantage of the support for weak references. Unlike an ordinary reference, the existence of a weak reference does not prevent the garbage collector from discarding the referenced object. This feature is useful because it is not uncommon for a collection to contain many objects to which only the collection has a reference. In such cases, the rest of the application has no interest in these objects, but they cannot be garbage-collected when any Java construct has ordinary object references for them. A collection that uses weak references does not stop the garbage collector from deleting objects to which only the collection refers.

Weak references and supporting classes in package **java.lang.ref** were introduced with Java 2. Previously, the Java platform had only the kind of reference now called a strong reference. Specifically, a **WeakHashMap** uses weak keys. When a **WeakHashMap** instance is the only object holding a reference to an object being used as a key in the map, the key becomes eligible for garbage collection. When the key is garbage-collected, it is removed from the map.

To avoid unexpected behavior, a **WeakHashMap** should only be used with key classes that are compared for equality using the == operator. With such classes, you cannot re-create a key after all references to it are gone. This is important because re-creating a key after its entry has been garbage-collected from the **WeakHashMap** is a potential source of error.

*Class*

## java.util.WeakHashMap

*Purpose*

Instances of the **WeakHashMap** class implement the **Map** interface using a hash table data structure. Objects of this class should be manipulated using methods from the **Map** interface.

*Constructors*

➤ **WeakHashMap()**
The no-argument constructor creates an empty set.

➤ **WeakHashMap( int** *initialCapacity* **)**
This constructor creates an empty map with the specified initial capacity. Setting a large initial capacity will improve performance for cases in which you know that the map will become very large.

➤ **WeakHashMap( int** *initialCapacity***, float** *loadFactor* **)**
The constructor creates an empty map with the specified initial capacity and load factor. Setting a large initial capacity improves performance when you know that the map will become very large. The load factor is a number between 0.0 and 1.0 and a measure of how full the map is allowed to become. A larger load factor uses memory more efficiently but can increase the time required to find keys.

The first half of the **main** method of the `MapsExample` class below demonstrates how to create and initialize a map and then iterate through the map by creating a view of its mappings as a set. The second half of the method shows how a **SortedMap** can be created with a **Comparator** object. In this case, the class implementing the **Comparator** interface is an anonymous inner class that simply reverses the natural ordering of the keys.

```
package examples.collections;
import java.util.*;
/** A class to demonstrate the use of the Map
  * and SortedMap interfaces in the java.util package
  */
```

```java
public class MapsExample {
    /** Test method for the class
     * @param args not used
     */
    public static void main( String[] args ) {
        // create a map and initialize it
        Map m1 = new HashMap();
        m1.put( "height", new Integer( 72 ) );
        m1.put( "weight", new Integer( 180 ) );
        m1.put( "age", new Integer( 21 ) );
        m1.put( "shoe", new Integer( 11 ) );
        m1.put( "sleeve", new Integer( 35 ) );
        // get a view of the map as a set
        Set s1 = m1.entrySet();
        // iterate to display the set values
        Iterator i1 = s1.iterator();
        while ( i1.hasNext() ) {
            Map.Entry me = (Map.Entry) i1.next();
            System.out.print( me.getKey() + ":"
                            + me.getValue() + " " );
        }
        System.out.println();
        // use an anonymous inner class to define the
        // Comparator for the SortedMap
        SortedMap m2 = new TreeMap( new Comparator() {
                public
                int compare( Object o1, Object o2 ) {
                    // reverse the natural ordering
                    Comparable c1 = (Comparable)o1;
                    Comparable c2 = (Comparable)o2;
                    return -( c1.compareTo( c2 ) );
                }
            }
        );
        m2.putAll( m1 );
        // get a view of the map as a set
        Set s2 = m2.entrySet();
        // iterate to display the set values
        Iterator i2 = s2.iterator();
        while ( i2.hasNext() ) {
            Map.Entry me = (Map.Entry) i2.next();
            System.out.print( me.getKey() + ":"
                            + me.getValue() + " " );
        }
        System.out.println();
    }
}
```

The output is similar to:

```
age:21 weight:180 sleeve:35 height:72 shoe:11
weight:180 sleeve:35 shoe:11 height:72 age:21
```

The actual output of the first line of output may vary because the sequence of keys in the unsorted map is undefined. However, the sequence of elements in a sorted map is defined, so the second line of output cannot vary. It is in reverse alphabetic order by key.

## Arrays as Collections

In recognition of the fact that arrays are also collections, the collections framework provides a method in the **Collection** interface for converting a **Collection** object into the array **Collection.toArray**. Because the reverse conversion is also commonly required, the class **Arrays** was added to the framework. This class defines the static method **asList** that converts an array of **Object**s into a **List** object.

---

*Class*

**java.util.Arrays**

---

*Purpose*

This class provides a number of static methods that operate on array objects.

---

*Methods*

➤ **List asList( Object[]** *a* **)**
This method returns a fixed-size list backed by the supplied array. The returned **List** object does not support operations that increase its size.

---

## Algorithms

Algorithms for sorting, searching, and reversing are commonly applied to collections. Because of the consistent design of the collections framework, the framework can include many polymorphic algorithms that you can apply to collections that implement the framework's interfaces.

The algorithms are not defined in an interface because all implementations would then have to provide them. Instead, the algorithms are collected into a single class, **Collections**, as static methods. Most of the algorithms take a **List** object as input because they require the indexed methods defined in the **List** interface, but some operate on **Collection** objects.

---

*Class*

**java.util.Collections**

---

*Purpose*

This class gathers together static methods that implement polymorphic algorithms on **List** and **Collection** objects.

*Methods*

➤ **int binarySearch( List** *list*, **Object** *target* **)**
**int binarySearch( List** *list*, **Object** *target*, **Comparator** *c* **)**
Before using the **binarySearch** method, the list must be sorted in ascending order using the elements' natural ordering or the **Comparator** object specified. Assuming the list is sorted, the method finds the *target* within the specified list and returns its index, if the target is found. If the target cannot be found, the value returned is (-(*insertion_point*) - 1), where *insertion_point* is defined as the place at which the target would be inserted into the list.

➤ **void copy( List** *target*, **List** *source* **)**
This method copies all of the elements of the *source* list into the *target* list.

➤ **void fill( List** *target*, **Object** *fill* **)**
This method replaces all of the elements of the list with the specified *fill* object.

➤ **Object max( Collection** *coll* **)**
**Object max( Collection** *coll*, **Comparator** *comp* **)**
This method returns the maximum object as defined by the elements' natural ordering or the **Comparator** object, if one is supplied.

➤ **Object min( Collection** *coll* **)**
**Object min( Collection** *coll*, **Comparator** *comp* **)**
This method returns the minimum object as defined by the elements' natural ordering or the **Comparator** object, if one is supplied.

➤ **void reverse( List** *list* **)**
This method reverses the order of the elements of the supplied list.

➤ **void shuffle( List** *list* **)**
**void shuffle( List** *list* **Random** *r* **)**
This method shuffles the order of the elements of the supplied list to create a random ordering. If a randomness source is supplied, it will be used.

➤ **void sort( List** *list* **)**
**void sort( List** *list*, **Comparator** *c* **)**
The **sort** method sorts the specified list in ascending order using the elements' natural ordering or the **Comparator** object specified. The sort algorithm used is a modified mergesort algorithm.

The `ArraySortExample` class below demonstrates how to create a **List** object from an array. This list can be sorted and traversed just like any other kind of list.

```java
package examples.collections;
import java.util.*;
/** A class to demonstrate the use of the sort and
  * search algorithms in the java.util package
  */
public class ArraySortExample {
    /** Test method for the class
      * @param args not used
      */
    public static void main( String[] args ) {
        // create a list and initialize it
        Object[] data = {   new Double( 3.45 ),
                            new Double( -0.2 ),
                            new Double( 100.3 ),
                            new Double( 89.67 ),
                            new Double( 11.0 ),
                            new Double( 23.132 )
                        };
        List list = Arrays.asList( data );
        // iterate to display the set values
        Iterator i1 = list.iterator();
        while ( i1.hasNext() ) {
            System.out.print( i1.next() + " " );
        }
        System.out.println();
        Collections.sort( list );
        Iterator i2 = list.iterator();
        while ( i2.hasNext() ) {
            System.out.print( i2.next() + " " );
        }
        System.out.println();
        for( int j=0; j<data.length; j++ ) {
            System.out.print( data[j] + " " );
        }
        System.out.println();
    }
}
```

The output looks like:

```
3.45 -0.2 100.3 89.67 11.0 23.132
-0.2 3.45 11.0 23.132 89.67 100.3
-0.2 3.45 11.0 23.132 89.67 100.3
```

Notice that the second and third lines of output match because the sort operation on the list also sorts its backing array object.

## Wrapper Implementations

Except for the legacy implementation classes, **Vector**, **Stack**, **Hashtable**, and **Properties**, none of the implementation classes supplied in the collections framework has built-in synchronization support that would allow them to be used safely by multiple concurrent threads of execution in the same program. Therefore, these collections are not considered **thread-safe**. The problems and solutions related to multithreaded programs are discussed in detail in Chapter 11. For now, take note that you can easily create a synchronized wrapper for a collection by using a method in the class **Collections**.

The **Collections** class has a set of static methods, one for each of the six interfaces, that take a collection as input and return a thread-safe collection that is backed by the original collection passed as input to the method. The definitions of the methods all follow the same pattern. The name of the method is the name of the interface prefixed with "synchronized". The input and output of the method is a single collection of the interface type. For example, the method to create a synchronized wrapper for a **SortedSet** is **synchronizedSortedSet**, and it takes a **SortedSet** as input and returns a **SortedSet** as output.

Another kind of collection wrapper that can be generated by methods of the **Collections** class is a read-only wrapper class. These methods take a collection as input and return a collection that will throw an **UnsupportedOperationException** if any method that modifies the collection is called. The definition of these methods also follows a pattern. Each method name is the name of the collection prefixed by the string "unmodifiable". So the method to create a read-only wrapper for a **TreeMap** is **unmodifiableTreeMap.** The method takes a **TreeMap** object as input and returns a read-only **TreeMap** as output.

The `ReadOnlyExample` class below demonstrates how to create a read-only **TreeMap** object from an existing **TreeMap** object. The result of the attempt to add a mapping to the read-only sorted map near the end of the **main** method is an **UnsupportedOperationException**.

```
package examples.collections;
import java.util.*;
/** A class to demonstrate the use of methods
  * to create read-only collections
  */
public class ReadOnlyExample {
   /** Test method for the class
     * @param args not used
     */
   public static void main( String[] args ) {
      // create a map and initialize it
      SortedMap m1 = new TreeMap();
```

```
m1.put( "beans", new Float( 2.99 ) );
m1.put( "carrots", new Float( 1.69 ) );
m1.put( "peas", new Float( 2.19 ) );
m1.put( "cabbage", new Float( 3.29 ) );
m1.put( "squash", new Float( 1.89 ) );
// create a read-only collection, then try to
// change it
m1 = Collections.unmodifiableSortedMap( m1 );
try {
    m1.put( "parsnips", new Float( 1.59 ) );
} catch ( UnsupportedOperationException x ) {
    System.out.println( x + " caught!" );
}
    }
}
```

The output looks like:

```
java.lang.UnsupportedOperationException caught!
```

## Extending the Abstract Implementations

If none of the implementation classes provided by the collections framework meets your requirements, you can define your own collection class. To simplify the process, the framework includes a number of abstract classes that have already done much of the work for you. These are the same abstract classes on which the framework's implementation classes were built. The classes are **AbstractCollection**, **AbstractList**, **AbstractSet**, **AbstractSequentialList**, and **AbstractMap**. The API documentation for the Java 2 platform describes in detail how to create an implementation class that extends each of the abstract classes.

## Legacy Collections Framework Classes

Before the collections framework was added in the Java 2 platform, there were several collection classes in the **java.util** package. The classes were useful but did not follow any particular pattern in their programming interfaces. Therefore, it was very difficult to switch implementations from one class to another. These classes have been retrofitted into the framework by modifying them to implement one of the interfaces in the framework. You can continue to use these classes, with the exception that the abstract **Dictionary** class is obsolete and replaced by the **Map** interface.

## Traversing Collections with Enumerations

Before the **Iterator** interface was introduced, using the **Enumeration** interface was the standard way to traverse collections. Just as with **Iterator** objects, you do not create **Enumeration** objects for collections directly. Instead, you call a method of the collection to obtain one. Do not write any new code using **Enumeration** objects. Using **Iterator** objects instead is strongly recommended.

---

*Interface*

## java.util.Enumeration

---

*Purpose*

This interface defines the methods you can use to traverse the objects in a collection.

---

*Methods*

➤ **boolean hasMoreElements()**
Call **hasMoreElements** to determine whether you can extract an object from the collection. The method returns **true** if an object is available and **false** if the collection is empty or has been completely traversed.

➤ **Object nextElement()**
Call **nextElement** to obtain the next object in a collection. If no object is available, the method throws the exception **NoSuchElementException**. You can prevent the exception by calling **hasMoreElements** first and then calling this method only if **hasMoreElements** returns **true**.

---

The legacy collection classes are summarized in Table 10-2. After you have created the collection class object, you can use any of the methods of the class. The most commonly used methods are listed in the detailed description of each class that follows the table.

**Table 10-2** Predefined collection classes

| | |
|---|---|
| BitSet | Use BitSet collections to contain sets of bits or true-false flags. The collection is dynamically sized so you can add elements without worrying about exceeding limits. Simply setting or clearing a value at an index value that is beyond the current size extends the set. When you extend a BitSet, all the added elements are given the default value of false. A BitSet never shrinks. |
| Dictionary | This abstract class defines methods for storing elements of type Object, according to key values that are also of type Object. It is the superclass of the Hashtable class. You also can extend Dictionary, but you cannot instantiate an object of the Dictionary class. |
| Hashtable | The Hashtable class extends Dictionary. Instances of this class are hash tables. Hash tables are an efficient way of storing large numbers of items that do not naturally lend themselves to storage in a stack, binary tree, or some other specialized structure. In hash tables, objects are put into locations called buckets, and each bucket has a unique identifier, or hash code. More than one object can fall into a bucket. |

**Table 10-2**  Predefined collection classes (continued)

| | |
|---|---|
| Properties | The Properties class extends Hashtable to create an even more specialized implementation of Dictionary. A Properties object is a collection of key-value pairs, where each key and each value is a String object. The key for each item in the Properties table is the name of a property. |
| Stack | The **Stack** class has methods to add and remove objects according to the last-in first-out rule. The **Stack** class extends **Vector** and adds methods for pushing, popping, and peeking into the stack. |
| Vector | A **Vector** is an indexed list of objects, much like an array. Use a **Vector** when you need greater flexibility than arrays provide. The main advantage is that a **Vector** can grow and shrink in size as required, but an array has a fixed size. The **Vector** class also has several methods that are not available for arrays. Because **Vector** objects are ordered, they are more efficient than **Hashtable** objects for enumeration purposes. |

*Class*

**java.util.BitSet**

**10**

*Purpose*

A **BitSet** contains a number of bits, each of which represents a **true** or **false** value.

*Constructors*

➤ **BitSet()**
**BitSet( int** *size***)**
The constructor created an empty set. You can optionally specify an initial size.

*Methods*

➤ **void and( BitSet** *b* **)**
The **and** method performs a logical AND on the bits in the current object and specified **BitSet**.

➤ **void andNot( BitSet** *b* **)**
The **andNot** method clears all of the bits in the current **BitSet** whose corresponding bit is set in the specified **BitSet**.

➤ **void clear( int** *position* **)**
The **clear** method clears the bit in the specified position so that its value, when returned by **get**, is **false**.

➤ **boolean get( int** *position* **)**
The **get** method returns **true** if the bit in the specified position is set and **false** otherwise.

➤ **int length()**
The **length** method returns the index of the highest bit set in the **BitSet** plus one.

➤ **void or( BitSet** *b* **)**
The **or** method performs a logical OR on the bits in the current object and specified **BitSet**.

➤ **void set( int** *position* **)**
The **set** method sets the bit in the specified position so that its value, when returned by **get**, is **true**.

➤ **int size()**
The **size** method returns the number of bits of space actually in use by the **BitSet**.

➤ **void xor( BitSet** *b* **)**
The **xor** method performs a logical EXCLUSIVE OR on the bits in the current object and specified **BitSet**.

---

*Class*

**java.util.Dictionary**

---

*Purpose*

The abstract class **Dictionary** is a superclass for collection classes that contain key-value pairs. This class is considered obsolete and should no longer be used. You should implement the **Map** interface instead of extending **Dictionary**.

---

*Constructors*

➤ **Dictionary()**
Only a no-argument constructor is available.

---

*Methods*

➤ **Enumeration elements()**
The **elements** method returns an **Enumeration** object to iterate through the values in the Dictionary.

➤ **Object get( Object** *key* **)**
The **get** method returns the value for the specified key.

➤ **boolean isEmpty()**
The **isEmpty** method returns **true** if no key mappings are contained in the collection and **false** otherwise.

➤ **Enumeration keys()**

The **keys** method returns an **Enumeration** object to iterate through the keys in the **Dictionary**.

➤ **Object put( Object** *key*, **Object** *value* **)**

The **put** method adds a key and value to the **Dictionary** or updates the value for a key that is already stored in the **Dictionary**. Both arguments must have non-**null** values. The return value is the value that was associated with the key before the method call or **null** if the key was not previously in the **Dictionary**.

➤ **Object remove( Object** *key* **)**

The **remove** method deletes a key and value from the Dictionary. The return value is the value associated with the removed key or **null** if the key was not in the **Dictionary**.

➤ **int size()**

The **size** method returns the number of entries in the **Dictionary**.

---

*Class*

**java.util.Hashtable**

---

*Purpose*

The **Hashtable** class extends **Dictionary** and implements **Map**. You can use a **Hashtable** for key-value pairs when the keys are instances of classes that implement the **hashCode** and **equals** methods.

---

*Constructors*

➤ **Hashtable()**
**Hashtable( int** *capacity* **)**
**Hashtable( int** *capacity*, **float** *load* **)**

When you create an empty **Hashtable**, you can optionally specify a capacity and load factor. The load factor must be a number between 0.0 and 1.0 and is a measure of how full the **Hashtable** is allowed to become. A larger load factor uses memory more efficiently but can increase the time required to look up keys.

---

The method **hashCode** returns an integer that identifies a bucket in a hash table. A default **hashCode** method is defined in the **Object** class. If you have a very good hash function, you can override the default **hashCode** method for objects in your hash table to increase its efficiency. Generally, if you define a class that overrides **Object.equals** and if objects of that class may be used in a hash table, you also should override the method **Object.hashCode** for your class. A correct **hashCode** method meets the following two criteria:

➤ The **hashCode** method must return the same integer value for two objects whenever comparing the two objects with the **equals** method returns **true**.

➤ The **hashCode** method must consistently return the same value for any particular object during the execution of an application.

If objects that satisfy the equality relationship have different **hashCode** values or if the **hashCode** for an object changes during the execution of a Java application, the **Hashtable** data structure can become corrupt.

---

*Class*

**java.util.Properties**

---

*Purpose*

The **Properties** class extends **Hashtable**. The key and value are both **String** objects, suitable for writing to or reading from I/O streams. A **Properties** object can contain another **Properties** object that gives default values.

---

*Constructors*

➤ **Properties()**
  **Properties( Properties default )**
  When you create a **Properties** object, you can optionally supply another **Properties** object to serve as a table of default values.

---

*Methods*

The **Properties** class indirectly implements the **Map** interface. Some very useful methods have been added to the **Properties** class that are not part of the interface.

➤ **String getProperty( String** *key* **)**
  **String getProperty( String** *key***, String** *default* **)**
  The **getProperty** first searches the property table, and then the default table, for an occurrence of the specified key. If it finds the key, it returns the associated value. Otherwise, it returns **null** or the default **String** specified in the optional second argument.

➤ **void load( InputStream** *in* **)**
  The **load** method reads a property list from an input stream.

➤ **Enumeration propertyNames()**
  The **propertyNames** method return an **Enumeration** object to iterate through the keys in **Properties** object.

➤ **void list( PrintStream** *out* **)**
 **void list( PrintWriter** *out* **)**
 The **list** method prints the property list on the specified output stream.

➤ **void save( OutputStream** *out*, **String** *header* **)**
 The save method outputs first the header **String** and then the contents of
 the **Properties** table to the specified output stream.

The JVM maintains a **Properties** collection of system information. Your code
can ask it questions such as "What version of the Java platform is running?"
or "What operating system is the JVM running under?" Applets have limited
access to this table, but applications can make full use of it.

Referring to the values contained in the system **Properties** collection is a standard way to determine information about the native
system in which your program is running.
Call the **load** and **save** methods of the **Properties** class for a
straightforward way of saving and restoring program attributes,
such as the current window size and window position.

## Class

**java.util.Vector**

## Purpose

The **Vector** class supports a dynamically resizable list of object references. The
**Vector** class implements the **List** interface.

## Constructors

➤ **Vector()**
 **Vector( int** *capacity* **)**
 **Vector( int** *capacity*, **int** *increment* **)**
 When you create a **Vector** collection, you can optionally specify an initial
 capacity, or the number of elements for which to reserve space, and by how
 much the capacity should be incremented every time the **Vector** must
 grow. The size of a **Vector** is the number of elements actually contained
 in the **Vector**. The capacity is always equal to or greater than the size.

## Methods

Because the **Vector** class implements the **List** interface, objects of the **Vector**
class should be manipulated using the methods of that interface. There are
many legacy methods of the **Vector** class that are not part of the **List** interface. Using any of them will eliminate the possibility of interchanging a
**Vector** implementation with any other implementation that uses the **List**
interface, so these legacy methods are not recommended.

If you know in advance approximately how many elements will be stored in the **Vector**, pass that number as the capacity argument of the constructor. This improves efficiency, especially if the **Vector** grows gradually to a large size. Every time a **Vector** grows, the object references it contains are copied into a new **Vector** and the old **Vector** space is left for garbage collection.

## Class

**java.util.Stack**

## Purpose

The **Stack** class extends **Vector** and adds methods for last-in first-out behavior. The **Stack** class indirectly implements the **List** interface through its superclass, **Vector**. For a **Stack** object to be useful, it needs to be manipulated with its own methods, such as **push**, **pop**, and **peek** that are defined outside of the **List** interface.

## Constructors

➤ **Stack()**
The Stack class has only the no-argument constructor.

## Methods

➤ **boolean empty()**
The **empty** method returns **true** if the **Stack** is empty and **false** if at least one element is in the **Stack**.

➤ **Object peek()**
The **peek** method returns an object reference last added to, but not removed from, the **Stack**. Unlike **pop**, this method does not remove the element from the **Stack**. If the **Stack** is empty, **peek** throws the exception **EmptyStackException**.

➤ **Object pop()**
The **pop** method returns the object reference last added to, but not removed from, the **Stack**. It also removes the element from the **Stack**. If the **Stack** is empty, **pop** throws the exception **EmptyStackException**.

➤ **Object push( Object** *object* **)**
The **push** method adds an element to the **Stack** and returns an object reference that is passed as an argument.

➤ **int search( Object** *object***)**
The search method returns the position of the specified object reference on the **Stack**, or minus one if the object reference is not stored on the **Stack**.

The following program, `LegacyLine`, is a reworked version of the `Line` example presented earlier in this chapter. This version demonstrates the **Vector** class and **Enumeration** interface. The class `LegacyLine` manipulates a **Vector** of **java.awt.Point** objects. The class **Point** stores the x and y coordinates of a two-dimensional point and implements the **toString** method to return a textual representation of a point.

```java
package examples.collections;
import java.util.Vector;
import java.util.Enumeration;
import java.io.PrintStream;
import java.awt.Point;
/** A class to demonstrate the use of the Vector and
  * Enumeration classes in the java.util package
  */
public class LegacyLine {
   private Vector points = new Vector();
   /** Set the starting point for a line
     * @param p the starting point
     */
   public void setStart( Point p ) {
      points.removeAllElements();
      points.addElement( p );
   }
   /** Set the next point in a line
     * @param p the next point
     */
   public void addPoint( Point p ) {
      points.addElement( p );
   }
   /** Print all the points in a line
     * @param ps the stream where the points
     *              will be printed
     */
   public void listPoints( PrintStream ps ) {
      Enumeration e = points.elements();
      while ( e.hasMoreElements() ) {
         ps.println( e.nextElement() );
      }
   }
   /** Test method for the class
     * @param args not used
     */
   public static void main( String[] args ) {
      LegacyLine x = new LegacyLine();
      x.setStart( new Point( 4, 11 ) );
      x.addPoint( new Point( -6, 1 ) );
      x.addPoint( new Point( 2, 3 ) );
      x.listPoints( System.out );
   }
}
```

**10**

The output is:

```
java.awt.Point[x=4,y=11]
java.awt.Point[x=-6,y=1]
java.awt.Point[x=2,y=3]
```

Do not be fooled into assuming that the declaration of **e** instantiates **Enumeration**. Instead, it declares an object reference for an object of unknown type that implements the **Enumeration** interface. The object is created by the method **Vector.elements** for the object **points**. The actual class of the object returned by **Vector.elements** is unimportant. All that matters is that it implements **Enumeration**.

---

**Mini Quiz 10-4**

When is the method **Point.toString** called during the execution of this sample program?

---

The following program demonstrates the **Properties** collection class:

```
package examples.collections;
import java.util.*;
/** A class to help demonstrate how to work with System
  * properties
  */
public class SystemProperties {
   /** Display the system properties specified as
     * input parameters or, if no input is given,
     * all the system properties
     * @param args the list of system properties
     *             to be displayed
     */
   public static void main( String[] args ) {
      if ( args.length > 0 ) {
         // dump selected system properties
         for ( int i=0; i<args.length; i++ ) {
            System.out.println( args[i] + ": " +
               System.getProperty( args[i],
                                      "not found" ) );
         }
      } else {
         // dump all system properties
         Properties sysProps = System.getProperties();
         Enumeration e = sysProps.propertyNames();
         while ( e.hasMoreElements() ) {
            String propName = (String)e.nextElement();
            System.out.println( propName + ": " +
               sysProps.getProperty( propName ) );
         }
      }
   }
}
```

```
      }
}
```

When no input arguments exist, the output describes the current native environment and the implementation of the JVM. If you run the program, you should see output similar to the lines below, except that several lines have been deleted from this listing and your results will reflect your installation of the Java platform:

```
user.language: en
file.encoding.pkg: sun.io
java.vm.name: Classic VM
java.class.version: 46.0
java.vm.version: 1.2
file.separator: \
user.region: US
file.encoding: Cp1252
path.separator: ;
```

You can specify specific properties as command-line arguments. For example, you can enter the following on one command line:

```
java examples.collections.SystemProperties user.timezone
```

If your system clock is set for Eastern Standard Time, the output is:

```
user.timezone: America/New_York
```

You can run the program again, by entering the following on one command line:

```
java examples.collections.SystemProperties file.encoding
not.a.property
```

If your operating system uses the default US character–encoding scheme, the output is:

```
file.encoding: Cp1252
not.a.property: not found
```

The bulk of this program is contained in the **main** method. If the user supplies the name of a system property as a command-line argument, the program prints the name and the value associated with the name in the system properties table. The JVM maintains the system properties table. The table is available to programs as a **Properties** collection in which the property names are the keys and the property values contain current settings. The **System** class provides the method **getProperty,** which returns the value of the property named in the argument.

When the user supplies no arguments, the program prints the entire system properties table. The method **System.getProperties** returns an object reference for the full system properties table, which is assigned here to the local variable sysProps. The **main** method next calls **propertyNames** to obtain an **Enumeration** object, **e**, to use as an iterator to step through the names of the properties. In the while loop, the program extracts property names one at a time by calling **nextElement** for **e**, as long as the method **hasMoreElements** returns **true** for **e**. It obtains the associated value by calling **System.getProperty** and prints each name-value pair.

---

**Mini Quiz 10-5**

In this sample program, why is each item in the collection `sysProps` cast to type `String` after it is returned from the method `nextElement` of the Enumeration **e**?

---

# SUMMARY

The Java platform provides classes that support a variety of data structures and other useful features in the package **java.util**.

Use the **Calendar**, **Date,** and **TimeZone** classes to store dates and times. With these classes, you can represent and manipulate date and time information as specified by the cultural environment in which your program runs.

If you have classes that depend on, or must react to, changes in the state of some other class, use **Observer** and **Observable** to set up an automatic event-notification mechanism. Classes that implement the interface **Observer** are notified when an object of a class that extends class **Observable** changes. The notification takes the form of a call to the method **update**, which is part of the **Observer** interface.

The collections framework defines interfaces that define standard programming interfaces for working with collection classes. The framework also provides general purpose implementations of the interfaces that are ready to use. The framework also defines interfaces for iterator classes that are used for traversing collections one element at a time.

To increase the usefulness of the collections framework, commonly used algorithms such as search, sort, and reverse are implemented in polymorphic methods that are gathered into the class **Collections**. This same class also provides methods for creating wrapper collections to add synchronization and read-only characteristics to existing collection objects.

There are a number of legacy collections classes still available. Where possible, these have been retrofitted into the new collections framework so that they may be manipulated using the same standard interfaces as the other implementation classes.

## QUESTIONS

1. Which of the following types can be stored in a **TreeSet** object? Select all that apply.

   a. **Integer**

   b. **int**

   c. **boolean**

   d. **Boolean**

   e. **String**

2. Which of the following are abstract classes? Select all that apply.

   a. **Collection**

   b. **Date**

   c. **Calendar**

   d. **TimeZone**

   e. **Observable**

3. Which of the following types have a fixed capacity? Select all that apply.

   a. **HashSet**

   b. **Hashtable**

   c. **int[ ]**

   d. **Vector[ ]**

   e. **LinkedList**

4. Examine the following code:

```
import java.util.List;
import java.util.ArrayList;
public class Quiz10_4 {
    public static void main( String[] args ) {
        List list = new ArrayList( 100 );
        double x = -34.678;
        list.add( x );
        System.out.println( list.get( 0 ) );
    }
}
```

   Which of the following statements are true when the code is compiled and run? Select all that apply.

   a. The compiler rejects the expression **new ArrayList( 100 )** because no constructor parameters are allowed when creating an **ArrayList** object.

   b. Compilation is successful, and the output is: **-34.678**.

   c. Compilation is successful, and the output is: **100.**

d. The compiler rejects the expression `list.add( x )` because **x** cannot be converted to the type **Object**.

e. The compiler rejects the expression `list.add( x )` because **List** objects can only contain integer values, not floating point values.

5. Which of the following methods are defined in the **Observer** interface? Select all that apply.

a. **observe**

b. **update**

c. **toString**

d. **hashCode**

e. **equals**

6. Which class is the best choice for storing **String** values that have a **String** key name?

7. Which of the following methods are defined in the **Iterator** interface? Select all that apply.

a. **hasMore**

b. **delete**

c. **add**

d. **next**

e. **removeAll**

8. True or False:

If a class definition overrides the **equals** method, it should not override the **hashCode** method.

9. Which of the following classes implement the **Collection** interface? Select all that apply.

a. **BitSet**

b. **Hashtable**

c. **Vector**

d. **TreeMap**

e. **LinkedList**

10. Examine the following code:

```
import java.util.StringTokenizer;
public class Quiz10_10 {
   private static final String text
      = "The quick, brown fox";
   public static void main( String[] args ) {
```

```
        StringTokenizer st
            = new StringTokenizer( text, "," );
        while( st.hasMoreTokens() ) {
            System.out.println( st.nextToken( " " ) );
        }
    }
}
```

Which of the following statements are true when the code is compiled and run? Select all that apply.

a. Compilation is successful, and the output is:

```
The
quick,
brown
fox
```

b. Compilation is successful, and the output is:

```
The quick,
brown
fox
```

c. Compilation is successful, and the output is:

```
The quick,
brown fox
```

d. The compiler rejects the expression
   `new StringTokenizer( text, "," )` because only **String**
   objects can be passed as parameters to **StringTokenizer** constructors.

e. The compiler rejects the use of the methods **hasMoreTokens** and
   **nextToken** because they are not defined in the **Enumeration** interface.

11. Which of the following interfaces do you implement for an unordered collection that allows duplicate elements?
    a. **Collection**
    b. **Set**
    c. **List**
    d. **Bag**
    e. **Map**

# EXERCISES

## Debugging

1. Correct all the errors in the following program:

```
package questions.c10;
import java.util.*;
```

```java
public class Debug10_1 {
    private static final int SIZE = 100;
    public static void main( String[] args ) {
        List list = new ArrayList( SIZE );
        for ( int i=0; i<=SIZE; i++ ) {
            list.add( new Integer( i*i ) );
        }
        Integer x = list.getLast();
        System.out.println( x.intValue() );
    }
}
```

2. Correct all the errors in the following program so that both output statements print `true`:

```java
package questions.c10;
public class Debug10_2 {
    private String name = "";
    public String getName() {
        return name;
    }
    public void setName( String newName ) {
        name = newName;
    }
    public boolean equals( Object other ) {
        return name.equals( ( (Debug10_2) other).name );
    }
    public static void main( String[] args ) {
        Debug10_2 x = new Debug10_2();
        Debug10_2 y = new Debug10_2();
        x.setName( "Bono" );
        y.setName( "Bono" );
        System.out.println( x.equals( y ) );
        System.out.println(
            x.hashCode() == y.hashCode() );
    }
}
```

3. Correct all the errors in the following program:

```java
package questions.c10;
public class Debug10_3 {
    public static void main( String[] args ) {
        Calendar c = new Calendar();
        Date d = c.getTime();
        System.out.println( d );
    }
}
```

4. Correct all the errors in the following program:

```java
package questions.c10;
```

```
public class Debug10_4 {
   private static final int SIZE = 3;
   public static void main( String[] args ) {
      BitSet myBits = new BitSet( SIZE );
      myBits.insertElementAt( true, 0 );
      myBits.insertElementAt( false, 1 );
      myBits.insertElementAt( true, 2 );
      System.out.println( myBits );
   }
}
```

5. Correct all the errors in the following program:

```
package questions.c10;
import java.util.Observable;
import java.util.Observer;
public class Debug10_5 {
   public static void main( String[] args ) {
      FireStation fs = new FireStation();
      FireAlarm fa = new FireAlarm();
      fa.addObserver( fs );
      fa.soundAlarm();
      fa.clearAlarm();
   }
   static private class FireAlarm {
      private boolean alarmOn;
      public boolean isAlarmOn() {
         return alarmOn;
      }
      public void soundAlarm() {
         alarmOn = true;
         setChanged();
         notifyObservers();
      }
      public void clearAlarm() {
         alarmOn = false;
         setChanged();
         notifyObservers();
      }
   }
   static private class FireStation
                        implements Observer {
      public void update( FireAlarm fa, Object arg ) {
         if ( fa.isAlarmOn() ) {
            System.out.println( "Go to fire!" );
         } else {
            System.out.println( "Go back to"
                              + "station." );
         }
      }
   }
}
```

**10**

## Complete the Solution

1. Extract the file questions.c10.Complete10_1.java from the question.jar file on the CD-ROM. Complete the class `Complete10_1` definition by adding an **ArrayList** object to hold the `Point` objects and by finishing the methods `addPoint` and `numberOfPoints`.

2. Add another method called `listIterator` to the definition of the `Complete10_1` class from Question 1. The new method returns a **ListIterator** object that can be used to iterate through the collection of `Point` objects. Add statements to the `main` method to test your `ListIterator` method and the **ListIterator** object it returns.

3. Extract the file questions.c10.Complete10_3.java from the question.jar file on the CD-ROM. Complete the definition of class `Complete10_3` by providing a correct **hashCode** method.

4. Extract the file questions.c10.Complete10_4.java from the question.jar file on the CD-ROM. Complete the definition of class `Complete10_4` by finishing the methods for setting and getting the address and phone number fields. Also, finish the methods that are used for saving the properties to disk and restoring them from disk.

5. Extract the file questions.c10.Complete10_5.java from the question.jar file on the CD-ROM. Complete the program `Complete10_5` by providing the missing class `Motorist`. This class should be defined as an observer of the `StopLight` class and should respond when the `StopLight` object that it observes changes color.

## Discovery

1. The **java.util** package has a subpackage called **java.util.zip**. Using the classes provided in this package, write your own unzip utility in the class `JUnzip`. Begin with the class **ZipFile,** and use its methods to obtain an array of **ZipEntry** objects that represent the contents of the file and the **InputStream** objects that correspond to each **ZipEntry**. For simplicity's sake, unzip the entire file contents in the current directory.

2. Create a collection class called `IntegerSet` that imposes the restriction that all elements in the collection must be integer values and that no duplicate values are allowed. The `IntegerSet` class should have methods for adding and removing values, checking to see if a value is already in the set, and removing all values. The class also should have a method that returns an **Iterator** object that will iterate through the set.

# MULTITHREADING

**In this chapter you will:**

➤ Understand how the Java platform supports threads and thread groups and how it uses the API provided to create multithreaded programs.

☕ Write code to define, instantiate, and start new threads using both **java.lang.Thread** and **java.lang.Runnable**.

☕ Recognize conditions that might prevent a thread from executing.

☕ Write code using **synchronized**, **wait**, **notify**, and **notifyAll** to protect against concurrent access problems and to communicate between threads.

☕ Define the interaction between threads and between threads and object locks when executing **synchronized**, **wait**, **notify**, or **notifyAll**.

## THREADS AND MULTITHREADING

If you draw a line through your code to trace how control moves from statement to statement as your program runs, you are tracing a **thread** of execution. All programs have at least one thread. A **multithreaded** program allows more than one thread to run through the code at once. In some programs, the flow of control splits and executes your program as though it were two or more separate processes, rather than sticking to the single sequential order. Multithreaded programs can execute more than one thread at once.

All the programs you have seen so far in this book are single-threaded. This chapter describes the features that the Java platform provides for creating multithreaded programs. Java is unlike many programming languages in that the language and API let you create, run, and manage threads in a wholly portable way. Under-standing the material in this chapter is essential for writing multithreaded programs.

When you launch a new path through your code, you start a thread. Typically, you use more than one thread to improve the performance or responsiveness of your application. For example, you can run the graphical user interface (GUI) for your application in one thread and separate processor-heavy or file manipulation tasks in other threads. You may want a separate thread for animation.

If you have created multithreaded programs in other environments, you may be familiar with the complications that multithreading introduces to your code. Threads can interfere with each other, especially when two or more threads that can run concurrently operate on the same variables or objects. At times, you must synchronize your threads so that they do not write to the same storage or contend for the same resources. You also want to eliminate the potential for threads to corrupt the values of objects used by other threads, or to go into deadlock when they all wait on the same condition or on each other. In short, you need a way for your threads to communicate with each other.

The Java programming language includes features for multithreading. You do not have to call an operating system API to manage threads or to use platform-dependent features for interthread communication. The close connection between the Java virtual machine (JVM) and the Java programming language breaks down traditional borders between the programming language, supporting libraries, and system APIs.

Even if you are familiar with the concepts of multithreading and have created multithreaded programs in other environments, you should read this chapter carefully. The Java platform provides a comprehensive set of services for managing threads that may be unlike operating system APIs or class libraries you have used in the past. The Java platform also introduces a feature that you may not have encountered before: You can gather threads into groups and operate on all threads in a group with a single method call.

## THE LIFE CYCLE OF A THREAD

Threads can come into being, start running, pause, and resume any number of times, and finally stop dynamically during program execution. One thread, the main thread, is launched by the JVM when you run an application or by a Web browser when it starts an applet. But how do other threads that you define in your Java source code come into being, start running, share the processor, and finally stop? The bulk of this chapter discusses the constructs in the Java programming language and the core classes that you use to manage threads. Before looking into the details, you may find it helpful to see an overview of the life cycle of threads.

After a single-threaded program starts, it has sole control of the process in which it runs until it ends. It may wait from time to time for user input or some I/O operation to complete, but no other activities occur in the JVM, with the possible exception of some internal operations, such as garbage collection, that run on other threads behind the scenes. The left side of Figure 11-1 represents this situation. Your program can explicitly create one or more objects that can run as separate threads. After an object capable of running as a thread is created, your program can call a method to begin running the thread. Your threads can also launch other threads. Your program can consist of several threads, all sharing the JVM.

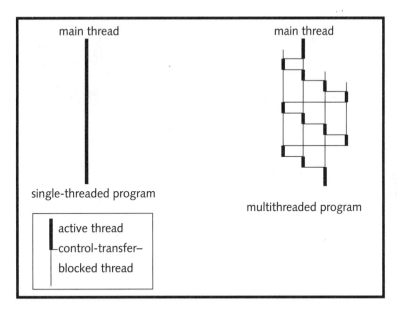

**Figure 11-1**   Single-threaded and multithreaded programs

How do threads share processing time? The simple story is that they each get a turn at running, and the JVM is in charge of scheduling processor time according to the priorities assigned to the threads. A more complete story depends on whether the native operating system uses preemptive or cooperative multitasking and whether you are running on a single-processor or a multiprocessor machine. Do not assume that threads are dispatched in the same way on all platforms and that they are given the same length of time every time they have an opportunity to run. For example, on a multiprocessor system, the JVM may be able to run more than one thread at the same time on different processors.

When a thread does not have control, it pauses like a movie when the projection freezes on a single frame and the JVM executes or tries to execute methods in another thread. The states of all threads except the thread that the JVM is currently executing cannot change, with the important exception that objects shared among threads may be modified by the executing thread or may be affected by external factors; for example, the state of I/O buffers can change. To the user, it may appear that all threads are running simultaneously, but the reality is more like that depicted on the right side of Figure 11-1.

By default, the JVM tries to distribute control equally to all threads. If you have some threads that require more immediate attention than others, such as threads that encapsulate the user interface and in which response time is very important, you can assign priority values to your threads. Threads with high priority values preempt lower priority threads.

# CREATING AND RUNNING THREADS

An object can be run as a thread if it is a **Runnable** object. In other words, any object that instantiates a class that implements the interface **Runnable** can be launched as a new thread by the main thread or by any other active thread.

*Interface*

**java.lang.Runnable**

*Purpose*

The **Runnable** interface defines the protocol that must be followed by all threads.

*Methods*

➤ **void run()** is the only method in the **Runnable** interface.

You must provide an implementation of the **run** method in every class that may be instantiated by an object that can run as a thread. This method is the entry point for the thread, and is analogous to **main** except that all threads, regardless of whether they are in applets or applications, must have a **run** method.

> **Mini Quiz 11-1**
>
> The definition of the **run** method in the **Runnable** interface lists no exceptions in its **throws** clause. What implications does this fact have for exception handling in threads?

The core class **Thread** implements **Runnable**, so you can create a thread by instantiating **Thread** or a subclass of **Thread**. The **Thread** class also defines a number of methods that you can use to manage the thread. The next sample program demonstrates extending the **Thread** class.

Generally, implementing **Runnable** is considered a better technique than extending **Thread**, for the following reasons:

➤ If your class already has a superclass other than **Object**, extending **Thread** is not an option.

➤ A class that implements **Runnable** inherits less overhead than one that extends **Thread**. This does not affect the efficiency of the code because you must always have a **Thread** object for each thread, but does reduce the number of inherited members.

You can always implement **Runnable**. The only catch is that you must wrap the **Runnable** object in a **Thread** object to use it as a thread. Do this by creating a **Thread** object and passing your **Runnable** object as an argument of the **Thread** constructor. When a **Thread** object is constructed with a **Runnable** object as input, the **Thread** object uses the **run** method of the **Runnable** object in place of its own **run** method.

When a class extends **Thread**, it inherits all the methods and fields required to be manipulated as a separate thread, with one important exception: The **Thread** class does have a **run** method, but it is empty. You must override the inherited **run** method with one from your class if your thread is to accomplish anything.

---

*Class*

**java.lang. Thread**

---

*Purpose*

The **Thread** class provides the infrastructure for multithreaded programs in the Java platform.

---

*Constructors*

➤ **Thread()**
   **Thread( Runnable** *object* **)**
   **Thread( String** *name* **)**
   **Thread( Runnable** *object*, **String** *name* **)**
   **Thread( ThreadGroup** *group*, **Runnable** *object* **)**
   **Thread( ThreadGroup** *group*, **String** *name* **)**
   **Thread( ThreadGroup** *group*, **Runnable** *object*, **String** *name* **)**

When you construct a **Thread** object, you can optionally specify a name for the thread in the argument of type **String**.

When you create a thread by instantiating a class that is defined to implement **Runnable**, you must provide the **Runnable** object as an argument of the constructor. Thread groups are discussed later in this chapter.

---

*Methods*

➤ **String getName()**
   The **getName** method returns the name of the **Thread** Object.

➤ **int getPriority()**
   The **int getPriority** method returns the priority of the thread.

➤ **void interrupt()**
   The interrupt method interrupts the current thread.

➤ **boolean isDaemon()**

The **isDaemon** method returns **true** if the **Thread** object is a daemon thread, and **false** otherwise.

➤ **boolean isAlive()**

The **isAlive** method returns **true** if the thread has been started and has not yet died, and **false** otherwise.

➤ **void join()**
**void join( long** *milliseconds* **)**

The **join** method waits for the thread object to terminate. You can optionally specify a maximum number of milliseconds to wait for the lifetime of the thread to end.

➤ **void setDaemon( boolean** *on* **)**

The **setDaemon** method determines whether the thread is a daemon thread. When the **boolean** argument has the value **true**, the **Thread** object becomes a daemon. If the argument is **false**, the thread runs as a regular thread.

➤ **void setPriority( int** *priority* **)**

The **setPriority** method sets the priority of a thread to the lesser of the specified value or the maximum allowed for the group to which the thread belongs. Threads with a higher integer priority value can preempt threads with a lower value.

➤ **void sleep( long** *milliseconds* **)**

The **sleep** method makes the thread pause for the specified number of milliseconds.

➤ **void start()**

The **start** method causes the thread to begin execution.

➤ **void yield()**

The **yield** method makes the thread pause so another thread can execute.

---

Three methods of the **Thread** class are deprecated in the Java 2 platform. Previous versions of the Java platform made the method **stop** available to terminate execution of a thread, **suspend** to suspend execution of a thread, and **resume to** restore a suspended thread to a runnable state. These methods are still available, but they are considered unsafe and you should not use them. If you call them or compile an existing class that calls them, the compiler produces a deprecation warning and you should rewrite the offending code to avoid calling **stop**, **suspend**, or **restore**. Later sections of this chapter explain the reason for the deprecation and give a safe way to stop execution of a thread.

You do not call the **run** method to start a thread. After you have created the thread, make it active by calling the **start** method. The JVM then passes control to the appropriate **run** method. After a thread starts, it can be in a runnable or blocked state. While it is runnable, the thread is either executing or ready to execute as soon as the JVM gives it control. The thread can be blocked as the result of a call to **sleep** or **Object.wait**, or because it is waiting for an I/O operation. Figure 11-2 shows how a thread can change state during its life cycle.

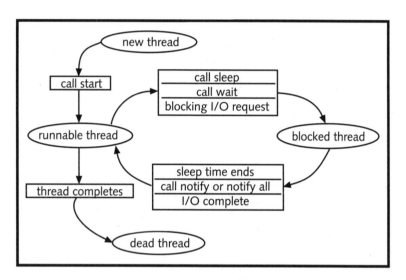

**Figure 11-2**  State Transition diagram for a thread

You can take two approaches in creating and running a thread, depending on whether you choose to implement the **Runnable** interface or extend the **Thread** class.

For an object that is **Runnable** but not a **Thread**:

1. Define a class that implements **Runnable**.

2. Implement the method **run** for your class.

3. Instantiate the class to create a **Runnable** object.

4. Create a **Thread** object, passing the **Runnable** object as an argument to the constructor of **Thread**.

5. Call the **start** method for the **Thread** object. Do not call the **run** method.

For an object that is a **Thread**:

1. Define a class that extends **Thread**.

2. Implement the method **run** for your class.

3. Instantiate the class to create a **Thread** object.

4. Call the method **start** for an instance of the class. Do not call the **run** method.

# STOPPING A THREAD

The **Thread** class provides the **start** method to begin the execution of a thread, but no methods to stop or suspend the execution. Moreover, the methods **stop**, **suspend**, and **resume** are deprecated. This situation poses two questions; this text answers both in turn.

## Why Were Stop and the Other Methods Deprecated?

The designers of the Java platform found the methods **stop** and **suspend** to be inherently unsafe because they can make the stopped thread leave data in an inconsistent state, if that data is accessed concurrently by more than one thread. The **resume** method is deprecated because, without **suspend**, you never need to call it.

Later in this chapter, you will learn how to protect threads from interfering with each other or corrupting data that different threads share, by applying locks to a class or an object. In the section "Writing Robust Multithreaded Programs," you learn how to set up locks so that only one thread at a time can alter the value of critical variables. Stopping an active thread asynchronously, from the outside by calling **stop** or **suspend**, releases all locks without giving the thread an opportunity to complete potentially critical operations. Because other threads may then pick up corrupt information, the integrity of all threads that share variables with a stopped or suspended thread is compromised.

## How Should You Stop a Thread?

A thread should run to its natural termination. In other words, you should let a thread return under its own control; you should never terminate it from the outside. What about threads that loop continuously? Without some signal to stop, some threads would run forever. Here is the recommended way to make all threads stop gracefully:

➤ Define an instance variable in the thread's class that acts as a flag indicating whether it is time to stop.

➤ Make sure that the variable itself is not affected by concurrent access from other threads. As explained later in this chapter, you can do this by declaring the variable with the keyword **volatile**, or by declaring all code that accesses it to be **synchronized**.

➤ In the thread, check the value of the variable frequently. Typically, you test the value in the condition controlling a loop. If the thread waits for long periods, you can call the **interrupt** method to interrupt the wait.

➤ Return from the **run** method as soon as possible when the flag indicates that the thread should stop.

The sample programs in this chapter use this approach. The following lines are taken from the first example, the `RepeatedMessage` class:

```
// declaration of a class that runs as a thread
// other fields declarations omitted
   private volatile boolean stopFlag;
// other methods omitted
   public void run() {
      stopFlag = false;
      try {
         while ( ! stopFlag ) {
         // body of main processing loop
         }
      } catch( InterruptedException ie ) {
         return;
      }
   }
   public void finish() {
      stopFlag = true;
      return;
   }
```

If you give the method that sets the flag the name `stop`, instead of giving it the name `finish`, you can use existing code that called the deprecated **stop** method for your thread. You may receive warnings that you are overriding the deprecated method **Thread.stop**, but this technique is safe and you can ignore these warnings.

The following simple program has three threads: a main thread and two threads launched by the main thread. As well as showing how to create and start threads, this program demonstrates one kind of problem that can occur when you do not synchronize your threads. This program uses the class `RepeatedMessage`. Because `RepeatedMessage` is a public class, it is found in a file called **RepeatedMessage.java**. The structure of packages mirrors the file system, so you will find this source code in the examples\threads subfolder of the folder in which you unpacked the JAR file **examples.jar**.

```
package examples.threads;
/**A class to demonstrate why synchronized methods
  * are needed by showing what can happen when they
  * are not synchronized.
  */
public class RepeatedMessage extends Thread {
   private String message;
   private int pauseTime;
   /** field stopFlag tells thread when to stop
          * declared volatile to ensure every thread sees
```

**11**

```
                         * change immediately
                         */
                  private volatile boolean stopFlag;
/** Construct a repeating message
      * @param inputMessage the message to be
      *      repeated
      * @param inputPauseTime the time, in ms,
      *      paused between each letter of the
      *      message
      */
     public RepeatedMessage( String inputMessage,
                              int inputPauseTime ) {
       message = inputMessage;
       pauseTime = inputPauseTime;
             }
     /** Display a repeating message
      * @param rm the message to be repeated
      * @exception InterruptedException if the thread
      *      does not sleep for the full time specified
      */
     public static
           void displayMessage( RepeatedMessage rm )
             throws InterruptedException {
       for( int i=0; i < rm.message.length(); i++ ) {
         System.out.print( rm.message.charAt( i ) );
         sleep( 50 );
       }
       System.out.println();
     }
     /** The workings of the thread
      */
     public void run() {
       stopFlag = false;
       try {
         while ( ! stopFlag ) {
           displayMessage( this );
           sleep( pauseTime );
         }
       } catch( InterruptedException ie ) {
         return;
       }
     }
       /** A method to set a flag to stop the thread
        */
       public void finish() {
         stopFlag = true;
         return;
       }
     /** The test method for the class
      * @param args not used
      */
```

```
public static void main( String[] args ) {
    try {
        RepeatedMessage m1
            = new RepeatedMessage( "bonjour!", 500 );
        m1.start();
        RepeatedMessage m2
            = new RepeatedMessage( "HELLO!", 111 );
        m2.start();
        // pause to let the threads run,
        // then stop them
        sleep( 5000 );
        m1.finish();
        m2.finish();
    } catch( InterruptedException ie ) {
        ie.printStackTrace();
    }
    finally {
        // flush the output buffer
        System.out.println();
    }
}
}
```

This program allows the output to be scrambled by printing messages one character at a time from different threads, and by pausing between characters. The output may look different on different installations of the Java platform, and may vary from run to run. Here is one possible output:

**11**

```
bHEoLnLjOo!u
r!
HELLO!
HEbLoLnOj!o
urH!E
LLO!
HELbLoOn!j
ouHrE!L
LO!
HELLOb!o
njHoEuLrL!O
!
HELLO!b
onHjEoLuLrO!!

HELLO!
bHoEnLjLoOu!r
!
```

In this program, two threads are instances of the class `RepeatedMessage`, and the main thread contains the **main** method of the class `RepeatedMessage`. **main** instantiates and starts the threads `m1` and `m2`. In these two threads, the **run** method repeatedly calls `displayMessage` to output a message and sleeps briefly after each call. The **sleep** method suspends execution for the specified number of milliseconds. Meanwhile, the main thread sleeps.

Notice that the **run** method is coded as an unending while loop. This looks like terrible programming style, but it is acceptable here because **main** stops the threads after five seconds, by calling **finish**. In fact, many event-driven applications rely on similar logic. Threads often loop continuously, monitoring their input buffers or waiting to be notified of an event.

In the code, you see try blocks, catch blocks, and a throws clause for **InterruptedException**. This exception can occur while **sleep** is running. The class **InterruptedException** extends the class **Exception**, so this is a checked exception. Because **run** cannot list any exceptions in a throws clause, the exception must be handled within the thread.

## CREATING SERVICE THREADS

Service threads typically contain a never-ending loop for the sole purpose of receiving and handling requests. You can convert such threads into daemon threads. A **daemon thread** runs continuously in the background. You can call the **setDaemon** method for a thread to specify that it is a daemon thread and call the **isDaemon** method to determine whether a thread is a daemon thread.

The JVM does not expect daemon threads, unlike regular user threads, to finish. However, a Java application is assumed to be complete when all its threads have terminated. How can a program that starts daemon threads ever end? The JVM can detect when your program reaches a point where only daemon threads are running. The JVM then assumes your application is finished and terminates the daemon threads.

In client-server configurations, one or several client processes make requests on a server process. Each server is usually a separate program from the clients and may reside on a different processor. A very common technique for programming servers that communicate over TCP/IP connections is to create a daemon thread to monitor each TCP/IP port for incoming client requests. When it receives a request, the server typically launches another thread to process it and then to return a response to the client. The threads dedicated to individual requests terminate when their response has been sent, but the monitoring thread is kept alive as long as the server is required.

Just as the Java platform provides API to simplify the task of creating multi-threaded programs, it provides core classes in the package **java.net** to support networking. In Chapter 16, you see how client and server programs can communicate over TCP/IP sockets. A sample server program is supplied and, like many servers, it is a multithreaded program.

# WRITING ROBUST MULTITHREADED PROGRAMS

Creating and running threads is straightforward. Making sure the threads work well together is a far more difficult task. The previous program demonstrates one way in which things can go wrong in multithreaded programs. The Java programming language has two keywords for the specific purpose of eliminating concurrent access problems:

➤ You can qualify variables with the keyword **volatile** to suppress compiler optimizations that might lose or ignore changes to the variables made by different threads. Changes made to a variable by another thread are called **asynchronous** changes because the flow of control through the current thread does not determine when the changes occur. Asynchronous changes are invisible to the compiler.

In reality, you rarely need to declare variables to be **volatile,** because the JVM updates memory frequently, at intervals known as **synchronization points**. However, you should use **volatile** for shared variables for which you adopt none of the synchronization techniques described in this chapter.

➤ If you qualify the declaration of a method with **synchronized**, the method can be run for a particular object or class by only one thread at a time. The Java platform provides features for synchronizing threads. You should use these features to avoid race situations in which threads share variables and the order in which they read or modify shared values can affect the results.

**11**

Deadlock can occur when all threads are in a blocked state, rather like gridlock in road traffic. Java provides no automatic way of detecting and resolving deadlock. To avoid deadlock, you can employ a number of design principles that are beyond the scope of this book. However, sometimes a good debugger is your best tool for detecting deadlock.

You are responsible for ensuring that your threads do not interfere with each other and that at least one thread is active until your program is meant to terminate.

# SYNCHRONIZING THREADS

Synchronizing threads involves setting **locks**. You can conceive of locks as flags that indicate whether objects or classes are available for threads to use or are already in use. Sometimes the term **monitor** is used to describe a lock. You can apply locks to methods or blocks of code to prevent them from running simultaneously in more than one thread. You do not have to apply locks to all methods. Use locks for code that requires exclusive access to an object or class while the code is running. Also you can use locks for code that cannot tolerate changes to fields while it executes.

The concept of locks is similar to that of semaphores, which you may have used in other programming languages for interthread communication. However, a lock is not quite the same thing as a semaphore. Two kinds of locks exist:

➤ **Object locks** apply to instance methods. The lock controls whether a method can be run when it is called for a particular object. Before the method can run, it must acquire the lock on the object, and may have to wait for the lock to become free. The method releases the lock automatically when it ends. Only one thread can have the lock at a time. Therefore, synchronized methods cannot operate on the same object in more than one thread at a time. Other objects of the same class and instance methods that do not require a lock are not affected. All class methods are also unaffected.

➤ **Class locks** apply to all the class methods. When a thread has the lock for a class, it is the only thread that can execute any of the class methods that require a lock. Class methods that do not require a lock are unaffected. All instance methods are also unaffected.

---

*Syntax*

[*access_specifier*] **synchronized** [*other_qualifiers*]
   *return_type method_name* ( *argument_list* )
   [*throws exception_list*]
   *block*

---

*Dissection*

➤ If the method is not declared with the qualifier **static**, the qualifier **synchronized** applies an object lock to the object for which the instance method is called.

➤ If the method is declared **static**, the qualifier **synchronized** applies a class lock to class methods.

---

This relatively simple locking mechanism is all that you need in the Java programming language—just qualify the declaration of methods with the keyword **synchronized**. You lock classes and objects independently by synchronizing class and instance methods separately.

You do not have to operate on the locks explicitly. The **synchronized** keyword tells the JVM that the method requires a lock in order to run. The JVM then creates the lock and manages the allocation of the lock to threads during execution, as follows:

➤ The request for the lock is automatic, and is always satisfied if no other thread has acquired the lock.

➤ A lock is always available unless a thread has requested and been granted the lock.

➤ When a synchronized method ends, it releases the lock. If another thread with a synchronized method is waiting for that lock, that thread acquires the lock and can proceed.

Synchronized methods are mutually exclusive in the sense that they can be run by only one thread at a time for the locked object. As a simple solution to the synchronization problem in the previous sample program, you can declare the `displayMessage` method to be synchronized so that the code is as follows:

```
public static synchronized
      void displayMessage ( RepeatedMessage rm )
                     throws InterruptedException {
   for( int i=0; i < rm.message.length(); i++ ) {
      System.out.print( rm.message.charAt( i ) );
      sleep( 50 );
   }
   System.out.println();
}
```

The `displayMessage` method is a class method in this example. As a result, the lock applies to the class `RepeatedMessage`.

You can also indicate that an object lock is required for a single statement or block of code, by using the **synchronized** statement.

**11**

*Syntax*

**synchronized (** *object_to_be_locked* **)**
   *statement_or_block*

*Dissection*

➤ When preceding a block or statement, the **synchronized** keyword synchronizes the code for the specified object. You can name any object, and a common technique is to declare a field specifically to act as a lockable object.

*Code Example*

```
// object used by all instances for its lock
private static Object sharedLock;
public static
      void displayMessage( RepeatedMessage rm )
throws InterruptedException {
   synchronized ( sharedLock ) {
      for( int i=0; i<rm.message.length(); i++ ) {
         System.out.print( rm.message.charAt( i ) );
         sleep( 50 );
      }
```

```
        System.out.println();
    }
}
```

---

*Code Dissection*

An alternate approach to the `displayMessage` problem is to acquire a lock just for the duration of the **for** statement that prints the messages one character at a time. The only reason for creating the object `sharedLock` is to apply its lock to this block of code.

---

## When to Synchronize Code

The most difficult aspect of the **synchronized** keyword is deciding when to use it. You pay a performance penalty for using synchronized methods. The Java 2 platform brings some new internal algorithms to the JVM to improve performance of multithreaded programs. The result is that synchronized methods now can run much closer to the speed of methods that have no locking considerations. Regardless of the size of the overhead for synchronization, it is a reasonable price to pay to ensure correctness of your program.

 The thread-local heap cache and the thread-local monitor cache, both of which affect multithreading, improve the performance of the Java 2 platform. A region of memory called the heap stores all objects, and the caches help the JVM manage memory on a thread-by-thread basis. The thread-local heap cache greatly reduces the need for locking in heap allocations. It also reduces the time and memory required by each run of the garbage collector. The thread-local monitor cache speeds up the process of synchronizing methods.

On the Solaris platform, the Java 2 platform also can take advantage of the operating system's support for threads for improved performance, particularly in a multi-processor environment.

To determine the level of synchronization that your application requires, consider how the threads within it share classes and objects. You can use one of the following approaches:

➤ The first and simplest level of synchronization is no synchronization at all. This is acceptable only for single-threaded programs and for multi-threaded programs that use all classes containing class methods only in a single thread. You need synchronization only when different threads share objects. If none of the class methods modifies any objects, maintaining object integrity does not require synchronization.

➤ In the second level of synchronization, you synchronize all class methods to safeguard the integrity of class variables that the methods use. If you adopt this approach, you can access class variables only by calling synchronized class methods, even from within methods of the same class. In this model, different threads can freely share class variables because they are protected from simultaneous access and modification. This level of synchronization is not adequate when instances of the class may be used by more than one thread.

➤ In the third level of synchronization, all class methods and instance methods are synchronized to protect the integrity of all fields. This allows different threads to share objects and classes because the fields have been protected from simultaneous access and modification.

> **Mini Quiz 11-2**
>
> Does synchronizing all class methods ensure the integrity of objects of that class in a multithreaded program?

Never synchronize a constructor. The JVM runs constructors only to create objects and you cannot use the **new** keyword to tell the JVM to create the same object on two different threads. Therefore, the compiler rejects a constructor qualified with the keyword **synchronized** as an error.

When you override a synchronized method, you do not have to synchronize the method in the subclass. The superclass method remains synchronized, even if the subclass method is not synchronized. The Java programming language has no rules about overriding synchronized methods beyond the usual rules about overriding methods.

**11**

> **Mini Quiz 11-3**
>
> Can you remember what parts of an overriding method definition must match the equivalent parts of the overridden method?

## Synchronizing Methods of Inner Classes

Inner classes can complicate the synchronization of methods. In Chapter 9, you saw that an inner class has access to the fields of the enclosing instances and that several inner class objects can share the same enclosing instance. Therefore, you should design inner class objects in such a way that they do not undermine the synchronization of the methods of the enclosing instances.

No special relationship exists between the synchronized methods of an inner class and its enclosing class. As a result, simply qualifying the methods of the inner and enclosing classes with the **synchronized** keyword does not provide proper synchronization between them. Using such an approach allows one thread to call a method of the enclosing class while another thread calls a method of the inner class. Potentially, these methods may access and modify the same fields.

Synchronizing access to fields of enclosing classes by inner classes is straightforward, if not automatic. The methods of the inner class that access the fields of the enclosing class can use a **synchronized** statement to obtain a lock on the enclosing instance before accessing or modifying the fields of the enclosing instance.

In the following example, both the inner and enclosing classes have methods for accessing the name field:

```java
package examples.threads;
/** Enclosing and inner classes to demonstrate how to
  * synchronize methods between them.
  */
public class Enclosing {
    private String name = "";
    /** get the name value
      * @return the name
      */
    public synchronized String getName() {
        return name;
    }
    /** set the name value
      * @param s the input name value
      */
    public synchronized void setName( String s ) {
        name = s;
    }
    /** Example inner class
      */
    public class Insider {

        /** convert the name to all upper case
          */
        public void upperCaseName() {
            synchronized( Enclosing.this ) {
                name = name.toUpperCase();
            }
        }
    }
    /** Test method for the class
      * @param args not used
      */
    public static void main( String[] args ) {
        Enclosing enc = new Enclosing();
        enc.setName( "Maria" );
        Insider ins = enc.new Insider();
        ins.upperCaseName();
        System.out.println( enc.getName() );
    }
}
```

The output is

MARIA

In this example, the methods of the inner class use a synchronized statement to obtain a lock on the enclosing instance, **Enclosing.this**, before accessing the **name** field and changing it.

Do the methods of the inner class need the synchronized qualifier in addition to the **synchronized** statement? In this simple case, the answer is no. Because the inner class does not define any fields of its own, you need to provide synchronization only for the enclosing class. In general, use the synchronization qualifier for methods of inner classes only when code running in more than one thread may use fields of the inner classes.

When you synchronize methods of both inner and outer classes and then run the classes in a multithreaded program, the principal of hierarchical locking specifies that the inner class acquires the lock first.

## COMMUNICATING BETWEEN THREADS

In multithreaded programs, you need some form of interthread communication so that threads can notify each other when conditions change. You often want threads to tell each other to wait or to stop waiting when a condition has been satisfied. Some of the methods for interthread communication are built into the **Object** class.

*Class*

**java.lang.Object**

*Purpose*

The common ancestor class **Object** defines the common behavior of all classes.

*Methods*

➤ **void wait()**
**void wait( long** *timeout* **)**
**void wait( long** *timeout,* **int** *nanoseconds* **)**
The **wait** methods put the current thread object into a blocked state. The method must own the lock when it calls **wait**. This method call releases the lock. If you do not specify a time period, the thread waits until notified by another thread. You can specify a timeout period, in milliseconds, after which the thread stops waiting, regardless of whether it has been notified. You can also specify a number of nanoseconds to add to the wait period.

➤ **void notify()**
The **notify** method wakes up a single thread that is blocked because it is in a wait state. The thread is put into a ready-to-run state, but does not automatically start running. A synchronized method must still wait for the lock on the class or object.

➤ **void notifyAll()**

The **notifyAll** method sends wake-up messages to all threads waiting for the lock. All the threads go into a runnable state, but only one can actually acquire the lock and start running. So which thread actually gets control? The JVM selects the thread to run. It may be the one that has been waiting longest, but there is no guarantee and you should not base the logic of your application on any assumptions about the order in which the JVM gives locks to threads. The other threads that have been awakened from their **wait** calls will continue as soon as they can reacquire the lock. In other words, you do not need to notify them again unless they call **wait** again.

---

You can use these methods for objects within single-threaded applications. However, no gain exists unless you are designing a class for use in either single-threaded or multithreaded programs.

The **wait**, **notify**, and **notifyAll** methods are final methods of the **Object** class. You cannot override them and can rest assured that no other class has overridden them. You can call these methods for a particular object only when the current thread has a lock on the object. Otherwise, the JVM throws an **IllegalMonitorStateException.** In this context, the term monitor refers to the locking mechanism.

The following program demonstrates correct and incorrect uses of the **notifyAll** method:

```
package examples.threads;
/** A class to demonstrate the run-time error that
  * occurs if wait, notify, or notifyAll are used
  * when no lock has been obtained.
  */
public class ShowThreadError {
   private int value;
   /** Set the value of an object
     * This method is synchronized
     * @param v the object's new value
     */
   public synchronized void setValue( int v ) {
      value = v;
      doTheNotificationThing();   // okay here
   }
   /** Get the value of the object
     * This method is synchronized
     * @return the object's value
     */
   public synchronized int getValue() {
      return value;
   }
```

```
/** Notify waiting objects of a change
  * This method is not synchronized
  */
public void doTheNotificationThing() {
   notifyAll();
}
/** Test method for the class
  * @param args not used
  */
public static void main( String[] args ) {
   ShowThreadError t = new ShowThreadError();
   t.setValue( 10 );
   System.out.println( "value has been set to "
                       + t.getValue() );
   // the next statement causes a run-time error
   t.doTheNotificationThing();
}
}
```

In the following output, some lines have been split and the indenting has been modified to fit on the printed page:

```
value has been set to 10
Exception in thread "main"
   java.lang.IllegalMonitorStateException:
   current thread not owner
   at
   java.lang.object.notifyAll(Native Method)
   at
   examples.threads.ShowThreadError.
      doTheNotificationThing(ShowThreadError.java:32)
   at
   examples.threads.ShowThreadError.
      main(ShowThreadError.java:45)
```

This program has only one thread, but can still use the locking mechanism for the ShowThreadError object that it creates in the **main** method. If this class is used in a multithreaded application, the accessor method getValue and mutator method setValue cannot run at the same time on more than one thread.

---

### Mini Quiz 11-4

Notice that the method **doTheNotificationThing**, which calls **notifyAll**, is not synchronized. Why is this method ever allowed to call **notifyAll**?

*Hint:* What is different about the methods on the call chain when the call of **notifyAll** succeeds and when it throws an exception?

## Making Threads Wait

The **wait** method suspends execution of the thread and releases the lock that the thread holds on the object for which **wait** is called. Call this method when your code must wait for a condition to be satisfied before it can continue. For example, your method may be waiting for input that is not yet available or for a numeric value to reach a certain threshold. For efficiency and to help avoid deadlock, you should call **wait** to suspend the thread, release the lock that it has on the object, and let other threads run during what otherwise might be wasted processor cycles.

Usually, the thread remains suspended until you call the **notify** or **notifyAll** method for the object from another thread. You can call **wait** with a time-out as an alternative to calling **sleep**, or use the time-out as a fail-safe measure in case the JVM does not always notify the thread as you intended.

Typically you put a call to **wait** in a loop, in the following form:

```
while ( condition ) {
    wait();
}
```

Using a loop is the safest approach. The thread may be awakened for many different reasons, and you should not assume that the value of the condition has changed. Every time you regain control, the while loop gives you an opportunity to check the reason you were waiting and wait again if the condition is still true.

Threads release locks when they call **wait.** Take care not to create opportunities for deadlock when you call **wait**. Consider what can happen when you program a design that allows access to one class, called B, from only synchronized methods of another class, called A. Suppose a synchronized method of A calls a synchronized method of B. All is well until the thread in which the method of B runs calls **wait**. The call of **wait** releases the lock on the instance of B, but the lock on the instance of A remains. Deadlock can result, because the synchronized methods of A are locked out and no other methods can access B to wake up the blocked thread.

## Waking a Single Thread

You can call **notify** to wake up a thread. You cannot specify which thread should be given control. The JVM decides what thread to notify. This method is most useful when all threads are waiting on the same condition.

Calling **notify** is more efficient than calling **notifyAll**. However the result of **notify** can be that the JVM wakes up a thread that should not be given control of the object at that moment, and leaves the thread that should have awakened waiting. When you use **notify**, be careful that deadlock is not a possible outcome.

## Waking All Threads

The **notifyAll** method wakes up all waiting threads for the object. If different threads are waiting on different conditions, you should call this method rather than **notify**. The threads should each check their conditions. At least one thread should be able to continue, and threads whose conditions are not yet satisfied should use the **wait** method to return to the blocked state.

It is important to note that even though more than one thread may be awakened by the **notifyAll** method, only one can obtain the lock for the object and be allowed to execute.

## An Example of Communicating Between Threads

The next example is a relatively long program. Setting up a multithreaded program often involves several classes. The sample program is a simple banking application. For demonstration purposes, it maintains a bank account and performs deposits and withdrawals against the same bank account on separate threads. It uses the **wait** method to force a withdrawal to wait until an account has enough money to maintain a positive bank balance. The program calls **notifyAll** whenever the bank balance changes so that all threads waiting on that bank account object receive notice of the change and can evaluate the situation to determine whether they can proceed.

The first of four classes encapsulates a bank account:

```
package examples.threads;
/** A class to demonstrate wait and notify methods
   */
public class BankAccount {
   private int balance = 0;
   private boolean isOpen = true;
   /** The method withdraws an amount from the
     * account. If funds are insufficient, it will
     * wait until the funds are available or the
     * account is closed.
     * @param amount The amount to be withdrawn from
     *     the account
     * @return true if the withdrawal is successful,
     *     false otherwise
     * @exception InterruptedException If another
     *     thread calls the <b>interrupt</b> method
     */
   public synchronized boolean withdraw( int amount )
               throws InterruptedException {
     while ( amount > balance && isOpen() ) {
        System.out.println( "Waiting for "
                            + "some money ..." );
           wait();
        }
```

**11**

```
         boolean result = false;
         if ( isOpen() ) {
            balance -= amount;
            result = true;
         }
         return result;
      }
      /** The method to deposit an amount into the
       * account, provided that the account is open.
       * When the deposit is successful, it will notify
       * all waiting operations that there is now more
       * money in the account
       * @param amount The amount to be deposited into
       *      the account
       * @return true if the deposit is successful,
       *      false otherwise
       */
      public synchronized boolean deposit( int amount ) {
         if ( isOpen() ) {
            balance += amount;
            notifyAll();
            return true;
         } else {
            return false;
         }
      }
      /** Check to see if the account is open
       * @return true if it is open, otherwise false
       */
      public synchronized boolean isOpen() {
         return isOpen;
      }
      /** Close the bank account */
      public synchronized void close() {
         isOpen = false;
         notifyAll();
      }
   }
```

The `BankAccount` class has the following characteristics:

➤ The methods `deposit` and `withdraw` are synchronized instance methods. Therefore, the JVM applies a lock to the `BankAccount` object for which they are called.

➤ If the account has insufficient funds, the method `withdraw` calls **wait** and prints a message. Because `withdraw` calls **wait**, an **InterruptedException** can occur, and must be listed in the throws clause.

➤ The `deposit` method calls **notifyAll** to alert all threads whenever the balance in the account changes.

The methods `isOpen` and `close` are also synchronized. The `BankAccount` class provides the `isOpen` method to check whether transactions are allowed on the `BankAccount` object. The `isOpen` method returns **true** until the method `close` is called to close an account. The `close` method is synchronized so that it can call **notifyAll** to stop any transactions that are in progress when the account is closed and to prevent the account from being closed in the middle of a transaction or while another thread is checking to see if the bank account is open.

The following listing is the thread that makes deposits. It contains a class called `Saver` that implements **Runnable**. The `Saver` object operates on a `BankAccount` object that the class `Banking` passes to the `Saver` constructor. The `Banking` class is the test program for the banking classes and is listed later in this chapter.

```java
package examples.threads;
/** A class to demonstrate wait and notify methods
  */
public class Saver implements Runnable {
   private BankAccount account;
   /** Class constructor method
     * @param ba The bank account where this saver
     *      puts the money
     */
   public Saver( BankAccount ba ) {
      account = ba;
   }
   /** The method the saver uses to put away money */
   public void run() {
      while( account.isOpen() ) {
         try {
            if ( account.deposit( 100 ) ) {
               System.out.println(
               "$100 successfully deposited." );
            }
            Thread.currentThread().sleep( 1000 );
         } catch ( InterruptedException iex ) {
            // display the exception, but continue
            System.err.println( iex );
         }
      }
   }
}
```

11

These classes demonstrate how the threads interact, rather than how a banking application should be designed. The **run** method of the `Saver` class tries repeatedly to deposit $100, as long as the account is open. After making a deposit, **run** sleeps for a second. The sleep staggers deposits and withdrawal transactions for demonstration purposes. If an **InterruptedException** is thrown while the thread sleeps, and that exception awakens the thread, the catch block catches but ignores the exception.

The following listing features the thread that makes withdrawals. It contains a class called Spender that extends **Thread**. It also could have implemented **Runnable** in the same manner that the Saver thread implements **Runnable**, but Spender extends **Thread** to demonstrate both techniques. Like the Saver class, Spender operates on a BankAccount object the Banking class passes as an argument to the constructor.

```java
package examples.threads;
/** A class to demonstrate wait and notify methods
  */
public class Spender extends Thread {
    private BankAccount account;
    /** Class constructor method
      * @param ba The bank account from which
      *     this spender takes the money
      */
    public Spender( BankAccount ba ) {
        account = ba;
    }
    /** The method the spender uses
      *   to take out money
      */
    public void run() {
        while( account.isOpen() ) {
            try {
                if ( account.withdraw( 500 ) ) {
                    System.out.println(
                    "$500 successfully withdrawn." );
                }
                sleep( 1000 );
            } catch ( InterruptedException iex ) {
                // display any interruptions but continue
                System.err.println( iex );
            }
        }
    }
}
```

Like the Saver class, the Spender class is not designed to model realistic banking activity. The **run** method of the Spender class tries repeatedly to withdraw $500 as long as the account is open. Like a Saver object, a Spender sleeps for a second after each withdrawal, and catches, but ignores, exceptions thrown during the sleep period.

The following listing is the test class for the banking application. The **main** method creates a BankAccount object ba. Then it creates a Spender thread

Use the **ThreadGroup** class to create and manipulate groups of threads.

## Class

java.lang.ThreadGroup

## Purpose

A **ThreadGroup** object represents a set of threads. It can include other groups and you can build a hierarchical structure of thread groups. Each **Thread** object can access information about its own group or its subgroups, but not about the parent groups, if any exist, or any other groups.

## Constructors

➤ **ThreadGroup( String** *name* **)**
**ThreadGroup( ThreadGroup** *parent*, **String** *name* **)**
When you create a thread group, you must specify the name of the group as a **String**. You cannot change the name after creating the group. If the new group is to be a subgroup of an existing group, supply the object reference for the parent group as the first argument of the constructor.

## Methods

➤ **int activeCount()**
The **activeCount** method returns an estimate of the number of active threads in the group.

➤ **int activeGroupCount()**
The **activeGroupCount** method returns an estimate of the number of groups in the current group.

➤ **void checkAccess()**
The **checkAccess** method is a security manager and is called by several other methods in the **ThreadGroup** class. If the thread does not have permission to modify the group, this method throws the exception **SecurityException**.

➤ **int enumerate( Thread[]** *list* **)**
**int enumerate( Thread[]** *list*, **boolean** *recurse* **)**
**int enumerate( ThreadGroup[]** *list* **)**
**int enumerate( ThreadGroup[]** *list*, **boolean** *recurse* **)**
The **enumerate** method copies object references for every active thread or thread group into the specified array. You should call **activeCount** or **activeGroupCount** before calling **enumerate,** and pass an array that has enough entries. If you supply a **boolean** argument with the value **true**, all threads or groups in subgroups of the current group are included, recursively. Due to the dynamic nature of threads, it is possible for the number

of threads and groups to change between the calling of **activeCount** or **activeGroupCount** and **enumerate**. It is wise to allocate an array larger than required because the list of threads will be truncated without any error indication if the array is too small.

➤ **int getMaxPriority()**
The **getMaxPriority** method returns the highest priority value allowed for the threads in the group.

➤ **String getName()**
The **getName** method returns the name of the group.

➤ **ThreadGroup getParent()**
The **getParent** method returns an object reference to the group that is the parent of the current group, or **null** if there is no parent group.

➤ **boolean isDaemon()**
The **isDaemon** method returns **true** if the group is a daemon thread group, or **false** otherwise.

➤ **interrupt()**
This method calls **interrupt** on all threads in this group.

➤ **void list()**
Call the **list** method to output information that is useful for debugging to the stream **System.out**.

➤ **void setDaemon( boolean** *daemon* **)**
Call the **setDaemon** method with a **boolean** value that establishes whether the group is a daemon group.

➤ **void setMaxPriority( int** *priority* **)**
Call **setMaxPriority** to set the highest priority value allowed for the threads in the group.

Beginning with the Java 2 platform, the methods stop, suspend, resume, and allowThreadSuspension of the ThreadGroup class are deprecated for the same reasons that stop, suspend, and resume are deprecated in the Thread class.

**ThreadGroup** objects provide security because a thread is allowed to modify another thread only if both threads reside in the same group, or if the modified thread resides in a group that is nested within the group of the modifying thread. For example, if a thread calls the **setPriority** method to lower the priority of a **Thread** object in another group that is not a subgroup, the JVM throws an exception.

Every thread belongs to a group. By default, a new thread is placed in the same group as the thread that created it. When you create a thread, you can assign it to a different group by supplying a **ThreadGroup** reference to the group as an argument to the constructor for the **Thread** object. After you create a thread, you cannot change its group.

The next sample program creates two **ThreadGroup** objects and creates one thread in each group. This program also demonstrates using piped input and output streams in multithreaded programs. Chapter 8 introduces piped input and output streams but does not include a multithreaded program to show their use.

```java
package examples.threads;
import java.io.*;
/** A class to demonstrate threads and piped streams
  */
public class PlumbingThreads implements Runnable {
   private PipedInputStream pipeIn;
   private PipedOutputStream pipeOut;
   /** Create a PlumbingThreads object to connect with
     * an existing PipedOutputStream
     */
   public PlumbingThreads( PipedOutputStream p ) {
     pipeOut = p;
   }
   /** Create a PlumbingThreads object to connect with
     * an existing PipedInputStream
     */
   public PlumbingThreads( PipedInputStream p ) {
     pipeIn = p;
   }
   /** Read from standard input and echo
     * the characters to the output pipe
     * @exception IOException general I/O error
     */
   public void sendKeystrokes() throws IOException {
     int c;
     while ( ( c = System.in.read() ) != -1 ) {
        pipeOut.write( c );
     }
     pipeOut.close();
   }
   /** Read characters from the input pipe
     * and echo them to standard out
     * @exception IOException general I/O error
     */
   public void receiveKeystrokes() throws IOException {
     int c;
     while ( ( c = pipeIn.read() ) != -1 ) {
        System.out.write( c );
     }
     pipeIn.close();
   }
```

11

```
    /** The workings of the threads
     */
    public void run() {
       try {
          // determine if this is an input or
          // output thread and go to work
          if ( pipeIn != null ) {
             receiveKeystrokes();
          } else if ( pipeOut != null ) {
             sendKeystrokes();
          }
       } catch ( IOException ioe ) {
          System.err.println( ioe );
       }
    }
    /** The test method for the class
      * @param args not used
      */
    public static void main( String[] args ) {
       try {
          // create the input and output pipes
          PipedInputStream istream
             = new PipedInputStream();
          PipedOutputStream ostream
             = new PipedOutputStream( istream );
          // construct the plumbing threads,
          // specifying the newly created pipes
          PlumbingThreads in
             = new PlumbingThreads( istream );
          PlumbingThreads out
             = new PlumbingThreads( ostream );
          // put the threads into separate groups
          ThreadGroup inputGroup
             = new ThreadGroup( "input thread group" );
          ThreadGroup outputGroup
             = new ThreadGroup( "output thread group" );
          // construct threads with existing
          // plumbing threads
          Thread inputThread
             = new Thread( inputGroup, in,
                              "input pipe" );
          Thread outputThread
             = new Thread( outputGroup, out,
                              "output pipe" );
          // start the threads and let them go!
          inputThread.start();
          outputThread.start();
       } catch ( IOException ioe ) {
          System.err.println( ioe );
       }
    }
}
```

The class `PlumbingThread` implements **Runnable** and does not extend **Thread**.

`PlumbingThread` objects communicate through a pipe. If the argument of the constructor is a **PipedInputStream** object, the thread reads from the pipe. If the argument of the constructor is a **PipedOutputStream** object, the thread writes to the pipe. Notice how the **run** method determines which end of the pipe is attached to the `PlumbingThread` object.

The **main** method creates two `PlumbingThread` objects, in and out. Then, **main** creates two **ThreadGroup** objects, `inputGroup` and `outputGroup`, and the **Thread** objects `inputThread` and `outputThread`. The constructor of **Thread** is called with three arguments:

➤ The **ThreadGroup** to which the JVM is to add the newly created thread

➤ The **Runnable** object

➤ A **String** that becomes the name of the thread

Finally, **main** starts the two threads. What they actually do is trivial. The input thread reads characters from **System.in** and puts them into the pipe. The output thread reads characters from the pipe and writes them to **System.out**.

The only complication that can occur is an **IOException**, which can be thrown during a read or write operation. The **run** method of `PlumbingThread` can catch the exception and print a message.

## SUMMARY

This chapter shows how to create threads, and gives some techniques for synchronizing threads and performing interthread communication.

A class can run as a separate thread if it extends the **Thread** class or implements the **Runnable** interface. The **Thread** class provides the full infrastructure for multithreading, and implements **Runnable**.

All classes that implement **Runnable** must implement the method **run**. This method is the entry point for the thread. Your multithreaded program must call **Thread.start** to launch all but the main thread. The **Thread** class provides many more methods that you can call to control your threads, including **yield, sleep,** and **setPriority**.

Programming for multithreading ensures that your threads do not interfere with each other or go into deadlock by entering a wait state. The Java programming language has features to help, but you are responsible for ensuring that your threads do not corrupt each other or create a deadlock.

You can declare variables to be **volatile** if other threads may change them. Do this if optimization may generate code that could lose or ignore the changes made to the variables on other threads.

Declare instance methods of a class with the keyword **synchronized** if only one thread at a time should be able to execute the method against a particular object. The **synchronized** qualifier on an instance method indicates that a thread must have a lock on the object before it can use the method on the object. While a synchronized method is active, no other synchronized methods defined for the same object can be executed until the lock becomes available.

Declare a class method with **synchronized** if only one thread at a time should be able to execute the method. In addition, no other synchronized class methods defined for the same class can run while the method is active. Use both the **synchronized** and **static** qualifiers to indicate that a thread must have a lock on the class before it can use a method. Object and class locks are independent.

Choosing to synchronize no methods, class methods, or all class and instance methods depends upon how threads share classes and objects.

No special relation exists between the synchronized methods of an inner class and its enclosing class. If a method of an inner class needs to participate in the synchronization of fields in the enclosing class, it should use a synchronized statement to obtain a lock for the enclosing class instance.

You can program one form of interthread communication by calling the methods **wait**, **notify** and **notifyAll**. These are final methods defined in the **Object** class.

Call the method **wait** if a thread reaches a condition in which it cannot continue. This method suspends the thread and gives other threads a chance to run. The best way to call **wait** is in a loop with the following form:

**while ( _condition_ ) { wait() }**

One thread can wake up another thread waiting for a lock on the same object by calling **notify.** It is safer to call **notifyAll** than **notify**. However, **notifyAll** is less efficient because it wakes up all threads that are waiting on a particular lock. Each thread can either call **wait** again or continue processing. Use **notifyAll** to reduce the risk of deadlock.

For greater security and convenience, you can collect **Thread** objects into **ThreadGroup** objects.

This chapter includes three example programs that demonstrate many features of the Java programming language that support multithreading. The last program also used a pipe to transfer data between threads. The sample code shows some common exceptions that can be thrown during multithreaded programs.

## QUESTIONS

1. Which of the following qualifiers is applied to a method to indicate that it requires exclusive access to an object or class? Select the best answer.

   a. **volatile**

   b. **final**

   c. **transient**

   d. **synchronized**

   e. **static**

2. Which method is used to initiate the execution of a **Thread**? Select the best answer.

   a. any **Thread** constructor

   b. **start**

   c. **go**

   d. **run**

   e. **begin**

3. Examine the following code:

```
public class Quiz11_3 {
    // —X—
}
```

   Which of the following definitions are valid when placed at the line marked —X— ? Select all that apply.

   a. `public synchronized Quiz11_3() {}`

   b. `private synchronized void b() {}`

   c. `public volatile void c() {}`

   d. `public static synchronized void d() {}`

   e. `public static volatile void d() {}`

4. In which of the following classes are the methods **wait**, **notify**, and **notifyAll** defined? Select all that apply.

   a. **Thread**

   b. **Runnable**

   c. **ThreadGroup**

   d. **System**

   e. **Object**

**11**

5. Examine the following code:

```
public class Quiz11_5 extends Thread {
   private int limit;
   public Quiz11_5( int l ) {
      limit = l;
   }
   public void run() {
      int i;
      for( i = 0; i <= limit - 1; i++ ) {
         System.out.print( i + ", " );
      }
      System.out.println( i );
   }
   public static void main( String[] args ) {
      Quiz11_5 x = new Quiz11_5( 5 );
      x.run();
   }
}
```

Which of the following statements are true when the code is compiled and run? Select all that apply.

a. The compiler rejects the definition of the **run** method because it does not have the **synchronized** keyword.

b. Compilation is successful and the output is

0, 1, 2, 3, 4, 5

c. The output of the program is written using a different thread than the thread executing the **main** method.

d. The compiler rejects the class definition because `Quiz11_5` does not implement the **Runnable** interface.

e. The output of the program is written using the same thread as that which executes the **main** method.

6. Which of the following methods are defined in the **Runnable** interface? Select all that apply.

a. **start**

b. **run**

c. **stop**

d. **getName**

e. **getDaemon**

7. Examine the following code:

```
public class Quiz11_7 implements Runnable {
    private int limit;
    public Quiz11_7( int l ) {
        limit = l;
    }
    public void run() {
        int i;
        for( i=0; i <= limit - 1; i++ ) {
            System.out.print( i + ", " );
        }
        System.out.println( i );
    }
    public static void main( String[] args ) {
        Quiz11_7 x = new Quiz11_7( 5 );
        Thread t = new Thread( x );
        t.start();
    }
}
```

Which of the following statements are true when the code is compiled and run? Select all that apply.

a. The compiler rejects the definition of the **run** method because it does not have the **synchronized** keyword.

b. Compilation is successful and the output is

0, 1, 2, 3, 4, 5.

c. The output of the program is written using a different thread than the one executing the **main** method.

d. The output of the program is written using the same thread as the one executing the **main** method.

e. The compiler rejects the expression **new Thread( x )** because the **Thread** class does not have any constructor that takes a `Quiz11_7` object as a parameter.

8. What kind of thread will the JVM stop if only threads of that kind are running?

9. Examine the following code:

```
public class Quiz11_9 {
   private String name;
   private int count;
   public Quiz11_9( String n, int c ) {
      name = n;
      count = c;
   }
   public static void main( String[] args ) {
      // -X-    }}
```

Which of the following statements are valid synchronized blocks if placed at the line marked –X–?

a. synchronized {}

b. synchronized ( String ) {}

c. synchronized ( a ) {}

d. synchronized ( a.name ) {}

e. synchronized ( a.count ) {}

10. Examine the following code:

```
public class Quiz11_10 {
   public Quiz11_10() throws InterruptedException {
      // A
   }
   public void f1() throws InterruptedException {
      // B
   }
   public static void f2()
                     throws InterruptedException {
      // C
   }
   private void f3() throws InterruptedException {
      // D
   }
   public synchronized void f4()
                     throws InterruptedException {
      // E
      f3();
   }
}
```

Which of the locations marked within the class definition are valid locations from which the **wait** method can be called?

a. A

b. B

c. C

d. D

e. E

# EXERCISES

## Debugging

1. Correct all the errors in the following program:

```java
package questions.c11;
public class Debug11_1 {
    private int count;
    public Debug11_1( int c ) {
        count = c;
    }
    public void run() {
        int powerOf2 = 1;
        for( int i=1; i < count; i++ ) {
            powerOf2 = 2*powerOf2;
            System.out.println( powerOf2 );
        }
    }
    public static void main( String[] args ) {
        Debug11_1 x = new Debug11_1( 10 );
        x.start();
    }
}
```

2. Correct all the errors in the following program, but do not change the fact that the class implements the **Runnable** interface:

```java
package questions.c11;
public class Debug11_2 implements Runnable {
    private int count;
    public Debug11_2( int c ) {
        count = c;
    }
    public void run() {
        int powerOf2 = 1;
        for( int i=1; i < count; i++ ) {
            powerOf2 = 2*powerOf2;
            System.out.println( powerOf2 );
        }
    }
    public static void main( String[] args ) {
        Debug11_2 x = new Debug11_2( 12 );
        x.start();
    }
}
```

**11**

3. Correct all the errors in the following program without removing the synchronized blocks:

```
package questions.c11;
public class Debug11_3 {
    private double balance = 0.0;
    public void increaseBalance( double increase ) {
        synchronized( balance ) {
            balance += increase;
        }
    }
    public void decreaseBalance( double decrease ) {
        synchronized( balance ) {
            balance -= decrease;
        }
    }
    public static void main( String[] args ) {
        Debug11_3 x = new Debug11_3();
        x.increaseBalance( 100.75 );
        x.decreaseBalance( 50.50 );
    }
}
```

4. Correct the following program so that all methods of the enclosing class and the inner class are synchronized:

```
package questions.c11;
public class Debug11_4 {
    private String name;
    class HomeAddress {
        private String street;
        private String city;
        public String getStreet() {
            return street;
        }
        public String getCity() {
            return city;
        }
        public void setStreet( String s ) {
            street = s;
        }
        public void setCity( String s ) {
            city = s;
        }
    }
    public synchronized String getName() {
        return name;
    }
    public synchronized void setName( String s ) {
        name = s;
    }
```

```java
    public static void main( String[] args ) {
        Debug11_4 person = new Debug11_4();
        HomeAddress address = person.new HomeAddress();
        person.setName( "Mike Edotsuc" );
        address.setStreet( "23 Elm Street" );
        address.setCity( "Toronto" );
        System.out.println( person.getName() );
        System.out.println( address.getStreet() );
        System.out.println( address.getCity() );
    }
}
```

5. Correct all the errors in the following program:

```java
package questions.c11;
public class Debug11_5 extends Thread {
    private int samples;
    private double average;
    public Debug11_5( int s ) {
        samples = s;
    }
    public synchronized void run() {
        java.util.Random r = new java.util.Random();
        double sum = 0.0;
        for( int i=0; i < samples; i++ ) {
            sum += r.nextDouble();
        }
        average = sum / samples;
    }
    public double getAverage() {
        while ( average == 0.0 ) try {
            wait();
        } catch ( InterruptedException ix ) {
            System.out.println( ix );
        }
        return average;
    }
    public static void main( String[] args ) {
        Debug11_5 x = new Debug11_5( 500000 );
        x.start();
        System.out.println( "Average = "
                          + x.getAverage() );
    }
}
```

## Complete the Solution

1. Extract the file **questions\c11\Complete11_1.java** from the file **question.jar** on the CD-ROM. Define the **main** method of the **Complete11_1** class to create and start a thread that executes the **run**

method of the `Complete11_1` class. The **main** method should let the thread run long enough to print its message approximately ten times. The **main** method should then request that the thread stop.

2. Extract the file **questions\c11\Complete11_2.java** from the file **question.jar** on the CD-ROM. Complete the definition of class `Complete11_2` by having the class extend **Thread** and by adding a **run** method. The **run** method should count characters and output the result to the console in a fashion similar to what the **main** method of the `Complete11_2` class does.

3. Start with version of class `Complete11_2` that is the answer to the previous exercise, and complete the solution by having the character counting operation take place on a different thread. But instead of having the top-level class extend **Thread**, add a method called `backgroundCount` that creates an anonymous inner class that extends **Thread**. The **run** method of the anonymous inner class should do the same thing as the method in Complete-the-Solution Question 2.

4. Extract the file **questions\c11\Complete11_4.java** from the file **question.jar** on the CD-ROM. Complete the definition of the class `Complete11_4` by providing a definition for the missing inner class `MessageReader` and by completing the method `addMessage`.

5. Extract the file **questions\c11\Complete11_5.java** from the file **question.jar** on the CD-ROM. The `Complete11_5` program uses graphical output to illustrate execution of three threads. It uses classes that you learn about in Chapter 12 and 13 to draw three rows of circles. A thread is dedicated to each row, and adds one circle at a time from the left of the output window until the preset window width is full. Figure 11-3 shows the output about half way through execution.

Do not worry about the code for the GUI. Fix this problem: When **run** in its current state, the program becomes deadlocked after each thread has drawn only one circle. The solution is to make each thread pause after calling **repaint**, which updates the display. Insert code in the **run** method to make each thread sleep. For added interest, set the sleep time to a random number from 0 to 1000 to simulate the threads doing variable amounts of background processing that takes, on average, half a second.

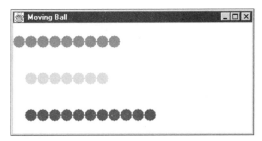

**Figure 11-3**   The Complete 11_5 solution while the program is running

## Discovery

1. Create a class called `FileWatcher` that can be given several filenames that may or may not exist. The class should start a thread for each filename. Each thread will periodically check for the existence of its file. If the file appears, the thread will write a message to the console and then end. Put all the threads within a new **ThreadGroup** object created by the `FileWatcher` class.

2. Write a program that finds all the prime numbers from 1 to 100. A positive integer is prime if the only positive integers that divide evenly into it are one and the number itself. To exercise multithreading, follow the algorithm presented here in pseudo code:

   ➤ Set up an array or **Vector** of 100 **boolean** elements and initialize every element to **true**. Each element is a flag and **true** indicates potential prime number. Set an element to **false** when its index is proven not to be prime.

   ➤ Loop through the array or **Vector**. If the element is true, meaning the number is a potential prime, launch a thread for the number and in that thread, set elements to **false** for all multiples of the number. For example, the first thread you launch this way eliminates multiples of 2 (4, 8, 16 …) from the set of potential primes. The next thread eliminates multiples of 3.

   ➤ When all the threads except the **main** thread have ended, print the numbers for which the corresponding element is still **true**. The output should start 1, 2, 3, 5, 7, 11, and so on.

**11**

# INTRODUCTION TO GRAPHICAL USER INTERFACES

---

**In this chapter you will:**

➤ Learn the characteristics of a graphical user interface (GUI).

➤ Explore the contents of the Java Foundation Classes (JFC).

➤ Discover how the JFC supports creating GUIs for the Java platform.

➤ Design GUIs with layouts that dynamically adjust to screen resolution and window size.

➤ Include predefined components such as text fields, buttons, and multimedia elements in your GUI.

➤ See how the JFC provide a framework for interacting with the user in event-driven programs.

➤ Use rapid application development (RAD) tools, such as IBM VisualAge for Java, to design GUIs visually and quickly.

---

## INTRODUCTION

This chapter explains the main elements of a GUI, gives an overview of the Java Foundation Classes (JFC) and shows by example how to program a GUI using the Abstract Windowing Toolkit (AWT) and the Swing APIs of the JFC. You can effectively use it in conjunction with Chapter 13, which presents the detailed descriptions for the classes and interfaces that constitute the APIs.

Software developers make extensive use of the tools for rapid application development (RAD) in order to create timely solutions for business and other application problems as well as to be competitive when bringing software products to market. RAD techniques are well-suited for building GUIs. Many proprietary RAD tools provide different forms of visual design aids and code generators. You may find that you use RAD tools extensively not only to design and generate the GUI portion of your programs, but also for many purposes that are beyond the scope of this book, such as the following:

➤ Accessing databases

➤ Creating objects that encapsulate business logic

➤ Supporting networking and distributed applications

To introduce the world of RAD tools, this chapter includes a brief tutorial on VisualAge for Java. Follow this tutorial to design a GUI-based program visually and use a code generator to build an application that conforms to Sun's 100% Pure Java™ initiative.

# THE CHALLENGE OF CREATING GUIs

Modern computer operating systems include presentation services that provide the user with a GUI. As a result, computer users now demand application programs that also provide GUIs. Fortunately, the Java platform provides extensive support for building them, and programmers have made the most of this support. For instance, in your studies of existing programs, have you ever downloaded sources for Java applets or applications that run in a windowing environment? You may be surprised by how much of that code is concerned with the user interface to the applet or application. When a program has a GUI, a large portion of the code services the GUI, even to the point where programming for the GUI sometimes becomes the largest part of the code.

GUIs display in graphical form on the screen. So far, you have used sample programs with console input and output. In other words, they were command-line programs with the look and feel of operating systems like DOS. The reason for this is simplicity—many aspects of the Java programming language and the packages in the Java platform are better explained without the distracting complexities of programming for a GUI. Programmers can use the forms of I/O described in Chapter 8 even when they are programming a GUI. For example, the program may open a file and write information into the file to be used to trace the flow of the program and as an aid for debugging errors.

To program a GUI, you must master event-driven programming because GUI-oriented programs are event-driven. The user initiates most events by moving and clicking the mouse or by pressing keys on the keyboard. Unlike command-line programs that operate in a batch-processing mode or perhaps pause occasionally to solicit user input, GUI-based programs must always be responsive to and take directions from the user.

The JFC provides a flexible and extensive set of GUI-building objects that are easy to use. For example, many features have been added since the original version of the Java platform in which support for GUI development was limited. Although some APIs of the JFC were first available in version 1.1 of the Java platform, the JFC did not exist as a complete set until the release of the Java 2 platform. The size of the JFC may be overwhelming at first, but these classes provide programmers with the objects necessary for creating powerful and polished GUIs that users demand.

# Main Features and Terminology of a GUI

All interactive output and input should pass through your program's GUI. Therefore, the GUI consists of what the user sees on the screen and code to process user actions such as clicking the mouse or typing on the keyboard. Your program must properly relate those actions to the elements displayed in the GUI and perform the appropriate activities in response.

To be consistent with object-oriented design, you should separate a program's GUI from a program's processing, just as you distinguish between the interface to a class and the implementation of the class. This design pattern, known as Model View Controller (MVC), structures your application effectively because all logic for an application is separated from visible elements and the controller controls all interactions between them. Later in this chapter, you will learn how to apply MVC when using RAD tools.

Model-view separation is the technique of separating a program's GUI from its data processing. It occurs when you run the GUI in one thread to give the user a quick response, or at least to acknowledge a user action, and then perform more time-consuming tasks, such as file I/O or number crunching, in other threads. The proportion of the program that is part of the GUI depends on the program's nature and purpose. For applets, which tend to be short and highly interactive, the GUI often makes up most of the code. For an application, the GUI could be a simple interface to a complex program.

Components comprise a major part of a GUI. In the Java platform, components are predefined standard elements such as buttons, text fields, frame windows, and dialog boxes. The Swing and AWT APIs provide a large repertoire of components. This chapter mentions a few of the most commonly used components. Discussions of additional components will come in the following chapters.

The display space on the screen is also a component. Like all GUI-based applications, a Java application window is a frame window. Frame windows have a title and a border; buttons for closing, minimizing, and maximizing the window; and can contain a menu bar. The browser or applet viewer that is used in a Java application controls the display space for an applet. Thus, applets run in a simpler and displayable component called a panel.

Controls such as check boxes, labels, scrollbars, text areas, dialog boxes, and list boxes are also components. Some components, such as buttons, are used individually. Others, aptly called containers, are components that house other components. Frame windows, panels, and dialog boxes are all containers.

Consider the dialog box, which is a window that opens to present information to or receive information from the user. A dialog box is a component as well as a container because it can have buttons, text fields, and other components

**12**

within it. A file dialog box is also a container. It lets you select or enter a file-name in a window. The Java platform has a class for file dialog boxes.

You can use one of the core classes—the layout managers—to control how components are arranged within a container. For each container, you select the layout manager that controls the size and position of components within the container. This separation of container classes from layout manager classes gives you the freedom to select the container you want, and then select a layout manager you want. Containers have no built-in limitations on how you can position components within them.

Swing and AWT components take responsibility for how they are drawn. However, your GUI is not limited to the available components. You can custom draw your own components directly onto the graphics context of a window or panel. The term *graphics* refers to drawing in the graphics context for a component. A graphics context is the area on the display screen where a component is positioned. You can obtain the graphics context from a window or panel and then call methods to draw entities such as lines, text, and images. To Java, images are graphical objects, such as pictures or icons, stored in a format supported by your implementation of the Java platform.

Painting is the process of displaying components or refreshing the display of components on the screen. Painting can occur when the GUI for an application or an applet starts; when you call methods to redraw the GUI; or when the application or applet window is resized, moved, or exposed on the screen after being covered. Objects of the component classes handle the painting of themselves. When you do custom drawing directly to a graphics context, your code must also handle the painting. To ensure that a program does not have to wait for every paint operation to complete, GUIs use a separate thread called the **event dispatch thread** for drawing and forwarding all paint requests to that thread.

Handling events is an important part of GUI programming. Events can be user actions, such as clicking or moving the mouse or pressing keys on the keyboard, and action events occur when the user acts on components. For example, the user may click a check box, select an item from a list, or type characters into a text field. Components encapsulate not only the look of visual elements of the GUI but also the set of events that the components generate.

You should structure your user interface so that it is directed by events. To do this, you provide handlers that react to events that can occur while your program runs. Chapter 6 introduced the concept of handlers in the discussion of catch clauses for exceptions. However, the JFC supports a much broader use of handlers than is used for exceptions. Exception handlers interrupt the usual flow of control to deal with an error or unexpected situation. In a GUI, event handlers let you pass control of the program to the user so that your program proceeds by responding to user activities.

The mechanism for event handlers is different from that of exception handlers. The GUI event-handling mechanism has been revised since the original version of the Java platform, and it now uses a set of interfaces called listeners, which are similar to the **java.util.Observer** interface explained in Chapter 10. Each listener interface is targeted for a specific type of GUI event, such as a mouse click. You create handlers for user-initiated events by defining classes that implement the listener interfaces. The appropriate listener interface method is called automatically whenever the component generates an event. You establish the relationship between each handler and an event by registering the listener with the component for which the event is generated.

Each listener interface that has more than one method also has a corresponding adapter class. The adapters are classes that implement the interfaces in a trivial way by providing empty methods. Thus, you can choose between implementing a listener or extending an adapter. The advantage of using an adapter is that you can provide implementations for only the events that are of interest and inherit the trivial handlers for the other events from the adapter class.

Programmers use the term 1.0.2 event model to describe GUI event handling in the original version of the Java platform that was based on the inheritance relationships of AWT API classes. The much-improved delegation event model described in this chapter was introduced in version 1.1 of the Java platform. The inheritance-based event model is still supported, but it has shortcomings. To avoid these shortcomings, you should use the delegation event model when you develop code. Do not mix the two event models within a single application; they are incompatible.

**12**

When you examine the code of existing applets or applications and find that any event handler implements an interface with a name that ends with "listener" or extends a class with a name that ends with "adapter", the programmer coded it using the delegation event model for version 1.1 or later of the Java platform. The use of the method **handleEvent** indicates that the program uses the original inheritance-based event model.

## INTRODUCING THE JAVA FOUNDATION CLASSES

The developers of the Java platform responded to popular demand and invested considerable effort into providing powerful and flexible support for creating GUIs for applications in the JFC. The goal of the JFC is to simplify the development of 100% Pure Java programs for network or standalone environments. The classes let you design GUIs that reflect the operating system that is host to the JVM, to create your own platform-independent interface, or to use a look and feel that is both defined for the Java platform and common across all implementations of the JVM.

Table 12-1 lists the five APIs that make up the JFC. This chapter and Chapter 13 focus on the Abstract Windowing Toolkit (AWT) API and the Swing API because they are fundamental for the creation of GUIs. The Java2D API, described in limited detail in Chapter 13, builds on the basic drawing support provided in the AWT to provide support for advanced graphics and imaging. The Accessibility API provides the programming interface necessary for assistive technologies, such as Braille screen readers and speech-recognition software, to interact with GUIs built with the JFC. This support is provided in the form of interfaces supported by GUI components that provide information about their current state and utilities that allow assistive technologies to easily plug into system services such as the user interface event queue. The Drag and Drop API provides support for transferring data within a Java application, between two Java applications, and between a Java application and a native application. A user performs a Drag and Drop operation by picking up an icon in one window, dragging it to another window, and dropping it. Both the Accessibility API and the Drag and Drop API are specialized topics that are beyond the scope of this text.

**Table 12-1**  The JFC APIs

| | |
|---|---|
| **Abstract Windowing Toolkit** | The Abstract Windowing Toolkit (AWT) API was the original toolkit for developing GUIs for the Java platform. It provides the foundation for the JFC with its support for colors, fonts, graphics, images, events, listeners, layout managers, and so forth. |
| **Swing** | Swing is an extensive set of mostly lightweight components built on top of the AWT component classes that feature a pluggable look-and-feel. Lightweight components do not have a window of their own but are drawn directly on their container's window. |
| Java2D | The Java2D API provides a variety of painting styles and features for defining complex shapes and controlling the rendering process. It provides enhanced font and drawing capabilites that build on those in the AWT. |
| **Accessibility** | The Accessibility API provides an interface that allows assistive technologies such as screen readers, screen magnifiers, and speech-recognition software to be easily integrated into applications. |
| **Drag and Drop** | The Drag and Drop API provides the ability to move data between programs created with the Java programming language. With applications developed in other languages, it provides for interoperability between applications. |

## Abstract Windowing Toolkit API

To program a GUI-oriented application or an applet, you need extensive support from your application development software. The Java platform provides a relatively simple set of GUI-building classes in the package **java.awt** and its subpackages.

This book cannot cover all the options of the AWT, and you could spend many weeks focusing on the AWT and Swing classes. The goal of this chapter and Chapter 13 is to show you the most commonly used features of the AWT and Swing classes. If you ultimately plan to write code based on the AWT or the Swing classes that are introduced in the next section of this chapter, you should become familiar with the JFC API documentation. Alternatively, you can assemble GUI programs by combining JavaBeans using RAD tools that will generate the code for you. Chapter 15 explains what JavaBeans are and how you can reuse them as building blocks for new programs.

This book discusses the most commonly used AWT classes so that you can confidently explore the rest of the package independently. This section and the next section of this chapter provide an overview of the classes and architecture of the AWT and Swing APIs. The rest of this chapter, Chapter 13, and Chapter 14 describe in detail how to use some of these classes and give simple examples.

We begin the discussion with the classes in the **java.awt** package and its subpackages. The classes fall into six major categories, as shown in Table 12-2.

**12**

**Table 12-2**  Categories of classes in the AWT

| Category | Description |
|----------|-------------|
| Graphics | This set of classes in **java.awt** encapsulate fonts, colors, images, polygons, and so forth. |
| Components and containers | This set of classes extends **Component** to provide objects such as buttons, check boxes, labels, scrollbars, and text components. The class **Container** extends **Component** for components that can contain other components, such as windows, panels, and dialog boxes. The AWT components make up a basic set of GUI building blocks. The Swing API provides a more extensive and flexible set of components. Although the Swing components are ultimately based on the AWT components, you should not mix Swing and AWT. Generally, the Swing set of components is replacing the AWT as the most popular GUI-building API. |

**Table 12-2** Categories of classes in the AWT (continued)

| Category | Description |
| --- | --- |
| Layout managers | To select a predefined strategy for positioning components in a container, set up an association between a class that extends **LayoutManager** or **LayoutManager2** and a container. You may set a wide range of format controls and let the layout manager dynamically determine where to put the components. With layout managers, you do not specify coordinate positions for components. To specify actual screen coordinates would make your program inflexible, probably build in dependence on a platform and screen resolution, and perhaps constrain your ability to translate labels into other languages. You can use the AWT layout managers for AWT and Swing containers. The Swing API adds some new layout managers for Swing containers only. |
| Events | This set of classes in the package **java.awt.event** extends **AWTEvent** to encapsulate the information about a user interaction with the application. For example, some classes are **MouseEvent**, **TextEvent**, and **FocusEvent**. Each kind of event has an associated listener interface. The Swing components use the AWT event model, although some of the Swing components add new types of events. |
| Listeners and adapters | Listeners and adapters handle events. To create a listener, implement one or more of the listener interfaces in the **java.awt.event** package. If you register an instance of a listener with one or more components, one of the listener methods is called whenever an event is generated by a component with which the event is registered. You can extend an adapter class rather than implement a listener. Extending an adapter can be more efficient because you need to override only the methods that are of interest and do not have to provide your own empty methods for the events to be ignored. As with events, listeners and adapters work in the same way for Swing and AWT components. |
| Peers | Peers are classes that implement the elements of a GUI built from AWT components on the platform that is host to your Java platform. You do not use these classes directly. Instead, you use the corresponding subclasses of **Component** classes. For example, a button peer on OS/2 uses an OS/2 Presentation Manager button and on Solaris uses a Motif button. You create a **Button** object and do not worry about the peer class behind the scenes. When your code runs on a different platform from the development platform, the look of AWT components adjusts automatically. |

Inside the package **java.awt**, the AWT encapsulates the platform specifics for the implementation of the AWT in the class **Toolkit**. This class is the bridge between the platform-dependent AWT classes and their corresponding peers. The class does have some useful methods that provide information on the screen size, screen resolution, available fonts, and so forth.

# EVENT MODEL

The AWT event model takes advantage of a hierarchy of event classes and associated listener interfaces. You can define any class to be an event handler, regardless of its superclass, by implementing a listener interface. Call a method of a component class to register the listener with the component. Chapter 13 describes how to do so and how to write the handler. When an event that relates to the component occurs, only the registered listeners are notified and passed a copy of the event. If no listeners are registered, the event is not delivered.

The event model is consistent with the JavaBeans interface. JavaBeans facilitate encapsulating GUI components in such a way that developers can easily build GUI-based programs, complete with event handling, by loading JavaBeans into tools and connecting them together.

## Swing API

The AWT API described in this chapter and Chapter 13 provides a user interface framework with which you can continue to develop GUIs. When the Java platform was introduced in 1995, the AWT was the only API for creating GUIs. The set of components provided by the AWT is adequate for simple tasks, but it has some significant limitations. For example, creating a new type of component by directly subclassing **Component** is difficult because you must also create a peer object. For components that are built on windows, the result is that each new component has its own opaque native window. This one-to-one mapping between components and native windows has disadvantages:

➤ Native windows can consume a lot of system resources. Therefore, you should create a minimum number of custom components.

➤ Native windows are handled differently across platforms. Therefore, maintaining a consistent view across varied platforms is difficult and error-prone.

In version 1.1 of the Java platform, the AWT introduced a framework for creating lightweight GUI components. The lightweight GUI framework lets you extend the **java.awt.Component** and **java.awt.Container** classes directly, without creating native peer objects. The Swing API builds upon this lightweight GUI framework to create a set of GUI components that are independent of the native windowing system. Because the components do not need native support, you don't have to supply any native code to process them. Therefore, handling lightweight components is 100% Pure Java. The result is common code and consistency across platforms.

Not every Swing component is a lightweight component. In order for a Java application to have a GUI that appears on the user's desktop, at least the top-level window on which the lightweight components are drawn must be a heavyweight component with a native peer. There are only a few heavyweight

**12**

Swing components: **JApplet**, **JDialog**, **JFrame**, and **JWindow**. They are based on **java.applet.Applet** and the AWT components **Dialog**, **Frame**, and **Window**, respectively.

The Swing API contains 100% Pure Java versions of the AWT components, plus many additional components that are also 100% Pure Java. Because Swing does not contain or depend on native code, none of the Swing components is constrained to conform to a single style. Instead, Swing components have a pluggable look-and-feel. They are adaptable to different operating system platforms or to a custom look and feel. The Swing API consists of more than 250 classes and 75 interfaces grouped into the following categories:

➤ A component named **JComponent** that extends the AWT class Container and a set of components that are subclasses of **JComponent**. All these components have names beginning with the letter J.

➤ Nonvisible support classes that provide important services, such as event classes, and that implement the model, or logic, portion of the Swing design model. These classes do not begin with the letter J.

➤ Swing includes a set of related interfaces that are implemented by its component and support classes.

Table 12-3 lists the most frequently used components of the Swing API and states which Swing components have a corresponding AWT component.

**Table 12-3**   Swing components

| Swing Component | Description |
| --- | --- |
| **JApplet** | The superclass of all Swing applets. It is a heavyweight component that implements the **RootPaneContainer** interface. It is an extension of the original applet superclass, java.applet.Applet. |
| **JButton** | A button that contains both text and graphics. The corresponding AWT component is **Button**. |
| **JCheckBox** | A check box that can contain both text and graphics. The corresponding AWT component is Checkbox. |
| **JCheckBoxMenuItem** | A check-box menu item. The corresponding AWT component is **CheckBoxMenuItem**. |
| **JColorChooser** | A component that provides the interface to allow a user to select a color with visual feedback of the color selected. |
| **JComboBox** | Combines a text field and drop-down list that lets the user either type in a value or select it from a list that appears in response to a user request. A **JComboBox** provides a superset of the functions provided by the AWT component Choice. |

**Table 12-3**   Swing components (continued)

| Swing Component | Description |
|---|---|
| **JDesktopPane** | A container intended to hold internal frame windows. |
| **JDialog** | The superclass of all Swing dialogs. **JDialog** is a heavyweight component that implements the **RootPaneContainer** interface. The corresponding AWT component is **Dialog**. |
| **JEditorPane** | Provides a text pane that lets the user edit content of various kinds. |
| **JFileChooser** | A component that provides the interface to allow a user to select a file. The corresponding AWT component is **FileDialog**. |
| **JFrame** | An external frame that encloses Java application GUIs. It is a heavyweight component that implements the **RootPaneContainer** interface. The corresponding AWT component is **Frame**. |
| **JInternalFrame** | Similar in function to a frame window but can be placed inside the top-level frame application. An internal frame is confined to the visible area of the container that holds it. It implements the **RootPaneContainer** interface. |
| **JLabel** | A label that can contain both text and graphics. The corresponding AWT component is **Label**. |
| **JList** | A component that presents a list of items for single or multiple selection. The corresponding AWT component is **List**. Unlike its AWT counterpart, a **JList** component does not have scrollbars and should be placed in a **JScrollPane** if scrollbars are required. |
| **JMenu** | A menu that can be attached to a menu bar or placed in another menu to create a cascading menu. The corresponding AWT component is **Menu**. |
| **JMenuBar** | A set of menus usually positioned beneath a frame window's title bar. The corresponding AWT component is **MenuBar**. |
| **JMenuItem** | An item in a menu. The corresponding AWT component is **MenuItem**. |
| **JOptionPane** | Provides a straightforward mechanism for creating commonly required dialog boxes. For example, use a **JOptionPane** to display a message, ask a yes-no question, or prompt for a single input. |
| **JPanel** | A basic container. The corresponding AWT component is **Panel**. |
| **JPasswordField** | A component that lets the user edit a single line of text. Feedback shows that characters are entered but does not display the input characters. |
| **JPopupMenu** | A popup menu component. The corresponding AWT component is **PopupMenu**. |

**12**

**Table 12-3** Swing components (continued)

| Swing Component | Description |
|---|---|
| **JProgressBar** | Can be used to indicate the progress of an activity by displaying its percentage of completion. |
| **JRadioButton** | Provides a round button with two possible states: selected or deselected. |
| **JRadioButtonMenuItem** | Provides a radio button item within a menu. |
| **JScrollBar** | A scroll-bar component. The corresponding AWT component is **Scrollbar**. |
| **JScrollPane** | A container with available vertical and horizontal scroll bars. The corresponding AWT component is **ScrollPane**. |
| **JSeparator** | A horizontal or vertical separator. |
| **JSlider** | Lets the user graphically select a value by graphically moving an indicator along a bounded range. |
| **JSplitPane** | A component intended to contain two components and divided horizontally or vertically. The user can interactively resize the split between the two components. |
| **JTabbedPane** | A component that lets the user switch from one group of components to another by clicking a tab with a given title or icon. |
| **JTable** | A component to present data in a two-dimensional table format. |
| **JTableHeader** | A heading for a table. |
| **JTextArea** | A component for entering and displaying multiple lines of text. The corresponding AWT component is **TextArea**. Unlike its AWT counterpart, a **JTextArea** component does not have scrollbars and should be placed in a **JScrollPane** if scrollbars are required. |
| **JTextField** | A component for entering a single line of text. The corresponding AWT component is **TextField**. |
| **JTextPane** | A simple text-editor component. |
| **JToggleButton** | Implements a two-state button that alternates between pressed and released. **JToggleButton** is the superclass of both **JRadioButton** and **JCheckBox**. |
| **JToolBar** | Displays commonly used actions or controls as a horizontal row or vertical column of buttons. |
| **JToolTip** | Creates a popup text window that can display a brief textual description of a component when the mouse pointer lingers over the component. |
| **JTree** | A component to display a set of hierarchical data as an outline. The display has branches that the user can expand and collapse. |

**Table 12-3**    Swing components (continued)

| Swing Component | Description |
| --- | --- |
| JViewport | A viewport for displaying scrollable components. |
| JWindow | A heavyweight component that implements the **RootPaneContainer** interface. The corresponding AWT component is **Window**. |

Table 12-3 does not list all the Swing components, but it includes the most notable. All the listed Swing components are in the package **javax.swing**. All AWT components are in the package **java.awt**.

GUI applications use Swing components and AWT components in much the same way. Swing components use the same layout managers, event objects, and listener interfaces as the AWT components. However, there are some notable differences. For example, it is not possible to add components directly to a container that implements the **RootPaneContainer** interface. Such containers have a content-pane container where all components are to be placed. The **RootPaneContainer** interface defines the method **getContentPane** for accessing this container. The **JFrame**, **JApplet**, **JDialog**, **JWindow**, and **JInternalFrame** classes all fall into this category. Another key difference is in the use of scrollbars. The AWT components **TextArea** and **List** both have available scrollbars, but the corresponding Swing components **JTextArea** and **JList** do not have scrollbars. If scrollbars are required, **JTextArea** and **JList** components can be placed in a **JScrollPane** container.

## Separable Model Architecture

A fundamental difference between the Swing architecture and AWT architecture is that Swing components separate the manipulation of data associated with a component from the rendering or graphical-representation component and its contents. The benefits are greatest for the more complicated containers, such as **JTree**, **JList**, and **JTable**, that contain structured data. However, the separation is implemented for all Swing components. One of the limiting factors of AWT-based GUIs is the absence of model and view separation.

The designers of the Swing API implemented prototypes that conformed fully to the MVC design pattern. Each component had a model object as well as view and controller objects that defined the component's look and feel. Experimentation with this separation led to the realization that a component's view and controller objects are tightly coupled and that it made sense to collapse these two objects into a single object. In the Swing API, this combined view-controller object is referred to as the component's UI delegate. Because Swing has these UI delegate objects in place of view and controller objects, it cannot be said to implement the true MVC separation. Instead, Swing is said to use a **separable model** architecture.

12

The separation of the model from its UI delegate gives programmers a great advantage over the AWT: Programmers can design their applications around operations on data rather than around operations that display data. The Swing API defines a set of model interfaces that are implemented by various components. Table 12-4 lists the various model interfaces and the components that use them.

**Table 12-4** Swing model interfaces

| Model Interfaces | Components |
| --- | --- |
| ButtonModel | JButton<br>JToggleButton<br>JCheckBox<br>JRadioButton<br>JMenu<br>JMenuItem<br>JCheckBoxMenuItem<br>JRadioButtonMenuItem |
| ComboBoxModel | JComboBox |
| BoundedRangeModel | JProgressBar<br>JScrollBar<br>JSlider |
| SingleSelectionModel | JTabbedPane |
| ListModel | JList |
| ListSelectionModel | JList |
| TableModel | JTable |
| TableColumnModel | JTable |
| TreeModel | JTree |
| TreeSelectionModel | JTree |
| Document | JEditorPane<br>JTextPane<br>JTextArea<br>JTextField<br>JPasswordField |

Because the models are separate from the components, several components can share the same model. For example, you can create a split-window view, similar to what is used in many word processors, by placing two **JTextPane** objects sharing the same model document into a **JSplitPane** object. Any changes made in one half of the split pane would be immediately reflected in the other half of the split pane because both are based on the same model.

Model objects must be able to notify their UI delegates whenever their data values change so that the user interface delegates always present current information. To do this, all Swing models use the JavaBeans event model. This event model is discussed in Chapter 15, when JavaBeans are presented in detail. For now, consider this event model similar in concept to the **Observer/Observable** model presented in Chapter 10.

Swing models use two different styles of notification: lightweight and stateful. **Lightweight notification** does nothing more than indicate that something in the model has changed, and provides no details. This means event objects used for lightweight notification can be reused, saving the cost of creating a new event object every time. **Stateful notification** provides the details of the change, saving the cost of calling the methods of the model to determine what changed. Event objects used for stateful notification are not reused.

The choice of notification style depends on the frequency of the events. For models such as the **BoundedRangeModel** used by sliders and scrollbars that can generate frequent events, a lightweight notification style is used to avoid the cost of creating many event objects. For most other models, the **DocumentModel** for example, stateful notification is used in order to provide as much information as possible in the event object and to avoid the need to call additional methods.

## JFC SAMPLE PROGRAMS

**12**

You can get a feel for what the JFC can do by looking at the small sample programs in this section. They introduce some of the most commonly used classes in the JFC. You can start to experiment by writing short programs that are similar to these samples and then expand your knowledge by trying to program variations that use different classes and methods.

The sample programs are applications, not applets. Chapter 14 explains that the main difference is that Swing-based applets extend the **javax.swing.JApplet** class, and Swing-based applications extend the **javax.swing.JFrame** class. Both **JApplet** and **JFrame** are indirect subclasses of Container. Similarly, an AWT-based applet extends **java.applet.Applet** and an AWT-based application extends **java.awt.Frame**.

As a further distinction between the two, you should know that a Web browser displays an applet as a panel within the browser window, so that the applet does not have a title bar or minimize, maximize, or close buttons. Also, applets do not have a **main** method, but are instead controlled by the browser using an event-driven mechanism that is also explained in Chapter 14. Apart from these differences, you can use the Swing or AWT classes in an applet just as you can in an application.

## A Java Hello World! Program

The first sample JFC program is a version of the classic starter program that most programmers write when they first work with a new language or programming environment. This program defines the class `HelloWorld`. Because `HelloWorld` is a public class, it is found in a file called **HelloWorld.java**. The structure of packages mirrors the file system, so you will find this source code in the examples\windows subfolder of the folder in which you unpacked the JAR file **examples.jar**. This program displays the string "Hello World!" centered in a window on the screen. As with most applications, the GUI for this program is contained in a frame window, which is an independent window with its own frame, title, and control boxes.

Although this is a simple program, the code is longer than a command-line version because it contains a minimal GUI:

```java
package examples.windows;
import javax.swing.JFrame;
import javax.swing.JLabel;
import java.awt.BorderLayout;
import java.awt.event.WindowAdapter;
import java.awt.event.WindowEvent;
/** An example of a very simple windowed program
  */
public class HelloWorld extends JFrame {
   /** Class constructor
     * @param titleText window's title bar text
     */
   public HelloWorld( String titleText ) {
      super( titleText );
      addWindowListener( new WindowAdapter() {
          /** End the program when the user
            * closes the window
            */
          public void
          windowClosing( WindowEvent e ) {
             HelloWorld.this.dispose();
             System.exit( 0 );
          }
       }
    );
      JLabel greeting = new JLabel( "Hello World!",
                               JLabel.CENTER );
      getContentPane().add( greeting,
                          BorderLayout.CENTER );
      setSize( 300, 100 );
      setVisible( true );
   }
   /** The test method for the class
     * @param args not used
```

```
        */
    public static void main( String[] args ) {
        new HelloWorld( "Hello World! Sample" );
    }
}
```

The output is similar on all platforms, but it does vary in small ways because the frame takes on the appearance and behavior of the application windows of the native operating system. Therefore, your output may look different from Figure 12-1, particularly in the buttons that are specific to the operating system and the borders of the frame.

**Figure 12-1**    Output from the Hello World! program

The Hello World! program is contained in one class, `HelloWorld`. The `HelloWorld` class extends **JFrame**. The **JFrame** class is a component class for frame windows, which are the usual top-level windows in which applications run. Because it extends **JFrame**, `HelloWorld` inherits functioning minimize, maximize, and close buttons, and a title bar. Below is the first line of the class definition that establishes the inheritance relationship:

```
public class HelloWorld extends JFrame {
```

Below are the first lines of the constructor for `HelloWorld`. The constructor has one argument, which is the string to be used in the title bar. It passes the string to the constructor of the superclass **JFrame** so that the string becomes the text in the title bar of the frame window:

```
public HelloWorld( String titleText ) {
    super( titleText );
```

You do not have to write the code for the event loop that controls a GUI program. The JFC APIs handle that. All you must do is plug in handlers for various events. The next statement is the most involved statement of the Hello World! program, and it deals with the only event of interest to this program: the WINDOW_CLOSING event that occurs when the user closes the application window. This event does not automatically terminate execution, but it is reported to the **JFrame** object so that the program has an opportunity to close down.

**12**

A call of **addWindowListener** registers an object to listen to window events for the current component. The argument becomes the registered handler for window events. In this call, the handler is an instance of the **WindowAdapter** class:

```
addWindowListener( new WindowAdapter() {
      /** End the program when the user
       * closes the window
       */
      public void
      windowClosing( WindowEvent e ) {
        HelloWorld.this.dispose();
        System.exit( 0 );
      }
   }
);
```

Similar lines of code appear in many GUI-based applications.

> **Mini Quiz 12-1**
>
> What kind of construct is used to create the **WindowAdapter** object? *Hint*: The object has no name, and its class id is defined completely within the argument list of the **addWindowListener** method.

An adapter class is appropriate because this program needs to handle only one of the events for which the WindowListener interface defines handlers. The method **windowClosing** overrides the default method of the **WindowAdapter** class to handle the WINDOW_CLOSING event. The method disposes of the current **JFrame** object and then calls **System.exit** to terminate the application.

The constructor of the HelloWorld class also sets the size of its window in pixels, by calling **setSize**. The width is 300 pixels, and the height is 100. The window appears at the upper-left corner of the screen because this constructor does not call **setLocation** to override the default location of the frame window. The constructor must call **setVisible** and pass the value **true** to make the window visible to the user and bring the window to the front of other windows.

```
setSize( 300, 100 );
setVisible( true );
```

The text message to be displayed is put into the **JLabel** object `greeting` and the justification of the text is set so that it is centered within the label. The label must be added to the **JFrame** object in order for it to appear within the frame window, but it cannot be added directly. Objects of the **JFrame** class have a **JRootPane** object to which they delegate control of the components they contain via the **JRootContainer** interface. You can access the container where components are placed by calling the **getContentPane** method defined in the **JRootContainer** interface. The method then adds the label to the content-pane container.

```
JLabel greeting = new JLabel( "Hello World!",
                                JLabel.CENTER );
getContentPane().add( greeting,
                      BorderLayout.CENTER );
```

By default, the content-pane container of a **JFrame** uses a **BorderLayout** object to arrange its components. A border layout can contain up to five components, arranged as shown on the left in Figure 12-2. This program uses only the center section. Therefore, the north, south, west and east drop out, the center component expands, and the arrangement is as shown on the right of Figure 12-2.

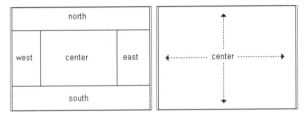

**Figure 12-2**    Border layouts

Because the `HelloWorld` class is an application, it must have a **main** method. For this application, **main** creates a `HelloWindow` object and passes the title of the frame window as an argument of the constructor.

```
public static void main( String[] args ) {
    new HelloWorld( "Hello World! Sample" );
}
```

After the **JFrame** object has been created, the application runs until the **windowClosing** method calls **System.exit**. The reason that the program does not end after calling the `HelloWorld` constructor is that the JFC APIs create an event dispatch thread when the **JFrame** class is instantiated. An application remains active as long as a nondaemon thread is running and the event dispatch thread is not a daemon thread.

## Three Panels Example

The Hello World! example is about as simple as a GUI program can be. The next program is a bit more complex. It makes greater use of layout managers; includes buttons with icons, a text field, and a check box; and has labelled borders.

**12**

The first program uses **JPanel** objects nested in the **JFrame** object's content-pane container to provide a more flexible approach to positioning components. The **JPanel** class, like **JFrame**, is a subclass of **java.awt.Container**, and instances of **JPanel** are the simplest objects that can hold other components. Panels are widely used to group objects. You can arrange one or more panels within a window using a layout manager.

The next program is called the Three Panels program because it has three **JPanel** objects. The panels are arranged vertically to occupy the top, middle, or bottom slices of a window. Often, event handling deals with user actions such as clicking a button. The Three Panels program demonstrates three buttons and one check box.

Three Panels is a simple application that displays the string "Change the color of this text" across the top panel of the frame window. The middle panel has three buttons labeled Black, Red, and Green. When the user clicks a button, the sentence above the buttons changes color accordingly. The bottom panel has a check box labeled Disable Changes. The user clicks the check box to disable or enable the buttons.

```
package examples.windows;

import javax.swing.*;
import java.awt.*;
import java.awt.event.*;
/** An example class used to demonstrate the basics of
  * creating components such as panels, arranging
  * components using layout objects, and nesting
  * components inside each other.
  */
public class ThreePanels extends JFrame {
    private JPanel upper, middle, lower;
    private JTextField text;
    private JButton black, red, green;
    private JCheckBox disable;
    /** Class constructor method
      * @param titleText Window's title bar text
      */
    public ThreePanels( String titleText ) {
        super( titleText );
        addWindowListener( new WindowAdapter() {
                /** End the program when the user
                  * closes the window
                  */
                public void
                windowClosing( WindowEvent e ) {
                    ThreePanels.this.dispose();
                    System.exit( 0 );
                }
            }
```

```
);
upper = new JPanel();
upper.setBorder(
   BorderFactory.createTitledBorder(
   "Sample text" ) );
upper.setLayout( new BorderLayout() );
text = new JTextField(
   "Change the color of this text" );
upper.add( text, BorderLayout.CENTER );
middle = new JPanel();
middle.setBorder(
   BorderFactory.createTitledBorder(
   "Text color control" ) );
middle.setLayout( new FlowLayout(
   FlowLayout.CENTER ) );
black = new JButton( "Black",
            new ColorIcon( Color.black ) );
black.addActionListener(
   new ButtonListener( Color.black ) );
middle.add( black );
red = new JButton( "Red",
            new ColorIcon( Color.red ) );
red.addActionListener(
   new ButtonListener( Color.red ) );
middle.add( red );
green = new JButton( "Green",
            new ColorIcon( Color.green ) );
green.addActionListener(
   new ButtonListener( Color.green ) );
middle.add( green );
lower = new JPanel();
lower.setLayout( new FlowLayout(
   FlowLayout.RIGHT ) );
disable = new JCheckBox( "Disable changes" );
disable.addItemListener( new ItemListener() {
      /** Disable and enable the buttons
       */
      public void
      itemStateChanged( ItemEvent e ) {
         boolean enabled
            = ( e.getStateChange()
               == ItemEvent.DESELECTED );
         black.setEnabled( enabled );
         red.setEnabled( enabled );
         green.setEnabled( enabled );
      }
   }
);
lower.add( disable );
Container cp = getContentPane();
cp.add( upper, BorderLayout.NORTH );
```

**12**

```
            cp.add( middle, BorderLayout.CENTER );
            cp.add( lower, BorderLayout.SOUTH );
            pack();
            setVisible( true );
        }
        /** The class representing the button event
          * listeners
          */
        class ButtonListener implements ActionListener {
            private Color c;
            /** Class constructor
              * @param c the color for this button
              */
            public ButtonListener( Color c ) {
                this.c = c;
            }
            /** Respond to the action events
              * @param e The click event
              */
            public void actionPerformed( ActionEvent e ) {
                text.setForeground( c );
            }
        }
        /** The class representing the colored icons on
          * the buttons
          */
        class ColorIcon implements Icon {
            private Color c;
            private static final int DIAMETER = 10;
            /** Class constructor
              * @param c the color for this button
              */
            public ColorIcon( Color c ) {
                this.c = c;
            }
            /** Paint the color icon with a black border
              * @param cp the component holding the icon
              * @param g the graphics context for the icon
              * @param x the x draw start position
              * @param y the y draw start position
              */
            public void paintIcon( Component cp, Graphics g,
                                   int x, int y ) {
                g.setColor( c );
                g.fillOval( x, y, DIAMETER, DIAMETER );
                g.setColor( Color.black );
                g.drawOval( x, y, DIAMETER, DIAMETER );
            }
            /** Get the icon's height
              * @return the height of the icon
              */
```

```
      public int getIconHeight() {
         return DIAMETER;
      }
      /** Get the icon's width
        * @return the width of the icon
        */
      public int getIconWidth() {
         return DIAMETER;
      }
   }
   /** The test method for the class
     * @param args not used
     */
   public static void main( String[] args ) {
      new ThreePanels( "Three Panels Sample" );
   }
}
```

The output looks similar to Figure 12-3.

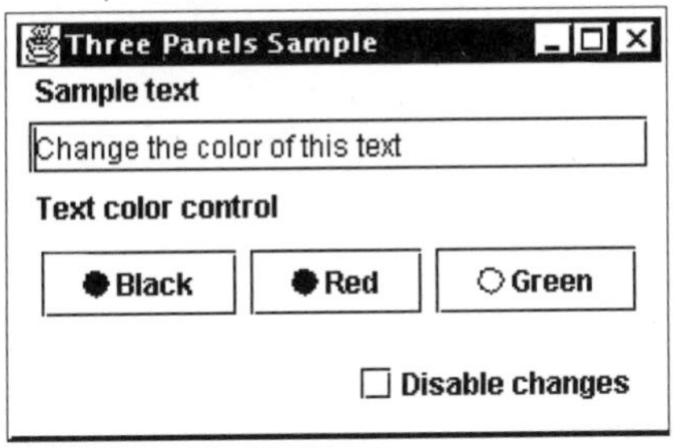

**Figure 12-3**   Output of the Three Panels application

The class of this application is called **ThreePanels**. Like the Hello World! application, it extends **JFrame**. The components used in this application are private fields of the **ThreePanels** class, as listed below:

```
public class ThreePanels extends JFrame {
   private JPanel upper, middle, lower;
   private JTextField text;
   private JButton black, red, green;
   private JCheckBox disable;
```

Also like the **HelloWorld** class, the constructor of **ThreePanels** passes the string that becomes the title of the frame window to the constructor of its super-class, **JFrame**:

```
   public ThreePanels( String titleText ) {
      super( titleText );
```

The next statement registers and creates a handler for the WINDOW_CLOS-ING event using the same technique as the Hello World! program:

```
addWindowListener( new WindowAdapter() {
    /** End the program when the user
     * closes the window
     */
    public void
    windowClosing( WindowEvent e ) {
        ThreePanels.this.dispose();
        System.exit( 0 );
    }

}
);
```

The rest of the constructor creates the components and sets their attributes and adds the components to the **JPanel** objects and the panels to the frame. The constructor assigns one **JPanel** field, upper, to a new **JPanel** object, sets its border to be a labelled border with the text "Sample text", and then gives the panel a border layout:

```
upper = new JPanel();
upper.setBorder(
    BorderFactory.createTitledBorder(
    "Sample text" ) );
upper.setLayout( new BorderLayout() );
```

The next object created is a **JTextField** object. The private field text is assigned the object reference to the **JTextField**. The **JTextField** class extends the **JTextComponent** class to define objects that hold a single line of text, and the method passes the text as a **String** to the constructor. The method add in these lines adds the text component to the upper container. Here, the argument **BorderLayout.CENTER** positions the component in the central area of the upper panel. Because only the center portion of the border layout for the upper panel has contents, the center portion expands to fill the entire area of the upper panel:

```
text = new JTextField(
    "Change the color of this text" );
upper.add( text, BorderLayout.CENTER );
```

The second of the three panels is assigned to the private field middle. Like the upper panel, the middle panel has its border set to be a labelled border with the text "Text color control". Unlike the upper panel, the middle panel has a flow layout. A flow layout places components side by side, from left to right, in the order they are added to the container, and wraps onto the next row as required. The argument of the constructor of a **FlowLayout** object is a constant provided by the **FlowLayout** class. Here, **FlowLayout.CENTER** specifies that the rows of components in middle panel be centered within the panel. By default, **JPanel** objects have a centered flow layout, so this statement was added for clarity:

```
middle = new JPanel();
middle.setBorder(
   BorderFactory.createTitledBorder(
   "Text color control" ) );
middle.setLayout( new FlowLayout(
   FlowLayout.CENTER ) );
```

You specify the label that appears on a **JButton** object as the argument of the constructor for the **JButton** object. The second constructor parameter specified for each of the buttons is a `ColorIcon` object. `ColorIcon` is an inner class that implements the **javax.swing.Icon** interface. It is described in detail below. The **class java.awt.Color** provides public-class variables for many colors, including **Color.red**, **Color.green**, and **Color.black**. Instead of using **Color** constants, you can alternatively construct a **Color** object from 8-bit values for red, green, and blue.

To handle button-click events, you must register an **ActionListener** object with each **JButton** object, by calling the method **JButton.addActionListener**. Here, instances of the inner class **ButtonListener** are constructed to specify the color associated with the button and are registered to handle the action events for the buttons:

```
black = new JButton( "Black",
          new ColorIcon( Color.black ) );
black.addActionListener(
   new ButtonListener( Color.black ) );
middle.add( black );
red = new JButton( "Red",
          new ColorIcon( Color.red ) );
red.addActionListener(
   new ButtonListener( Color.red ) );
middle.add( red );
green = new JButton( "Green",
          new ColorIcon( Color.green ) );
green.addActionListener(
   new ButtonListener( Color.green ) );
middle.add( green );
```

The last of the three panels is assigned to the object reference `lower`. This panel also has a flow layout, but this flow layout is right justified. As a result,

**12**

the **JCheckBox** component labeled "Disable changes" that is placed in the panel appears on the lower right of the application frame window:

```
lower = new JPanel();
    lower.setLayout( new FlowLayout(
        FlowLayout.RIGHT ) );
```

The **JCheckBox** object disable requires an **ItemListener** so that it can enable or disable the buttons as the user checks or unchecks the box:

```
disable = new JCheckBox( "Disable changes" );
disable.addItemListener( new ItemListener() {
        public void
        itemStateChanged( ItemEvent e ) {
            boolean enabled
                = ( e.getStateChange()
                    == ItemEvent.DESELECTED );
            black.setEnabled( enabled );
            red.setEnabled( enabled );
            green.setEnabled( enabled );
        }
    }
);
lower.add( disable );
```

Now that the three panels are complete, the next four statements can add them to the content-pane container of the frame window:

```
Container cp = getContentPane();
cp.add( upper, BorderLayout.NORTH );
cp.add( middle, BorderLayout.CENTER );
cp.add( lower, BorderLayout.SOUTH );
```

The final statements in this rather long constructor are calls to **pack** and **setVisible**. Call **pack** to give the layout managers a chance to arrange all components for optimal size. When you call **pack**, the layout managers determine how much space each of the components needs and dynamically adjusts the component positions. Call **setVisible** to make the `ThreePanels` object and all the contained panels and components visible and available for display:

```
pack();
setVisible( true );
```

The ButtonListener class implements the **ActionListener** interface. It also implements the **actionPerformed** method to handle the **ActionEvent** objects for button clicks. When an instance of the **ButtonListener** class is created, the color of its button is specified. Because each **ButtonListener** object is associated with only one button, when its **actionPerformed** method is called, the appropriate action is to set the foreground color for the **JTextField** text by calling the method **JComponent.setForeground**. The **JTextField** class inherits this method from the **JComponent** class:

```
class ButtonListener implements ActionListener {
   private Color c;
   public ButtonListener( Color c ) {
      this.c = c;
   }
   public void actionPerformed( ActionEvent e ) {
      text.setForeground( c );
   }
}
```

**Mini Quiz 12-2**

Can you deduce from this code how many methods the **ActionListener** interface has?

The `ColorIcon` class implements the **Icon** interface and its three methods: **paintIcon**, **getHeight**, and **getWidth**. Its purpose is to draw a very simple color icon that consists of a solid circle of a specified color with a black border. The size of the circle is fixed by the class constant DIAMETER, and the color of the circle is set by the constructor parameter:

```
class ColorIcon implements Icon {
   private Color c;
   private static final int DIAMETER = 10;
   public ColorIcon( Color c ) {
      this.c = c;
   }
```

**12**

Both **getHeight** and **getWidth** are simple methods that return the circle's diameter. The **paintIcon** method is more involved. It must draw the circle and its border using the provided graphics context at the specified x and y coordinates. An object of the class **java.awt.Graphics** represents the graphics context. This class provides many methods for doing basic drawing operations. In this case, the two methods used are **fillOval** and **drawOval**, which are used to draw a solid circle and an outline of a circle, respectively:

```
public void paintIcon( Component cp, Graphics g,
                       int x, int y ) {
   g.setColor( c );
   g.fillOval( x, y, DIAMETER, DIAMETER );
   g.setColor( Color.black );
   g.drawOval( x, y, DIAMETER, DIAMETER );
}
public int getIconHeight() {
   return DIAMETER;
}
```

```
public int getIconWidth() {
   return DIAMETER;
}
```

The main method of the `ThreePanels` class, shown below, has very little to do. It simply creates a `ThreePanels` object. This instance of **JFrame** contains all the panels set up in the constructor. The driving force behind the application is the user who triggers events by clicking one of the three color buttons or the check box:

```
public static void main( String[] args ) {
   new ThreePanels( "Three Panels Sample" );
}
```

All of the coding and GUI design for the `ThreePanels` class was done by entering Java source statements into a text file using an editor. Using this approach, it can be difficult to visualize how the resulting GUI will look when the program executes, which means getting the right look for the GUI can become a trial-and-error process. In the next section, we will discuss how a GUI can be designed visually to get the right look—the first time—for the GUI.

# DESIGNING A PROGRAM VISUALLY WITH VISUALAGE FOR JAVA

Some Java development products include features that can greatly increase your productivity when developing Java programs. Among the most popular are Rapid Application Development (RAD) tools that generate code for you, under your direction. IBM VisualAge for Java includes a Visual Composition Editor (VCE). The VCE is a RAD tool for building GUIs interactively. It generates pure Java code.

In the VCE, you can design a GUI for your applet or application by visually positioning and connecting instances of AWT or Swing components. You can use the VCE to manipulate any class that conforms to the JavaBeans specification. Chapter 15 introduces the concept and usage of JavaBeans. The AWT and Swing component classes are bean classes and the AWT event model is consistent with the JavaBeans specification.

You also can define invisible beans with the VCE and use the invisible beans to tie the visually built GUI to classes that process data or that perform the part of an application that is not visible to the user. In this way, you can add a GUI to an existing program. You also can very quickly create a prototype user interface for a program that does not yet exist. The VCE not only generates code to build the screen that you design but also can automatically provide the event-handling framework that makes the GUI responsive to the user.

The Composition Editor gives you a palette of beans for many of the core classes. The palette is divided into categories including AWT components, Swing components, and specialized beans that become Available when you load VisualAge features such as the Database Access Beans. You select beans from the palette, drag them with the mouse, and then drop them onto a work surface. VisualAge lets you connect the beans and represents the connections by drawing arrows between connected beans. Connections encapsulate the interactions between the beans.

Two kinds of beans exist in the Visual Composition Editor:

➤ **GUI beans** map onto the classes that have graphical representations. These beans represent the visual elements in your GUI. Often, you do not need to do any hand coding to generate classes based on the AWT or Swing components.

➤ **Invisible beans** usually represent logic classes for objects in your program that are not part of the GUI. Use invisible beans for the interface between your GUI and the classes that you create in other ways. For example, if handling the event that occurs when the user clicks a button involves calling a method to process data, you can connect the GUI bean for the button to the invisible bean for a class that does the processing.

In short, you can create whole applets or small applications with the Visual Composition Editor. Alternatively, you can create the GUI portion of applications that use other classes.

**12**

Describing the Visual Composition Editor in detail is beyond the scope of this book, but working through a scenario of building a simple program with VisualAge for Java should give you an idea of the power of RAD tools such as the Visual Composition Editor.

## Temperature Conversion Program

Follow this scenario to create a program that gives similar functionality to the `TempConvert` class of Chapter 1. The first class you encountered in this book accepted as command-line arguments a number of degrees followed by the name of a temperature scale, Celsius or Fahrenheit. The program converted the temperature from Celsius to Fahrenheit or from Fahrenheit to Celsius and printed the result on the console. This exercise produces a `TempConvert` program that has a GUI and looks like Figure 12-4.

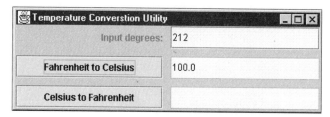

**Figure 12-4** The Temperature Conversion Utility

This temperature-conversion program has one text field, beside the label **Input degrees**, in which users can enter a number. There are buttons labeled **Fahrenheit to Celsius** and **Celsius to Fahrenheit**, and beside each button is another text field. If the user clicks the **Fahrenheit to Celsius** button, the number in the input text field is interpreted as degrees C and the equivalent temperature in degrees F is displayed in the textbox beside the button. The **Celsius to Fahrenheit** button performs and displays the result of the opposite conversion.

This program is simple but gives an opportunity to apply some good design principles:

➤ Consistently use components based on Swing or AWT classes. The VCE uses a different framework for event handling for Swing and AWT components. If you mix both kinds in one GUI class, the class may look correct but may not respond as expected to user input. In this case, either component set is adequate for the job and you use the Swing set to see that it can be just as easy to use as AWT classes.

➤ Follow the MVC design pattern. Create nonvisual classes to encapsulate the model: the logic and objects that belong to your problem domain. The GUI should provide the user with a view of the model and the controller that lets the user interact with the program. For example, the view should never alter the state of the model, but should be updated whenever the state of the model changes in a way that affects what is displayed. Controller-view separation is subtler than model-view separation. In a GUI-driven program such as this one, the connections can provide the controller for the events that the user initiates. In this case, it is appropriate to combine the view and controller in one class.

➤ Try to eliminate opportunities for the user to provide input that is not valid or to initiate actions that do not make sense. Create your own exception types if necessary, and handle all exceptions that may occur and affect your program. In this example, you will take a simple approach to recover when the user enters a value for input degrees that is not a valid number.

➤ Avoid the null layout manager unless you know the user's screen resolution and can prevent the user from resizing the window. The temperature conversion utility uses a simple **GridLayout**.

➤ Minimize the number of connections. Often, that is achieved by connecting events, such as button clicks, to one method rather than to several other components.

➤ Design for flexibility by building your GUI out of **Panel** or **JPanel** objects. Create a separate panel class for each part of the GUI you may want to use again. You can run a panel in the VCE to test it. When the panel is ready, you can add it to a **Frame** or **JFrame** for use in an application or to an **Applet** or **JApplet** for use in an applet.

## Creating the View for the Temperature-Conversion Program

This exercise starts much like the scenario in Chapter 1 in which you entered the `TempConvert` class manually. You will create a new class called `TCPanel` in the `examples.windows` package in the `learning` project.

To open the Visual Composition Editor for a new class:

1. Click **Start**. Select **Programs, IBM VisualAge for Java for Windows**, and then click **IBM VisualAge for Java**.

2. The VisualAge for Java banner window appears, followed by the **Quick Start** window. Select **Go to the Workbench**, if necessary, and then click **OK**.

3. The workbench opens to the **Projects** window. If you already have a `learning` project, select it.

4. If you do not have a `learning` project, create it now. Right-click in the **All Projects** pane, Select **Add** and then **Project...** from the popup menus. In the **Add Project** SmartGuide, make sure the **Create a new project named:** button is selected, type the name **learning** into the text box, and then click **Finish**.

5. If you already have an `examples.windows` package in the `learning` project, select it.

6. If you do not have an `examples.windows` package in the `learning` project, create it now. Right-click on the **learning** project. Select **Add** and then **Package...** from the popup menus. In the **Add Package** SmartGuide, make sure the **Create a new package named:** button is selected, type the name `examples.windows` into the text box, and then click **Finish**.

7. Back in the **Projects** window with the `examples.windows` package highlighted, right-click and select **Add** and then **Class...** from the popup menus.

8. In the **Create Class** SmartGuide, check that the correct project and package are named in the top two text boxes. Make sure the **Create a new class** button is selected and type the name **TCPanel** into the class name text field.

**12**

9. Enter the superclass name **com.sun.java.swing.JPanel**. Note that the fully qualified class name for **JPanel** is **javax.swing.JPanel** in the Java 2 SDK. This version of VisualAge uses version 1.1.6 of the Java platform. One of the few notable changes to the Swing classes in the Java 2 platform is that package names have changed.

10. Select **Compose the class visually** and **Browse the class when finished**. Then click **Finish**. The **Class browser** opens to **Visual Composition** window.

The starting position for designing a panel looks like Figure 12-5.

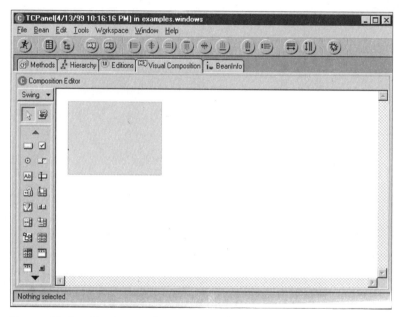

**Figure 12-5**   Starting to design a panel visually

The large white area is your work surface, and the gray box represents the panel you are building. At the left of the window, under the word **Swing**, is the palette of Swing components. You can click on the word **Swing** to see a drop-down list of other palettes, but do not select any of the other palettes. Hold the mouse over each icon in the palette, without clicking, until the tool tip pops up telling you what kind of component each icon represents. As you can see, the palette is extensive, and you can scroll up and down through the Swing components by clicking on the up and down arrowheads above and below the displayed icons. Find the elements that you will use in this exercise: the **Choose Bean** tool directly under the word **Swing**, and the **JButton**, **JLabel**, and **JTextField** components near the top of the palette.

Now, you are ready to design the `TCPanel` class to contain the GUI for the temperature-conversion utility.

To design the `TCPanel` class visually:

1. Click on the gray box to select it. Small black boxes, called anchors, on the corners and sides of the component joined by dashed lines indicate that it is selected. Notice that the name of a selected component and its type is displayed in the status line at the bottom of the VCE window. The status line should say "TCPanel(com.sun.java.swing.JPanel) selected", indicating that the gray box is a `TCPanel` object.

2. Drag one of the anchors on the right side of the panel to the right to widen the panel. Notice how the cursor takes different shapes to move or expand the panel. Experiment until you are comfortable selecting and sizing a component with the mouse.

3. Before adding components to the `TCPanel`, set properties for this component. Right-click on the **TCPanel** and select **Properties** from the popup menu. A **TCPanel – Properties** sheet similar to Figure 12-6 appears. You may have to expand the property sheet window and click the **Show expert features** box on the bottom left of the window to see all the entries listed in Figure 12-6. Properties are listed in alphabetic order in the first column of the property sheet. The value of the property appears in the second column.

**12**

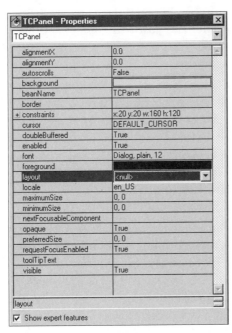

**Figure 12-6**    A property sheet for a Visual Bean

4. Select the **layout** property and click the down arrow beside the value **<null>** to see a list of layout managers. Select **GridLayout**. Now a + (plus) sign appears to the left of the word *layout* and the word *GridLayout* is the value of the layout property.

5. Click the **+** sign to expand a list of parameters of the layout. Change the entry for **rows** to **3**, for **columns** to **2**, for **hgap** to **10**, and for **vgap** to **10**. The result will be a 3 by 2 grid with horizontal and vertical gap of 10 pixels between cells.

6. In the **Properties** window, click the close box on its upper-right corner.

7. The next step is to drop the components onto the panel. Select the **JLabel** component from the palette. You can glance at the status line to see that you have picked the right type of component. Move the mouse over the `TCPanel` without pressing a mouse button and when the + cursor appears, click to drop a component labeled `JLabel1` into place. The label temporarily occupies a whole row of the panel. Its size will adjust as you add more components.

8. If you make a mistake in the VCE, you can select **Undo** from the **Edit** menu to back out of your most recent changes.

9. Select a **JButton** from the palette, and drop it onto the `TCPanel` in the same way. Repeat for a second **JButton**. Do not worry what cells components occupy at this stage. You can rearrange them after they are all present.

10. In the same way, add three **JTextField** components to the `TCPanel`. The `TCPanel` is now full. The **JLabel** and **JButton** components have default labels `JLabel1`, `JButton1`, and `JButton2`. Select each component in turn, and look at the VCE status line.

11. Rearrange the components. Select **JLabel1** first. Drag it, holding down the mouse button. A dotted outline moves with the mouse. When a component is dragged over a place where it can be dropped, a vertical bar appears. When you see the vertical bar on the top of the right edge of the `TCPanel`, release the mouse button to drop the **JLabel** into place. Repeat this process until the `TCPanel` looks like Figure 12-7. Make sure `JTextField1` is in the top row, `JTextField2` is in the second row, and `JTextField3` is in the third row.

12. Set the properties for each component. Do this much as you set the properties for the `TCPanel`. Right-click on each component, and select **Properties** from its popup menu. Then click **Show expert features** in each **Properties** window. The properties are different for different types of component, and some kinds of properties have special editors. For example, set foreground and background colors by choosing a color scheme and then a color from popup window. In the property sheets, make the changes listed in Table 12-5. In a large program, you also would change the bean names to be more meaningful, but for this small exercise the default names are adequate.

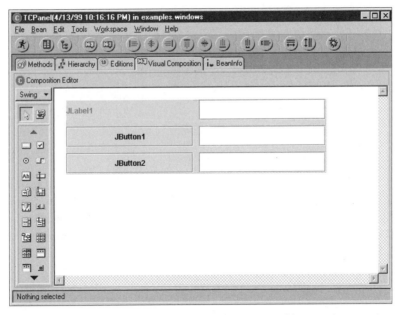

**Figure 12-7**   Arranging the components in a grid layout

**Table 12-5**   Properties settings for the components in the TCPanel container

| Component | Property | Value |
|---|---|---|
| JLabel1 | horizontalAlignment<br>text | Select **RIGHT** from drop-down list<br>**Input degrees:** |
| JTextField1 | background<br>columns<br>text<br>toolTipText | Click **Basic** radio button, then **white**<br>**22**<br>**0**<br>**Enter temperature in degrees F or C** |
| JButton1 | background<br>text<br>toolTipText | Click **Basic** radio button, then **yellow**<br>**Fahrenheit to Celsius**<br>**Convert input degrees F to C** |
| JTextField2 | background<br>columns<br>editable | Click **Basic** radio button, then **white**<br>**22**<br>Select **False** from drop-down list |
| JButton2 | background<br>text<br>toolTipText | Click **Basic** radio button, then **yellow**<br>**Celsius to Fahrenheit**<br>**Convert input degrees C to F** |
| JTextField3 | background<br>columns<br>editable | Click **Basic** radio button, then **white**<br>**22**<br>**Select** False from drop-down list |

**12**

It is time for the first test. You can run a **Panel** or **JPanel** from the VCE.

To test the `TCPanel` design:

1. Click the **Run** button, which is the rightmost button in the Toolbar. A window pops up to inform you the VisualAge is generating code. VisualAge also saves your bean automatically every time you run it.

2. Examine the `TCPanel` displayed in a test frame provided by VisualAge. Verify that it looks like the `TCPanel` shown in Figure 12-8. You should be able to type characters into the first text field and click both buttons. If you can type into the second or third text field, you probably did not set the component's **editable** property to **false**. The buttons do nothing because you have not yet provided a controller to go with this view. If you hold the mouse over the first text field or either button, the tool tip text may pop up or some error messages may be printed to the **Console** window. You can ignore this behavior because tool tips do not work until you have added the panel to an application or applet.

3. If the behavior of your `TCPanel` differs from what is described in the previous step, close the test frame exactly as you close any window, and return to the VCE. Correct the component properties, and test again until you achieve the desired behavior.

4. Close the VCE, and return to the **Project** window of the workbench.

## Creating the Model for the Temperature-Conversion Program

Now that you have finished the view, it is time to create the model for the `TempConvert` program. You will return to the `TCPanel` class to add the controller later.

The model for this program is simple. A class that holds a temperature value and has methods for getting and setting its value as a number on the Fahrenheit scale and on the Celsius scale is required. The only catch is that the class must be a JavaBean to be useable in the VCE. How can you create a JavaBean before you read about beans in Chapter 15? Just as VisualAge for Java provides the VCE for creating GUIs without writing Java source code, it also gives a way of generating classes that conform to the bean standard without requiring detailed knowledge of that standard.

You will use the **BeanInfo** window of the class browser to add methods and fields to a class in such a way that the class conforms to the JavaBean standard. The **BeanInfo** window for the completed `TCModel` class is shown in Figure 12-8. This window has three panes:

➤ The upper-left pane is labeled **Features** and lists fields, methods, and other features of the bean.

➤ The upper-right pane is labeled **Definitions** and lists methods that support the feature selected in the **Features** pane.

➤ The bottom pane, **Property Feature Information**, is an editor for the bean features. Chapter 15 explains bean properties and features.

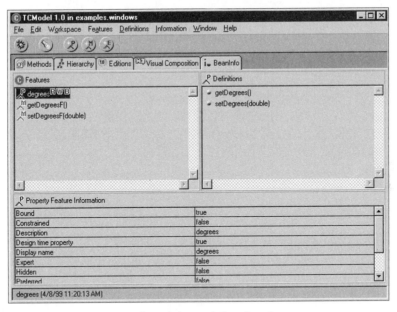

**Figure 12-8**   A BeanInfo window of the class browser

## Creating an Invisible JavaBean

**12**

The model for this program is an invisible bean class called TCModel.

To create this class:

1. Back in the **Projects** window with the examples.windows package highlighted, right-click and select **Add**, and then **Class...** from the popup menus.

2. In the **Create Class** SmartGuide, check that the learning project and examples.windows package are named in the top two text boxes. Make sure the **Create a new class** button is selected, and then type the name TCModel into the class name text field. Accept the default superclass **java.lang.Object**.

3. Deselect **Compose the class visually**. Select **Browse the class when finished**. Then click **Finish**.

4. The Class browser opens to **Methods** window. Click the **BeanInfo** tab to open the **BeanInfo** window on the TCModel Class. This window looks like Figure 12-13, except that the **Features** and **Definitions** panes are empty, and the third pane below them is called "Bean Reflection Information".

5. Right-click in the **Features** pane to bring up the popup menu. To add a field to the class, select **New Property Feature...** from the popup menu. The **New Property Feature** SmartGuide opens.

6. In the **Property name:** text box, enter the name of the field, which is `degrees`. In the **Property type:** text box, enter **double**, or click the down arrow and select **double** from the drop-down list. Take care not to select the array form **double[ ]**. Click **Finish**.

7. Back in the **BeanInfo** window, verify that the `degrees` feature is now listed in the **Features** pane. Methods `setDegrees()` and `getDegrees()` have been created and are listed in the **Definitions** pane. According to the bean standard, you should always use methods to get and set the values of fields and never refer to a field directly by name. If you decide to always store the temperature in degrees Celsius, you already have methods to set and return the temperature using the Celsius scale.

The `TCModel` bean needs two more methods to convert between Celsius and Fahrenheit scales.

To add custom methods to the `TCModel` JavaBean:

1. Create a method to set the temperature given a number of degrees Fahrenheit. Right-click in the **Features** pane, and select **New Method Feature...** from the popup menu. The **New Method Feature** SmartGuide opens.

2. In the **Method name:** text box, enter `setDegreesF`. Accept the **Return type:** void. In the **Parameter count:** text box, enter **1** or use the up arrow to increase the count to **1**. Click **Next**.

3. The **Parameter 1** SmartGuide appears. Beside **Parameter name:**, enter `value` and beside **Parameter type:**, enter or select **double**. Click **Finish**.

4. Back in the **BeanInfo** window, the method `setDegreesF` is now listed in the **Features** pane. Click **setDegreesF** to list it also in the **Definitions** pane. Click setDegreesF in the Definitions pane to display its source in the **Source** pane.

5. Edit the `setDegreesF` method in the **Source** pane so that it looks like the following lines of code (new code shown in bold):

```
/**
 * Perform the setDegreesF method.
 * @param value double
 */
public void setDegreesF(double value) {
/* Perform the setDegreesF method. */
   setDegrees( 5.0 * ( value - 32.0 ) / 9.0);
   return;
}
```

6. Save the method by right-clicking in the **Source** pane, and selecting **Save** from the popup menu, or by pressing **Ctrl+S**. If no errors are reported,

the method has compiled successfully and is saved. Correct compilation errors and save again if necessary, until the method compiles successfully.

7. Create a method to return the temperature in degrees Fahrenheit. Right-click in the **Features** pane, and select **New Method Feature...** from the popup menu. The **New Method Feature** SmartGuide opens.

8. In the **Method name:** text box, enter **getDegreesF**. In the **Return type:** text box, enter **double**, or click the down arrow and select **double** from the drop-down list. Accept the default **Parameter count: 0**. Click **Finish**.

9. Back in the **BeanInfo** window, the method `getDegreesF` is now listed in the **Features** pane. Click **getDegreesF** to list it also in the **Definitions** pane. Click **getDegreesF** in the **Definitions** pane to display its source.

10. Edit the `getDegreesF` method in the **Source** pane so that it looks like the following lines of code (new code shown in bold):

```
/**
Perform the getDegreesF method.
@return double
*/
public double getDegreesF() {
/* Perform the getDegreesF method. */
    return 9.0 * getDegrees() / 5.0 + 32.0;
}
```

11. Compile and save the method by pressing **Ctrl+S** in the **Source** pane. Correct compilation errors, if necessary.

12. The `TCModel` class is now complete. If you click in the **Features** pane, the **BeanInfo** window should look like Figure 12-13. Close the window.

Back in the **Projects** window of the workbench, you can expand the `TCModel` class to see that VisualAge has generated more methods in the `TCModel` class than you explicitly created. These methods add support for events to the bean. Another class, `TCModelBeanInfo`, has also been added to the `examples.windows` package. Chapter 15 describes **BeanInfo** classes.

## Creating the Controller for the Temperature-Conversion Program

It is time to pull the program together by adding the controller to the model and view. You do this visually by adding connections between the `TCPanel` and `TCModel` classes and between the components that make up the GUI in the `TCPanel` class.

To load the `TCPanel` and `TCModel` classes into the VCE:

1. In the **Projects** window of the workbench, select the **TCPanel** class in the `examples.windows` package of the `learning` project. Right-click, and select **Open To** and **Visual Composition** from the popup menus. The VCE opens.

2. Add the invisible bean `TCModel` to the VCE. Click the **Choose Bean** tool from the palette. It is located immediately under the word **Swing**.

3. When the **Choose Bean** window opens, make sure the radio button **Class** is selected for the bean type. Enter **examples.windows.TCModel** in the text box near **Class Name:**, or click the **Browse** button to use a browser to locate the class. Click **OK**.

4. Back in the VCE, the cursor has the form of a cross when you move it over the unused area of the work surface. Click to the right of the `TCPanel` to drop the `TCModel` bean on the work surface. It looks like a puzzle piece, as shown in Figure 12-9.

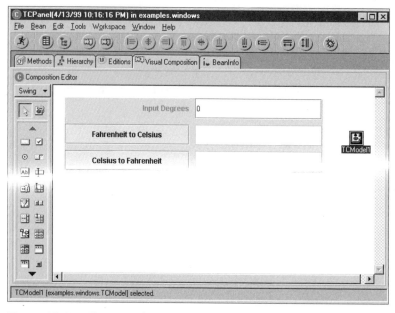

**Figure 12-9**   The VCE showing a GUI bean and an invisible bean

It is time to start making connections. All connections have a source and target. The source is often an event for a component. For example, when the user presses a button that is enabled, an **actionPerformed** event occurs. The target may be a property—usually a field whose value is set or a method that is called. Many connections need parameters, such as the value to assign to the target property, and you can set these values as properties of the connection or by connecting to values stored in other beans.

If you made a mistake following the next set of instructions, you can select **Undo** from the **Edit** menu, or remove a connection by right-clicking it and selecting **Delete** from its popup menu. You can then try to remake the connection.

To make connections so that when the user presses the `Celsius to Fahrenheit` button the input value is stored in the `TCModel` in degrees Celsius and then displayed in `JTextField3` in degrees Fahrenheit, follow these steps:

1. To set the source for the first connection, right-click on the button labeled **Celsius to Fahrenheit**, select **Connect**, and then select **actionPerformed** from its popup menu.

2. A dotted line with one end attached to the button appears. The other end moves with the mouse and has a spider-like shape. Position the spider over the target of the connection, the `TCModel` bean, and click. When a popup menu appears, select **Connectable Features** to display the **End connection to** window.

   The **End connection to** window lists bean features that can be the target of the connection, as shown in Figure 12-10. To set the value of the `degrees` property, make sure the **Method** radio button is selected, select **degrees** from the list, and click **OK**.

Figure 12-10   The VCE showing the TCPanel GUI bean

3. The connection is drawn in the VCE as a dashed line because the connection is incomplete. The purpose of the connection is to set the value of the `degrees` property when the button is pressed, but it does not specify a value

to set. Another connection can fetch the value: right-click on the incomplete connection and select **Connect** and then **value** from the connection's popup menu. When the "spider" appears, drag it over the `JTextField1` component and click. Select **text** from the popup menu. The value in the text field is now the parameter of the `TCModel.setDegrees( )` method, and VisualAge automatically takes care of the conversion from type **String** to **double**.

The first connection is complete, and the VCE looks like Figure 12-11. Complete connections show as solid lines. A small solid circle indicates the source of each connection and an arrowhead indicates the target. As with components, you can click on a connection to display its details in the VCE status line. Check, for example, that the name of the first connection is `connEtoM1`. The VCE implements the connection by generating a method with this name.

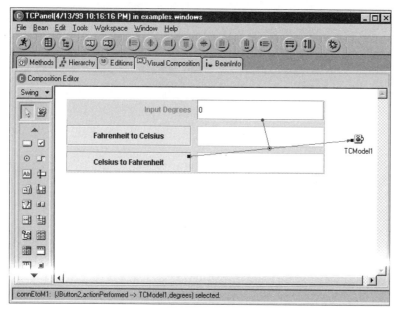

**Figure 12-11** The VCE showing connections between GUI and invisible beans

4. The second operation after the user presses **Celsius to Fahrenheit** is to display the temperature in degrees Fahrenheit. Make another connection by right-clicking the **Celsius to Fahrenheit** button and selecting **Connect** and then **actionPerformed** from its popup menu.

5. A dashed line and draggable spider reappear. Position the spider over the `JTextField3` component and click. When a popup menu appears, select **text** to make the contents of this text field the target of the connection. Another connection is drawn as a dashed line in the VCE.

6. Right-click on the dashed connection, select **Connect**, and then select **value** from its popup menu. Drag the spider over the `TCModel` bean, click, and select **Connectable Features** from the popup menu. In the **End connection to** window, select the **Method** radio button to display the list of methods and then select **getDegreesF( )** from the list. When you click **OK**, you return to the VCE and see the complete connections drawn as solid lines.

You can test again at this stage by clicking the **Run** button in the VCE toolbar. The **Celsius to Fahrenheit** button should work for valid input. If you have been deleting and remaking connections, the program may not work because the connections fire in the wrong order.

To check the order of connections from a component:

1. Right-click on the **Celsius to Fahrenheit** button and select **Reorder Connections From** in the popup menu.

2. A **Reorder Connections** window appears and should show two connections from this component. If the connection with target bean `TCModel1` is not listed on the line above the connection with target bean `JTextField3`, click and hold the mouse button to drag the **TCModel1** connection. Release the mouse to drop the connection into the first row, if necessary.

3. Close the window to accept the new order, and return to the VCE.

4. **Run** the bean to save, and test again, if necessary.

Make connections so that when the user presses the `Fahrenheit to Celsius` button, the input value is interpreted as degrees Fahrenheit, stored in the `TCModel`, and then displayed in `JTextField3` in degrees Celsius.

To make the connections:

1. To set the **Fahrenheit to Celsius** button as the source for the next connection, right-click the button, select **Connect**, and then select **actionPerformed** from its popup menu.

2. A dashed line representing the new connection and draggable spider appear. Position the spider over the target of the connection, the `TCModel` bean, and click. When the popup menu appears, select **ConnectableFeatures** to display the **End connection to** window.

3. Make sure the **Method** radio button is selected in the **End connection to** window, select **setDegreesF(double)** from the list, and click **OK**.

4. The connection is drawn as a dashed line. To fetch the argument for the `setDegreesF` method, right-click on the incomplete connection, select **Connect**, and then click **value** from the connection's popup menu. When

the spider appears, drag it over the `JTextField1` component, and click. Select **text** from the popup menu. The complete connection is drawn in the VCE.

5. The second operation after the user presses **Fahrenheit to Celsius** is to display the temperature in degrees Celsius. Make another connection from the button by right-clicking the **Fahrenheit to Celsius** button, selecting **Connect**, and then selecting **actionPerformed** from its popup menu.

6. The dashed line and draggable spider appear again. Position the spider over the `JTextField2` component, and click. When a popup menu appears, select **text** to make the contents of this text field the target of the connection.

7. Right-click on the dashed connection, and select **Connect** and then **value** from its popup menus. Click the spider on `TCModel1`, and select **Connectable features** from the popup menu. In the **End connection to** window, make sure the **Property** radio button is selected, click **degrees**, and then click **OK**.

8. The VCE should now look like Figure 12-12, except that the positions of your connections may not be exactly like those in Figure 12-12. To make your connections easier to see, you can drag the midpoint of each connection to another position. As long as you do not change the target or source, you can reposition connections without affecting the generated code.

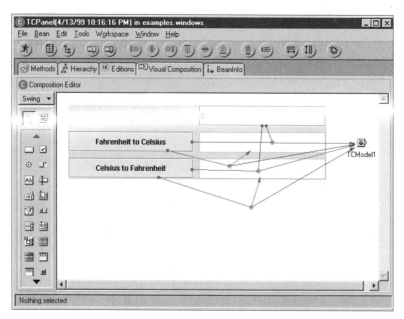

**Figure 12-12** The VCE showing connections between GUI and invisible beans

The **TCPanel** class should now have the required basic functionality. You can test again at this stage by clicking the **Run** button in the VCE toolbar. Both buttons should work for valid input.

## Improving the User Interface

If you test the **TCModel** class for more than one input value, you may notice that the numbers in **JTextField2** and **JTextField3** can temporarily display values that are not correct for the input displayed in **JTextField1**. This happens because the output text fields are not updated until the user presses the appropriate button. You will improve the user interface by clearing all text fields automatically whenever the user starts to enter new input. You can achieve this improvement with a single connection by making use of an event-to-code connection.

To make one connection that clears all text fields:

1. Right-click on the source of the connection, **JTextField1**, select **Connect**, and then click **Connectable Features** from the popup menus. When the **Start connection from** window opens, make sure the **Event** radio button is selected, and then click **Show expert features**. Select **focusGained** from the list of events that can originate from a **JTextField**. This event occurs whenever the user clicks in or tabs to the **JTextField**. Click **OK**.

2. Rather than connecting to another component, make the target a new method. When the spider appears, click over an empty area of the work surface. Select **Event to Code** from the popup menu.

   The **Event-to-Code Connection** window opens and displays the skeleton of a new method, as shown in Figure 12-13.

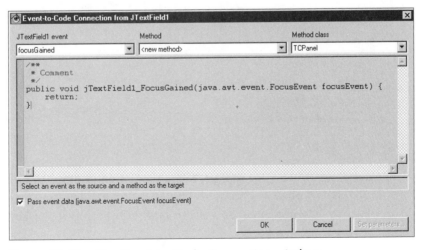

**Figure 12-13** The Event-to-Code Connection window

3. Edit the method in the **Event-to-Code Connection** window. Deselect the **Pass event data( )** checkbox in the lower left, and verify that the argument for the connection is removed. Add lines of code to the method to clear **JTextField1**, **JTextField2**, and **JtextField3**. The finished method should look like the following lines of code, except that the lines you enter are shown here in bold:

```
/**
 * Clear all text fields on new input
 */
public void jTextField1_FocusGained() {
    getJTextField1().setText("");
    getJTextField2().setText("");
    getJTextField3().setText("");
return;
}
```

4. Compile and save the code by pressing **Ctrl+S**. Correct compilation errors, if necessary. Click **OK**. The VCE displays the new method, as shown in Figure 12-14.

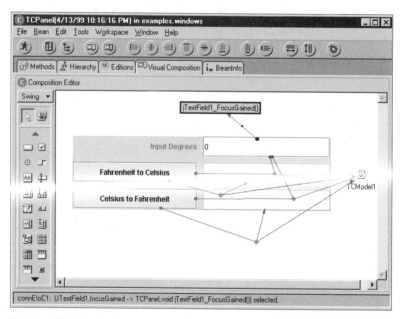

**Figure 12-14**   An Event-to-Code connection in the VCE

5. Click **Run** on the VCE toolbar. When the test frame appears, enter a value in the input text field. Press both buttons. Enter a different value in the input text field. See the text fields clear as soon as you change the input.

Try typing input that is not a number into the input text field. For example, enter **cold**, and then click **Celsius to Fahrenheit**. The program appears not to see the new input and uses the previous temperature value. The VCE generates code with exception handling. That is why this program does not terminate when it tries to interpret "cold" as a number. A **NumberFormatException** occurs, but the catch clauses in the connections that call methods `TCModel.setDegrees` and `TCModel.setDegreesF` ignore it.

One way to make this program robust is to subclass **JTextField** to create a bean that prevents non-numeric input. Many specialized input beans are available from a variety of sources. For this exercise, you will use the standard `JTextField` class and modify the generated code to handle the exception.

To handle exceptions caused by user-input errors:

1. Identify the two connections affected by user input errors. Click on the connection from the **Celsius to Fahrenheit** button to `TCModel`. In the status line, see that its name is `connEtoM1`. Click on the connection from the **Fahrenheit to Celsius** button to `TCModel`. In the status line, see that its name is `connEtoM3`. If you created connections in a different order, your connections may have different names and you should substitute your names in the following steps.

2. Click on the **Methods** tab to open the Methods window of the class browser. The window has two panes, as shown in Figure 12-15. The top pane lists all methods in the current class starting with constructors and then in alphabetic order. The bottom pane displays the source of the selected method. Click **connEtoM1** in the Method pane.

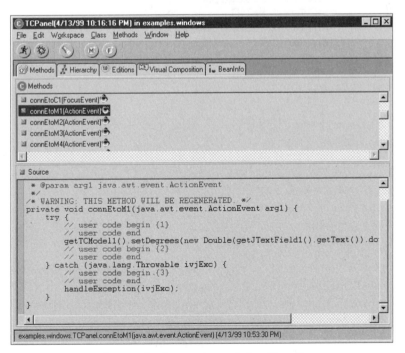

**Figure 12-15** The Methods Window of the Class Browser

In the source, verify that the body of the method is enclosed in a try block. The catch clause accepts all `Throwable` exceptions and calls an empty method `handleException`. The comments indicate places where you can safely insert your own code. Modify the catch clause by inserting the lines shown in bold:

```
catch (java.lang.Throwable ivjExc) {
   // user code begin {3}
   if ( ivjExc instanceof NumberFormatException ) {
      getJTextField1( ).setText(
       "numeric input required" );
      getTCModel1( ).setDegreesF( 0 );
   }
   // user code end
   handleException(ivjExc);
}
```

3. Press **Ctrl+S** to compile and save the method. Correct compilation errors, if necessary.

4. Click method **connEtoM3** in the top pane of the **Methods** browser. When method connEtoM3 is displayed in the **Source** pane, locate the catch clause and modify it by inserting the lines shown in bold here:

```
catch (java.lang.Throwable ivjExc) {
   // user code begin {3}
   if ( ivjExc instanceof NumberFormatException ) {
      getJTextField1().setText(
       "numeric input required" );
      getTCModel1().setDegrees(0);
   }
   // user code end
   handleException(ivjExc);
}
```

5. Press **Ctrl+S** to compile and save the method. Correct compilation errors, if necessary.

6. Close the Class browser, and return to the **Projects** window of the workbench.

7. Test `TCPanel` class again. Right-click on **TCPanel** in the `examples.examples` package of the `learning` project. Select **Run** and then **Run main...** from the popup windows. VisualAge provides a test frame and runs the class.

The job is complete, except that you cannot run a **Panel** or **JPanel** outside the VisualAge for Java IDE. Before deploying, you must wrap the **TCPanel** in a **JFrame** or **JApplet** object. The instructions for a **JFrame** follow. Creating an applet version is left as an exercise for the reader.

## Deploying the Temperature-Conversion Program

To create an application from the `TCPanel` class:

1. In the **Projects** window of the workbench, right-click on the **examples.windows** package in the `learning` project. Select **Add** and then **Class...** from the popup menu.

2. In the **Create Class** SmartGuide, make sure **Create a new class** is selected. Enter **TempConvert** into the **Class name:** text field. Enter **com.sun.java.swing.JFrame** into the **Superclass:** text field. Select both **Browse the class when Finished** and **Compose the class visually**. Click **Finish** to open the new class in the VCE.

3. You see the outline of a frame window in the VCE. Open the **Properties** window for the frame by right-clicking on its title bar and selecting **Properties** from the popup window.

4. In the **TempConvert-Properties** window, enter the string **Temperature Conversion Utility** as the value of the **title** property. Close the **Properties** window, and verify that the title is displayed.

5. Open the **Properties** window for the content area by right-clicking on the gray area and selecting Properties from its popup window.

6. In the **JFrameContentPane Properties** window, set the layout to **BorderLayout**. Close the **Properties** window.

7. Click the **Choose Bean** tool on the palette. In the **Choose Bean** window, make sure the **Class** radio button is selected. Enter **examples.windows.TCPanel** in the **Class name:** text field. Click **OK**.

8. When the cross-hair cursor appears in the VCE, click in the middle of the contents area of the frame. The `TCPanel` appears. It occupies the entire contents area because it is the only component in a **BorderLayout**. The `TCModel` bean does not appear.

9. Make an Event-to-Code connection to terminate the program when the user closes the frame. Right-click on the title of the frame. Select **Connect** and then **windowClosed** from the popup menu. When the spider appears, click on a clear area of the work surface, and select **Event to Code**.

10. In the **Event-to-code Connection** window, deselect the **Pass event data( )** check box, and then modify the code to insert the lines shown in bold below:

```
/**
 * Stop when the user closes the JFrame
 */
public void tempConvert_WindowClosed() {
```

```
      this.dispose();
      System.exit(0);
      return;
   }
```

11. Compile and save by pressing **Ctrl+S**. Correct compilation errors, if necessary. Click **OK** to return to the VCE.

12. Click **Run** to test the frame and its contents.

13. Close the VCE, and return to the **Projects** window.

The final step is to deploy outside VisualAge for Java. You will export only the source code for the `TempConvert`, `TCPanel`, and `TCModel` classes, and then recompile and run them with the Java 2 SDK.

To export the `examples.windows.TempConvert` program:

1. Version your new classes. Right-click on the **examples.windows** package, and select **Manage** and **Version ...** from the popup menus. In the **Versioning Selected Items** window, select **Automatic**, if necessary, and click **OK**.

2. Highlight the **examples.windows** package and then select **Export** from the **File** menu. On the first window of the **Export SmartGuide**, select **Directory**, if necessary, and click **Next**.

3. In the **Export to a directory** SmartGuide, select **.java** and **.class** and deselect the other check box in the group. Click **Details** to the right of the **.java** check box. The next window, **.java export**, lists projects and types. Figure 12-16 shows this SmartGuide on top of the **Export SmartGuide**.

4. Make sure **learning** is selected in the Projects list of the **.java export** window. In the **Types** list, select **TCModel::examples.windows**, **TCPanel::examples.windows**, and **TempConvert::examples.windows** only. Click **OK**.

5. Back in the **Export to a directory** SmartGuide, enter the full path to a destination folder in the **Directory:** text field. For example, you could export to **D:\myJava**. Click **Finish**.

6. If you do not want to do any more work in VisualAge for Java, close the IDE by clicking on **Exit VisualAge** in the File menu.

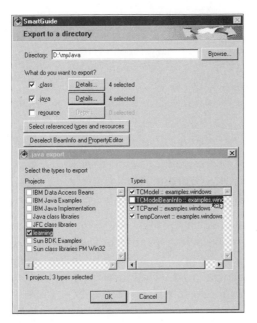

**Figure 12-16**   The Export to a directory SmartGuide

The Java source files you just exported now reside in an \examples\windows subfolder on your file system. The name of the package that holds the Swing classes has changed since the version implemented in VisualAge for Java, so you must update reference to this package name in the source before compiling and testing with the command line tools of the Java 2 SDK.

To run the TempConvert application with the command line tools of the Java 2 SDK:

1. Go to the directory where you exported the files. Open the file **examples\windows\TempConvert.java** in any plain text editor that has a global find-and-replace feature. Replace all occurrences of the string **com.sun.java.swing** with **javax.swing**. Save.

2. Open the file **examples\windows\TCPanel.java** in any flat text file editor that has a global find-replace feature. Replace all occurrences of the string **com.sun.java.swing** with **javax.swing**. Save changes to both files.

3. Open a command-line window and go to the directory to which you exported the source files. Compile the three classes with the commands:

```
javac examples\windows\TCModel.java
javac examples\windows\TCPanel.java
javac examples\windows\TempConvert.java
```

4. Run the program with the command:

```
java examples.windows.TempConvert
```

# SUMMARY

This chapter and the next are complementary. Chapter 13 builds on the understanding that you gain in this chapter to provide more comprehensive coverage of the JFC. This chapter explained that the JFCs are part of the Java platform. The JFC consists of five major APIs, including the classes and interfaces in the AWT and Swing APIs that you use to program a GUI for an application or applet.

The Swing API includes classes for the standard elements of GUIs, many of which are components. For example, **JButton**, **JCheckBox**, and **JTextField** are Swing component classes. You build the GUI for your program with components.

To make a class into an application that runs in a top-level window, define your class to extend the class **javax.swing.JFrame** or **java.awt.Frame**. Coding the GUI for an applet is similar to coding a GUI-based application except that the applet class must extend the class **javax.swing.JApplet** or **java.applet.Applet** and does not need a **main** method.

You can add components to containers by creating objects of the component class and calling the add method of the container, passing the component as an argument.

Use layout managers to arrange the components in a way that adjusts for screen resolutions and window resizings. Specify a layout manager by calling the **setLayout** method for the container.

An equally important aspect of programming GUIs consists of responding when the user moves the mouse, clicks the mouse, or types on the keyboard. These kinds of user input are events. Each component class supports a number of events that are appropriate to its type of component.

To handle an event, define a class to implement the appropriate listener interface. Call a method for the component to register the listener with the component. The methods in the listener interface are automatically called when events occur and receive an event object as an argument. Therefore, the listener can interrogate and handle the event.

You can use adapter classes that implement the interfaces to reduce the number of methods that you must implement to only those events that are of interest. Also, you can code for the AWT and Swing APIs manually or use RAD tools to program much more productively. There are a variety of proprietary development environments with RAD features.

VisualAge for Java from IBM provides an integrated development environment that includes a Visual Composition Editor. You can use the Visual Composition

Editor to design the visual elements of your program and to connect the visual elements to nonvisual elements.

You can create complete programs with the VisualAge for Java Visual Composition Editor by entering a minimum of code manually. VisualAge for Java generates 100% Pure Java code. You can develop, test, and debug within the VisualAge environment and then export packages for use in other implementations of the Java platform.

## QUESTIONS

1. Which of the following major groups of the AWT API are responsible for the strategy of placing GUI elements within an interface? Select the best answer.

   a. Graphics

   b. Components

   c. Layout managers

   d. Events

   e. Listeners and adapters

2. Name the class in the AWT API that is the superclass of events generated by all classes that extend **java.awt.Component**.

3. Which of the following are subpackages of the **java.awt** package? Select all that apply.

   a. **java.awt.components**

   b. **java.awt.event**

   c. **java.awt.image**

   d. **java.awt.graphics**

   e. **java.awt.peer**

4. Which classes are superclasses of Swing applets? Select all that apply.

   a. **java.lang.Object**

   b. **javax.swing.JFrame**

   c. **java.awt.Panel**

   d. **javax.swing.JApplet**

   e. **java.awt.Window**

5. How many components can be added to a container using a **BorderLayout** layout manager?

6. Which are heavyweight Swing components? Select all that apply.

    a. **JApplet**

    b. **JPanel**

    c. **JInternalFrame**

    d. **JDialog**

    e. **JFrame**

7. Which Swing components implement the **RootPaneContainer** interface? Select all that apply.

    a. **JFrame**

    b. **JOptionPane**

    c. **JApplet**

    d. **JPanel**

    e. **JDesktopPane**

8. What interface must a class implement if it needs to handle the event that occurs when a user clicks a push button?

9. What class in the **java.awt.event** package implements all of the methods defined in the **WindowListener** interface?

10. Which method is used to obtain a reference to the content-pane container of a frame window?

---

# EXERCISES

## Debugging

1. Correct all the errors in the following program:

```
package questions.c12;
import javax.swing.*;
import java.awt.*;
import java.awt.event.*;

public class Debug12_1 {
   public Debug12_1( String titleText ) {
      addWindowListener( new WindowAdapter() {
            public void
            windowClosing( WindowEvent e ) {
               e.getWindow().dispose();
               System.exit( 0 );
            }
         }
      }
```

```
        );
        JLabel greeting = new JLabel( "Debug Question",
                                      JLabel.CENTER );
        getContentPane().add( greeting,
                              BorderLayout.CENTER );
        setSize( 300, 100 );
        setVisible( true );
    }
    public static void main( String[] args ) {
        new Debug12_1( "Debug Question" );
    }
}
```

2. Correct all the errors in the following program:

```
package questions.c12;
import javax.swing.*;
import java.awt.*;
import java.awt.event.*;

public class Debug12_2 extends JFrame {
    public Debug12_2( String titleText ) {
        super( titleText );
        addWindowListener( new WindowAdapter() {
                public void
                windowClosing( WindowEvent e ) {
                    e.getWindow().dispose();
                    System.exit( 0 );
                }
            }
        );
        JLabel greeting = new JLabel( "Debug Question",
                                      JLabel.CENTER );
        getContentPane().add( greeting,
                              BorderLayout.CENTER );
    }
    public static void main( String[] args ) {
        new Debug12_2( "Debug Question" );
    }
}
```

3. Correct all the errors in the following program:

```
package questions.c12;
import javax.swing.*;
import java.awt.*;
import java.awt.event.*;

public class Debug12_3 extends JFrame {
    public Debug12_3( String titleText ) {
        super( titleText );
        addWindowListener( new WindowAdapter() {
```

**12**

```
                    public void
                    windowClosing( WindowEvent e ) {
                        e.getWindow().dispose();
                    }
                }
            );
            JLabel greeting = new JLabel( "Debug Question",
                                        JLabel.CENTER );
            setSize( 300, 100 );
            setVisible( true );
        }
        public static void main( String[] args ) {
            new Debug12_3( "Debug Question" );
        }
    }
```

4. Correct all the errors in the following program so that a single button with the label "Debug" appears in the middle of the frame window:

```
package questions.c12;
import javax.swing.*;
import java.awt.*;
import java.awt.event.*;

public class Debug12_4 extends JFrame {
    private JButton debugButton;
    public Debug12_4( String titleText ) {
        super( titleText );
        addWindowListener( new WindowAdapter() {
                public void
                windowClosing( WindowEvent e ) {
                    e.getWindow().dispose();
                    System.exit( 0 );
                }
            }
        );
        Container cp = getContentPane();
        cp.setLayout( new BorderLayout() );
        cp.add( debugButton, BorderLayout.CENTER );
        pack();
        setVisible( true );
    }
    public static void main( String[] args ) {
        new Debug12_4( "Debug Question" );
    }
}
```

5. Correct all the errors in the following program so that the three buttons appear within the frame in a single row:

```
package questions.c12;
import javax.swing.*;
import java.awt.*;
import java.awt.event.*;

public class Debug12_5 extends JFrame {
    private JButton black, red, green;
    public Debug12_5( String titleText ) {
        super( titleText );
        addWindowListener( new WindowAdapter() {
                public void
                windowClosing( WindowEvent e ) {
                    e.getWindow().dispose();
                    System.exit( 0 );
                }
            }
        );
        black = new JButton( "Black" );
        red = new JButton( "Red" );
        green = new JButton( "Green" );
        Container cp = getContentPane();
        cp.add( black );
        cp.add( red );
        cp.add( green );
        pack();
        setVisible( true );
    }
    public static void main( String[] args ) {
        new Debug12_5( "Debug Question" );
    }
}
```

**12**

## COMPLETE THE SOLUTION

1. Extract the file **questions\c12\Complete12_1.java** from the file **question.jar** on the CD-ROM. Complete the `Complete12_1` class definition by adding a **JLabel** object with the string, "I completed the solution!".

2. Extract the file **questions\c12\Complete12_2.java** from the file **question.jar** on the CD-ROM. Complete the `Complete12_2` class definition by adding a **JTextField** that can hold 40 characters in the center of the frame window.

3. Extract the file **questions\c12\Complete12_3.java** from the file **question.jar** on the CD-ROM. Complete the `Complete12_3` class definition by creating a **JPanel** object and a **JCheckBox** object. Put the check box into

the center of the panel and put the panel into the North section of the frame window.

4. Extract the file **questions\c12\Complete12_4.java** from the file **question.jar** on the CD-ROM. Complete the `Complete12_4` class definition by adding code to the **actionPerformed** method that will change the label of the button to "Thanks!" when the user clicks it.

5. Extract the file **questions\c12\Complete12_5.java** from the file **question.jar** on the CD-ROM. Complete the `Complete12_5` class definition by putting a check box in the middle of the window. When the check box is selected, the text should be green; when the check box is not selected, the text should be red.

# DISCOVERY

1. Create a class called `SquareRoots` that implements a special-purpose calculator that finds only square roots. The user interface for this calculator should have an entry field where the user enters the input number for the calculation and a second entry field that displays the answer. Put two buttons in the window: one called Calculate that causes the square root to be calculated and displayed and another called Cancel that ends the program.

2. Add a user interface to the `JUnzip` class described in the Discovery questions in Chapter 10. Call the new class `JUnzip2`. The user interface should display the files contained in a zip file and provide two buttons: one to unzip the file and the other to end the program. The name of the zip file is passed as a command-line argument.

# PROGRAMMING WINDOWS AND EVENTS

---

### In this chapter you will:

➤ Create a graphical user interface (GUI) for your application or applet.

➤ Become familiar with the extensive library of GUI components offered by the Swing API.

☞ Write code to implement listener classes and methods.

☞ Call listener methods to extract information from the event about the affected component, mouse position, and the nature and time of the event.

☞ State the name of the event class for any specified listener interface in the **java.awt.event** package.

☞ Write code using component, container, and layout manager classes of the AWT and Swing APIs to present a GUI with specified appearance and resize behavior, and to distinguish the responsibilities of layout managers from those of containers.

➤ Write code that uses the methods of the **javax.swing.JComponent** class.

➤ Draw directly on the surface of a component using the methods of the **Graphics** class.

➤ Know what classes and methods affect the look and feel of Swing components and what classes or methods affect the model or data displayed.

➤ Identify the sequence of **JComponent** methods involved in redrawing areas of a GUI.

➤ Distinguish between methods invoked by the user thread and those normally invoked by the event dispatch thread.

➤ Write code to implement the **paintComponent** method of a **javax.swing.JComponent**.

---

## PROGRAMMING WITH THE JFC

If you are planning to write applets or applications that have GUIs, you will be using the Java Foundation Classes (JFC) of the Java platform. The JFC consists of a set of classes that supports the programming of a GUI. Comprehensive coverage of the JFC is beyond the scope of this book. This chapter, however, builds on the introduction to writing a GUI that was given in Chapter 12, describes the classes that implement the concepts introduced in that chapter, and demonstrates how to use many of them in small sample programs.

This chapter focuses on the following four categories drawn from the JFC:

➤ Components and facilities

➤ Layouts

➤ Event handling

➤ 2D graphics

You do not have to use the JFC if you are programming only for console I/O, but users of applications usually demand GUI operation, and the nature of applets mandates that you program for a windowing environment. Therefore, many, if not all, of your programs are likely to use the JFC.

Java 2 gives you a choice between using the AWT or Swing component classes to build your GUI, whereas previously the AWT was the only option. The AWT has been available since the original Java platform, although the event-handling model was radically redesigned for version 1.1 of the Java platform. For applets, you may decide to build a simple GUI based on AWT components because they are supported by most current web browsers without requiring a plug-in. A sophisticated GUI needs the flexibility and power of Swing because Swing provides support for borders, icons, pluggable look-and-feel, and advanced components such as tool bars, tabbed panes, and tables.

One of the advantages of the Java platform is that core classes and interfaces provide support for creating a GUI. The AWT, Drag and Drop, and Java 2D APIs are contained in the core package java.awt and related packages, as shown in Table 13–1.

**Table 13-1**  Packages of the AWT

| Package Name | Description |
| --- | --- |
| **java.awt.color** | A part of the Java 2D API, it provides classes for color spaces. |
| **java.awt.datatransfer** | Provides classes that support data transfer between applications. For example, you can give users access to the operating system clipboard and let them perform cut-and-paste operations to and from the clipboard. |
| **java.awt.dnd** | Provides interfaces and classes for supporting drag-and-drop operations for the Drag and Drop API. |
| **java.awt.event** | Provides classes that encapsulate the various kinds of user activities. Other classes and interfaces provide the framework within which you create customized handlers for the events. |

*continued*

**Table 13-1** Packages of the AWT (continued)

| Package Name | Description |
|---|---|
| **java.awt.font** | A part of the Java 2D API that provides enhanced support for fonts. |
| **java.awt.geom** | A part of the Java 2D API that provides classes for defining and performing operations on objects related to two-dimensional geometry. |
| **java.awt.im** | Provides classes and an interface for the input method framework used for entering characters for languages such as Japanese. |
| **java.awt.image.renderable** | A part of the Java 2D API that provides classes and interfaces for producing rendering-independent images. |
| **java.awt.image** | Contains classes that support different color models and image filters for image processing. However, the **Image** class itself is in the **java.awt** package. |
| **java.awt.peer** | The classes that bridge between the AWT classes and their implementations that depend on the native operating system. Usually, you do not use the classes in this package directly.<br>The component classes in the Swing API do not use peers and have no native code. AWT components always adopt the look-and-feel of the native operating system. An advantage of Swing is greater flexibility in designing the look-and-feel of a GUI than is possible with the AWT. |
| **java.awt.print** | A part of the Java 2D API that provides classes and interfaces for a general printing. |

**13**

The Swing and Accessibility APIs are contained in the core package **javax.swing** and its related packages, as shown in Table 13–2.

**Table 13-2** The Swing packages

| Package Name | Description |
|---|---|
| **javax.swing** | The base Swing package, and provider of all the Swing components. |
| **javax.swing.border** | Provides classes and an interface for drawing specialized borders around Swing components. |
| **javax.swing.colorchooser** | Contains classes and interfaces used by **JColorChooser** objects. However, the **JColorChooser** class is in the **javax.swing** package. |
| **javax.swing.event** | This package provides for events used by Swing components. |

*continued*

**Table 13-2**   The Swing packages (continued)

| Package Name | Description |
|---|---|
| **javax.swing.filechooser** | Contains classes and interfaces used by the **JFileChooser** objects. However, the **JFileChooser** class is in the **javax.swing** package. |
| **javax.swing.plaf** | Provides one interface and many abstract classes that Swing uses to provide its pluggable look-and-feel capabilities. |
| **javax.swing.plaf.basic** | Provides user interface objects built according to the **Basic** look-and-feel. |
| **javax.swing.plaf.metal** | Provides user interface objects built according to the cross-platform look-and-feel called **metal**. |
| **javax.swing.plaf.multi** | Provides the multiplexing look-and-feel used by the Accessibility API to combine auxiliary look-and-feels (e.g., audio, large type, etc.) with the default look-and-feel. |
| **javax.swing.table** | Provides classes and interfaces for dealing with the **JTable** component.  However, the **JTable** class is in the **javax.swing** package. |
| **javax.swing.text** | Provides classes and interfaces that deal with editable and noneditable text components. |
| **javax.swing.text.html** | Provides the classes for creating HTML text editors. |
| **javax.swing.tree** | Provides classes and interfaces for dealing with the **JTree** component.  However, the **JTree** class is in the **javax.swing** package. |
| **javax.swing.undo** | Provides support for undo/redo capabilities in an application such as a text editor. |

# SWING API COMPONENTS

The Java platform provides two sets of classes that implement the Swing and AWT visual components. These visual components common in GUIs include buttons, check boxes, text areas, and windows. Using them you do not need to design your own classes for standard elements.

This chapter focuses on the components in the Swing API because these components represent the future of GUI development for the Java platform. Their design and implementation is much improved over the original AWT API components, and the functionality of Swing components is more extensive. Mostly, the functionality provided by AWT components is a subset of what you can do with Swing components. If you learn how to develop GUIs with Swing components, you can transfer this skill to AWT components.

Each component includes the support required to draw itself. For example, if you create an instance of the **JButton** class and add it to a container, the button appears fully rendered on the screen when the object is displayed. Components also support the framework for GUI interaction that is appropriate for the component. For example, the **JButton** class can generate events when the user clicks a **JButton** object.

Component classes do all this for you, and more. That is why most GUI applications and applets make heavy use of the component classes provided by the Java platform. The following sections discuss commonly used Swing component classes, beginning with the **JComponent** class.

# JCOMPONENT CLASS

The **JComponent** class is the superclass of all Swing components. The **JButton** objects, **JCheckbox**, and **JTextField** that you saw in the `ThreePanels` program of Chapter 12 are all examples of **JComponent** subclasses.

The **JComponent** class is a direct subclass of the **java.awt.Container** class that, in turn, is a direct subclass of **java.awt.Component**. This inheritance hierarchy establishes two important facts for all Swing components: they are all containers, and they are all connected to the original AWT component hierarchy.

In addition to their overloaded constructors, the various subclasses of the **JComponent** class inherit a number of methods that establish the common behavior of all components. The following description of the **JComponent** class lists several of the most frequently used methods. In addition, for each method listed for the **JComponent** class that sets the value of a property, there is a method to retrieve the value of the property. For example, you can call **setSize** and pass a **Dimension** object to specify the exact size of a component in pixels. To find out the size of a component, call **getSize**, which returns a **Dimension** object.

*Class*

**javax.swing.JComponent**

*Purpose*

The **JComponent** class is the abstract superclass for all Swing components.

*Methods*

➤ **void add**xxx**Listener(** xxx**Listener** *object* **)**
  All components have a set of methods in which the name of each method begins with the word **add** and ends with **Listener.** Each add**xxx**Listener method registers a listener for a specific type of event with the component.

Use listeners to handle user–initiated events that relate to the component. Different listeners handle different types of events. The *xxx* in the method name varies, depending on the type of the listener. Events and listeners are discussed later in this chapter.

➤ **void repaint()**
**void repaint( long** *msec* **)**
**void repaint( int** *x*, **int** *y*, **int** *height*, **int** *width* **)**
**void repaint( long** *msec*, **int** *x*, **int** *y*, **int** *height*, **int** *width* **)**
You can call the **repaint** method to have the current component repainted. If you do not supply a parameter, the **repaint** request is sent immediately to the AWT thread. You can schedule the repainting operation by specifying that the repaint begins in *msec* milliseconds. If it is not necessary to repaint the entire component, it is possible to specify the area to be repainted.

➤ **void setBackground( Color** *c* **)**
Call **setBackground** to set the background color. For the argument, you can use one of the constants defined in the class **java.awt.Color**. Several color constants are available, including **red**, **green**, **blue**, **yellow**, **black**, and **white**. Also, you can specify colors as 24–bit values in which the first eight bits are the intensity of red, the middle eight bits are the intensity of green, and the last eight bits are the intensity of blue. To do that, use **Color** objects created by passing integer values in the range zero to 255 for the red, green, and blue integer arguments to the **Color** constructor.

➤ **void setBorder( Border** *b* **)**
Call **setBorder** to add a border to the component. Use a border to outline a component, add a title to a component, or to create space around a component. By default, components have no border. The simplest way to create a border is to use one of the many static methods defined in the **javax.swing.BorderFactory** class. The **BorderFactory** class defines static methods to create all of the styles of borders that Swing supports.

➤ **void setDoubleBuffered( boolean** *b* **)**
Call **setDoubleBuffered( true )** to let a component prepare component updates in an off-screen buffer before they are copied to the screen. Double buffering helps eliminate screen flicker. Components are enabled for double buffering by default. Specify the argument **false** to turn off double buffering.

➤ **void setEnabled( boolean** *b* **)**
Call **setEnabled( true )** to enable the component to respond to user input and to generate events. Components are enabled by default. When the argument is **false**, the component does not respond to events.

➤ **void setFont( Font** *f* **)**
Call **setFont** to specify the font for all textual data in the component. The argument should be an instance of the class **java.awt.Font**. When you

create a **Font** object, you specify the name of the font, the style, and the point size in arguments of the constructor. The FontSlider program later in this chapter demonstrates creating and modifying **Font** objects.

➤ **void setForeground( Color** *c* **)**
Call **setForeground** to set the foreground color. Specify the argument exactly as you would specify the argument to the method **setBackground**.

➤ **void setPreferredSize( Dimension** *d* **)**
Call **setPreferredSize** to specify the ideal size for the component. The argument should be an instance of the class **java.awt.Dimension**. You can create a **Dimension** object with an **int** argument for width, followed by an **int** argument for height, or just one argument for a square shape. Layout managers use the preferred size when positioning and shaping components.

➤ **void setSize( Dimension** *d* **)**
Call **setSize** to set the size of a component in pixels.

➤ **void setToolTipText( String** *s* **)**
Call **setToolTipText** to associate a string with a component. This string is displayed in a popup window near the component when the user's mouse pauses over the component for a short time.

➤ **void setVisible( boolean** *b* **)**
Call **setVisible** and pass the value **true** to show the component. Pass **false** to hide it.

➤ **void update( Graphics** *context* **)**
The **update** method calls **paint** to repaint the component. Later sections of this chapter and Chapter 14 describe how to use this method.

**13**

## WINDOWS, DIALOGS, AND PANELS

Generally, graphical designers do not place windows, dialogs, and panels in user interfaces. However, these containers are key for programmers because containers organize and, with the help of layout managers, establish the visual design of a GUI by providing the surfaces on which other components are placed.

Although all Swing components inherit from the **java.awt.Container** class, only certain components can hold other Swing components. A container can also hold other containers because every container is a component. The ability to nest components within containers, and containers within containers, gives you flexibility to create an enormous variety of designs for your user interface. Adding a component to a container involves calling the method **add** for the container object and passing the **JComponent** object as the argument of **add**.

---

*Class*

**java.awt.Container**

---

*Purpose*

The **Container** class provides a number of methods to add and remove components or to work with layouts.

---

*Methods*

➤ **void add( Component** *comp* **)**

➤ **void add( Component** *comp***, Object** *constraint* **)**
The **add** method adds the specified component to the container using default placement rules. For some layout managers, you should specify an object that constrains where the layout manager places the component. For example, if your container has a border layout, specify the area in which to put the component as a **String** in the second argument of the **add** method. Border layouts and other layout managers are described later in this chapter. Some overloaded **add** methods return the object reference passed as an argument to the method.

➤ **Component[ ] getComponents()**
The **getComponents** method returns an array containing all the components within the container.

➤ **LayoutManager getLayout()**
The **getLayout** method returns the layout manager for the container.

➤ **void remove( Component** *comp* **)**
The **remove** method removes the component from the container.

➤ **void setLayout( LayoutManager** *mgr* **)**
The **setLayout** method determines which layout manager controls the arrangement of components as they are added to the container.

---

Swing has several top-level container components that you will use as the basis for your GUI programs: **JApplet**, **JDialog**, **JFrame**, and **JWindow**. These heavyweight components extend components in the AWT API. (A heavyweight component is one that has a peer component in the underlying native windowing support of the operating system.) The **JApplet** class will be discussed in detail in Chapter 14 because of its special browser environment.

Unlike their AWT counterparts, top-level Swing containers have a separate container called the **content pane** to which all components are added. To add a component to a **JApplet**, **JDialog**, **JFrame**, or **JWindow**, you must first call the method **getContentPane** and add the component to the returned object, as shown in the examples in this section. At first, this content pane may seem an unnecessary complication, but Swing containers use it to provide flexibility in positioning other components in layers and in controlling mouse events.

Descriptions of the **JDialog**, **JFrame**, and **JWindow** classes as well as the details of the constructors that are available for creating objects of these classes follow.

## Class

**javax.swing.JDialog**

## Purpose

The **JDialog** class extends **java.awt.Dialog**. Typically, you use a dialog to solicit input from the user. You can display labels and other information, provide components in which users enter data or select items from a list, and add buttons that users can click to submit or cancel their input.
By default, the layout manager for a **JDialog** object is a **BorderLayout.**

## Constructors

➤ **JDialog( Frame** *parent* **)**
**JDialog( Frame** *parent,* **boolean** *modal* **)**
**JDialog( Frame** *parent,* **String** *title* **)**
**JDialog( Frame** *parent,* **String** *title,* **boolean** *modal* **)**
A **JDialog** object must have a parent window, which usually is the **JFrame** for an application. By default, **JDialog** windows are not modal. If you want to prevent the user from interacting with other windows while the **JDialog** is visible, include the **boolean** argument with the value **true**. To give the **JDialog** a title, specify it with the **String** argument.

**13**

## Class

**javax.swing.JFrame**

## Purpose

The **JFrame** class extends **java.awt.Frame**. A **JFrame** object is a window with borders and a title bar. It can have a menu bar also. All the sample programs in this and the previous chapter are created and displayed as **JFrame** objects. A GUI-driven application usually has at least one frame window, and the main class of the application often extends **JFrame**. Applets and applications can open additional frame windows.
By default, the layout manager for a **Frame** object is a **BorderLayout**.

*Constructors*

➤ **JFrame()**
**JFrame( String** *title* **)**
If you pass a **String** object to the constructor, the content of the string appears in the title bar of the frame window.

*Class*

**javax.swing.JWindow**

*Purpose*

**JWindow** objects are empty windows that have no title or menu bar. Typically, Swing programmers use them as the basis for creating custom components. By default, the layout manager for a **JWindow** object is a **BorderLayout.**

*Constructors*

➤ **JWindow( Frame** *parent* **)**
You usually specify the **JFrame** for your application as the parent of a **JWindow** object. In this context, the parent is the owner of the window. When a parent window is closed, its child windows are also closed automatically. The parent-child relationship does not place any constraints on the positioning of child windows, as the case in some windowing systems that require the placement of child windows on top of parent windows.

There are other container components that Swing programs use within the top-level containers just described. **JDesktopPane**, **JInternalFrame**, **JOptionPane**, and **JPanel** are lightweight components that extend **JComponent**.

*Class*

**javax.swing.JDesktopPane**

*Purpose*

The **JDesktopPane** class is a container for **JInternalFrame** objects. You can use this class to give your GUI  a work area that resembles the desktop provided by a native GUI-oriented operating system.

*Constructors*

➤ **JDesktopPane()**
No parameters are allowed when constructing a **JDesktopPane**. By default, a **JDesktopPane** object uses a null layout manager that requires the user to control absolute positioning.

*Class*

**javax.swing.JInternalFrame**

*Purpose*

The **JInternalFrame** class extends **JComponent**, but not any heavyweight AWT component. A **JInternalFrame** object does not have its own window and is almost always contained in a window within a **JDesktopPane**. You can add several panels to the internal frame's window to divide the area of the window into regions, as you did in the `ThreePanels` program in Chapter 12. You can use layout managers and nested panels to create almost any arrangement of components on the screen.       .

*Constructors*

➤ **JInternalFrame()**
**JInternalFrame( String** *title* **)**
**JInternalFrame( String** *title*, **boolean** *resizable* **)**
**JInternalFrame( String** *title*, **boolean** *resizable*, **boolean** *closable* **)**
**JInternalFrame( String** *title*, **boolean** *resizable*, **boolean** *closable*,
        **boolean** *maximizable* **)**
**JInternalFrame( String** *title*, **boolean** *resizable*, **boolean** *closable*,
        **boolean** *maximizable*, **boolean** *iconifiable* **)**

If you pass a **String** object to the constructor, the content of the string appears in the title bar of the internal frame window. The **boolean** constructor parameters set the allowable actions for the window. The default is **false** in all cases. When a frame or internal frame is iconifiable, the user can minimize it so that an icon, but not the whole object, is displayed on the desktop or desktop pane.

**13**

*Class*

**javax.swing.JOptionPane**

*Purpose*

The **JOptionPane** class provides an easy way to create and display the most common kinds of dialog boxes. It supports message dialogs, confirmation dialogs, input dialogs, and combinations of dialog types.

*Constructors*

➤ **JOptionPane()**
**JOptionPane( Object** *message* **)**
**JOptionPane( Object** *message*, **int** *messageType* **)**
**JOptionPane( Object** *message*, **int** *messageType*, **int** *optionType* **)**
**JOptionPane( Object** *message*, **int** *messageType*, **int** *optionType*, **Icon** *icon* **)**

> **JOptionPane( Object** *message,* **int** *messageType,* **int** *optionType,* **Icon** *icon,*
>      **Object[]** *options* **)**
> **JOptionPane( Object** *message,* **int** *messageType,* **int** *optionType,* **Icon** *icon,*
>      **Object[]** *options,* **Object** *initialValue***)**

**JOptionPane** objects are highly configurable. The constructor builds a dialog based on the specified message, type, options, icon, and an initially selected option.

---

*Class*

## javax.swing.JPanel

---

*Purpose*

The **JPanel** class extends **JComponent** but is not a heavyweight component. A **JPanel** object does not have its own window and is almost always contained in a window. You can add several panels to a panel's window to divide the area of the window into regions, as you did in the **ThreePanels** program in Chapter 12. You can use layout managers and nested panels to create almost any arrangement of components on the screen.

---

*Constructors*

> ➤ **JPanel()**
>   **JPanel( boolean** *isDoubleBuffered* **)**
>   **JPanel( LayoutManager** *layout* **)**
>   **JPanel( LayoutManager** *layout,* **boolean** *isDoubleBuffered* **)**

If you do not want the default arrangement of components on a panel, specify one of the **LayoutManager** classes described later in this chapter. It is also possible to specify whether double buffering is turned on or off. By default, a **JPanel** object uses a **FlowLayout** layout manager.

---

The following is a program that exercises several of the classes described above. A breakdown of this code follows the output. This program defines the class `DesktopAndDialog`. Because `DesktopAndDialog` is a public class, it is found in a file called **DesktopAndDialog.java**. The structure of packages mirrors the file system, so you will find this source code in the examples\windows subfolder of the folder in which you unpacked the JAR file **examples.jar**:

```
package examples.windows;
import javax.swing.*;
import java.awt.*;
/** An example class used to demonstrate the use of
  * the JDesktopPane, JInternalFrame, and
  * JOptionPane components
  */
```

```
public class DesktopAndDialog extends JFrame {
    private static final boolean RESIZABLE = true;
    private static final boolean CLOSABLE = true;
    private static final boolean MAXIMIZABLE = true;
    private static final boolean ICONIFIABLE = true;
    private static final boolean MODAL = false;
    /** Class constructor method
      * @param titleText Window's title bar text
      */
    public DesktopAndDialog( String titleText ) {
        super( titleText );
        addWindowListener( new WindowCloser() );
        JInternalFrame ifrm = new JInternalFrame(
            "Internal Frame",
            RESIZABLE, CLOSABLE, MAXIMIZABLE, ICONIFIABLE );
        ifrm.setPreferredSize( new Dimension( 375, 300 ) );
        JDesktopPane dt = new JDesktopPane();
        dt.setLayout( new FlowLayout() );
        dt.add( ifrm );
        getContentPane().add( dt, BorderLayout.CENTER );

        setSize( 500, 400 );
        setVisible( true );
        JOptionPane.showMessageDialog(
            ifrm, "This is a JOptionPane" );
    }
    /** The test method for the class
      * @param args not used
      */
    public static void main( String[] args ) {
        new DesktopAndDialog(
            "Example Desktop with Dialog" );
    }
}
```

**13**

Allowing for differences in operating systems, the output should be similar to Figure 13-1. You may notice that the internal frame does not look like a native frame on your platform. That is because, by default, Swing uses a cross-platform look-and-feel known as the **Metal look-and-feel** for its components. The Metal look-and-feel was designed to be distinctive from existing look-and-feels provided by Windows, MacOS, and Motif. Its name comes from the fact that it is reminiscent of embossing on sheets of metal.

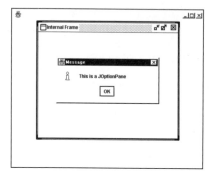

**Figure 13-1**    Output of the DesktopAndDialog class

The class encapsulating the drawing program is called `DesktopAndDialog`. The constructor, as usual, begins by passing the title for the **JFrame** to the constructor of the **JFrame** superclass:

```
public DesktopAndDialog( String titleText ) {
   super( titleText );
```

An object of the class `WindowCloser` is created and registered as a window event handler by calling addWindowListener:

```
addWindowListener( new WindowCloser() );
```

The class `WindowCloser` is created for convenience. You can find it in the package as the `WindowCloser` example class. All the sample programs in this chapter use this simple class to close a **JFrame** and exit the JVM. Here is the entire class definition:

```
public class WindowCloser extends WindowAdapter {
   public void windowClosing( WindowEvent e ) {
      e.getWindow().dispose();
      System.exit( 0 );
   }
}
```

The next two statements create a **JInternalFrame** object that can be resized, closed, maximized, and iconified. They also set the preferred size of the object:

```
JInternalFrame ifrm = new JInternalFrame(
   "Internal Frame",
   RESIZABLE, CLOSABLE, MAXIMIZABLE, ICONIFIABLE );
ifrm.setPreferredSize( new Dimension( 375, 300 ) );
```

A **JDesktopPane** is needed to contain the internal frame, and the following lines create the pane and give it a flow layout manager before adding the internal frame to the pane:

```
JDesktopPane dt = new JDesktopPane();
dt.setLayout( new FlowLayout() );
dt.add( ifrm );
```

The desktop pane is then added to the center of the **JFrame** object's content pane that is retrieved using the method **getContentPane**:

```
getContentPane().add( dt, BorderLayout.CENTER );
```

The next step is to set the size of the **JFrame** and to make it visible:

```
setSize( 500, 400 );
setVisible( true );
```

The last statement of the constructor uses a static method of the **JOptionPane** class to display a message dialog. This dialog is created using the internal frame object as its parent. The text of the message is also provided. You can use this static method to create a **JOptionPane** that contains a **JDialog** object and display it with one method call:

```
JOptionPane.showMessageDialog(
    ifrm, "This is a JOptionPane" );
```

The **main** method simply creates a `DesktopAndDialog` object and provides it with the text for the **JFrame** object's title bar:

```
public static void main( String[] args ) {
    new DesktopAndDialog(
        "Example Desktop with Dialog" );
}
```

# LAYOUT MANAGERS

Layout managers automate the positioning components within containers. They free you from the tricky task of figuring out how much space each component requires and at what pixel coordinates to position it. Usually, the exact position of components isn't important, but they should be arranged neatly. For example, you probably want components such as buttons and labels to be aligned and not to overlap or crowd into one area of the screen.

Layout managers make optimal use of space and automatically align buttons and similar components. Moreover, they adjust for factors such as different screen resolutions, platform-to-platform variations in the appearance of components, and font sizes. It would be very difficult to program a GUI if you could not depend on layout managers to figure out the best layout on the target platform at run time.

In the Java platform, two interfaces—**java.awt.LayoutManager** and **java.awt.LayoutManager2**—provide the base for all layout manager classes. As its name implies, the **LayoutManager2** interface is an extension of **LayoutManager**. It has additional layout management methods to support layout constraints that are typically used in the more complicated layout managers.

**13**

These interfaces define the methods necessary for arranging **JComponent** objects inside containers. The relationship between the layout manager interfaces and classes that implement them is shown in Figure 13-2. Note that ovals represent interfaces.

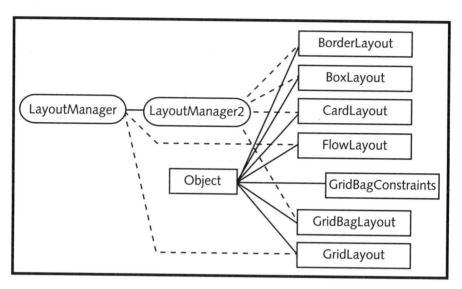

**Figure 13-2**    Layout managers and related interfaces

Each layout manager supports a different strategy for arranging components within a container component. Of course, the individual components can, in turn, be containers, which gives you the option of nesting layout managers within layout managers. You can nest a layout of one kind within a layout of a different kind, which means you can create an amazing variety of effects by manipulating just a few layout manager classes.

When you create a new container component, you should call the method **setLayout** for it, specifying an object of one of the classes that implement **LayoutManager**. Each container class has a default layout manager, but the defaults are not the same for all types of containers. Therefore, it is best to set the layout manager for a container explicitly.

While the AWT API provides five layout manager classes to give you five different layout strategies, the Swing API adds one more: the **BoxLayout**. In addition, two containers in the Swing API—**javax.swing.JTabbedPane** and **javax.swing.JSplitPane**—have built-in layout characteristics that make it easy to create effects not possible with the AWT alone. You also can create your own layout manager class by defining a class that implements the **LayoutManager** interface.

The following is a program that exercises several of the available layout managers by positioning **JButton** objects. A **JTabbedPane** is used to organize the different layouts. For a breakdown of this code, see the following description of each layout manager:

```java
package examples.windows;
import javax.swing.*;
import java.awt.*;
import java.awt.event.*;
/** An example class used to demonstrate the basics of
  * creating components such as panels, arranging
  * components using layout objects, and nesting
  * components inside each other.
  */
public class ExampleLayouts extends JFrame {
    private JPanel flow
        = new JPanel( new FlowLayout( FlowLayout.CENTER ) );
    private Box box = new Box( BoxLayout.Y_AXIS );
    private JPanel boxPanel = new JPanel();
    private JPanel grid
        = new JPanel( new GridLayout( 3, 2 ) );
    private JPanel gridBag
        = new JPanel( new GridBagLayout() );
    private JPanel border
        = new JPanel( new BorderLayout() );
    /** Class constructor method
      * @param titleText Window's title bar text
      */
    public ExampleLayouts( String titleText ) {
        super( titleText );
        addWindowListener( new WindowCloser() );
        // Add the buttons to the flow layout
        flow.add( new JButton( "One" ) );
        flow.add( new JButton( "Two" ) );
        flow.add( new JButton( "Three" ) );
        flow.add( new JButton( "Four" ) );
        // Add the buttons to the box
        box.add( new JButton( "One" ) );
        box.add( new JButton( "Two" ) );
        box.add( new JButton( "Three" ) );
        box.add( new JButton( "Four" ) );
        // Add the buttons to the grid layout
        grid.add( new JButton( "One" ) );
        grid.add( new JButton( "Two" ) );
        grid.add( new JButton( "Three" ) );
        grid.add( new JButton( "Four" ) );
        grid.add( new JButton( "Five" ) );
        grid.add( new JButton( "Six" ) );
        // Add the buttons to the gridbag layout
        GridBagConstraints c = new GridBagConstraints();
```

**13**

```java
        c.fill = GridBagConstraints.BOTH;
        c.weightx = 1.0;
        c.weighty = 1.0;
        c.gridwidth = GridBagConstraints.REMAINDER;
        gridBag.add( new JButton( "One" ), c );
        c.gridy = 1;
        c.gridx = 1;
        gridBag.add( new JButton( "Two" ), c );
        c.gridy = 2;
        gridBag.add( new JButton( "Three" ), c );
        c.gridy = 1;
        c.gridx = 0;
        c.gridheight = 2;
        c.gridwidth = 1;
        gridBag.add( new JButton( "Four" ), c );
        // Add the buttons to the border layout
        border.add( new JButton( "One" ),
                BorderLayout.NORTH );
        border.add( new JButton( "Two" ),
                BorderLayout.WEST );
        border.add( new JButton( "Three" ),
                BorderLayout.CENTER );
        border.add( new JButton( "Four" ),
                BorderLayout.EAST );
        border.add( new JButton( "Five" ),
                BorderLayout.SOUTH );
        // create a tabbed pane and put the panels into it
        JTabbedPane tp = new JTabbedPane();
        tp.addTab( "Flow", flow );
        boxPanel.add( box );
        tp.addTab( "Box", boxPanel );
        tp.addTab( "Grid", grid );
        tp.addTab( "GridBag", gridBag );
        tp.addTab( "Border", border );
        setContentPane( tp );
        setSize( 250, 175 );
        setVisible( true );
    }
    /** The test method for the class
      * @param args not used
      */
    public static void main( String[] args ) {
        new ExampleLayouts( "Example Layouts" );
    }
}
```

## Border Layouts

The class **BorderLayout** class implements the **LayoutManager2** interface to support a container that holds up to five components. The components are sized to fill all the space in the container and arranged, as shown in Figure 13-3.

The relative sizes of the areas are determined at run time from the contents of each area. If you do not fill all areas, the empty ones collapse so that they take up no space, and the other areas expand to fill the container.

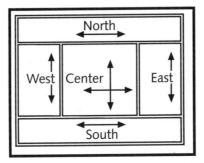

**Figure 13-3**  The BorderLayout strategy

When a container with a **BorderLayout** is resized to be wider or narrower, the north and south regions change in width, but the sizes of the west and east regions do not change. When the window is stretched vertically, the west and east regions get taller or shorter, but the north and south regions do not change. The central region can expand and contract in both directions.

When you add a component to a container using a **BorderLayout** object, you specify in which area of the layout to place the component, using one of the constants (NORTH, SOUTH, EAST, WEST, and CENTER) that are defined in the **BorderLayout** class. For example, the following lines of code give a container a border layout and add a component called `newPanel` to the center of the layout:

```
setLayout( new BorderLayout() );
add( newPanel, BorderLayout.CENTER );
```

You can put only one component into each area, and the size of the component adjusts to fill the area. This is not as restrictive as it might seem because each component can also be a container. That container can have its own layout manager and can hold any number of components. When the window is displayed, the border layout manager investigates the component in each area to see how much space it needs. If the component is a container, the sizing algorithm recursively determines how much space the components within the container need. As a result, border layouts give you great flexibility to group components and create a wide variety of arrangements.

By default, the **JWindow**, **JFrame**, and **JDialog** containers have border layouts.

**13**

In the preceding `ExampleLayouts` example, the following lines were used to implement the border layout strategy shown in Figure 13-3 and to produce the output that appears in Figure 13-4.

```
private JPanel border
    = new JPanel( new BorderLayout() );
// Add the buttons to the border layout
border.add( new JButton( "One" ),
            BorderLayout.NORTH );
border.add( new JButton( "Two" ),
            BorderLayout.WEST );
border.add( new JButton( "Three" ),
            BorderLayout.CENTER );
border.add( new JButton( "Four" ),
            BorderLayout.EAST );
border.add( new JButton( "Five" ),
            BorderLayout.SOUTH );
```

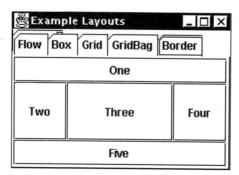

**Figure 13-4**   A BorderLayout

**Mini Quiz 13-1**

Draw diagrams of how the pane with a border layout would look with components in:

Only North and South areas

Only East and West areas

Only North and Center areas

Only East, Center, and South areas

Only North, East, and West areas

## Flow Layouts

The class **FlowLayout** implements the **LayoutManager** interface to support flow layouts. If the container uses a flow layout, components are arranged in a row across the area of the container. When you add a component, it is added to become the rightmost component in the row. If there is not enough room, the row wraps so that the new component starts a new row. Figure 13-5 shows one possible effect of positioning four buttons in a container with a flow layout, with alignment set to **FlowLayout.CENTER**.

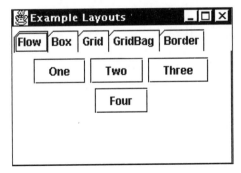

**Figure 13-5**   A FlowLayout

When you create a **FlowLayout** object, you can specify with an argument to the constructor whether components are centered, right-justified, or left-justified. By default, the components are centered. The following line of code gives a container a centered flow layout, and adds a button labeled "Cancel" to the container:

```
setLayout( new FlowLayout( FlowLayout.CENTER ) );
add( new Button( "Cancel" ) );
```

Unlike a component in a border layout that expands to fill the area in which it is placed, components in a flow layout retain their preferred size. Resizing the window does not change the size of the components in a flow layout but may adjust their positions.

By default, **JPanel** objects have flow layouts.

In the preceding `ExampleLayouts` example, the following lines were used to implement the **FlowLayout** strategy shown in Figure 13-5:

```
private JPanel flow
    = new JPanel( new FlowLayout( FlowLayout.CENTER ) );
// Add the buttons to the flow layout
flow.add( new JButton( "One" ) );
flow.add( new JButton( "Two" ) );
flow.add( new JButton( "Three" ) );
flow.add( new JButton( "Four" ) );
```

## Grid Layouts

The class **GridLayout** implements the **LayoutManager2** interface to support grid layouts. This layout manager divides the area of the container into a grid of equally sized rows and columns. When you add a component to the container, it automatically goes into the next cell in the grid. Components are put into cells in row order, as shown in Figure 13-6.

13

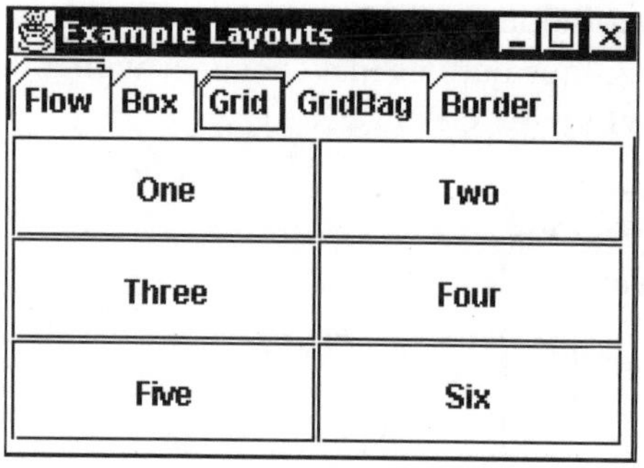

**Figure 13-6**  A GridLayout

When you set up a grid layout, you specify the number of rows and columns as arguments to the constructor. You can specify zero to mean an unlimited number. However, you cannot specify a row or column position when you add a component to the container. Components are automatically put into the next cell, in a left to right order, filling rows from top to bottom. You cannot skip cells or insert a component into an arbitrarily selected cell. When the user resizes a window that has a grid layout, the cells in the grid change size uniformly, and the appearance of components in those cells adjusts accordingly.

In the preceding `ExampleLayouts` example, the following lines were used to implement the **GridLayout** strategy shown in Figure 13-6:

```
private JPanel grid
   = new JPanel( new GridLayout( 3, 2 ) );
// Add the buttons to the grid layout
grid.add( new JButton( "One" ) );
grid.add( new JButton( "Two" ) );
grid.add( new JButton( "Three" ) );
grid.add( new JButton( "Four" ) );
grid.add( new JButton( "Five" ) );
grid.add( new JButton( "Six" ) );
```

## Grid-Bag Layouts

The class **GridBagLayout** implements the **LayoutManager2** interface to support grid-bag layouts. This layout manager is more flexible than a grid layout because components can be put in any cell and can span more than one row or column. A grid-bag layout is based on a rectangular grid, just like a grid layout, but it uses a helper class, **GridBagConstraints**, to specify how each component should be located within the grid. With the grid-bag layout, you can create effects such as the arrangement shown in Figure 13-7.

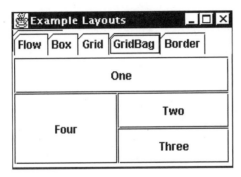

**Figure 13-7**  A GridBagLayout

Using a grid-bag layout is not as simple as using a grid, border, or flow layout. You should create a **GridBagConstraints** object for each component that you put in the container. In the **GridBagConstraints** object, you set fields to indicate factors such as the following:

➤ How many vertical or horizontal cells to span.

➤ Where to position the component in the container, and whether that position should be relative to that of the previous component.

➤ Where to orient the component if it does not fill its cell.

➤ How to display a component that is too big for its cell.

The Java platform documentation describes the full set of methods for the **GridBagLayout** class and fields in the **GridBagConstraints** class.

You must do some extra work to take advantage of the power of a grid-bag layout. For instance, in the preceding `ExampleLayouts` example, the following lines implemented the **GridBagLayout** strategy shown in Figure 13-7. Note that the constraints apply to the next cell put into the container. For example, the button labeled "One" goes into the default cell (0, 0) and fills the row because its width is set to the remainder of the row. Then, the button labeled "Two" goes into cell (1, 1) and button "Three" goes into cell (2, 1). Finally, the button labeled "Four" goes into cell (0, 1) but is two rows high. You can vary the **weightx** constraint from row to row and **weighty** constraint from column to column. The **weightx** field controls relative height of rows and **weighty** controls the relative width of columns. Setting both to 1.0, as in this example, makes all rows and columns expand uniformly to fill the container:

```
private JPanel gridBag
   = new JPanel( new GridBagLayout() );
// Add the buttons to the gridbag layout
GridBagConstraints c = new GridBagConstraints();
c.fill = GridBagConstraints.BOTH;
c.weightx = 1.0;
```

**13**

```
c.weighty = 1.0;
c.gridwidth = GridBagConstraints.REMAINDER;
gridBag.add( new JButton( "One" ), c );
c.gridy = 1;
c.gridx = 1;
gridBag.add( new JButton( "Two" ), c );
c.gridy = 2;
gridBag.add( new JButton( "Three" ), c );
c.gridy = 1;
c.gridx = 0;
c.gridheight = 2;
c.gridwidth = 1;
gridBag.add( new JButton( "Four" ), c );
```

## Card Layouts

The class **CardLayout** implements the **LayoutManager2** interface to support card layouts. If a container has a card layout, the components are stacked on top of each other, like a deck of cards, so that only one component is visible at a time. This layout is not used frequently, but it may work when you want users to be able to view the components in a container one component at a time, and in order. The **CardLayout** class provides the methods first, last, and next that you can call to make a component visible.

---

### Mini Quiz 13-2

The AWT component set has no equivalent to the **JTabbedPane**. Can you design a scheme using panels and a combination of card layouts and border layouts that creates an effect similar to that of a tabbed pane?

---

## Box Layouts

The class **Box** is a Swing container that uses the **BoxLayout** strategy. **BoxLayout** implements the **LayoutManager2** interface to define a layout strategy that is similar to the **FlowLayout** strategy. However, the two-box layout does not wrap to create additional lines. All components are placed in a single line, which may be arranged horizontally or vertically. Figure 13-8 shows a **BoxLayout** with the components stacked vertically.

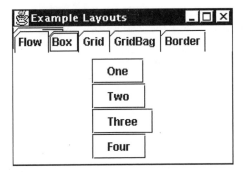

**Figure 13-8**    A BoxLayout

In the preceding `ExampleLayouts` example, the following lines implemented the **BoxLayout** strategy shown in Figure 13-8:

```
private Box box = new Box( BoxLayout.Y_AXIS );
private JPanel boxPanel = new JPanel();
// Add the buttons to the box
box.add( new JButton( "One" ) );
box.add( new JButton( "Two" ) );
box.add( new JButton( "Three" ) );
box.add( new JButton( "Four" ) );
```

## Tabbed Panes

The class **JTabbedPane** isn't a true layout manager in the sense that it does not implement the **LayoutManager** interface. However, from the point of view that a tabbed pane does control the positioning and presentation of components, it can be considered a type of layout manager.

In the preceding `ExampleLayouts` example, the following lines positioned the panels containing the button layouts shown in Figures 13-6 through 13-10:

```
// create a tabbed pane and put the panels into it
JTabbedPane tp = new JTabbedPane();
tp.addTab( "Flow", flow );
boxPanel.add( box );
tp.addTab( "Box", boxPanel );
tp.addTab( "Grid", grid );
tp.addTab( "GridBag", gridBag );
tp.addTab( "Border", border );
setContentPane( tp );
```

## Split Panes

Similar to the class **JTabbedPane**, the class **JSplitPane** is not a true layout manager because it does not implement the **LayoutManager** interface. However, from the point of view that a split pane does control the positioning and presentation of components, it can be considered a type of layout manager.

For an example program later in the chapter that includes a split pane, refer to the example program in the section "Text-Entry Components" and its output.

## Positioning Components Manually

If you want to position components manually, you can suppress the layout manager with the following method call:

```
setLayout( null );
```

If you turn off the layout manager by specifying a null layout manager, you must position and shape all the components in the container. The **Component** class provides methods for doing this. In particular, you can call **setBounds** to specify the height, width, and upper-left corner of a component. You can use the **setLocation** method to reposition a component relative to the upper left of its container, and **setSize** to resize a component. All of these methods operate on pixel addresses. You may want to undertake the considerable effort of arranging components for the following reasons:

➤ To gain more precise control than an available layout manager provides.

➤ As part of creating a layout manager of your own.

# LABELS, BUTTONS, AND CHECK BOXES

Labels, buttons, and check boxes are fundamental parts of a GUI. Labels add text that typically explains the purpose of the other elements of a user interface. They can also display a message, such as a status line, to the user. Buttons and check boxes provide the opportunity to make selections and trigger actions.

The **JLabel** class inherits directly from **JComponent**, but all the button classes extend the class **AbstractButton**. The **AbstractButton** class extends **JComponent** and provides the implementation of behavior that is common to all button classes. Figure 13-9 shows **AbstractButton** and its button subclasses.

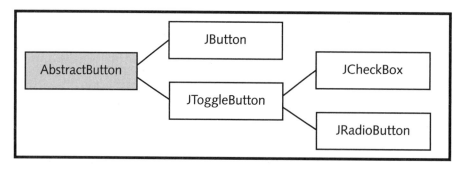

**Figure 13-9**  AbstractButton and its subclasses

Details about each of the Swing label, button, and check box classes are provided next. Lists of all the constructors that are available for creating objects of these classes are provided also.

---

*Class*

**javax.swing.JLabel**

---

*Purpose*

A **JLabel** object is a single line of read-only text. A common use of **JLabel** objects is to position descriptive text above or beside other components.

---

*Constructors*

➤ **JLabel()**
**JLabel( Icon** *icon* **)**
**JLabel( Icon** *icon,* **int** *horizontalAlignment* **)**
**JLabel( String** *text* **)**
**JLabel( String** *text,* **int** *horizontalAlignment* **)**
**JLabel( String** *text,* **Icon** *icon,* **int** *horizontalAlignment* **)**
The constructor with no arguments creates a horizontally left-justified, empty **JLabel**. Use the **String** argument to specify the contents of the **Jlabel** and the **Icon** argument to add a graphic picture. The alignment is an integer, and you can specify any one of the following fields: **JLabel.LEFT**, **JLabel.CENTER**, **JLabel.RIGHT**, **JLabel.LEADING**, or **JLabel.TRAILING**. Use the methods **setHorizontalTextPosition** and **setVerticalTextPosition** to specify the position of the text relative to the graphic.

---

*Class*

**javax.swing.JButton**

---

*Purpose*

A **JButton** object is a push button with a text label.

---

*Constructors*

➤ **JButton()**
**JButton( Icon** *icon* **)**
**JButton( String** *label* **)**
**JButton( String** *label,* **Icon** *icon* **)**
When you create a button, you can specify the text that appears on the button as a **String** argument of the constructor. It is also possible to add a graphic to the button by specifying an **Icon** object. Use the methods **setHorizontalTextPosition** and **setVerticalTextPosition** to specify the position of the button label relative to the graphic.

---

**13**

---

*Class*

### javax.swing.JToggleButton

---

*Purpose*

A **JToggleButton** object is a push button with a text label. Clicking on the button causes the button to alternate between the pressed and released states.

---

*Constructors*

➤ **JToggleButton()**
**JToggleButton( Icon** *icon* **)**
**JToggleButton( String** *label* **)**
**JToggleButton( String** *label*, **Icon** *icon* **)**
**JToggleButton( Icon** *icon*, **boolean** *pressed* **)**
**JToggleButton( String** *label*, **boolean** *pressed* **)**
**JToggleButton( String** *label*, **Icon** *icon*, **boolean** *pressed* **)**
When you create a button, you can specify the text that appears on the button as a **String** argument of the constructor. Use the boolean parameter to specify whether the button is initially pressed or released. Also, you can add a graphic to the button by specifying an **Icon** object. Use the methods **setHorizontalTextPosition** and **setVerticalTextPosition** to specify the position of the button label relative to the graphic. You also can create groups of toggle buttons. A **ButtonGroup** object may contain a set of **JToggleButton** objects and permit the user to select only one button in the group at a time. To combine a **JToggleButton** with others in a group, construct a **ButtonGroup** and add the toggle button to the group. Toggle buttons in a **ButtonGroup** are mutually exclusive, which means that when the user selects one, all others in the same group are deselected automatically.

---

*Class*

### javax.swing.JCheckBox

---

*Purpose*

A **JCheckBox** object is a check box with a text label.

---

*Constructors*

➤ **JCheckBox()**
**JCheckBox( Icon** *icon* **)**
**JCheckBox( String** *label* **)**
**JCheckBox( String** *label*, **Icon** *icon* **)**

**JCheckBox( Icon** *icon,* **boolean** *selected* **)**
**JCheckBox( String** *label,* **boolean** *selected* **)**
**JCheckBox( String** *label,* **Icon** *icon,* **boolean** *selected* **)**
The **String** contains the text that labels the check box. The **boolean** indicates whether the check box is on or off, and it is set to off, or **false,** by default. You also can add a graphic to the check box by specifying an **Icon** object or create groups of check boxes. A **ButtonGroup** may contain a set of **JCheckBox** objects from which the user can check only one box in the group at a time. To combine a **JCheckBox** with others in a group, construct a **ButtonGroup** and add the check box to the group. Check boxes in a **ButtonGroup** are mutually exclusive, which means that when the user selects one, all others in the same group are deselected automatically.

*Class*

**javax.swing.JRadioButton**

*Purpose*

A **JRadioButton** object is a radio button with a text label.

*Constructors*

➤ **JRadioButton()**
**JRadioButton( Icon** *icon* **)**
**JRadioButton( String** *label* **)**
**JRadioButton( String** *label,* **Icon** *icon* **)**
**JRadioButton( Icon** *icon,* **boolean** *selected* **)**
**JRadioButton( String** *label,* **boolean** *selected* **)**
**JRadioButton( String** *label,* **Icon** *icon,* **boolean** *selected* **)**
The **String** contains the text that labels the radio button. The **boolean** indicates whether the radio button is on or off, and it is set to off, or **false**, by default. It is also possible to add a graphic to the button by specifying an **Icon** object. You can create groups of radio buttons. A **ButtonGroup** may contain a set of **JRadioButton** objects from which the user can select only one button in the group at a time. To combine a **JRadioButton** with others in a group, construct a **ButtonGroup** and add the button to the group. Radio buttons in a **ButtonGroup** are mutually exclusive, which means that when the user selects one, all others in the same group are deselected automatically.

**13**

*Class*

**javax.swing.ButtonGroup**

---

*Purpose*

A **ButtonGroup** object is a group of mutually exclusive buttons. A **ButtonGroup** may contain a set of button objects from which the user can check only one box in the group at a time. You can mix **JToggleButton**, **JRadioButton**, and **JCheckbox** objects in one group, but groups usually contain sets of radio buttons. Buttons in a **ButtonGroup** are mutually exclusive, which means that when the user selects one, all others in the same group are deselected automatically.

---

*Constructors*

➤ **ButtonGroup()**
  Only the default constructor is available. Use the **add** method to add a button to the group.

---

*Class*

**javax.swing.ImageIcon**

---

*Purpose*

The **ImageIcon** class defines objects representing small fixed-size pictures that are used typically to decorate components. This class implements the **Icon** interface.

---

*Constructors*

➤ **ImageIcon()**
  **ImageIcon( byte[]** *imageData* **)**
  **ImageIcon( byte[]** *imageData***, String** *description* **)**
  **ImageIcon( Image** *image* **)**
  ImageIcon( Image *image*, **String** *description* )
  **ImageIcon( String** *filename* **)**
  **ImageIcon( String** *filename***, String** *description* **)**
  **ImageIcon( URL location )**
  **ImageIcon( URL location, String description )**
  You can build **ImageIcon** objects from binary data by supplying an array of bytes from an existing **Image** object, from an image stored in a file (typically, in .gif format), or from a URL. Also, you can supply a **String** that contains a description of the image to the constructor.

---

The following is a program that exercises many of the classes described previously. A breakdown of this code follows the output. This program defines the class `ButtonsAndBoxes` to demonstrate the use of radio buttons, check boxes, and toggle buttons. Each type of button has its own panel, and the panels have titled borders to indicate the type of button. The program uses colorful icons to show the flexibility of these classes and to make the GUI more appealing. Before you run this program, copy all the .gif files from the folder into which you unpacked the **examples.jar** file into the current directory. If the JVM cannot find the .gif files, the program runs, but the icons do not display.

```java
package examples.windows;
import javax.swing.*;
import java.awt.*;
import java.util.Enumeration;
/** An example class used to demonstrate the use of
  * the JToggleButton, JCheckBox, and JRadioButton
  * components
  */
public class ButtonsAndBoxes extends JFrame {
   /** Class constructor method
     * @param titleText Window's title bar text
     */
   public ButtonsAndBoxes( String titleText ) {
      super( titleText );
      addWindowListener( new WindowCloser() );
      JPanel left = new JPanel( new GridLayout( 0, 1 ) );
      left.setBorder(
         BorderFactory.createTitledBorder(
            "Button group" ) );
      ButtonGroup bg = new ButtonGroup();
      bg.add( new JRadioButton( "ribeye" ) );
      bg.add( new JRadioButton( "filet mignon" ) );
      bg.add( new JRadioButton( "T-bone" ) );
      Enumeration e = bg.getElements();
      while( e.hasMoreElements() ) {
         JRadioButton rb = (JRadioButton) e.nextElement();
         rb.setIcon( new ImageIcon( "bulb1.gif" ) );
         rb.setSelectedIcon(
            new ImageIcon( "bulb2.gif" ) );
         left.add( rb );
      }
      JPanel right = new JPanel( new GridLayout( 0, 1 ) );
      right.setBorder(
         BorderFactory.createTitledBorder(
            "Independent check boxes" ) );
      right.add( new JCheckBox( "cake" ) );
      right.add( new JCheckBox( "pie" ) );
      right.add( new JCheckBox( "soft drink" ) );
      right.add( new JCheckBox( "fries" ) );
      JPanel bottom = new JPanel();
      bottom.setBorder(
         BorderFactory.createTitledBorder(
            "Toggle buttons" ) );
```

**13**

```
        bottom.add( new JToggleButton(
            "burger", new ImageIcon( "burger.gif" ) ) );
        bottom.add( new JToggleButton(
            "hot dog", new ImageIcon( "hotdog.gif" ) ) );
        bottom.add( new JToggleButton(
            "pizza", new ImageIcon( "pizza.gif" ) ) );
        Container cp = getContentPane();
        cp.setLayout( new GridBagLayout() );
        GridBagConstraints c = new GridBagConstraints();
        c.fill = GridBagConstraints.BOTH;
        c.weightx = 1.0;
        c.weighty = 1.0;
        cp.add( left, c );
        c.gridwidth = GridBagConstraints.REMAINDER;
        cp.add( right, c );
        cp.add( bottom, c );
        pack();
        setVisible( true );
    }
    /** The test method for the class
      * @param args not used
      */
    public static void main( String[] args ) {
        new ButtonsAndBoxes(
            "Example Buttons and Check Boxes" );
    }
}
```

When you run this program, you will see that the **ButtonsAndBoxes** GUI could be the menu of a fast-food outlet. The radio buttons display as labeled images instead of the default labeled circle, and the buttons have icons showing pictures of menu items. Allowing for differences in operating systems, the output should be similar to Figure 13-10.

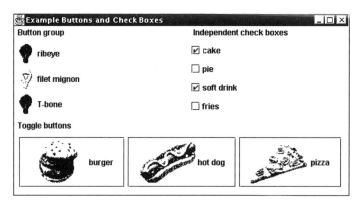

**Figure 13-10**   Output of the ButtonsAndBoxes class

The class encapsulating the menu-drawing program is called
`ButtonsAndBoxes`. The structure of this example is similar to the preceding
examples in this chapter, so only those program statements that pertain to the
classes presented in this section are discussed in the code breakdown.

First, a panel is created with a one-column grid layout and a border titled "Button
group". This panel will be put in the upper-left part of the frame window.

```
JPanel left = new JPanel( new GridLayout( 0, 1 ) );
left.setBorder(
   BorderFactory.createTitledBorder(
      "Button group" ) );
```

A button group is created to hold a mutually exclusive set of buttons. In this
case, three radio buttons are created and added to the group. These buttons are
initially created with only a text label:

```
ButtonGroup bg = new ButtonGroup();
bg.add( new JRadioButton( "ribeye" ) );
bg.add( new JRadioButton( "filet mignon" ) );
bg.add( new JRadioButton( "T-bone" ) );
```

The radio buttons must then be added to the panel. A while loop uses an
**Enumeration** object to iterate through the list of radio buttons in the group
and place each one into the panel. At the same time, each of the radio buttons
is assigned two images: one to be used when the button is selected and the
other when the button is not selected. The images are pictures of lightbulbs. A
lighted bulb indicates the selected button.

```
Enumeration e = bg.getElements();
while( e.hasMoreElements() ) {
   JRadioButton rb = (JRadioButton) e.nextElement();
   rb.setIcon( new ImageIcon( "bulb1.gif" ) );
   rb.setSelectedIcon(
      new ImageIcon( "bulb2.gif" ) );
   left.add( rb );
}
```

**13**

Another panel with a single-column grid layout is created to hold the list of
check boxes that appear in the upper-right part of the frame window. This
panel is also given a border titled "Independent check boxes" because these
boxes are not in a group:

```
JPanel right = new JPanel( new GridLayout( 0, 1 ) );
right.setBorder(
   BorderFactory.createTitledBorder(
      "Independent check boxes" ) );
```

Four check boxes are created and added to the panel. Because they are not part of a button group, any number of the check boxes may be selected at the same time. These check boxes do not have associated images:

```
right.add( new JCheckBox( "cake" ) );
right.add( new JCheckBox( "pie" ) );
right.add( new JCheckBox( "soft drink" ) );
right.add( new JCheckBox( "fries" ) );
```

The panel to be used at the bottom of the window is created with the panel's default flow layout and is given a border titled "Toggle buttons". Three toggle buttons are added to the panel, each with a text description and a graphic image.

```
JPanel bottom = new JPanel();
bottom.setBorder(
   BorderFactory.createTitledBorder(
      "Toggle buttons" ) );
bottom.add( new JToggleButton(
   "burger", new ImageIcon( "burger.gif" ) ) );
bottom.add( new JToggleButton(
   "hot dog", new ImageIcon( "hotdog.gif" ) ) );
bottom.add( new JToggleButton(
   "pizza", new ImageIcon( "pizza.gif" ) ) );
```

After the panels are created and filled, they must be added to the frame window's content pane. A grid bag layout is used for the frame window and a constraints object is created to hold positioning information:

```
Container cp = getContentPane();
cp.setLayout( new GridBagLayout() );
GridBagConstraints c = new GridBagConstraints();
```

The default constraints are accepted for use by the method with a few exceptions. First, the fill attribute is set so that the components will stretch to fill the frame in both directions. The weighting of 1.0 for both the $x$ and $y$ direction causes all components to share equally when the frame is stretched or shrunk:

```
c.fill = GridBagConstraints.BOTH;
c.weightx = 1.0;
c.weighty = 1.0;
```

The upper-left panel is added first. Then, the grid width constraint is set so that the next two components added will stretch to fill the two rows of the layout.

```
cp.add( left, c );
c.gridwidth = GridBagConstraints.REMAINDER;
cp.add( right, c );
cp.add( bottom, c );
```

# EVENTS

A user interface usually displays components and graphics, but it is not just output. It must interact with user input as well.

In a GUI for a Java application, **events** are objects that encapsulate changes in state that are initiated by the user. Generally, the user triggers events by pressing and releasing keys on the keyboard or by moving and clicking the mouse. Some events, such as button clicks or text entry, have meaning only for specific components in your GUI. Others, such as resizing a window or moving focus from window to window, also are recognized by the native operating system.

The AWT API includes the package **java.awt.event** in which you will find the classes from this API that encapsulate the events that relate to the GUI components in your application or applet. All classes in this package that define events are subclasses of the class **java.awt.event.AWTEvent** which is a subclass of **java.util.EventObject**. **EventObject** is the superclass of all Java platform classes that define events, whether they are GUI events or not.

The Swing API separates its event-related classes into a package called **javax.swing.event**. It is worth noting that most Swing event classes are direct subclasses of **EventObject**, not **AWTEvent**.

A large part of programming a GUI involves providing handlers for events. In the Java programming language, this task is straightforward because you create event handlers by implementing predefined listener interfaces or extending predefined adapter classes. Listeners and adapters are described later in this chapter.

To catch and handle events, you adopt the "Hollywood model" of programming: "Don't call us, we'll call you." In other words, you do not poll the environment looking for events. When an event occurs, the event dispatch thread calls you. In parts of your code not directly related to events, you can ignore events. Like different threads in a multithreaded application, these parts of your code just carry on with their usual business. When events occur, the JVM or your Web browser receives messages from the operating system. The classes in the **java.awt.event** package determine the nature of the event and identify the appropriate component. The JVM calls the object that implements the listener interface registered for the event. Through listeners, events call you.

Table 13-3 lists the types of common AWT events. Table 13-4 lists common Swing events.

**13**

**Table 13-3** Description of common AWT event classes

| Event class | Description |
|---|---|
| **AWT Event class** | Description |
| **AdjustmentEvent** | Adjustment events indicate a change to an object of a class that implements the **Adjustable** interface. The **JScrollBar** class is an example of an **Adjustable** class of objects. |
| **ComponentEvent** | Component events occur when a component has been moved, resized, shown, or hidden. The event dispatch thread typically handles such events. |
| **ContainerEvent** | Container events occur when the contents of a container have changed or when a component has been added or removed. Use this event as notification only because the event dispatch thread handles these events. |
| **FocusEvent** | Multitasking operating systems let a user open more than one window simultaneously, but only one window at a time can be highlighted and brought to the foreground. The foreground window is said to have **focus**, and the user usually brings a window into focus by clicking the mouse over it. A focus event occurs when a component gets or loses focus. |
| **InputEvent** | The **InputEvent** class is the superclass for both keyboard and mouse events. It has no corresponding listener interface. |
| **ItemEvent** | Item events occur when the state of an item within a component that implements the **ItemSelectable** interface has changed. **JCheckBox**, **JComboBox**, and **JList** are examples of selectable components. The **JComboBox** and **JList** classes are discussed later in this chapter. |
| **KeyEvent** | A key event occurs when the user releases a key on the keyboard. |
| **MouseEvent** | The events encapsulated by this class are pressing the mouse button, releasing the button, dragging the mouse, and moving the mouse. |
| **PaintEvent** | Paint events indicate that a component should have its **update** method invoked. The event dispatch thread handles these events automatically. |
| **TextEvent** | When the user edits the text value in components such as **JTextField** or **JTextArea**, a text event occurs. The classes that provide text components are discussed later in this chapter. |
| **WindowEvent** | User actions relating to windows generate instances of this event class. |

**Table 13-4**   Description of common Swing event classes

| Event class | Description |
|---|---|
| Swing Event class | Description |
| ChangeEvent | **ChangeEvent** objects are used to notify interested parties that the state has changed in the event source. It carries no details about the change that has happened. |
| InternalFrameEvent | The **InternalFrameEvent** class inherits from **AWTEvent** and adds support for **JInternalFrame** objects as the event source. |
| ListSelectionEvent | This event class is used to indicate a change in the current list selection. |
| MenuEvent | **MenuEvent** is used to notify interested parties that the menu which is the event source has been posted, selected, or canceled. It carries no details about the change that has happened. Menus are described later in this chapter. |
| TableModelEvent | A **TableModelEvent** object is used to notify listeners that a date in a table model has changed. Like all Swing components, there is a separate model class to hold the data displayed in the component. For tables, lists, and trees, the ability to deal with the model separately from the component adds great power to the Swing classes. The **JTable** class and its model are explained later in this chapter. |
| TreeSelectionEvent | This event indicates a change in the current tree selection. |

Each event object contains the appropriate data for the event. You can call methods of the event classes to access this information. Table 13-5 shows some methods you can call to get information about an event in an event handler.

**13**

**Table 13-5**   Select methods of the event classes

| Class | Method | Description |
|---|---|---|
| AWTEvent | int getID() | This superclass method returns the type of the current event. |
| ComponentEvent | Component getComponent() | This method returns the component involved in the event. |
| ItemEvent | Object getItem() | This method returns the object that was either selected or deselected. |
| ItemEvent | int getStateChange() | The return value is **ItemEvent.SELECTED** or **ItemEvent.DESELECTED**. A method to indicate the change of state is required because the only handler in the **ItemListener** interface, **itemStateChanged**, does not make this distinction. |

*continued*

**Table 13-5**  Select methods of the event classes (continued)

| Class | Method | Description |
|-------|--------|-------------|
| KeyEvent | int getKeyChar() | This method returns the Unicode character that was typed. |
| MouseEvent | int getClickCount() | This method distinguishes between single and double mouse clicks. |
| InputEvent | int getModifiers() | The return value indicates which mouse button is involved. Different operating systems support one, two, or three mouse buttons. |
| MouseEvent | Point getPoint() | This method returns the location for the mouse event. |
| PaintEvent | Rectangle getUpdatedRect() | This method returns the rectangle representing the area to be painted. |
| WindowEvent | Window getWindow() | This method returns the window that is the source of the event. |

To make the method **AWTEvent.getID** easier to use, each event that sub-classes it defines integer constants for events associated with the class. For example, the **FocusEvent** class defines the two constants **FOCUS_GAINED** and **FOCUS_LOST**. Very often, the context of each event handler gives you the same information as the **getID** method, so you do not have to call this method. For example, there are two handlers for **FocusEvent** objects in the **FocusListener** interface: **focusGained** and **focusLost**.

## Listeners and Adapters

The AWT and Swing APIs define a set of interfaces called listeners. Each kind of event has a listener interface, and each listener has methods for every event that can occur in its event class. For example, the TextListener interface corresponds to the TextEvent class. The only thing a user can do to a TextField or TextArea object is change the contents of the text component. Thus, the only method in the TextListener interface is textValueChanged.

Use listener interfaces to create handlers for events. You must complete two steps to create a handler for an event:

1. Define a class that implements the appropriate listener interface. Your class provides the handler by implementing the methods that are declared in the interface.

2. Register an instance of the class with the component affected by the event.

The following syntax boxes give details on the methods used to register listener objects with a component and also on the listener interfaces. They are presented using generic names because all of these methods and interfaces follow the same naming pattern.

*Class*

*Any component class*

*Methods*

➤ **void add***xxx***Listener(** *xxx***Listener** *object* **)**
The **add***xxx***Listener** methods register a listener with a component; they all return **void**. The *xxx* is the type of the listener. All components have the methods **addComponentListener**, **addFocusListener**, **addMouseListener**, and **addMouseMotionListener**.

*Code Example*

```
class myHandler implements TextListener {
    public void textValueChanged( TextEvent e ) {
        // implementation of textValueChanged omitted
    }
}
TextListener tl = new myHandler();
JTextArea t = new JTextArea();
t.addTextListener( tl );
```

*Code Dissection*

These lines of code are excerpts from a program that handles text events.

**13**

The structure of the listener interfaces is regular and predictable. All the methods of all the interfaces follow the same form.

*Interface*

*xxx***Listener**

*Dissection*

Each event class has an associated listener interface. The *xxx* represents the name of an event class.

*Methods*

➤ **void** *xxx***Event(** *xxx***Event** *E* **)**

➤ All listener methods have return type **void.**

➤ All listener methods take one argument: an object of an event class.

➤ All listener methods begin with the same word as the listener.

➤ For example, all the methods in the **ComponentListener** interface begin with **component**, have an argument of type **ComponentEvent**, and return **void**. The methods in a **ComponentListener** are **componentMoved, componentShown**, and **componentHidden**.

➤ Mouse events are the one exception to this pattern. Mouse event handlers are split over two interfaces: **MouseListener** and **MouseMotionListener**. The methods in these two interfaces all begin with **mouse**, and all take a single **MouseEvent** object as a parameter. The **MouseListener** methods are **mouseClicked, mousePressed, mouseReleased, mouseEntered**, and **mouseExited**. The **MouseMotionListener** methods are **mouseDragged** and **mouseMoved**.

---

You can implement a listener interface directly. For listener interfaces with more than one method, you can alternatively implement the listener indirectly by extending its adapter class.

The AWT and Swing APIs provide several adapter classes that implement listener interfaces for you. The adapters provide empty implementations of all the methods in the interface. The advantage of the adapter classes is that classes that extend them can implement only the handlers of interest and inherit the empty implementations of all other methods.

The adapter classes follow a similar naming pattern to the listener interfaces, except that the names are *xxx*Adapter rather than *xxx*Listener, where *xxx* is the type event for which the interface is listening.

Generally, extending adapter classes is preferable when a minority of the methods in the interface are of interest. Using an adapter simplifies the coding but does not change the mechanism. The example programs in Chapter 12 and this chapter use adapter classes.

The listener interfaces in **java.awt.event** all extend the interface EventListener from the package **java.util**, just as the adapter classes extend Object from **java.lang**. The predefined adapter classes for listeners are all abstract classes.

Any class can handle events, not just GUI components; a class only needs to implement the appropriate interface and register itself with the object that generates the events.

## Events That Start Long Operations

At times, a user action will begin a long operation. For example, clicking a menu item that causes the contents of a file to be retrieved from another computer somewhere on the Internet starts an operation that could take a minute or longer. In such cases, it is important that the long operation be executed on a separate thread and not on the event dispatch thread. Failing to do so will cause the user interface to become unresponsive because no other events can be handled until the long operation completes and frees the event dispatch thread.

However, using separate threads to handle long operations can cause problems because Swing components are not thread-safe. If more than one thread attempts to access a Swing component at the same time, errors will result. This is because, for the sake of speed, the methods of Swing components are not synchronized. So, if the thread that retrieves the contents of a file from the Internet attempts to write those contents into a text area in the user interface, it may conflict with the event dispatch thread as it updates the same text area.

What is the solution? The solution is to make sure that all updates to the user interface are made by the event dispatch thread. Obviously, if only one thread updates the user interface, no conflicts will occur. In the **javax.swing.SwingUtilities** class, the **invokeLater** and **invokeAndWait** methods allow other threads to define updates to Swing components for the event dispatch thread to execute. The only difference between these two methods is that **invokeAndWait** blocks the thread that calls it until the event dispatch thread completes the updates. The **invokeLater** method does not block. Both **invokeLater** and **invokeAndWait** take a single **Runnable** object as input.

Below is the outline of a class that would execute on a thread separate from the event dispatch thread. In its **run** method, it uses the **invokeLater** method to update a text field to indicate when the operation begins and when it ends. Anonymous inner classes are used to create the **Runnable** objects that are passed as input to the **invokeLater** method:

```
package examples.windows;
import javax.swing.*;
public class ReadFromInternet extends Thread {
   private JTextField status;
   public ReadFromInternet( JTextField tf ) {
      status = tf;
   }
   public void run() {
      SwingUtilities.invokeLater( new Runnable() {
            public void run() {
               status.setText(
                  "Beginning the operation" );
            }
         }
      );

      // read the file from the Internet
```

**13**

```
        SwingUtilities.invokeLater( new Runnable() {
            public void run() {
                status.setText( "Operation complete" );
            }
        }
    );
    }
}
```

# MENUS, TOOLBARS, AND ACTIONS

Even before GUIs became commonplace in application software, applications
have had menu bars and menu items for organizing the functions available
within the application. As GUIs proliferated and became more sophisticated,
another element for organizing function, the toolbar, also became very common. So it should come as no surprise that the Swing API would have components for implementing menu systems and toolbars.

Because many of the functions available on toolbars also are available in the
menu system, Swing provides a mechanism, the **Action** interface, for defining
objects that can be put into both toolbars and menus. These action objects
provide a single point of control and avoid duplication.

Within the Swing component hierarchy, menus and menu items are subclasses
of the **AbstractButton** class. Figure 13-11 shows how the menu classes fit
within this hierarchy.

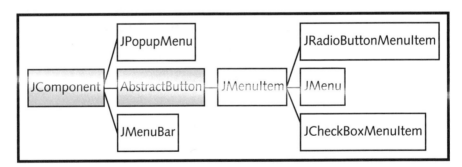

**Figure 13-11**   Menu classes in javax.swing

You can create instances of all the classes in the following syntax discussions
and combine them into menus by using these guidelines:

➤ To create a main menu for an application, use a **JMenuBar** object. Use
  the add method to add menus to the menu bar and the **setJMenuBar**
  method to add the menu bar to its window.

➤ For a menu that is associated with a component and pops up when the
  user clicks a component, create a **JPopupMenu** object.

➤ For every item in a menu, use an instance of **JMenuItem** or a subclass of **JMenuItem**.

➤ To nest menus, use **JMenu** objects. A **JMenu** object is a **JMenuItem** that is itself a menu.

➤ For a menu item that is also a check box, use a **JCheckBoxMenuItem** object.

➤ For a menu item that is also a radio button, use a **JRadioButtonMenuItem** object.

*Class*

**javax.swing.JMenuBar**

*Purpose*

The **JMenuBar** encapsulates the sort of menu bars you often see directly under the title of the **Frame** for an application. Items in the menu are arranged side-by-side starting on the left. Often each item is itself a pull-down menu.

*Constructors*

➤ **JMenuBar()**

A **JMenuBar** object can be set for the top-level containers **JApplet**, **JDialog**, **JFrame**, or **JInternalFrame**. Use the method **setJMenuBar** to associate a **JMenuBar** with one of these top-level containers.

*Class*

**13**

**javax.swing.JMenuItem**

*Purpose*

The **JMenuItem** encapsulates standard menu items that do not take the form of a check box or a radio button.

*Constructors*

➤ **JMenuItem()**
**JMenuItem( Icon** *icon* **)**
**JMenuItem( String** *label* **)**
**JMenuItem( String** *label*, **Icon** *icon* **)**
**JMenuItem( String** *label*, **int** *mnemonic* **)**
Usually, you give every item a label, an icon, or both so users can identify the menu item. You pass the label to the constructor as a **String** and the icon as an **Icon** object. A mnemonic character can be specified also. Use the method **setMnemonic** to add or change the mnemonic character after constructing the object. The mnemonic character is underlined when

the menu item is displayed, and then the user can type that key as an alternative of clicking on the item. If you want to set up an accelerator key (such as Ctrl+S for save) that is available regardless of whether the menu item is visible, use the method **setAccelerator** and specify a **java.awt.Keystroke** object as input.

*Class*

**javax.swing.JMenu**

*Purpose*

A **JMenu** object is a **JMenuItem** that is itself a pull-down menu from a **JMenuBar**.

*Constructors*

➤ **JMenu()**
**JMenu( String** *label* **)**
**JMenu( String** *label*, **boolean** *tearoff* **)**
The **String** is the label of the **JMenu** in the **JMenuBar** or other **JMenu** of which this object is a submenu. By default, **JMenu** objects disappear when the user releases the mouse button. If your native operating system supports tear-off menus, you can create a tear-off menu by setting the **boolean** argument to **true**. Tear-off menus are pull-down menus that can be detached from the menu bar and dragged to another position for convenient access.

*Class*

**javax.swing.JPopupMenu**

*Purpose*

A **PopupMenu** object is a menu that is not tied to the menu bar and can appear at a dynamically determined position within a component.

*Constructors*

➤ **PopupMenu()**
**PopupMenu( String name )**
When you create a **PopupMenu**, you can optionally give it a specific name by supplying a **String** argument to the constructor. Associate a popup menu with a component by calling the following method:

```
Component.add( PopupMenu popup )
```

The **add** method of **Component** class adds the specified **PopupMenu** object to the component.

*Class*

**javax.swing.JCheckboxMenuItem**

*Purpose*

A **JCheckboxMenuItem** object is a **JMenuItem** object that includes a check box.

*Constructors*

➤ **JCheckBoxMenuItem()**
**JCheckBoxMenuItem( Icon** *icon* **)**
**JCheckBoxMenuItem( String** *label* **)**
**JCheckBoxMenuItem( String** *label***, Icon** *icon* **)**
**JCheckBoxMenuItem( String** *label***, boolean** *selected* **)**
**JCheckBoxMenuItem( String** *label***, Icon** *icon***, boolean** *selected* **)**
When you create a **JCheckboxMenuItem**, you can optionally specify a label, a graphic, or both to appear beside the check box. The **boolean** argument indicates whether the check box is checked initially. Include this argument with the value **true** to override the default state, in which the check box is not checked.

*Class*

**javax.swing.JRadioButtonMenuItem**

*Purpose*

A **JRadioButtonMenuItem** object is a **JMenuItem** object that includes a radio button.

*Constructors*

➤ **JRadioButtonMenuItem()**
**JRadioButtonMenuItem( Icon** *icon* **)**
**JRadioButtonMenuItem( Icon** *icon***, boolean** *selected* **)**
**JRadioButtonMenuItem( String** *label* **)**
**JRadioButtonMenuItem( String** *label***, Icon** *icon* **)**
**JRadioButtonMenuItem( String** *label***, boolean** *selected* **)**
**JRadioButtonMenuItem( String** *label***, Icon** *icon***, boolean** *selected* **)**
When you create a **JRadioButtonMenuItem**, you can optionally specify a label, a graphic, or both to appear beside the check box. The **boolean** argument indicates whether the check box is initially checked. Include this argument with the value **true** to override the default state, in which the check box is not checked.

13

---

*Class*

**javax.swing.JToolBar**

---

*Purpose*

The **JToolBar** encapsulates the list of buttons you often see directly under the title or the menu bar for an application. By default, items in the toolbar are arranged side-by-side starting on the left.

---

*Constructors*

➤ **JToolBar()**

➤ **JToolBar( int** *orientation* **)**
When a **JToolBar** object is created, specifying its orientation is optional. The two possible values are **JToolBar.HORIZONTAL** and **JToolBar.VERTICAL**. The default orientation is horizontal.

---

*Class*

**javax.swing.AbstractAction**

---

*Purpose*

The **AbstractAction** class implements the **Action** interface and provides default implementations of all methods except the **actionPerformed** method. Subclassing **AbstractAction** greatly simplifies the job of defining classes that implement the **Action** interface.

---

*Constructors*

➤ **AbstractAction()**
**AbstractAction( String** *name* **)**
**AbstractAction( String** *name*, **Icon** *icon* **)**
**AbstractAction** is an abstract class and must be extended to be used. It is not possible to construct instances of this class. When you construct a subclass of **AbstractAction**, you can call the superclass constructor and optionally specify the name of the action, an icon for the action, or both.

---

The following is a program that exercises many of the classes described previously. A breakdown of this code follows the output. This program defines the class `MenusToolbar` and five inner classes that extend **AbstractAction** to represent actions for creating and saving files, as well as the clipboard operations of cut, copy, and paste. The constructor creates instances of each of these

**AbstractAction** subclasses and puts each object into both a tool bar and a menu. If the JVM cannot find the .gif files, the program runs, but the icons do not display.

```java
package examples.windows;
import javax.swing.*;
import java.awt.*;
import java.awt.event.*;
/** An example class used to demonstrate the use of
  * menus and toolbars
  */
public class MenusToolbar extends JFrame {
    private JLabel actionInfo
       = new JLabel( "Action information", JLabel.CENTER );
    /** Class constructor method
      * @param titleText Window's title bar text
      */
    public MenusToolbar( String titleText ) {
        super( titleText );
        addWindowListener( new WindowCloser() );
        JToolBar tb = new JToolBar();
        JMenu file = new JMenu( "File" );
        JMenu edit = new JMenu( "Edit" );
        JMenuBar mb = new JMenuBar();
        mb.add( file );
        mb.add( edit );
        NewAction na = new NewAction();
        file.add( na ).setMnemonic( 'N' );
        tb.add( na );
        SaveAction sa = new SaveAction();
        KeyStroke ks
           = KeyStroke.getKeyStroke( KeyEvent.VK_S,
                                     Event.CTRL_MASK );
        file.add( sa ).setAccelerator( ks );
        tb.add( sa );
        tb.addSeparator();
        CutAction cta = new CutAction();
        edit.add( cta );
        tb.add( cta );
        CopyAction cpa = new CopyAction();
        edit.add( cpa );
        tb.add( cpa );
        PasteAction pa = new PasteAction();
        edit.add( pa );
        tb.add( pa );

        setJMenuBar( mb );
        Container cp = getContentPane();
        cp.add( tb, BorderLayout.NORTH );
        cp.add( actionInfo, BorderLayout.CENTER );
        setSize( 350, 200 );
```

**13**

```java
            setVisible( true );
        }
        class NewAction extends AbstractAction {
            public NewAction() {
                super( "new", new ImageIcon( "new.gif" ) );
            }
            public void actionPerformed( ActionEvent e ) {
                actionInfo.setText( "new selected" );
            }
        }
        class SaveAction extends AbstractAction {
            public SaveAction() {
                super( "save", new ImageIcon( "save.gif" ) );
            }
            public void actionPerformed( ActionEvent e ) {
                actionInfo.setText( "save selected" );
            }
        }
        class CutAction extends AbstractAction {
            public CutAction() {
                super( "cut", new ImageIcon( "cut.gif" ) );
            }
            public void actionPerformed( ActionEvent e ) {
                actionInfo.setText( "cut selected" );
            }
        }
        class CopyAction extends AbstractAction {
            public CopyAction() {
                super( "copy", new ImageIcon( "copy.gif" ) );
            }
            public void actionPerformed( ActionEvent e ) {
                actionInfo.setText( "copy selected" );
            }
        }
        class PasteAction extends AbstractAction {
            public PasteAction() {
                super( "paste", new ImageIcon( "paste.gif" ) );
            }
            public void actionPerformed( ActionEvent e ) {
                actionInfo.setText( "paste selected" );
            }
        }
        /** The test method for the class
          * @param args not used
          */
        public static void main( String[] args ) {
            new MenusToolbar( "Example Menus and Toolbar" );
        }
    }
```

Allowing for differences in operating systems, the output should be similar to Figure 13-12.

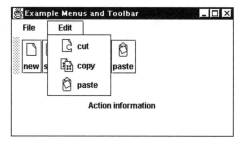

**Figure 13-12**   Output of the MenusToolbar class

The class encapsulating the drawing program is called **MenusToolbar**. The structure of this example is similar to the preceding examples, so only those program statements that pertain to the classes presented in this section are discussed in the code breakdown.

Consider the following code. In order to demonstrate that an action has been invoked without going to all the trouble of actually implementing the actions, a label object called **actionInfo** is created. It appears in the center of the frame window and reports which menu item or toolbar button was last selected.

```
private JLabel actionInfo
   = new JLabel( "Action information", JLabel.CENTER );
```

This example uses a toolbar, so, with the following code, a toolbar object is created with the default horizontal orientation.

```
JToolBar tb = new JToolBar();
```

Two menus for file-related and edit-related actions are created. Then a menu bar object is created and the menus are added to the menu bar, with the following code:

```
JMenu file = new JMenu( "File" );
JMenu edit = new JMenu( "Edit" );
JMenuBar mb = new JMenuBar();
mb.add( file );
mb.add( edit );
```

Then, an instance of the **NewAction** class is created and added to both the File menu and the toolbar. This is possible because the NewAction class extends **AbstractAction**. The **add** method for the menu returns a **JMenuItem** that is used to set the mnemonic character for the menu item. Similarly, the toolbar's **add** method returns a **JButton**, but it is not used.

```
NewAction na = new NewAction();
file.add( na ).setMnemonic( 'N' );
tb.add( na );
```

Consider the following code. The `SaveAction` class also extends **AbstractAction**, so the `SaveAction` object also can be added to both the menu bar and the toolbar. For the save action, an accelerator key is set to be Ctrl+S. The difference between an accelerator key and a mnemonic is that an accelerator key is always active, even if the menu is not visible. Mnemonic keys are only active when the menu is displayed. The **getKeyStroke** method is a static method of the **KeyStroke** class that returns a **KeyStroke** object given a base key and any modifying keys with which it must be combined. Here, its first argument is the constant for the character "S" and the second argument is a key modifier that specifies the control key must be pressed also:

```
SaveAction sa = new SaveAction();
KeyStroke ks
   = KeyStroke.getKeyStroke( KeyEvent.VK_S,
                              Event.CTRL_MASK );
file.add( sa ).setAccelerator( ks );
tb.add( sa );
```

To separate the file-related actions from the edit-related actions on the toolbar, a separator is added to the toolbar between the Save and Cut buttons.

```
tb.addSeparator();
```

Then, an instance of the **CutAction** class is created and added to the edit menu and the toolbar. Similarly, instances of the **CopyAction** and **PasteAction** also are added in both places.

```
CutAction cta = new CutAction();
edit.add( cta );
tb.add( cta );
```

Once the menu bar is complete, it is added to the frame window:

```
setJMenuBar( mb );
```

Toolbars have no special method for adding them to a container. Typically, they are added to the **NORTH** section of the container's border layout, as the following code shows:

```
Container cp = getContentPane();
cp.add( tb, BorderLayout.NORTH );
```

All the classes that extend **AbstractAction** take the same form. Each defines a default constructor that passes its text and icon to its superclass. Also, each must define the **actionPerformed** method that will be invoked when the toolbar button is clicked or the menu item is selected. Only the `NewAction` class is shown here. The `SaveAction`, `CutAction`, `CopyAction`, and `PasteAction` classes are similar to `NewAction`.

```
class NewAction extends AbstractAction {
   public NewAction() {
      super( "new", new ImageIcon( "new.gif" ) );
   }
   public void actionPerformed( ActionEvent e ) {
      actionInfo.setText( "new selected" );
   }
}
```

## SLIDERS, PROGRESS BARS, AND SCROLLBARS

Most of the GUI components discussed in the preceding sections, such as buttons and menu items, are useful for selecting among a fixed set of choices that are few in number. Usually, a different approach is more appropriate for selecting or displaying a value within a range of values, especially if the number of selections between the minimum and maximum values is very large. Swing provides three controls—**JProgressBar**, **JScrollbar**, and **JSlider**—that allow users to select or display a value within a bounded range. The **JScrollPane** control uses **JScrollbar** controls to specify the visible portion of a viewport.

Details about each of these classes are provided next. Lists of all the constructors that are available for creating objects of these classes are provided also.

**13**

*Class*

**javax.swing.JProgressBar**

*Purpose*

Use a **JProgressBar** object to display a value within a bounded range. Most commonly, programs use **JProgressBar** objects to indicate the progress (for example, percent completed) of a long-running operation.

*Constructors*

➤ **JProgressBar**()
  **JProgressBar**( **BoundedRangeModel** *brm* )
  **JProgressBar**( **int** *orientation* )
  **JProgressBar**( **int** *min*, **int** *max* )
  **JProgressBar**( **int** *min*, **int** *max*, **int** *value* )

**JProgressBar( int** *orientation*, **int** *min*, **int** *max*, **int** *value* **)**
By default, a slider is created with a vertical orientation, a minimum value
of zero, a maximum value of 100, and an initial value in the middle of the
range at 50. If you choose to specify the *orientation*, supply either of
**JProgressBar.HORIZONTAL** or **JProgressBar.VERTICAL**.

---

*Class*

**javax.swing.JScrollBar**

---

*Purpose*

Use a **JScrollBar** object to control the visible contents of a component. This
component is not usually used on its own, but is used indirectly as part of a
JScrollPane component.

---

*Constructors*

➤ **JScrollBar()**
   **JScrollBar( int** *orientation* **)**
   **JScrollBar( int** *orientation*, **int** *value*, **int** *extent*, **int** *min*, **int** *max* **)**
   By default, a scrollbar is created with a vertical orientation, a value of
   zero, an extent of 10, a minimum value of zero, and a maximum value
   of 100. If you choose to specify the *orientation*, its value should be one of
   **JScrollBar.HORIZONTAL** or **JScrollBar.VERTICAL**. The initial
   position of the sliding knob is on the top or left. The *extent* is a measure of
   how much of the component is visible when the knob is in any particular
   position.

---

*Class*

**javax.swing.JScrollPane**

---

*Purpose*

Use a **JScrollPane** object to display a component with contents that are likely
to exceed the available visible area. The **JScrollPane** class adds scrollbars automatically to control scrolling operations. A common use of this component is
to contain **JTextArea** objects and **JList** objects because these classes do not
provide scrollbars.

---

*Constructors*

➤ **JScrollPane()**
   **JScrollPane( Component** *view* **)**
   **JScrollPane( int** *vsbPolicy*, **int** *hsbPolicy* **)**
   **JScrollPane( Component** *view*, **int** *vsbPolicy*, **int** *hsbPolicy* **)**
   By default, scrollbars are included as needed so the user can view the entire
   component by scrolling. You also can specify an integer representing the

horizontal and vertical scrollbar display policies. The *hsbPolicy* value should be one of **JScrollPane.HORIZONTAL_SCROLLBAR_ALWAYS**, **JScrollPane. HORIZONTAL_SCROLLBAR_AS_NEEDED**, or **JScrollPane. HORIZONTAL_SCROLLBAR_NEVER**. The *vsbPolicy* value should be one of **JScrollPane.VERTICAL_SCROLLBAR_ALWAYS**, **JScrollPane. VERTICAL _SCROLLBAR_AS_NEEDED**, or **JScrollPane.- VERTICAL _SCROLLBAR_NEVER**.

*Class*

**javax.swing.JSlider**

*Purpose*

Use a **JSlider** object to allow selection of a value within a bounded range. **JSlider** objects support labels for their minimum and maximum values as well as major and minor ticks along their range.

*Constructors*

➤ **JSlider()**
**JSlider( BoundedRangeModel** *brm* **)**
**JSlider( int** *orientation* **)**
**JSlider( int** *min*, **int** *max* **)**
**JSlider( int** *min*, **int** *max*, **int** *value* **)**
**JSlider( int** *orientation*, **int** *min*, **int** *max*, **int** *value* **)**
By default, a slider is created with a vertical orientation, a minimum value of zero, a maximum value of 100, and an initial value in the middle of the range at 50. If you choose to specify the *orientation*, its value should be one of **JSlider.HORIZONTAL** or **JSlider. VERTICAL**.

**13**

The following is a program that uses the **JSlider** class to change the size of the text in a **JLabel** that is centered in a frame window. For an example that uses a **JScrollPane**, refer to the "Text-Entry Components" section later in this chapter. A breakdown of this code follows the output. This program defines the class FontSlider:

```
package examples.windows;
import javax.swing.*;
import javax.swing.event.*;
import java.awt.*;
import java.awt.event.*;
/** An example class used to demonstrate the use of
  * the JSlider component
  */
public class FontSlider extends JFrame {
   private JLabel text = new JLabel( "Sample Text",
                                     JLabel.CENTER );
```

```java
    private static final int MIN_POINTS = 8;
    private static final int MAX_POINTS = 36;
    private JSlider sizer = new JSlider();
    /** Class constructor method
      * @param titleText Window's title bar text
      */
    public FontSlider( String titleText ) {
        super( titleText );
        addWindowListener( new WindowCloser() );
        getContentPane().add( text, BorderLayout.CENTER );
        sizer.setMinimum( MIN_POINTS );
        sizer.setMaximum( MAX_POINTS );
        sizer.setValue( text.getFont().getSize() );
        sizer.setMajorTickSpacing( 4 );
        sizer.setMinorTickSpacing( 1 );
        sizer.setPaintLabels( true );
        sizer.setPaintTicks( true );
        sizer.addChangeListener( new ChangeListener() {
                public void stateChanged( ChangeEvent e ) {
                    Font of = text.getFont();
                    Font nf = new Font( of.getName(),
                                        of.getStyle(),
                                        sizer.getValue() );

                    text.setFont( nf );
                    text.repaint();
                }
            }
        );
        JPanel sliderPanel
            = new JPanel( new BorderLayout() );
        sliderPanel.setBorder(
            BorderFactory.createTitledBorder( "Font size" ));
        sliderPanel.add( sizer, BorderLayout.SOUTH );
        getContentPane().add( sliderPanel,
                            BorderLayout.SOUTH );
        setSize( 250, 175 );
        setVisible( true );
    }
    /** The test method for the class
      * @param args not used
      */
    public static void main( String[] args ) {
        new FontSlider( "Example Slider Usage" );
    }
}
```

Allowing for differences in operating systems, the output should be similar to Figure 13-13.

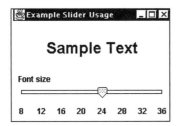

**Figure 13-13**   Output of the FontSlider class

The class encapsulating the drawing program is called `FontSlider`. The structure of this example is similar to the preceding examples, so only those program statements that pertain to the classes presented in this section will be discussed in the following code breakdown.

This program uses a slider to control the font size of a **JLabel** object, `text`, which is centered in the window above the slider. With the following code, this label object is created with default horizontal centering and with vertical centering explicitly specified as the second constructor parameter:

```
private JLabel text = new JLabel( "Sample Text",
                                  JLabel.CENTER );
```

Consider the following code. The minimum and maximum value for this font size slider are defined as class constants, and the **JSlider** object is created. No constructor parameters are specified because the initial value has not yet been calculated and the default initial value, 50, is not within the valid range. Using an initial value that is outside of the valid range would cause an exception when the program runs:

```
private static final int MIN_POINTS = 8;
private static final int MAX_POINTS = 36;
private JSlider sizer = new JSlider();
```

Within the constructor, the minimum, maximum, and initial values of the slider control can now be set. The initial value is the current font size of the label object:

```
sizer.setMinimum( MIN_POINTS );
sizer.setMaximum( MAX_POINTS );
sizer.setValue( text.getFont().getSize() );
```

The difference between the minimum and maximum values is 24, so setting the major ticks to be 4 units apart will yield a reasonable number of major ticks, as the following code shows. Minor ticks don't have labels and can be

**13**

closer together, so the minor tick spacing is set at one. These tick marks are not painted by default, so the **setPaintTicks** method is used to enable painting:

```
sizer.setMajorTickSpacing( 4 );
sizer.setMinorTickSpacing( 1 );
sizer.setPaintLabels( true );
sizer.setPaintTicks( true );
```

As the knob of the slider is moved, the slider fires **ChangeEvent** objects. The following statements define an anonymous inner class that implements the **ChangeListener** interface and register it to handle the events. The interface has only one method, **stateChanged**, and this method is implemented to get the current font of the label. Then, the method creates a new font with the same font name and style, but with a font size that is taken from the current value of the slider. **Font** objects are immutable, so you cannot simply change the size of the current font. The new **Font** object is set for the label, and the label is repainted:

```
sizer.addChangeListener( new ChangeListener() {
    public void stateChanged( ChangeEvent e ) {
        Font of = text.getFont();
        Font nf = new Font( of.getName(),
                            of.getStyle(),
                            sizer.getValue() );
        text.setFont( nf );
        text.repaint();
    }
  }
);
```

The following statements give the user an explanation of the slider control by placing the slider in a panel with a titled border. They give the panel a border layout and add the slider to the SOUTH area so that the slider stretches horizontally, but not vertically, with the window:

```
JPanel sliderPanel
    = new JPanel( new BorderLayout() );
sliderPanel.setBorder(
    BorderFactory.createTitledBorder( "Font size" ) );
sliderPanel.add( sizer, BorderLayout.SOUTH );
```

Finally, the panel containing the slider is added to the SOUTH section of the frame window so that it is positioned beneath the text that is being controlled:

```
getContentPane().add( sliderPanel,
                    BorderLayout.SOUTH );
```

# LISTS AND COMBO BOXES

Swing provides two components for presenting lists from which the user can select single or multiple items. The **JComboBox** component is a drop-down list that is useful for lists with a small number of items because it does not have scrolling capability. The **JComboBox** can provide an entry field where users enter values not present in the list. For long lists of items, you should use **JList** class because **JList** objects can be contained within a **JScrollPane** and scrolled to view the entire list. Users cannot directly enter new values into a **JList** object.

Details about the list and combo box classes are provided next. Lists of all the constructors that are available for creating objects of these classes are provided also.

## Class

**javax.swing.JComboBox**

## Purpose

A **JComboBox** object displays a drop-down list of choices from which the user can select one or more items. A combo box can provide an entry field into which the user can enter a value instead of selecting from the presented list.

## Constructors

➤ **JComboBox()**
**JComboBox( ComboBoxModel** *model* **)**
**JComboBox( Object[]** *items* **)**
**JComboBox( Vector** *items* **)**
You can specify that the list be built from an existing model, or the list of items can be specified and a new model will be created to contain them. If no parameter is specified, an empty default model is created.

**13**

## Class

**javax.swing.JList**

## Purpose

A **JList** object displays a list of choices from which it is possible to select one or multiple items. List contents cannot be edited by the user. Because lists can be long, they are typically contained within JScrollPane objects so scrollbars are available for controlling the visible portion of the list.

## Constructors

➤ **JList()**
**JList( ListModel** *model* **)**

**JList( Object[]** *items* **)**
**JList( Vector** *items* **)**
The model for a list is a separate object that contains the data displayed in the list. You can specify that the list be built from an existing model or provide data from which a new model will be created. If no parameter is specified, an empty default model is created.

---

The following is a program that exercises both **JComboBox** and **JList** classes. A breakdown of this code follows the output. This program defines the class **ListsAndComboBoxes** to create a GUI for ordering a pizza. A list is used to present the available toppings because the number of choices is large and because selecting more than one topping is possible. A combo box is used to present the pizza crust choices. A combo box is appropriate because the number of choices is small, and only one of the choices can be selected. The button used to place the order includes a colorful icon to make the GUI more appealing. When the order button is clicked, a confirmation dialog is presented so that the customer has one last chance to verify that the order is correct.

Before you run this program, copy all the pizza.gif file from the folder into which you unpacked the examples.jar file into the current directory. If the JVM cannot find the .gif file, the program runs, but the icon on the button does not display:

```
package examples.windows;
import javax.swing.*;
import java.awt.*;
import java.awt.event.*;
/** An example class used to demonstrate the use of
  * the JList and JComboBox components
  */
public class ListsAndComboBoxes extends JFrame {
    private JComboBox crustBox;
    private JList toppingList;
    /** Class constructor method
      * @param titleText Window's title bar text
      */
    public ListsAndComboBoxes( String titleText ) {
        super( titleText );
        addWindowListener( new WindowCloser() );
        crustBox = new JComboBox( new Object[] {
                "thick and chewy",
                "thin and crispy",
                "Chicago deep dish"
            }
        );
        toppingList = new JList( new Object[] {
                "pepperoni",
```

```
                "sausage",
                "ham",
                "grilled chicken",
                "mushrooms",
                "green peppers",
                "hot peppers",
                "black olives",
                "tomato slices",
                "sun-dried tomatoes",
                "extra cheese",
                "pineapple",
                "anchovies"
        }
);
toppingList.setSelectionMode(
    ListSelectionModel.MULTIPLE_INTERVAL_SELECTION );
JScrollPane scrollToppingList
    = new JScrollPane( toppingList );
JPanel lists = new JPanel( new GridBagLayout() );
GridBagConstraints c = new GridBagConstraints();
c.fill = GridBagConstraints.HORIZONTAL;
c.anchor = GridBagConstraints.NORTHWEST;
c.insets = new Insets( 10, 10, 10, 10 );
c.weightx = 0.0;
c.weighty = 0.0;
lists.add( new JLabel( "Toppings:" ), c );
c.gridwidth = GridBagConstraints.REMAINDER;
c.weightx = 1.0;
c.weighty = 1.0;
lists.add( scrollToppingList, c );
c.gridwidth = 1;
c.weightx = 0.0;
c.weighty = 0.0;
lists.add( new JLabel( "Crust type:" ), c );
c.gridwidth = GridBagConstraints.REMAINDER;
c.weightx = 1.0;
c.weighty = 1.0;
lists.add( crustBox, c );
JPanel buttons = new JPanel();
JButton order = new JButton( "Place order",
    new ImageIcon( "pizza.gif" ) );
order.addActionListener( new ActionListener() {
        public void actionPerformed( ActionEvent e ) {
            confirmOrder();
        }
    }
);
buttons.add( order );
Container cp = getContentPane();
cp.add( lists, BorderLayout.CENTER );
```

**13**

```
            cp.add( buttons, BorderLayout.SOUTH );
            setSize( 400, 350 );
            setVisible( true );
      }
      /** Confirm a customer's order
        */
      public void confirmOrder() {
         StringBuffer question = new StringBuffer();
         question.append( "Order a " +
             crustBox.getSelectedItem() +
             " crust pizza topped with" );
         Object[] toppings = toppingList.getSelectedValues();
         for ( int i=0; i < toppings.length; i++ ) {
            question.append( " " + toppings[i] );
            question.append ( ( i + 1 < toppings.length)
               ? " and" : "?" );
         }
         JOptionPane.showConfirmDialog( this,
                                        question );
      }
      /** The test method for the class
        * @param args not used
        */
      public static void main( String[] args ) {
         new ListsAndComboBoxes(
             "Example Lists and Combo Boxes" );
}}
```

Allowing for differences in operating systems, the output should be similar to
Figure 13-14.

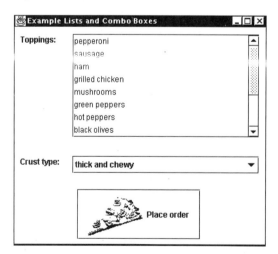

**Figure 13-14**   Output of the ListsAndComboBoxes class

The class encapsulating the drawing program is called `ListsAndComboBoxes`. The structure of this example is very similar to the preceding examples, so only those program statements that pertain to the classes presented in this section are discussed in the following code breakdown.

The program defines a combo box called `crustBox` for presenting a list of possible pizza crust types and a list called `toppingList` that will contain a list of all the available pizza toppings. These are fields of the class so that they are accessible to both the constructor and the `confirmOrder` method defined next:

```
private JComboBox crustBox;
private JList toppingList;
```

When the combo box is constructed, it is initialized with an anonymous array of three **String** objects:

```
crustBox = new JComboBox( new Object[] {
        "thick and chewy",
        "thin and crispy",
        "Chicago deep dish"
    }
);
```

Another anonymous array initializes the contents of the list with all the possible pizza toppings:

```
toppingList = new JList( new Object[] {
        "pepperoni",
        "sausage",
        "ham",
        "grilled chicken",
        "mushrooms",
        "green peppers",
        "hot peppers",
        "black olives",
        "tomato slices",
        "sun-dried tomatoes",
        "extra cheese",
        "pineapple",
        "anchovies"
    }
);
```

**13**

Because we want to let users select as many pizza toppings as they want, the multiple-selection mode is set for the list:

```
toppingList.setSelectionMode(
    ListSelectionModel.MULTIPLE_INTERVAL_SELECTION );
```

**JList** objects do not have any scrollbars of their own, so the topping list is wrapped in a **JScrollPane** object that will provide the scrollbars and handle the scrolling operations:

```
JScrollPane scrollToppingList
   = new JScrollPane( toppingList );
```

A grid-bag layout is used to position the combo box and the list along with their labels. All four objects are put into a single panel called `lists`. Within the grid bag, all four objects are set to stretch horizontally and anchored in the northwest corner of their cells. They also have a 10-pixel border around them, as the following code shows:

```
JPanel lists = new JPanel( new GridBagLayout() );
GridBagConstraints c = new GridBagConstraints();
c.fill = GridBagConstraints.HORIZONTAL;
c.anchor = GridBagConstraints.NORTHWEST;
c.insets = new Insets( 10, 10, 10, 10 );
```

The $x$ and $y$ weights for the label are set to zero so that it will not stretch with the window. This will allow the combo box to do the stretching, as the following code shows:

```
c.weightx = 0.0;
c.weighty = 0.0;
lists.add( new JLabel( "Toppings:" ), c );
```

The combo box takes the remainder of the first row and is given $x$ and $y$ weightings so that it will stretch:

```
c.gridwidth = GridBagConstraints.REMAINDER;
c.weightx = 1.0;
c.weighty = 1.0;
lists.add( scrollToppingList, c );
```

The gridwidth value is reset to its default value of 1 and, again, the weightings are set so that the label won't stretch:

```
c.gridwidth = 1;
c.weightx = 0.0;
c.weighty = 0.0;
lists.add( new JLabel( "Crust type:" ), c );
```

The last component that the method puts into the layout is the list, which is set to take the remainder of the second row:

```
c.gridwidth = GridBagConstraints.REMAINDER;
c.weightx = 1.0;
c.weighty = 1.0;
lists.add( crustBox, c );
```

Then, a panel is created for the "Place order" button and the button is created with both text and a graphic of a piece of pizza:

```
JPanel buttons = new JPanel();
JButton order = new JButton( "Place order",
   new ImageIcon( "pizza.gif" ) );
```

The next statement defines an action listener as anonymous inner class and adds it to the button, so that the `confirmOrder` method is invoked when the user clicks the button:

```
order.addActionListener( new ActionListener() {
      public void actionPerformed( ActionEvent e ) {
         confirmOrder();
      }
   }
);
```

The button is added to the panel and then both of the panels are added to the frame window's content pane. The lists are set in the center of the window and the button at the bottom, as the following code shows:

```
buttons.add( order );
Container cp = getContentPane();
cp.add( lists, BorderLayout.CENTER );
cp.add( buttons, BorderLayout.SOUTH );
```

The `confirmOrder` method begins by creating a string with the type of crust the user selected:

```
public void confirmOrder() {
   StringBuffer question = new StringBuffer();
   question.append( "Order a " +
      crustBox.getSelectedItem() +
      " crust pizza topped with" );
```

Then, the list of toppings that were selected is added to the string so that all the details of the order are now in the string:

```
Object[] toppings = toppingList.getSelectedValues();
for ( int i=0; i < toppings.length; i++ ) {
   question.append( " " + toppings[i] );
   question.append ( ( i + 1 < toppings.length)
      ? " and" : "?" );
}
```

Presenting a dialog to the user so that the order can be confirmed is a simple matter of calling the static **showConfirmDialog** method of the **JOptionPane** class. The two parameters are the parent window for the dialog

**13**

and the question to be displayed. Although it is not shown in this example, this method returns an integer that indicates the user's action:

```
JOptionPane.showConfirmDialog( this,
                              question );
```

## TEXT-ENTRY COMPONENTS

No set of GUI components would be complete without components that allowed the user to enter text. Swing provides several such components from the most basic single-line text field to the sophisticated multiline components that understand and support HTML and RTF. Swing also provides a convenience class of entry fields specifically suited for entering passwords.

Figure 13-15 shows **TextComponent** and its subclasses. Following the figure, the syntax discussion gives details about each of the text components. Lists of all the constructors that are available for creating objects of these classes are provided also.

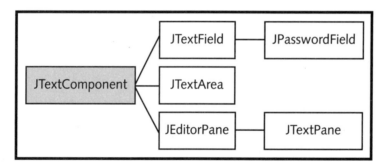

**Figure 13-15**   TextComponent and its subclasses

*Class*

**javax.swing.JEditorPane**

*Purpose*

A **JEditorPane** is a region that is designed to parse and edit specific types of structured text content. If a scrollable region is required, this component should be placed inside a **JScrollPane** object.

## Constructors

➤ **JEditorPane()**
**JEditorPane( String** *url* **)**
**JEditorPane( String** *mimeType***, String** *text* **)**
**JEditorPane( URL** *url* **)**

The text pane requires that a MIME type be specified for its content. If a URL is given as input to the constructor, the MIME type will be determined by the URL. However, it is possible to construct a **JEditorPane** specifying both the MIME type and the actual text to be displayed. By default, three MIME types of content are known:

**text/plain:** Plain text, which is the default the type given isn't recognized. This produces a wrapped plain text view.

**text/html:** HTML text as defined by HTML version 3.2.

**text/rtf:** A limited support of the Rich Text Format (RTF) is supported.

## Class

**javax.swing.JPasswordField**

## Purpose

A **JPasswordField** can display a single line of text and lets the user enter or edit the text. The field provides feedback as characters are entered, but the actual characters typed are not displayed.

## Constructors

➤ **JPasswordField()**
**JPasswordField( String** *text* **)**
**JPasswordField( int** *columns* **)**
**JPasswordField( String** *text***, int** *columns* **)**
**JPasswordField( Document** *docModel***, String** *text***, int** *columns* **)**

If you supply an initial text string, it is displayed in the **JPasswordField**; otherwise, the **JPasswordField** is initially empty. The text field will use a **Document** model object if one is specified; otherwise, a new model is constructed. The **int** argument is the width of the **JPasswordField** expressed as the number of feedback characters that can be displayed. For a fixed-pitch or monospace font, the width is equivalent to the number of columns of characters that fit on the line. For a variable-pitch or proportional font, the width is an approximation based on medium-size letters. You may see more letters if the feedback string contains several occurrences of narrow letters, such as *l* or *i,* and fewer characters if the string contains several occurrences of wide letters, such as *m* or *w.* If you do not specify a width, the **JPasswordField** is wide enough to display either the specified **String** object or a minimum of one character.

**13**

---

*Class*

**javax.swing.JTextArea**

---

*Purpose*

A **JTextArea** is a region that can contain several lines of text. If a scrollable region is required, this component should be placed inside a **JScrollPane** object.

---

*Constructors*

► **JTextArea()**
  **JTextArea( String** *text* **)**
  **JTextArea( Document** *docModel* **)**
  **JTextArea( int** *rows*, **int** *columns* **)**
  **JTextArea( String** *text*, **int** *rows*, **int** *columns* **)**
  **JTextArea( Document** *docModel*, **String** *text*, **int** *rows*, **int** *columns* **)**
  You can specify the size of the **JTextArea** in terms of the number of rows and the number of characters or columns that are displayable at once. The text area will use a **Document** model object if one is specified; otherwise, a new model is constructed. As with a **JTextField**, the number of columns is exact for a fixed-pitch font and approximate for a variable-pitch font. If you specify a string to the constructor, the content of the string is displayed when the **JTextArea** is displayed.

---

*Class*

**javax.swing.JTextField**

---

*Purpose*

A **JTextField** can display a single line of text and lets the user enter or edit the text.

---

*Constructors*

► **JTextField()**
  **JTextField( String** *text* **)**
  **JTextField( int** *columns* **)**
  **JTextField( String** *text*, **int** *columns* **)**
  **JTextField( Document** *docModel*, **String** *text*, **int** *columns* **)**
  If you supply an initial text string, it is displayed in the **JTextField**; otherwise, the **JTextField** is initially empty. The text field will use a **Document** model object if one is specified; otherwise, a new model is constructed. The **int** argument is the width of the **JTextField** expressed as the number of characters that can be displayed. For a fixed-pitch or monospace font, the width is equivalent to the number of columns of characters that fit on

the line. For a variable-pitch or proportional font, the width is an approximation based on medium-size letters. You may see more letters if the string contains several occurrences of narrow letters such as *l* or *i,* but fewer characters if the string contains several occurrences of wide letters such as *m* or *w.* If you do not specify a width, the **JTextField** is wide enough to display either the specified **String** object or a minimum of one character.

*Class*

### javax.swing.JTextPane

*Purpose*

A **JTextPane** is a region that can contain several lines of text. This text can be given styles that can be represented graphically. If a scrollable region is required, this component should be placed inside a **JScrollPane** object.

*Constructors*

➤ **JTextPane()**
**JTextPane( StyledDocument** *docModel* **)**
The text pane will used a **StyledDocument** model object if one is specified; otherwise, a new model is constructed.

The following is a program that exercises the **JTextField** and **JTextArea** classes described previously. A breakdown of this code follows the output. This program defines the class `TextExamples` to create a GUI in which the user enters a filename in the text field at the top of the frame window and the contents of the file are displayed in two text areas. The text areas are put into a **JSplitPane** object that is split horizontally. The two text areas share the same underlying document model, so any change that is made in one text area will be immediately reflected in the other text area:

```
package examples.windows;
import javax.swing.*;
import java.awt.*;
import java.awt.event.*;
import java.io.*;
/** An example class used to demonstrate the use of
  * the JTextField and JTextArea components
  */
public class TextExamples extends JFrame {
   /** Class constructor method
     * @param titleText Window's title bar text
     */
   public TextExamples( String titleText ) {
      super( titleText );
      addWindowListener( new WindowCloser() );
```

**13**

```
        final JTextArea upper = new JTextArea();
        final JTextArea lower
            = new JTextArea( upper.getDocument() );
        JScrollPane upperScroll = new JScrollPane( upper );
        JScrollPane lowerScroll = new JScrollPane( lower );
        JSplitPane sp
            = new JSplitPane( JSplitPane.VERTICAL_SPLIT,
                              upperScroll,
                              lowerScroll );
        sp.setOneTouchExpandable( true );
        sp.setDividerLocation( 0.5 );
        final JTextField fName = new JTextField();
        fName.setToolTipText( "Enter a file name" );
        fName.addActionListener( new ActionListener() {
            public void actionPerformed( ActionEvent e ) {
                if ( fName.getText() != null ) try {
                    FileReader fr
                        = new FileReader( fName.getText() );
                    upper.setText( "" );
                    char[] buffer = new char[4096];
                    int count = fr.read( buffer, 0,
                                            buffer.length );
                    while ( count != -1 ) {
                        upper.append( new String( buffer, 0,
                                                    count ) );
                        count = fr.read( buffer, 0,
                                            buffer.length );
                    }
                } catch( IOException ioe ) {
                    System.out.println( ioe );
                }
            }
        }
        );
        JPanel entry = new JPanel( new BorderLayout() );
        entry.add( new JLabel( "File: " ),
                   BorderLayout.WEST );
        entry.add( fName, BorderLayout.CENTER );
        getContentPane().add( entry, BorderLayout.NORTH );
        getContentPane().add( sp, BorderLayout.CENTER );
        setSize( 500, 400 );
        fName.requestFocus();
        setVisible( true );
    }
    /** The test method for the class
      * @param args not used
      */
    public static void main( String[] args ) {
        new TextExamples( "Example Text Components" );
    }
}
```

Allowing for differences in operating systems, the output should be similar to Figure 13-16.

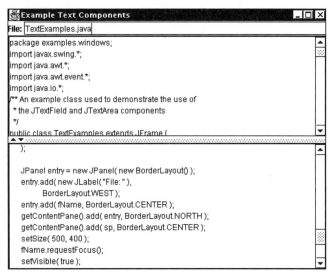

**Figure 13-16**   Output of the TextExamples class

The class encapsulating the drawing program is called **TextExamples**. The structure of this example is similar to the preceding examples, so only those program statements that pertain to the classes presented in this section are discussed in the code breakdown below.

Consider the following code, which uses two **JTextArea** objects that share a single document model. The first **JTextArea** object is constructed using all the defaults, and then the second **JTextArea** is constructed specifying the document model of the first **JTextArea** as input. The result is two text areas that are two different views on the same document model:

```
final JTextArea upper = new JTextArea();
final JTextArea lower
   = new JTextArea( upper.getDocument() );
```

The two text-area components are put into **JScrollPane** objects so that they will have scrollbars if they are needed:

```
JScrollPane upperScroll = new JScrollPane( upper );
JScrollPane lowerScroll = new JScrollPane( lower );
```

Then, the two scroll panes are put into a split pane, one on top of the other:

```
JSplitPane sp
   = new JSplitPane( JSplitPane.VERTICAL_SPLIT,
                     upperScroll,
                     lowerScroll );
```

13

Examine the following code. By setting the **oneTouchExpandable** property of the split pane to true, a control is added to the bar that divides the split pane. This makes it easy to expand the split pane to show one component or the other. The **dividerLocation** property is set so that it is initially in the middle of the pane:

```
sp.setOneTouchExpandable( true );
sp.setDividerLocation( 0.5 );
```

A text field is created to be used for inputting the name of the file to be displayed in the two text-area components. A tooltip is associated with the entry field to help the user to know its use:

```
final JTextField fName = new JTextField();
fName.setToolTipText( "Enter a file name" );
```

Then, an action listener is needed for the text area so that when the Enter key is pressed, the value in the text field can be used as a filename for loading the text areas:

```
fName.addActionListener( new ActionListener() {
     public void actionPerformed( ActionEvent e ) {
```

As long as the specified string isn't null, the string will be used to create a file reader and the file will be read in 4Kb chunks:

```
if ( fName.getText() != null ) try {
   FileReader fr
      = new FileReader( fName.getText() );
   upper.setText( "" );
   char[] buffer = new char[4096];
   int count = fr.read( buffer, 0,
                         buffer.length );
```

As long as something is successfully read from the file, the method will append it to the text area:

```
while ( count != -1 ) {
   upper.append( new String( buffer, 0,
                             count ) );
   count = fr.read( buffer, 0,
                    buffer.length );
}
```

If an I/O exception occurs, the contents of the I/O exception object will be written to the standard output stream:

```
} catch( IOException ioe ) {
   System.out.println( ioe );
}
```

A panel is created for combining the entry field along with its label. This panel is added to the NORTH section of the frame window and the split pane with the two text area objects is put into the center of the frame window, as shown next:

```
JPanel entry = new JPanel( new BorderLayout() );
entry.add( new JLabel( "File: " ),
          BorderLayout.WEST );
entry.add( fName, BorderLayout.CENTER );
getContentPane().add( entry, BorderLayout.NORTH );
getContentPane().add( sp, BorderLayout.CENTER );
```

Finally, just before the window is made visible, a request is made to have the focus put on the entry field so that if the user begins typing, it will go into the entry field:

```
fName.requestFocus();
```

# CHOOSERS

Some panels are used so commonly that they have been added to Swing as standard components. This is just as well because both the **JColorChooser** and **JFileChooser** standard components are complex panels that would be difficult for most programmers to create on their own. Like the panels of the **JOptionPane** class, the **JColorChooser** and **JFileChooser** components typically are imbedded in with **JDialog** components. (Another possibility is to embed them in an internal frame.) Both classes provide convenient static methods that do the work of creating the panel, creating the dialog, and putting the panel into the dialog and making it visible.

Details about these chooser classes are provided next. Lists of all the constructors that are available for creating objects of these classes are provided also.

*Class*

**javax.swing.JColorChooser**

*Purpose*

The **JColorChooser** is a panel that allows users to browse a palette of available colors and select one.

*Constructors*

➤ **JColorChooser()**
**JColorChooser( Color** *initialSelection* **)**
**JColorChooser( ColorSelectionModel** *model* **)**
If the default constructor is used, a dialog is displayed with white as the initial selection. If a color is specified, it will be indicated to be the initial

selection. By default, a new selection model is created for the chooser, but it is possible to specify that the chooser use an existing selection model at construction time.

*Class*

**javax.swing.JFileChooser**

*Purpose*

The **JFileChooser** is a panel that allows users to browse the contents of the file system and select a file to open or a file to save.

*Constructors*

➤ **JFileChooser()**
**JFileChooser( File** *currentDirectory* **)**
**JFileChooser( FileSystemView** *fsView* **)**
**JFileChooser( String** *currentDirectoryPath* **)**
**JFileChooser( File** *currentDirectory*, **FileSystemView** *fsView* **)**
**JFileChooser( String** *currentDirectoryPath*, **FileSystemView** *fsView* **)**
The file selection begins in the user's home directory if no current directory is specified as either a **File** object or a string. The **FileSystemView** object is an object that encapsulates the details of the host system's file system. To display the chooser, typically either the method **showOpenDialog** or the **showSaveDialog** is used.

Next is a program that exercises both of the chooser classes described previously. A breakdown of this code follows the output. The program defines the class `Choosers` to implement a simple file browser program. The file to be displayed is selected using a **JFileChooser** object that is invoked from the item "File open..." on the File menu. The browser allows the text color to be changed using a **JColorChooser** object that is placed within a **JDialog** object. The menu item used to change the text color is found on the Edit menu:

```
package examples.windows;
import javax.swing.*;
import java.awt.*;
import java.awt.event.*;
import java.io.*;
/** An example class used to demonstrate the
  * use of the color and file choosers
  */
public class Choosers extends JFrame {
   private JTextArea text = new JTextArea();
   private JFileChooser fileChoose
      = new JFileChooser();
   private JDialog colorDlg;
```

```java
private JColorChooser colorChoose
   = new JColorChooser();
/** Class constructor
 * @param titleText Title bar text
 */
public Choosers( String titleText ) {
   super( titleText );
   addWindowListener( new WindowCloser() );
   setJMenuBar( buildMenuBar() );
   text.setEditable( false );
   Container cp = getContentPane();
   cp.add( new JScrollPane( text ),
           BorderLayout.CENTER );
   setSize( 500, 400 );
   setVisible( true );
}
/** Present a dialog box to have the user select
 * the file for browsing */
public void loadFile() {
   int result = fileChoose.showOpenDialog(
      Choosers.this );
   File file = fileChoose.getSelectedFile();
   if ( file != null
        && result == JFileChooser.APPROVE_OPTION )
   try{
      FileReader fr = new FileReader( file );
      text.setText( "" );
      char[] charBuffer = new char[4096];
      int charsRead = fr.read( charBuffer, 0,
                                 charBuffer.length );
      while ( charsRead != -1 ) {
         text.append( new String( charBuffer, 0,
                                 charsRead ) );
         charsRead = fr.read( charBuffer, 0,
                                 charBuffer.length );
      }
   } catch( IOException ioe ) {
      ioe.printStackTrace();
   }
}
/** Build the menu bar, menus, and menu items for
 * the file browser */
public JMenuBar buildMenuBar() {
   JMenuBar menuBar = new JMenuBar();
   JMenu fileMenu = new JMenu( "File" );
   JMenu editMenu = new JMenu( "Edit" );
   JMenuItem exitItem = new JMenuItem( "Exit" );
   JMenuItem fileOpenItem
      = new JMenuItem( "File open..." );
   JMenuItem colorsItem
      = new JMenuItem( "Change Color..." );
```

**13**

```java
            fileMenu.setMnemonic( KeyEvent.VK_F );
            editMenu.setMnemonic( KeyEvent.VK_E );
            fileOpenItem.setMnemonic( KeyEvent.VK_O );
            exitItem.setMnemonic( KeyEvent.VK_X );
            colorsItem.setMnemonic( KeyEvent.VK_C );
            fileOpenItem.addActionListener(
                new ActionListener() {
                    public void actionPerformed( ActionEvent e ) {
                        loadFile();
                    }
                }
            );
            exitItem.addActionListener(
                new ActionListener() {
                    public void actionPerformed( ActionEvent e ) {
                        dispose();
                        System.exit( 0 );
                    }
                }
            );
            colorsItem.addActionListener(
                new ActionListener() {
                    public void actionPerformed( ActionEvent e ) {
                        if ( colorDlg == null ) {
                            colorDlg = JColorChooser.createDialog(
                                Choosers.this,
                                "Select Text Color",
                                true,
                                colorChoose,
                                new ColorOKListener(),
                                null
                            );
                        }
                        colorChoose.setColor(
                            text.getForeground() );
                        colorDlg.setVisible( true );
                    }
                }
            );
            menuBar.add( fileMenu );
            menuBar.add( editMenu );
            fileMenu.add( fileOpenItem );
            fileMenu.add( exitItem );
            editMenu.add( colorsItem );
            return menuBar;
        }
        class ColorOKListener implements ActionListener {
            public void actionPerformed( ActionEvent e ) {
                Color c = colorChoose.getColor();
                text.setForeground( c );
                text.repaint();
            }
```

```
}
/** The test method for the class
 * @param args not used
 */
public static void main( String[] args ) {
    new Choosers( "File and Color Choosers" );
}
}
```

Allowing for differences in operating systems, Figure 13-17 represents what you will see if you choose the Change Color item from the Edit menu.

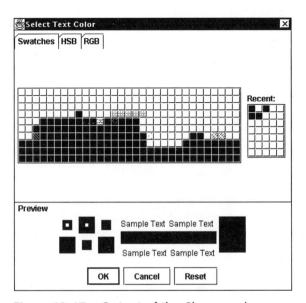

**Figure 13-17**   Output of the Choosers class

The class encapsulating the drawing program is called **Choosers**. The structure of this example is very similar to the preceding examples, so only those program statements that pertain to the classes presented in this section are discussed in the following code breakdown.

Consider the following code that defines the fields for the **Choosers** class that will be used throughout the program. The fields are the text-area component where the file contents will be shown, the file-chooser panel, and a color-chooser panel and the dialog in which it will be displayed:

```
private JTextArea text = new JTextArea();
private JFileChooser fileChoose
    = new JFileChooser();
private JDialog colorDlg;
private JColorChooser colorChoose
    = new JColorChooser();
```

**13**

The menu bar for this class is built and returned by the `buildMenuBar` method and then it is set for the frame window:

```
setJMenuBar( buildMenuBar() );
```

Examine the following code. You are working with a file-browser program, so editing is disabled for the text area. Text areas do not have scroll bars, so the text-area object is placed in a scrollpane and then positioned in the center of the frame window's content pane:

```
text.setEditable( false );
Container cp = getContentPane();
cp.add( new JScrollPane( text ),
        BorderLayout.CENTER );
```

The `loadFile` method is invoked when the "File open..." menu item is selected. It begins by using the file chooser's **showOpenDialog** method to allow the user to select a file. This is a modal dialog, so when the method completes, the user has either selected a file or quit from the dialog:

```
public void loadFile() {
   int result = fileChoose.showOpenDialog(
      Choosers.this );
   File file = fileChoose.getSelectedFile();
```

Consider the following code. If the user did not select a file, the `file` string will be null. The int value returned from the **showOpenDialog** method call can be used to determine what action the user took to close the dialog. If the "Open" button was selected, then the result will equal **JFileChooser.APPROVE_OPTION**:

```
if ( file != null
     && result == JFileChooser.APPROVE_OPTION )
try {
```

Assuming that a file was selected successfully, a **FileReader** object is constructed to read the file and the text area is cleared. A buffer for reading from the file is created and the first read operation is performed, as shown in the following code:

```
FileReader fr = new FileReader( file );
text.setText( "" );
char[] charBuffer = new char[4096];
int charsRead = fr.read( charBuffer, 0,
                         charBuffer.length );
```

As long as characters are being read successfully, data will continue to be read from the file and appended to the contents of the text area until the whole file has been processed:

```
while ( charsRead != -1 ) {
   text.append( new String( charBuffer, 0,
                            charsRead ) );
```

```
        charsRead = fr.read( charBuffer, 0,
                             charBuffer.length );
}
```

The menu bar for the program consists of one **JMenuBar** object, two **JMenu** objects for "File" and "Edit", and three **JMenuItem** objects for the actions:

```
public JMenuBar buildMenuBar() {
    JMenuBar menuBar = new JMenuBar();
    JMenu fileMenu = new JMenu( "File" );
    JMenu editMenu = new JMenu( "Edit" );
    JMenuItem exitItem = new JMenuItem( "Exit" );
    JMenuItem fileOpenItem
        = new JMenuItem( "File open..." );
    JMenuItem colorsItem
        = new JMenuItem( "Change Color..." );
```

Mnemonic characters are set for both menus and all the menu item objects:

```
fileMenu.setMnemonic( KeyEvent.VK_F );
editMenu.setMnemonic( KeyEvent.VK_E );
fileOpenItem.setMnemonic( KeyEvent.VK_O );
exitItem.setMnemonic( KeyEvent.VK_X );
colorsItem.setMnemonic( KeyEvent.VK_C );
```

Action listeners must be created and added for each of the three menu items. Anonymous inner classes are used in all cases. The action listener for the "Open file..." menu item calls the `loadFile` method, as shown in the following code:

```
fileOpenItem.addActionListener(
    new ActionListener() {
        public void actionPerformed( ActionEvent e ) {
            loadFile();
        }
    }
);
```

**13**

The action listener for the "Exit" item disposes the frame window and exits the JVM:

```
exitItem.addActionListener(
    new ActionListener() {
        public void actionPerformed( ActionEvent e ) {
            dispose();
            System.exit( 0 );
        }
    }
);
```

Then, as shown in the following code, the action listener for the "Change Color..." item creates a dialog to hold the color chooser panel, if one does not already exist. This approach avoids creating a new dialog every time, which would be very expensive. The last two parameters of the **createDialog** method are the listeners for the dialog's OK and Cancel buttons. Because this program will take no action if Cancel is selected, that handler is set to null:

```
colorsItem.addActionListener(
   new ActionListener() {
      public void actionPerformed( ActionEvent e ) {
         if ( colorDlg == null ) {
            colorDlg = JColorChooser.createDialog(
               Choosers.this,
               "Select Text Color",
               true,
               colorChoose,
               new ColorOKListener(),
               null
            );
         }
```

The current color of the text is set as the initial color for the color chooser, and then the dialog is made visible:

```
         colorChoose.setColor(
            text.getForeground() );
         colorDlg.setVisible( true );
      }
   }
);
```

The last group of statements in the **buildMenuBar** method adds the menu items to the menus and then the menus to the menu bar. The finished product is returned:

```
   menuBar.add( fileMenu );
   menuBar.add( editMenu );
   fileMenu.add( fileOpenItem );
   fileMenu.add( exitItem );
   editMenu.add( colorsItem );
   return menuBar;
}
```

The **ColorOKListener** class is defined for use as the action listener for the OK button for the color chooser dialog. The selected color is determined and used as the foreground color of the text area. A call to **repaint** causes the change to take effect:

```
class ColorOKListener implements ActionListener {
   public void actionPerformed( ActionEvent e ) {
```

```
        Color c = colorChoose.getColor( );
        text.setForeground( c );
        text.repaint( );
    }
}
```

# TABLES AND TREES

The two most ambitious components in Swing are the **JTable** and **JTree** components. Each of these components is very complex. In fact, both classes have an entire package of their own support classes. This section outlines what is possible with these components. Specifically, you will learn how to use these controls to present information.

The **JTable** component is useful for presenting information of a tabular nature. This section presents the JTable syntax and a sample program first. Then, the section presents the syntax and sample program for the **JTree** component.

*Class*

**javax.swing.JTable**

*Purpose*

The **JTable** is a component that displays information in tabular format.

*Constructors*

➤ **JTable()**
  **JTable( int** *rows*, **int** *columns* **)**
  **JTable( Object[][]** *rowData*, **Object[]** *columnNames* **)**
  **JTable( Vector** *rowData*, **Vector** *columnNames* **)**
  **JTable( TableModel** *model* **)**
  **JTable( TableModel** *model*, **TableColumnModel** *tcModel* **)**
  **JTable( TableModel** *model*, **TableColumnModel** *tcModel*,
        **ListSelectionModel** *lsModel* **)**
  By default, default models are created for the table, but it is possible to specify that the chooser should use existing model objects.

The following is a program that uses the **JTable** class just described. A breakdown of this code follows the output. This program defines the class TableExample to create a GUI that displays a table of statistics for five baseball players:

```
package examples.windows;
import javax.swing.*;
import javax.swing.event.*;
```

**13**

```
import java.awt.*;
/** An example class used to demonstrate the use of
  * the JTable component
  */
public class TableExample extends JFrame {
    /** Class constructor method
      * @param titleText Window's title bar text
      */
    public TableExample( String titleText ) {
        super( titleText );
        addWindowListener( new WindowCloser() );
        JTable stats = new JTable( new Object[][] {
                { "Gonzalez",   ".295", "34", "12", "6",  "10" },
                { "Carter",     ".302", "27", "12", "2",  "15" },
                { "Fernandez", ".285", "30", "12", "11", "1"  },
                { "Greene",     ".321", "41", "12", "0",  "10" },
                { "Delgado",    ".298", "34", "12", "1",  "20" },
            } ,
            new Object[] {
                "Player", "avg", "1B", "2B", "3B", "HR"
            }
        );
        JScrollPane scrollStats = new JScrollPane( stats );
        getContentPane().add( scrollStats,
                              BorderLayout.CENTER );
        setSize( 500, 200 );
        setVisible( true );
    }
    /** The test method for the class
      * @param args not used
      */
    public static void main( String[] args ) {
        new TableExample( "Table Example" );
    }
}
```

Allowing for differences in operating systems, the output should be similar to Figure 13–18.

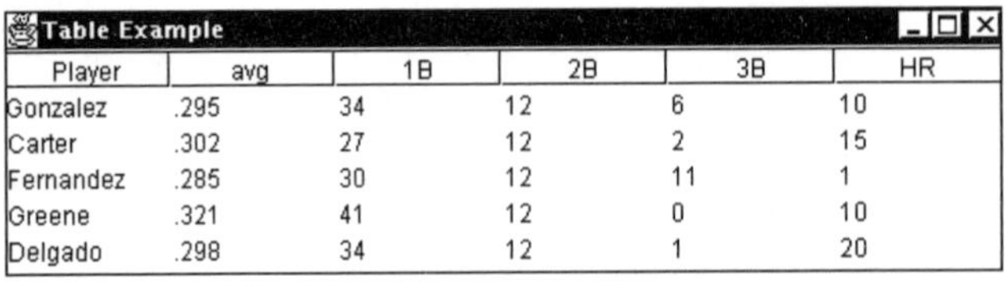

| Player | avg | 1B | 2B | 3B | HR |
|--------|-----|----|----|----|----|
| Gonzalez | .295 | 34 | 12 | 6 | 10 |
| Carter | .302 | 27 | 12 | 2 | 15 |
| Fernandez | .285 | 30 | 12 | 11 | 1 |
| Greene | .321 | 41 | 12 | 0 | 10 |
| Delgado | .298 | 34 | 12 | 1 | 20 |

**Figure 13-18**   Output of the TableExample class

The class encapsulating the drawing program is called **TableExample**. The structure of this example is similar to the preceding examples, so only those program statements that pertain to the classes presented in this section are discussed in the following code breakdown.

Consider the following code. The table is constructed by providing two array objects as input. The first is an anonymous two-dimensional array of **String** objects containing the table data. The second array contains the column titles defined as an anonymous array of **String** objects:

```
JTable stats = new JTable( new Object[][] {
        { "Gonzalez",  ".295", "34", "12", "6",  "10" },
        { "Carter",    ".302", "27", "12", "2",  "15" },
        { "Fernandez", ".285", "30", "12", "11", "1"  },
        { "Greene",    ".321", "41", "12", "0",  "10" },
        { "Delgado",   ".298", "34", "12", "1",  "20" },
    } ,
    new Object[] {
        "Player", "avg", "1B", "2B", "3B", "HR"
    }
);
```

Then, the table object is put into a scroll pane. This serves two purposes: it provides the table with scrollbars, and it gives the table column headers a place to reside. The scroll pane is then set in the center of the frame window's content pane:

```
JScrollPane scrollStats = new JScrollPane( stats );
getContentPane().add( scrollStats,
                      BorderLayout.CENTER );
```

---

*Class*

**javax.swing.JTree**

**13**

---

*Purpose*

The **JTree** is a component that displays information in hierarchical format.

---

*Constructors*

➤ **JTree()**
**JTree( Hashtable** *hashtable* **)**
**JTree( Object[]** *value* **)**
**JTree( TreeModel** *model* **)**
**JTree( TreeNode** *root* **)**
**JTree( TreeNode** *root,* **boolean** *asksAllowsChildren* **)**
**JTree( Vector** *value* **)**
By default, default models are created for the tree, but it is possible to specify that the tree should use existing model objects.

---

The following program exercises many of the classes described previously. A breakdown of this code follows the output. This program defines the class `TreeExample` that creates a very simple tree-structured GUI with three branches under the root node and a few leaf nodes under each of these three branches:

```java
package examples.windows;
import javax.swing.*;
import javax.swing.event.*;
import javax.swing.tree.*;
import java.awt.*;
/** An example class used to demonstrate the use of
 * the JTree component
 */
public class TreeExample extends JFrame {
    /** Class constructor method
     * @param titleText Window's title bar text
     */
    public TreeExample( String titleText ) {
        super( titleText );
        addWindowListener( new WindowCloser() );
        DefaultMutableTreeNode everything
            = new DefaultMutableTreeNode( "everything" );
        JTree avm = new JTree( everything );
        DefaultMutableTreeNode animal
            = new DefaultMutableTreeNode( "animal" );
        everything.add( animal );
        animal.add( new DefaultMutableTreeNode( "cat" ) );
        animal.add( new DefaultMutableTreeNode( "dog" ) );
        animal.add( new DefaultMutableTreeNode( "fish" ) );
        DefaultMutableTreeNode vegetable
            = new DefaultMutableTreeNode( "vegetable" );
        everything.add( vegetable );
        vegetable.add(
            new DefaultMutableTreeNode( "onion" ) );
        vegetable.add(
            new DefaultMutableTreeNode( "lettuce" ) );
        vegetable.add(
            new DefaultMutableTreeNode( "carrot" ) );
        DefaultMutableTreeNode mineral
            = new DefaultMutableTreeNode( "mineral" );
        everything.add( mineral );
        mineral.add(
            new DefaultMutableTreeNode( "quartz" ) );
        mineral.add(
            new DefaultMutableTreeNode( "feldspar" ) );
        avm.addTreeSelectionListener(
            new TreeSelectionListener() {
                public void
                valueChanged( TreeSelectionEvent e ) {
                    JOptionPane.showMessageDialog(
                        TreeExample.this,
                        "You selected " + e.getPath() );
```

```
            }
        }
    );
    getContentPane().add( avm, BorderLayout.CENTER );
    setSize( 200, 300 );
    setVisible( true );
}
/** The test method for the class
 * @param args not used
 */
public static void main( String[] args ) {
    new TreeExample( "Tree Example" );
}
}
```

Allowing for differences in operating systems, the output should be similar to Figure 13-19.

**Figure 13-19**   Output of the TreeExample class

The class encapsulating the drawing program is called **TreeExample**. The structure of this example is similar to the preceding examples, so only those program statements that pertain to the classes presented in this section are discussed in the following code breakdown.

The tree containing the information to be displayed is built one node at a time, beginning with the root node "everything". This root node object is passed as the tree's constructor input.

```
DefaultMutableTreeNode everything
    = new DefaultMutableTreeNode( "everything" );
JTree avm = new JTree( everything );
```

Next, the node for animals is created and it is added as a child node of the root node. In turn, three animal nodes are added to the "animal" node:

```
DefaultMutableTreeNode animal
   = new DefaultMutableTreeNode( "animal" );
everything.add( animal );
animal.add( new DefaultMutableTreeNode( "cat" ) );
animal.add( new DefaultMutableTreeNode( "dog" ) );
animal.add( new DefaultMutableTreeNode( "fish" ) );
```

Next, a node for vegetables is created and added as a child node of the root node. Then, three nodes are added as children of the "vegetable" node:

```
DefaultMutableTreeNode vegetable
   = new DefaultMutableTreeNode( "vegetable" );
everything.add( vegetable );
vegetable.add(
   new DefaultMutableTreeNode( "onion" ) );
vegetable.add(
   new DefaultMutableTreeNode( "lettuce" ) );
vegetable.add(
   new DefaultMutableTreeNode( "carrot" ) );
```

Consider the following code. A node for minerals is created and added as a child node of the root node, and then two nodes are added as children of the "mineral" node.

```
DefaultMutableTreeNode mineral
   = new DefaultMutableTreeNode( "mineral" );
everything.add( mineral );
mineral.add(
   new DefaultMutableTreeNode( "quartz" ) );
mineral.add(
   new DefaultMutableTreeNode( "feldspar" ) );
```

It is possible to detect when the user makes a selection in the tree. To do this, a tree selection listener object is added to the tree, as shown in the following code. The **valueChanged** method for this anonymous inner class displays an informational message dialog with the path of the **TreeSelectionEvent** object, for instructional purposes:

```
avm.addTreeSelectionListener(
   new TreeSelectionListener() {
      public void
      valueChanged( TreeSelectionEvent e ) {
         JOptionPane.showMessageDialog(
            TreeExample.this,
            "You selected " + e.getPath() );
      }
   }
);
```

Finally, the **JTree** object is added to the center of the frame window's content pane:

```
getContentPane().add( avm, BorderLayout.CENTER );
```

## PAINTING

Painting is the act of producing the graphics image of windows and everything that they contain on the screen. This is a different task from making a window visible by calling the **setVisible** method. A window can be fully rendered, or painted, and, at the same time, not visible because it is minimized or hidden behind another window. Painting occurs every time the display is updated. For example, when the window is resized or covered by another window and then uncovered, it must be repainted.

All paint operations are performed by a central thread: the event dispatch thread. When your code requests that a component be painted or repainted, the JVM passes the request to the event dispatch thread. Your code then continues to execute in its own thread while the event dispatch thread does the actual painting.

All objects that are instances of subclasses of **java.awt.Component** handle their own painting. Unless your application has special requirements for graphics, such as drawing directly on the graphics context or performing animation, you do not have to implement the paint method. Generally, it is better to let the Java platform use its own methods for the painting of components.

Four key methods are involved in painting components:

➤ A Swing component should override the following method to control how it is displayed:

**void paintComponent( Graphics** *context* **)**

The **paintComponent** method provides control over how the component itself is displayed but maintains the default behavior for displaying the component's border and child components. It draws the entire component automatically when the component is first displayed, exposed after being covered, resized, or scrolled into view. Unless the component is intended to be transparent, the first statement in a component's **paintComponent** method should be a call to **super.paintComponent**.

Do not call **paintComponent** directly. Only the event dispatch thread schedules the painting of objects. It does this to make sure that painting operations always complete and do not have unpredictable results, such as leaving half of a window on the screen while the application does something else.

**13**

➤ The method of the component class that renders components for display is the following:

**void paint( Graphics** *context* **)**

The **paint** method draws the entire component automatically when the component is first displayed, exposed after being covered, resized, or scrolled into view. Do not call **paint** directly. Only the event dispatch thread schedules the painting of objects. It does this to make sure that painting operations always complete and do not have unpredictable results, such as leaving half of a window on the screen while the application does something else.

➤ To make sure a component is painted, you can call the following method:

**void repaint( long** *time* **)**

When you call **repaint**, the JVM calls update and then paint for the current component. Unlike paint, repaint can be called directly. You can call the overloaded version of the repaint method with no arguments to request that the repaint begin immediately. Because painting occurs on a separate event dispatch thread, specifying a time interval in milliseconds before the next paint is to begin can give better performance than tying up the processor by repainting frequently in a tight loop.

➤ The fourth essential painting method is the following:

**void update( Graphics** *context* **)**

Unlike **paint**, which must be able to render the entire component, update can be used to update selective areas. One reason to override **update** is to create smooth animations. The default implementation can produce a flickering image because it floods the entire area of the component with the background color before calling paint.

The **JComponent** class overrides the **update** method to call **paint** directly in order to reduce flicker when drawing.

When you override the **paint**, **paintComponent**, or **update** methods, make sure that your code can execute very quickly. Include all the statements you need for painting, but no more. For example, try to remove all calculations and retain only the drawing statements. You do not want to slow down the event dispatch thread by making it perform any operations that you can do elsewhere. If the **paint** or **paintComponent** methods for one component hog time, they can prevent other components from being painted in a timely fashion and potentially cause a situation in which the display for a program does not match its internal state.

# 2D Graphics

Many programs produce graphical output. Lines, characters, and any shapes drawn directly onto a component's display area make up graphical output. Graphical output can be part of your GUI. The AWT API provides basic two-dimensional (2D) graphics support through the class **Graphics**, which includes many methods you can use for drawing. This class is one of many utility classes that reside in the package java.awt.

The drawing methods are instance methods of the **Graphics** class, and each instance of **Graphics** is the **graphics context** for a component. The **paint** and **update** methods provide a **Graphics** object as an argument of the method for you to use when you override the method.

The next sample program defines the `Drawings` class and provides a demonstration of using the methods of the Graphics class.

Drawing in the graphics context of a component is a very different process than adding a component to a container. The main differences are the following:

➤ No core Java platform layout manager class can work with graphics, and you must specify coordinates.

➤ Components automatically redraw themselves when the window in which they appear is displayed, resized, or uncovered on the screen. You must redraw graphical output as required. Usually, you effect redraw operations by including in the **paint** method the method calls for drawing.

➤ If your program uses only components and never draws to the graphics context, there is no need to implement **paint**.

Details about the **Graphics** class are provided next. A list of commonly used methods defined in this class are provided also.

**13**

---

*Class*

**java.awt.Graphics**

---

*Purpose*

The **Graphics** class provides a number of methods for drawing onto a component.

---

*Methods*

➤ **void drawString( String** *str*, **int** *x*, **int** *y* **)**
The **drawString** method draws the string provided by the first argument so that the lower-left corner of the first character is at pixel coordinate ( *x*, *y* ). The characters appear in the current font and color, which you can set with other methods of the **Graphics** class.

➤ **void drawLine( int** *x1*, **int** *y1*, **int** *x2*, **int** *y2* **)**
The **drawLine** method draws a line from ( *x1*, *y1* ) to ( *x2*, *y2* ), in the coordinates of the graphics context.

➤ **void drawRect( int** *x*, **int** *y*, **int** *width*, **int** *height* **)**
The **drawRect** method draws the outline of a rectangle from ( *x, y* ) to ( *x+width, y+height* ).

➤ **void drawPolygon( int[]** *xPoints*, **int[]** *yPoints*, **int** *nPoints* **)**
The **drawPolygon** method draws the closed polygon defined by the arrays of *x* and *y* coordinates. It is also possible to create an instance of the **Polygon** class and use the version of **drawPolygon** with a single **Polygon** parameter.

➤ **void drawArc( int** *x*, **int** *y*, **int** *width*, **int** *height*, **int** *startAngle*,
        **int** *arcAngle* **)**
The **drawArc** method draws an arc of an ellipse or circle bounded by the coordinates *x* and *y* and the specified *width* and *height* arguments. The arc rotates counterclockwise from *startAngle* degrees to *startAngle* + *arcAngle* degrees.

➤ **boolean drawImage( Image** *img*, **int** *x*, **int** *y*, **ImageObserver**
*observer* **)**
The **drawImage** method draws an image at the coordinates specified. The **Image** class is defined in **java.awt** for GIF files, JPEG files, and URLs. Images are most frequently used in applets, and the **Image** and **ImageObserver** classes are described in Chapter 14, along with other applet topics. Loading an image can take some time. Therefore, the method returns without waiting, and a return value of **false** indicates the image is not completely loaded. The **ImageObserver** object is notified when the operation is complete. Chapter 14 describes how to display **Image** objects.

➤ **void fillRect( int** *x*, **int** *y*, **int** *width*, **int** *height* **)**
**void fillPolygon( int** *xPoints*[], **int** *yPoints*[], **int** *nPoints* **)**
**void fillArc( int** *x*, **int** *y*, **int** *width*, **int** *height*, **int** *startAngle*, **int** *arcAngle* **)**
These methods of the **Graphics** class fill areas of the screen with color rather than draw outlines. The result of a draw or fill operation depends on various settings that you can specify by calling the following methods of the **Graphics** class:

➤ **void setColor( Color** *c* **)**
The **setColor** method sets the color used for subsequent drawing and fill coloring.

➤ **void setFont( Font** *f* **)**
This method sets the font for subsequent text operations.

➤ **void setPaintMode()**
**void setXORMode( Color *c* )**
The **setPaintMode** and **setXORMode** methods set alternatives paint modes. Call **setPaintMode** to overwrite whatever is already drawn on the screen. Call **setXORMode** to display pixels in the color that results from an EXCLUSIVE OR ( XOR ) operation between the current color and the color specified in the argument. Predicting the resulting colors from XOR mode is difficult, and this mode can create bizarre effects. However, the colors are reversible, and you can restore pixels to the original color by redrawing the same area.

---

It is important to note that the values set for a particular **Graphics** object used in a **paint** method are lost at the end of the paint method. This is because each **paint** method gets a fresh **Graphics** object with which to work. To make such changes last, you should make them to the component object.

Although the **Graphics** class is useful, it does have limitations. For example, you cannot specify the width of a line or use a fill pattern. The Java 2D API introduces a new class called **Graphics2D** that extends the original **Graphics** class and addresses the shortcomings of the basic 2D graphics support in the AWT API. A discussion of the Java 2D API is beyond the scope of this text.

The following is a program that exercises several methods of the **Graphics** class. It also demonstrates using the **java.awt.Font** class to set the size of characters to draw, and working with the **java.awt.Color** class. The program does not have much substance, pretense to art, or even amusing output, but it exercises a representative sample of the methods in the **Graphics** class. As with the other sample programs, a breakdown of this code follows the output.

This program defines the class `Drawings`:

```java
package examples.windows;
import java.awt.*;
import javax.swing.*;
/** An example class used to demonstrate various
  * drawing techniques including text, lines,
  * shapes, and filled shapes.
  */
public class Drawings extends JFrame {
   /** Class constructor method
     * @param titleText name to be put in the
     *    window's title bar
     */
   public Drawings( String titleText ) {
     super( titleText );
     addWindowListener( new WindowCloser() );
     DrawingPanel dp = new DrawingPanel();
```

**13**

```
            getContentPane().add( dp, BorderLayout.CENTER );
            setSize( 500, 500 );
            setVisible( true );
        }
    public class DrawingPanel extends JPanel {
        /** Class constructor
          */
        public DrawingPanel() {
            setBackground( Color.white );
            setBorder( BorderFactory.createTitledBorder(
                "Sample output from drawing methods:" ) );
        }
        /** Draws the text, lines, and shapes in the
          * specified graphics context
          * @param g the component's graphics context
          */
        public void paintComponent( Graphics g ) {
            super.paintComponent(g);
            g.drawString( "Hello World!", 100, 60 );
            Font cFont = g.getFont();
            Font newFont = new Font( cFont.getName(),
                                     cFont.getStyle(),
                                     cFont.getSize() + 20 );
            g.setFont( newFont );
            g.drawString( "Here I am!", 200, 80 );
            g.drawLine( 50, 50, 100, 200 );
            g.setColor( Color.blue );
            g.drawRoundRect( 150, 300, 100, 125, 15, 15 );
            g.setColor( Color.red );
            g.fillOval( 400, 200, 50, 180 );
        }
    }
    /** The test method for the class
      * @param args not used
      */
    public static void main( String[] args ) {
        new Drawings( "Drawings Sample" );
    }
}
```

Allowing for differences in operating systems, the output should be similar to Figure 13-20.

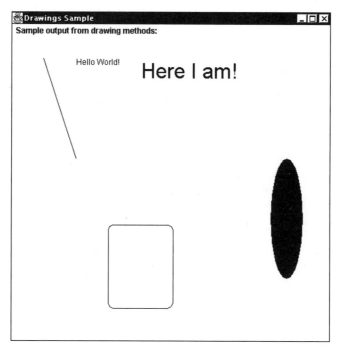

**Figure 13-20** Output of the Drawings class

The class encapsulating the drawing program is called **Drawings**. The constructor, as usual, begins by passing the title for the **JFrame** to the constructor of the **JFrame** superclass:

```
public Drawings( String titleText ) {
    super( titleText );
```

As with the other sample programs in this chapter, an instance of the class **WindowCloser** is created and registered to handle window events, as shown next:

```
addWindowListener( new WindowCloser() );
```

Then, an instance of the **DrawingPanel** class is constructed. This object is positioned in the center section of the border layout of the frame window:

```
DrawingPanel dp = new DrawingPanel();
getContentPane().add( dp, BorderLayout.CENTER );
```

The last statements of the constructor call two methods that are inherited from the **Component** class. The first sets the size of the **JFrame**, in pixels. The second sets the background color, using a constant defined in the **Color** class.

Finally, the **JFrame** is displayed by a call to **setVisible**. The **setVisible** method is implemented in the **JComponent** class to make the component visible:

```
setSize( 500, 500 );
setVisible( true );
```

A nested class defines the component where the actual drawing will take place. This class extends the **JPanel** class. The constructor sets the background color for the panel and adds a titled border to it:

```
public class DrawingPanel extends JPanel {
    public DrawingPanel() {
        setBackground( Color.white );
        setBorder( BorderFactory.createTitledBorder(
            "Sample output from drawing methods:" ) );
    }
```

This application just draws some shapes, so most of the action occurs in the **paintComponent** method. The first statement calls the **paintComponent** of the superclass:

```
public void paintComponent( Graphics g ) {
    super.paintComponent(g);
```

The **paintComponent** method draws two strings—"Hello World!" and "Here I am!"—in different sizes. The "Hello World!" string is drawn in the default font. To be bigger than "Hello World!", "Here I am!" must be drawn with a different font. The **Font** class is a utility class in **java.awt** that encapsulates fonts, and the **Font** constructor has arguments for the name, style, and size of the required font. Here, the new font is a variation on the default font because only the size changes, so the paint method creates a **Font** object and specifies it as the font for the graphics context. The **paint** method executes the following steps in the order presented:

➤ Obtains an object reference for the current font of the graphics context, by calling **Graphics.getFont**.

➤ Retrieves the current **Font** object to determine its name, style, and size by calling **getName**, **getStyle**, and **getSize**. The name of a font is specified in a **String**. You can call the method **getAvailableFontFamilyNames** using an instance of the class **GraphicsEnvironment** to get the names of the fonts available on your installation of the Java platform. The possible styles are **Font.PLAIN**, **Font.BOLD**, and **Font.ITALIC**. The size is expressed in points.

➤ Uses the **new** keyword to create a new **Font** object with the same characteristics as the current font, except that the size is increased by 20 points.

➤ Calls **Graphics.setFont** to set the new font as the current font for the current graphics context.

The following lines of the **paint** method draw the two strings using the process described previously:

```
g.drawString( "Hello World!", 100, 60 );
Font cFont = g.getFont();
Font newFont = new Font( cFont.getName(),
                         cFont.getStyle(),
                         cFont.getSize() + 20 );
g.setFont( newFont );
g.drawString( "Here I am!", 200, 80 );
```

The remaining lines of the **paint** method draw a line in the default foreground color, a rounded rectangle in blue, and a solid oval shape in red:

```
g.drawLine( 50, 50, 100, 200 );
g.setColor( Color.blue );
g.drawRoundRect( 150, 300, 100, 125, 15, 15 );
g.setColor( Color.red );
g.fillOval( 400, 200, 50, 180 );
```

The **main** method for the Drawings class simply creates a Drawings object and passes the title bar text as the parameter for the constructor:

```
public static void main( String[] args ) {
   new Drawings( "Drawings Sample" );
}
```

## CHAPTER SUMMARY

Support for the development of GUIs for the Java platform is provided by combination of the AWT and Swing APIs.

The AWT API provides the infrastructure for layout manage a con listeners, and basic 2D graphics support. The Swing API pro hensive set of GUI components that can be assembled applications.

The most basic Swing class is **JComponent**, wh Swing components and provides the basic fu components.

Components that are containers hold container components. Especially **JDialog**, **JFrame**, and **JWindow**

An application runs in a **JFra** GUI adding containers an panel of an applet.

Swing provides several class of buttons and check boxes that can be used to provide selection lists and triggers for events.

Each container has a layout manager that arranges components dynamically. Standard layout managers include **BorderLayout**, **FlowLayout**, **GridLayout**, **GridBagLayout**, **Box**, and **CardLayout**. You can nest components and layout managers for flexible arrangements. **JPanel** objects are useful containers for this purpose.

Use the classes **JMenuBar**, **JMenuItem**, **JMenu**, **JPopupMenu**, **JRadioButtonMenuItem**, and **JCheckboxMenuItem** to add menus to your GUI. Swing also provides support for toolbars through the **JToolBar** class. Actions that are common to both menus and toolbars can be created as subclasses of **AbstractAction** to provide a single point of control.

The classes **JSlider**, **JProgressBar**, and **JScrollBar** provide adjustable components to be added to GUIs. The classes **JList** and **JComboBox** provide selection lists to be added to GUIs. In addition, Swing provides several text entry classes with a wide variety of complexity: **JTextField**, **JTextArea**, **JPasswordField**, **JEditorPane**, and **JTextPane**.

Because selecting files and colors are such common operations, Swing includes the standard classes **JFileChooser** and **JColorChooser** that implement panels and that can be embedded in dialogs or internal frames.

Swing provides two sophisticated controls for structured information: **JTable** and **JTree**. The **JTable** class is best-suited for tabular information, and **JTree** is ideal for hierarchical information.

Painting is the act of drawing onto the graphics context of a component. Use paint you call drawing methods of the **Graphics** class in overloaded component, **paint**, and **update** methods of a component. The graphics call p **Graphics** object passed as an argument to these methods. Do not The A **intComponent**, or **update** directly.

initiated ns a hierarchy of event classes for different kinds of user **ItemEve** h as **ComponentEvent**. **MouseEvent**, **KeyEvent**, Create ha **nt**, and **ActionEvent**.

implement various kinds of events by instantiating classes that where xxx i compes. The listener interfaces are named xxx**Listener** ing the comp nt. Register a listener with a component by calling the comp ld xxx**Listener**, where xxx is the kind of event. For most listen

nient to extend ciated adapter class. Often, it is more convenient to extend n to implement the interface.

# REVIEW QUESTIONS

1. Which of the following classes are subclasses of **javax.swing.AbstractButton**? Select all that apply.

   a. **JButton**

   b. **JComboBox**

   c. **JRadioButton**

   d. **JMenu**

   e. **JMenuItem**

2. Which method of the **JComponent** class allows a component to respond to user input and generate events? Select the best answer.

   a. **setVisible**

   b. **setEnabled**

   c. **setReady**

   d. **addListener**

   e. **setActive**

3. Which of the following classes are subclasses of **javax.swing.text.JTextComponent**? Select all that apply.

   a. **JList**

   b. **JTextField**

   c. **JFileChooser**

   d. **JEditorPane**

   e. **JScrollPane**

**13**

4. Which of the following statements construct a **JTextArea** object that can display 20 lines of text of approximately 60 characters each? Select all that apply.

   a. `JTextArea t = new JTextArea( 60, 20 );`

   b. `JTextArea t = new JTextArea( 20, 60 );`

   c. `JTextArea t = new JTextArea( "Sales Projections:",`
      `                            60, 20 );`

   d. `JTextArea t = new JTextArea( "Sales Projections:",`
      `                            20, 60 );`

   e. `JTextArea t = new JTextArea( 60, 20,`
      `                            "Sales Projections:" );`

5. Which of the following classes implement the **LayoutManager** interface? Select all that apply.

   a. **Container**

   b. **Canvas**

   c. **FlowLayout**

   d. **BoxLayout**

   e. **GridLayout**

6. Which of the following classes is the default **LayoutManager** class for the **JPanel** class? Select the best answer.

   a. **BorderLayout**

   b. **CardLayout**

   c. **FlowLayout**

   d. **GridBagLayout**

   e. There is no default.

7. Which of the following method definitions can be used to override the **paintComponent** method of the **JComponent** class? Select all that apply.

   a. `protected void paintComponent( ) { }`

   b. `protected boolean paintComponent( ) { return false; }`

   c. `public boolean paintComponent( ) { return false; }`

   d. `public void paintComponent( ) { }`

   e. `protected void paintComponent( ) throws Throwable { }`

8. Assuming that g is a **Graphics** object, what does the following statement do when executed? Select the best answer.

   `g.drawString( "Hello!", 100, 60 );`

   a. It writes the string "Hello!" into g in an area 100 pixels wide by 60 pixels high.

   b. It writes the string "Hello!" into g in an area 60 pixels wide by 100 pixels high.

   c. It writes the string "Hello!" into g in an area 60 pixels from the top edge of the area and 100 pixels from the left edge of the area.

   d. It writes the string "Hello!" into g in an area 100 pixels from the top edge of the area and 60 pixels from the left edge of the area.

   e. It writes the string "Hello!" into g in an area 100 pixels from the top edge of the area and 60 pixels from the right edge of the area.

9. Which of the following statements draws a horizontal line 100 pixels long into a **Graphics** object g? Select all that apply.

   a. `g.drawLine( 50, 50, 150, 50 );`

   b. `g.drawLine( 50, 50, 100 );`

   c. `g.drawLine( 100 );`

   d. `g.drawLine( 50, 50, 50, 150 );`

   e. `g.drawLine( 100, 50, 50 );`

10. What is the return type of all methods defined in the **TreeSelectionListener** interface? Select the best answer.

    a. **void**

    b. **boolean**

    c. **TreeSelectionEvent**

    d. **TreeSelectionListener**

    e. **TreeSelection**

11. What is the parameter type of all methods defined in the **KeyListener** interface? Select the best answer.

    a. These methods have no parameters.

    b. **boolean**

    c. **KeyEvent**

    d. **KeyListener**

    e. **KeyAdapter**

12. In which positions in a **BorderLayout** will components stretch horizontally as the container is stretched? Select all that apply.

    a. North

    b. South

    c. Center

    d. East

    e. West

13. In which positions in a **BorderLayout** will components stretch vertically as the container is stretched? Select all that apply.

    a. North

    b. South

    c. Center

    d. East

    e. West

# Exercises

## Debugging

1. Correct all the errors in the following program so that the text in the label is green when the window appears:

```
package questions.c13;
import javax.swing.*;
import java.awt.*;
import java.awt.event.*;
public class Debug13_1 extends JFrame {
    public Debug13_1( String titleText ) {
        super( titleText );
        addWindowListener( new WindowAdapter() {
                public void
                windowClosing( WindowEvent e ) {
                    e.getWindow().dispose();
                    System.exit( 0 );
                }
            }
        );
        JLabel l = new JLabel( "Debug question" );
        l.setColor( green );
        getContentPane().add( l, BorderLayout.CENTER );
        setSize( 300, 100 );
        setVisible( true );
    }
    public static void main( String[] args ) {
        new Debug13_1( "Debug Question" );
    }
}
```

2. Correct all the errors in the following program so that when the frame window appears it contains a text area with 80 columns and 25 rows:

```
package questions.c13;
import javax.swing.*;
import java.awt.*;
import java.awt.event.*;
public class Debug13_2 extends JFrame {
    public Debug13_2( String titleText ) {
        super( titleText );
        addWindowListener( new WindowAdapter() {
                public void
                windowClosing( WindowEvent e ) {
                    e.getWindow().dispose();
                    System.exit( 0 );
                }
```

```
            }
        );
        JTextArea ta
            = new JTextArea( 80, 25, "Sample Text" );
        getContentPane().add( ta, BorderLayout.CENTER );
        pack();
        setVisible( true );
    }
    public static void main( String[] args ) {
        new Debug13_2( "Debug Question" );
    }
}
```

3. Correct all the errors in the following program so that the nine buttons are displayed in a three-by-three grid no matter how the frame window is resized:

```
package questions.c13;
import javax.swing.*;
import java.awt.*;
import java.awt.event.*;
public class Debug13_3 extends JFrame {
    public Debug13_3( String titleText ) {
        super( titleText );
        addWindowListener( new WindowAdapter() {
                public void
                windowClosing( WindowEvent e ) {
                    e.getWindow().dispose();
                    System.exit( 0 );
                }
            }
        );
        JButton[] buttons = new JButton[9];
        for( int i=0; i<buttons.length; i++ ) {
            buttons[i]
                = new JButton( String.valueOf( i+1 ) );
            add( buttons[i] );
        }
        pack();
        setVisible( true );
    }
    public static void main( String[] args ) {
        new Debug13_3( "Debug Question" );
    }
}
```

**13**

4. Correct all the errors in the following program so that the handler defined for the **JTextField** converts any lowercase character entered to uppercase when the Enter key is pressed:

```
package questions.c13;
import javax.swing.*;
import java.awt.*;
import java.awt.event.*;
public class Debug13_4 extends JFrame {
    public Debug13_4( String titleText ) {
        super( titleText );
        addWindowListener( new WindowAdapter() {
                public void
                windowClosing( WindowEvent e ) {
                    e.getWindow().dispose();
                    System.exit( 0 );
                }
            }
        );
        final JTextField tf = new JTextField( 40 );
        tf.addListener( new Listener() {
                public void eventHappened( Event e ) {
                    tf.setText(
                        tf.getText().toUpperCase() );
                }
            }
        );
        getContentPane().add( tf, BorderLayout.NORTH );
        pack();
        setVisible( true );
    }
    public static void main( String[] args ) {
        new Debug13_4( "Debug Question" );
    }
}
```

5. Correct all the errors in the following program so that a pattern of alternating black and white squares begins with a black square in the upper-left corner of the window:

```
package questions.c13;
import javax.swing.*;
import java.awt.*;
import java.awt.event.*;
// extend the Frame class
public class Debug13_5 extends JFrame {
    public Debug13_5( String titleText ) {
        super( titleText );
        addWindowListener( new WindowAdapter() {
                public void
                windowClosing( WindowEvent e ) {
```

```
                e.getWindow().dispose();
                System.exit( 0 );
            }
        }
    );
    setSize( 500, 300 );
    setVisible( true );
    }
    public void paintComponent( Graphics g ) {
        int squareSize = 30;
        Dimension d = getSize();
        g.setColor( Color.white );
        g.fillRect( 0, 0, d.width, d.height );
        g.setColor( Color.black );
        for( int y=0; y<d.height; y+=squareSize*2 ) {
            for( int x=0; x<d.width; x+=squareSize*2 ) {
                g.fillRect( x, y,
                            squareSize, squareSize );
            }
        }
    }
    public static void main( String[] args ) {
        new Debug13_5( "Debug Question" );
    }
}
```

## Complete the Solution

1. Extract the file **questions\c13\Complete13_1.java** from the file **question.jar** on the CD-ROM. Complete the `Complete13_1` class defin- ition by defining an inner class called `CheckboxHandler`. Objects of this class will handle events generated by the `disableCheck` object. When `disableCheck` is selected, all the **JButton** objects should be disabled.

2. Extract the file **questions\c13\Complete13_2.java** from the file **question.jar** on the CD-ROM. Complete the `Complete13_2` class defin- ition by adding statements that create a label, a list, and a panel with two buttons. Put the label in the north position of the frame, the list in the center position, and the button panel in the south position. It isn't neces- sary to add event handlers for these components.

3. Extract the file **questions\c13\Complete13_3.java** from the file **question.jar** on the CD-ROM. Complete the `Complete13_3` class defin- ition by adding statements to the empty `centerOnDesktop` method so that the method centers the window on the user's desktop. Look to the **Toolkit** class for methods that provide information about the desktop.

**13**

4. Extract the file **questions\c13\Complete13_4.java** from the file **question.jar** on the CD-ROM. Complete the `Complete13_4` class definition by writing a paint method that draws a chessboard pattern of eight rows and eight columns of black and white squares with a black outline around the entire board.

5. Extract the file **questions\c13\Complete13_5.java** from the file **question.jar** on the CD-ROM. Complete the `Complete13_5` class definition by adding a **MouseEvent** handler that responds to mouse clicks and puts their locations into either the `singleClicks` or the `doubleClicks` **Vector** object depending upon whether or not they are single or double clicks. The definition provides a **paint** method that draws blue dots (for single clicks) and green dots (for double clicks) at the click location.

## Discovery

1. Create a class called `ColoredScribble` that lets the user click, drag, and release with the mouse to draw lines in a window. Include menu items that let the user select the color of the line to be drawn, save the drawing to a file, and retrieve the drawing from a file. (*Hint:* Use object serialization for saving and retrieving the drawing.)

2. Continue the enhancement of your `JUnzip` class from the previous chapter's Discovery questions to allow the user either to extract all files or extract files selectively from the Zip archive.

3. Enhance the `Choosers` sample program to provide the ability to change the font used to display the file contents. Swing currently has no font chooser class, so create your own using a **JOptionPane** to display a list of fonts from which the user can select. (*Hint:* Investigate the **GraphicsEnvironment** class to find a method that will return a list of all the available fonts.)

## CHAPTER FOURTEEN

# CLIENT-SIDE JAVA AND APPLETS

### In this chapter you will:

➤ Learn what applets are and how they are different from Java applications.

➤ Use the core classes **java.applet.Applet** and **javax.swing.JApplet**.

➤ Invoke applets from HTML documents.

➤ Pass information between a web browser and an applet and between applets in the same HTML document.

➤ Add special effects such as animation and sound clips to applets.

➤ Learn what you cannot do in an applet and why these limitations are important for security reasons.

➤ Learn how signing an applet can allow it to have additional authority granted to it.

➤ Learn how to create a security-policy file and understand how to use this file to control the authority of Java programs.

➤ Use .jar (Java archive) files to reduce data-transmission time when loading applets and related files over a network.

## APPLETS: AN OVERVIEW

This chapter explains how to write and run Java applets. Some aspects of applets, such as calling them from HTML documents, do not involve the Java programming language. HTML provides all the control you need to tell a web browser how to embed a compiled applet into a web page. No feature of the Java programming language is exclusively for applets. In fact, the opposite is true: Some features cannot be used in applets and are only for applications.

In applets, programmers frequently use certain core classes and interfaces of the Java platform. These include the **java.applet.Applet** and **javax.swing.JApplet** classes. In addition, programmers use the features of the Swing and the Abstract Windowing Toolkit (AWT) APIs in applets. All of these features are described in this chapter.

With the Java platform, programmers can add applets to web pages—a fact that contributed to the Java platform's early popularity. Many books that teach Java programming, particularly those that have been available for a few years, begin with discussions of applets. You might wonder whether you can start with this chapter without plowing through all the preceding chapters. Well, the answer is a qualified maybe.

Experimenting with applets is a fun way of exploring the Java platform. With a copy of the Software Development Kit (SDK) documentation, and some sample applets, you may manage to write some handy or amusing applets. What you can do in applets is a subset of what you can do in a Java application, so you certainly do not have to know all aspects of the Java platform in depth before you start coding applets. On the other hand, if you want to program applets well, you need grounding in the Java programming language and some of the core classes. Most applets have a large visual component, so you should become familiar with the JFC Swing and AWT APIs early in your applet-writing career.

Your understanding of the nuances of the previous paragraph should tell you whether you are ready to start programming applets. At the very least, review Chapters 2, 3, 4, 5, 12, and 13, which cover the essentials of the Java programming language and the JFC APIs, before you begin to write your first applet.

## WHAT ARE APPLETS?

Java applets are Java programs designed to be run from HTML documents in the context of a web browser. Usually, an applet is a small piece of code that performs a specific task. Unlike applications, applets must have graphical user interfaces (GUI) because they always run in a graphical environment. An applet is a class that extends the core class **Applet** from the package **java.applet**. Instead of using the method **main** as an entry point (as is the case with Java applications), an applet is initialized, started, and stopped when its methods are called by the browser that is displaying the HTML document.

Applets can do most of the things that applications can do but are limited by some security restrictions described later in this chapter. Balancing this limitation, however, is the ease with which you can distribute a program on a web page to a large audience that does not have to do anything more than view an HTML document in order to run the program. No installation of any kind is required, and updates made by the programmer are automatically available the next time the HTML document is opened. This is true for HTML documents on the Internet as well as for those on an intranet.

## Viewing HTML Documents

When you browse the World Wide Web (WWW), each web page that you view is an HTML document. An HTML document is a text file that contains a mixture of ordinary text and tags that control how text and other elements appear on a computer screen. The **tags** are character sequences enclosed in angle brackets. For example, **<hr>** inserts a horizontal line. Other tags come in on-off pairs; for example, the HTML coding to display "some text" in italics is the following:

```
<i>some text</i>
```

Many tags have attributes. For example, within **<a>** and **</a>**, which are the pair of tags that enclose hypertext links, the attribute **href** must be assigned a value that represents the location to which to link, usually a URL. The following HTML excerpt defines a link to the IBM home page that the user activates by clicking the phrase "the IBM home page":

```
<a href="http://www.ibm.com">the IBM home page</a>
```

If you have used the WWW, or a private corporate intranet, you have probably used applets, because your web browser loaded them from the Internet and ran them on your workstation. Part of the great business potential for applets comes from the fact that they require no expertise of the user and are easily accessible by everyone who has learned to surf the web. As a rule of thumb, when you encounter the following situations, an applet is usually running:

➤ You are viewing a web page that contains extensive animation beyond an image that merely moves through a relatively small number of prerecorded frames. These images, such as rotating balls and flickering lights, can be stored in files called **animated GIFs** and do not require applets.

➤ You are reading a table of data on a web page that appears to be updated in real time.

➤ A web page that you are viewing lets you complete some interactive sequence other than filling in a form.

However, you cannot always be sure that an applet is running. The web page may contain code that is written in an interpreted language called **JavaScript**, which has superficial similarities to the Java programming language. One of the differences between applets and JavaScript is that the code that makes up an applet is not stored in the HTML document but is kept separately on the web server in the bytecode files created by the Java language compiler. Your web browser downloads the applet's bytecode files and loads them into the web browser's JVM when you view the HTML document. JavaScript code must be available as source statements that are typically embedded in **<script>** tags in the HTML document. The web browser interprets the JavaScript statements

**14**

when the HTML document is loaded. This process is sometimes referred to as **Dynamic HTML (DHTML)**. In addition, some browsers provide animation-like features through extensions to HTML. For example, a ticker-tape message may be produced by an applet or it could be produced by the Internet Explorer–specific tag **<marquee>**.

Another web programming technology that you may mistake for an applet is a mechanism called the **Common Gateway Interface (CGI)**. CGI is a standard for interfacing external applications with information servers and is commonly used to provide features such as forms processing. Essentially, a CGI program runs when a web server treats a URL as the name of a program to run on the server and not as the name of a file to be sent back to the client. The output of the CGI program is then sent to the client web browser for display. CGI programs are often written using the programming languages Perl or Tcl, or command processor shell scripts, but can be written in any language. **Servlets**, which are discussed in Chapter 18, are similar in function to CGI programs.

## HTML Support for Applets

All browsers, including Netscape Navigator, Microsoft Internet Explorer, and HotJava from Sun, recognize (that is, run) HTML tags. Before proceeding with this chapter, you should check the configuration of your browser to make sure that all the settings that enable applets are selected. Most browsers provide a setting to enable support for Java applets in a preferences or options menu. If you can find no such setting, you may have an old browser and should consider updating it.

You can run applets without a web browser, if necessary, in the following two ways:

➤ Load the HTML document that invokes one or more applets into the **appletviewer** program supplied with the Java 2 SDK. The **appletviewer** ignores all HTML tags, except the applet tags, and thus displays only the applet. This is an excellent way to test applets because of the environment's simplicity.

➤ Test your applet in the proprietary Java development package that you used to develop it. VisualAge for Java, and most other proprietary Java development packages, provides features for loading, running, and debugging applets, all without requiring an HTML document. VisualAge can automatically generate an HTML document that you can export with the applet class and use to test the applet in a web browser.

## Creating Applets

You produce and distribute an applet through web pages by defining a class that extends the class **Applet** or **JApplet** and then inserting applet tags in an HTML document. The tags instruct the browser to load the applet bytecode files, embed the applet in the web page, and run the applet in the browser's JVM. To pass security checks put in place by the web browser, use only the features of the Java platform that are permitted in applets. The details on applet security are presented later in this chapter.

When programming applets for the WWW, you may encounter web browsers that do not support the same level of the Java platform that you used to develop your applet. For your applet to work for a wide range of users, who might have different or older web browsers, you may have to restrict your usage of the latest classes and methods. Try to minimize the size of the applet and the amount of data it downloads to reduce transmission time.

The major web browser providers have been slow to adopt the new Java platform versions. To reduce the impact of these delays, Sun developed the **Java Plug-in** to let users install Sun's implementation of the Java Runtime Environment (JRE) in Microsoft Internet Explorer 3.02 or later and in Netscape Navigator 3.0 or later. This plug-in replaces the browser's default JVM. Sun keeps the Java Plug-in current with the most recent Java platform versions and provides a migration utility to convert existing web pages to use the plug-in.

## SAMPLE APPLET

The following code is a simple applet. This program defines the class `SimplestApplet`. Because `SimplestApplet` is a public class, it is found in a file called SimplestApplet.java. The structure of packages mirrors the file system, so you will find this source code in the examples\applet subfolder of the folder in which you unpacked the file examples.jar. This applet places a label with the text "SimplestApplet" into the content pane of the applet panel. The HTML and sample output follow in the section describing how to test the applet:

```
package examples.applet;
import java.awt.BorderLayout;
import javax.swing.JApplet;
import javax.swing.JLabel;
/** A class to demonstrate how simple an applet can be
  */
public class SimplestApplet extends JApplet {
    public void init() {
        JLabel msg = new JLabel( "SimplestApplet",
                              JLabel.CENTER );
        getContentPane().add( msg, BorderLayout.CENTER );
    }
}
```

To run an applet with a web browser or the SDK **appletviewer**, you must create an HTML document. Be careful where you put the HTML document.

By default, browsers look for files used by applets in the location from which the browser loaded the HTML document. Therefore, you should create your HTML document in the same folder as the top-level package that contains the applet.

Many browsers, and the **appletviewer** as well, use the CLASSPATH environment variable to find applet files. If you are using such a browser, make sure that the CLASSPATH includes the parent folder of the top-level package containing your applet. If you do this, you can then put the HTML document anywhere on your file system.

All the files required to run the `SimplestApplet` and other applets in this chapter are included in the .jar file **examples.jar** on the CD-ROM that accompanies this book. The multimedia applets use sound and image files. Therefore, the easiest way to run all the sample applets is from the examples folder that is created when you unpack the .jar file. Before you run any of the applets, do the following:

To prepare to run an applet:

1. Unpack the **examples.jar** file, if you have not done so already. Instructions for unpacking the .jar file are in the ReadMe file on the CD-ROM.

2. Make sure the CLASSPATH environment variable lists the parent folder of the examples subfolder.

Once you have prepared an applet, you should test it.

To test the SimplestApplet class:

1. Open the folder **examples\applet**. The file **TestSimplestApplet.html** contains the following HTML document. You can edit it to add additional text and tags to the HTML, or use this minimal web page to run the applet.

```
<html>
<applet code="examples.applet.SimplestApplet.class"
        codebase="../.." width=300 height=100>
</applet>
</html>
```

2. Either load the file **TestSimplestApplet.html** into your web browser or issue the following command:

```
appletviewer TestSimplestApplet.html
```

3. If you have installed the Java Plug-in, you can open the file **TestSimplestAppletPlugin.html** with your Netscape Navigator or Microsoft Internet Explorer browser, and the plug-in will be used to display the applet. (The file **TestSimplestAppletPlugin.html** was generated from the file **TestSimplestApplet.html** using the **HTMLConverter** tool available from the Sun web site.)

4. If you used the **appletviewer** utility, you should see a window that looks like Figure 14-1. (If this is the first time you have used **appletviewer**, you will need to first click to accept the copyright notice.) Close the **appletviewer** window the same way you close any window. If you used a web browser, the output includes any extra text that you added to the HTML document. Close the applet by closing the browser or moving to another page.

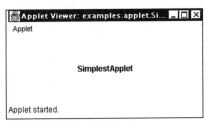

**Figure 14-1**  Output of SimplestApplet

If the applet does not display in your browser, the problem may be one of the following:

➤ The browser may not be configured to enable applets. Check the browser settings.

➤ The browser may not support the Java platform or it supports an out-of-date version. This is the most likely cause with older browsers. The solution is to get a new browser or install the Java Plug-in.

➤ The browser may not find the applet because it does not use the CLASSPATH environment variable. In this case, copy the HTML document into the parent folder of examples and try loading the copy into the browser.

**14**

# USING HTML APPLET TAGS

The simple HTML page TestSimplestApplet.html contains only two pairs of HTML tags, **<html> </html>** and **<applet> </applet>**. Like all HTML documents, TestSimplestApplet.html begins with **<html>** and ends with **</html>**. These tags identify an HTML document and are required, regardless of whether the page contains applets.

To insert an applet into an HTML document, use the tag pair **<applet>** and **</applet>**. You can control how a browser handles the applet by including attributes in the **<applet>** tag. The simple applet page has the three mandatory attributes for every **<applet>** tag: **code**, **width**, and **height**. It also has one optional attribute, **codebase**. The structure of the **<applet>** tag and the use of its attributes are detailed next.

---

*HTML Tag*

**<applet** *attributes***>***alternative content***</applet>**

---

*Purpose*

The start and end tags for an applet are **<applet>** and **</applet>**, respectively.

You can insert alternative content for browsers that do not support applets by inserting any valid HTML after the **<applet>** tag and before the **</applet>** tag. Web browsers ignore tags they do not understand. Therefore, browsers that do not recognize the applet tags skip over them, but they do process whatever comes between the tags. The alternative content is also used when a browser that recognizes the applet tags does not display the applet, which can occur for a number of reasons. For example, some browsers do not have graphics facilities (some produce alternative forms of output such as Braille), and sometimes the user has set options to turn graphics off.

---

*Attributes*

➤ **code** = "*appletFile*"
The **code** attribute is required in all **<applet>** tags. It specifies the name of the .class file that contains the applet bytecode. By default, the browser assumes that the compiled bytecode is in a file in the same folder as the HTML file. You can prefix the file with a relative path. Also, you can specify a different folder with the **codebase** attribute. Enclosing the filename in double quotation marks is required only if the filename contains spaces, punctuation, or characters other than letters and digits. However, the safest approach is always to include the quotation marks.

➤ **width** = *pixels*
The **width** attribute is required in all **<applet>** tags. It sets the horizontal size of the panel occupied by the applet, in pixels. The author of the HTML document, rather than the creator of the applet, controls the viewable area of the applet with the **width** and **height** attributes.

➤ **height** = *pixels*
The **height** attribute is required in all **<applet>** tags. It sets the vertical size of the panel occupied by the applet, in pixels.

➤ **codebase** = "*codebaseURL*"
The optional **codebase** attribute specifies a folder in which the browser should look for the applet bytecode. Use this attribute if the applet files reside in a different folder from the HTML file, and if the folder cannot be specified in the **code** attribute with the relative folder name. If your applet is defined within a package, the **codebase** attribute is used to direct the browser to the parent directory for the package. For example, the **code-base** attribute in the `SimplestApplet` example uses the directory "..\.."

to direct the browser up two directory levels to the parent directory for the examples.applet package.

➤ **alt** = "*string*"
The **alt** attribute is used by browsers that recognize the **<applet>** tag but that do not load and run the applet. The **alt** tag specifies the text to appear in place of the applet. Typically, the text is a message to inform users that the page contains a nonvisible applet. You can supply only a simple string. For more flexible alternative content, include any valid HTML between the **<applet>** and **</applet>** tags.

➤ **name** = *name*
The **name** attribute assigns a name to the applet. Include this attribute if two or more applets that run from the same HTML document may try to communicate with each other. If an applet has a name, other applets can ask, and be told, the name. JavaScript statements also can use names specified by this attribute for communicating with the applets.

➤ **vspace** = *pixels*
The **vspace** attribute specifies the depth of borders above and below the applet. Specify the number of pixels that the browser should leave empty between the surrounding elements in the HTML document and the applet panel.

➤ **hspace** = *pixels*
The **hspace** attribute specifies the width of borders to the left and right of the applet. Specify the number of pixels that the browser should leave empty between the surrounding elements in the HTML document and the applet panel.

➤ **align** = **left | right | top | texttop | middle | absmiddle | baseline | bottom | absbottom**
Use the **align** attribute when an applet occupies less screen space than the HTML file gives it. Include this attribute, and specify one of the alignment values to control the positioning of the applet within the space provided. If the applet requires more space than it is given, the panel is clipped and no errors result.

➤ **archive** = "*JARfilename*"
The **archive** attribute identifies an archive file that stores all the files required by the applet. The value is the URL identifying the archive and usually specifies a .zip or .jar file. Creating a .jar file is an excellent way to package the .class files and other files the applet uses. To considerably reduce the time to download the files required by an applet, use an archive file.

**14**

The CLASSPATH environment variable (described in Chapter 1) also plays a role in how applets are located. If your applets do not run as expected and your browser is configured to run applets, the browser may be unable to find the applet because it is not searching the folder in which the applet resides. When you are running applets from the local file system, the browser searches for files in every folder listed in the CLASSPATH. The file and path specified in the code attribute and the folders specified in the codebase attribute are treated as relative to the folders listed in your CLASSPATH. It is always a good idea to include the current folder, specified by a simple dot, in the CLASSPATH.

You also can specify parameters for the browser to pass to the applet with the **\<param\>** tag. To pass parameters to an applet, include **\<param\>** tags after the **\<applet\>** tag and before the **\</applet\>** tag. Because the use of **\<param\>** tags is optional, you can have none, one, or several of them. Details of the **\<param\>** tag follow.

---

*HTML Tag*

---

**\<param** *attributes*>

---

*Purpose*

---

Include one **\<param\>** tag for each parameter to be passed from the browser or applet viewer to the applet.

---

*Attributes*

➤ **name** = "*parameter name*"
You must include the **name** attribute because it specifies the name of a parameter of the applet. Double quotation marks around the parameter name are required only when the name contains embedded blanks, but it is safest to include the quotation marks.

➤ **value** = "*parameter value*"
You must include the **value** attribute because it assigns a value to the parameter named in the same **\<param\>** tag. Double quotation marks around the value are required only when the value contains embedded blanks, but it is safest to include the quotation marks. The value is always passed to the applet as a **String** object.

---

# USING THE JAVA.APPLET PACKAGE

The package java.applet supports writing applets. This package has only the class **Applet** and three interfaces. Figure 14-2 shows how the applet class is related to other Java classes. Shaded boxes represent abstract classes, and ovals represent interfaces.

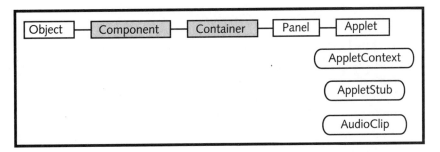

**Figure 14-2** The java.applet package

The superclasses **Panel**, **Container**, and **Component** of the **Applet** class are in the package **java.awt**. **AppletContext**, **AppletStub**, and **AudioClip** are interfaces in the **java.applet** package.

The class **Applet** extends the class **Panel** from the package **java.awt**. Therefore, an applet is a container, but not a frame. The fact that an applet is a **Panel** object is a significant design criterion. An applet is intended to look like part of an HTML page, and not like a standalone application. The size of the applet window is fixed and set by the height and width attributes of the HTML **<applet>** tag. This gives HTML authors control over the layout of their pages, but puts considerable restraints on the developers of applets.

Security is an important issue when it comes to loading applets from the Internet. By extending **Panel** rather than **Frame**, the **Applet** class prevents mischievous or malicious programmers from spoofing users. For example, if a particular applet is a **Frame**, it could be made to resemble an application that resides on the client systems. A user might be tricked into entering data that the applet could transmit back to its host system.

Although an applet cannot be a frame window, an applet can create a frame window by instantiating the **Frame** or **JFrame** class. However, the browser adds a warning message to such frame windows opened by applets in order to foil spoofing. The form of the warning varies from browser to browser. Such a warning may be enough to deter unsophisticated users and to warn others about the activities of the applet.

The life cycle of an applet is unlike that of a Java application. Applets respond to events, but cannot take the initiative. They do not have a main method to drive them. Instead, they live within the web page and are under the control of a browser or an applet-viewer utility, to which they must respond. The class **Applet** provides the methods you need to make applets work in the required way.

**14**

# EXTENDING THE APPLET CLASS

The **Applet** class is extended by the Swing class **JApplet**. The **JApplet** class is a top-level Swing container, similar to **JFrame**, that uses a content pane to contain its components. Although it is possible to use the **Applet** class in combination with the components of the AWT API to build applets, this text focuses on the use of the combination of the **JApplet** class and Swing components to create applets because of the additional GUI components and supporting classes that the Swing API offers.

All applets in this chapter extend the **JApplet** class. However examples that use only the AWT are provided in the examples.jar file. Look in the package examples.awt. The class names are the same as class names of applets in this chapter.

Not all web browsers support the Java 2 platform. Many Java programmers continue to use the AWT classes for applets so that the applets can be used by the widest-possible range of browsers. A similar phenomenon occurred after the release of version 1.1 of the Java platform: Programmers didn't upgrade from version 1.0 to version 1.1—in some cases, for as long as a year. Widespread use of the Java Plug-in should reduce programmers' reluctance to switch to the latest version of the Java platform.

To create an applet, define a class that extends the **JApplet** class and override some, or all, the methods of the **Applet** class that are inherited by **JApplet**. Usually you accept the default, no-argument constructor for your applet class. However, you can define a constructor if you want to make your class useable in some other way than as an applet. If you provide a constructor that has one or more arguments, make sure that you also explicitly provide a constructor that has no arguments. Details of the **Applet** and **JApplet** classes and their most commonly used methods are given below.

---

*Class*

**java.applet.Applet**

---

*Purpose*

The **Applet** class provides all the methods that you need to program an applet.

---

*Constructors*

➤ **Applet()**
    To create an applet class, you extend, rather than instantiate, the **Applet** class.

---

*Methods*

➤ **void init()**
    The browser or applet-viewer utility calls **init** after loading the applet and before the first call of **start**. There is a default **init** method, but you usually

override it to set up objects used by your applet. You should use **init** rather than the constructor to initialize your applet. If you define a constructor for your applet class, the constructor runs before **init**.

➤ **void start()**
The browser or applet viewer calls **start** to tell the applet to start processing. There may be an interval between the call to **init** and the call to **start**. In this method, code the applet to do its job.

➤ **void stop()**
The **stop** method tells the applet to stop processing. This method may be called because the page that contains the applet has been replaced by another page or the **destroy** method is about to be called. The browser also calls **stop** when the user scrolls up or down the page so that the applet is no longer visible. Usually, you want to suspend processing to avoid wasting CPU cycles when the applet is outside the viewing area. For example, there is no point in maintaining an animation that the user cannot see.

➤ **void destroy()**
The **destroy** method gives the applet an opportunity to deallocate resources before it is destroyed. For example, you can use this method to close a socket that had been opened for communication purposes and is no longer required. Usually, you do not need to implement this method, but it is available in case you have objects that you want to clean up. The browser calls **destroy** after **stop**, but not necessarily after every call to **stop**. If you depend on the **destroy** method, you should allow for the fact that not all browsers use it in the same way. Some browsers call **destroy** for all loaded applets when they are shutting down or unloading a page that contains applets.

➤ **String getAppletInfo()**
The **getAppletInfo** method is called by the browser and gives you an opportunity to return the name of the author, copyright information, the version number, and so forth for your applet. Return the information in a **String** object. The format and content of the string are up to you.

➤ **String getParameter( String** *parameterName* **)**
If your applet has parameters, you call the **getParameter** method to access the parameter values specified in the **<param>** tag in the HTML markup. You supply the name of a parameter as a **String** object. If the string matches the value of the **name** attribute in a **<param>** tag, the return value is the contents of the **value** attribute of the **<param>** tag. Typically, this method is used in the **init** method. Do not try to call **getParameter** in the constructor because the parameters are not yet available when the constructor for the applet runs.

**14**

➤ **String[][] getParameterInfo()**
The browser can call the **getParameterInfo** method. If your applet has any parameters, you can override the **getParameterInfo** method to provide the user with documentation about the parameters of the applet. Return the name, the type, and a description of each parameter in a two-dimensional array of strings, as shown in Figure 14-3.

➤ **AudioClip getAudioClip( URL** *url* **)**
**AudioClip getAudioClip( URL** *url***, String name )**
The **getAudioClip** method returns an **AudioClip** object. Use the object to add sound to your applet, as described later in this chapter. The audio clip is retrieved from a URL specified by an object of type **java.net.URL**. You also can supply a **String** object that contains the location of the audio clip relative to the URL.

➤ **URL getDocumentBase()**
The **getDocumentBase** method returns the **URL** object that represents the URL of the HTML document in which the applet is used. If the document resides in the local file system, the URL consists of a filename and a path name.

➤ **Image getImage( URL** *url* **)**
**Image getImage( URL** *url***, String** *name* **)**
The **getImage** method returns an **Image** object. You can display the image in your applet, as described later in this chapter. The image is retrieved from a URL specified by an object of type **java.net.URL**. You also can supply a **String** object that contains the location of the image file relative to the URL.

➤ **AudioClip newAudioClip( URL** *url* **)**
This method retrieves an **AudioClip** object from the specified URL. This is a class method that can be used to obtain an audio clip without requiring an applet instance, making it much more convenient for non-applet programs to get audio clips.

*Class*

**javax.swing.JApplet**

*Purpose*

The **JApplet** class extends the **Applet** class and provides a top-level Swing container that is similar in function to a **JFrame**. The **JApplet** class brings the power of programming with Swing components to applets. For example, a **JApplet** object can have a menu bar, but an **Applet** object cannot.

*Constructors*

➤ **JApplet()**

Typically, objects of the **JApplet** class are constructed by a web browser and not by the user.

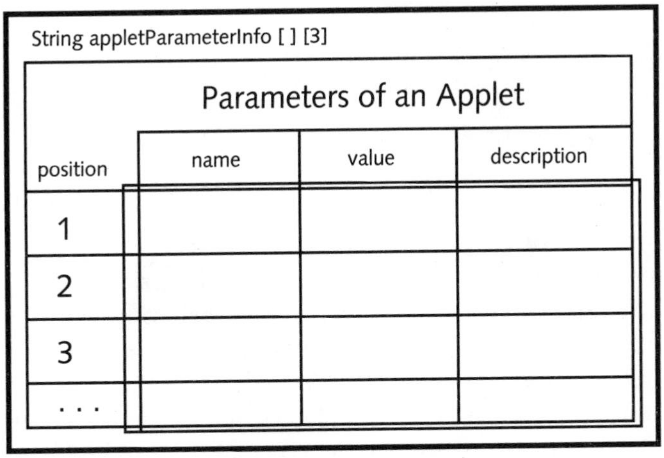

String appletParameterInfo [ ] [3]

## Parameters of an Applet

| position | name | value | description |
|----------|------|-------|-------------|
| 1 | | | |
| 2 | | | |
| 3 | | | |
| . . . | | | |

**Figure 14-3**  Applet parameter information

The methods **init, start, stop**, and **destroy** control the life cycle of the applet. During the applet's life cycle, **start** and **stop** may be called several times as the user moves up and down the page or back and forth between pages. Structure the logic of your start and stop methods accordingly.

The methods **getAppletInfo**, **getParameterInfo**, and **getParameter** pass information between the applet and the browser. The default implementation of these methods returns null. Use **getParameter** to obtain the parameter values specified in the HTML document that embeds the applet. Implementing the other two methods is optional. You can override **getAppletInfo** to provide general information about the applet to the user and getParameterInfo to document the parameters of the applet. How users access the applet and parameter information varies from browser to browser. The SDK **appletviewer** displays this information when you choose **Info** from the **Applet** menu.

**14**

> **Mini Quiz 14-1**
>
> How can you use **getParameter** to determine the values of parameters when values have types, such as **int** and **double**, other than **String**?

You can use parameters to generalize an applet so that you can use it in many different web pages. For example, the sample applet `TickerMessage` in the following section demonstrates receiving a parameter from the HTML document. The content of the message to display is a parameter of the applet.

Creating animations is an extremely popular use for applets. To create animations, use the painting methods of the **JComponent** class. The `TickerMessage` example demonstrates how to use the **paintComponent** method in an applet. The following is a review of the painting methods that are described in Chapter 13.

*Class*

**javax.swing.JComponent**

*Methods*

➤ **void paintComponent( Graphics** *context* **)**
The **paintComponent** method provides control over how the component itself is displayed but maintains the default behavior for displaying the component's border and child components. It draws the entire component automatically when the component is first displayed, exposed after being covered, resized, or scrolled into view. Unless the component is intended to be transparent, the first statement in a component's **paintComponent** method should be a call to **super.paintComponent**. Do not call **paintComponent** directly. Only the event dispatch thread schedules the painting of objects, to make sure that painting operations always complete and do not have unpredictable results such as leaving half of a window on the screen while the application does something else.

➤ **void paint()**
The **paint** method draws the entire component automatically when the component is first displayed, exposed after being covered, resized, or scrolled into view. Do not call paint directly. Only the event dispatch thread schedules the painting of objects, to make sure that painting operations always complete and do not have unpredictable results such as leaving half of a window on the screen while the application does something else.

➤ **void repaint()**
**void repaint( long** *milliseconds* **)**
When you call **repaint**, the JVM calls update and then paint for the current component. Unlike **paint**, **repaint** can be called directly. You can call the overloaded version of the repaint method with no arguments to request that the repaint begin immediately. Because painting occurs on a separate event dispatch thread, specifying an interval in milliseconds before the next paint is to begin can give better performance than tying up the processor by repainting frequently in a tight loop.

# TICKER MESSAGE APPLET

This sample applet creates a fairly simple but common form of animation. Like a ticker tape, it prints a message on the screen, and animates the message by moving it from right to left across the panel occupied by the applet.

The HTML required to run the applet and some of the interesting points in the code are described after the code:

```java
package examples.applet;
import javax.swing.*;
import java.applet.*;
import java.awt.*;
import java.awt.event.*;
/** A class to demonstrate how an applet can use
  * a thread and parameters specified in HTML
  */
public class TickerMessage extends JApplet
                            implements Runnable {
    private int delay;
    private Thread scrollingThread;
    private boolean keepScrolling;
    /** Initialize the applet and prepare to start
      */
    public void init() {
        String message = getParameter( "message" );
        if ( message == null ) {
            message = "missing parameter 'message'";
        }
        String p = getParameter( "period" );
        int period;
        if ( p == null ) {
            period = 20;
        } else {
            period = Integer.parseInt( p );
        }
        // Calculate the delay between repaints based
        // on the size and specified period. This
        // calculation is only very approximate because
        // the time needed to do the painting is not
        // accurately accounted for. Dividing the delay
        // by an adjustment factor is a simple attempt.
        delay = ( 1000 * period / getSize().width ) / 2;
        TickerPanel tp = new TickerPanel( message );
        tp.setBorder( BorderFactory.createTitledBorder(
                    "Ticker Message" ) );
        setContentPane( tp );
    }
    /** Start the ticker applet running, creating a
      * new thread as necessary
      */
```

**14**

```java
public void start() {
   if ( scrollingThread == null ) {
      scrollingThread = new Thread( this );
      keepScrolling = true;
      scrollingThread.start();
   }
}
/** Stop the ticker applet running
 */
public void stop() {
   if ( scrollingThread != null ) {
      keepScrolling = false;
      scrollingThread = null;
   }
}
/** Run the ticker. This method repaints the
 * message repeatedly, which will cause it to
 * move across the display. To save CPU, it
 * sleeps between repaint operations.
 */
public void run() {
   while ( keepScrolling ) {
      repaint();
      try {
         Thread.sleep( delay );
      } catch ( InterruptedException e ) {
         e.printStackTrace();
      }
   }
}
/** A very brief description of the applet
 * @return the applet description
 */
public String getAppletInfo() {
   return "Demonstration applet";
}
/** Provide information about the applet parameters
 * @return a two-dimensional array containing
 *     parameter names, types, and
 *     descriptions
 */
public String[][] getParameterInfo() {
   return new String[][] {
      { "message",
        "String",
        "The message to be displayed"
      },
      { "period",
        "int",
        "The time (in sec) to display the message"
      }
   };
```

```java
}
/** Implements the applet's panel where the message
  * will be scrolled.
  */
public class TickerPanel extends JPanel {
    private int strWidth, strHeight, x, y;
    private final int pixelShift = 1;
    private String msg;
    private final Color textColor = Color.black;
    private Rectangle clip;
    private Insets i;
    /** Class constructor
      * @param message The ticker message
      */
    public TickerPanel( String message ) {
        msg = message;
        Font f = new Font( "Helvetica", Font.BOLD, 18 );
        setFont( f );
        FontMetrics fm = getFontMetrics( f );
        strWidth = fm.stringWidth( msg );
        strHeight = fm.getHeight();
        addComponentListener( new ComponentAdapter() {
                public void
                componentResized( ComponentEvent e ) {
                    y = getSize().height/2 + strHeight/2;
                    x = getSize().width/2 - strWidth/2;
                    i = getInsets();
                    clip = new Rectangle( i.left, i.top,
                        getSize().width - i.left
                                        - i.right - 1,
                        getSize().height - i.top
                                        - i.bottom - 1 );
                }
            }
        );
    }
    /** Paint the panel with the message text
      * @param g The panel's graphics context
      */
    public void paintComponent( Graphics g ) {
        super.paintComponent( g );
        Rectangle clipOrig = g.getClipBounds();
        g.setClip( clip );
        g.setColor( getBackground() );
        g.drawString( msg, x, y );
        g.setColor( textColor );
        x -= pixelShift;
        if ( x < ( -strWidth + i.left ) ) {
            x = getSize().width - i.right;
        }
```

**14**

```
        g.drawString( msg, x, y );
        g.setClip( clipOrig );
    }
  }
}
```

Here is the code in the HTML page that runs the `TickerMessage` applet:

```html
<html>
<applet code="examples.applet.TickerMessage.class"
        codebase="../.."
        width=400 height=90>
<param name=message value="Your Message Here!">
<param name=period value="10">
</applet>
</html>
```

To run the `TickerMessage` applet, use the same method you used to run the simple applet earlier. Load either the file examples\applet\TestTickerMessage.html or examples\applet\TestTickerMessagePlugin.html into your web browser, or make the subfolder examples\applet the current folder and issue the following command:

```
appletviewer TestTickerMessage.html
```

At one point during execution, the output looks like Figure 14-4.

**Figure 14-4** Output of the TickerMessage applet

The first thing you may notice is that the class `TickerMessage` implements the **Runnable** interface. Running in a separate thread is desirable for animations because you can use the features of multithreading to ensure that they do not take up a lot of processor time:

```java
public class TickerMessage extends JApplet
                                implements Runnable {
```

The next notable part of the applet is the **init** method, which is where the parameters are read. One parameter is the text of the message, and a default message is available. A second parameter controls the animation speed, and the default period for the message to cross the screen is 20 seconds. The delay between repaints is calculated based on the period parameter and the width of the applet area:

```
public void init() {
   String message = getParameter( "message" );
   if ( message == null ) {
      message = "missing parameter 'message'";
   }
   String p = getParameter( "period" );
   int period;
   if ( p == null ) {
      period = 20;
   } else {
      period = Integer.parseInt( p );
   }
   // Calculate the delay between repaints based
   // on the size and specified period. This
   // calculation is only very approximate because
   // the time needed to do the painting is not
   // accurately accounted for. Dividing the delay
   // by an adjustment factor is a simple attempt.
   delay = ( 1000 * period / getSize().width ) / 2;
```

At the end of the **init** method, the panel in which the animation will take place is constructed, given a titled border, and set as the applet's content pane. The class `TickerPanel` is a nested class of `TickerMessage` and is described next:

```
   TickerPanel tp = new TickerPanel( message );
   tp.setBorder( BorderFactory.createTitledBorder(
                "Ticker Message" ) );
   setContentPane( tp );
}
```

Consider the following code. The methods **start** and **stop** override **start** and **stop** of the **Applet** class. Here, the animation thread is launched in **start** and terminated in **stop**. The **if** statements check whether `scrollingThread` is a running thread and use the value of the object reference as a flag:

```
public void start() {
   if ( scrollingThread == null ) {
      scrollingThread = new Thread( this );
      keepScrolling = true;
      scrollingThread.start();
   }
}
/** Stop the ticker applet running
 */
public void stop() {
   if ( scrollingThread != null ) {
      keepScrolling = false;
      scrollingThread = null;
   }
}
```

**14**

**Mini Quiz 14-2**

Why does the program pass **this** to the constructor of **Thread**? (*Hint*: Does the class `TickerMessage` extend the class **Thread**?)

The **run** method is the entry point of the thread. This method repaints continually, relying on the overloaded **update** method to modify the drawing and create the effect of animation. Here, the call to **sleep** controls the speed of the animation, but that is not the only reason for calling **sleep** between repeated calls of **repaint**. The **repaint** method is asynchronous, which means it returns without waiting for the **paint** operation that it requests to complete. The CPU can be kept so busy scheduling **paint** requests that the event dispatch thread cannot keep up. The sleep method gives the event dispatch thread, as well as other threads in your program, a chance to run.

```java
public void run() {
   while ( keepScrolling ) {
      repaint();
      try {
         Thread.sleep( delay );
      } catch ( InterruptedException e ) {
         e.printStackTrace();
      }
   }
}
```

**Mini Quiz 14-3**

Why is the **sleep** method in a try block? What exception might the catch clause handle?

The two methods **getAppletInfo** and **getParameterInfo** provide information about the applet and its parameters so that a browser can retrieve on demand:

```java
public String getAppletInfo() {
   return "Demonstration applet";
}
/** Provide information about the applet parameters
 * @return a two-dimensional array containing
 *    parameter names, types, and
 *    descriptions
 */
public String[][] getParameterInfo() {
   return new String[][] {
      { "message",
        "String",
        "The message to be displayed"
      },
```

```
      { "period",
        "int",
        "The time (in sec) to display the message"
      }
   };
}
```

**Mini Quiz 14-4**

Why does an implementation of the **repaint** method, which this class uses, not appear in the program listing?

The class **TickerPanel** implements the actual scrolling of the ticker message. The class constructor takes the message as input. To set the font for the message, it is necessary to create an appropriate **Font** object to pass to the **setFont** method that the applet inherits from **Container**. The class **java.awt.FontMetrics** provides information about the rendering of a font on a specific screen. Here, the method **FontMetrics.stringWidth** returns the number of pixels required to display the message:

```
public TickerPanel( String message ) {
   msg = message;
   Font f = new Font( "Helvetica", Font.BOLD, 18 );
   setFont( f );
   FontMetrics fm = getFontMetrics( f );
   strWidth = fm.stringWidth( msg );
   strHeight = fm.getHeight();
```

Next, a component listener is registered for the panel so that the component will be notified whenever its size changes. Several of the scrolling parameters must be adjusted if the component's size changes. The value of **y** is calculated to position the message exactly halfway down the panel. The value of **x** is set to initially center the message horizontally in the panel. The insets for the panel are retrieved in order to determine the boundaries for drawing the message. These values are needed to establish a clip area for drawing, which will prevent the message from being painted over the component's titled border:

```
addComponentListener( new ComponentAdapter() {
      public void
      componentResized( ComponentEvent e ) {
         y = getSize().height/2 + strHeight/2;
         x = getSize().width/2 - strWidth/2;
         i = getInsets();
         clip = new Rectangle( i.left, i.top,
            getSize().width - i.left
                              - i.right - 1,
            getSize().height - i.top
                              - i.bottom - 1 );
      }
   }
);
```

Consider the following code. The `TickerPanel` class's **paintComponent** method is used to do the actual animation. The method begins by chaining to its superclass's method in order to correctly paint the component's border and any child components. The initial clip area for the entire component is saved, and then the clip area for the scrolling message is set:

```
public void paintComponent( Graphics g ) {
    super.paintComponent( g );
    Rectangle clipOrig = g.getClipBounds();
    g.setClip( clip );
```

Consider the impact of the following code. The message is first drawn using the background color to erase the currently visible message. Then the message is shifted on the *x*-axis and a check is made to see if the message has disappeared off the left side of the window. If the message has disappeared to the left, it is then repositioned at the right side of the window. Once the position of the message has been established, it is drawn with the text color. The last statement of the method restores the original clip area of the component. If this isn't done, the component's border will not be drawn properly:

```
    g.setColor( getBackground() );
    g.drawString( msg, x, y );
    g.setColor( textColor );
    x -= pixelShift;
    if ( x < ( -strWidth + i.left ) ) {
        x = getSize().width - i.right;
    }
    g.drawString( msg, x, y );
    g.setClip( clipOrig );
}
```

If you run this applet in the **appletviewer**, and choose **Info** from the **Applet** menu, you see the information displayed in Figure 14-5.

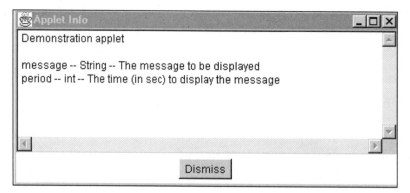

**Figure 14-5** TickerMessage applet information

# ADDING MULTIMEDIA TO APPLETS

Many programmers include applets in their web pages to add sounds and images, two common elements of multimedia. By combining multimedia and animation, programmers can create appealing special effects. As you go through this section of the chapter, remember that these same multimedia effects can be applied to Java applications.

 The Java 2 platform enhanced the support for sound. New features include playback support for wav, aiff, and au files. In addition, the Java 2 platform supports the MIDI-based song file formats of MIDI TYPE 0, MIDI TYPE 1, and RMF. The sound quality is also much improved. As a simpler way of obtaining an audio clip, applications can call a new class method, **newAudioClip**, in the **Applet** class.

## Adding Sound

Adding sound to an applet is simple: Call the method **getAudioClip** of the **Applet** class to get an object that implements the interface **java.applet.AudioClip**. Support for audio clips is available only from the **java.applet** package. Java applications as well can use this support by applying the **newAudioClip** method in the **Applet** class.

*Interface*

java.applet.AudioClip

*Methods*

➤ **AudioClip getAudioClip( URL** *url* **)**
**AudioClip getAudioClip( URL** *url*, **String** *name* **)**
These methods retrieve an **AudioClip** object from the specified URL. The method returns immediately, regardless of whether the audio clip exists. You can use the methods of this interface for the audio clip in your applet.

➤ **void play()**
The **play** method plays an audio clip or restarts a playing audio clip from the start. If the data for the audio clip is not yet loaded, it is loaded after you call this method.

➤ **void loop()**
The **loop** method plays the audio clip repeatedly in a loop.

➤ **void stop()**
The **stop** method stops playing the audio clip.

**14**

The following is a simple applet that loads an audio clip from the folder in which the HTML document resides and then plays the audio clip once. The name of the audio clip file is a parameter of the applet called sound:

```java
package examples.applet;
import java.applet.AudioClip;
import javax.swing.JApplet;
/** An example applet that loads and plays an audio clip
 */
public class SoundApplet extends JApplet {
   private AudioClip sound;
   public void init() {
      sound = getAudioClip( getDocumentBase(),
                               getParameter( "sound" ) );
   }
   public void start() {
      sound.play();
   }
   public void stop() {
      sound.stop();
   }
   public String getAppletInfo() {
      return "Demonstration applet";
   }
   public String[][] getParameterInfo() {
      String pInfo[][] = {
         { "sound", "String",
            "The file containing the sound clip"  }
      };
      return pInfo;
   }
}
```

Here is the code, taken from HTML document, that runs the SoundApplet class:

```html
<html>
<applet code="examples.applet.SoundApplet.class"
        codebase="../.."
        width=300 height=300>
<param name=sound value="youhink.au">
</applet>
</html>
```

The audio clip for this applet is included in the examples\applet folder. To run the applet, load either the file examples\applet\TestSoundApplet.html or examples\applet\TestSoundAppletPlugin.html into your browser or go to the subfolder examples\applet and issue the following command:

```
appletviewer TestSoundApplet.html
```

When this applet runs in the applet viewer, you see an empty applet viewer window. In a browser, you see an empty web page. However, if your workstation is enabled for sound, you should hear a few bars of guitar music while the audio clip is playing.

## Adding Images

Use the **Image** class to work with pictorial data stored in a known graphics format. For example, the source for an image can be a GIF or JPEG file that you load into your application from a file or any data that you download into your applet from a URL on the web. The **Image** class is in the package java.awt.

 The original version of the Java platform accepted files only in GIF format. Support for JPEG files was added in version 1.1.

Adding images to applets is similar to adding sound clips. As with **AudioClip**, you cannot simply create an **Image** object because **Image** is an abstract class. Instead, call a method that returns an **Image** object. You can call a **getImage** method of the **Applet** or **Toolkit** class. The **Applet** class provides two methods for getting an image from a URL:

```
Image getImage( URL url )
Image getImage( URL url, String name )
```

You also can call instance methods of the **Toolkit** class. In an applet, the **Applet.getImage** methods are usually more convenient because you do not have to create a **Toolkit** object. However, in an application, you can use the **Toolkit** methods without having to create an **Applet** object. Details of the **Toolkit** class and its **getImage** methods follow.

*Class*

**java.awt.Toolkit**

*Purpose*

The **Toolkit** class contains the methods that join the platform-independent classes of the AWT with the platform-specific implementations of peer classes. This class has many methods, but usually you do not call them directly. However, the **Toolkit** methods are useful in some specific circumstances, such as when you want to load an image from a file.

To get the **Toolkit** object for a component, use the **Component.getToolkit** method. The **getToolkit** method has no argument and returns a **Toolkit** object. Then you can use the **Toolkit** object to call instance methods of the **Toolkit** class, including **getImage**.

14

*Methods*

➤ **Image getImage( String** *filename* **)**
**Image getImage( URL** *url* **)**
The **getImage** method returns an **Image** object. You can specify the location of the image as either a URL encapsulated in a **URL** object or a filename in a **String**.

*Code Example*

**Image babycats = getToolkit().getImage( "kittens.gif" );**

*Code Dissection*

This statement accesses the file kittens.gif.

To display the image in a graphics context, use one of the **drawImage** methods of the **Graphics** class. Of the several overloaded **drawImage** methods, the simplest follows:

```
boolean drawImage( Image img,
                        int x, int y,
                        Color bgcolor,
                        ImageObserver observer )
```

The image is drawn so that its upper-left corner is at the specified coordinates. If the image contains transparent pixels, they are drawn in the color specified by the **Color** argument. Images can take time to load, and the **ImageObserver** objects are notified about image-drawing progress. You also can use objects of the **java.awt.MediaTracker** class to monitor the loading of several images with a single object. Using a **MediaTracker** is much more convenient than using several **ImageObserver** objects.

The following is a sample applet that retrieves and displays an image that is frequently used in demonstrations of Java technology:

```
package examples.applet;
import javax.swing.*;
import java.awt.*;
/** An example applet that loads and displays an image
  */
public class ImageApplet extends JApplet {
    public void init() {
        Image image = getImage( getDocumentBase(),
                                getParameter( "image" ) );
        ImagePanel ip = new ImagePanel( image );
        setContentPane( ip );
    }
    public String getAppletInfo() {
        return "Demonstration applet";
```

```
        }
    public String[][] getParameterInfo() {
        String pInfo[][] = {
            { "image", "String",
              "The file containing the image."  }
        };
        return pInfo;
    }
    public class ImagePanel extends JPanel {
        private Image image;
        public ImagePanel( Image image ) {
            this.image = image;
        }
        public void paintComponent( Graphics g ) {
            Insets ins = getInsets();
            g.drawImage( image, ins.right, ins.top, this );
        }
    }
}
```

Here is the code, taken from the HTML document, to test the applet:

```
<html>
<applet code="examples.applet.ImageApplet.class"
        codebase="../.."
        width=300 height=300>
<param name=image value="Juggler0.gif">
</applet>
</html>
```

The image file for this applet, Juggler0.gif, is included in the examples\applet folder. To run the applet, load one of the following files into your browser

examples\applet\TestImageApplet.html
examples\applet\TestImageAppletPlugin.html:

Or, go to the subfolder examples\applet and issue the following command:

```
appletviewer TestImageApplet.html
```

The output looks like Figure 14-6.

---

**Mini Quiz 14-5**

What is the role of a Graphics object when drawing in a component? (*Hint:* You may need to combine your knowledge of applets with what you learned in Chapters 12 and 13.)

**Figure 14-6** Output of the image applet

 One advantage of Swing applets is that the images are double-buffered by default. Double buffering involves drawing the image off-screen first and then transferring the complete image to the screen. This reduces flicker because drawing the image becomes one operation that does not depend on file I/O. If you do not use the Swing classes, you can program double buffering yourself, using "off-screen images." Before Swing classes were available, Java programmers often explicitly programmed double buffering. This technique is not described in this book, but an example is included in the examples.jar file. See the source file examples\awt\BufferedTickerMessage.java.

# SECURITY

Security is a serious concern because many Java programs (notably, applets) are designed to be loaded from the WWW. Because many of these programs originate from untrusted host systems, the worry about viruses and other unwanted side-effects is valid. The JVM puts many restrictions on applets, which severely limits their activity. Nevertheless, most users welcome the limitations as good safety precautions.

## Understanding Applet Security

You do not have to do anything to provide a security envelope for applets that run in your browser. The Java platform provides a default security manager for applets that protect your system from downloaded applets and another security manager that lets applications do almost anything. When you load an HTML document from the web into your web browser, you are operating in a client-server environment. Your browser, which displays the page, is the client. The host from which the web page is accessed is the server. The client and server can both be on the same workstation or thousands of miles apart on the Internet. Generally, security is an issue only when you are running applets that have been downloaded from other sites.

By default, bytecode files for applets loaded over the network are passed through the bytecode verifier, which ensures that the bytecode conforms to the Java virtual machine specification. The verifier reduces the chance that a saboteur can hand-code bytecode and trick the JVM into performing actions it would not otherwise allow. The verifier is not called for applets loaded from local disk storage unless the user specifically requests the verifier.

During execution, the applet security manager enforces applet security restrictions. All browsers define their own subclass of the **java.lang.SecurityManager** to enforce their security policy, as does the **appletviewer** that comes with the JDK. The **SecurityManager** class provides many methods with names that start with the word "**check**". Each **check***xxx* method corresponds to an action that can possibly be disallowed. For example, every time a user attempts to delete a file, the method **checkDelete** is called. You can set arguments that determine whether the method decides to allow or disallow the operation by throwing a **java.lang.SecurityException** object. Because different browsers implement the check methods differently, sometimes the same applet may execute without an error within one browser but trigger a security exception within another browser.

Security managers typically impose the following restrictions:

➤ An applet cannot read and write files on the client file system. However, it can read and write files on the system on which the applet originated. Some browsers let applets use certain folders. Exactly what files your applet can access vary from client to client.

➤ An applet can access only a subset of the system property values returned by the method **System.getProperty.**

➤ An applet may make network connections only with sockets on the computer from which the applet was loaded. This restriction prevents applets from becoming "Trojan horse" attackers. For example, an applet cannot move inside a firewall and then set up connections on the intranet where the applet would otherwise not be allowed to establish connections.

➤ An applet cannot start other programs on the client.

➤ An applet cannot shut down the web browser by calling the **System.exit** method.

➤ The **System** class defines the method **loadLibrary**, which is used to bring in a shared code library. This method is not available to applets.

**14**

➤ An applet cannot use native methods. Native methods are used to run code written in other languages than the Java programming language that run outside the JVM. Appendix B describes how to create native methods. Native methods are considered unsafe because there is no way to know what they have been programmed to do.

➤ Applets cannot provide their own versions of classes from any package that begins with the word "java". For example, an applet cannot create its own version of **java.lang.String** and have it downloaded to the client system.

## Signed Applets

Many people find the preceding security restrictions unacceptably limiting. Of course, where there is a "way," there is a security hole. Nonetheless, what if you wanted to use the features of a particular applet, even if that applet would be considered dangerous by conservative security measures?

If that were your goal, you would use signed applets. They let you relax the security rules for applets that are signed by people you trust. The signature is a digital signature applied to a .jar file. A browser that supports signed applets recognizes the digital signature. When a signed applet requires a special privilege, a dialog box is presented to the user indicating the privilege requested and the name of the person who signed the applet. It is then up to the user to decide whether or not to grant this special privilege.

The SDK includes tools for generating and managing digital signatures. They are listed briefly in Table 14-1. Unfortunately, each of the popular web browsers support this technology in different ways. There is no standard implementation that will work with them all. This technology is bound to be important in the future. In particular, companies with their own intranets may want to use applets as applications and give the applets special privileges on employee workstations.

**Table 14-1**   Tools provided by the Java 2 platform for managing security

| Tool | Description |
|------|-------------|
| keytool | Maintains a database of digital signatures and certificates called the keystore. Typically, an individual who is responsible for administering security for your organization uses this tool. It is password-protected. |
| jarsigner | Assigns a digital signature to a .jar file or verifies digital signatures. Make sure the signature is registered in the keystore before assigning it to a .jar file. |
| policytool | Creates or modifies policy configuration files that determine the security policy enforced by your organization. Typically, the security administrator for your organization uses this tool. |

The Java 2 platform introduced some major changes to the security model. With the 1.1 version of the Java platform, applets were either trusted or not trusted. Java 2 gives finer-grained control through **policies** that you can set up to let named users or groups use specific resources. The next section discusses policies. The implementation of the **PolicyManager** class has changed. The **jarsigner** tool of version 1.1 has been redesigned to work with the new **keytool** and **policytool** tools.

## Permissions and Policy Files

With the release of the Java 2 platform, an object of the **java.security.Policy** class now represents the security policy for all kinds of Java programs. The information used to build the **Policy** object is taken from a default, systemwide policy file and an optional user policy file. The default name for these files is java.policy. The default location of the systemwide file is the directory *java.home*\lib\security, where *java.home* is the directory where the Java runtime is installed, as defined in the system property called java.home. Use the system property *user.home* in the directory *user.home*\lib\security to locate the user policy file.

The contents of the systemwide and user **java.policy** files is one or more of the **grant entry** statements in the form below. The square brackets are not part of the statement syntax but are used to indicate which parts of the statement are optional. Italicized text represents values that are replaced by actual user information:

```
grant [signedBy "signer_names",] [codeBase "URL"] {
    permission permission_class_name
        "target_name", ["action"]
        [, signedBy "signer_names"];
}
```

The **signedBy** and **codeBase** clauses of the statement identify the code to which the permissions listed inside the brace brackets { } apply. The **signedBy** clause is used to indicate that the permissions apply to code signed by the names inside the double quotes that follow. The **codeBase** clause is used to indicate that the permissions apply to code from the URL specified inside the double quotes that follow. These can be used singly or together. If both are omitted, the permissions will apply to all code, regardless of origin and who may have signed it.

The contents of an example policy file are shown below. Two grant statements are included: The first applies to code signed by ACME Software, and the second applies to code from the URL www.mycompany.com. The dash at the end of the URL indicates that the statement also applies to all files in all subdirectories.

**14**

If an asterisk were used in place of the dash, it would apply to all files in the specified directory, but not to any subdirectories:

```
grant signedBy "ACME Software" {
    permission java.io.FilePermission
        "c:\\autoexec.bat", "read";
    permission java.lang.RuntimePermission
        "queuePrintJob";
}
grant codeBase "http://www.mycompany.com/-" {
    permission java.util.PropertyPermission
        "java.*", "read";
    permission java.util.PropertyPermission
        "user.*", "write";
    permission java.lang.RuntimePermission
        "exitVM";
}
```

The Java 2 security model is a more fine-grained model than the security model of earlier versions of the Java platform because you can now specify the permissions that you grant. Table 14-2 lists the available permission class names that can be used in a grant statement and describes the purpose for each class. Example target names are also given as well as any applicable actions.

**Table 14-2**   Policy file permission class names and descriptions

| Permission Type Class Name | Description |
| --- | --- |
| java.security.AllPermission | This permission implies all other permissions. It is granted to allow code the ability to run without any security restrictions, so it should be used cautiously. |
| java.awt.AWTPermission | This permission is granted to allow code special privileges with respect to GUI operations. Examples of targets for this type are **accessClipboard**, which allows information to be placed upon and taken from the AWT clipboard and **showWindowWithoutWarningBanner**, which allows frame windows created by applets to appear without any warning message. |
| java.io.FilePermission | This permission is granted to allow code access to read and write files. Targets of this type are specific files, directories, or directory trees. Actions that can be controlled are read, write, execute, and delete. |
| java.net.NetPermission | This permission is granted to allow code to perform certain network-related operations. Examples of targets for this type are **setDefaultAuthenticator**, which allows the ability to set the way authentication information is retrieved when a proxy or HTTP server asks for authentication and **requestPasswordAuthentication**, which allows the ability to ask the authenticator for a password. |

**Table 14-2**   Policy file permission class names and descriptions (continued)

| Permission Type Class Name | Description |
| --- | --- |
| java.util.PropertyPermission | This permission is granted to allow code to access property values. Targets for this type are specific properties or groups of properties specified with a wildcard match. Actions that can be controlled are read and write. |
| java.lang.ReflectPermission | This permission is granted to allow code to query information about classes. An example target for this type is **suppressAccessChecks** that allows the ability to find out about public, private, and protected fields and methods. |
| java.lang.RuntimePermission | This permission is granted to allow code the ability to perform operations related to the functioning of the JVM. Example targets for this type are **exitVM**, which allows the ability to halt the JVM; **loadLibrary**, which allows the dynamic linking of a specified library; and **queuePrintJob**, which allows a print job request to be initiated. |
| java.security.SecurityPermission | This permission is granted to allow code to perform operations related to the enforcement of security policy. Example targets for this type are **getPolicy**, which allows the retrieval of the system-wide security policy, and **setPolicy**, which allows the setting of the systemwide security policy. |
| java.io.SerializablePermission | This permission is granted to allow code to perform operations related to serializing and deserializing objects. Example targets for this type are **enableSubclassImplementation**, which allows the default implementations of **ObjectOutputStream** and **ObjectInputStream** to be replaced with a user-defined subclass, and **enableSubstitution**, which allows one object to be substituted for another during a serialization or deserialization operation. |
| java.net.SocketPermission | This permission is granted to allow code to perform operations related to establishing connections to host systems. The targets for this type are port numbers or ranges of port numbers on specific host systems. Actions that can be controlled are accept, connect, listen, and resolve. |

**14**

# PACKAGING APPLETS IN .JAR FILES

Files with a .jar extension provide a packaging mechanism for Java classes and for resource files used by Java classes. For applets, the files address the inefficiencies that result from each bytecode file, image file, and sound file being downloaded separately in its own HTTP request. By bundling everything that an applet needs into a single file, a .jar file ensures that only one HTTP request is needed.

The .jar files can be compressed files that use the same format as the zip files. You can create a .jar file with the **jar** tool that comes with the JDK.

*Syntax*

**jar** *options* **[***manifest***]** *destination file_list*

*Dissection*

Control the activities of the **jar** utility with options. The fields you include in a **jar** command depend on the actions to be performed.

➤ When you specify more than one option, concatenate them into one token.

➤ The optional manifest file holds information about the .jar file. A default manifest is included in the .jar file if you do not specify one of your own. Usually, the default manifest is adequate.

➤ You can use the wildcard characters **\*** and **?** when listing files. You can also specify folder names.

➤ The **jar** command recursively processes subfolders when the input file is a folder.

➤ Options of the **jar** command are the following:

➤ The option **c** creates a new or empty .jar file.

➤ Include option **f** to indicate that the .jar file to create is named on the command line. Without this option, the command sends the output to standard output. When combined with the x or **t** options, option **f** indicates that the second field on the command line is the name of an existing .jar file to process.

➤ To include information from an existing manifest, include the **m** option and list the manifest file on the command line.

➤ If you do not want a manifest file, include option **m** to suppress creation of a manifest.

➤ The option **t** lists the table of contents for the archive.

➤ The option **v** generates additional output, such as the size of files and when they were created.

➤ The option **x** extracts the files named on the command line, or all files if no specific files are listed.

➤ The **0** (digit zero) option tells the **jar** utility to store the files only when creating a .jar file and not to apply any compression.

---

*Code Examples*

```
jar cf mystuff.jar *.class *.au *.gif *.jpg
jar cmf mymanifest.txt mystuff.jar *.class
jar tf newjar.jar
```

---

*Code Dissection*

The first command creates a .jar file called mystuff.jar and adds to the .jar file all files in the current folder with the extension .class, .au, .gif, or .jpg.

The second command creates a .jar file called mystuff.jar, using an existing manifest mymanifest.txt, and adds all .class files in the current folder to the .jar file.

The third command lists all the files in the .jar file newjar.jar.

 The Java 2 platform provides an API for reading and writing .jar files in the package **java.util.jar** that was not available previously. The security mechanism relating to jars also has been enhanced. The implementation of the **jarsigner** tool has changed. The policy manager now has a mechanism for dealing dependencies on extensions and third-party libraries that are packaged .jar files.

# SUMMARY

Applets are small programs that can run from HTML web pages. Applets run only in web browsers, application-development environments, or special utilities such as the **appletviewer** of the SDK.

To run an applet from an HTML document, you specify the name of the applet and its size in an **<applet>** tag. Use the **<param>** tag to pass parameters to the applet.

The **java.applet** package supports applets. It contains the **Applet** class, which all applets must extend and which extends **java.awt.Panel.** The Swing class **javax.swing.JApplet** extends the **Applet** class and defines a top-level container with a content pane that brings the power of Swing GUI components to applet programming.

Use methods of the **Applet** class to initialize, start, and stop your applet as well as to pass parameters between the applet and the browser.

Most applets are small and many have a high graphics content, such as animation, images, and multimedia objects. Therefore, applet programming usually makes heavy use of the AWT and Swing APIs.

Use the **AudioClip** interface for sound. In addition, you should use the **Image** class for pictures stored on file.

Applications can do everything that applets can do. To access the methods of the **Applet** class, an application must create an **Applet** or **JApplet** object.

**14**

Security is such a major concern with applets that most people welcome the restrictions put on applets for protection against viruses, spoofing, and other forms of malicious code. With applets, code downloaded from a network is verified, the security manager prevents the downloaded code from accessing the local file system, and other security measures are implemented.

Applets that originate locally and applets that are signed have relaxed security limitations. Tools have been developed for managing signatures, but the popular web browsers support signed applets in different, and incompatible, ways.

The Java 2 platform introduced a new, fine-grained security policy that is defined by grant entry statements in policy files. Each grant entry statement is applied to code that is signed by a particular name, or that originates from a particular URL. With grant entry statements, a wide range of permissions, targets, and actions are available for the user to build an effective security policy.

The **jar** tool compresses and packages files into .jar files, which are a convenient and efficient way to distribute sets of files required by applets.

# QUESTIONS

1. Which of the following classes is a superclass of **javax.swing.JApplet**? Select all that apply.
    a. **Container**
    b. **Panel**
    c. **ContentPane**
    d. **JFrame**
    e. **JComponent**

2. Which method of the **JApplet** class is called when the applet is loaded? Select the best answer.
    a. **init**
    b. **start**
    c. **begin**
    d. **play**
    e. **load**

3. Which methods of the **JApplet** class are called when the HTML page on which an applet is defined is removed from the browser's window and then brought back? Select the best answer.
    a. **init**
    b. **start**
    c. **destroy**
    d. **stop**
    e. **load**

4. Which of the following HTML tags load the applet class `Hello`? Select all that apply.
    a. `<applet code=Hello.class>`

b. `<applet code=Hello.class width=300 height=100>`

c. `<applet code=Hello width=300 height=100>`

d. `<applet code=Hello>`

e. `<applet code=Hello.class width=300 height=100`
`        name=Hello>`

5. Which of the following are valid attributes for the **<applet>** HTML tag? Select all that apply.

   a. **param**

   b. **archive**

   c. **vspace**

   d. **alt**

   e. **value**

6. Examine the following HTML statements:

```
<applet code="TickerTape.class" width=400 height=90>
<param name=speed value="1">
</applet>
```

Which of the following Java statements successfully retrieve the specified parameter for the class `TickerTape`? Select all that apply.

   a. `String speed = getParameter( "speed" );`

   b. `String speed = getParameter( speed );`

   c. `String speed = getValue( "speed" );`

   d. `int speed = getParameter( "speed" );`

   e. `int speed = getValue( "speed" );`

7. In which of the following situations is the **paintComponent** method called for a component? Select all that apply.

   a. The component is resized.

   b. A method of the component calls the **repaint** method without any arguments.

   c. A method of the component calls the **repaint** method with an **int** argument.

   d. The component is constructed and made visible.

   e. A method of the component calls the **drawImage** method.

8. Which interface of the **java.applet** package defines the behavior of objects used to manipulate sound?

9. What does the following statement do when executed within an applet? Select the best answer.

```
getImage( getDocumentBase(), "duke.jpg" );
```

   a. Returns an **Image** object called duke.jpg, located at the same URL as the applet, that can be painted in a **Graphics object**.

   b. Returns a **Graphics object** called duke.jpg, located at the same URL as the current HTML document, that can be painted in an **Image** object.

**14**

    c. Returns an **Image** object called duke.jpg, located at the same URL as the current HTML document, that can be painted in a **Graphics** object.

    d. Returns a **Graphics** object called duke.jpg, located at the same URL as the applet, that can be painted in an **Image** object.

    e. Displays an image called duke.jpg, located at the same URL as the HTML document.

10. Given that `img` is a valid Image object and `g` is a valid **Graphics** object, which of the following statements draw the image 20 pixels from the top edge of the container and 30 pixels from the left edge of the container? Assume that the method is called from within an instance method of an applet. Select all that apply.

    a. `g.drawImage( img, 30, 20, this );`

    b. `g.drawImage( img, 20, 30, this );`

    c. `g.drawImage( img, 30, 20 );`

    d. `g.drawImage( img, 30, 20, 100, 100, this );`

    e. `g.drawImage( img, 20, 30, 100, 100, this );`

11. True or False: The **drawImage** method returns only after the **Image** object has been drawn.

## EXERCISES

### Debugging

1. Correct any errors in the following HTML document:
```
<html>
<applet code="questions.c14.Debug14_1.class"
        width=300 height=100>
</applet>
</html>
```
Also correct any errors in the following class definition:
```
package questions.c14;
public class Debug14_1 {
    public void init() {
        getContentPane().add(
            new JLabel( "Debug question." ) );
    }
}
```

2. Correct any errors in the following HTML document:
```
<html>
<applet code="questions.c14.Debug14_2.class"
        width=300 height=100>
</applet>
</html>
```
Also correct any errors in the following class definition:
```
package questions.c14;
import javax.swing.*;
```

```java
import java.awt.*;
public class Debug14_2 extends JApplet {
    public void init( Graphics g ) {
        JLabel l = new JLabel( "Label text" );
        getContentPane().add( l );
    }
}
```

3. Correct any errors in the following HTML document:

```html
<html>
<applet code="questions.c14.Debug14_3.class"
        width=500 height=600>
</applet>
</html>
```

Also correct any errors in the following class definition:

```java
package questions.c14;
import javax.swing.*;
import java.awt.*;
import java.applet.*;
public class Debug14_3 extends JApplet {
    public void init() {
        JLabel l = new JLabel( "TextArea Label" );
        JTextArea ta = new JTextArea( 25, 40 );
        add( ta, BorderLayout.CENTER );
        add( l, BorderLayout.NORTH );
    }
}
```

4. Correct any errors in the following HTML document:

```html
<html>
<applet code="questions.c14.Debug14_4.class"
        width=400 height=400>
<param Choice1="pepperoni">
<param Choice2="extra cheese">
<param Choice3="sweet peppers">
<param Choice4="hot peppers">
<param Choice5="mushrooms">
<param Choice6="tomatoes">
<param Choice7="sausage">
<param Choice8="black olives">
</applet>
</html>
```

Also correct any errors in the following class definition:

```java
package questions.c14;
import javax.swing.*;
import java.awt.*;
public class Debug14_4 extends JApplet {
    public void init() {
        JLabel label = new JLabel( "Please choose your "
                                 + "pizza toppings:" );
        JList list = new JList( 10, true );
        JPanel buttonPanel = new JPanel();
        JButton order = new JButton( "Order Pizza" );
```

**14**

```
            JButton cancel = new JButton( "Cancel Order" );
            buttonPanel.add( order );
            buttonPanel.add( cancel );
            int index = 1;
            String choice = getParameter( Choice + index );
            while ( choice != null ) {
                list.add( choice );
                ++index;
                choice = getParameter( Choice + index );
            }
            Container cp = getContentPane();
            cp.setLayout( new BorderLayout( 10, 10 ) );
            cp.add( label, BorderLayout.NORTH );
            cp.add( list, BorderLayout.CENTER );
            cp.add( buttonPanel, BorderLayout.SOUTH );
            setSize( 200, 300 );
        }
    }
```

5. Correct any errors in the following HTML document:

```
<html>
<applet code="questions.c14.Debug14_5.class"
        width=500 height=300>
</applet>
</html>
```

Also correct any errors in the following class definition so that the animation sequence is displayed properly. The animation sequence uses the 10 files T1.gif to T10.gif that are located in the same folder as the HTML file and the Java source file:

```
package questions.c14;
import javax.swing.*;
import java.awt.*;
import java.applet.*;
public class Debug14_5 extends JApplet
                        implements Runnable {
    private static final int NUM_IMAGES = 10;
    private static final int ID_VALUE = 0;
    private static final int PAUSE_MS = 250;
    private Image[] images = new Image[NUM_IMAGES];
    boolean keepGoing;
    Thread  animate;
    public void init() {
        MediaTracker tracker = new MediaTracker( this );
        for ( int i=0; i < NUM_IMAGES; i++ ) {
            images[i]
                = getImage( getDocumentBase(),
                        "T" + (i+1) + ".gif" );
            tracker.addImage( images[i], ID_VALUE );
        }
        try {
```

```
            tracker.waitForAll();
        } catch ( InterruptedException ix ) {
            ix.printStackTrace();
        }
    }
    public void start() {
        keepGoing = true;
        animate = new Thread( this );
        animate.start();
    }
    public void stop() {
        keepGoing = false;
    }
    public void run() {
        while ( keepGoing ) {
            repaint();
            try {
                sleep( PAUSE_MS );
            } catch ( InterruptedException ix ) {
                ix.printStackTrace();
            }
        }
    }
    public class ImagePanel extends JPanel {
        private int currentImage = 0;
        public void updateComponent( Graphics g ) {
            Insets insets = getInsets();
            g.drawImage( images[currentImage],
                        insets.left, insets.top, this );
            ++currentImage;
        }
    }
}
```

## Complete the Solution

1. Extract the file **questions\c14\Debug14_5.java** from the file **question.jar** on the CD-ROM. Complete the `Debug14_5` class defined in the last exercise (after you've fixed the errors in it) by adding support for three parameters that can be passed from the HTML document into the applet. The first parameter, `fileroot`, is the part of the image filename that comes before the number. The second parameter, `fileext`, is the extension of all the image files. The third parameter, `numfiles`, is the number of image files in the sequence. The default values for these parameters should be "T", ".gif", and 10.

2. Extract the files **questions\c14\Complete14_2.html** and **questions\c14\Complete14_2.java** from the file **question.jar** on the CD-ROM. Complete the HTML document and the `Complete14_2` class definition by defining an anonymous inner class that extends **MouseAdapter** and

14

creating an object of this class called **ml**. The class definition should override the **mouseEntered** and **mouseExited** methods so that the label text changes to red when the mouse moves over the labels. The labels are arranged in a single column to give the appearance of a menu of choices, and the color feedback lets the user know which choice is active.

3. Extract the files **questions\c14\Complete14_3.html** and **questions\c14\Complete14_3.java** from the file **question.jar** on the CD-ROM. Complete the HTML document and the **Complete14_3** class definition by providing **ActionEvent** handlers for the two buttons. This applet converts measurements between feet and meters. One button converts the value entered from feet to meters, and the other converts from meters to feet. After the conversion operation is complete, the focus should return to the entry field and the value in the field should be selected so that it is easy for the user to enter another value. Make sure that your conversion operations can gracefully handle cases in which the user enters a string that is not a number.

4. Extract the files **questions\c14\Complete14_4.html** and **questions\c14\Complete14_4.java** from the file **question.jar** on the CD-ROM. Complete the HTML document and the **Complete14_4** class definition by adding an **ActionEvent** handler for the **playSound** button that retrieves the selected audio clip and plays it. You also need to add code that reads the names of the audio clips from the parameters in the HTML document and puts the names into the list box, where the user can select them.

5. Extract the files **questions\c14\Complete14_5.html** and **questions\c14\Complete14_5.java** from the file **question.jar** on the CD-ROM. Complete the HTML document and the **Complete14_5** class definition by completing the **start**, **stop**, and **run** methods so that the simple animation of an expanding circle runs.

## Discovery

1. Create a class called **SpyApplet** that lets the user enter the name of a Java class and can display a list of that class's fields, constructors, and methods in a text area. (You will need to use the Reflection API to get this class information.) Use a set of check boxes to let the user select whether to display the fields, constructors, or methods.

2. Create a class called **SpreadSheetApplet** that implements a very basic spreadsheet consisting of 10 rows, A to J, and 10 columns, 1 to 10. Cell names are identified by their row and column (for example, B7). Cells in this spreadsheet can contain a string inside double quotes, a number, or a formula. Formulas are distinguished from strings because they are not enclosed in quotes. To keep the class simple, allow only addition operations in the formulas.

# JAVABEANS

---

**In this chapter you will:**

➤ Learn what the JavaBeans component model is.

➤ Create your own JavaBean components.

➤ Learn how beanboxes consume beans.

➤ Learn the characteristics of a JavaBean, including how to define the properties, methods, and events for your own beans.

➤ Add custom event types to your beans.

➤ Use JavaBeans information classes to make all features available to beanboxes that operate on your beans.

➤ Provide customized editors so that properties of your beans can be edited in a beanbox.

➤ Use the BeanContext API to create JavaBeans that can search their environment for available services.

➤ Gain a basic understanding of what an Enterprise JavaBean is.

---

## INTRODUCTION

With a grounding in JavaBeans, you can create better software because it forces you to think and design in a modular fashion. Two groups of Java programmers need to understand the JavaBeans architecture:

➤ Programmers who create **beanboxes**, which are the tools that consume JavaBeans and allow them to be connected.

➤ Developers who create the actual JavaBeans.

This chapter focuses on the latter, and larger, group. Much of the discussion centers on using the Java programming language and the core classes and interfaces in the package **java.beans** to create beans. Because understanding how beans are used to create applications is essential for designers of beans, this chapter includes an introduction to the Beans Development Kit (BDK) and BeanBox from Sun.

# JavaBeans Component Model

For many years, software developers have strived to achieve modularity and reusability of software components. The goal of software developers is to make the integration of software components a reality, so that they can build applications from existing components, or entire programs. The goal of creating reusable and interchangeable software components is emerging through the development of software component models. The Java platform's designers have taken a bold step by proposing the platform's own component model—JavaBeans. The JavaBeans component model provides a framework for creating reusable, embeddable software components.

Increasingly, Integrated Development Environments (IDEs) for the Java platform, such as IBM's VisualAge for Java, are being designed to accept JavaBean components. These packages provide environments in which the programmer can easily connect one JavaBean component to another, slowly building complex software applications. It is in such IDEs that JavaBeans really shine. For a good example of how easily components can be connected, see the section "Designing a Class Visually" in Chapter 12.

When you use a visual development environment, the distinguishing feature of components such as JavaBeans becomes clear: The components are manipulated at design time as binary executables. You are not modifying source statements or working with the Java platform APIs.

By no means is JavaBeans the first component model, but it is the first component model for the Java platform. Recognizing that other component models are in use, the creators of the JavaBeans component model designed the model for interoperability with other component frameworks. For example, the ActiveX bridge, which is available on 32-bit Windows platforms, can turn a bean into an ActiveX control for embedding in ActiveX-aware software such as Lotus WordPro.

It is possible to define classes that conform to the specification of the JavaBeans component model and are also compatible with other Java programming models. For example, you can create a class that can function both as an applet and as a JavaBean. Indeed, you may already be more familiar with the JavaBeans specification than you realize. All of the Swing and AWT components that are described in Chapters 12 and 13 are JavaBeans.

# What Makes a Class a Bean

The core classes and interfaces in the packages **java.beans** and **java.beans.beancontext** provide the support for creating JavaBeans. However, there is no JavaBean superclass that all JavaBeans extend and no interface that all JavaBeans implement. Creating a class of JavaBeans largely involves adhering to the standards of the JavaBeans component model.

Support for the JavaBeans component model was added to the
Java platform with version 1.1.

Many method names in the AWT API were changed between versions 1.0 and 1.1 to follow the JavaBeans convention. The original
GUI event model was deprecated, and the current model was
introduced to make JavaBeans possible.

Creating a reusable, embeddable piece of software such as a JavaBean requires
some planning. Enough of the workings of the JavaBean must be exposed to
make it useful, but not so much that the user becomes overwhelmed with its
complexity or hopelessly dependent on the details of the bean's inner workings. Each item of a JavaBean interface falls into one of the three categories
listed in Table 15–1.

A full description of the JavaBeans specification is beyond the scope of this
book. The programming conventions are summarized in Table 15-2, and the
full specifications are available from the Sun Web site at the following URL:
http://java.sun.com/beans/docs/spec.html.

The latest news about JavaBeans and many related documents are available
from the JavaBeans home page on the Sun Web site at the following URL:
http://java.sun.com/beans.

**Table 15-1**  Elements of a JavaBean interface

| Element | Description |
| --- | --- |
| Methods | A method represents some action that can be executed against the JavaBean. For example, a JavaBean that contains an animation may have methods to start and stop the animation. |
| Properties | A property represents an attribute of the JavaBean, such as its color or font. The property does not have to be a visible attribute. For exam-ple, a property can be an abstract quality, such as a **boolean** flag that indicates whether a component is enabled for input.<br>Properties can be single entities or indexed elements of a set. They can be passive or bound. A **passive** property cannot initiate any activity. A **bound** property can notify other beans when they change. If a property is **constrained**, other beans can prevent it from changing value. |
| Events | JavaBean objects use events to notify other JavaBean objects that some event has occurred. These objects use the same event-handling mechanism as Swing and AWT components. JavaBeans that must be aware of a certain event register as a listener with the JavaBean that generates the event. Listener JavaBeans must implement the interface that corresponds to the event class of interest. Source JavaBeans pro-vide registration methods for the event. When the event occurs, the source JavaBean sends a copy of the event to each registered listener. Many of the events generated by beans are **PropertyChangeEvent** objects, but you can define custom events. |

**15**

Some of the main characteristics of JavaBeans follow:

➤ If a bean has a property named X, it can have public methods named **setX** or **getX**, to assign and return the value of the property X. A variation on this convention is allowed for properties of type **boolean**, for which the methods are named **setX** and **isX**. A read-only or write-only property has only one method of the pair. A read-only property is not necessarily constant; a change to another property might change a read-only property indirectly.

➤ If a bean can generate events of the class **YEvent**, it should have public methods of the following forms:

```
void addYListener( YEvent )
void removeYListener( YEvent )
```

Other public methods of the class are actions that the JavaBean can execute.

➤ All beans should have a constructor that takes no arguments because most beanboxes call this constructor. When the superclass constructor has required arguments, the bean constructor must call the superclass constructor and pass literal constants as arguments.

➤ A JavaBean class must implement the marker interface **Serializable** because beanboxes use serialization to save the state of beans. (Chapter 8 describes object serialization.) As a result, fields that are instances of classes that do not support serialization must be qualified with the keyword **transient**. In general, attributes that depend on system-specific features such as font sizes should also be qualified with **transient** so that they can be recalculated when the bean is deserialized. Table 15-2 gives a more complete list of the programming conventions for declarations in a bean.

**Table 15-2**   Programming conventions for JavaBeans

| Element of the Bean | Form of Declaration |
| --- | --- |
| Property X of type C | |
| Accessor | **public C getX()** |
| Mutator | **public void setX( C** *value* **)** |
| Boolean property X | |
| Accessor | **public boolean getX()** or **public boolean isX()** |
| Mutator | **public void setX( boolean** *value* **)** |
| Indexed property X of type C[ ] | |
| Group accessor | **public C[] getX()** |
| Group mutator | **public void setX( C[]** *value* **)** |
| Element accessor | **public C getX( int** *index* **)** |
| Element mutator | **public void setX( int** *index*, **C** *value* **)** |

*continued*

**Table 15-2**  Programming conventions for JavaBeans (continued)

| Element of the Bean | Form of Declaration |
| --- | --- |
| **Bound property X of type C** | |
| Accessor | **public C getX()** |
| Mutator | **public void setX( C** *value* **)** |
| Listener registration | **public void addPropertyChangeListener** <br> ( **PropertyChangeListener** *listener* ) |
| Listener removal | **public void removePropertyChangeListener** <br> ( **PropertyChangeListener** *listener* ) |
| **Constrained property X of type C** | |
| Accessor | **public C getX()** |
| Mutator | **public void setX( C** *value* **)  throws** <br> **PropertyVetoException** |
| Listener registration | **public void addVetoableChangeListener** <br> ( **VetoableChangeListener** *listener* ) |
| Listener removal | **public void  RemoveVetotableChangeListener** <br> ( **VetoableChangeListener** *listener* ) |
| **Event Y** | |
| Class name | **YEvent** |
| Listener interface name | **YListener** |
| Listener registration | **public void addYListener( YListener** *listener* ) |
| Listener removal | **public void removeYListener( YListener** *listener* ) |
| **BeanInfo class for class JB** | |
| Class name | **JBBeanInfo** |
| **Property editor for type C** | |
| Class name | **CEditor** |
| Constructor | Must have a no-argument constructor. |
| **Customizer for class JB** | |
| Class name | Any, but **JBCustomizer** is common. |
| Superclass | Must be **java.awt.Component** or a subclass, <br> usually **Panel** or **JPanel**. |
| Constructor | One constructor must have no arguments. |

# BEAN DEVELOPMENT ENVIRONMENTS

When you are creating JavaBeans, it is helpful to understand how development environments operate on JavaBeans. To that end, Sun created a demonstration development environment called the **BeanBox**. This book uses this capitalized term when referring to this specific environment to distinguish it from a generic beanbox environment.

You can download the most recent version from the Sun Web site by following the instructions in the ReadMe file. Because the BDK is freely available, it

15

is used as the reference point for the JavaBean examples in this chapter. When using the BeanBox, keep in mind that it is not a production IDE and that you should not use it to create JavaBean applications. Instead, you should perform production development using tools such as IBM VisualAge for Java.

You can load beans into the Sun BeanBox directly from a .jar file. You create and manipulate these files using the **jar** utility, as described Chapter 14. A .jar file should contain all the class files that the bean needs. The manifest file indicates which of these class files contain a JavaBean class. A single .jar file can have more than one JavaBean class.

In general, a beanbox uses the classes of the **java.lang.reflect** package to analyze the classes contained within the .jar file. This package supports run-time type information, as described in Chapter 7. If the beanbox finds public methods of the form **setX**, **getX**, or **isX**, it assumes that X is a property of the JavaBean. If the beanbox finds public methods of the form **addYListener** and **removeYListener**, both of which return **void** and take a single argument of type **YEvent**, it assumes that the JavaBean fires events of the class **YEvent**. Some beanboxes, including the version of the Sun BeanBox described in this chapter, have a limitation that prevents them from handling other methods, unless the methods take no arguments and return **void**. This restriction is not part of the JavaBeans specification.

## USING THE SUN BEANBOX

To follow the examples in this chapter, install the Sun BeanBox by following the instructions in the ReadMe file on the CD-ROM.

To start the BeanBox:

1. Open a command-line window and go to the folder in which you installed the BDK.

2. Make the subfolder **beanbox** the current folder.

3. Enter **run**.

The **run** command executes a batch file that sets up the environment for the BDK, loads the JVM, and loads the BeanBox Java application. When the BeanBox starts, you see four windows similar to those shown in Figures 15-1, 15-2, 15-3, and 15-4.

The Toolbox window serves as a palette of the available beans. Beans are loaded when the BeanBox automatically opens and processes all .jar files that reside in the reserved subfolder called jars. If you start with only the files supplied with the BDK, the Toolbox window lists the demonstration beans included with the BDK, as shown in Figure 15-1.

**Figure 15-1** The BDK BeanBox Toolbox window

The window labeled BeanBox is the Composition window in which you can arrange and connect the beans. You can load a .jar file into the Toolbox window after the BeanBox has started by choosing Load Jar from the File menu of the window in Figure 15-2.

**Figure 15-2** The BDK BeanBox composition window

The Properties window, shown in Figure 15-3, lists the properties of a selected bean and lets you edit those properties.

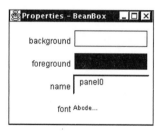

**Figure 15-3** The BDK BeanBox Properties window

The Method Tracer window, shown in Figure 15-4, displays the output from the method tracing service provided by the BeanBox. JavaBeans use the **BeanContext** API to locate and use the method tracing service. An example of how this is done will be presented later in this chapter.

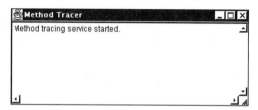

**Figure 15-4** The BDK BeanBox Method Tracer window

Before developing this chapter's example bean, try positioning a demonstration bean in the Composition window and then removing the bean.

To position a demonstration bean in the Composition window:

1. Select the OrangeButton bean from the Toolbox window by clicking the word **OrangeButton** with the mouse. The cross-hair cursor appears.

2. Position the cross-hair cursor on the BeanBox window. Click the **BeanBox** window, and the OrangeButton bean drops into place.

   The bean is surrounded by a hatched black and gray border, which indicates the bean is selected. When a bean is selected, its properties are displayed and editable in the Properties window.

3. Try changing some properties. Click the **background** box in the Properties window. The window called sun.beans.editors.ColorEditor pops up. Figure 15-5 shows the ColorEditor window.

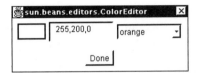

**Figure 15-5** The BeanBox Property Editor window

4. Change the color of the bean by selecting a color from the drop-down list on the right of the window or by changing the red, green, or blue intensity values in the middle of the window. The color on the left of the ColorEditor and the color of the bean in the BeanBox window change immediately.

Now, you are ready to remove the bean from the BeanBox window.

To remove the bean from the BeanBox window:

1. Make sure the bean is selected.

2. Click **Edit** from the BeanBox menu bar, and then click **Cut**.

3. Click **File** from the BeanBox menu bar, and then click **Exit** to close the BeanBox window.

   The BeanBox comes with its own documentation in a web of HTML documents, including more complete instructions for using the BeanBox than this chapter can include. You can experiment with the BeanBox until you have a feel for how it works.

When a bean is instantiated in a beanbox, the bean's methods are called in the following order:

➤ The constructor with no arguments is called to set up the bean.

➤ The **preferredSize** method, which you encounter again later in this chapter, returns the display dimensions of the bean.

➤ The **paint** method draws the bean on the BeanBox window. Recall that for Swing components the **paint** method calls the **paintComponent** method.

## CREATING A JAVABEAN CLASS

As a programmer, you may be expected to build beans that other developers load into a beanbox and use to build an application. Thus, in this section, you will learn how to create a JavaBean, package it into a .jar file, and then load it into the BeanBox so that it can be connected with other JavaBean components.

An example JavaBean is developed throughout this chapter. The bean displays an image on a panel. The first version is a class called ImageBean1. It extends the class **Panel** and manipulates an object of type **Image**. The default image is a GIF file that is provided by the Sun BeanBox and that contains the same picture loaded by the `ImageApplet` of Chapter 14—the familiar juggler.

The ImageBean1 bean has three properties:

➤ The properties `fileName` and `fillColor` have mutator methods `setFileName` and `setFillColor`, and accessor methods `getFileName` and getFillColor. They are read-write properties.

➤ ImageBean1 has a **getPreferredSize** method but no **setPreferredSize** method. The property **preferredSize** is a read-only property of the bean.

If the image chosen is smaller than the panel, the empty space is painted using a specified fill color.

Here is the complete source code for the ImageBean1 JavaBean. Because ImageBean1 is a public class, it is found in a file called ImageBean1.java. The structure of packages mirrors the file system, so you will find this source code in the examples\beans subfolder of the folder in which you unpacked the file examples.jar:

```java
package examples.beans;
import javax.swing.JPanel;
import java.awt.*;
import java.io.*;
import java.awt.image.ImageObserver;
/** A very simple JavaBean class that displays an image
  * and allows the user to specify the file containing
  * the image and the fill color to be used if the
  * image is smaller than the panel
  */
public class ImageBean1 extends JPanel {
    private String fileName = "";
    private transient Image image;
    private int width = 200;
    private int height = 150;
    private Color fill = Color.lightGray;
    /** No-argument constructor; sets the filename to a
      * default value.
      */
    public ImageBean1() {
        setFileName( "..\\demo\\sunw\\demo\\juggler\\"
                   + "Juggler0.gif" );
    }
    /** Accessor for the filename property.
      * @return The current image's filename
      */
    public String getFileName() {
        return fileName;
    }
```

```java
/** The preferred size of the panel
  * @return The size of the current image
  */
public Dimension getPreferredSize() {
   return new Dimension( width, height );
}
/** Accessor for the fillColor property
  * @return The current fill color
  */
public Color getFillColor() {
   return fill;
}
/** Method for monitoring the progress of the
  * loading of the current image.
  */
public boolean imageUpdate( Image img,
                            int infoflags,
                            int x, int y,
                            int w, int h ) {
   if ( (infoflags & ImageObserver.ALLBITS) != 0 ) {
      width = img.getWidth( null );
      height = img.getHeight( null );
      repaint();
      return false;
   } else {
      return true;
   }
}
/** Paint the fill color if the panel is bigger than
  * the image and then draw the image.
  * @param g the panel's graphics context
  */
public void paintComponent( Graphics g ) {
   super.paintComponent( g );
   Dimension panelSize = getSize();
   Insets ins = getInsets();
   int actWidth = panelSize.width - ins.right
                     - ins.left - 1;
   int actHeight = panelSize.height - ins.top
                     - ins.bottom - 1;
   if ( panelSize.width > width ||
        panelSize.height > height ) {
      g.setColor( fill );
      g.fillRect( ins.left, ins.top,
                  actWidth, actHeight );
   }
   if ( image != null ) {
      g.drawImage( image, ins.left, ins.top, this );
   }
}
/** Deserialization method called for the JavaBean.
```

**15**

```
 *   This is necessary because Image objects can be
 *   serialized and must be regenerated manually.
 * @exception IOException if an error occurs
 *             reading the serialized JavaBean.
 * @exception ClassNotFoundException if the
 *             serialized JavaBean can't be found.
 */
private void readObject( ObjectInputStream ois )
        throws IOException, ClassNotFoundException {
   ois.defaultReadObject();
   image = getToolkit().getImage( fileName );
   repaint();
}
/** Mutator method for the fillColor property.
  * @param c the new fill color value
  */
public void setFillColor( Color c ) {
   fill = c;
   repaint();
}
/** Mutator method for the fileName property.
  * @param fn the new image filename
  */
public void setFileName( String fn ) {
   fileName = fn;
   image = getToolkit().getImage( fileName );
   repaint();
}
}
```

## Breakdown of the ImageBean1 Class

The ImageBean1 class is in the package examples.beans. The `ImageBean1` class uses the **JPanel class** in the package **javax.swing**, several classes in the packages **java.awt** and **java.io**, as well as the **ImageObserver** class in the package **java.awt.image:**

```
package examples.beans;
import javax.swing.JPanel;
import java.awt.*;
import java.io.*;
import java.awt.image.ImageObserver;
```

The class `ImageBean1` inherits its serialization behavior from its superclass, **JPanel**. Therefore, `ImageBean1` does not have to declare explicitly that it implements the interface **Serializable:**

```
public class ImageBean1 extends JPanel {
```

The fields of the `ImageBean1` class record the state of the JavaBean. They are all given default values except for the **Image** instance. Notice that the image instance variable is qualified as **transient**. The **Image** class does not implement the interface **Serializable**. Therefore, the image field cannot be serialized with the other fields in an `ImageBean1` object. Because the **Image** class is not serializable, any attempt to serialize an **Image** object results in an exception:

```
private String fileName = "";
private transient Image image;
private int width = 200;
private int height = 150;
private Color fill = Color.lightGray;
```

> **Mini Quiz 15-1**
>
> The majority of core classes implement **Serializable**. Some do not for a good reason. Can you name at least two core classes, other than **Image**, that do not implement **Serializable**?

The `ImageBean1` has a constructor with no arguments. The beanbox calls this constructor when an object of this class is dropped on the beanbox canvas. This constructor initializes the `fileName` property of the JavaBean. The default filename has a relative path, ..\demo\sunw\demo\juggler\juggler0.gif, and is set on the assumption that a .jar file containing the `ImageBean1` class is in the jars subfolder of the folder in which the BDK is installed. You can edit the `fileName` property to point to any other valid file containing an image:

```
public ImageBean1() {
    setFileName( "..\\demo\\sunw\\demo\\juggler\\"
                 + "Juggler0.gif" );
}
```

The next three methods are accessor methods that return the current values of the three properties of the JavaBean: `fileName`, `preferredSize`, and `fillColor`:

```
public String getFileName() {
    return fileName;
}
public Dimension getPreferredSize() {
    return new Dimension( width, height );
}
public Color getFillColor() {
    return fill;
}
```

The **imageUpdate** method is part of the **ImageObserver** interface that all AWT components implement. When a method is called to draw an image, the

**15**

method may return before the image is fully available. For this reason, the methods to draw images take a reference to an **ImageObserver** object. Periodically, the bean's **imageUpdate** method is called to update the status of the image. As long as **imageUpdate** returns true, the updates continue.

As listed following, this implementation of **imageUpdate** waits until the information flags have the **ALLBITS** flag set on. When that condition indicates that the entire image is drawn, the actual width and height of the image are requested and the image is repainted. The method returns **false** to indicate that no further updates are required.

```java
public boolean imageUpdate( Image img,
                            int infoflags,
                            int x, int y,
                            int w, int h ) {
   if ( (infoflags & ImageObserver.ALLBITS) != 0 ) {
      width = img.getWidth( null );
      height = img.getHeight( null );
      repaint();
      return false;
   } else {
      return true;
   }
}
```

Looking at the code that follows this paragraph, you will note that the **paintComponent** method for this JavaBean compares the size of the panel to the size of the image. If the panel is bigger, the **paintComponent** operation begins by filling the panel with the specified fill color. Then, if the image is not null, it is drawn starting in the upper-left corner of the panel. By retrieving and using the inset values of the panel, care is taken not to draw the image over any border that the panel may have.

```java
public void paintComponent( Graphics g ) {
   super.paintComponent( g );
   Dimension panelSize = getSize();
   Insets ins = getInsets();
   int actWidth = panelSize.width - ins.right
                     - ins.left - 1;
   int actHeight = panelSize.height - ins.top
                     - ins.bottom - 1;
   if ( panelSize.width > width ||
        panelSize.height > height ) {
      g.setColor( fill );
      g.fillRect( ins.left, ins.top,
                  actWidth, actHeight );
   }
   if ( image != null ) {
      g.drawImage( image, ins.left, ins.top, this );
   }
}
```

The instance variable image must be qualified with the **transient** keyword so that the image is not saved when the bean is serialized and not restored when the bean is deserialized. As a result, the image must be reloaded from the GIF file when this bean is deserialized. Deserializing the bean is accomplished using the **readObject** method, as shown below:

```
private void readObject( ObjectInputStream ois )
      throws IOException, ClassNotFoundException {
  ois.defaultReadObject();
  image = getToolkit().getImage( fileName );
  repaint();
}
```

> **Mini Quiz 15-2**
>
> Why is the **readObject** method a suitable place to reload the image, and why does the **readObject** method call **defaultReadObject** first? (*Hint:* Review the description of the Serializable interface in Chapter 9.)

The last two methods of the JavaBean class are the mutator methods that allow the read-write properties `fileName` and `fillColor` to be changed. Both of these methods trigger a **repaint** operation. A change of the filename also causes a new image to be loaded, which may cause the `preferredSize` property to change.

```
public void setFillColor( Color c ) {
    fill = c;
    repaint();
}
public void setFileName( String fn ) {
    fileName = fn;
    image = getToolkit().getImage( fileName );
    repaint();
}
```

15

## ImageBean1 Class Used in a Beanbox

Before you can access a JavaBean in a beanbox, you must put it in a .jar file. There is an additional requirement: The .jar file must include a manifest that specifies which .class files in the .jar file are JavaBeans. To do this, you simply set the **JavaBean** property in the manifest to be true for the JavaBean class.

To load this example bean into the BeanBox window of the BDK:

1. Create a minimal manifest file for the bean `ImageBean1`. In a text editor, create a flat text file that contains the following two lines, followed by a blank line. Spaces are significant, so make sure both lines start in the first character position of each line.

```
Name: examples/beans/ImageBean1.class
Java-Bean: True
```

2. Save the file with filename **ImageBeans.manifest** in the folder that is the parent of the folder that contains the package examples.

3. Make sure the current folder is the one that contains the file ImageBeans.manifest and the examples folder. Type the following command on one line to create a .jar file named ImageBeans.jar:

```
jar cfm ImageBeans.jar ImageBeans.manifest
                       examples\beans\*.class
```

4. Copy the file ImageBeans.jar into the **jars** subfolder of the folder in which you installed the BDK.

5. To start the beanbox, make the subfolder **beanbox** the current folder, and enter the command **run**.

   When the four windows appear, you should see ImageBean1 listed in the Toolbox window, as shown in Figure 15-6.

6. Using the same method described earlier in this chapter, load the ImageBean1 bean into the BeanBox.

7. Select the **ImageBean1** bean from the Toolbox window by clicking the word **ImageBean1** with the mouse. The cross-hair cursor appears. (Notice that the position of **ImageBean1** in the list may not be exactly as shown in Figure 15-6.)

**Figure 15-6** The ImageBean1 in the Toolbox window

8. Position the cross-hair cursor on the BeanBox window. Click the **BeanBox** window, and the ImageBean1 bean drops into place so that it looks like Figure 15-7.

**Figure 15-7** The ImageBean1 in the BeanBox window

The Properties window for the ImageBean1 bean looks like Figure 15-8 and shows many fields, although the `ImageBean1` class defines only two read-write properties. All the other fields are inherited from the superclass, **JPanel**. In the Properties window, you can enter different values for the `fillColor` and the `fileName` properties of the JavaBean. If you try this, you will see the changes immediately reflected in the BeanBox window.

| | |
|---|---|
| doubleBuffered | True |
| opaque | True |
| autoscrolls | False |
| background | |
| alignmentY | 0.5 |
| alignmentX | 0.5 |
| fileName | ..\demo\sunw\demo\juggler\Juggler0.gif |
| debugGraphicsOptions | 0 |
| fillColor | |
| foreground | |
| requestFocusEnabled | True |
| font | Abcde... |

Properties – ImageBean1

**Figure 15-8** The Properties window for the ImageBean1 bean

15

You can bind a property of the `ImageBean1` bean to a property of another bean, if the properties have the same type.

To tie a property from the JellyBean JavaBean to the ImageBean1 JavaBean:

1. The BeanBox ships a JellyBean JavaBean that has a color property. Select the **JellyBean** bean from the Toolbox window, and then drop the bean on the BeanBox composition window.

2. The JellyBean should be surrounded by a hatched black and gray border to indicate it is selected. If it is not, click the **JellyBean** to select it.

3. Click **Edit** on the menu bar of the BeanBox window, and then click **Bind property.**

4. The PropertyNameDialog box appears, as shown in Figure 15-9. It lists properties of the JellyBean. Select **color**, and click **OK** to close the dialog box.

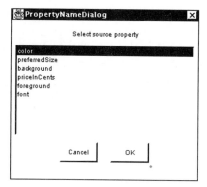

**Figure 15-9** The PropertyNameDialog box

5. A red line appears. One end of the line is attached to the JellyBean and the other end follows the mouse. Drag the moving end of the line over the `ImageBean1` bean, and click.

6. The PropertyNameDialog box appears again, now showing the properties of the `ImageBean1` bean. Select **fillColor**, and click **OK**.

   The `ImageBean1` is selected, and its fill color is the same as the color of the JellyBean.

If you select the JellyBean and change its color using the Properties window, the fill color of the ImageBean1 changes to match. The reason is that the `fillColor` property of the `ImageBean1` bean is now **bound** to the color property of the JellyBean.

You cannot do much more with the `ImageBean1` bean. It is limited to being a passive participant in a beanbox. Enabling this bean to be wired more actively to other components involves adding events and more methods. The next version of this bean, `ImageBean2`, can be a more active participant in an application or applet.

The following section discusses JavaBean property types beyond the basic property type used in the `ImageBean1` class. The following major section discusses a class, `ImageBean2`, that uses one of these more advanced property types.

# EXPLORING MORE PROPERTY TYPES

The bean `ImageBean1` has the simplest type of property. For more flexibility, you can use properties that are indexed, bound, or constrained.

## Indexed Properties

Properties are not limited to individual values. They can be indexed under a single name with an integer index value. For example, to alter the `ImageBean1` to display an animated sequence, you might have to supply several filenames for the sequence of images. In that case, `fileName` must become an **indexed property**. In addition to providing the methods for reading and writing the entire indexed property, you can provide methods for reading and writing individual elements of the property.

*Syntax*

*property_type* **get***property_name*( **int** *index* )
**void set***property_name*( *property_type* **x, int** *index* )

*Dissection*

The mutator and accessor methods for an indexed property must have the arguments, names, and return types shown here. Beanboxes also recognize method signatures with these patterns and add them to the list of properties for the JavaBean. To be usable, the methods must be public.

*Code Example*

```
myBean.setFileName( "Juggler0.gif", 0 );
String fn = myBean.getFilename( 0 );
```

*Code Dissection*

These are the accessor and mutator methods for an indexed property called fileName of type **String**.

## Bound Properties

Bound properties provide notification when they change so that other JavaBeans can listen for these changes and act accordingly. For example, the

**15**

properties of the ImageBean1 class are passive but are tied to the bound properties of a demonstration JavaBean of the JellyBean class. The `fillColor` property of the `ImageBean1` class is not bound. However, the color property of the JellyBean class is bound.

The package **java.beans** includes a class for use with bound properties, **PropertyChangeSupport**, that is detailed next.

## Class

**java.beans.PropertyChangeSupport**

## Purpose

You can create an instance of this class for a JavaBean class and delegate to it the tasks of maintaining a list of interested listeners and sending **java.beans.PropertyChangeEvent** objects.

## Constructors

➤ **PropertyChangeSupport( Object** *sourceBean* **)**
You can create a **PropertyChangeSupport** object for a JavaBean.

## Methods

➤ **void addPropertyChangeListener( PropertyChangeListener** *listener* **)**
The **addPropertyChangeListener** method adds the specified object to the list of listeners for the bean.

➤ **void firePropertyChange( String** *propertyName***,**
**Object** *oldValue***,**
**Object** *newValue* **)**
The **firePropertyChange** method informs all listeners of a change to a bound property. The method generates no event if the new value equals the old value.

➤ **void removePropertyChangeListener( PropertyChangeListener**
*listener* **)**
The **removePropertyChangeListener** method removes the specified object from the list of listeners for the bean.

The next example program shows how these methods are used typically:

➤ A class defines its own **addPropertyChangeListener** and **removePropertyChangeListener** methods that do little more than pass the **PropertyChangeListener parameter** they receive along to the **PropertyChangeSupport** instance.

➤ The **set** methods for the properties are modified to call the **firePropertyChange** method to indicate that the value has changed.

# Constrained Properties

The JavaBeans component model allows for the possibility that one or more of the listening objects might not allow some changes to the value of a property. This variation is known as a **constrained property**. In this case, each listener can veto a change and stop it from happening.

The difference between implementing support for a constrained property and a bound property is mostly in the support class that is chosen. To implement a constrained property, a JavaBean class should use a **VetoableChangeSupport** object. The details of this class are given next:

### Class

**java.beans.VetoableChangeSupport**

### Purpose

Use a **VetoableChangeSupport** object for constrained properties much like you use a **PropertyChangeSupport** object for bound properties.

### Constructors

➤ **VetoableChangeSupport( Object** *sourceBean* **)**
You can create a **VetoableChangeSupport** object for a JavaBean.

### Methods

➤ **void addVetoableChangeListener( PropertyChangeListener** *listener* **)**
The **addVetoableChangeListener** method adds the specified object to the list of listeners for the bean.

➤ **void firePropertyChange( String** *propertyName*,
                    **Object** *oldValue*,
                    **Object** *newValue* **)**
The **firePropertyChange** method informs all listeners of a change to a bound property. The method generates no event if the new value equals the old value. Listeners can veto the change by throwing a **java.beans.PropertyVetoException** object. When this happens, the **VetoableChangeSupport** object catches this exception, re-notifies the other listeners that the property is reverting back to its original value, and then re-throws the exception.

➤ **void removeVetoableChangeListener( PropertyChangeListener**
                        *listener* **)**
The **removeVetoableChangeListener** method removes the specified object from the list of listeners for the bean.

**15**

The event object type is **PropertyChangeEvent** for both constrained and bound properties because the information contained in the event object is the same. Only the mechanism for delivering the event differs. Write the **set** method for a constrained property to catch the **PropertyVetoException** object and undo the change.

# ADDING CUSTOM EVENT TYPES

JavaBeans are not limited to just the **PropertyChangeEvent** event type. They can use any event type, even custom event types. Unfortunately, implementing custom event types requires more work because there is no core class analogous to **PropertyChangeSupport** to support such events.

To create and use a custom event:

1. Define the event class that extends **java.util.EventObject** or one of its subclasses. The rest of this discussion refers to this class as class X.

2. Define the interface, **XListener**, that the event listeners must implement. This interface should extend the marker interface **java.util.EventListener**. The methods of this interface are the event handlers. They should return **void** and take one parameter of type **X**. They have the following form:

   ```
   void handleX( X event )
   ```

   The **JavaBean** class that can fire the event should define the methods `addXListener` and `removeXListener`, both taking a single parameter of type `XListener`. An instance of the **Vector** class can be used to hold the list of registered listeners updated by these two methods.

3. The JavaBean class should define a method, `fireX`, that goes through the list of registered listeners and calls the `handleX` method, passing an **X** object for each of them.

   Follow these conventions so that a beanbox can detect the presence of the custom event type and allow it to be connected to other JavaBeans. The `ImageBean2` class that follows contains an example of a custom event type called `FillColorEvent`.

# CREATING A JAVABEAN CLASS WITH EVENTS

The second JavaBean class, `ImageBean2`, is an enhancement of the `ImageBean1` class. This class converts all the properties into bound properties and adds a custom event type, `FillColorEvent`. The code for the `FillColorEvent` follows the discussion of the `ImageBean2` class.

The class adds two methods, `makeFillGreen` and `makeFillRed`, as conveniences to the users of the JavaBean. In a beanbox, it is very simple to add a button JavaBean and then connect the button's click action to one of these methods.

> **Mini Quiz 15-3**
>
> What conventions for the arguments and return type must be used to enable a bean-box to recognize the two new methods, `makeFillGreen` and `makeFillRed`, and add them to the list of available methods?

Much of the following code is identical to the Java source `ImageBean1`. Therefore, the changes are highlighted in boldface. The details of the changes made from `ImageBean1` to `ImageBean2` are described in the breakdown after the complete source code:

```java
package examples.beans;
import javax.swing.JPanel;
import java.awt.*;
import java.io.*;
import java.util.*;
import java.awt.image.ImageObserver;
import java.beans.*;
/** A very simple JavaBean class that displays an image
  * and allows the user to specify the file containing
  * the image and the fill color to be used if the
  * image is smaller than the panel
  */
public class ImageBean2 extends JPanel {
   private String fileName;
   private transient Image image;
   private int width = 200;
   private int height = 150;
   private Color fill = Color.lightGray;
   private PropertyChangeSupport
      myListeners = new PropertyChangeSupport( this );
   private Vector fillColorListeners = new Vector();
   /** No-argument constructor; sets the filename to a
     * default value.
     */
   public ImageBean2() {
      setFileName( "..\\demo\\sunw\\demo\\juggler\\"
                  +"Juggler0.gif" );
   }
   /** Send an event to all registered listeners */
   public void fireFillColorEvent( FillColorEvent e ) {
      Vector snapshot
         = (Vector) fillColorListeners.clone();
      Enumeration cursor = snapshot.elements();
      while( cursor.hasMoreElements() ) {
         FillColorListener fcl
```

15

```
                    = (FillColorListener) cursor.nextElement();
            if ( e.getID()
                        == FillColorEvent.COLOR_CHANGE ) {
                fcl.fillColorChange( e );
            }
        }
    }
    /** Accessor for the filename property.
      * @return The current image's filename
      */
    public String getFileName() {
        return fileName;
    }
    /** The preferred size of the panel
      * @return The size of the current image
      */
    public Dimension getPreferredSize() {
        return new Dimension( width, height );
    }
    /** Accessor for the fillColor property
      * @return The current fill color
      */
    public Color getFillColor() {
        return fill;
    }
    /** Method for monitoring the progress of the
      * loading of the current image.
      */
    public boolean imageUpdate( Image img,
                                int infoflags,
                                int x, int y,
                                int w, int h ) {
        if ( (infoflags & ImageObserver.ALLBITS) != 0 ) {
            int oldWidth = width;
            int oldHeight = height;
            width = img.getWidth( null );
            height = img.getHeight( null );
            if ( oldWidth != width
                 || oldHeight != height ) {
                myListeners.firePropertyChange(
                    "preferredSize",
                    new Dimension( oldWidth, oldHeight ),
                    new Dimension( width, height ) );
            }
            repaint();
            return false;
        } else {
            return true;
        }
    }
    /** Set the image fill color to green.  The Sun
      * BeanBox recognizes only methods without
```

```
 * parameters that return void.
 */
public void makeFillGreen() {
   setFillColor( Color.green );
}
/** Set the image fill color to red.  The Sun
 * BeanBox recognizes only methods without
 * parameters that return void.
 */
public void makeFillRed() {
   setFillColor( Color.red );
}
/** Paint the fill color if the panel is bigger than
 * the image and then draw the image.
 * @param g the panel's graphics context
 */
public void paintComponent( Graphics g ) {
   super.paintComponent( g );
   Dimension panelSize = getSize();
   Insets ins = getInsets();
   int actWidth = panelSize.width - ins.right
                       - ins.left - 1;
   int actHeight = panelSize.height - ins.top
                       - ins.bottom - 1;
   if ( panelSize.width > width ||
        panelSize.height > height ) {
      g.setColor( fill );
      g.fillRect( ins.left, ins.top,
               actWidth, actHeight );
   }
   if ( image != null ) {
      g.drawImage( image, ins.left, ins.top, this );
   }
}
/** Deserialization method called for the JavaBean.
 * This is necessary because Image objects can be
 * serialized and must be regenerated manually.
 * @exception IOException if an error occurs
 *            reading the serialized JavaBean.
 * @exception ClassNotFoundException if the
 *            serialized JavaBean can't be found.
 */
private void readObject( ObjectInputStream ois )
        throws IOException, ClassNotFoundException {
   ois.defaultReadObject();
   image = getToolkit().getImage( fileName );
   repaint();
}
/** Mutator method for the fillColor property.
 * @param c the new fill color value
 */
public void setFillColor( Color c ) {
```

**15**

```
                Color oldFill = fill;
                fill = c;
                myListeners.firePropertyChange( "fillColor",
                                                  oldFill,
                                                  fill );
                fireFillColorEvent( new FillColorEvent( this,
                                   FillColorEvent.COLOR_CHANGE,
                                   c ) );
                repaint();
        }
        /** Mutator method for the fileName property.
          * @param fn the new image filename
          */
        public void setFileName( String fn ) {
            String oldFileName = fileName;
            fileName = fn;
        image = getToolkit().getImage( fileName );
            myListeners.firePropertyChange( "fileName",
                                              oldFileName,
                                              fileName );
            repaint();
        }
        /** Add a listener interested in FillColorEvent
          * objects
          */
        public void
        addFillColorListener( FillColorListener l ) {
            fillColorListeners.addElement( l );
        }
        /** Add a listener interested in property change
          * events
          */
        public void addPropertyChangeListener(
            PropertyChangeListener l ) {
            myListeners.addPropertyChangeListener( l );
        }
        /** Remove a listener no longer interested in
          * FillColorEvent objects
          */
        public void removeFillColorListener(
            FillColorListener l ) {
            fillColorListeners.removeElement( l );
        }
        /** Remove a listener no longer interested in
          * property change events
          */
        public void
        removePropertyChangeListener(
            PropertyChangeListener l ) {
            myListeners.removePropertyChangeListener( l );
        }
    }
```

## Breakdown of the ImageBean2 Class

The two new fields support the handling of events. The field `myListeners` provides the support for creating bound properties. The field `fillColorListeners` is the list of listeners registered to receive `FillColorEvent` objects:

```
public class ImageBean2 extends JPanel {
   private String fileName;
   private transient Image image;
   private int width = 200;
   private int height = 150;
   private Color fill = Color.lightGray;
   private PropertyChangeSupport
      myListeners = new PropertyChangeSupport( this );
   private Vector fillColorListeners = new Vector();
```

The method `fireFillColorEvent` sends a `FillColorEvent` object to all registered listeners. It begins by cloning the list of registered listeners to avoid any problems that could arise if the list changed while the events were being delivered. Using an **Enumeration** object, the program visits all items in the list and calls the handler method `fillColorChange` for each one.

```
public void fireFillColorEvent( FillColorEvent e ) {
   Vector snapshot
      = (Vector) fillColorListeners.clone();
   Enumeration cursor = snapshot.elements();
   while( cursor.hasMoreElements() ) {
      FillColorListener fcl
         = (FillColorListener) cursor.nextElement();
      if ( e.getID()
         == FillColorEvent.COLOR_CHANGE ) {
         fcl.fillColorChange( e );
      }
   }
}
```

**15**

The methods for accessing the properties have not changed, but the **imageUpdate** method has changed to fire a **PropertyChangeEvent** if the image loaded has a size different from the previous image. The method also saves the old width and height at the beginning of the method so that the old and new values can be put into the event object. Because the **preferredSize** property is returned as a **Dimension** object, two **Dimension** objects are created to hold the old and new values, as shown next:

```
public boolean imageUpdate( Image img,
                        int infoflags,
                        int x, int y,
                        int w, int h ) {
   if ( (infoflags & ImageObserver.ALLBITS) != 0 ) {
      int oldWidth = width;
```

```
            int oldHeight = height;
            width = img.getWidth( null );
            height = img.getHeight( null );
            if ( oldWidth != width
                 || oldHeight != height ) {
                myListeners.firePropertyChange(
                    "preferredSize",
                    new Dimension( oldWidth, oldHeight ),
                    new Dimension( width, height ) );
            }
            repaint();
            return false;
        } else {
            return true;
        }
    }
```

The convenience methods `makeFillGreen` and `makeFillRed` simply call
the `setFillColor` method and pass the appropriate constant value. These do
not set the field fillColor directly because that would bypass the property-
change reporting that has been added to this class:

```
public void makeFillGreen() {
    setFillColor( Color.green );
}
public void makeFillRed() {
    setFillColor( Color.red );
}
```

The painting and deserialization methods do not change, but the mutator
methods are altered to add change reporting. Both methods now begin by saving the old value of the property before changing it to the new value. After
the change is made, the **firePropertyChange** method is used to fire the
**PropertyChangeEvent**. The `setFillColor` method not only reports a
property-change event, it also fires a `FillColorEvent` with an ID value of
COLOR_CHANGE, as shown next:

```
public void setFillColor( Color c ) {
    Color oldFill = fill;
    fill = c;
    myListeners.firePropertyChange( "fillColor",
                                    oldFill,
                                    fill );
    fireFillColorEvent( new FillColorEvent( this,
                        FillColorEvent.COLOR_CHANGE,
                        c ) );
    repaint();
}
public void setFileName( String fn ) {
    String oldFileName = fileName;
    fileName = fn;
```

```
image = getToolkit().getImage( fileName );
myListeners.firePropertyChange( "fileName",
                                oldFileName,
                                fileName );

repaint();
}
```

The last four methods of the class are for adding and removing event listeners. The method addFillColorListener puts the given listener object into the **vector** of listeners:

```
public void
addFillColorListener( FillColorListener l ) {
    fillColorListeners.addElement( l );
}
```

The **addPropertyChangeListener** method delegates to the **PropertyChangeSupport** object, myListeners, the handling of the bound property listeners:

```
public void addPropertyChangeListener(
    PropertyChangeListener l ) {
    myListeners.addPropertyChangeListener( l );
}
```

To remove themselves from the list, listeners no longer interested in FillColorEvent objects use the method removeFillColorListener. This method then removes the element from the **vector** holding the list:

```
public void removeFillColorListener(
    FillColorListener l ) {
    fillColorListeners.removeElement( l );
}
```

The method **removePropertyChangeListener** delegates to the **PropertyChangeSupport** object the removal of the specified **PropertyChangeListener** object from the list:

```
    public void
    removePropertyChangeListener(
        PropertyChangeListener l ) {
        myListeners.removePropertyChangeListener( l );
    }
}
```

## Custom Event Class for the ImageBean2 Bean

A separate class defines the custom event used in the ImageBean2 class. The constructor takes three inputs: a reference to the object that is the source of the event, an integer constant that is the event identifier, and the color associated with the event. The source reference is passed along to the superclass constructor,

**EventObject.** The other methods of the class are defined so that the receiving objects can extract information from the event, as follows:

```java
package examples.beans;
import java.awt.Color;
import java.util.EventObject;
/** A user-defined event class
  */
public class FillColorEvent extends EventObject {
    /** event type identifier */
    public static final int COLOR_CHANGE = 0;
    private int id;
    private Color color;
    /** Construct an event object
      * @param source the object initiating the event
      * @param id the event identifier
      * @param c the color for the event
      */
    public FillColorEvent( Object source, int id,
                           Color c ) {
      super( source );
      id = id;
      color = c;
    }
    /** Return the color associated with the event
      * @return The color
      */
    public Color getColor() {
      return color;
    }
    /** Return the event identifier
      * @return The event identifier
      */
    public int getID() {
      return id;
    }
}
```

## Listener Interface for the Custom Event Class

The last piece of code needed for this example is the definition of the FillColorListener interface. It adds just one empty method to the **EventListener** interface:

```java
package examples.beans;
import java.util.EventListener;
public interface FillColorListener extends EventListener {
    /** The method called when a FillColor change occurs
      */
    public void fillColorChange( FillColorEvent e );
}
```

## ImageBean2 Used in a BeanBox

You can test the bean, or change roles from that of a bean provider to an application developer who uses predefined beans, by loading the bean into a beanbox. To load the ImageBean2 JavaBean into the BDK BeanBox, follow the same process you used for `ImageBean1`.

To load ImageBean2 into the BDK BeanBox:

1. Add lines to the **ImageBeans.manifest** file in the folder into which you unpacked the examples.jar file, so that the file lists both `ImageBean1` and `ImageBean2`. One .jar file can list any number of beans. The BDK BeanBox requires a blank line between the entries for each bean and a blank line after the last entry. The manifest file should now look like the following:

   ```
   Name: examples/beans/ImageBean1.class
   Java-Bean: True

   Name: examples/beans/ImageBean2.class
   Java-Bean: True
   ```

2. Type the following command, on one line, from the parent folder of the examples folder to create a .jar file **ImageBeans.jar**:

   ```
   jar cfm ImageBeans.jar ImageBeans.manifest
                          examples\beans\*.class
   ```

3. Copy the file **ImageBeans.jar** into the **jars** subfolder of the folder in which you installed the BDK.

4. Start the BeanBox. See that `ImageBean2` is now listed in the Toolbox window.

5. You can have a little fun with this bean. Drop an `ImageBean2` bean onto the BeanBox window.

6. Drop two BlueButton beans on to the BeanBox window and position them near, but not on top of, the `ImageBean2`. These beans look like buttons labeled "press".

7. Change the background property of one BlueButton to red and the other BlueButton to green. Use the Properties window and ColorEditor the same way as when you changed the color of a JellyBean object earlier in this chapter.

8. Click the **red** button. While it is selected, click **Edit** on the menu bar, and then select **Events**. From the cascading menus, select **button push** and then click **action performed**.

   A red line appears from the bean to the current mouse position.

9. Move over the area of the `ImageBean2` bean, and click.

15

10. The EventTargetDialog appears, inviting you to select a target method. Click **makeFillRed**, and then click **OK**. Briefly, a message box appears saying that an adaptor class is being generated and compiled.

11. Now, try clicking the **red** button. The fill color of the ImageBean2 should turn red.

12. In a similar fashion, make the green button change the fill color of the ImageBean2 to green. Depending on how you arrange the beans, your BeanBox window may look similar to Figure 15-10.

**Figure 15-10** The ImageBean2 in the BDK BeanBox

13. Now, you can use the bound properties of the ImageBean2. Drop a JellyBean onto the BeanBox window.

14. Select the **ImageBean2**. Click **Edit** from the menu bar and then click **Bind property**. When the PropertyNameDialog pops up, select **fillColor** and then **OK**.

15. Connect the red line from the ImageBean2 to the JellyBean. When the PropertyNameDialog pops up, select **color** and then click **OK**.

    Now, click the **red** and **green** buttons and see what happens. Feel free to experiment.

## SUPPLYING ADDITIONAL JAVABEAN INFORMATION

Beanboxes generally can use the Reflection API to determine what they need to know about a JavaBean. But you cannot deduce some pieces of information from a JavaBean definition, and in some cases you cannot follow the programming conventions for beanboxes. For these reasons, the JavaBeans specification allows for the definition of additional information classes to accompany a JavaBean class: **BeanInfo** classes.

**BeanInfo** classes are used only when beans are being connected in a beanbox. They have no role when the bean is executing, so you do not have to include them in the .jar file when you package JavaBeans into an application. The **BeanInfo** classes implement the **java.beans.BeanInfo** interface.

A beanbox finds the information classes as follows:

➤ For each JavaBean class, the beanbox looks for a class with a name formed by appending the suffix **BeanInfo** onto the name of the JavaBean class. For example, if the JavaBean class is named **JB**, the beanbox looks for class JBBeanInfo.

➤ If a class satisfies the naming convention, the beanbox next checks whether the class implements the **BeanInfo** interface. For example, the beanbox accepts the following class:

```
class JBBeanInfo implements java.beans.BeanInfo
```

➤ If a class satisfies these requirements, the beanbox can call its methods to collect detailed information about the JavaBean. Some of the information is encapsulated in instances of other classes in the **java.beans** package that are listed in Table 15-3.

**Table 15-3**  JavaBean information classes

| Class | Description |
|---|---|
| **FeatureDescriptor** | **FeatureDescriptor** is the superclass for all the other descriptor classes. It contains methods for reading and writing information that is common to all features of a JavaBean, such as **name**, **shortDescription**, and **value**. |
| **BeanDescriptor** | The **BeanDescriptor** class contains high-level information for the entire JavaBean class. |
| **EventSetDescriptor** | The **EventSetDescriptor** class provides detail about the set of events that are gathered under a single listener interface. Each listener interface supported by the JavaBean can have its own **EventSetDescriptor** object. |
| **MethodDescriptor** | The **MethodDescriptor** class describes one of the methods supported by a JavaBean. |
| **ParameterDescriptor** | **ParameterDescriptor** objects are associated with **MethodDescriptor** objects. Each **ParameterDescriptor** describes one argument of a method. |

**15**

*continued*

**Table 15-3** JavaBean information classes (continued)

| Class | Description |
|---|---|
| PropertyDescriptor | A **PropertyDescriptor** object describes a single property of a JavaBean. If your bean has a property for which the read and write methods do not follow the JavaBeans naming convention, use the **PropertyDescriptor** object to identify the read and write methods. |
| IndexedPropertyDescriptor | The **IndexedPropertyDescriptor** class extends **PropertyDescriptor** and adds methods for the indexed read and write methods. |

*Class*

**java.beans.BeanInfo**

*Purpose*

You can optionally define a class that implements this interface, to provide information about the methods, events, properties, and other characteristics of your JavaBean class. Development tools that consume JavaBean classes may use the classes that implement this interface. Programs that use the JavaBean class do not use BeanInfo classes.

*Methods*

➤ **BeanInfo[] getAdditionalBeanInfo()**
Implement the **getAdditionalBeanInfo** method to specify an array of additional **BeanInfo** objects that provide information about the JavaBean.

➤ **BeanDescriptor getBeanDescriptor()**
Implement **getBeanDescriptor** to return general information in a **BeanDescriptor** object.

➤ **int getDefaultEventIndex()**
Implement **getDefaultEventIndex** to tell the beanbox which element in the **EventSetDescriptor** array to treat as the default event when a user interacts with the JavaBean.

➤ **int getDefaultPropertyIndex()**
Implement the **getDefaultPropertyIndex** method to tell the beanbox which element in the **PropertyDescriptor** array to treat as the default when a user interacts with the JavaBean.

➤ **EventSetDescriptor[] getEventSetDescriptors()**
Implement **getEventSetDescriptors** to return an array of **EventSetDescriptor** objects that describes the events generated by this bean.

➤ **Image getIcon( int** *iconKind* **)**
Implement the **getIcon** method to return an icon that can be used to represent the JavaBean in toolbars and the like. The argument specifies the kind of icon required.

➤ **MethodDescriptor[] getMethodDescriptors()**
Implement the **getMethodDescriptors** method to return an array of **MethodDescriptor** objects that describe the externally visible methods of the JavaBean.

➤ **PropertyDescriptor[] getPropertyDescriptors()**
Implement the **getPropertyDescriptors** method to return an array of **PropertyDescriptor** objects that describe the properties of the JavaBean.

---

You can define a class that implements the **BeanInfo** interface and supply implementations of all the **BeanInfo** methods. A simpler approach is to define a class that extends the class java.beans.SimpleBeanInfo. This class implements the BeanInfo interface and provides methods in which the return values indicate that no information is available.

You can extend the **SimpleBeanInfo** class and override selected methods. For example, if an icon can represent your JavaBean class, you can implement the **BeanInfo.getIcon** method to return the icon. Some of the classes in the **java.beans** package that provide information about JavaBean classes are listed in Table 15-3.

## Providing a Custom Property Editor

Beanboxes can provide property editors for several different types of properties, including **String**, **Font**, and **Color**. However, a programmer who creates JavaBeans must provide a property editor for other kinds of properties. All property editors must implement the interface **java.beans.PropertyEditor**. Property editors must keep track of all objects that are interested in the property and notify all these objects when a property changes.

The class **java.beans.PropertyEditorSupport** provides a trivial property editor. For many cases, all you must do to create a custom property editor is extend this class and override a few of its methods. For example, if the editor only needs to present a list of valid choices for the property value, the support **PropertyEditorSupport** provides is sufficient. The next example program demonstrates a customized editor class that takes this approach.

For cases requiring something more complex, a class that directly implements the **PropertyEditor** interface and provides implementation of all its methods may be more appropriate.

**15**

Beanboxes usually provide a dialog box containing a list of all the JavaBean properties and a field for editing each one. Often, this dialog box is sufficient. Nevertheless, a complex JavaBean may require that you efficiently customize a specialized user interface. A special purpose customizer can treat the JavaBean as a whole because it can understand the dependencies between fields and makes sure that they are respected.

A customizer class must meet the following criteria:

➤ The class must implement the **java.beans.Customizer** interface.

➤ An instance of the class must be an AWT component that can be embedded in a dialog box. Typically, you define a customizer class to extend the **Panel** or **JPanel** classes.

➤ The class must have a constructor that has no arguments.

When you create a customizer class, you must also provide the method **getBeanDescriptor** in the **BeanInfo** class associated with the JavaBean. The **BeanDescriptor** associates the customizer class with a particular JavaBean. To instantiate the **BeanDescriptor** class, use the form of the constructor that has two arguments so that you can specify both the JavaBean object and the customizer object.

---

*Syntax*

**BeanDescriptor myBeanDescriptor**

    **= new BeanDescriptor(** *beanClass*, *customizerClass* **);**

---

*Dissection*

The first argument of the constructor is the **Class** object for the JavaBean class.

The second argument of the constructor is the **Class** object for the customizer class.

---

# CREATING A JAVABEAN CLASS WITH A BEANINFO CLASS

The third version of the example JavaBean, the `ImageBean3` class, is expanded further by the addition of another property called scaling. It allows the image to appear at its original size or scaled to fit the panel that contains it. This property has only two allowable values, the constants `ORIGINAL_SIZE` and `SCALED_TO_FIT`, both of which are defined in the class. A custom property editor is created for this property that lets the user choose between these two values without having to know the integer values used within the class.

`ImageBean3` also has an accompanying **BeanInfo** class. Following the prescribed naming convention, this class is called `ImageBean3BeanInfo`. The source for the scaling property editor class and the `ImageBean3BeanInfo` class follow the breakdown of the `ImageBean3` class.

Here is the complete source code for this third version of the ImageBean example. The differences between this version and the previous version are highlighted in boldface and described in detail after the source code:

```
package examples.beans;
import javax.swing.JPanel;
import java.awt.*;
import java.io.*;
import java.util.*;
import java.awt.image.ImageObserver;
import java.beans.*;
/** A very simple JavaBean class that displays an image
 *  and allows the user to specify the file containing
 *  the image and the fill color to be used if the
 *  image is smaller than the panel.  There is also a
 *  scaling property that allows the image to be shown
 *  in its original size or scaled to fit in the panel.
 */
public class ImageBean3 extends JPanel {
    private String fileName;
    private transient Image image;
    private int width = 200;
    private int height=150;
    private Color fill = Color.lightGray;
    private PropertyChangeSupport
       myListeners = new PropertyChangeSupport( this );
    private Vector fillColorListeners = new Vector();
    /** Specify how the image is drawn, must be one of
     *  the constants defined below */
    private int scaling;
    /** Draw the image in its original size */
    public static final int ORIGINAL_SIZE = 0;
    /** Scale the image to fit in the panel */
    public static final int SCALED_TO_FIT = 1;
    /** No-argument constructor; sets the file name to a
     *  default value.
     */
    public ImageBean3() {
        setFileName( "..\\demo\\sunw\\demo\\juggler\\"
                   + "Juggler0.gif" );
    }
    /** Send an event to all registered listeners */
    public void fireFillColorEvent( FillColorEvent e ) {
        Vector snapshot
           = (Vector) fillColorListeners.clone();
        Enumeration cursor = snapshot.elements();
        while( cursor.hasMoreElements() ) {
```

```
            FillColorListener fcl
               = (FillColorListener) cursor.nextElement();
            if ( e.getID()
               == FillColorEvent.COLOR_CHANGE ) {
               fcl.fillColorChange( e );
            }
      }
}
/** Display the image at its original size.  The Sun
  * BeanBox recognizes only methods without
  * parameters that return void.
  */
public void displayOriginalSize() {
   setScaling( ORIGINAL_SIZE );
}
/** Display the image scaled to fit the panel.  The
 * Sun BeanBox recognizes only methods without
  * parameters that return void.
  */
public void displayScaledToFit() {
   setScaling( SCALED_TO_FIT );
}
/** Accessor for the filename property.
  * @return The current image's filename
  */
public String getFileName() {
   return fileName;
}
/** Accessor for the fillColor property
  * @return The current fill color
  */
public Color getFillColor() {
   return fill;
}
/** The preferred size of the panel
  * @return The size of the current image
  */
public Dimension getPreferredSize() {
   return new Dimension( width, height );
}
/** How the image is drawn within the panel
  */
public int getScaling() {
   return scaling;
}
/** Method for monitoring the progress of the
  * loading of the current image.
  */
public boolean imageUpdate( Image img,
                            int infoflags,
                            int x, int y,
                            int w, int h ) {
```

```java
        if ( (infoflags & ImageObserver.ALLBITS) != 0 ) {
            int oldWidth = width;
            int oldHeight = height;
            width = img.getWidth( null );
            height = img.getHeight( null );
            if ( oldWidth != width
                || oldHeight != height ) {
                myListeners.firePropertyChange(
                    "preferredSize",
                    new Dimension( oldWidth, oldHeight ),
                    new Dimension( width, height ) );
            }
            repaint();
            return false;
        } else {
            return true;
        }
    }
    /** Set the image fill color to green.  The Sun
      * BeanBox recognizes only methods without
      * parameters that return void.
      */
    public void makeFillGreen() {
        setFillColor( Color.green );
    }
    /** Set the image fill color to red.  The Sun
      * BeanBox recognizes only methods without
      * parameters that return void.
      */
    public void makeFillRed() {
        setFillColor( Color.red );
    }
    /** Paint the fill color if the panel is bigger than
      * the image and the image will be displayed
      * original size.  Then draw the image according to
      * the selected scaling type.
      * @param g the panel's graphics context
      */
    public void paintComponent( Graphics g ) {
        super.paintComponent( g );
        Dimension panelSize = getSize();
        Insets ins = getInsets();
        int actWidth = panelSize.width - ins.right
                        - ins.left - 1;
        int actHeight = panelSize.height - ins.top
                        - ins.bottom - 1;
        if ( scaling == ORIGINAL_SIZE &&
            ( panelSize.width > width ||
              panelSize.height > height ) ) {
            g.setColor( fill );
            g.fillRect( ins.left, ins.top,
                        actWidth, actHeight );
```

**15**

```
        }
        if ( image != null ) {
            if ( scaling == SCALED_TO_FIT ) {
                g.drawImage( image, ins.left, ins.top,
                             actWidth, actHeight,
                             fill, this );
            } else {
                g.drawImage( image, ins.left, ins.top, this );
            }
        }
    }
    /** Deserialization method called for the JavaBean.
      * This is necessary because Image objects can be
    * serialized and must be regenerated manually.
      * @exception IOException if an error occurs
      *              reading the serialized JavaBean.
      * @exception ClassNotFoundException if the
      *              serialized JavaBean can't be found.

      */
    private void readObject( ObjectInputStream ois )
            throws IOException, ClassNotFoundException {
        ois.defaultReadObject();
        image = getToolkit().getImage( fileName );
        repaint();
    }
    /** Mutator method for the fillColor property.
      * @param c the new fill color value
      */
    public void setFillColor( Color c ) {
        Color oldFill = fill;
        fill = c;
        myListeners.firePropertyChange( "fillColor",
                                        oldFill,
                                        fill );
        fireFillColorEvent( new FillColorEvent( this,
                            FillColorEvent.COLOR_CHANGE,
                            c ) );
        repaint();
    }
    /** Mutator method for the fileName property.
      * @param fn the new image filename
      */
    public void setFileName( String fn ) {
        String oldFileName = fileName;
        fileName = fn;
        image = getToolkit().getImage( fileName );
        myListeners.firePropertyChange( "fileName",
                                        oldFileName,
                                        fileName );

        repaint();
    }
```

```
/** Mutator method for the image-scaling property
  * used to specify how the image should be drawn
  * within the panel.
  * @param s the scaling type, either ORIGINAL_SIZE
  *           or SCALED_TO_FIT
  */
public void setScaling( int s ) {
   int oldScaling = scaling;
   scaling = s;
   myListeners.firePropertyChange( "scaling",
      new Integer( oldScaling ),
      new Integer( scaling ) );
}
/** Add a listener interested in FillColorEvent
  * objects
  */
public void
addFillColorListener( FillColorListener l ) {
   fillColorListeners.addElement( l );
}
/** Add a listener interested in property change
  * events
  */
public void addPropertyChangeListener(
   PropertyChangeListener l ) {
   myListeners.addPropertyChangeListener( l );
}
/** Remove a listener no longer interested in
  * FillColorEvent objects
  */
public void removeFillColorListener(
   FillColorListener l ) {
   fillColorListeners.removeElement( l );
}
/** Remove a listener no longer interested in
  * property change events
  */
public void
removePropertyChangeListener(
   PropertyChangeListener l ) {
   myListeners.removePropertyChangeListener( l );
}
}
```

**15**

## Breakdown of the ImageBean3 Class

The ImageBean3 class is a variation on the ImageBean1 class that has a
BeanInfo class. The differences between this version and the previous version
are highlighted in boldface:

```
public class ImageBean3 extends Panel {
```

Three fields are added to the class. One is the field for holding the scaling, and the other two are the constant values to be assigned to the scaling field.

```
private int scaling;
public static final int ORIGINAL_SIZE = 0;
public static final int SCALED_TO_FIT = 1;
```

Two more convenience methods are added for changing the scaling of the image. Because they return no value and take no input, they are very easy to connect to the events of other JavaBeans.

```
public void displayOriginalSize() {
   setScaling( ORIGINAL_SIZE );
}
public void displayScaledToFit() {
   setScaling( SCALED_TO_FIT );
}
```

An accessor method for the scaling property is then added:

```
public int getScaling() {
   return scaling;
}
```

The **paintComponent** method is changed to handle the choices of image scaling. If the scaling property has the value ORIGINAL_SIZE, the image is drawn as before. If the value is SCALED_TO_FIT, a different version of the **drawImage** method is used. This version takes the size that the image should become, which is the size of the panel after taking the panel's insets into account.

```
public void paintComponent( Graphics g ) {
   super.paintComponent( g );
   Dimension panelSize = getSize();
   Insets ins = getInsets();
   int actWidth = panelSize.width - ins.right
                       - ins.left - 1;
   int actHeight = panelSize.height - ins.top
                       - ins.bottom - 1;
   if ( scaling == ORIGINAL_SIZE &&
        ( panelSize.width > width ||
          panelSize.height > height ) ) {
      g.setColor( fill );
      g.fillRect( ins.left, ins.top,
                  actWidth, actHeight );
   }
   if ( image != null ) {
      if ( scaling == SCALED_TO_FIT ) {
         g.drawImage( image, ins.left, ins.top,
                      actWidth, actHeight,
                      fill, this );
```

```
      } else {
         g.drawImage( image, ins.left, ins.top, this );
      }
   }
}
```

A mutator method for the scaling type has been added.

```
public void setScaling( int s ) {
   int oldScaling = scaling;
   scaling = s;
   myListeners.firePropertyChange( 'scaling',
      new Integer( oldScaling ),
      new Integer( scaling ) );
}
```

None of the other methods in the `ImageBean3` class are new or have been updated. However, this class uses two additional classes:

➤ The property editor class.

➤ The bean information class.

## Property Editor Class for the ImageBean3 Class

The scaling property of the `ImageBean3` class requires a customized editor, and the `ScalingEditor` class provides it. This simple property editor only needs to present a list of two choices for users. Therefore, the `ScalingEditor` can be defined as a subclass of **PropertyEditorSupport** and can use most of the inherited method implementations.

```
package examples.beans;
import java.beans.*;
/** This class provides the editing support for the
  * scaling property of the ImageBean3 class.
  */
public class ScalingEditor extends PropertyEditorSupport {
   /** Provide the names of the allowable values.
     * Don't put spaces in these tags
     * for the Sun BeanBox, ensure that no
     * spaces appear in these tags.
  * @return An array of strings containing the
     *            allowable values
     */
   public String[] getTags() {
      return new String[] { "original_size",
                            "scaled_to_fit" };
   }
   /** Convert a tag string into a tag name into a
     * value.  The default is to set the value to
     * the ORIGINAL_SIZE value.
     * @param s The tag string
     */
```

**15**

```
      public void setAsText( String s ) {
         if ( s.equals( "scaled_to_fit" ) ) {
            setValue( new Integer(
                       ImageBean3.SCALED_TO_FIT) );
         } else {
            setValue( new Integer(
                       ImageBean3.ORIGINAL_SIZE) );
         }
      }
   }
   /** For a given property value, return a string
    * that can be used for code generation.  The
    * default value returned is the string for the
    * ORIGINAL_SIZE value.
    * @return The string put into the generated code
    */
   public String getJavaInitializationString() {
      switch( ( (Number) getValue() ).intValue() ) {
         default:
         case ImageBean3.ORIGINAL_SIZE:
            return "examples.beans.ImageBean3."
                   +"ORIGINAL_SIZE";
         case ImageBean3.SCALED_TO_FIT:
            return "examples.beans.ImageBean3."
                   +"SCALED_TO_FIT";
      }
   }
}
```

The `ScalingEditor` class overrides three methods of the
**PropertyEditorSupport** class that relate to the names and values of the
allowable choices. The **getTags** method returns the names of the value scaling
for the property:

```
public String[] getTags()
```

The **setAsText** method is overridden to convert the tag strings into the actual
integer values they represent:

```
public void setAsText( String s )
```

The **getJavaInitializationString** method returns a string in a form suitable for
putting into a class definition. This method is used when a beanbox is generating a class definition and is preparing Java statements for inclusion in the class:

```
public String getJavaInitializationString()
```

## Information Class for the ImageBean3 Class

To make the `ImageBean3` class usable as a bean, a **BeanInfo** class is required.
The primary reason to create this class is to associate the `ScalingEditor`
class with the scaling property of `ImageBean3`. Here is the complete source

code for the `ImageBean3BeanInfo` class. Following the listing is a detailed breakdown of the code:

```java
package examples.beans;
import java.beans.*;
import java.lang.reflect.Method;
/** The class contains information about the ImageBean3
  * class in a format that is understood by JavaBean
  * builder programs like Sun's BeanBox
  */
public class ImageBean3BeanInfo extends SimpleBeanInfo {
    /** Create an array of PropertyDescriptor objects
      * representing each of the class's properties
      * @return The array of PropertyDescriptor objects
      */
    public PropertyDescriptor[] getPropertyDescriptors() {
        PropertyDescriptor[] pds = null;
        try {
            pds = new PropertyDescriptor[] {
                new PropertyDescriptor( "fillColor",
                                        ImageBean3.class ),
                new PropertyDescriptor( "fileName",
                                        ImageBean3.class ),
                new PropertyDescriptor( "scaling",
                                        ImageBean3.class ),
                new PropertyDescriptor( "preferredSize",
                                        ImageBean3.class,
                                        "getPreferredSize",
                                        null )
            };
            pds[0].setShortDescription(
                "The fill color around the image" );
            pds[1].setShortDescription(
                "The file containing the image" );
            pds[2].setShortDescription(
                "How the image should be drawn" );
            pds[3].setShortDescription(
                "The preferred size of the panel" );
            // all properties of this bean are bound
            for ( int i = 0; i < pds.length; i++ ) {
                pds[i].setBound( true );
            }
            pds[2].setPropertyEditorClass(
                ScalingEditor.class );
        } catch( IntrospectionException ix ) {
            System.out.println( ix );
            return super.getPropertyDescriptors();
        }
        return pds;
    }
```

**15**

```
     /** Indicate that the fileName property is the
       * default property to be updated by returning
       * its index in the PropertyDescriptor array
       * obtained from the method
       * getPropertyDescriptors
       * @return The index of the fileName array
       *         element
       */
    public int getDefaultPropertyIndex() {
       return 1;   // the filename property index
    }
}
```

## Breakdown of the ImageBean3BeanInfo Class

The first method of the class, **getPropertyDescriptors**, returns an array of objects in which each element describes a different property of the ImageBean3 class:

```
public class ImageBean3BeanInfo extends SimpleBeanInfo {
   public PropertyDescriptor[] getPropertyDescriptors() {
```

The method begins by declaring the array and then initializing it using an anonymous array that has the descriptor objects in it. The descriptor objects must be created inside a try block because their constructor may throw an **IntrospectionException** that can be caught and handled. The minimum constructor arguments required are the name of the property and the class to which the property belongs. These constructor arguments suffice for all of the properties except **preferredSize**. Because **preferredSize** is a read-only property, additional arguments of the constructor are specified for the methods that read and write **preferredSize**. The null indicates that the property has no write method:

```
PropertyDescriptor[] pds = null;
   try {
      pds = new PropertyDescriptor[] {
         new PropertyDescriptor( "fillColor",
                                 ImageBean3.class ),
         new PropertyDescriptor( "fileName",
                                 ImageBean3.class ),
         new PropertyDescriptor( "scaling",
                                 ImageBean3.class ),
         new PropertyDescriptor( "preferredSize",
                                 ImageBean3.class,
                                 "getPreferredSize",
                                 null )
      };
```

The next group of statements sets the short descriptions for the properties. Not all beanboxes make use of these short descriptions, but they can be helpful:

```
pds[0].setShortDescription(
    "The fill color around the image" );
pds[1].setShortDescription(
    "The file containing the image" );
pds[2].setShortDescription(
    "How the image should be drawn" );
pds[3].setShortDescription(
    "The preferred size of the panel" );
```

The **for** loop marks each property as a bound property:

```
for ( int i = 0; i < pds.length; i++ ) {
    pds[i].setBound( true );
}
```

---

**Mini Quiz 15-4**

Why is the variable pds declared outside the try block in the **getPropertyDescriptors** method?

---

The method **setPropertyEditorClass** makes the association between the scaling property and its editor class. In the **pds** array, the scaling property has the index value two:

```
pds[2].setPropertyEditorClass(
    ScalingEditor.class );
```

The **catch** block is required to handle any errors that may occur because the introspection process could not be completed for the JavaBean. This **catch** clause recovers by printing a message to the console and returning the default list of property descriptors, as determined by the superclass `SimpleBeanInfo`. If no errors occur, the array calculated in this method is returned:

**15**

```
    } catch( IntrospectionException ix ) {
        System.out.println( ix );
        return super.getPropertyDescriptors();
    }
    return pds;
```

The other method in this **BeanInfo** class is used to indicate the default property for the JavaBean. It does this by returning the index of a property in the array prepared by **getPropertyDescriptors**. It is assumed that the beanbox will give this property some sort of preferential treatment. Returning a value of negative one (–1) indicates that there is no default. In this case, the default property is the filename for the image file:

```
public int getDefaultPropertyIndex() {
    return 1;    // the filename property index
}
```

To load the `ImageBean3` JavaBean into the BDK BeanBox, follow the same process you used for `ImageBean1` and `ImageBean2`.

To load the ImageBean3 into the BeanBox:

1. Add lines to the **ImageBeans.manifest** file in the folder into which you unpacked the **examples.jar** file, so that the manifest file lists the three image beans, as follows, with a blank line after the last entry:

```
Name: examples/beans/ImageBean1.class
Java-Bean: True

Name: examples/beans/ImageBean2.class
Java-Bean: True

Name: examples/beans/ImageBean3.class
Java-Bean: True
```

2. Issue the following command, on one line, from the parent folder of the examples folder to create a .jar file named **ImageBeans.jar**:

```
jar cfm ImageBeans.jar ImageBeans.manifest
                       examples\beans\*.class
```

3. Copy the file **ImageBeans.jar** into the jars subfolder of the folder in which you installed the BDK.

4. Start the beanbox. See that the Toolbox window now lists `ImageBean3`.

   The interesting feature of this bean is the scaling property and the customized property editor, `ScalingEditor`.

5. Drop an `ImageBean3` bean onto the BeanBox window, and make sure that the bean is selected.

6. You may have to resize the Properties window to see all of it. Click the **down arrow** beside the scaling property or on the scaling entry field. The drop-down menu that is shown in Figure 15-11 appears.

7. Select **scaled_to_fit**, and see the image in the bean expand to fill the dimensions of the bean. Select **original_size**, and the image is redrawn at the original size.

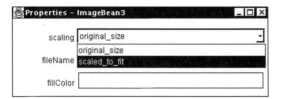

**Figure 15-11** The scaling editor for ImageBean

# CREATING A JAVABEAN CLASS THAT USES THE BEANCONTEXT API

The fourth and final version of the example JavaBean, the `ImageBean4` class, is expanded further using the BeanContext API to dynamically query its run-time environment to discover and use services offered by other JavaBeans. This is a significant step because, up to this point, all the features of the JavaBeans have focused on identifying and interconnecting JavaBeans at design time.

The BeanContext API was added as a core API in the Java 2 Standard Edition SDK. It contains two parts: a containment hierarchy for JavaBean components and support for the discovery of services provided by JavaBeans within the hierarchy.

The BeanContext API has two parts. The first is a logical containment hierarchy for JavaBeans that describes JavaBeans as being located within something called a **BeanContext container**. In the case of the `ImageBean4` example, the BeanContext container is the BeanBox itself. All the JavaBeans that are added to the BeanBox are said to exist within its BeanContext. Having a context gives the JavaBeans a focal point for requesting information about other JavaBeans and the services they provide. To take advantage of the fact that it contains BeanContext, a JavaBean must implement the **BeanContextChild** interface or implement the **BeanContextProxy** interface. A JavaBean that implements the **BeanContextProxy** acts as a proxy for the object that does implement the **BeanContextChild** interface.

JavaBeans that have a service to publish and make available to other JavaBeans must implement the **BeanContextServiceProvider** interface. The BeanBox implements this interface and publishes a method-tracing interface to which JavaBeans can connect and use to trace their own methods.

Few substantial changes were made to the `ImageBean3` class to create the `ImageBean4` class. Therefore, only the statements that have changed from `ImageBean3` to `ImageBean4` are shown next. However, the **ImageBeanContextChildSupport** class, where most of the interesting statements are located, are provided in full.

**15**

In addition to all the other packages already used in `ImageBean3`, `ImageBean4` imports the contents of the java.beans.beancontext package.

```
import java.beans.beancontext.*;
```

`ImageBean4` implements the **BeanContextProxy** interface which has only a single method, **getBeanContextProxy**, which returns an object that implements the **BeanContextChild** interface. In this case, the object returned is of the class **ImageBeanContextChildSupport**:

```
public class ImageBean4 extends JPanel
                        implements BeanContextProxy {
```

One field is added, and that is an object of the **ImageBeanContextChildSupport** class that will provide the support for implementing the **BeanContextChild** interface on behalf of `ImageBean4`. The definition of the class **ImageBeanContextChildSupport** is given next. The constructor parameter is used to associate the object with the `ImageBean4` object:

```
private ImageBeanContextChildSupport
   ibccs = new ImageBeanContextChildSupport( this );
```

One method is added, and that is the one method of the **BeanContextProxy** interface, **getBeanContextProxy.** It is written to return the **ImageBeanContextChildSupport** object. When an `ImageBean4` object is added to the BeanBox, the BeanBox will recognize that `ImageBean4` implements the **BeanContextProxy** interface and will call the **getBeanContextProxy** to get the **BeanContextChild** object for the JavaBean. The **if** statement found at the beginning of this method is put at the beginning of each method in the `ImageBean4` class to enable the tracing of the method. The test that protects the call to **getMethodTracer** is required in case the method tracing service could not be provided for some reason:

```
public BeanContextChild getBeanContextProxy() {
   if ( ibccs.getMethodTracer() != null ) {
      ibccs.getMethodTracer().traceMethod();
   }
   return ibccs;
}
```

## Context Child Support Class for the ImageBean4 Class

Most of the work done to use the BeanContext API is found in the **ImageBeanChildContextSupport** class. The complete source code for the **ImageBeanChildContextSupport** class follows. After the listing is a detailed breakdown of the code:

```
package examples.beans;
import java.beans.beancontext.*;
import sunw.demo.methodtracer.MethodTracer;
```

```
/** This class provides the BeanContextChild support
 * used by the ImageBean4 class
 */
public class ImageBeanContextChildSupport
             extends BeanContextChildSupport
             implements BeanContextServicesListener {
   private Object requestor;
   private MethodTracer tracerService;
   /** Class constructor
    */
   public
   ImageBeanContextChildSupport( BeanContextProxy r ) {
      requestor = r;
   }
   protected void initializeBeanContextResources() {
      try {
         BeanContextServices bcs
            = (BeanContextServices) getBeanContext();
         if ( bcs.hasService( MethodTracer.class ) ) {
            tracerService
               = (MethodTracer) bcs.getService(
                     this,
                     requestor,
                     MethodTracer.class,
                     null,
                     this );
         } else {
            bcs.addBeanContextServicesListener( this );
         }
      } catch ( ClassCastException x ) {
         // The BeanContext of this object is not a
         // BeanContextServices object, so there's nothing
         // to do
      } catch ( Exception x ) {
         x.printStackTrace();
      }
   }
   protected void releaseBeanContextServices() {
      if ( tracerService != null ) {
         tracerService = null;
      }
      try {
         BeanContextServices bcs
            = (BeanContextServices) getBeanContext();
         bcs.removeBeanContextServicesListener( this );
      } catch ( ClassCastException x ) {
         // The BeanContext of this object is not a
         // BeanContextServices object, so there's nothing
         // to do
      } catch ( Exception x ) {
         x.printStackTrace();
      }
```

**15**

```
    }
    public void
    serviceRevoked( BeanContextServiceRevokedEvent e ) {
        if ( e.getServiceClass() == MethodTracer.class ) {
            tracerService = null;
        }
    }
    public void
    serviceAvailable( BeanContextServiceAvailableEvent e ){
        try {
            if ( e.getServiceClass() == MethodTracer.class ){
                BeanContextServices bcs
                    = e.getSourceAsBeanContextServices();
                tracerService
                    = (MethodTracer) bcs.getService(
                        this,
                        requestor,
                        MethodTracer.class,
                        null,
                        this );
            }
        } catch ( Exception x ) {
            x.printStackTrace();
        }
    }
    /** Return the tracer service object
      * @return the MethodTracer for this context
      */
    public MethodTracer getMethodTracer() {
        return tracerService;
    }
}
```

## Breakdown of the ImageBeanContextChildSupport Class

The support for method tracing provided by the BeanBox is implemented in a
demonstration class that is included with the BDK in the file methodtracer.jar.
This .jar file must be added to the CLASSPATH environment variable in
order to be able to successfully compile this class:

```
import sunw.demo.methodtracer.MethodTracer;
```

This class extends the class **BeanContextChildSupport** that is part of the
**java.beans.beancontext** package. The advantage of extending
**BeanContextChildSupport** is that it provides methods that implement the
**BeanContextChild** interface, greatly reducing the work required. All that is
left for the class **ImageBeanChildContextSupport** to do is to override the
methods that are of interest for its situation. These methods are

**initializeBeanContextResources** and **releaseBeanContextServices**. The implementations of these two methods are given next:

```
public class ImageBeanContextChildSupport
            extends BeanContextChildSupport
            implements BeanContextServicesListener {
```

The class constructor takes an **Object** as input and saves it for use later as the service requestor. For this example, the object will be an ImageBean4 object:

```
public ImageBeanContextChildSupport( Object r ) {
   requestor = r;
}
```

The **initializeBeanContextResources** method overrides the method inherited from **BeanContextChildSupport**. It gets the **BeanContext** object and casts it to be a **BeanContextServices** object. This is successful because the BeanBox is acting as both a BeanContext and a **BeanContextServices** object. If the MethodTracer service is available, then the service is retrieved and a reference to it is saved in the field `tracerService`. If it is not available, then this object adds itself as a listener to be notified when the service does become available:

```
protected void initializeBeanContextResources() {
   try {
      BeanContextServices bcs
         = (BeanContextServices) getBeanContext();
      if ( bcs.hasService( MethodTracer.class ) ) {
         tracerService
            = (MethodTracer) bcs.getService(
                 this,
                 requestor,
                 MethodTracer.class,
                 null,
                 this );
      } else {
         bcs.addBeanContextServicesListener( this );
      }
   } catch ( ClassCastException x ) {
      // The BeanContext of this object is not a
      // BeanContextServices object, so there's nothing
      // to do
   } catch ( Exception x ) {
      x.printStackTrace();
   }
}
```

The **releaseBeanContextServices** method overrides the method inherited from **BeanContextChildSupport**. This method will be called by the **BeanContext** to request that the JavaBean release the services that it is using.

15

The only service is the method tracing service, so the field referencing this service is set to **null**. Then, the object removes itself as a listener for the service:

```
protected void releaseBeanContextServices() {
    if ( tracerService != null ) {
        tracerService = null;
    }
    try {
        BeanContextServices bcs
            = (BeanContextServices) getBeanContext();
        bcs.removeBeanContextServicesListener( this );
    } catch ( ClassCastException x ) {
        // The BeanContext of this object is not a
        // BeanContextServices object, so there's nothing
        // to do
    } catch ( Exception x ) {
        x.printStackTrace();
    }
}
```

The **serviceRevoked** method is part of the **BeanContextServicesListener** interface and is called when a service is revoked. The response from this object is to check to see if the service being revoked is the method tracing service, and if it is, the object sets the reference to the service to **null**:

```
public void
serviceRevoked( BeanContextServiceRevokedEvent e ) {
    if ( e.getServiceClass() == MethodTracer.class ) {
        tracerService = null;
    }
}
```

The **serviceAvailable** method is part of the **BeanContextServicesListener** interface and is called when a service becomes available. The response from this object is to check to see if the service being made available is the method-tracing service, and if it is, then the object gets a reference to the **BeanContextServices** object and then retrieves the service and saves a reference to it:

```
public void
serviceAvailable( BeanContextServiceAvailableEvent e ){
    try {
        if ( e.getServiceClass() == MethodTracer.class ){
            BeanContextServices bcs
                = e.getSourceAsBeanContextServices();
            tracerService
                = (MethodTracer) bcs.getService(
                    this,
                    requestor,
```

```
            MethodTracer.class,
            null,
            this );
      }
   } catch ( Exception x ) {
      x.printStackTrace();
   }
}
```

This accessor method is used by the **ImageBean4** class to get a reference to the method tracing service so that the object can use the service to trace its method calls:

```
public MethodTracer getMethodTracer() {
   return tracerService;
}
```

To load the **ImageBean4** JavaBean into the BDK BeanBox, follow the same process you used for **ImageBean1**, **ImageBean2**, and **ImageBean3**.

To load the ImageBean4 into the BeanBox:

1. Add lines to the **ImageBeans.manifest** file in the folder into which you unpacked the **examples.jar** file, so that the manifest file lists all four image beans, as follows, with a blank line after the last entry:

   ```
   Name: examples/beans/ImageBean1.class
   Java-Bean: True

   Name: examples/beans/ImageBean2.class
   Java-Bean: True

   Name: examples/beans/ImageBean3.class
   Java-Bean: True

   Name: examples/beans/ImageBean4.class
   Java-Bean: True
   ```

2. Issue the following command, on one line, from the parent folder of the examples folder to create a .jar file named **ImageBeans.jar**:

   ```
   jar cfm ImageBeans.jar ImageBeans.manifest
                          examples\beans\*.class
   ```

3. Copy the file **ImageBeans.jar** into the jars subfolder of the folder in which you installed the BDK.

4. Start the beanbox. See that the Toolbox window now lists **ImageBean4**.

5. Drop an **ImageBean4** bean to the BeanBox window and make sure that the bean is selected.

**15**

6. Examine the contents of the Method Tracer window which should be similar to what is shown in Figure 15-12. Every time a method of the **ImageBean4** class is called, a trace entry appears in the Method Tracer window. Try changing the values of one or more properties to see the trace entries that are generated.

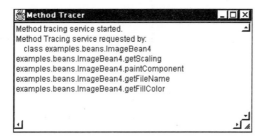

**Figure 15-12** The Method Tracer output for ImageBean4

Explore the BeanBox and try other demonstration beans before you close the BeanBox window and proceed to Chapter 16.

# ENTERPRISE JAVABEANS

The Enterprise JavaBeans (EJB) specification describes a model for Java components that is designed to be installed on and made available from servers. The connection between EJB components and JavaBeans is that both are component models for the Java programming language. Except for the similarity in the names—JavaBeans and Enterprise JavaBeans—there are few similarities between the actual components.

The EJB specification does not include the same programming conventions listed in Table 15-2 for JavaBeans. EJB components are components intended for use in the **multi-tier networks** of large enterprises that need a specification for sharing objects between many systems. Java programs that run on a single workstation or that use a simple client/server model do not require the use of EJBs.

An EJB component does not use any system-level services directly and does not have a user interface. EJB components contain only the logic required to run business processes. Typically, they are made available from a server called an **application server**. User workstations connect to application servers to run a program, and the application server handles all the details of accessing and updating information stored in databases that are usually located on separate servers.

On the application server, EJB components are located within an EJB **container**. The container handles all the details of creating, activating, and destroying EJB component instances. It also deals with the complex issues related to transactions and security. The great advantage of EJBs over other distributed programming frameworks is that EJB developers focus on the business logic and are relieved of responsibility for difficult tasks, such as ensuring the integrity of transactions.

To create an EJB, you define a class that performs your business logic and then add the methods that clients can call to an EJB interface. The server must provide implementations that conform to the EJB specification. Your EJB is then deployed in the server. Many different software companies supply EJB application servers. Until the EJB specification was available, every application server defined a different way to create and install components.

Client programs that use EJB components do not have to know that the components are located in remote containers, but they do use two interfaces that interact with the EJB components. The **home interface** provides methods to find particular instances of an EJB component. The **remote interface** provides access to the business logic methods of the component.

A simple example of an EJB component is a stock portfolio component developed by a financial services company. Its home interface provides methods for creating a new portfolio and for finding an existing portfolio given an account number. The remote interface provides methods for buying and selling stocks, bonds, and mutual funds. Stock portfolio components are available from an application server to which the customers of the financial services component connect from their personal workstations. The container holding the stock portfolio objects provides security for the portfolios and executes all the buy and sell operations on the central database. To maintain the integrity of the information in the database and in the stock portfolios, all database operations are completed as atomic transactions.

## SUMMARY

**15**

The JavaBeans component model is a framework for creating reusable Java classes. Classes that conform to the JavaBeans specification can be loaded into development tools called beanboxes, with which developers can create applications by positioning and connecting beans. This new and emerging technology may become the dominant software technique.

The following facts are key to understanding this chapter:

➤ The interface to a JavaBean consists of methods, properties, and events.

➤ The package **java.beans** provides the core classes and interfaces that support beans.

➤ A bean must implement the interface **java.io.Serializable** because beanboxes use object serialization.

➤ A bean must have a constructor that has no arguments. You must make provisions to pass arguments, if necessary, to the superclass of a bean.

➤ Beanboxes use the Reflection API in the package **java.lang.reflect** to interrogate a bean.

➤ Properties are the attributes of a bean, commonly implemented as the fields of a Java class.

➤ Properties may be single entities or indexed properties, which are arrays of values.

➤ Bound properties can notify other beans when their value changes. Use the class **PropertyChangeSupport** to implement support for bound properties.

➤ Constrained properties are bound properties with the additional characteristic that other listeners can prevent a change in value from occurring. Use the class **VetoableChangeSupport** to implement support for constrained properties.

➤ Event handling follows the same model as event handling for components in the Swing and AWT APIs. If a bean can generate an event `Y`, the class for the event is `YEvent`. A listener class `YListener` should handle `YEvent` objects.

➤ Changes to properties trigger events of the class **PropertyChangeEvent** objects. You can add custom events for other kinds of events.

➤ If the Reflection API cannot provide all the information that a beanbox needs about a bean, you can supply an additional information class that implements the interface **BeanInfo**. In simple cases, you can extend the class **SimpleBeanInfo** rather than implementing the interface.

➤ Beanboxes provide property editors for **String**, **Font**, and **Color** properties. You can provide customized editors for other kinds of properties by defining a class that extends **PropertyEditorSupport** or implements the **PropertyEditor** interface.

➤ If the property editor dialog box of the beanbox is not adequate, you can supply a customizer class for the bean.

➤ By using the BeanContext API, a JavaBean object dynamically queries its runtime environment to discover and use services offered by other JavaBeans.

➤ The Enterprise JavaBeans specification defines a model for components that are located on a server and shared across networks.

# QUESTIONS

1. Which of the following represent a major category of the JavaBeans interface? Select all that apply.

   a. properties

   b. events

   c. menus

   d. methods

   e. streams

2. Which of the following describe a category of JavaBeans events? Select all that apply.

   a. restrained

   b. indexed

   c. bound

   d. controlled

   e. reversible

3. If a JavaBean has a property called `X` with type `T`, which of the following are possible mutator methods for that property in the absence of any other information? Select all that apply.

   a. `T isX( )`

   b. `void setXValue( T newValue )`

   c. `T getX( )`

   d. `void setX( T newValue )`

   e. `void putX( T newValue )`

4. Which class can be used as the basis for supporting bound properties in a JavaBean?

5. If a JavaBean has a property called `X` with type `T`, which of the following are possible accessor methods for that property in the absence of any other information? Select all that apply.

   a. `T isX( )`

   b. `void getXValue( T newValue )`

   c. `T getX( )`

   d. `void setX( T newValue )`

   e. `T getX( int index )`

**15**

6. For a JavaBean class named **A**, which of the following would be the name of its associated **BeanInfo** class? Select the best answer.

   a. `BeanInfo`

   b. `SimpleBeanInfo`

   c. `ABeanInfo`

   d. `AInfo`

   e. `ASimpleBeanInfo`

7. Which of the following are classes that can be used to describe features of a JavaBean? Select all that apply.

   a. **ParameterDescriptor**

   b. **IndexedPropertyDescriptor**

   c. **MethodDescriptor**

   d. **ConstructorDescriptor**

   e. **EventSetDescriptor**

8. What class can be used to provide a basic editor for a JavaBean property with values that must be chosen from a list?

9. Which interface must all JavaBeans implement? Select the best answer.

   a. **Runnable**

   b. **Beanable**

   c. **Cloneable**

   d. **Serializable**

   e. **PropertyChangeListener**

10. How does a listener object veto a proposed property change?

---

# EXERCISES

## Debugging

1. Correct all the errors in the following JavaBean class to create a bean that draws a square of a specified size:

```
package questions.c15;
import javax.swing.JPanel;
import java.awt.*;
public class Debug15_1 extends JPanel {
    private String sideLength = "10";
    private static final Point START
        = new Point( 20, 20 );
    void setSideLength( String sideLength ) {
        this.sideLength = sideLength;
    }
```

```
   String getSideLength() {
      return sideLength;
   }
   public Dimension getPreferredSize() {
      return new Dimension( 100, 100 );
   }
   public void paintComponent( Graphics g ) {
      super.paintComponent( g );
      int sl = Integer.parseInt( sideLength );
      g.drawRect( START.x, START.y, sl, sl );
   }
}
```

Use the following entry in the manifest file Debug15_1.manifest of your .jar file:

```
Name: questions/c15/Debug15_1.class
Java-Bean: True
```

Then, execute the following command (entered on a single line) from the parent folder of the questions folder to create the .jar file:

```
jar cfm0 questions/c15/Debug15_1.jar
           questions/c15/Debug15_1.manifest
           questions/c15/Debug15_1.class
```

2. Correct all the errors in the following JavaBean class to create a bean that draws a circle of a specified radius:

```
package questions.c15;
import javax.swing.JPanel;
import java.awt.*;
public class Debug15_2 extends JPanel {
   private String radius = "25";
   private static final Point START
      = new Point( 20, 20 );
   public void radius( String radius ) {
      this.radius = radius;
   }
   public String radius() {
      return radius;
   }
   public Dimension getPreferredSize() {
      return new Dimension( 100, 100 );
   }
   public void paintComponent( Graphics g ) {
      super.paintComponent( g );
      int r = Integer.parseInt( radius );
      g.fillOval( START.x, START.y, r, r );
   }
}
```

**15**

Use the following entry in the manifest file Debug15_2.manifest of your .jar file:

```
Name: questions/c15/Debug15_2.class
Java-Bean: True
```

Then, execute the following command (entered on a single line) from the parent folder of the questions folder to create the .jar file:

```
jar cfm0 questions/c15/Debug15_2.jar
        questions/c15/Debug15_2.manifest
        questions/c15/Debug15_2.class
```

3. Correct all the errors in the following JavaBean class to create a bean that draws the given text and provides notification when the text changes:

```
package questions.c15;
import javax.swing.JPanel;
import java.awt.*;
import java.beans.*;
public class Debug15_3 extends JPanel {
    private String text = "Default text";
    private static final Point START
        = new Point( 20, 20 );
    private PropertyChangeSupport listeners
        = new PropertyChangeSupport( this );
    public void setDrawText( String text ) {
        this.text = text;
    }
    public String getDrawText() {
        return text;
    }
    public Dimension getPreferredSize() {
        return new Dimension( 100, 40 );
    }
    public void paintComponent( Graphics g ) {
        super.paintComponent( g );
        g.drawString( text, START.x, START.y );
    }
    public void addPropertyChangeListener(
            PropertyChangeListener l ) {
        listeners.addPropertyChangeListener( l );
    }
    public void removePropertyChangeListener(
            PropertyChangeListener l ) {
        listeners.removePropertyChangeListener( l );
    }
}
```

Use the following entry in the manifest file Debug15_3.manifest of your .jar file:

```
Name: questions/c15/Debug15_3.class
Java-Bean: True
```

Then, execute the following command (entered on a single line) from the parent folder of the questions folder to create the .jar file:

```
jar cfm0 questions/c15/Debug15_3.jar
         questions/c15/Debug15_3.manifest
         questions/c15/Debug15_3.class
```

4. Correct all the errors in the following JavaBean class to create a bean that draws ovals and provides vetoable notification when the height or width of the oval changes:

```
package questions.c15;
import javax.swing.JPanel;
import java.awt.*;
public class Debug15_4 extends JPanel {
    private String ovalHeight = "25";
    private String ovalWidth = "50";
    private static final Point START
        = new Point( 20, 20 );
    public void setOvalHeight( String ovalHeight ) {
        try {
            listeners.fireVetoableChange( "ovalHeight",
                                          this.ovalHeight,
                                          ovalHeight );

            this.ovalHeight = ovalHeight;
        } catch ( PropertyVetoException pve ) {
            // change was vetoed, nothing to do
        }
    }
    public String getOvalHeight() {
        return ovalHeight;
    }
    public void setOvalWidth( String ovalWidth ) {
        try {
            listeners.fireVetoableChange( "ovalWidth",
                                          this.ovalWidth,
                                          ovalWidth );

            this.ovalWidth = ovalWidth;
        } catch ( PropertyVetoException pve ) {
            // change was vetoed, nothing to do
        }
    }
    public String getOvalWidth() {
        return ovalWidth;
    }
    public Dimension getPreferredSize() {
        return new Dimension( 100, 100 );
    }
    public void paintComponent( Graphics g ) {
        super.paintComponent( g );
        int h = Integer.parseInt( ovalHeight );
        int w = Integer.parseInt( ovalWidth );
```

**15**

```
            g.fillOval( START.x, START.y, w, h );
        }
    }
```

Use the following entry in the manifest file Debug15_4.manifest of your .jar file:

```
Name: questions/c15/Debug15_4.class
Java-Bean: True
```

Then, execute the following command (entered on a single line) from the parent folder of the questions folder to create the .jar file:

```
jar cfm0 questions/c15/Debug15_4.jar
           questions/c15/Debug15_4.manifest
           questions/c15/Debug15_4.class
```

5. Correct all the errors in the following JavaBean class and its associated **BeanInfo** and editor classes to create a bean that draws a rectangle with either sharp or rounded corners:

```
package questions.c15;
import javax.swing.JPanel;
import java.awt.*;
public class Debug15_5 extends JPanel {
    public static final int SHARP = 0;
    public static final int ROUNDED = 1;
    private String sideLength = "60";
    private int corners = SHARP;
    private static final Point START
        = new Point( 20, 20 );
    private static final int ROUNDING = 20;
    public void setCorners( int corners ) {
        this.corners = corners;
    }
    public int getCorners() {
        return corners;
    }
    public Dimension getPreferredSize() {
        return new Dimension( 100, 100 );
    }
    public void paintComponent( Graphics g ) {
        super.paintComponent( g );
        int sl = Integer.parseInt( sideLength );
        if ( corners == SHARP ) {
            g.drawRect( START.x, START.y, sl, sl );
        } else {
            g.drawRoundRect( START.x, START.y, sl, sl,
                             ROUNDING, ROUNDING );
        }
    }
}
package questions.c15;
```

```
import java.beans.*;
public class Debug15_5BeanInfo extends SimpleBeanInfo {
    public PropertyDescriptor[]
    getPropertyDescriptors()  {
        PropertyDescriptor[] pds = null;
        try {
            pds = new PropertyDescriptor[] {
                new PropertyDescriptor( "corners",
                                        Debug15_5.class ),
            };
            pds[0].setShortDescription(
                "The shape of the rectangle's corners" );
            pds[0].setBound( false );
        } catch( IntrospectionException ix ) {
            ix.printStackTrace();
            return super.getPropertyDescriptors();
        }
        return pds;
    }
}
package questions.c15;
import java.beans.*;
public class Debug15_5Editor
    extends PropertyEditorSupport {
    public String[] getTags() {
        return new String[] { "sharp", "rounded" };
    }
    public String getJavaInitializationString() {
        switch( ( ( Number ) getValue() ).intValue() ) {
            default:
            case Debug15_5.SHARP:
                return "questions.c15.Debug15_5.SHARP";
            case Debug15_5.ROUNDED:
                return "questions.c15.Debug15_5.ROUNDED";
        }
    }
}
```

Use the following entry in the manifest file Debug15_5.manifest of your
.jar file:

```
Name: questions/c15/Debug15_5.class
Java-Bean: True
```

Then, execute the following command (entered on a single line) from the
parent folder of the questions folder to create the .jar file:

```
jar cfm0 questions/c15/Debug15_5.jar
         questions/c15/Debug15_5.manifest
         questions/c15/Debug15_5*.class
```

**15**

## Complete the Solution

1. Extract the file **questions\c15\Complete15_1.java** from the file **question.jar** on the CD-ROM. Complete the `Complete15_1` JavaBean class by adding another property, `messageFont`, which defines the font used to display the message. Then, execute the following command (entered on a single line) from the parent folder of the questions folder to create the .jar file:

```
jar cfm0 questions/c15/Complete15_1.jar
            questions/c15/Complete15_1.manifest
            questions/c15/Complete15_1*.class
```

2. Beginning with the JavaBean class shown in Exercise 1, change the `message` property so that it is a bound message that provides notification when it changes.

3. Extract the file **questions\c15\Complete15_1.java** from the file **question.jar** on the CD-ROM. Complete the `Complete15_1` JavaBean class that implements a progress bar by adding the methods required to make the current position and upper limit into properties that the user can customize. Then, execute the following command (entered on a single line) from the parent folder of the questions folder to create the .jar file:

```
jar cfm0 questions/c15/Complete15_3.jar
            questions/c15/Complete15_3.manifest
            questions/c15/Complete15_3*.class
```

4. Beginning with the JavaBean class shown in Exercise 3, add the support needed to make the current position and upper limit into constrained properties.

5. Beginning with the JavaBean class shown in Exercise 3, add a corresponding **BeanInfo** class that gives short descriptions of the properties, indicates that the properties are constrained, and identifies the position property as the default property for customization.

## Discovery

1. Create a JavaBean class called `Prompter` that displays a prompting message and provides an entry field where users can enter their response to the prompt. This bean should also include an OK button so users can indicate they are finished entering their response.

2. Create a JavaBean class called `Counter` that counts upward from 0 to some limit. The increment and the interval between ticks should be properties of this bean, and the actual count should be a bound property. Try connecting this bean to the progress bar bean from the Complete the Solution exercises so that the count and the progress bar move in unison to the same upper limit.

3. Create a JavaBean class called `BarGraph` that draws a simple bar graph for the data given as five separate bar height properties.

# NETWORK PROGRAMMING

## In this chapter you will:

➤ Perform network I/O using the core classes in the package java.net.

➤ Write programs that establish connections to URLs and perform stream I/O between URLs.

➤ Read and write data to local and remote sites using TCP/IP sockets and datagram sockets.

➤ Use Remote Method Invocation (RMI) to develop classes of objects that are accessible from a server.

➤ Learn the steps involved in compiling and deploying an application that uses RMI.

➤ Be introduced to the Java Naming and Directory Interface (JNDI).

➤ Discover the relationship between RMI and the Java Interface Definition Language (IDL).

## INTRODUCTION

Input and output (I/O) is not restricted to your workstation or the personal computer (PC) that hosts the Java platform. There is a high probability that you are connected to a network. If you are not on a local area network (LAN), you may have a dial-up connection to the Internet. For many programmers, the need to program for the Internet or web-oriented HTML browsers is among the main reasons for learning the Java programming language. Unlike most other programming languages, the Java programming language is designed for use in just such an environment. The Java 2 Platform SDK includes a package **java.net**, specifically so that you can make connections and perform I/O to and from other stations on the network.

A program can communicate with another program on the same host or on a different host. Often, the programs have a client-server relationship with each other. For example, if you are reading an HTML document in a web browser, the system from which the document originates is the server, and your work-station is the client. When you are developing and testing applets written in the Java programming language locally, your workstation is both server and client. Client-server relationships and networking protocols are beyond the scope of this book, but the relationship between the client and server for applets is discussed in Chapter 14.

You can perform network programming at different levels. For example, you can work with URLs and sockets. A socket is an abstraction of the end points of connections between processes or applications. The term *socket* originated in the UNIX environment, where it applies to communication between unrelated processes. Using the Java platform, you can set up connections and communicate over TCP/IP sockets. With a little more programming effort, you can send and receive packets of data using datagram sockets.

Most of the classes in **java.net** can be categorized by whether they support URLs, TCP/IP sockets, or datagram sockets. Some classes are used by all supported protocols. For example, instances of the **InetAddress** class represent Internet Protocol (IP) addresses. An IP address is a 32-bit binary value that identifies one host on the Internet. To be human-readable, an IP address can be represented as four decimal numbers separated by dots, as in 9.21.105.214, or by a string, such as torolab.ibm.com.

# WORKING WITH URLS

You are probably used to specifying URLs to your web browser. As you know, URLs begin with a protocol specification such as http (for Hypertext Transfer Protocol) or ftp (for File Transfer Protocol), followed by ":://" and the host name, along with optional file and port information.

The **java.net** package contains classes that are designed around URLs. The next sample program demonstrates two of these: **URL** and **URLConnection**. Use these classes for creating and manipulating URLs. You can get the file associated with a URL and process the contents in any manner in which you choose to program. Also, you can connect to the host of a URL and perform more complex operations.

The safest way to communicate with the host of a URL is through a **URLConnection**. After you connect, you can request and receive information. However, a **URLConnection** closes after one exchange, and you cannot sustain a long-running conversation. You must reestablish the link for every exchange. To create a connection that can stay open, you should use a TCP/IP socket.

Here is a simple program that connects to the home page for the IBM VisualAge for Java product:

```
package examples.network;
import java.net.*;
import java.util.Date;
/** An example class to demonstrate the use of URL
  * class objects
  */
```

```
public class TryURLObjects {
   /** The test method for the class
    * @param args not used
    */
   public static void main( String[] args ) {
      try {
         URL vajavaPage
            = new URL( "http://www.software.ibm.com"
                       + "/ad/vajava" );
         URLConnection vajavaConn
            = vajavaPage.openConnection();
         Date lastModified
            = new Date( vajavaConn.getLastModified() );
         System.out.println( vajavaPage
                             + " was last modified "
                             + lastModified );

      }
      catch( Exception x ) {
         System.out.println( x );
      }
   }
}
```

The output is of the following form:

```
http://www.software.ibm.com/ad/vajava was last modified
Fri Oct 29 15:20:40 EST 1999
```

Notice how easy it is to construct a **URL** object by passing to the constructor a **String** containing a URL. To open a connection, you call the method **openConnection** for the **URL** object. This method creates and then returns a **URLConnection** object.

This program simply asks when the page was last modified by calling **getLastModified** for the **URLConnection**. To store the information returned, the program creates a **Date** object and then prints the date in a readable format by taking advantage of the fact that the **Date** class overrides the **Object.toString** method in a meaningful way.

This simple program demonstrates how easy it is to set up a connection with systems that host URLs. You can do many meaningful activities with URL connections. For example, using the methods shown in this sample, you could write an application to monitor when URLs on your site are updated. You also can send information to the URL, if the page has a form that has been set up in some other way to receive data.

This program is a rudimentary web browser. All that is required to convert it to a usable, though limited, web browser is logic to read the page, to interpret and display its contents, and to follow the hypertext links code in the page.

**16**

# WORKING WITH SOCKETS

Different programs can communicate through communications channels called "sockets." You can use sockets to transfer data between unrelated processes that can be running on the same workstation or on different hosts on a network. The concept of sockets originated in UNIX environments but is now supported on a wide range of operating systems. The Java platform supports two types of sockets: TCP/IP and datagram, including multicast datagram.

## TCP/IP Sockets

A TCP/IP socket is connection-oriented. When you create a socket, you create an endpoint for a connection between two processes. This is analogous to plugging a telephone into a suitable outlet in the wall. The system at the other end of the "conversation" must also be plugged into a suitable outlet, and the telephone company plays the role of the network by connecting the points. The programs at the two ends of the socket can write to and read from the socket. This is analogous to using a pipe to pass data between streams in a multithreaded program.

You can easily read and write to TCP/IP sockets using stream I/O. All you need to do is set up the socket by creating a **Socket** object, ask the socket for its input stream and output stream, and use these streams like any other input or output stream. The next example program demonstrates this process.

The ease of use of TCP/IP sockets is one of the most appealing features of network programming in the Java programming language. Because sockets are connection-oriented, you can use them as two-way communication channels over a period of time. If you are sending more than a brief message—for example, if you are transferring a file—you can be sure that no parts of the transmission are lost and fail to reach the destination.

However, TCP/IP sockets impose an overhead that datagram sockets do not have. A connection requires setup time before and shutdown time after you transfer any data. Therefore, delivery of information is slower than datagram sockets, but more reliable.

A sample program that creates a TCP/IP socket with a server side and a client side follows. In this case, the client and server reside on the same host. Nevertheless, they run as separate processes, just like client and server programs on different hosts. To identify its server, the client side uses a combination of a server-host name and a port number that makes up a unique identifier to the server. The server is not hardcoded for a particular port because the socket is created with the port number as an argument of the socket constructor.

Here is the server class, `AdditionServer`. A detailed breakdown of the class follows the code:

```java
package examples.network;
import java.io.*;
import java.net.*;
import java.util.StringTokenizer;
/** An example class that uses the server socket class
 */
public class AdditionServer {
   private int port;
   // This is not a reserved port number
   static final int DEFAULT_PORT = 8189;
   /** Constructor
    * @param port The port where the server
    *             will listen for requests
    */
   AdditionServer( int port ) {
      this.port = port;
   }
   /** The method that does the work for the class */
   public void run() {
      try {
         ServerSocket ss = new ServerSocket( port );
         Socket incoming = ss.accept();
         BufferedReader in;
         in = new BufferedReader(
            new InputStreamReader(
            incoming.getInputStream() ) );
         PrintWriter out
            = new PrintWriter(
            incoming.getOutputStream(), true );
         String str;
         while ( !( str = in.readLine() ).equals( "" ) ) {
            double result = 0;
            StringTokenizer st
               = new StringTokenizer( str );
            try {
               while( st.hasMoreTokens() ) {
                  Double d = new Double( st.nextToken() );
                  result += d.doubleValue();
               }
               out.println( "The result is " + result );
            }
            catch( NumberFormatException nfe ) {
               out.println( "Sorry, your list "
                              + "contains an "
                              + "invalid number" );
            }
         }
         incoming.close();
```

**16**

```
        }
     catch( IOException iox ) {
        System.out.println( iox );
        iox.printStackTrace();
     }
  }
  /** The test method for the class
   * @param args[0] Optional port number in place of
   *          the default
   */
  public static void main( String[] args ) {
     int port = DEFAULT_PORT;
     if ( args.length > 0 ) {
        port = Integer.parseInt( args[0] );
     }
     AdditionServer addServe
        = new AdditionServer( port );
     addServe.run();
  }
}
```

The following breakdown of the code does not follow the order of statements in the program listing, so that explanation can follow more closely the order in which statements are executed.

The constructor of an **AdditionServer** object, shown next, stores the port number that it receives as an argument.

```
public class AdditionServer {
   private int port;
   static final int DEFAULT_PORT = 8189;
   AdditionServer( int port ) {
      this.port = port;
   }
```

The **main** method creates an **AdditionServer** object, **addServe**, using a port number that can be either supplied as a command–line argument or taken from an arbitrarily chosen default.

The client and server must use the same port, and that port must not be used or reserved by another process. A convention on UNIX and some other operating systems is to reserve port numbers zero to 1023 for system services. If you run the server and client in separate threads of one multithreaded program, the client thread can create the server thread object and pass the port number to the server constructor. Otherwise, the programmers of the client and server sides must agree on a port number to use.

The main method starts the server by calling the run method of this class:

```
public static void main( String[] args ) {
   int port = DEFAULT_PORT;
   if ( args.length > 0 ) {
```

```
      port = Integer.parseInt( args[0] );
   }
   AdditionServer addServe = new AdditionServer( port );
   addServe.run();
}
```

The **run** method does all the work of this server. It creates a **ServerSocket** object for the port and then calls the method **accept**. This is an important method defined by the **ServerSocket** class. The nature of a server is to listen passively to its port. The **accept** method puts the server into a wait state until input arrives and then it returns a socket.

```
public void run() {
   try {
      ServerSocket ss = new ServerSocket( port );
      Socket incoming = ss.accept();
```

When the connection is established, the server asks the socket for its input stream by calling the method **getInputStream**. Notice that in the code that follows, you use buffered, character-oriented input by wrapping a **BufferedReader** object and an **InputStreamReader** object around the **InputStream** object returned by **getInputStream**. Similarly, on the output side, you ask the socket for its output stream and wrap a **PrintWriter** object around the **OutputStream** object returned. The second argument of the constructor for **PrintWriter** is a **boolean** set to **true** when you want every call of **println** to flush the output buffer.

```
BufferedReader in;
in = new BufferedReader(
   new InputStreamReader(
   incoming.getInputStream() ) );
PrintWriter out
   = new PrintWriter(
   incoming.getOutputStream(),true );
```

After setting up the streams, you can use ordinary stream I/O to and from the socket. This server only reads and adds numbers. It reads from the socket, one line at a time. An empty line indicates the end of the input. The method uses the classes **StringTokenizer** and **Double** to extract numbers from the input and convert them to type **double** so that it can add them. After handling the last token, the server writes the sum of the numbers to the output stream:

**16**

```
String str;
   while ( !( str = in.readLine() ).equals( "" ) ) {
      double result = 0;
      StringTokenizer st
         = new StringTokenizer( str );
      try {
         while( st.hasMoreTokens() ) {
            Double d = new Double( st.nextToken() );
            result += d.doubleValue();
```

```
        }
        out.println( "The result is " + result );
        }
```

Finally, the server closes the socket. The server also contains handlers for the two types of exceptions that may occur. It has nested try blocks with catch blocks for **NumberFormatException** and **IOException**.

```
        catch( NumberFormatException nfe ) {
            out.println ( "Sorry, your list "
                            + "contains an "
                            + "invalid number" );
        }
    }
    incoming.close();
}
catch( IOException iox ) {
    System.out.println( iox );
    iox.printStackTrace();
}
}
```

Here is the client-side class. Again, the detailed breakdown follows the class:

```
package examples.network;
import java.io.*;
import java.net.*;
/** A client-side class that uses a TCP/IP socket
  */
public class AdditionClient {
    private InetAddress host;
    private int port;
    // This is not a reserved port number
    static final int DEFAULT_PORT = 8189;
    /** Constructor
      * @param host Internet address of the host
      *         where the server is located
      * @param port Port number on the host where
      *         the server is listening
      */
    public AdditionClient( InetAddress host, int port ) {
        this.host = host;
        this.port = port;
    }
    /** The method used to start a client object
      */
    public void run() {
        try {
            Socket client = new Socket( host, port );
            BufferedReader socketIn;
            socketIn
                = new BufferedReader(
```

```
                 new InputStreamReader(
                    client.getInputStream() ) );
            PrintWriter socketOut
               = new PrintWriter(
                    client.getOutputStream(), true );
            String numbers = "1.2 3.4 5.6";
            System.out.println( "Adding the numbers "
                                  + numbers
                                  + " together" );
            socketOut.println( numbers );
            System.out.println( socketIn.readLine() );
            socketOut.println ( "" );
         }
      catch( IOException iox ) {
         System.out.println( iox );
         iox.printStackTrace();
      }
   }
   /** The test method for the class
    * @param args Optional port number
    *           and host name
    */
   public static void main( String[] args ) {
      try {
         InetAddress host = InetAddress.getLocalHost();
         int port = DEFAULT_PORT;
         if ( args.length > 0 ) {
            port = Integer.parseInt( args[0] );
         }
         if ( args.length > 1 ) {
            host = InetAddress.getByName( args[1] );
         }
         AdditionClient addClient
            = new AdditionClient( host, port );
         addClient.run();
      }
      catch ( UnknownHostException uhx ) {
         System.out.println( uhx );
         uhx.printStackTrace();
      }
   }
}
```

**16**

The structure of the client class, `AdditionClient`, is complementary to that of the server. The constructor stores the host address, which is of type **InetAddress**, as well as the port number. The class **InetAddress** is defined in the **java.net** package to represent IP addresses:

```
public class AdditionClient {
   private InetAddress host;
   private int port;
```

```
// This is not a reserved port number
static final int DEFAULT_PORT = 8189;
public AdditionClient( InetAddress host, int port ) {
   this.host = host;
   this.port = port;
}
```

As on the server, let the port number be either a command-line parameter or a stored arbitrary default value. Here, the default value is 8189.

**Mini Quiz 16-1**

Why does the client, but not the server, enclose the body of the **main** method in a try block and have an exception to catch?

The main method of the `AdditionClient` class gets the IP address for the server host by calling the method **InetAddress.getLocalHost** to serve as the default value. The user can override this default by specifying a different host address as the second command-line parameter. With these two pieces of information, the main method can create a client object, `addClient`, and then start the client by calling its **run** method:

```
public static void main( String[] args ) {
   try {
      InetAddress host = InetAddress.getLocalHost();
      int port = DEFAULT_PORT;
      if ( args.length > 0 ) {
         port = Integer.parseInt( args[0] );
      }
      if ( args.length > 1 ) {
         host = InetAddress.getByName( args[1] );
      }
      AdditionClient addClient
         = new AdditionClient( host, port );
      addClient.run();
   }
   catch ( UnknownHostException uhx ) {
      System.out.println( uhx );
      uhx.printStackTrace();
   }
}
```

Like the server, the client has its work performed by its **run** method. The first job of this method is to create the client end of the socket. Next, **run** sets up a **BufferedReader** object for input and a **PrintWriter** object for output, much like the server does, except that these objects are associated with the sides of the socket that are opposite those of the server end.

```
public void run() {
   try {
      Socket client = new Socket( host, port );
      BufferedReader socketIn;
      socketIn
         = new BufferedReader(
            new InputStreamReader(
            client.getInputStream() ) );
      PrintWriter socketOut
         = new PrintWriter(
            client.getOutputStream(), true );
```

The processing is simple: The client writes a textual representation of three numbers to the socket. Then, it reads whatever the server sends back and outputs that line to **System.out**:

```
String numbers = "1.2 3.4 5.6";
System.out.println( "Adding the numbers "
                    + numbers + " together" );
socketOut.println( numbers );
System.out.println( socketIn.readLine() );
socketOut.println( "" );
}
```

Like the server, the client catches **IOException** objects that can occur during any kind of stream I/O:

```
catch( IOException iox ) {
   System.out.println( iox );
   iox.printStackTrace();
}
}
```

For this application to work, TCP/IP must be installed and running on your system. A working Internet connection is proof that TCP/IP is running. You must start the server class in one window and then start the client in a different window.

To run this application:

1. Open two command–line windows.

2. If you are running from the .jar file that contains all sample programs, go to the folder in which the file **examples.jar** resides in both windows. Make sure the .jar file is part of your path by entering the following command in both windows:

```
SET CLASSPATH=examples.jar;%CLASSPATH%
```

3. In one window, start the server by entering the following command:

```
java examples.network.AdditionServer
```

**16**

4. In the other window, start the client by entering the following command, optionally adding a port number to the end of this command string:

```
java examples.network.AdditionClient [port]
```

5. If you run and receive a message saying the connection is refused, try running the client again with a different port number.

If you cannot open a connection successfully, you may have to stop the server by pressing Ctrl+C in the window in which you started the server.

If the connection is successful, the output appears in the client window as follows:

```
Adding the numbers 1.2 3.4 5.6 together
The result is 10.2
```

Then, both the client and server programs stop.

## Datagram Sockets

Datagram sockets are not connection-oriented. Instead of establishing a two-way connection, you send self-contained packets of data whenever necessary. Each packet contains information that identifies the network destination in addition to the content of your message. The class **DatagramPacket** represents these packets. The amount of data transmitted is less than over a TCP/IP socket because TCP/IP sockets transmit additional packets for connection setup and teardown and also transmit checksum data to detect data corruption. However, while a connection is open, datagram sockets give no advantage in speed. On the other hand, delivery of datagram packets is not guaranteed. The intended recipient might miss a packet due to some network error or congestion, and neither the sender nor recipient may be aware of the loss. The UDP protocol used by these sockets makes no attempt to recover from lost or damaged packets.

Datagram sockets provide an alternative communications interface to TCP/IP sockets. For example, the Simple Network Management Protocol (SNMP) uses datagrams, and games played across a network often use datagrams. Use datagram sockets, rather than TCP/IP sockets, if your application meets the following criteria:

➤ You want to avoid the overhead of opening and closing connections.

➤ The nodes in the network periodically send relatively short messages to each other.

➤ Losing the occasional packet does not have serious repercussions.

Here is a sample program that uses datagrams for communication between the client and server. The classes **DatagramAdditionServer** and

`DatagramAdditionClient` perform exactly the same function as
`AdditionServer` and `AdditionClient` did in the previous TCP/IP socket
example, except that they use datagrams. The data being transferred between
client and server has not changed. Because the only difference between the
client-server examples is the transport mechanism, only the **run** methods of
the two classes have changed.

Here is the run method of the server class, `DatagramAdditionServer`.
Only the **run** method is shown because the rest of the class is exactly the same
as `AdditionServer`. A detailed breakdown of the method follows the code:

```java
public void run() {
    try {
        DatagramSocket ss = new DatagramSocket( port );
        byte[] buffer = new byte[256];
        DatagramPacket inDgp
            = new DatagramPacket( buffer,
                                  buffer.length );
        String req, rsp;
        do {
            ss.receive( inDgp );
            InetAddress senderAddress = inDgp.getAddress();
            int senderPort = inDgp.getPort();
            req = new String( inDgp.getData(), 0,
                              inDgp.getLength() );
            if ( ! req.equals( "" ) ) {
                double result = 0;
                StringTokenizer st
                    = new StringTokenizer( req );
                try {
                    while( st.hasMoreTokens() ) {
                        Double d
                            = new Double( st.nextToken() );
                        result += d.doubleValue();
                    }
                    rsp = "The result is " + result;
                } catch( NumberFormatException nfe ) {
                    rsp = "Sorry, your list contains an "
                            + "invalid number";
                }
                DatagramPacket outDgp
                    = new DatagramPacket( rsp.getBytes(),
                                          rsp.length(),
                                          senderAddress,
                                          senderPort );
                ss.send( outDgp );
            }
        } while( ! req.equals( "" ) );
        ss.close();
    }
    catch( IOException iox ) {
```

**16**

```
        System.out.println( iox );
        iox.printStackTrace();
    }
}
```

The **run** method of the server begins by creating a datagram socket on the
prearranged port number that is known by the client:

```
DatagramSocket ss = new DatagramSocket( port );
```

In preparation for the arrival of the first request datagram, the server allocates a
buffer for the incoming requests and creates an incoming **DatagramPacket**
object that will use this buffer. This is necessary because **DatagramPacket**
objects do not have buffers of their own. The request and response will be handled as **String** objects, so the references `req` and `rsp` are declared for later use:

```
byte[] buffer = new byte[256];
DatagramPacket inDgp
    = new DatagramPacket( buffer,
                             buffer.length );
String req, rsp;
```

A **do**-**while** loop begins the server's loop for receiving requests and returning
responses. The first statement within the loop receives the incoming request
datagram. The address and port of the client that sent the request are extracted
and saved for later use. The request data is taken from the datagram and put
into a **String** object for easier manipulation:

```
do {
    ss.receive( inDgp );
    InetAddress senderAddress = inDgp.getAddress();
    int senderPort = inDgp.getPort();
    req = new String( inDgp.getData(), 0,
                         inDgp.getLength() );
```

If a non-null request string was received, the processing of the request begins.
The processing in this example is similar to the processing in the TCP/IP
example, with the main difference being that the response string cannot be
sent to the client by stream I/O, but instead is put into a **String** object for
later transmission in a datagram:

```
if ( ! req.equals( "" ) ) {
    double result = 0;
    StringTokenizer st
        = new StringTokenizer( req );
    try {
        while( st.hasMoreTokens() ) {
            Double d
                = new Double( st.nextToken() );
            result += d.doubleValue();
        }
        rsp = "The result is " + result;
```

```
      } catch( NumberFormatException nfe ) {
        rsp = "Sorry, your list contains an "
                + "invalid number";
      }
```

After the response string is determined, an output **DatagramPacket** object is created, and the response, along with the client's address and port, is put into it. After the outgoing datagram is constructed, it is sent to the client using the same socket that was used to receive the original request:

```
      DatagramPacket outDgp
        = new DatagramPacket( rsp.getBytes(),
                              rsp.length(),
                              senderAddress,
                              senderPort );
      ss.send( outDgp );
    }
```

The server loop is terminated when a datagram containing an empty string is received. Then the datagram socket is closed and the server is finished:

```
  } while( ! req.equals( "" ) );
  ss.close();
```

Here is the run method of the client-side class, `DatagramAdditionClient`. Only the **run** method is shown because the rest of the class is exactly the same as `AdditionClient`. A detailed breakdown of the method follows the code:

```
public void run() {
  try {
    DatagramSocket client = new DatagramSocket();
    String numbers = "1.2 3.4 5.6";
    DatagramPacket outDgp
        = new DatagramPacket( numbers.getBytes(),
                              numbers.length(),
                              host,
                              port );
    client.send( outDgp );
    System.out.println( "Adding the numbers "
                        + numbers + " together" );
    byte[] buffer = new byte[256];
    DatagramPacket inDgp
        = new DatagramPacket( buffer,
                              buffer.length );
    client.receive( inDgp );
    String rsp = new String( inDgp.getData(), 0,
                             inDgp.getLength() );
    System.out.println( rsp );
    String quit = "";
    outDgp.setData( quit.getBytes() );
    outDgp.setLength( quit.length() );
```

16

```
        client.send( outDgp );
        client.close();
   }
   catch( IOException iox ) {
        System.out.println( iox );
        iox.printStackTrace();
   }
}
```

The **run** method of the client begins by constructing the datagram socket needed for sending and receiving information. It does not specify a port number because a default port will be assigned. The server address and port are not provided because that information is put into each **DatagramPacket** object and is not kept with the datagram socket:

```
DatagramSocket client = new DatagramSocket();
```

The data to be sent to the server is defined in a **String** object. The **DatagramPacket** to be used for sending the information is created and the data, in the form of a byte array, is put into the **DatagramPacket** along with the host address and port number:

```
String numbers = "1.2 3.4 5.6";
DatagramPacket outDgp
   = new DatagramPacket( numbers.getBytes(),
                         numbers.length(),
                         host,
                         port );
```

The outgoing **DatagramPacket** is sent, and a message is written to the console:

```
client.send( outDgp );
System.out.println( "Adding the numbers "
                    + numbers + " together" );
```

In preparation for receiving a response, a buffer is created for the response and the incoming **DatagramPacket** object is created with the buffer and its length as constructor parameters. The same socket that was used to send the request datagram is then used to receive the response datagram.

```
byte[] buffer = new byte[256];
DatagramPacket inDgp
   = new DatagramPacket( buffer,
                         buffer.length );
client.receive( inDgp );
```

The response is extracted from the incoming datagram data and put into a **String** object. The response is then written to the console:

```
String rsp = new String( inDgp.getData(), 0,
                         inDgp.getLength() );
System.out.println( rsp );
```

To stop the server, the client puts the empty string and its length into the outgoing **DatagramPacket** and sends it. It isn't necessary to set the host address and port because that is unchanged from the previous outgoing **DatagramPacket** object. After the final **DatagramPacket** object is sent, the socket is closed:

```
String quit = "";
outDgp.setData( quit.getBytes() );
outDgp.setLength( quit.length() );
client.send( outDgp );
client.close();
```

For this application to work, UDP must be installed and running on your system. Typically, a working Internet connection is proof that UDP is installed and running. You must start the server class in one window and then start the client in a different window.

To run this application:

1. Open two command-line windows.

2. If you are running from the .jar file that contains all sample programs, go to the folder in which the file **examples.jar** resides in both windows. Make sure the .jar file is part of your path by entering the following command in both windows:

   ```
   SET CLASSPATH=examples.jar;%CLASSPATH%
   ```

3. In one window, start the server by entering the following command. If you do not specify a port, 8189 is used:

   ```
   java examples.network.DatagramAdditionServer [port]
   ```

4. In the other window, start the client by entering the following command on one line, optionally adding a port number to match the port on the server. You also can specify the local host name.

   ```
   java examples.network.DatagramAdditionClient [port]
   [localhost]
   ```

5. If you run and receive a message saying the connection is refused, try running the client again with a different port number. If the message indicates that there is no route to the host, try entering an alias such as local host or whatever is set up in your operating system. When you cannot open a connection successfully, you may have to stop the server by pressing **Ctrl+C** in the window in which you started the server. If the connection is successful, the output appears in the client window as follows:

   ```
   Adding the numbers 1.2 3.4 5.6 together
   The result is 10.2
   ```

Then, both the client and server programs stop.

**16**

# REMOTE METHOD INVOCATION (RMI)

You will find that the techniques in the preceding sections that describe how to use URLs and sockets are very useful when you want to move data from one point to another. For example, socket programming easily solves the problem of copying the contents of a file from System A to System B. However, there are many occasions when you will want to directly invoke the methods of objects located on other systems. This problem is not easily solved with URL objects or sockets, though it can be done. To do so, you could create and install a server that runs on the other system; establish a TCP/IP connection to it; and then send and receive messages using a format that would indicate the object, method, parameters, and return value for each invocation. After all of your hard work, you would have merely created a subset of the functionality already provided by Java RMI.

RMI is a technology that allows programmers to directly call the methods of Java objects that reside on other systems. The fact that you are using remote objects is nearly transparent to you as a programmer when you are developing your application. You must take one additional step to locate the object within your network after your application starts, but after you do have the object reference, you use it just as you would use any other object reference.

What makes this an interesting aspect of application development is the fact that you do not have a reference to the object on the remote system itself. Instead, you have a reference to a **stub object** that is a local surrogate for the remote object. This stub is returned by the local **Object Request Broker (ORB)** in response to your request to locate the object. The stub object has all the same methods supported by the remote object but, instead of executing the methods independently, it forwards the parameters to the remote object and passes back any return value for the method. The technique used to forward the parameters to the remote object is called **marshaling**. After marshaling, the parameters are serialized into a byte stream and sent to the remote system. Only primitive types and reference types that implement the **Serializable** interface can be used as parameter types for remote methods.

On the remote system, a **skeleton object** receives this byte stream and uses a technique called **unmarshaling** to deserialize the contents of the parameter list. The skeleton object passes the parameters to the remote object, and the method is executed. If there is a return value, it is serialized and returned using the same process, but in reverse. Figure 16-1 summarizes the execution flow of a remote method call.

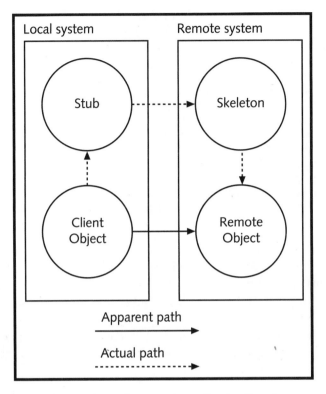

**Local system**

**Remote system**

Stub

Skeleton

Client
Object

Remote
Object

Apparent path

Actual path

**Figure 16-1** Flow of a remote method call

## Developing a Remote Class of Objects

Start developing a remote class of objects by answering the following question: "What methods will my class expose to clients?" Define these methods, and place them into an interface definition. Remember that static methods cannot be part of the interface, and neither can any fields. Only nonstatic methods are allowed. You can define the interface just as you would any other Java interface definition, but with a couple of additional requirements: The interface must extend the interface **java.rmi.Remote**, and all methods in the interface must indicate that they may throw a **java.rmi.RemoteException**. The **Remote** interface is a marker interface and defines no methods. Its sole purpose is to identify interfaces that are to be made available to clients.

As an example of a remote interface, suppose that you were developing a remote class of objects to represent students enrolled at a college. Such a class could expose many potential methods to clients. These methods would get the ID number for a student, retrieve and update the student's name, and retrieve

**16**

and update the number of credits the student has accumulated. Following the preceding rules, a remote interface for the **Student** class would look like this:

```
package examples.network;
import java.rmi.Remote;
import java.rmi.RemoteException
public interface Student extends Remote {
    public int getID() throws RemoteException;
    public void setName( String name )
                    throws RemoteException;
    public String getName() throws RemoteException;
    public int getCredits() throws RemoteException;
    public int addCredits( int credits )
                    throws RemoteException;
}
```

This remote interface definition defines the interface that a client would use to manipulate the student objects, but the job to define the class that implements this interface remains to be done. You will locate this class of objects on the server and make them available to the client. However, the client will never access this class directly but will instead use the interface defined previously. The convention is to give this class the name of the interface with the characters "Impl" as a suffix. In this class, "Impl" is short for implementation because this class is an implementation of the interface.

In addition to implementing the **Student** interface, the **StudentImpl** class must also extend the class **java.rmi.server.RemoteObject**. The **RemoteObject** class is the superclass for all remote classes just as **Object** is the superclass for all classes. In particular, **RemoteObject** overrides the methods **equals**, **hashCode**, and **toString** to make sense for remote objects. But the **RemoteObject** class does not implement a particular remote behavior, instead leaving that for its subclasses. One such subclass, **java.rmi.server.UnicastRemoteObject**, implements a remote object that supports point-to-point active object references using TCP streams. Because this behavior is suitable for most cases, implementation classes extend **UnicastRemoteObject**, by convention. The **StudentImpl** class definition that follows this convention is shown here:

```
package examples.network;
import java.rmi.RemoteException;
import java.rmi.server.UnicastRemoteObject;
public class StudentImpl extends UnicastRemoteObject
                        implements Student {
    private int ID;
    private String name;
    private int credits = 0;
    public StudentImpl( int ID, String name )
                    throws RemoteException {
        this.ID = ID;
        this.name = name;
```

```
   }
   public int getID() throws RemoteException {
      return ID;
   }
   public void setName( String name )
                      throws RemoteException {
      this.name = name;
   }
   public String getName() throws RemoteException {
      return name;
   }
   public int getCredits() throws RemoteException {
      return credits;
   }
   public int addCredits( int credits )
                         throws RemoteException {
      return ( this.credits += credits );
   }
}
```

After the implementation class has been defined and compiled successfully, you must create the stub and skeleton classes required by RMI. Fortunately, this is easy because the Java 2 SDK includes the utility **rmic** to automate this job. The **rmic** tool takes the name of the implementation class as input and generates the two .class files for the stub and skeleton. The names of these generated classes are the same as the implementation class, but with the suffixes _Stub and _Skel. For example, executing the command:

```
rmic examples.network.StudentImpl
```

creates the files StudentImpl_Stub.class and StudentImpl_Skel.class and causes them to contain the stub and skeleton classes, respectively.

## Developing an RMI Server Class

You can use a combination of server and client program classes to put the remote class of objects to work. Essentially, the server program creates the remote objects and registers them with a naming service, and the client program looks for these objects using a naming service to obtain object references. The content of a server program class and a detailed breakdown of the class follows:

**16**

```
package examples.network;
import java.rmi.Naming;
import java.rmi.RMISecurityManager;
/** A server-side program that creates and registers
  * StudentImpl objects with the RMI registry for use
  * by clients
  */
public class StudentEnrollment {
   public static void main( String[] args ) {
```

```
         if ( System.getSecurityManager() == null ) {
            System.setSecurityManager(
               new RMISecurityManager() );
         }
         try {
            StudentImpl[] students = {
               new StudentImpl( 1001, "Elaine Jones" ),
               new StudentImpl( 1002, "Patricia Hartswell" ),
               new StudentImpl( 1003, "Darius Smith" ),
               new StudentImpl( 1004, "Mary Bagshaw" ),
               new StudentImpl( 1005, "Henry Miller" )
            };
            for ( int i = 0; i < students.length; i++ ) {
               int id = students[i].getID();
               Naming.rebind( "Student" + id , students[i] );
            }
            System.out.println( "Student objects bound." );
         } catch ( Exception x ) {
            x.printStackTrace();
         }
      }
   }
}
```

Consider the following line of code. Unlike the **Student** interface and the
**StudentImpl** class, this server program class has neither interfaces that it must
implement nor a prescribed base class:

```
public class StudentEnrollment {
```

As shown next, the server program class contains only a **main** method. This
method creates the remote objects and registers them with a naming service.
The class has no additional purpose, so no other methods exist:

```
   public static void main( String[] args ) {
```

Because the server is opening up an interface to its objects and allowing programs on other systems to access them, there are security risks. It would be
most unwise to make the objects available within a JVM that has no
**SecurityManager** object installed, so the server program first checks to see if
a **SecurityManager** has been installed. In fact, the class loader used by RMI
will not download any classes from remote locations unless a
**SecurityManager** has been installed.

The **SecurityManager** object used in the following code is an instance of the
**java.rmi.RMISecurityManager** class. This class is as an example of a
**SecurityManager** for applications that use downloaded code:

```
if ( System.getSecurityManager() == null ) {
   System.setSecurityManager(
      new RMISecurityManager() );
}
```

As shown next, the `StudentImpl` objects are created and loaded into an array for convenient access. In a more realistic program, this information would not be hardcoded into the server program, but would be read from an existing file or a database. The "Java Database Connectivity Section" of Chapter 17 describes how to access a relational database from Java programs:

```
StudentImpl[] students = {
    new StudentImpl( 1001, "Elaine Jones" ),
    new StudentImpl( 1002, "Patricia Hartswell" ),
    new StudentImpl( 1003, "Darius Smith" ),
    new StudentImpl( 1004, "Mary Bagshaw" ),
    new StudentImpl( 1005, "Henry Miller" )
};
```

After the method creates the array of `StudentImpl` objects, the method uses a **for** loop to iterate through the list and register each object with the naming service. In a Java program, the naming service is represented by the class **java.rmi.Naming**. The method **rebind** takes two parameters—the name of the object as a string and a reference to the object—and binds the object reference using the given name.

In this chapter's program, the names being used to uniquely identify `StudentImpl` objects are a concatenation of the word "Student" and the student's ID number. For example, the first element in the array is bound to the name "Student1001". The client program must follow the same naming scheme to locate the student objects.

```
for ( int i = 0; i < students.length; i++ ) {
    int id = students[i].getID();
    Naming.rebind( "Student" + id , students[i] );
}
```

By default, the names are registered and available from a registry service on the local host. The registry service listens for requests from clients on port 1099. (The RMI registry uses port 1099 by default.) To specify a different host name or port number for the registry service, the name should be provided in the format `//host:port/name`:

Because it can take some time for the registry service to create and bind all the `StudentImpl` objects, the method uses the statement shown next to display an information message when the process completes. After this message appears on the host, you can safely run the client programs that remotely access the objects:

```
System.out.println( "Student objects bound." );
```

## Developing an RMI Client Class

If the client program is an application or enabling class, it needs a **main** method to lookup the remote objects using a naming service and to obtain references to the objects of interest. After the program obtains these references, it uses them just like any other object reference. Only the need to catch potential **RemoteException** objects indicates the program is working with remote objects. Below is the content of a client program class. A detailed breakdown of the class follows:

```
package examples.network;
import java.rmi.Naming;
import java.rmi.RMISecurityManager;
/** A client program that accesses and updates Student
  * objects on the server
  */
public class StudentClient {
   private static final String HOST_NAME = "localhost";
   public static void main( String[] args ) {
      if ( System.getSecurityManager() == null ) {
         System.setSecurityManager(
            new RMISecurityManager() );
      }
      try {
         Student s1001
            = (Student) Naming.lookup( "//" + HOST_NAME
                                       + "/Student1001" );
         Student s1005
            = (Student) Naming.lookup( "//" + HOST_NAME
                                       + "/Student1005" );
         System.out.println( s1001.getName() );
         System.out.println( s1005.getName() );
         System.out.println( s1001.getCredits() );

         s1001.addCredits( 3 );
         s1001.setName( "Elaine Goldman" );
         System.out.println( s1001.getName() );
         System.out.println( s1001.getCredits() );

      } catch ( Exception x ) {
         x.printStackTrace();
      }
   }
}
```

Consider the following code. The **StudentClient** class that makes up the client program and that uses the remote objects has no requirement to extend a particular superclass or implement specified interfaces:

```
public class StudentClient {
```

When the program uses the naming service to lookup the remote objects, a host name can be specified to indicate where to find the registry in which the objects have been bound. In order to make it very easy to change the host name, this class contains a constant that holds the registry's host name, as the following code shows:

```
private static final String HOST_NAME = "localhost";
```

Because the client is opening up and accepting stubs for remote objects, there are security risks. It would be unwise to load and execute these stubs within a JVM that has no **SecurityManager** object installed, so the server program first checks for one. In fact, the class loader used by RMI will not download any classes from remote locations unless a **SecurityManager** has been installed. The **SecurityManager** used in this case is an instance of the **java.rmi.RMISecurityManager** class. This class is an example of a **SecurityManager** for applications that use downloaded code:

```
public static void main( String[] args ) {
    if ( System.getSecurityManager() == null ) {
      System.setSecurityManager(
        new RMISecurityManager() );
    }
```

The calls to the naming service and the calls to the methods of the remote objects are enclosed in a try block so that any exceptions they may throw may be caught. An alternative to this would be to list the exceptions thrown in the main method's throws clause.

References to two remote objects are obtained using the **lookup** method of the **Naming** class. The input to the **lookup** method is a URL string of the form //host:port/name. The host indicates the system on which the registry for the remote objects is found, and the port is the port number to which the registry is listening for requests. The default host is **localhost**, and the default port number is 1099. The **rmiregistry** program that comes with the Java Platform SDK uses this port number as well. The provided name must match the name to which the object was originally bound.

In the example below, the name is a concatenation of the word "Student" and the student number. The **lookup** method returns a reference of the type **Remote**. You should cast the return value to the expected object type before using the reference:

**16**

```
try {
  Student s1001
    = (Student) Naming.lookup( "//" + HOST_NAME
                               + "/Student1001" );

  Student s1005
    = (Student) Naming.lookup( "//" + HOST_NAME
                               + "/Student1005" );
```

Consider the following code. To see if the client program obtained references to the objects that it expected, the client program calls a few accessor methods and echoes the return values to the console, where you can see them:

```
System.out.println( s1001.getName() );
System.out.println( s1005.getName() );
System.out.println( s1001.getCredits() );
```

The next two remote method calls make changes to the remote objects. The inputs to these methods are serialized and sent to the remote system, where they are deserialized and used:

```
s1001.addCredits( 3 );
s1001.setName( "Elaine Goldman" );
```

Finally, a check is made to see if the changes of the preceding methods have actually occurred. The **main** method uses accessor methods to retrieve the values. The values are then echoed to the console.

```
System.out.println( s1001.getName() );
System.out.println( s1001.getCredits() );
```

## Running the Server and Client Programs

We have now reached the point where all classes have been defined, and the gratifying part of compiling and running the programs has now arrived.

To compile and run the files for the student remote object example:

1. Open the folder examples\network under the folder where you installed the **examples.jar** file.

2. Compile the file **Student.java** using the command:

   ```
   javac Student.java
   ```

3. Compile the file **StudentImpl.java** using the command:

   ```
   javac StudentImpl.java
   ```

4. Create the stub and skeleton classes for the examples.network.StudentImpl class using the command:

   ```
   rmic examples.network.StudentImpl
   ```

5. Compile the file **StudentEnrollment.java** using the command:

   ```
   javac StudentEnrollment.java
   ```

6. Compile the file **StudentClient.java** using the command:

   ```
   javac StudentClient.java
   ```

7. Open a command line window and start the RMI registry. No messages are displayed to indicate that the registry is running. The only indication

you will get is that the window's title bar text will change. Start the registry using the command:

```
rmiregistry
```

You can now minimize the registry window.

8. Start the server program that will construct and register the `StudentImpl` objects.

   In addition to supplying the class name to the JVM, two other parameters are required. The first specifies the codebase from which the stub and skeleton files will be made available. The stub class files will be automatically downloaded to client programs from this location as needed. The second specifies the file in which the user security policy for the program is located. The option –D is used in both cases to set the appropriate system properties. Here, it is assumed that the parent folder of the examples\network folder is D:\jars. The file RMISecurity.policy can be found in the examples\network folder. The entire contents of this file are:

```
grant {
  permission java.net.SocketPermission "*:1024-65535",
      "connect,accept";
};
```

   The one statement contained in this file will give the code loaded over the network the ability to listen and connect on sockets with port numbers between 1024 and 65535. Granting this permission is necessary for RMI to work successfully. For more details on the structure and content of security policy files such as this one, refer to the security section of Chapter 14.

9. Open a command-line prompt window and start the server program by entering the following command on one line:

```
java -Djava.rmi.server.codebase=file:/..\..\
        -Djava.security.policy=RMISecurity.policy
        examples.network.StudentEnrollment
```

If your operating system does not allow you to enter the command as shown, you can use the batch file called **StudentEnrollment.bat**. It is provided in the examples\network directory. Make the directory examples\network the current directory before executing the command or running the batch file.

10. Wait until the message "Student objects bound." appears in the window to indicate that the server has successfully constructed and registered the `StudentImpl` objects.

11. Start the client program that locates and uses the remote objects. In addition to supplying the class name to the JVM, you must specify the file in which the user security policy for the program is located. This is the same file that was used in the previous step to start the server program. The option –D is used to set the **java.security.policy** system property.

**16**

12. Open an MS-DOS prompt window and start the client program with the following command:

```
java -Djava.security.policy=RMISecurity.policy
          examples.network.StudentClient
```

If your operating system does not allow you to enter the command as shown, you can use the batch file called **StudentClient.bat**. It is provided in the examples\network directory. Make the directory examples\network the current directory before executing the command or running the batch file.

13. The client program terminates after it runs, but the server and the **rmiregistry** programs will run forever. To end the server program or the **rmiregistry** program, make the window in which the program is running the active window, and then press **Ctrl+C** to end the program.

## JNDI

The **rmiregistry** program, which is supplied with the Java platform SDK, is a useful program and works well for small applications such as the one described earlier in this chapter. However, the **rmiregistry** program does not scale well when applications become large and are spread across many host systems.

In anticipation of this problem, Sun developed a standard Java platform extension: Java Naming and Directory Interface (JNDI). JNDI is not itself a naming or directory service, but is a unified interface to multiple naming and directory services that already exist for enterprise development. It gives Java programmers easy access to heterogeneous enterprise naming and directory services. Table 16-1 lists the JNDI packages.

**Table 16-1**  JNDI Packages

| Package | Description |
|---|---|
| **javax.naming** | This package is the core of JNDI and defines the basic operations of binding names to objects and looking up objects for a given name. |
| **javax.naming.directory** | This package defines methods for making changes to directories such as examining and updating the attributes of a directory object. |
| **javax.naming.spi** | This package contains the server provider interface that is intended to be used by companies and organization for integrating their existing naming and directory service products into JNDI. |

## Java IDL and CORBA

Java RMI provides support that makes it easy to define and use remote objects, but it does have a drawback: It only works with remote objects that are developed using the Java programming language. CORBA (Common Object Request Broker Architecture) is a more generic architecture for defining and using remote objects. It allows for the mixing of objects developed using different programming languages. A consortium of companies known as the OMG (Object Management Group) developed the CORBA standard.

CORBA and RMI are similar. The concepts of stubs, skeletons, and ORBs that you have already learned for RMI also apply to CORBA. One important difference between the two, however, is the way in which the ORBs communicate with each other. RMI ORBs use a protocol called JRMP (Java Remote Method Protocol), but CORBA ORBs use IIOP (Internet Inter-ORB Protocol), which is based on the standard TCP/IP protocol. Unfortunately, this means that RMI ORBs and CORBA ORBs cannot communicate with each other. Sun and IBM have announced plans to enable RMI to use the IIOP protocol to communicate with CORBA-compliant remote objects.

Another important difference between CORBA and RMI is that the interfaces of CORBA objects are defined using a special language called Interface Definition Language (IDL). To make it easier for programmers that have already defined their object interfaces using CORBA IDL, the Java platform SDK provides a tool called **idl2java** that generates Java interfaces and stub and skeleton classes.

A CORBA-compliant ORB called **Java IDL** is included in the SDK. You can use it for those cases where you must develop remote objects that can interact with objects created using programming languages other than Java.

The development process you follow with Java IDL is similar to the Java RMI development process that has been described in this chapter. The process begins by using IDL to define the interfaces that will be distributed and registered for use by CORBA client programs. The **idl2java** tool generates the Java interface, and stub and skeleton classes. The implementation of the class is then defined and compiled, just as was done for Java RMI.

## SUMMARY

The Java platform includes core classes with which you can communicate with URLs and create TCP/IP and datagram sockets.

Objects of the **URL** class hold the details of URLs such as the protocol and host. To exchange information with a URL, you must create a **URLConnection** object. Do this by calling the method **openConnection** for a URL.

For a connection that remains open, you can connect to a system on your network with a TCP/IP socket. A number of classes, including **Socket**, support TCP/IP sockets. To perform ordinary stream I/O to and from a TCP/IP socket, use the methods **Socket.getInputStream** and **Socket.getOutputStream**.

**16**

You can use the **ServerSocket** class to create the server side of a TCP/IP socket. Datagram sockets are also useful. Some extra programming is required, but this may be worthwhile if you intermittently send short messages and do not need the reliability of a TCP/IP connection.

Java RMI makes it possible to define and implement classes of objects that can be accessed remotely from client programs running on different systems within a network. Only the interfaces of these objects are exposed to the client programs.

Classes of objects that implement remote interfaces are constructed on the server systems, and then they are bound to names that are registered with a naming service. Client programs lookup these names using ORBs (Object Request Brokers) in order to obtain references to these remote objects.

Local stub classes that act as local surrogates for the remote objects provide access to remote objects. Stub classes communicate with skeleton classes on the server. Skeleton classes marshal and unmarshal parameters and return values between the stub and the remote object.

Security is a concern when using RMI. RMI server and client programs must install a **SecurityManager** object to protect against unauthorized access.

JNDI is not a naming and directory service, but it provides Java applications a unified interface to multiple naming and directory services.

The Java 2 Platform SDK provides a CORBA-compliant ORB called Java IDL for those cases in which it is necessary to define and implement remote objects that must integrate with remote objects written in programming languages other than Java.

## QUESTIONS

1. True or False: A **URLConnection** object closes after one read/write operation.

2. Which of the following classes can be passed as a parameter to the constructor of the **Socket** class? Select all that apply.
   a. **InetAddress**
   b. **URL**
   c. **URLConnection**
   d. **ServerSocket**
   e. **DatagramSocket**

3. True or False: TCP/IP sockets have input and output streams that can be used just like any other I/O streams.

4. True or False: Datagram sockets are connection-oriented and guarantee the delivery of all packets sent through them.

5. Examine the following code:

```java
import java.io.*;
import java.net.*;
public class Quiz16_5 {
    public static void main( String[] args ) {
        Socket client = new Socket();
        BufferedReader socketIn;
        PrintWriter socketOut
            = new PrintWriter( client.getOutputStream(),
                               true );
        socketOut.println( "Quiz question 16_5" );
        client.close();
    }
}
```

Which of the following statements are true when the code is compiled and run? Select all that apply.

a. The compiler rejects the method `Quiz16_5.main` because of missing socket constructor parameters.

b. Compilation is successful, and the method `Quiz16_5.main` establishes a TCP/IP socket and sends one message before closing the socket.

c. Compilation is successful, and the method `Quiz16_5.main` establishes a datagram socket and sends one message before closing the socket.

d. The compiler rejects the method Quiz16_5.main because the possible **IOException** is not caught.

e. Compilation is successful, and the method `Quiz16_5.main` establishes a TCP/IP socket and receives one message before closing the socket.

6. Examine the following code:

```java
import java.io.*;
import java.net.*;
public class Quiz16_6 {
    private static byte[] buffer;
    private static DatagramSocket ss;
    private static DatagramPacket inDgp;
    public static void main( String[] args ) {
        try {
            ss = new DatagramSocket( 9002 );
            inDgp = new DatagramPacket( buffer,
                                        buffer.length );
            ss.receive( inDgp );
            ss.close();
        }
        catch( IOException iox ) {
            System.out.println( iox );
```

**16**

```
                        iox.printStackTrace();
                }
        }
}
```

Which of the following statements are true when the code is compiled and run? Select all that apply.

a. The compiler rejects the method `Quiz16_6.main` because of missing datagram socket constructor parameters.

b. Compilation is successful, and the method `Quiz16_6.main` establishes a datagram socket and receives one datagram before closing the socket.

c. Compilation is successful, and the method `Quiz16_6.main` establishes a TCP/IP socket and receives one datagram before closing the socket.

d. Compilation is successful, but the method `Quiz16_6.main` causes a **NullPointerException** because the field buffer does not refer to a **byte[]** object.

e. Compilation is successful, and the method `Quiz16_6.main` establishes a datagram socket and sends one datagram before closing the socket.

7. Which of the following are methods defined within the interface **java.rmi.Remote**? Select all that apply.

a. `public void remote()`

b. `public void rebind( String, Object )`

c. `public void bind( String, Object )`

d. `public void lookup( String )`

e. `public void remote() throws java.rmi.RemoteException`

8. True or False: The class loader used by RMI will not download any classes from remote locations if no **SecurityManager** has been installed.

9. Examine the following command:

```
rmic questions.c16.EmployeeImpl java
```

Which of the following statements are true when the command is executed, assuming that the file questions.c16.EmployeeImpl has previously compiled successfully? Select all that apply.

a. The command completes successfully, and the file EmployeeImpl_Stub.class is generated.

b. The command completes successfully, and the file Employee_Stub.class is generated.

c. The command completes successfully, and the file EmployeeImpl_Skel.class is generated.

    d. The command completes successfully, and the file Employee_Skel.class is generated.

    e. The command does not complete successfully because the .java file extension is missing from the input parameter.

10. Which of the following are valid superclasses for a class of remote objects that are accessible by RMI? Select all that apply.

    a. **java.rmi.Naming**

    b. **java.rmi.server.RemoteObject**

    c. **java.rmi.RemoteException**

    d. **java.rmi.server.UnicastRemoteObject**

    e. **java.rmi.Remote**

# EXERCISES

## Debugging

1. Correct all the errors in the following program so that it returns the type of content located at the specified URL:

```java
package questions.c16;
import java.net.*;
public class Debug16_1 {
    public static void main( String[] args ) {
        if ( args.length >= 1 ) {
            URL x = new URL( args[0] );
            URLConnection xConnect = x.openConnection();
            System.out.println( x + " has content type "
                                + xConnect.getType() );
        } else {
            System.out.println( "Please enter a URL" );
        }
    }
}
```

2. Correct all of the errors in the following program so that the **run** method successfully opens and then closes a server TCP/IP socket:

```java
package questions.c16;
import java.io.*;
import java.net.*;
public class Debug16_2 {
    private int port;
    Debug16_2( int port ) {
        this.port = port;
    }
    public void run() {
        try {
```

16

```
               ServerSocket ss = ServerSocket.accept( port );
               ss.close();
           }
           catch( IOException iox ) {
               iox.printStackTrace();
           }
       }
       public static void main( String[] args ) {
           Debug16_2 server = new Debug16_2( 8189 );
           server.run();
       }
   }
```

3. Correct all the errors in the following program so that the **run** method successfully opens a TCP/IP socket to the **host** and **port** values in its fields, and then writes a test message to the socket:

```
package questions.c16;
import java.io.*;
import java.net.*;
public class Debug16_3 {
   private InetAddress host;
   private int port;
   public Debug16_3( InetAddress host, int port ) {
       this.host = host;
       this.port = port;
   }
   public void run() {
       try {
           Socket client = new Socket();
           PrintWriter socketOut
             = client.getPrintWriter();
           socketOut.println( "Test message" );
           client.close();
       }
       catch( IOException iox ) {
           System.out.println( iox );
           iox.printStackTrace();
       }
   }
   public static void main( String[] args ) {
       try {
           InetAddress host = InetAddress.getLocalHost();
           Debug16_3 client
             = new Debug16_3( host, 8189 );
           client.run();
       }
       catch ( UnknownHostException uhx ) {
           uhx.printStackTrace();
       }
   }
}
```

4. Correct all the errors in the following program so that the **run** method successfully opens a datagram socket to the host and port values in its fields, and then sends one datagram and receives one datagram.

```java
package questions.c16;
import java.io.*;
import java.net.*;
public class Debug16_4 {
    private InetAddress host;
    private int port;
    public Debug16_4( InetAddress host, int port ) {
        this.host = host;
        this.port = port;
    }
    public void run() {
        try {
            DatagramSocket client = new DatagramSocket();
            String testData = "Test Data";
            DatagramPacket outDgp
                = new DatagramPacket( testData.getBytes(),
                                          testData.length() );
            client.send( outDgp );
            byte[] buffer = new byte[256];
            DatagramPacket inDgp = new DatagramPacket();
            client.receive( inDgp );
            client.close();
        }
        catch( IOException iox ) {
            iox.printStackTrace();
        }
    }
    public static void main( String[] args ) {
        try {
            InetAddress host = InetAddress.getLocalHost();
            Debug16_4 client
                = new Debug16_4( host, 8189 );
            client.run();
        }
        catch ( UnknownHostException uhx ) {
            uhx.printStackTrace();
        }
    }
}
```

5. Correct all the errors in the following interface and class definitions so that the instances of the **Employee** class can be used successfully as remote objects accessible by RMI:

```java
package questions.c16;
import java.rmi.RemoteException;
public interface Employee {
```

16

```
        public int getSerial() throws RemoteException;
        public void setName( String name )
                        throws RemoteException;
        public String getName() throws RemoteException;
        public void setSalary( double salary )
                        throws RemoteException;
        public double getSalary() throws RemoteException;
}

package questions.c16;
import java.rmi.RemoteException;
public class EmployeeImpl implements Employee {
    private int serial;
    private String name;
    private double salary;
    public EmployeeImpl( int serial, String name,
                        double salary ) {
        this.serial = serial;
        this.name = name;
        this.salary = salary;
    }
    public int getSerial() throws RemoteException {
        return serial;
    }
    public void setName( String name )
                        throws RemoteException {
        this.name = name;
    }
    public String getName() throws RemoteException {
        return name;
    }
    public void setSalary( double salary )
                        throws RemoteException {
        this.salary = salary;
    }
    public double getSalary() throws RemoteException {
        return salary;
    }
}
```

## Complete the Solution

1. Extract the file **questions\c16\Complete16_1.java** from the file **question.jar** on the CD-ROM. Complete the `Complete16_1` class definition by finishing the method `printPage`. This method should construct a **URL** object, get the input stream for the **URL**, and then wrap it in a **BufferedReader** object so that the contents of the **URL** can be read and printed to the console.

2. Extract the file **questions\c16\Complete16_2.java** from the file **question.jar** on the CD-ROM. Complete the `Complete16_2` class definition by finishing the method `waitForMessage`. This method should open a server TCP/IP socket for the port number specified and wait for a connection. When the connection is made, it should read a string from the connection, echo it to the console, and then close the socket.

3. Extract the file **questions\c16\Complete16_3.java** from the file **question.jar** on the CD-ROM. Complete the `Complete16_3` class definition by finishing the method `waitForDatagram`. This method should open a server datagram socket for the port number specified and wait for a datagram to arrive. When a datagram arrives, it should read a string from it, echo the string to the console, and then close the socket.

4. Extract the file **questions\c16\Complete16_4.java** from the file **question.jar** on the CD-ROM. Complete the `Complete16_4` class definition by adding code to the main function that will create in separate threads an instance of both the client and server classes. The **main** method should give the client enough time to send about 20 messages to the server, and then it should end.

5. Extract the files **questions\c16\RemoteEcho.java, questions\c16\RemoteEchoImpl.java, questions\c16\EchoServer.java,** and **questions\c16\EchoClient.java,** from the file **question.jar** on the CD-ROM. Complete the class definitions by adding code to the main functions of the classes `EchoServer` and `EchoClient`. The **main** method of `EchoServer` should create an instance of `RemoteEchoImpl` and register it with the naming service. The **main** method of `EchoClient` should use the naming service to locate the `RemoteEchoImpl` object and obtain a reference to it of type `RemoteEcho`. The client should then use the `echo` method to send strings to the remote object that will be echoed to the console by the remote object.

**16**

## Discovery

1. Create a class called `URLMonitor` that can be used to monitor a list of URLs for changes. Objects of this class will provide support to check the modification dates of a list of URLs and print a report of which URLs have changed since the last time they were checked. You will probably find it useful to serialize the **Date** objects collected by the objects to simplify the storing and retrieval of the information for later comparison. The URL list should be read from a file.

2. Create a pair of classes called `ImmediateMessage` and `ImmediateMessageServer`. Objects of the `ImmediateMessageServer` class should listen on a specified port for connection from other systems, and then display the information received on the connection. Objects of the `ImmediateMessage` class will connect to these server objects and send a single message to be displayed at the server system.

3. Create a pair of classes called `TemperatureServer` and `TemperatureClient`. Objects of the `TemperatureServer` class contain a table of current temperatures for a number of cities around the world. They receive requests from `TemperatureClient` objects in the form of datagrams. Each datagram contains the name of a city which the server looks up in its table. The current temperature for the city is returned by the `TemperatureServer` to the `TemperatureClient` in a datagram. If the requested city cannot be found, an empty string is returned.

4. Take the `Employee` interface and `EmployeeImpl` class that you corrected in the debugging exercises previously and write a **main** method that creates and registers many `EmployeeImpl` objects as part of a `HumanResources` class. Then, write a client class that provides a GUI interface to update the name and salary of a remote employee object that is found based on a serial number that the user enters in a text field of the GUI.

## CHAPTER SEVENTEEN

# PROGRAMMING SERVER-SIDE JAVA

---

**In this chapter you will:**

➤ Learn how to generate dynamic content for web pages in the web server

➤ Become familiar with the servlet API

➤ Consider some of the design issues relating to building a web site that is open for business

➤ Write servlets and Java Server Pages (JSPs)

➤ Use Java DataBase Connectivity (JDBC)

➤ Write programs that read, write, update, and delete records in a relational database

---

## INTRODUCTION

The Internet and Java Programming Language have matured together. The Internet has evolved from a worldwide forum used primarily for the exchange of free information into an infrastructure supporting the essential operation of many organizations. Companies now use the web for more than advertising. It has become a medium for conducting business operations, coordinating activities with cooperating companies, and providing information to employees. Similarly, academic institutions, government agencies, and other organizations are building web-based activities into their everyday operations. As a result, designing a web site and providing functionality that is accessible through that site may have a profound impact on how a company or organization operates. The very success of the commercial venture may be determined by a company's ability to effectively take advantage of the web.

Java has become the de facto programming language for supporting web sites. Although HTML remains the tagging language that turns text documents into pages that web browsers can display, it can only display static information. In Chapter 14, you learned how to add flair to web pages by writing applets to include multimedia and animation. Such applets contributed to the early success of the Java platform.

Applets are good at enhancing the look and feel of a web page, but are they adequate for conducting business? Can a customer browse a catalog, place orders, track the status of an account or transaction, and perform other typical business operations using applets? Generally, the answer is no. These sorts of activities require a program that can access databases and perform complex processing. Web sites now must let clients initiate operations that may update databases and trigger other operations. These web sites must display information that is changing dynamically while the client is interacting with the site.

This chapter discusses how the Java platform is evolving to meet requirements for dynamic web sites. Here, the word **dynamic** refers to the content displayed on individual web pages, and to the interaction between the web site and the software infrastructure supporting an organization. Dynamic content is content that adjusts programmatically in response to actions of the web client. For example, a web site for a retail outlet may display a shopping cart for the customer and automatically position the customer in the department where he or she most frequently makes purchases. As the customer selects items for purchase, the contents of the cart changes.

In Chapter 16, you learned how to distribute classes over a network and make those classes communicate and cooperate. In this chapter, you explore the Java features that support distributing programs that communicate over a web. This chapter introduces a new kind of program, the **servlet**, that runs on the web server rather than on the web browser, and a new kind of web document, called a **Java Server Page (JSP)**, that is processed by the web server before the page is sent to the browser. As you will see, JSPs are closely related to servlets.

This chapter also shows how Java programs can use relational databases through the **Java Database Connectivity (JDBC)** feature of the Java platform. You also can use JDBC locally from an application or remotely from a distributed application. Read the JDBC discussion here if you want to program for relational databases regardless whether of you are programming applications or servlets. JDBC is included in this chapter because, in practice, servlets often access databases.

## Deciding to Build a Dynamic Web Site

When a company decides to do business over a web, the software architects must design a system that allows for factors such as the following:

➤ Can you build the user interface for your clients in pure HTML, or HTML plus some small applets and JavaScript? If the answer is no, a web site may not be the best way for you to distribute your application. Web technology may change radically in the near future when the **Extensible Markup Language (XML)** becomes widely used, but for now, webs transmit HTML files over TCP/IP connections using the HTTP protocol.

➤ Does the system rely on legacy software such as an existing database or trusted program that supports essential business operations? If the answer is yes, what is the bridge between the legacy code and new Java programs?

➤ Who is the target audience? Is this an internal site for employees? Are business partners such as suppliers, distributors, or agents going to use the site? Or is the site open to the general public?

➤ Can this organization provide an adequate web server? It may be more appropriate to publish to an Internet Service Provider (ISP) who can provide the bandwidth required by a popular site.

➤ Can the site developers dictate what web browsers the clients use and set requirements such as the speed of the communication line and local processing power on the client workstation?

➤ How important is visual appeal and ease of use? Is the site a form of advertising, or does it represent the company to the outside world? If clients are all employees or associates, is it reasonable to expect them to undertake some training to be able to use the site correctly?

➤ Will clients keep coming back because they must in order to access the data or to do their own jobs? Alternatively, will this site fail if clients lose interest and stop visiting?

➤ Does the company have people skilled in web design, graphic arts, user-interface design, HTML, and Java programming? Do these people work well as a team? A strong team is necessary to create a consistent look and feel for all web pages and a standardized user interface.

Often the underlying characteristics of a web site depend on the type of network to which the web site will be deployed. Table 17-1 gives some guidelines for the three main types of networks:

The ways in which web pages use Java classes and run Java programs on the web server is the main topic of this chapter. Also, this chapter describes using JDBC as a way of accessing relational databases, where the database management system comes with a JDBC or ODBC driver. The very important matter of security is mentioned briefly but often is a function of the web server—not a programming concern. Later, this chapter explains how you can use servlets to leverage Java programming skills or JSPs to leverage web authoring tools and skills when building dynamic pages for the web. Deploying and maintaining a web site—tasks directly related to the topics in this chapter—depend largely on the web server and distribution vehicle and, therefore, are beyond the scope of this book.

**17**

**Table 17-1**  Three types of Networks

| | |
|---|---|
| **Internet** | The Internet is synonymous with the World Wide Web (WWW). Generally, you want to create HTML pages that a wide range of browsers can handle and that are of reasonable size for download-ing. Assume that minimal processing power is available on the client. Web pages should be appealing and self-explanatory. A web site is most effective if it has a common look and feel on all pages. |
| | Program for thin clients by placing as much of the processing on the server side as possible. Processing done on the server side can be behind the company firewall so that you do not have to distribute code that accesses databases or other internal processes. |
| **Extranet** | An extranet is a web that connects a set of cooperating organiza-tions, such as distributors and suppliers of goods, institutions and their agents, service providers and their subcontractors. Typically, one organization sets up a web site for its own employees and its part-ners. For example, an insurance company may maintain a web that insurance agents use to create policies on behalf of their customers. |
| | How much control the web provider has over the web users depends on the relationship between them. Some of the characteris-tics of the Internet and some of an intranet may apply. For example, the company may not be able to control the client's processing power or choice of browser, but may insist that the client take some training. A fancy look and feel may not be necessary, but a stan-dardized user interface may be important. |
| **Intranet** | An intranet is a web that is accessible only by authorized users. Usually, the users are employees of the organization that owns the web site. They may be using hardware and software provided by their employer and may be behind the company's firewall. |
| | In certain circumstances, fat clients capable of significant processing may be appropriate. You can create a fat client by downloading signed applets that do the processing or by invoking other programs stored on the client workstations. |
| | On an intranet, visual appeal, ease of use, and a standard page design may be less important than quick and accurate access to information. |
| | On the other hand, a web site designed for the intranet of a large organization may have many of the characteristics of a web site intended for the Internet. |

# Understanding the HTTP Protocol

The HyperText Transfer Protocol (HTTP) is the communication protocol over which web browsers and servers communicate. HTTP operates over TCP/IP sockets, which you learned about in Chapter 16. You also should be familiar with Uniform Resource Locators (URLs) from the discussion in Chapter 16. The full form of a URL is:

## Syntax

*protocol***://***hostname***[:***port***]/***identifers*

## Dissection

➤ The protocols most web servers and browsers use are HTTP and HTTPS. HTTPS is a variant of HTTP with security provided by the Secure Socket Layer (SSL). Another protocol is File Transfer Protocol (FTP).

➤ The hostname identifies the server and may be a name or a TCP/IP address. In this chapter, one workstation hosts both client and server, so the hostname for the examples is either the name of your workstation or the common alias "localhost".

➤ The port identifies the TCP/IP socket at which the server listens for requests. Usually, port numbers are reserved for different protocols. For example, the web server provided with this book listens at port 8080. Often, you do not see the port number because a default is in use.

➤ The identifiers specify a specific resource. Typically, you supply a filename, including a path relative to the folder used by the server.

## Code Example

`HTTP://localhost:8080/skiclub/index.html`

## Code Dissection

This is the URL for the main page of the sample web page provided with this book:

HTTP is a stateless request–response protocol. In other words, the client sends a request, and the server responds. The state of the client and server are not altered by the exchange and no record of the request is kept, except possibly in the history list of URLs and the cache of the web browser. Statelessness raises the question of how to provide some continuity in conversation that consists of several request–response exchanges. One of the challenges of designing an effective web site is allowing for a natural flow from web page to web page and letting clients navigate easily to the desired pages. Techniques for recording and recalling what clients did on previous pages are discussed throughout this chapter and are the focus of the section "Storing State Data in Sessions."

On the web, the most common HTTP request is to get a resource, such as a web page. The server responds by finding the resource in its file system and sending it back to the client. The web page is an HTML document, and it becomes the body of an HTTP response.

**17**

HTTP requests have a method, an optional number of headers, and then the body. Table 17-2 lists the common methods. Possible HTTP methods are defined in the HTTP protocol and are not the same as Java methods. GET and POST are the HTTP methods of interest in this chapter. Headers give control information, such as the MIME type of the document. HTTP allows for a number of MIME types, including "text/HTML" for HTML text files and "image/gif" for images in the .gif format. HTTP responses have a status line, headers, and a body.

**Table 17-2**  HTTP request methods

| Method | Description |
| --- | --- |
| DELETE | Deletes a resource. |
| GET | Requests a resource. |
| POST | Transmits information, usually data entered in an HTML form. |
| PUT | Stores a resource, usually used with FTP. |

Not all web servers can handle servlets or JSPs. You need a Java-enabled web server that contains what is sometimes called a **servlet engine**. Usually, you install an ordinary HTTP server and a Java web server. The Java web server often comes in the form of a plug-in to the HTTP server. Most organizations install proprietary web servers such as Sun Microsystems' Java Web Server or IBM's WebSphere.

The examples in this chapter use a simple, free server from Sun Microsystems included in the **JavaServer Web Development Kit (JSWDK)**. It is adequate for these examples but lacks many features that are required to conduct business using a web application.

# INTRODUCTION TO SERVLETS

On the web, a client requests a web page by issuing an HTTP request that specifies the URL of a page that the web server returns. Servlets are Java programs that run in a web server. They are not contained in HTML pages, as are applets. A servlet runs in response to an HTTP request that specifies a servlet name to a Java-enabled web server. The web server runs the servlet, and the servlet outputs an HTML page that the server returns to the client.

If you think the preceding description of servlets sounds much like the **Common Gateway Interface (CGI)**, you are right. For years, programmers have been providing dynamic content for web sites by calling CGI programs. Servlets do much the same thing that CGI programs do, but they do it better. Servlet technology is replacing CGI technology for the following reasons:

➤ CGI programs can be written in any language. Perl, C, and C++ are popular for this purpose. Servlets are always written in Java. Compiled CGI programs may have a slight advantage in performance but are not portable. Servlets, like all Java programs, can boast to be "write once, run anywhere."

➤ The marginal performance advantage of compiled programs is more than offset by the overhead of loading and starting CGI programs. CGI programs must run as separate processes on the host of the web server, unlike servlets, which run in the JVM of the web server. CGI programs must be loaded and started every time they are called. After a servlet has been loaded into the JVM, it remains available for subsequent uses. This is a tremendous performance enhancement for frequently used programs.

➤ **FastCGI**, a recent development based on CGI technology, does reuse a single copy of a FastCGI program for many client requests. FastCGI requires one process for every FastCGI program, instead of one process for every client request. The result is a great performance improvement over CGI. In contrast, servlets need no extra processes because they run within the single JVM on the server.

➤ Most Java-enabled web servers let the server administrator specify that servlets be preloaded when the server starts or loaded on demand at the first request. Therefore, the overhead of even the first load can be eliminated or moved to the time when the web server starts up.

➤ Java servlets run in a JVM and can, therefore, be subject to a security manager. Chapter 14 introduces the security managers applied by default to applets. By default, servlets are subject to the same restrictions as Java applications.

➤ Many commercial Java web servers provide value-add features such as pooling of database connections for improved performance, site-use monitoring, and much more. Also, they usually provide API so you can access each feature programmatically.

➤ For continuity between calls to different CGI programs, programmers encode parameters in the URL, and then parameters are passed back and forth between client and server. Sometimes, sensitive data must be transferred this way. Servlets can share information by sharing session objects that reside in the server. Only an identifier for the session must be transferred between the server and the client. This process is explained in the section "Storing State Data in Sessions."

Figure 17-1 shows the flow of a hypothetical client-server interchange. A discussion of its points follow the figure.

**17**

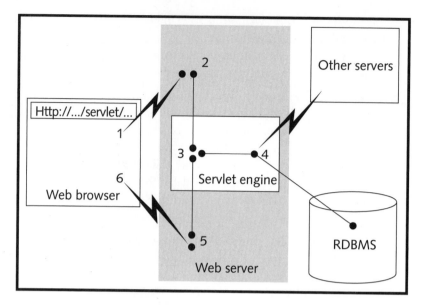

**Figure 17-1** How web servers handle HTTP requests for servlets

Here is what happens at the numbered points in the diagram:

1. The client issues an HTTP request, and the URL includes the reserved folder name /servlet. The user could have entered the URL in the browser's navigation bar or clicked a link that issued the URL.

2. The web server intercepts the request and loads the class named in the URL. The class name follows the "/servlet/" in the URL. The browser passes objects encapsulating the HTTP request and a response object to the servlet.

3. The servlet can interrogate the request to get parameters and other information about the request and its source. It can call other classes loaded or available on the web server.

4. The servlet can optionally communicate with database management software or another server. In a three-tier, distributed architecture, a common arrangement is to have a database server or legacy system on the third tier. The servlet engine resides on the second tier, and the client browser is the first tier. Any protocol available to Java programs can be used, including Remote Method Invocation (RMI) and Internet Inter-ORB Protocol (IIOP).

5. After gathering data and processing, the servlet creates an HTML document by writing to an output stream acquired from the response object.

6. The server redirects the output from the servlet to the client.

A servlet is simply a class that resides in the servlet folder of the web server and implements certain methods. The sole purpose of a servlet is to receive one HTTP request and prepare a complete HTML page that becomes the response.

You may have encountered web pages containing <servlet> and </servlet> tags. These are analogous to <applet> and </applet> tags and relate to a technology called **server-side includes (SSI)**. Much like the <applet> tag, the <servlet> tag provides the name of a class to run. Files that contain SSI must end with the extension .jhtml, instead of .html. Before a server that supports SSI serves a .jhtml file to the client, it runs the class specified in each <servlet> in a server-side JVM. The output of the servlet class then replaces the <servlet> tag in the document, and the server sends an ordinary HTML document to the client. The key difference between the <servlet> and <applet> tags is that an SSI runs on the server rather than in the browser, and no Java classes are downloaded. SSI technology was an early attempt to meet the need for dynamic content generated on the server side. Servlets as described in this chapter provide a much more powerful solution. Many Java-enabled web servers still support SSI, but you should consider it a deprecated technology.

## Your First Servlet

Before getting into the details of the Servlet API, look at a simple servlet that prints the current date and time. You can find the file that contains this class and all the other examples in this chapter in the file **examples.jar** on the CD-ROM that accompanies this book. The **ReadMe.html** file on the CD-ROM explains how to extract the file from the JAR and install the servlet. An explanation of the servlet follows the listing:

```java
import java.io.*;
import java.util.Date;
import javax.servlet.*;
import javax.servlet.http.*;
public class TodayServlet extends HttpServlet {
    public void doGet( HttpServletRequest request,
                       HttpServletResponse response )
        throws IOException, ServletException {
        response.setContentType( "text/HTML" );
        response.setHeader( "Pragma", "no cache" );
        response.setHeader( "Cache-Control", "no cache" );
        response.setHeader( "Expires", "0" );
        PrintWriter out = response.getWriter();
        out.println( "<HTML>" );
        out.println( "<head>" );
        out.println( "<title>Today</title>" );
        out.println( "</head>" );
        out.println( "<body>" );
        out.println(
            "<h1>The current date and Time is:</h1>" );
        Date today = new Date();
```

**17**

```
        out.println( "<p>" + today + "</p>" );
        out.flush();
        out.println( "</body>" );
        out.println( "</HTML>" );
    }
```

The output of this servlet is an HTML page similar to Figure 17-2.

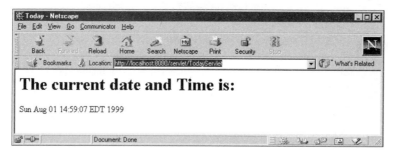

**Figure 17-2**   Output of the TodayServlet class

Most servlet classes that reply to an HTML **GET** request look similar in structure to `TodayServlet`, except that they may have additional methods and do different processing in the **doGet** method. Therefore, you can use this class as a template for your own servlets. The following paragraphs provide a detailed breakdown of the code.

Like any file that contains a class, the file **TodayServlet.java** starts with a package statement and import statements. However, this servlet is in the default, nameless package. All servlets should import the packages **javax.servlet** and **javax.servlet.http** to have access to the classes that support servlets. The **java.io** package is also required because servlets direct their character output stream **java.io.PrintWriter**:

```
import java.io.*;
import javax.servlet.*;
import javax.servlet.http.*;
import java.util.Date;
```

Servlets that use the HTTP protocol extend the class **javax.servlet.http.HttpServlet**. There is a superclass **javax.servlet.Servlet** that allows for the possibility of other protocols, but for now, all servlets are **HttpServlet** objects:

```
public class TodayServlet extends HttpServlet {
```

This servlet prepares the response to an HTTP **GET** method. **GET** methods are forwarded to the **doGet** method of the **HttpServlet**. The web server encapsulates the request in an instance of **HttpServletRequest** and also gives the servlet an **HttpServletResponse** object to use when building the HTML output page. Of course, things can go wrong. Any IO can cause an exception, so the **doGet** method must list an **IOException** in its throws clause. Similarly, the servlet mechanism may encounter an unexpected condition, and the **doGet** must include a **ServletException** in its throws clause:

```
public void doGet(HttpServletRequest request,
    HttpServletResponse response)
        throws IOException, ServletException {
```

The first step in preparing an HTML response is to set the MIME type for the contents of the response to tell the browser what kind of document is coming:

```
response.setContentType( "text/HTML" );
```

The next three lines tell the browser not to cache this page by adding headers to the HTTP response. Including them is optional; if you omit them, the servlet still works. However, if the users run the servlet, move on to another page, and then return by pressing the browser's **Back** button, the old time still shows. By turning off caching, you force the browser to retrieve the page again from the server. There are three lines instead of one to supply headers recognized by a wide range of browsers.

```
response.setHeader( "Pragma", "no cache" );
response.setHeader( "Cache-Control",
"no cache" );
response.setHeader( "Expires", "0" );
```

A servlet needs a character output stream to send the HTML output to. Most servlets call the **getWriter** method to acquire a reference to the **PrintWriter** from the **HttpServletResponse** object:

```
PrintWriter out = response.getWriter();
```

The contents of the HTML page are written with ordinary stream output. The **PrintWriter** class implements the same methods as **PrintStream**, including **print** and **println**. The servlet must create a complete HTML document:

```
out.println( "<HTML>" );
out.println( "<body>" );
```

**17**

```
out.println( "<head>" );
out.println( "<title>Today</title>" );
out.println( "</head>" );
out.println( "<body>" );
out.println(
    "<h1>The current date and Time is:</h1>" );
```

The next two lines create the dynamic content of this web page. Just to show that you can mix any valid Java statements with the statements that create output, the **Date** object today is instantiated in a separate statement from the method call that inserts the date as a string into the HTML. You can call other methods and do as much processing as you want:

```
Date today = new Date();
out.println( "<p>" + today + "</p>" );
```

The final lines output the tags to end the HTML document and then make sure all characters are flushed from the output stream. Calling **flush** is optional but always a good idea at the end of a servlet:

```
    out.println( "</body>" );
    out.println( "</HTML>" );
    out.flush();
  }
}
```

---

**Mini Quiz 17-1**

If the web client and web server are in different type zones, which time does the `TodayServlet` print?

---

## Installing and Running the Servlet Examples

To run the servlets, you need a web server that contains a servlet engine. Many suitable servers are available from a variety of vendors. Some are called **application servers**. Usually, the web server resides on a different host from the client, but you can configure a single workstation to act as both web server and web client. You already have the client-side software installed in the form of your web browser. The file **ReadMe.html** on the CDROM that accompanies this book gives detailed instructions for installing a simple web server and all the software required to run all the examples in this chapter.

The rest of this chapter assumes you have installed the JSWDK, following the instructions in **ReadMe.html**. Where you see the path *X:\jswdk*, substitute the actual drive and folder into which you installed the JSWDK. For example, *X:\jswdk* may represent C:\jswdk-1.0. Also, make sure **localhost** is recognized by your operating system as the name of your workstation or substitute the name your operating system does recognize or your TCP/IP address wherever you see *localhost* in this chapter.

Deploying servlets and JSPs involves copying files that contain them into the correct subfolders of *X:\jswdk*. The sample web server looks in locations relative to the folder *X:\jswdk\* for classes, HTML files, .gifs, and other resources. The installation instructions in the **ReadMe.html** file step you through deploying the Today servlet and other examples in this chapter.

To run the TodayServlet class:

1. Start the web server in any of a number of ways. The most convenient may be to create a shortcut for the file **X:\jswdk\startserver.bat** on your desktop. Then you can start the server by simply clicking on the icon. You can also enter *X:\jswdk*\`startserver` at a command line or use the Windows **Start > Run** dialog.

2. Open your web browser. Enter the URL:

   `HTTP://localhost:8080/servlet/TodayServlet`

3. You should now see a page that looks like Figure 17-2, except that the date and time should reflect real time. If your browser reports a problem connecting to the server, check your browser options for proxy servers. You may have to turn off all proxies or specify not to use proxies for domains starting `localhost:8080`.

4. To stop the web server, run the file **X:\jswdk\stopserver.bat** from the command line, the start menu, or from a shortcut you have placed on the desktop. If the batch file does not work, you can also type **Ctrl+C** in the window that opened when you started the server.

Before you run examples that use a database, such the example ski club web, you must make sure that DB2 is running.

To start DB2:

1. Open a DB2 command window by selecting **Start > Programs > DB2 for Windows > Command Window**.

**17**

2. When the prompt **SQLLIB\BIN>** appears, enter the command:

```
db2start
```

3. You can now close the command window.

Servlets rarely work in isolation. Unlike the `TodayServlet`, most servlets are designed to work in a web site. Therefore, most of the examples in this chapter are excerpts from a web site created for a hypothetical ski club. You can try the web site by starting DB2, your web server, and web browser, and then loading this URL:

```
HTTP://localhost:8080/skiclub
```

The ski club web site should be self-explanatory. It offers one-day ski trips to its members and provides bus transportation to a local resort called Near Hills. You can use the web site to join the club and book ski trips.

DB2 is a fairly large program and may slow your machine noticeably. Therefore, you should keep it running only when you are using the database.

To stop DB2:

1. Return to the Command window if it is open, or open it again from the Start menu.

2. When the prompt **SQLLIB\BIN>** appears, enter this command:

```
db2stop
```

## DEVELOPING YOUR OWN WEB AND SERVLETS

You can write your own servlets and complete the end-of-chapter exercises for this chapter using the JSWDK and the command-line tools of the Java 2 SDK. VisualAge for Java has a popular feature called the WebSphere Test Environment for developing, testing, and debugging servlets in the VisualAge IDE. However, the WebSphere Test Environment is not included in the version of VisualAge on the CD-ROM that accompanies this book. For the .html and .jsp files that also make up your web, use your favorite text editor. If you use a WYSIWYG HTML editor or another authoring tool, you must be able to read and edit the files your tool generates with an ordinary text editor.

When you build your web, it is a good idea to put all the HTML and JSP pages for one web into one folder and group classes for that web into Java packages. You should not have to worry about the final destination of the files if you build your web using relative paths for all filenames in HTML links and the like. Alternatively, you can build a small web in the local deployment folders.

To deploy your web:

1. Put all .html, .gif, or other multimedia files as well as .jsp files into the folder *X:\jswdk*\webpages. You can create subfolders to organize the files.

2. Copy the servlet .class files into the folder *X:\jswdk*\webpages\WEB-INF\ servlets. If the classes are in Java packages, they go into subfolders of the servlets folder.

3. You can put additional classes that support the servlets and JSPs into the directory *X:\jswdk*\classes. As always, classes in the same package must be in the same subfolder of the classes folder.

When you call a servlet, include the word "servlet" in the URL after the server name and port, as in:

**http://localhost:8080/servlet/***ServletClassName*

Note that the singular form of servlet appears in the URL, whereas the folder containing servlets is named with the plural form "servlets".

Unlike standalone JVMs and many proprietary Java-enabled web servers, the JSWDK server does not reload classes automatically when you place a version with a later timestamp in the *X:\jswdk*\webpages\WEB-INF\ servlets folder or the *X:\jswdk*\classes folder. If you change a class used by a servlet or JSP, you must stop the server and restart it for the changes to take effect.

## SERVLET API

The Java 2 platform does not include the servlet API. This API and its documentation are packaged separately in the Java Server Development Kit (JSDK) and JSWDK. Both kits are freely downloadable from Sun. You can use them with the Java 2 platform or versions 1.1.6 and later of the Java 1.1 platform.

The Java 2 enterprise edition (J2EE) will support servlets. The JSWDK, which became available in August 1999, includes support for servlets and JSPs as described in version 1.0 of the JSP specification. At the time of writing, the JSP specification is still volatile and Sun has not integrated support for JSPs into the JSDK.
The servlet API has been subject to changes even during its brief history, and minor changes to a new API are to be expected. This chapter uses version 1.0 of the JSWDK which, in turn, is based on version 2.1 of the servlet specification. This description of the API does not mention many of the small refinements made to the API prior to version 2.1.

Two packages provide the servlet API: **javax.servlet** and **javax.servlet.http**. The classes and interfaces they contain are shown in Figure 17-3.

**17**

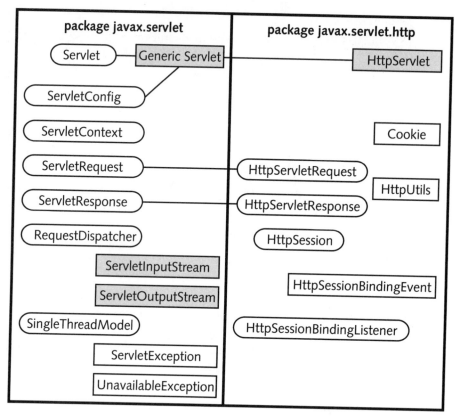

**Figure 17-3** The Servlet API

Except where Figure 17-3 indicates that a class implements and interface or extends a class, all the classes extend **java.lang.Object** except the following:

➤ **ServletInputStream** extends **java.io.InputStream**

➤ **ServletOutputStream** extends **java.io.OutputStream**

➤ **ServletException** extends **java.lang.Exception**

➤ **UnavailableException** extends **java.lang.Exception**

➤ **HTTPSessionBindingEvent** extends **java.util.EventObject**

➤ **interface HTTPSessionBindingListener** extends **java.util.EventListener**

Generally, you use the classes in **javax.servlet.http** because they support the HTTP protocol. The classes of most interest are briefly described in Table 17-3. Only the most important classes are described in detail in this chapter.

**Table 17-3**   Some types in the Servlet API

| Type | Description |
|------|-------------|
| HttpServlet | Is the class most frequently extended to create servlets. |
| HttpServletRequest | Encapsulates information from the HTTP request in a form accessible by the servlet. |
| HttpServletResponse | Is the object through which the servlet returns HTTP headers and body to the client. |
| HttpSession | Provides a mechanism for sharing data between servlets visited by one user during a browser session. |
| Cookie | Encapsulates small amounts of data to be tranferred autotmatically between web server and browser as part of the request header. |
| HttpSessionBindingEvent | Defines an event that occurs when the contents of a session change. |
| HttpSessionBinding Listener | Provides a listener for session-binding events. |
| SessionConfig | Passes initialization parameters from the servlet engine to the servlet. |
| SessionContext | Allows for communication between the servlet and the servlet engine. |
| RequestDispatcher | Wraps a resource, such as a servlet or JSP, and is most often used to redirect HTTP request and responses. |
| ServletInputStream | Is a binary input stream for reading data from the client request. |
| ServletOutputStream | Is a binary output stream for writing binary data to the client. |
| HttpUtils | Provides a set of useful methods. |
| SingleThreadModel | Is an interface that forces a servlet to run only in single-threaded mode. |

# Life Cycle of a Servlet

**17**

The life cycle of a servlet is different from that of applications and applets. By default, servlet classes reside in a JVM in the server from the time they are first loaded until the server process stops. Many servers have a feature that administrators use to specify which servlets are loaded automatically when the server process starts and which are loaded on demand. It is also possible to explicitly unload a servlet. Some servers automatically unload a servlet and reload it if they detect that the servlet class has changed. So, the life cycle of a servlet often is the same as the life cycle of the server in which it runs.

The methods that the server class uses to load and unload a servlet resemble the methods that a web browser calls to load and unload applets. They are declared in the **Servlet** interface.

---

*Interface*

**javax.servlet.Servlet**

---

*Purpose*

The **Servlet** interface declares methods that control the life cycle of a servlet.

---

*Methods*

➤ **void init (ServletConfig)** *config*
The **init** method initializes a servlet and puts it into service. If the servlet cannot be loaded, it throws a **ServletException**. Initialization parameters are passed by in the **ServletConfig** object. These parameters are set up by the administrator of the web server.

➤ **void service( ServletRequest** *request***, ServletResponse** *response* **)**
The **service** method performs the work of the servlet. This is the method that the server calls, passing the request and response objects.

➤ **ServletConfig getServletConfig( )**
The **getServletConfig** method gives access to the initialization and start-up parameters, including the **ServletContext** object.

➤ **String getServletInfo()**
The **getServletInfo** method returns a **String** that typically includes the name of the author, version number, copyright, and the like.

➤ **void destroy()**
The **destroy** method unloads the servlet as soon as all active threads end or after a timeout period.

---

The **GenericServlet** and **HttpServlet** classes provide implementations of the **Servlet** methods. The most frequently used methods are introduced here:

➤ At load time, the **init** method runs. Use **init**—not the constructor—to prepare your servlet. Often, the implementation provided by **HttpServlet** is adequate, but you can override the **init** method to perform specialized initialization. For example, this may be a good place to open a database connection.

➤ In response to a client request, the server calls the **service** method. Therefore, **service** is analogous to the **start** method of a thread or applet. The **HttpServlet** class overrides **service** with an implementation that looks at the HTTP request and then calls **doGet, doPost, doPut, doDelete**, or **doTrace** accordingly. **HttpServlet** also supplies empty implementations of the **do***Xxx* methods. When you extend an **HttpServlet**, you have a choice of overriding **service** or the **do***Xxx* methods of interest.

➤ You can override the **destroy** method to perform specialized cleanup, such as releasing resources opened by **init**. Usually, the **destroy** method provided by **HttpServlet** is adequate.

# WRITING SERVLETS TO RECEIVE REQUESTS AND SEND RESPONSES

Most servlets that supply a web page to a client implement the **doGet** method or the **service** method. Most servlets that accept input from an HTML form implement the **doPost** method, as described in the next session. Almost always, servlets implement at least one of these three methods. The most common reason for implementing two of the methods is to generate a form in **doGet** and then process the form in **doPost**.

To understand how these three methods relate to each other and to http requests and responses, you must become familiar with the **HttpServlet** class and **HttpServletRequest** and **HttpServletResponse** interfaces in the **javax.servlet.http** package as well as the class and interfaces they extend in the **javax.servlet** package.

The abstract class **GenericServlet** implements the methods in the **Servlet** interface and adds more methods.

*Class*

**javax.servlet.GenericServlet**

*Purpose*

The **GenericServlet** class provides a blueprint for servlets that are not specific to any protocol. Future subclasses of **GenericServlet** may support other protocols.

*Methods*

➤ **String getInitParameter( String** *name* **)**
The **getInitParameter** method returns a **String** containing the named initialization parameter.

➤ **Enumeration getInitParameterNames( )**
Use this method to get the names of the initialization parameters. It returns a collection of string objects. Then, you can call **getInitParameter** to find the value of a specific initialization parameter.

➤ **ServletContext getServletContext( )**
For some operations, such as forwarding a request to another servlet, you need to know about the servlet engine. This convenience method returns an object that encapsulates the context of the servlet engine.

**17**

➤ **void log( String** *message* **)**
**void log( String** *message***, Throwable** *t* **)**
The **log** methods write a message to the servlet log file. The one-argument
form writes the servlet name and a servlet message. The two-argument
form writes a system exception message.

In practice, all servlets extend the abstract class **HttpServlet**. This class adds
more methods to the set inherited from **GenericServlet**. The classes specific
to the HTTP protocol are in the package **javax.servlet.http**.

*Class*

➤ **javax.servlet.http.HttpServlet**

*Purpose*

Extend the abstract class **HttpServlet** to create a servlet for use with the
HTTP protocol.

*Methods*

➤ **void doDelete( HttpServletRequest** *request***, HttpServletResponse**
*response* **)**
**void doGet( HttpServletRequest** *request***, HttpServletResponse**
*response* **)**
**void doOptions( HttpServletRequest** *request***, HttpServletResponse**
*response* **)**
**void doPost( HttpServletRequest** *request***, HttpServletResponse**
*response* **)**
**void doPut( HttpServletRequest** *request***, HttpServletResponse**
*response* **)**
**void doTrace( HttpServletRequest** *request***, HttpServletResponse**
*response* **)**
Override the **do***Xxx* methods to handle the HTTP request *Xxx*. Usually,
an **HttpServlet** has a **doGet** or **doPost** method or both. The other
**do***Xxx* methods are less frequently used, and the default implementations
are often adequate. All of these methods can throw a **ServletException** or
an **IOException**.

➤ **void service( HttpServletRequest** *request***, HttpServletResponse**
*response* **)**
**void service( ServletRequest** *request***, ServletResponse** *response* **)**

The **HttpServlet** class overrides and overloads the **service** method. The arguments of the overloaded version supply the servlet with information about the HTTP request and response. The implementation provided calls one of the **do***Xxx* methods according to the method in the HTTP request. Overriding this method is a valid alternative to overriding the **do***Xxx* methods. Usually, you do not override the method with arguments of type **ServletRequest** and **ServletResponse**.

➤ **long getLastModified( HttpServiceRequest** *request* **)**
The **getLastModified** returns the time the **HttpServletRequest** object was last modified, measured in milliseconds since January 1, 1970 GMT.

---

A request object is essential for receiving information the client. The server passes an **HttpRequest** to the servlet. This object can hold data provided by the user, such as entries into an HTML form, as well as information about the request itself. The request object implements the **HttpServletRequest** interface. The **HttpServletRequest** interface extends the **ServletRequest** interface.

*Interface*

**javax.servlet.ServletRequest**

---

*Purpose*

The **ServletRequest** interface provides access to the servlet context and defines a large number of methods that give information about the request.

---

*Methods*

➤ **Object getAttribute( String** *name* **)**
**Enumeration getAttributeNames( )**
**setAttribute( String** *name*, **Object** *attribute* **)**
An object that can be stored in the session context is an attribute of the context. For example, you can store beans to make them available to other servlets and JSPs. Attributes and their values are stored as name–value pairs. Call **setAttribute** to add an attribute to the context. Call **getAttributeNames** to get the names of stored attributes. Then you can call **getAttribute** to retrieve a named attribute.

**17**

➤ **String getCharacterEncoding( )**
**int getContentLength( )**
**String getContentType( )**
These methods may be useful if you must read the request directly. The **getContentLength** method returns the number of bytes in the request. The **getContentType** method returns the MIME type. The **getCharacterEncoding** returns the name of the request's character-encoding scheme.

➤ **ServletInputStream getInputStream( )**
The **getInputStream** method returns binary data from the body of the request as a **ServletInputStream**.

➤ **Enumeration getParameterNames( )**
**String[ ] getParameterValues( String** *name***)**
**String getParameter( String** *name* **)**
Use these methods to get information from the body of the request. Typically, you use them in a **doPost** method to read the information a user has entered into an HTML form. Call **getParameterNames** to get an array containing the names of all the parameters. Parameter names usually match the names of input elements on forms. Then you can call either **getParameterValues** supplying the name of a parameter that may have more than one value or **getParameter** supplying the name of a parameter that can have only one value.

➤ **BufferedReader getReader( )**
The **getReader** method returns the body of the request as a **BufferedReader**. Characters are translated according to the character encoding of the request.

➤ **String getScheme( )**
**String getServerName( )**
**String getServerPort( )**
These and other methods return a wealth of information about the nature and origin of the request. For example, **getScheme** can tell you whether the protocol is HTTP or HTTPS. You can use **getScheme**, **getServerName**, and **getServerPort** to programmatically build up the full URL for the client. These methods cannot correct for redirection by a proxy server, and often the safest approach is to use relative URLs whenever possible.

*Interface*

**javax.servlet.http.HttpServletRequest**

*Purpose*

The **HttpServletRequest** interface adds a large number of accessor methods that supply information specific to an HTTP request.

*Methods*

➤ **String getAuthTypes( )**
The **getAuthType** method indicates the authentication scheme used by the server. It returns "BASIC" for basic authentication, "SSL" for Secure Socket Layer, and null for no server authentication.

➤ **Cookie[ ] getCookies( )**
The **getCookies** method returns an array containing all the cookies sent by the browser.

➤ **Enumeration getHeaderNames( )**
**String getHeader( String** *name* **)**
**long getDateHeader( String** *name* **)**
**int getIntHeader( String** *name* **)**
Use these methods to get fields from the HTTP headers. Each field is a name-value pair. The **getHeaderNames** method returns a collection of the header names. You can call it first and then the **getHeader**, **getDateHeader**, or **getIntHeader** to get the value for a named field. Dates are given in milliseconds since January 1, 1970 GMT.

➤ **String getMethod( )**
The **getMethod** method returns the name of the HTTP method with which the request was made, which is usually **GET** or **POST**.

➤ **String getRemoteUser( )**
If the user was logged in using HTTP authentication, you can call **getRemoteUser** to get the user's name.

➤ **HttpSession getSession( )**
**HttpSession getSession( boolean** *create* **)**
Use a session object to store information that relates to any individual client. The session resides on the server but is identified by an id supplied with the HTTP request. Different servlets can access the same session by calling the **getSession** method. If you do not provide an argument or set the **boolean** argument to **true** and no session exists, a new session is created. If you do not want to start a new session, supply an argument with the value **false**.

➤ **boolean isRequestedSessionIdFromCookie( )**
**boolean isRequestedSessionIdFromURL( )**
**boolean isRequestedSessionIdValid( )**
The server may get a session id from a Cookie or URL rewriting or because you created a new session by calling **getSession**. Use the first two of these methods if you need to know the source of the session id and the last to check whether the session context has a session with the id for the requested session.

**17**

To send a response to send back to the client, servlets must use the Http response object that the **do***Xxx* and service methods receive as an input argument. The response object implements the **HttpServletResponse** interface. The **HttpServletResponse** interface extends the **ServletResponse** interface.

*Interface*

**javax.servlet.ServletResponse**

---

*Purpose*

The **HttpServletResponse** interface defines five methods that all servlet response classes must implement.

---

*Methods*

➤ **String getCharacterEncoding( )**
The **getCharacterEncoding** method returns the name of the character encoding of the body of the response.

➤ **ServletOutputStream getOutputStream( )**
The **getOutputStream** method returns a binary output stream object to which the servlet can write binary data.

➤ **PrintWriter getWriter( )**
The **getWriter** method returns a character output stream object to which the servlet can write character data.

➤ **void setContentLength( int** *length* **)**
The **setContentLength** method sets the length of the content the server returns to the client.

➤ **void setContentType( String** *type* **)**
The **setContentType** method sets the type of the response. Specify a MIME type and optionally include the type of character encoding. For example, a web document in the Latin-1 character set may be specified as "`text/html charset=ISO-8859-1.`"

---

*Interface*

**javax.servlet.http.HttpServletResponse**

---

*Purpose*

The **HttpServletResponse** interface defines a large number of constants as well as the methods listed here.

---

*Fields*

➤ **SC_OK**
A large number of static fields hold integer values that indicate the status codes for HTTP requests. The field **SC_OK** has the value 200, which is the code for success.

---

*Methods*

➤ **void addCookie( Cookie** *cookie***)**
Call the **addCookie** method to return a cookie to the client in the response. If you add a cookie that already exists in the response, you replace the old cookie, and effectively change its value.

➤ **boolean containsHeader( String** *name* **)**
The **containsHeader** method checks whether the response header has a field with the specified name. Use the **setHeader**, **setDateHeader**, or **setIntHeader** to add fields to the header.

➤ **String encodeURL( String** *url* **)**
**String encodeRedirectURL ( String** *url* **)**
These methods encode a URL when encoding is required. If the client does not accept cookies, you can encode session-tracking information into the URL. This technique is called URL rewriting and adds the session id to the supplied URL. If the URL is to be the destination of a redirect, use the **encodeRedirectURL** method.

➤ **void sendError( int** *statusCode*, **String** *message* **)**
**void sendError( int** *statusCode* **)**
The **sendError** method sends an error response to the client. You can use the two-arguments form to supply a message.

➤ **void sendRedirect( String** *location* **)**
The **sendRedirect** method redirects the client to the specified location. The location must be an absolute URL.

➤ **void setHeader( String** *name*, **String** *value* **)**
**void setDateHeader ( String** *name*, **long** *date* **)**
**void setIntHeader( String** *name*, **int** *value* **)**
Http headers can contain fields. Each field is a name-value pair. Use one of these methods to add a field to the header. Specify the date in milliseconds since January 1, 1970 GMT. If a header already contains the named field, its value is overwritten.

➤ **void setStatus( int** *statusCode* **)**
The **setStatus** method sets the status code for the response.

## Writing Servlets To Process HTML Forms

Usually, the dynamic content in an HTML page produced by a servlet is based on some input from the client. The web site first gives the user an opportunity to supply input. For example, the user may be adding items to a shopping cart, selecting items from a menu, or entering data. The HTML mechanism for accepting user input is a form. Typically, the user completes the form and then presses its submit button. This triggers an HTTP **POST** method and a request that contains data extracted from the form. A servlet processes the form and sends a dynamically generated response to give appropriate feedback to the user.

HTML forms are enclosed in **<form>** and **</form>** tags. The **<form>** tag has a **METHOD** attribute that specifies the HTTP method the browser sends when the user submits the form. Use the **POST** method to call a servlet to process the form. You can put any valid HTML between the **<form>** and

**17**

**</form>** tag. Often, forms are presented as tables. HTML provides a number of tags specifically for forms, and some of the most common ones are listed in Table 17-4 along with their most important attributes.

**Table 17-4** HTML FormTags

| Tag and Attributes | Description |
|---|---|
| FORM | Starts a new form: |
| • NAME=string | • Specifies a name for the form. |
| • METHOD=GET | • Generates a GET method when a user submits the form. Encodes input values in the URL to pass as parameters to a CGI script. |
| • METHOD=POST | • Generates a POST method when the user submits the form. Puts input values into the body of the request to pass as parameters to a servlet. |
| • ACTION=url | • Specified the target servlet or CGI script to process the form. |
| INPUT | Creates an area for user input: |
| • NAME=string | • Specifies a name of the item. |
| • TYPE=TEXT | • The item is a text input field. The specified value is displayed initially but is overwritten when user enters characters. |
| • TYPE=PASSWORD | • The item is text-input field, but user input is echoed as * characters. |
| • TYPE=CHECKBOX | • The item is a check box. The value is returned to the server only if the check box is checked. |
| • CHECKED | • Sets a check box to initially checked. |
| • TYPE=HIDDEN | • The item is not displayed, but the value is passed back to the server. |
| • VALUE=string | • The *string* is the value returned to the server and for **TEXT** appears in the input field. |
| BUTTON | Creates a button that the user can click to initiate an action: |
| • NAME=string | • Specifies the name of the button. |
| • TYPE=SUBMIT | • Submits the input data from the form to the server. |
| • TYPE=RESET | • Resets all input items to initial settings. |
| • VALUE=string | • Specifies the label on the button. |
| /FORM | Ends the form. |

It is time to introduce the ski club sample web site. Most of the examples in this chapter are taken from this collection of web documents and classes. Feel free to explore the site, starting at URL http://localhost:8080/skiclub. The first page is an ordinary HTML document shown in Figure 17-4. At the bottom of the page are two links—one is to a registration page for new members, and the other goes to a log in page for established members.

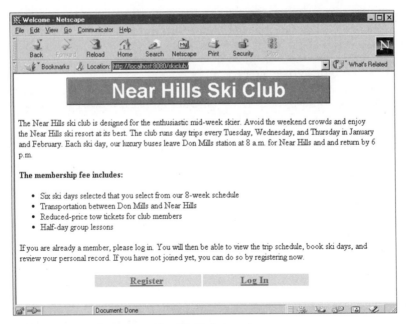

**Figure 17-4** The Near Hills Ski Club home page

The Ski club web site includes a number of forms. One of the simplest is the login form. You can reach it by clicking the **Log in** link on the page shown in Figure 17-4. The HTML page that produces the form is listed here, and Figure 17-5 shows the web page it produces. Notice that the form contains two tables. The first table arranges the input fields beside labels, and the second form contains a submit button labeled "Log in" and a reset button labeled "Clear". Most of the tagging deals with the layout and look of the tables. The lines specific to the login form are in bold font.

```
<HTML>
<HEAD>
<META HTTP-EQUIV="ContentType" CONTENT="text/html; >
<META NAME="Pragma" CONTENT="no-cache">
<META NAME="Cache-Control" CONTENT="nocache">
<META NAME="Expires" CONTENT="0">
<TITLE>Log In</TITLE>
</HEAD>
<BODY  BGCOLOR="#FFFFFF" LINK="#0000FF"
                VLINK="#990099" 0>
<CENTER>
<IMG  SRC="./images/SkiClub.gif"
     ALT="Near Hills Ski Club " >
</CENTER>
<h3>Members, please log in</H3>
<p>The information you enter here must exactly match our
records. Enter your last name and the ID you were
assigned when you registered. <em>Your ID is your
```

17

```
password.</em> If you are not a member, please return to
<a href="/skiclub/index.html">Near Hills Ski Club
home page</a>.</p>
<CENTER>
<FORM METHOD=POST ACTION=
    "http://localhost:8080/servlet/skiclub.LoginServlet" >
<TABLE BORDER=0 BGCOLOR="#DDDDFF" CELLPADDING=10 >
<TR>
<TD><strong>Last name</strong></TD>
<TD><INPUT TYPE="text" NAME="LNAME" VALUE="" SIZE=30
    MAXLENGTH=30></TD>
</TR>
<TR>
<TD><strong>ID</strong></TD>
<TD><INPUT TYPE="password" NAME="ID" VALUE="" SIZE=5
    MAXLENGTH=5></TD>
</TR>
</TABLE>
<TABLE BORDER=0 CELLSPACING=20 >
<TR>
<TD><INPUT TYPE="submit" VALUE="   Log in    "></TD>
<TD><INPUT TYPE="reset"  VALUE="   Clear    "></TD>
</TR>
</TABLE>
</FORM>
</CENTER>
<p> Please wait after pressing <strong>Log in</strong>
while we retrieve your record from the database. </p>
</BODY>
</HTML>
```

**Figure 17-5**  The Near Hills Log In form

Here is the servlet that processes the log in form. This servlet class has other methods, but only the method **doPost** and a method that retrieves the user input from the form, getMemberData, are shown. A breakdown of the **doPost** and CheckMemberData methods follows the listing:

```java
package skiclub;
import java.io.*;
import javax.servlet.*;
import javax.servlet.http.*;
import java.sql.SQLException;
public class LoginServlet
    extends javax.servlet.http.HttpServlet {
    public void doPost( HttpServletRequest req,
            HttpServletResponse res)
            throws ServletException, IOException {
        HttpSession session = req.getSession( false );
        if ( session != null ) {
            session.invalidate();
        }
        ClubMember skier = null;
        try {
            skier = getMemberData( req );
            confirmLogin( req, res, skier );
        } catch( BadDataException e ) {
            SkiClubUtils.sendInputErrorPage( req, res, e );
        } catch( Exception e ) {
            SkiClubUtils.sendErrorPage( req, res, e );
        }
        return;
    }

    private ClubMember
        getMemberData( HttpServletRequest req )
        throws DBopException, SQLException,
            BadDataException {
        int id;
        String lastName = req.getParameter( "LNAME" );
        if ( lastName.length() == 0 ) {
            throw new BadDataException(
            "Last Name Required" );
        }
        String sid = req.getParameter( "ID" );
        try {
            id = Integer.parseInt( sid );
        } catch( NumberFormatException e ) {
            throw new BadDataException(
                "ID must be an integer" );
        }
        ClubMember skier = SkiClubDB.getMemberByID( id );
        if ( skier == null ) {
            throw new BadDataException(
                "The ID " + id + " is not correct." );
```

**17**

```
        }
        if ( ! ( skier.getLastName().equals( lastName ) ) )
        {
            throw new BadDataException(
                "Last name does not match records." );
        }
        return skier;
}
```

The **doPost** method is called when the user presses the **Submit** button on the form. As with all the **do***Xxx* methods, the web server passes the request and response objects to the servlet. Like all **do***Xxx* methods, **doPost** must allow for I/O exceptions and servlet exceptions:

```
public void doPost( HttpServletRequest req,
    HttpServletResponse res)
    throws ServletException, IOException {
```

The next four lines relate to API that are discussed in the section "Storing State Data in Sessions." For now accept that they make sure the user is starting a new session with the ski club web site. In case the member returned to the log in page using the browser's **Back** button or using a bookmark stored in the browser, these lines clear any stored data so that the member can start again or someone else can log in:

```
        HttpSession session = req.getSession( false );
        if ( session != null ) {
            session.invalidate();
        }
```

The rest of the **doPost** method itself makes little use of the servlet API. It creates an object of type `ClubMember` to encapsulate the data about a person who joins the club. Then, it delegates the task of reading the input parameters and validating the user input to the method `getMemberData`. If the input is good, the `getMemberData` method returns a `ClubMember` object called `skier`. Then, the **doPost** method calls a `confirmLogin` method to generate and send a confirmation page. You will see the `confirmLogin` method in the discussions of sessions and cookies:

```
        ClubMember skier = null;
        try {
            skier = getMemberData( req );
            confirmLogin( req, res, skier );
```

The `getMemberData` method signals errors by throwing exceptions. If it detects illegal input, it throws an exception of type `BadDataException`. `BadDataException` is one of the supporting classes and subclasses **Exception**. If a `BadDataException` or another **Exception** occurs, catch clauses handle them by calling methods `sendInputErrorPage` and `sendErrorPage` from the supporting class `SkiClubUtils` to produce html error pages instead of the login confirmation. These methods are passed the request and response objects so that they can generate alternative HTML responses. They are also given the **Exception** object so that their dynamic output can include the message stored in the exception. The structure of `sendInputErrorPage` and `sendErrorPage` is similar to the **toGet** methods of the `TodayServlet`, so they are not included in this listing:

```
    } catch( BadDataException e ) {
       SkiClubUtils.sendInputErrorPage( req, res, e );
    } catch( Exception e ) {
       SkiClubUtils.sendErrorPage( req, res, e );
    }
    return;
}
```

The method `getMemberData` processes the **HttpRequest** from the submitted form. It creates and throws a `BadDataException` if it cannot accept the user input and also allows for a problem accessing the ski club database. The core JDBC classes can throw exceptions of type **SQLException**. A `DBopException` is created and thrown by the classes in the `skiclub` package that issues database queries for this application:

```
private ClubMember
    getMemberData( HttpServletRequest req )
    throws DBopException, SQLException,
        BadDataException {
```

Because the developer of the servlet knows the names of input controls in the HTML form, the easiest way to get the string the user typed into the last name field is to call **getParameter**, passing the parameter name `"LNAME"`. In a large web-development project, good communication or naming conventions between the HTML author and the servlet programmer are essential:

```
    int id;
    String lastName = req.getParameter( "LNAME" );
```

Next, the `getMemberData` method makes sure the user did enter a last name and throws an exception if the input string is empty:

```
    if ( lastName.length() == 0 ) {
       throw new BadDataException(
           "Last Name Required" );
    }
```

Similarly, the `getMemberData` method retrieves the value the user entered in the id input control and checks that it is an integer value. Each member is assigned a unique id on joining the ski club. When they return to the web site,

**17**

members must log in by supplying their last name and using their id like a password:

```
String sid = req.getParameter( "ID" );
try {
    id = Integer.parseInt( sid );
} catch( NumberFormatException e ) {
    throw new BadDataException(
        "ID must be an integer" );
}
```

In this case, the id plays double duty as password and the primary key of member's record on the database. The method **getMemberByID** of the class **SkiClubDB** retrieves a skier record from the database and returns an object containing the information stored about the member. If there is no record with the specified id in the database, **getMemberData** throws a **BadDataException**. The method also throws the exception if there is a record in the database but it does not belong to a person with the supplied last name:

```
ClubMember skier = SkiClubDB.getMemberByID( id );
if ( skier == null ) {
    throw new BadDataException(
        "The ID " + id + " is not correct." );
}
if ( ! ( skier.getLastName().equals( lastName ) ) )
{
    throw new BadDataException(
        "Last name does not match records." );
}
```

If the name and id match, the log in is successful. The **getMemberData** method returns the **ClubMember** object called **skier** that contains this member's personal data:

```
    return skier;
}
```

The registration form, shown in Figure 17-6, is similar to the log in form except that it contains more fields. In Figure 17-6, and some subsequent figures, the browser button bar and address bar are not displayed. This was done in order to save space.

**Figure 17-6** The Near Hills Ski Club registration form

## Redirecting Servlet Output

As a rule of thumb, you can associate one servlet with every HTML page that has dynamic content. A servlet can send only one response, and it must be a complete page. However, the servlet can choose between alternative responses. Often, you want to send an error page instead of the standard output, or depending on the user input, you may want to direct your user to different parts of your web site. For example, the Near Hills Ski Club log in servlet either responds to the log in request with an error page or sends the user to the member home page. The way the member home page is produced by a JSP is discussed later in this chapter. The three options for producing a response page from a servlet are covered in the following sections.

### Output the HTML Response Page

The `TodayServlet` is an example of this common approach. You can provide alternative outputs by using if statements to write different HTML content. Essentially, `LoginServlet` does this when it calls `SendErrorPage` or `SendInputErrorPage`.

### Redirect the Request and Response to Another Resource

Sometimes, the response is not itself dynamic and can be an ordinary HTML page. The role of the servlet may be simply to select the appropriate page. The trick is to route the request and response through the server so that the server can serve the correct page to the right client. Do this by obtaining a request dispatcher object from the servlet context for the destination URL and then transferring the HTTP request and response through the request dispatcher. First, use the inherited method **GenericServlet.getServletContext** to access the servlet engine, and then call **ServletContext.getRequestDispatcher**. Both **ServletContext** and **RequestDispatcher** are interfaces defined in the **javax.servlet** package. Finally, use the method **RequestDispatch.forward** to transfer the request and response. For example, when the `LoginServlet` in the ski club web admits a member to the web site, it sends the member to the member home page with the following lines:

```
RequestDispatcher rd = getServletContext().
    getRequestDispatcher(
        "/skiclub/MemberHome.jsp" );
rd.forward( req, res );
```

The URL can be for any appropriate resource such as an HTML document or JSP. In this case, the destination is a JSP. Specify a URL relative to the base location for web pages in your server. The object references `req` and `res` refer to the **HttpServletRequest** and **HttpServletResponse** objects passed to the **doGet** or **doPost** servlet methods.

## Delegate the Response to Another Servlet

You also can pass the request and response on to another servlet. Only one servlet can generate the response, but the first servlet can delegate the job of creating that response. For example, if there are several different paths through an online shopping web, the user may give the command to place the order for the items in the user's virtual shopping cart to any one of a number of servlets. Those servlets can all redirect the request on to one ordering servlet by calling the **HttpServletResponse.sendRedirect** method with a statement such as:

```
res.sendRedirect(
"http://localhost:8080/servlet/shopping.PlaceOrder" );
```

The URL in a sendRedirect must be an absolute address. Often, this technique is used to transfer the client to another web site.

Early versions of the JSDK, precursor to the JSWDK, provided a method **HttpServiceResponse.callPage** instead of the request dispatcher to forward requests and responses. You may see lines such as the following in early servlets:

```
( ( com.sun.server.http.HttpServiceResponse) res ) .
    callPage( "/folder/resource.jsp" , req );
```

The **HttpServletResponse** object `res` is cast to an **HttpServiceResponse**, and the **HttpServletRequest** object `req` is passed as an argument of the method. The **callPage** method, **HttpServiceResponse** class, and **com.sun.server.http** package are no longer available.

Do not use the deprecated interface
**javax.servlet.http.HttpSessionContext** or method
**javax.servlet.http.HttpSesssion.getSessionContext**.

## Storing State Data in Sessions

One challenge of building a web site with servlets is maintaining continuity between the different servlets and HTML documents. The HTTP protocol is stateless, so every request and response is a complete, independent transaction. However, web clients usually want to carry on a conversation with the entire web site. For example, in a shopping site, a customer usually visits several pages and expects all purchases to be added to a single virtual shopping cart. When they decide to confirm their orders, customers expect the site to remember the contents of the shopping cart.

The art of converting distinct web pages into an effective web site comes into play when you create the look and feel of the pages and when you design for flow from page to page, allowing for the various paths clients may take through your site. The larger topic of web design is beyond the scope of this book. Fortunately, the servlet API provide a simple mechanism for supporting your design by letting you save and share information between servlets.

The key concept in this activity is the **session**. A session is a place to store state information about the client and client activities. It is associated with one client but spans many HTTP requests. Typically, you start a session when a client first reaches your site. The end of a session is not as easy to pinpoint, but the important task is to maintain the session as long as the customer is active at the site. You can leave the task of terminating a session up to the web server. Usually, the web administrator configures the server to discard sessions based on a time interval since the last activity.

To the servlet programmer, a session is an object provided by the server and accessible through the **HttpServletRequest** object. You can access or create a session for a client by calling the **HttpServletRequest.getSession** method. This method is overloaded to have one optional argument of type **boolean**. If you call the no-argument version or supply a value of **true**, the server gives you the session for this client, if there is one, and creates a new session object otherwise. Specify **false** to get an existing session without giving the server permission to create a new one. If called with **false** when no session exists, **getSession** returns **null**.

A **Session** object contains a collection of name–value pairs. The name is a **String** identifying a value of an object of type **Object**. When you add objects to the session, you supply the object reference and a name as a **String**. To retrieve the object, ask for it by name. One very important proviso: The objects in a session must be serializable. You may want to review the discussion of object serialization in Chapter 8. Save any information that your servlet

**17**

knows and that might be useful to other servlets in the **Session** object. Other servlets run by the same client can then get the information from the **Session** object.

*Interface*

**javax.servlet.http.HttpSession**

*Purpose*

The **HttpSession** interface defines the methods a servlet can use to manipulate a session object for the purpose of maintaining state information that spans a series of HTTP requests and responses.

*Methods*

➤ **long getCreationTime( )**
  **long getLastAccessedTime( )**
  **long getMaxInactiveInterval( )**
  **set MaxInactiveInterval( int** *interval* **)**
  The first two of these methods tell you when the session was created or last used, in milliseconds, since January 1, 1970. You can programmatically control how long the server must keep an inactive session using the accessor and mutator methods for the maximum inactive interval, in seconds.

➤ **String getId( )**
  The **getId()** method returns the identifier assigned to this session. The return value is a unique value generated by the server.

➤ **String[] getValueNames( )**
  **Object getValue( String** *name* **)**
  **void putValue( String** *name*, **Object** *value*)
  **Object removeValue( String** *name* **)**
  The primary role of a session is to hold information as name-value pairs. You can add any serializable object to a session by calling **putValue**. Also, you can ask a session what named values it holds by calling **getValueNames**. To retrieve individual objects, call **getValue** and supply the name. You also can remove objects from the session.

➤ **void invalidate( )**
  You do not have to wait for a session to time out and be destroyed by the server. Instead, you can tell the server to invalidate a session by calling **invalidate**.

➤ **boolean isNew( )**
  If you need to know whether the client has just joined the session, call **isNew**. Until the session id has been sent to the client and returned in a subsequent request, the session is new.

Now it is time to look at more of the `LoginServlet` from the ski club web site. A member of the ski club usually visits the log in page only once because the site has no links to the log in form from other pages. However, a member may have an existing session object by returning to the log in page using the browser's **Back** button or by revisiting the ski club's web site before the previous session times out. The `LoginServlet.doPost` method first checks for an existing session and invalidates the session if it finds one, so that every log in starts a fresh conversation with the client:

```
HttpSession session = req.getSession( false );
if ( session != null ) {
   session.invalidate();
}
```

Later, after the member has logged in, the `LoginServlet.`**doPost** instantiates a session object and adds information about the member to the session. The member data is encapsulated in a `ClubMember` object skier. The method `confirmLogin` is called by **doPost** to send confirmation back to the member.

```
public void confirmLogin( HttpServletRequest req,
   HttpServletResponse res, ClubMember skier )
   throws IOException
{
   try {
      HttpSession session = req.getSession( true );
      session.putValue( "member", skier );
      RequestDispatcher rd = getServletContext().
         getRequestDispatcher(
         "/skiclub/MemberHome.jsp");
      rd.forward( req, res );
   } catch ( Exception e ) {
      SkiClubUtils.sendErrorPage( req, res, e );
   }
}
```

You may lose a session in the middle of a conversation. This can happen if the server invalidates a session because it has timed out or a servlet explicitly invalidates a session. You can never predict whether you will lose a session before the client next visits your site. Therefore, you should design all conversations so that each request-response could be the last exchange in the conversation. For example, if your servlets update a database, consider committing all changes when you send the HTTP response and at least make sure the database is in a consistent state.

Adding an object to a session binds the object to the session. Conversely, removing an object from the session unbinds it. When the session is invalidated,

**17**

all its objects are unbound. The servlet API provides an event and listener mechanism in the **HttpSessionBindingEvent** class and the **HttpSessionBindingListener** interface for monitoring the binding and unbinding of objects to and from sessions. Usually, you need to use this mechanism only in the following situations:

➤ You need to provide a recovery mechanism for the loss of a session.

➤ The objects that servlets may add to a session must track how they are used.

You can make objects sensitive to binding events by defining the class that the objects instantiate to implement **HttpSessionBindingListener.** Provide implementations for the two methods defined in this interface: **valueBound** and **valueUnBound**. The session context generates **HttpSessionBindingEvents** when the object is added to or removed from the session and notifies the object by calling **valueBound** or **valueUnBound**, passing the **HttpSessionBindingEvent** as the argument of the method.

How do sessions provide continuity during stateless HTTP request-and-response sequences? Do the web server and web browser pass the **Session** object back and forth? The answer is an emphatic "no." Sessions reside on the server. Instead, an identifying key passes between server and client using a web technology that predates Java: cookies. If the client has a session, the server automatically adds a cookie containing the session ID to the response generated by the servlet. The mechanism is secure because no client-specific data is sent except the session ID; that is, a computer-generated identifier with no meaning to human readers. When subsequent servlets asks for the **Session** object for this client, the server uses the cookie to identify and supply the correct session.

> **Mini Quiz 17-2**
>
> Why must **Session** objects, and therefore all the objects stored in sessions, be serializable?

## Providing Continuity with Cookies

Web browsers have supported cookies for several years, and the cookie mechanism is used extensively by CGI programs. The developers of the servlet API incorporated the de facto industry standard for cookies into the servlet specification. A cookie is a name-value pair that is included in an HTTP header. Both the name and value are strings. Browsers store cookies locally and tag each cookie with the domain name or IP address that sent the cookie. Every time the browser sends a request, it includes all cookies stored for that domain. In other words, if several servlets in your web send cookies, each servlet gets back all the cookies from all the servlets. But no other site ever gets the cookies that originated on your site. You can specify how long a browser should retain a cookie by calling **Cookie.setMaxAge**, specifying the number of seconds after which the cookie will expire.

Sessions provide state data only as long as the client is actively navigating through your web site. What if you want to store information one day so that it is available when the client returns to your site a day or a month later? You can program cookies explicitly. First, consider that the data you send to the client may not be secure and that cookies are limited in size. However, cookies provide a handy way to store information such as customer preferences. For example, your welcome servlet can interrogate the cookie and then redirect the request to a page written in the client's native language. All cookies are stored as name-value pairs, for example, `"language"="Français"`.

To send a cookie, call the **HttpServletResponse.addCookie** method supplying a **Cookie** object. To receive cookies, call the **HttpServletRequest.getCookies** method. This method has no arguments but returns an array of **Cookie** objects.

---

*Class*

**javax.servlet.http.Cookie**

---

*Purpose*

Instances of the **Cookie** class represent the objects known to web browsers and servers as cookies. The class provides a number of methods that give information about the cookie as a whole as well as the methods listed here to get and set the name, value, comment, or lifetime of a cookie.

---

*Constructor*

➤ **Cookie( String** *name*, **String** *value* **)**
The cookie class has no default constructor. You must supply a name and a value when you create the cookie.

---

*Methods*

➤ **String getComment( )**
**void setComment( String** *value***)**
You can attach a descriptive comment to a cookie. The **getComment** method returns the comment for a cookie or **null** if it has no comment. The **setComment** method adds a comment or changes an existing comment.

➤ **String getName( )**
The **getName** method returns the name of this cookie. Note that you can change the value, but not the name, of a cookie.

**17**

➤ **String getValue( )**
**void setValue( String** *value* **)**
The **getValue** method returns the value of a cookie, and the **setValue** method assigns a value to an existing cookie.

➤ **int getMaxAge( )**
**void setMaxAge( int** *expiry* **)**
The **setMaxAge** method tells the browser how long to keep a cookie. A negative number means that the cookie lives only as long as the browser runs. A positive number is the number of seconds the browser must keep the cookie. Specify a positive number to make the cookie persistent on the client machine for the specified time. An input value of zero tells the browser to delete the cookie immediately. The **getMaxAge** method returns the positive or negative age assigned to a cookie. It never returns zero because such a cookie must have been deleted.

In the sample ski club web, new members join the club by running the `RegistrationServlet` class. This servlet is similar in structure to the `LoginServlet` except that it reads more data from the input form and uses the data to add a new member to the database, rather than extracting information about an existing member. The `RegistrationServlet.`**doPost** method calls the `confirmRegistration` method that is listed after this paragraph. The `confirmRegistation` method adds a cookie to the HTTP response to indicate that this member is new to the club, adds the member data to the **Session** object, and redirects the member to a confirmation page.

```
public void confirmRegistration(
    HttpServletRequest req, HttpServletResponse res,
    ClubMember skier )
    throws IOException
{
    try {
        HttpSession session = req.getSession( true );
        session.putValue( "member", skier );
        res.addCookie(
            new Cookie( "NewMember", "yes" ) );
        RequestDispatcher rd = getServletContext().
        getRequestDispatcher(
            "/skiclub/newMember.jsp" );
        rd.forward( req, res );
    } catch ( Exception e ) {
        SkiClubUtils.sendErrorPage( req, res, e );
    }
}
```

The cookie named NewMember is used by the servlet that lets members book ski trips. The first time a member books trips, the BookingServlet outputs some descriptive sentences. On subsequent visits to the BookingServlet, these sentences do not appear. The BookingServlet.**doGet** method inserts the extra sentences into the top of its response page when it executes the following lines:

```
Cookie[] cookies = req.getCookies();
for( int i = 0; i < cookies.length; i ++ ) {
    if( cookies[i].getName().equals("NewMember")
        && cookies[i].getValue().equals("yes") ) {
        res.addCookie(
        new Cookie( "NewMember", "no" ) );
      out.println( "<p>" +
        // paragraph containing descriptive
        // sentences are here in the code
        "</p>" );
      break;
    }
}
```

To see what the descriptive sentences say, run the ski club web site, register, and then select to book ski trips. Note that the descriptive sentences appear only the first time you run the **BookingServlet,** regardless of whether you first book trips during your initial visit to the ski club web site or a subsequent visit. Adding the **NewMember** cookie again, this time with the value **"no"**, overrides the value **"yes"**.

With the API, you can put any information you want into a cookie, but you should never put in sensitive information that compromises the security of conversations with your clients. People with expertise and tools have little trouble intercepting and decoding Internet communications. As a result, many web users are uncomfortable with cookies. Some are simply misguided and fear that cookies may give remote programs access to their local file system or provide information that is securely stored in a session on the server. Other web users have justified concerns about scripts or servlets including sensitive or inappropriate information in cookies. Imagine a possibly unencrypted HTTP header containing your credit card account number, user id, password, or other private information in a cookie being sent back and forth over the public communication line! Hopefully, cookies will be more widely accepted as servlet programmers use them more wisely.

## URL Rewriting

Most browsers let users disable cookies, and you may have to make provisions for users who turn cookies off. There is an alternative way to send a cookie: **URL rewriting.** This approach uses the same technique that HTML forms use to send parameters to CGI scripts: The cookie data is appended to the URL. You should use URL rewriting only as a fallback for browsers that do not support

**17**

cookies. Before each of your servlets returns the response to the client, ask the server to encode the session ID and other cookies in every local URL that is contained in the response: by calling **HttpServletResponse.encodeURL** or **HttpServletResponse.encodeRedirectURL**. Pass the URL as a **String** in the argument and receive the resulting URL as a **String** as the return value. Both methods check whether the client supports cookies and returns the unaltered URL if rewriting is not necessary. Use **encodeRedirectURL** when you are redirecting the request and response to another resource and **encodeURL** when replying directly to the client.

Two methods of the **HttpServletResponse** class that perform URL rewriting have been changed in version 2 of the Servlet API. The older versions remain part of the API but are deprecated. You should call **encodeURL** and not **encodeURL** or **encodeRedirectURL** and not **encodeRedirectURL**.

# GUIDELINES FOR SERVLET-DRIVEN WEBS

There are additional factors that you should take into consideration when you start to build a servlet-driven web site. Some factors relate to programming techniques, and others are design principals. The five most important issues—multithreading, combining servlets and applets, MVC design, browser caching, and security—are discussed in the following sections.

## Program Servlets for Multithreading

When the web server loads a servlet class—either at startup time or the first time the servlet is called by a client—it instantiates one instance of the class. By default, the server creates a new thread for every client request and runs the called servlet's **service** method on a separate thread for each client. Therefore, only one instance of the servlet exists, but several different threads may be sharing that instance at any particular time. As a result, servlets should be designed for multithreaded use.

Be sure you understand the multithreading concepts explained in Chapter 11 and program your servlets to allow mulithreaded use. In practical programming terms, it means that you do not have to provide a **run** method because that method is provided by the server-generated **Thread** object and is the method that calls your servlet. Methods **wait**, **notify**, and **notifyAll** generally are not relevant because the different client threads should not be aware of each other, and inter-thread communication is not an issue. The important issue is thread safety of variables. You do not want the threads to interfere with each other by altering variables used by one another.

Generally, you can achieve thread safety by following some guidelines:

▶ Do not use fields of the servlet class as working storage. The threads share the same instance variables. Therefore, all active clients share instance variables much like they share class variables of the servlet class.

▶ Use **Session** objects rather than fields to store state data. Each client has a separate session, so session data is thread-safe.

▶ Local variables are thread-safe because the JVM maintains a separate stack frame for each thread.

▶ Declare methods that should run for only one client at a time to be **synchronized**. For example, `ClubMember.store` method in the ski club web is synchronized. `ClubMember.store` is called by the register servlet when a new member registers, and it assigns an id to the member. To calculate the next id, it asks the database for the last id used and adds one. If this method was not synchronized, two members might simultaneously receive the same id.

---

**Mini Quiz 17-3**

If a method of a servlet class or method called by a servlet creates an object using the **new** keyword, is that object thread-safe?

---

If you must use instance variables, or for some reason cannot make your servlets thread-safe, declare them to implement the **SingleThreadModel** interface. The web server does create a separate instance of **SingleThreadModel** servlets for every client. The resulting overhead may degrade the performance, especially if the servlet is in high demand, so use the **SingleThreadModel** only when necessary.

## Use Applets Judiciously

One of the desirable results of creating dynamic content on the server in servlets rather than on the client in applets is that overhead on the client is reduced. Download time is less if you do not have to send applets and supporting JAR files to the client JVM, and demands on the client's processor are decreased. In client-server jargon, you can create very **thin clients**. In contrast, you create **fat clients** when you distribute much of the processing to clients. Thin clients improve the performance of your web, especially for clients who may have little local processing power. If you eliminate applets altogether, the user does not even need a Java-enabled browser!

Applets or JavaScript can still play a key role in your web, and there is no suggestion that they are inherently undesirable. Some kinds of processing must be

**17**

done on the client. Animation, and any display effects that cannot be coded in HTML, fall into this category. Sometimes, adding a little fat to clients saves transmission time and aggravation. Input validation that does not require database lookup can fall into this category as well. For example, it may be better to program a form as an applet so that you can check that the telephone number is all digits and do similar first-pass checking before submitting the result, than to require a sequence of HTML requests and responses.

A servlet can write an HTML document that includes any valid HTML, including **<APPLET>** and **<SCRIPT>** tags. **<APPLET>** tags are described in Chapter 14. **<SCRIPT>** tags run scripts that are written in the JavaScript language and embedded in the HTML page. The servlet can pass parameters to an applet by including **<PARAM>** tags. Of course, an applet called in an HTML page generated by a servlet can do anything applets in any web page can do, including opening a TCP/IP connection to perform two-way communication with the server and use RMI. As a rule of thumb, if your web is destined for the Internet, a thin client is preferable.

## Apply the MVC Design Pattern

When deciding how to distribute processing tasks through your web and supporting classes, apply the Model-View-Controller (MVC) design principals introduced in Chapter 12. The rule of thumb is that the client side should be concerned only with the view, including the user interface and all display processing such as multimedia. The model is the core of the application, usually the business logic and classes that model the real-world problem. The model should be contained in a set of server-side classes apart from the servlet classes. Database managers and connectors to legacy systems may form another layer of classes behind the model.

So where do the servlets fit in? Servlets naturally become the controller. Consider the job of servlets to that of a broker for client requests. The servlet receives client input, calls methods in the model layer, and prepares the response. A breakdown of MVC occurs when the servlet generates HTML because displaying the response to the client request should be delegated to the view layer. In the next section, you see that JSPs can allow truer implementation of MVC principals.

## Be Wary of the Browser Back Button

You may design a web that is easy to navigate and lets users reach only pages that are appropriate from any particular page, only to be undermined by the **Back** button. Consider what happens when a shopper in a virtual store visits the shirt department and puts a shirt in the shopping cart. Then the shopper visits the shoe department and adds a pair of shoes to the shopping cart. The shopper then presses the **Back** button to look for another shirt. Should the shoes disappear from the shopping cart?

The problem is that browsers support the **Back** feature by caching pages and redisplaying the cached pages. You cannot turn off the browser's **Back** button. However, you can tell the browser not to cache a page, by including **<META>** tags in the HTML response header. Different browsers understand different meta tags, so you usually have to provide a number of them. Here is the start of an HTML page that tells Netscape, Internet Explorer, and some other browsers not to cache this page:

```
<HTML>
<HEAD>
<META NAME="Pragma" CONTENT="no-cache">
<META NAME="Cache-Control" CONTENT="no-cache">
<META NAME="Expires" CONTENT="0">
</HEAD>
```

What actually happens when the user presses the **Back** button? If the previous page is in the cache, the browser displays it. If the page is not in the cache, the browser refreshes it from its URL. This is exactly what you want to happen when the page is the output of an HTTP **GET** request. If the request is directed to a servlet, the servlet runs again and generates the page to reflect the current state of the user's session. If the page were the output of an HTTP **Post** method, the browser cannot retrieve the data that accompanied the POST request and prints a message saying the page cannot be displayed. This behavior may not be the ideal, but it is better than displaying an outdated page.

Generally, you should turn off caching for all pages that contain dynamic content.

## Security

Security can be of paramount importance, especially for an Internet site that is accessible by the general public. Consider these facets of web security:

➤ **Authentication**: Who is the client? The most common way to confirm the client's identity is to issue a user id and password challenge.

➤ **Authorization**: What is this client allowed to do? You can let some clients perform a limited set of activities. For example, anyone can shop at your store. Other clients can do more — an employee can get a list of customers.

➤ **Data Integrity**: Has the data been corrupted during transmission? Is the data encrypted to ensure privacy?

➤ **Accountability**: Is there a log of transmissions in case you need to trace the history of a transaction?

**17**

The good news is that the web server, not the servlet programmer, handles most of these concerns. Commercial web servers provide a basic functionality for security and boast of many additional security-related features. With these features, these servers often provide API so that you can bring security under program control. Often, setting up security options of the web server is a job for the server administrator. Most web servers support the following features and much more:

➤ **Basic Authentication**: In basic authentication, the browser and server cooperate. When the server receives an HTTP request, it sends back to the browser a command to issue a standard password challenge. The browser pops up a window prompting the user for a user id and password and sends the user input back to the server. The server checks the user id and password and then either proceeds with the request or returns a security error code to the browser.

➤ **Data Encryption**: The bytes transferred can be subject to 64- or 128-bit encryption to protect the data while it is being transferred. However, 64-bit encryption is not very secure because decoding packages are widely available.

➤ **HTTPS protocol**: HTTPS is a combination of HTTP and the Secure Socket Layer (SSL). SSL is based on digital certificates. Usually certificate authorities, such as VeriSign, AT&T, and some other organizations, issue certificates. The certificates pass between server and client and contain keys required to decode encrypted messages.

# JAVA SERVER PAGES

JSPs provide a way to write dynamic web pages as HTML documents, rather than as output from a servlet. Essentially, a JSP is an HTML document with embedded Java code. A file that contains a JSP must have the extension .jsp. To use JSPs, you need a web server that supports JSPs as well as servlets. Suitable proprietary servers are becoming available. IBM's WebSphere Application Server supports servlets and JSPs, and VisualAge for Java has a test environment for WebSphere so you can debug servlets and monitor JSPs in the VisualAge IDE. The JVM in servers that support JSPs includes the package **javax.servlet.jsp.** You do not use the types defined in this package directly; the server uses them to process JSPs.

To deploy a JSP in a web, put it in the same folder as the HTML documents in that web. Unlike an applet that is downloaded and run on the client, a JSP is preprocessed on the server before the page is served to the client. The Java inserts are enclosed in tags such as those listed in Figure 17-5. Output from the Java inserts replaces the JSP tagging in the resultant HTML page. A JSP serves the same purpose as a servlet: to produce HTML pages with dynamic content. Everything you can do with a servlet, you can do with a JSP, and everything you can do with a JSP, you can do with a servlet. Why, then, would you use JSPs? They help solve the following problems that are inherent to servlets:

➤ Calling print methods to write HTML is clumsy. You cannot use HTML editors and must write a large volume of tedious code. Using templates for the HTML content is difficult and the HTML content is hard to maintain. For example, it takes a programmer to correct a spelling mistake in the HTML output. A JSP is written in HTML so you can use your favorite HTML authoring tools to create at least the static portions of the page.

➤ Developing a large web site requires a team of people with a variety of skills. Programmers, graphic designers, HTML authors, user-interface designers, and others may be involved. When programmers write servlets, they start doing the jobs of HTML authors and all the others who have a hand in designing web pages. This may be a misuse of human resources and prove to be an expensive way to produce content for a web site. Using a JSP gives the job of designing and writing web pages back to the people whose primary skill is in web development rather than programming.

➤ Using JSPs can provide much cleaner implementation of MVC design than servlets allow. The JSP and HTML pages become the view layer, the logic layer behind the scenes remains as always the model, and servlets can continue to be the controller. You can achieve this by using servlets to receive HTTP requests, determine what action to take and perhaps call methods of the business or model layer, and then call HTML pages or JSPs to produce the HTTP response.

In short, JSPs let you write your HTML in HTML rather than in Java. Nevertheless, you have to know some Java to write a JSP, because the inserts that create dynamic content are snippets of Java code. The JSP tags that enclose the Java inserts follow the syntax of HTML tags. They start with **<%** and end with **%>** and are summarized in Table 17-5. Use them like an extension to HTML.

Here is a JSP page that gives exactly the same output as the `TodayServlet` from earlier in this chapter. The JSP tagging is shown in bold:

```
<html>
<head>
<META NAME="Pragma" CONTENT="no-cache">
<META NAME="Cache-Control" CONTENT="no-cache">
<META NAME="Expires" CONTENT="0">
<title>Today</title>
</head>
<%@ page import="java.util.*" %>
<body >
<H1> The current date and time is:</h1>
<p> <%= new Date( ) %> </p>
</body>
</html>
```

**17**

**Table 17-5**   JSP tags for Java code

| JSP element | Description | Examples |
|---|---|---|
| `<%@ page`<br>`attribute=value`<br>`... %>` | Directive:<br>Defines attributes of the page, such as packages to import and whether page participates uses an HttpSession object. | `<%@ page info=`<br>`  "An example JSP" %>`<br>`<%@ page import=`<br>`  "skiclub.*" %>`<br>`<%@ page lang="java`<br>`  session="true" %>` |
| `<%@ include`<br>`file=`<br>`"relativeURL" %>` | Directive:<br>Substitutes text or code from specified file. | `<%@ include file=`<br>`  "banner.html" %>` |
| `<%@ taglib uri=`<br>`"uri" ...%>` | Directive:<br>Declares a library of custom tags to extend the JSP set. | `<%@taglib uri=`<br>`  "myTagLibrary" %>` |
| `<%! ... %>` | Declaration:<br>Declares a variable for use in this JSP. | `<%! Double intRate=`<br>`  2.32 ; %>`<br>`<%! skier = new`<br>`  ClubMember(); %>`<br>`<%! Vector v =`<br>`  new Vector(); %>` |
| `<%= ... %>` | Expression:<br>Inserts value of the Java expression into page. | `<% skier.getName()%>`<br>`<% Math.sqrt`<br>`  ( a * a + b * b) %>`<br>`<% (int)`<br>`  session.getValue(`<br>`        "id" ) %>` |
| `<% ... %>` | Scriptlet:<br>Execute enclosed Java code. | `<% // items is declared`<br>`  // and holds data`<br>`  for ( int m=0;`<br>`       m< items.length;`<br>`       m++ ) {`<br>`     System.out.println(`<br>`       "Item: " +`<br>`     items[m].getName( )`<br>`        );`<br>`  }`<br>`%>` |

For a convincing argument for using JSP instead of servlets, compare this listing to the `TodayServlet`. Only two lines are not standard HTML: The first makes all classes in the package **java.util** available for the rest of the page. The second is an expression with a value of the current date. The value returned by calling **toString** on this **Date** object is printed in the page in place of this expression:

```
<%@ page import="java.util.*" %>
...
<p> <%= new Date( ) %> </p>
```

To call a JSP, you give the URL to the browser, just as you would to request any HTML page. The only difference is that the extension is .jsp, not .htm or .html. Like any HTML page or servlet, it can be called directly by the user, by a hyperlink in an HTML document, or by a servlet. For example, to run the today JSP, enter the following URL in your browser:

```
http://localhost:8080/today.jsp
```

The output looks like Figure 17-2.

 Java Server Pages are a new technology. They are so new that the specification is still evolving. This discussion is based on the JSP 1.0 specification but a draft of 1.1 specification is available for public review. A goal of ongoing development is to make JSP tags more accessible to non-Java programmers by introducing a syntax that depends less on knowledge of Java. Some of the tags have changed between releases and may still be subject to change.

## How the Server Processes JSPs

The Server recognizes a JSP by its file extension and calls a process called **page compile** to convert it into a servlet. The process creates a servlet class, builds a **service** method from the contents of the .jsp file, and then compiles the servlet. It generates pure Java for JSP declarations and definitions. All straight HTML is wrapped in calls to **print** or **output** methods. Java scriptlets and expressions are left alone, except that the surrounding **<%** or **<%=** and **%>** are stripped off. These elements are added to the **service** method in the order in which they appear in the JSP, and then the server runs the servlet. The servlet, like all servlets, must create an HTTP response, and the server sends the page to the client.

Unlike ordinary servlets, the servlet generated from JSPs cannot be preloaded. The JSP must be compiled when it is first called. If you change the .jsp file between calls, the server reads the source, page-compiles, loads, and runs it again. After it is loaded, the JSP remains in the JVM on the server until its source is changed again, the JSP is destroyed, or the server process stops. Therefore, the overhead of page compile usually happens only the first time the servlet is used, and the life cycle of a JSP-generated servlet is different in that way only from the life cycle of an ordinary servlet.

Combining JSPs and servlets in a web can be very effective. Figure 17-7 shows how servlets, JSPs, browsers, and supporting classes the server can relate to each other. The numbers in Figure 17-7 correspond to the following numbered steps:

1. Usually, the interaction starts with the client entering the URL of a servlet, clicking a hyperlink to a servlet, or submitting a form.

**17**

2. The browser submits an HTTP request with a **GET** or **POST** method.

3. The server runs the servlet, calling the **service** method. In an ordinary servlet, the default **service** method often passes the request and response on to the **doGet** or **doPost** method. The servlet may process the input from a form, manipulate session data, retrieve data from databases, decide to redirect the output to an error page, or complete other processing required to prepare to answer.

4. Then the servlet can redirect the HTTP request and response to the JSP.

5. If necessary, the page-compile process converts the JSP to a servlet and page-compiles it. Then, the server loads and runs the JSP-generated servlet, calling the **service** method.

6. The HTML page produced by the JSP-generated servlet is returned to the client's browser.

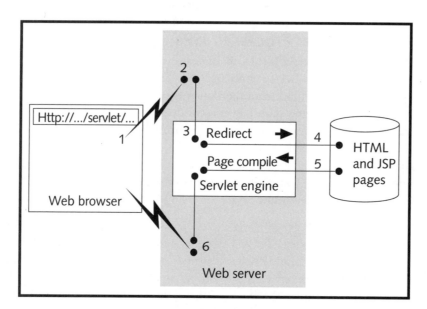

**Figure 17-7** The interaction between servlets and JSPs

## Programming Java in JSPs

Unlike the `Today` JSP, most JSPs do not stand on their own. They usually are responsible for producing the dynamic pages in a web. How do you pass information between your servlets and your JSPs? Scriptlets and Java expressions in JSPs can access all classes loaded in the server JVM. Also, the server makes the objects listed in Table 17-6 available to the JSP. The obvious way to pass information between servlets and JSPs is in the **Session** object.

**Table 17-6**   Implicit objects in JSPs

| Variable name | Type | Description |
|---|---|---|
| request | javax.servlet.http. HttpServletRequest | The HTTP request originally sent to the server. |
| response | javax.servlet.http. HttpServletResponse | The HTTP response to the request. |
| pageContext | javax.servet.jsp. PageContext | An object encapsulating the context for this page. |
| session | javax.servlet.http. HttpSession | The **Session** object associated with the request and response. |
| application | javax.servlet. ServletContext | The object returned by **getServletConfig().getContext().** |
| out | javax.servlet.jsp. JspWriter | An object that writes to the response output stream. |
| config | javax.servlet. ServletConfig | The **ServletConfig** object for this JSP. |
| page | java.lang.Object | The **this** object reference in this JSP. |

You can use the objects listed in Table 18-6 without declaring them. The sample ski club web contains JSPs. When a new member registers with the ski club, the registration servlets set up a session and then redirect the HTTP request and response to the page shown with sample data in Figure 17-8. This page is generated by a JSP stored at the URL skiclub/newMember.jsp. The source for this page is not shown here because you can see all the JSP tags it demonstrates in a page that is dissected later in this chapter.

JSPs can call servlets through ordinary HTML hyperlinks. The option **Update your registration information** that you see in Figure 17-8 is a link to the URL /servlet/skiclub/UpdateServlet. The **UpdateServlet** has **doGet** and **doPost** methods. The **doGet** method checks that the member has a session and throws an exception if the HTTP request has no session. Otherwise, it forwards the HTML request to the JSP with the URL skiclub/update.jsp. This JSP displays the member's session data in a form suitable for editing. Listings of the **UpdateServlet.doGet** method and then **update.jsp** file follow Figure 17-8. The **doPost** method of the **skiclub.UpdateServlet** class processes the data the user enters on the form.

**17**

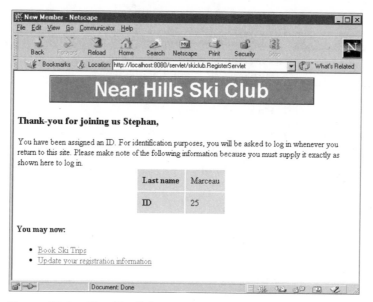

**Figure 17-8** The Ski Club new member confirmation page

Below is the **doGet** method for the `UpdateServlet` class. It contains no features that have not already been described in this chapter.

```
// extract from public class UpdateServlet
   public void doGet( HttpServletRequest req,
                      HttpServletResponse res)
     throws IOException, ServletException
   {
     try {
       HttpSession session = req.getSession(false);
       if ( session == null ) {
          throw new NoSessionException(
            "No session: " +
            "have you registered or Logged in?" );
       }
       RequestDispatcher rd = getServletContext().
          getRequestDispatcher("/skiclub/Update.jsp");
       rd.forward( req, res );
     } catch ( noSessionException e ) {
       SkiClubUtils.sendErrorPage( req, res, e );
     }
   }
```

---

**Mini Quiz 17-4**

List three ways a user can call the `UpdateServlet` servlet without first creating a session. Try to do it yourself using the Near Hills Ski Club example web.

The page that displays registration information is an HTML form so that the user can modify the data that is stored in the ski club database. Figure 17-9 shows sample output of this JSP.

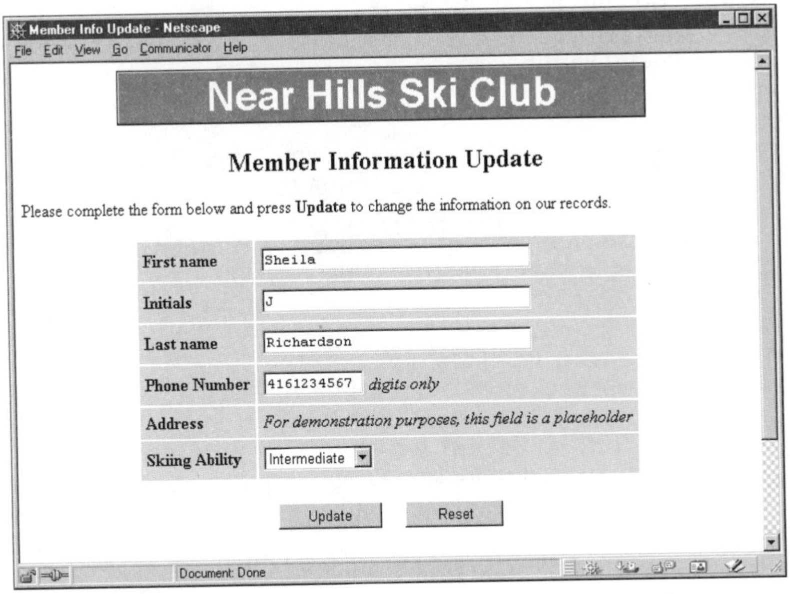

**Figure 17-9** Sample output from the ski club update JSP

Here is a listing of the update JSP with the JSP tags in bold. A breakdown of the code follows the listing:

```
<HTML>
<HEAD>
<META NAME="Pragma" CONTENT="no-cache">
<META NAME="Cache-Control" CONTENT="no-cache">
<META NAME="Expires" CONTENT="0">
<TITLE>Member Info Update</TITLE>
</HEAD>
<%@ page import="skiclub.*" %>
<BODY  BGCOLOR="#FFFFFF" LINK="#0000FF" VLINK="#990099" >
<CENTER>
<IMG  SRC="/skiclub/images/SkiClub.gif"
    ALT="Near Hills Ski Club " >
<h2>Member Information Update</H2>
</CENTER>
<p>Please complete the form below and press
    <strong>Update</strong> to change
    the information on our records.
</p>
<CENTER>
<FORM METHOD=POST ACTION=
    "http://localhost:8080/servlet/skiclub.UpdateServlet">
```

17

```
<TABLE BORDER=0 BGCOLOR="#DDDDFF" CELLPADDING=5 >
<TR>
<TD><strong>First name</strong></TD>
<TD><INPUT TYPE="text" NAME="FNAME"
    VALUE="<%= ( (ClubMember)
        session.getValue( "member" ) ).getFirstName() %>"
     SIZE=30 MAXLENGTH=30 > </TD>
</TR>
<TR>
<TD><strong>Initials</strong></TD>
<TD><INPUT TYPE="text" NAME="MNAME"
    VALUE="<%= ( (ClubMember)
        session.getValue( "member" ) ).getMiddleName() %>"
     SIZE=30 MAXLENGTH=30 > </TD>
</TR>
<TR>
<TD><strong>Last name</strong></TD>
<TD><INPUT TYPE="text" NAME="LNAME"
    VALUE="<%= ( (ClubMember)
        session.getValue( "member" ) ).getLastName() %>"
     SIZE=30 MAXLENGTH=30 > </TD>
</TR>
<TR>
<TD><strong>Phone Number</strong></TD>
</TD>
<TD><INPUT TYPE="text" NAME="PHONE"
    VALUE="<%= ( (ClubMember)
        session.getValue( "member" ) ).getPhoneNumber() %>"

     SIZE=10 MAXLENGTH=10 >
      <em>digits only</em>
</TD>
</TR>
<TR>
<TD><strong>Address</strong></TD>
<TD><em>For demonstration purposes,
     this field is a placeholder</em></TD>
</TR>
<TR>
<TD><strong>Skiing Ability</strong></TD>
<TD>
<%! String[] levels = { "Novice",
                        "Intermediate",
                        "Advanced",
                        "Expert" };
%>
<% String ability = ( (ClubMember)
     session.getValue( "member" ) ).getAbility();
  out.println( "<SELECT NAME=\"ABILITY\" >" );
  for ( int i = 0; i < levels.length; i++ ) {
     out.print( "<OPTION VALUE=\"" + levels[i] + "\"");
```

```
        if ( ability.equals( levels[i] ) ) {
            out.print( " SELECTED>" );
        } else {
            out.print( ">" );
        }
        out.println( levels[i] + "</OPTION>" );
    }
    out.println("</SELECT>");
%>
</TD>
</TR>
</TABLE>
<TABLE BORDER=0 CELLSPACING=20 >
<TR>
<TD><INPUT TYPE="submit" VALUE="    Update    "></TD>
<TD><INPUT TYPE="reset"  VALUE="    Reset    " ></TD>
</TR>
</TABLE>
</CENTER>
<p>If this information is correct, you may:
<ul>
<li><a href="/servlet/skiclub.BookingServlet">
    Update ski trip bookings</a></li>
<li><a href="/skiclub/skiclub/memberHome.jsp">
    Return to your member home page</a></li>
</ul>

</FORM>

</p>
</BODY>
</HTML>
```

A large portion of this page is ordinary HTML and is not explained here. The first JSP tag is a directive that translates into a Java import statement. The Java code in this JSP can access all classes in the skiclub package using unqualified class names:

```
<%@ page import="skiclub.*" %>
```

The following lines write one row of an HTML form. The first column contains the text "First name", and the second column displays the member's first name. A JSP expression extracts the name from the session:

```
  <TR>
<TD><strong>First name</strong></TD>
<TD><INPUT TYPE="text" NAME="FNAME"
    VALUE="<%= ( (ClubMember)
        session.getValue( "member" ) ).getFirstName() %>"
    SIZE=30 MAXLENGTH=30 > </TD>
</TR>
```

The form contains rows for middle name, last name, and phone number that are similar to the row for first name and, therefore, are not repeated here. The JSP must set up an array of String objects describing ability levels before it can output the row of the table that provides the drop-down list of abilities. The following JSP declaration creates and initializes an array called `levels`:

```
<%! String[] levels = { "Novice",
                        "Intermediate",
                        "Advanced",
                        "Expert" };
%>
```

In the row for ability, a following Java scriptlet outputs the HTML **OPTION** tag and inserts the **SELECTED** attribute beside the correct option. Note that the Java code in the scriptlet writes HTML to the object **out**:

```
<% String ability = ( (ClubMember)
      session.getValue( "member" ) ).getAbility();
   out.println( "<SELECT NAME=\"ABILITY\" >" );
   for ( int i = 0; i < levels.length; i++ ) {
       out.print( "<OPTION VALUE=\"" + levels[i] + "\"");
       if ( ability.equals( levels[i] ) ) {
          out.print( " SELECTED>" );
       } else {
          out.print( ">" );
       }
       out.println( levels[i] + "</OPTION>" );
   }
   out.println("</SELECT>");
%>
```

## Applying MVC Principles Using JSPs and JavaBeans

JSPs offer an opportunity for creating a clear separation between Model-View-Controller (MVC) aspects of a web-based application. You can take advantage of JSPs to separate programming tasks from HTML authoring. For MVC, you should create classes or JavaBeans to provide the business or core application logic. Let the servlets act as controller, and delegate view functionality to HTML pages and JSPs. The ski club's update servlet is an example of this approach because it uses other classes to perform update operations on member registration information and then transfers the HTTP request and response to JPSs to generate output. One benefit of this approach is that individuals on a team creating a web can apply their different skills and use different tools designed for their specialized contributions to the overall web.

Ideally, HTML authors should be able to create JSPs without having Java programming skills, and programmers should not be responsible for writing HTML. To achieve this goal, more JSP features are required. The JSP specification is moving in that direction.

Currently, the JSP specification includes tags that let you access instances of JavaBeans and use features of those beans. These tags have a different syntax from the JSP tags you have already seen and are listed in Table 17-7. These tags begin with **<jsp** and end with **/>**. Unlike HTML tags, JSP tags are case-sensitive and follow Java conventions for upper- and lowercase.

**Table 17-7**   JSP tags for JavaBeans

| Tag and Attributes | Description |
|---|---|
| **<jsp:useBean**<br>• **"id="***name*"<br>• **scope="page"**<br>        **"request"**<br>        **"session"**<br>        **"application"**<br>• **class=** "*classname*" | Instantiates or returns an object of the class named with the CLASS attribute. The identifier for the object reference is specified by the **id** attribute. SCOPE attribute specifies that the object has one of the following scopes:<br>• **scope="page"**<br>The object is local to this JSP page. This is the default.<br>• **scope="request"**<br>The object may be obtained by calling the method **ServletRequest.getAttribute(** *name* **)** and is discarded when the request is completed.<br>• **scope="session"**<br>The object may be obtained by calling the method **HttpSession.getValue(** *name* **)** and lives as long as the session is valid.<br>• **scope="application"**<br>The object may be obtained by calling the method **ServletContext.getAttribute(** *name* **)** and is discarded when the server reclaims the servlet's context. |
| **jsp:setProperty**<br><br>**name="***beanName*"<br>**property="***propertyName*"<br>**value="***value*" | Sets the value of a property in the named beans, in one of four ways:<br>• You can name the property and supply a value in the tag. The value may be a Java expression. |
| **name="***beanName*"<br>**property="***propertyName*"<br>**param="***parameterName*" | • Name a parameter in the request to assign the value of that parameter to the property. |
| **name="***beanName*"<br>**property="***propertyName*" | • If you omit both the value and parameter name, the value of the parameter with the same name as the property is assigned to the property. |
| **name="***beanName*"<br>**property="***\****"<br>**/>** | • To read all parameters into properties with matching names specify * as the property name. |
| **<jsp:getProperty**<br>**name="***beanName*"<br>**property="***propertyName*"<br>**/>** | Returns the value of the named property in the named bean. |

**17**

When processing a **<jsp:useBean>** tag, the server first looks for an existing object. If there is none, it instantiates a new object by calling the default constructor of the class. Make sure that classes you use this way have no-argument constructors. The **<jsp:setProperty>** and **<jsp:getProperty>** tags use accessor and mutator (get and set) methods. Make sure all properties of classes that you use this way have these methods. Accessor and mutator methods and other JavaBean standards are described in Chapter 15. The beans used by JSPs do not have to conform to every part of the JavaBean specification but must at least provide a no-argument constructor and accessor and mutator methods for properties that the JSPs use.

The Near Hills Ski Club web directs members to a customized member home page after they log In. The page looks like Figure 17-10.

**Figure 17-10**  Near Hills Ski Club member home page

The member home page is produced by a JSP that uses JavaBeans. It uses the `skiclub.ClubMember` class extracted from the session object to get the member's name and a helper class called `skiclub.SkierInfo` to extract information about ski trips that the member has booked.

The next listing shows the `skiclub/memberHome.jsp` page with the JSP tags in bold. You can see that the bulk of the work to retrieve the list of trips that a member has booked is done by the `SkierInfo` bean and not by the JSP itself. This is another example of MVC because the `SkierInfo` class belongs to the model layer of this web application, and the JSP is part of the view layer. An explanation of the JSP tagging follows the listing:

```
<HTML>
<HEAD>
<META NAME="Pragma" CONTENT="no-cache">
<META NAME="Cache-Control" CONTENT="no-cache">
<META NAME="Expires" CONTENT="0">
<@ page import="skiclub.*" %>
<jsp:useBean id="tripInfo" class="skiclub.SkierInfo"
    scope="session" />
<jsp:useBean id="member" class="skiclub.ClubMember"
    scope="session" />
<% tripInfo.setId( member.getId() ); %>
<TITLE>Ski Club Member Home Page</TITLE>
</HEAD>
<BODY  BGCOLOR="#FFFFFF" LINK="#0000FF" VLINK="#990099" >
<CENTER>
<IMG  SRC="/skiclub/images/SkiClub.gif"
     ALT="Near Hills Ski Club ">
</CENTER>
<h3>Hello
<%= member.getFirstName()+ "," %>
</h3>
<CENTER>
<TABLE BORDER=0 WIDTH=300 BGCOLOR=#DDDDFF>
<TR><TD ALIGN=CENTER>
You have booked <strong>
<jsp:getProperty name="tripInfo" property="numTrips" />
</strong>trips.</p>
<PRE><STRONG>
<%= tripInfo.getTripList() %>
</STRONG></PRE>
</TR></TD></TABLE>
</CENTER>
<jsp:setProperty name="tripInfo" property="id"
    value="0" />
<p>
<strong>You may now:</strong>
<ul>
<li><a href="/servlet/skiclub.BookingServlet">
    Update ski trip bookings</a></li>
<li><a href="/servlet/skiclub.UpdateServlet">
    Update your registration information</a></li>
<li><a href="/skiclub/index.html">
    Return to Near Hills Ski Club home page</a></li>
</ul>
</p>
</BODY>
</HTML>
```

**17**

The first JSP tag in this page imports all classes from the `skiclub` package:

```
<@ page import="skiclub.*" %>
```

The member home page uses two JavaBean classes from the `skiclub` package, `ClubMember` and `SkierInfo`. Note that the **<jsp:useBean>** tag requires the fully qualified class name. The `ClubMember` class encapsulates registration data for a club member and the `SkierInfo class` provides information about trip bookings. A `SkierInfo` object called `tripInfo` is instantiated as a result of the first **<jsp:useBean>** tag because it is not available from the **Session** object. The `ClubMember` object member in the second **<jsp:useBean>** tag is retrieved from the `Session` object, as a result of the following lines:

```
<jsp:useBean id="tripInfo" class="skiclub.SkierInfo"
   scope="session" />
<jsp:useBean id="member" class="skiclub.ClubMember"
   scope="session" />
```

Because this page is interested in trips booked by the current member, it gets the member's id from the `ClubMember` bean and assigns its value to the id property in the `tripInfo` bean. You cannot nest **<jsp:getProperty>** and **<jsp:setProperty>** tags in this version of the JSP standard, so a scriptlet is required to get the member's id from the `member` bean and set the value in the `tripInfo` bean:

```
<% tripInfo.setId( member.getId() ); %>
```

In the following line, expression syntax is used to get the name of the member as a convenience for appending the comma using Java string concatenation. The current version of the JSWDK inserts a space before the comma if the comma follows the expression tag:

```
<%= member.getFirstName()+ "," %>
```

The next line uses the **<jsp:getProperty>** tag to get the `numTrips` property from the `tripInfo` object. The `tripInfo` bean finds this value by looking up the bookings for the member in the ski club's database:

```
<jsp:getProperty name="tripInfo" property="numTrips" />
```

You can call any method of a bean in an expression or scriptlet. This `SkierInfo` class is designed to support this JSP, and the `SkierInfo.getTripList` method returns a string containing the list of trips booked by the current member:

```
<%= tripInfo.getTripList() %>
```

The last line that contains JSP tagging resets the property that stores the id of the current member in the `tripInfo` object to zero. This line is required to force the list of booked trips to be updated every time this JSP runs:

```
<jsp:setProperty name="tripInfo" property="id"
   value="0" />
```

> **Mini Quiz 17-5**
>
> The SkierInfo class queries the database to get an updated list of trips booked by the current member every time this JSP runs. This approach lets the ski club web demonstrate more JSP features and database operations than a more efficient approach that returns to the database less often. How might the more efficient approach work?

You have now seen the entire Near Hills Ski Club sample web, except for error pages and the page that contains the form for booking ski trips. The trip-booking page is shown in Figure 17-11. These pages are produced with features that have already been covered in this chapter, so the source code is not listed here. Indeed, the source is rather ugly and does not conform to MVC because the pages are output by servlets rather than by JSPs.

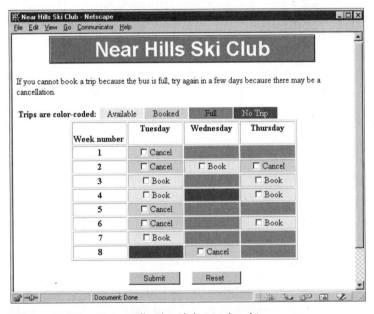

**Figure 17-11**   Near Hills Ski Club trip-booking page

## Keeping Abreast of the JSP Specification

The description of JSPs in this chapter does not cover every tag and attribute. For example, this chapter does not describe how to use the **<jsp:forward>** to redirect the HTTP request and response to another URL and how to use the **<jsp:request>** tag to access information from the server about the context of the page.

17

The set of available JSP tags is growing. The following are expected future versions of the JSP specification:

➤ Tags that support loops and let you set specify a loop counter with a start and end value. With a loop tag, you can use indexed properties of beans and perform more processing without using Java scriptlets. For example, you will be able to programmatically generate rows of a table by adding one row with each pass through the loop.

➤ An extensible tag-set feature that lets you define your own tags. In part, this feature addresses a need created by the changes in the early versions of the JSP specification. Many webs are already working to the versions .91 or .92 of the JSP specification, which became available in 1998, and several tags have changed name since then. Defining tag extensions that map the obsolete tags onto their new names may provide a migration path for these webs. Ultimately, tag extensions may let you define customized tags for elements or styles that are standards for web pages your company produces.

The format of some JSP tags, including **<jsp:useBean>**, **<jsp:setProperty>**, and **<jsp.getProperty>**, now conforms to XML grammar. Ultimately, all tags will have forms that are compatible with XML conventions, and JSPs will be valid XML documents. The eXtensible Markup Language(XML) is an emerging technology that provides a way to transfer files containing any sort of data as character files. It has great potential to become the preferred language for data transfer over the web. XML has a tagging syntax similar to HTML because both languages are derived from the Standard Generalized Markup Language (SGML). HTML provides a fixed repertoire of tags that mostly specify how to display text. XML is really a language for specifying what tags may appear in a document, what attributes the tags may have, and how tags relate to each other. Usually, XML tags describe data and relationships between data elements, rather than how to display the data. A discussion of XML is beyond the scope of this book. However, Table 17-8 lists some of the XML forms for current JSP tags.

**Table 17-8** XML forms of JSP tags

| XML Form | JSP Form |
| --- | --- |
| <jsp:directive. page ... /> | <%@page ... %> |
| <jsp:directive. include file= ... /> | <%@include file=... %> |
| <jsp:decl> ... </jsp:decl> | <%! ... %> |
| <jsp:scriptlet> ...</jsp:scriptlet> | <% ... %> |
| <jsp:expr> ... </jsp:expr> | <%= ... %> |

When you look at JSPs, notice what level of the JSP specification they use. Prior to the publication of the JSP1.0 standard, some web servers supported release .91 or .92 of the JSP specification. As a result, you may see some sample JSPs that are not old but that already contain tags that have been dropped from the standard. Some tags have been renamed. For example, the obsolete **<script>** and **</script>** tag-pair has been replaced with the **<%! ... %>** tag, the **<BEAN>** tag now has the form **<jsp:usebean>**, and the **<REPEAT>** tag for loops has temporarily disappeared.

# DATABASE CONNECTIVITY

Any Java program can use a database. Most commercial programs depend heavily on data that resides in databases. The Java 2 platform provides a set of core classes that you can use to access data in relational databases, provided you have a suitable relational database manager (RDBM) installed, and that your RDBM provides a driver you can call from the Java classes. The **Java Database Connectivity (JDBC)** API is composed of the methods defined by the interfaces and classes in the package **java.sql**.

Why does this book discuss databases in the chapter on server-side Java? The reason is that most companies install their database on a server or mainframe. Security and reliability of the database is of the utmost importance to most companies and institutions, so the database server is almost always protected from the outside world by the company's firewall. Apart from prototypes, demonstrations, and workstations set up for testing or learning purposes, Java applications rarely run on a single computer in a standalone configuration. Most distributed systems have client and server processes. The RDBM is always on the server side and often resides on the tier of a multitier architecture that is farthest removed from end users.

The use of databases is such a wide topic that a single chapter or portion of a chapter can only introduce it. The goal of this section is to show you how to program simple operations to:

➤ Retrieve rows of data from a table or a simple inner join.

➤ Insert a row into a table.

➤ Update a row in a table.

➤ Delete a row from a table.

Before reading this section, you should understand the basic concepts of RDBM systems (RDBMS). Also, you should know how to write simple Structured Query Language (SQL) statements and understand the meaning of the terms and SQL keywords listed in Table 17-9.

**17**

**Table 17-9**   Basic RDBMS and SQL terminology

| RDBMS Concepts | SQL Keywords |
| --- | --- |
| Tables | CONNECT |
| Rows or Records | DISCONNECT |
| Columns or Fields | SELECT |
| Joins | INSERT |
| Foreign keys | UPDATE |
| Primary keys | DELETE |
| Commit | FROM |
| Rollback | WHERE |
| SQL data types | AND |
| Precompiled statements | OR |
| Stored Procedures | ORDER BY |

This chapter explores the JDBC API using the Near Hills Ski Club sample web as an example. The discussion does not touch on many major concerns that affect all programs that access databases, including performance, data integrity, transactional integrity, security, stored procedures and precompiled SQL, and many SQL types (including BLOBs, CLOBs, ARRAYs, structured types, and custom data-types). For detailed discussions of these items, consult the documentation for your RDBM software. All SQL statements described in this chapter are dynamic SQL. **Dynamic SQL** consists of statements that are compiled and then run by the RDBMs as you issue them at run time.

The Ski Club example uses only simple data types, **VARCHAR** and **INTEGER**, and accepts the default mappings from SQL types to Java types. **VARCHAR** columns are mapped onto **String** objects, and the values of **INTEGER** columns are given as values of Java type **int**. You can manipulate rows that contain the full set of SQL types with the JDBC API. Table 17-10 lists the default mappings.

**Table 17-10**   Default SQL to Java type mappings

| SQL Type | Java Type |
|----------|-----------|
| CHAR | String |
| VARCHAR | String |
| LONGVARCHAR | String |
| NUMERIC | java.math.BigDecimal |
| DECIMAL | java.math.BigDecimal |
| BIT | boolean |
| TINYINT | byte |
| SMALLINT | short |
| INTEGER | int |
| BIGINT | long |
| REAL | float |
| DOUBLE | double |
| BINARY | byte[] |
| VARBINARY | byte[] |
| LONGVARBINARY | byte[] |
| DATE | java.sql.Date |
| TIME | java.sql.Time |
| TIMESTAMP | java.sql.Timestamp |

Using servlets and JDBC is just one of many possible ways to access databases from Java programs. Chapter 16 describes some other architectures for distributing applications, such as using RMI. Chapter 15 introduced a definition of Enterprise JavaBeans (EJB), and a large part of the EJB specification specifies ways EJBs can access persistent data from the EJB server. Even an applet can access a database that resides on its web server by using a database driver that supports TCP/IP connections to the database clients. You can use the JDBC API in Java applications, applets, and servlets to access a database.

None of the servlets or JSPs in the ski club web accesses the database directly. Other classes loaded on the server do that. In a layered architecture in which model, view, and controller functionality is separated, a separate persistence layer usually lies behind the model. The `skiclub` package developed for the sample web follows this layered approach. This project is so small that the persistence layer consists of one class: the `SkiClubDB` class. The classes that model the ski club operations, such as the `ClubMember`, `SkiTrip`, and

**17**

`Booking` classes, use the sample database by calling methods of the `SkiClubDB` class.

## JDBC API

Table 17-11 lists the interfaces, and Table 17-12 lists the classes in the package **java.sql**. Not all of these types are described in this chapter or used in the ski club sample database. For a full description of the JDBC API, refer to the SDK documentation or the help system that comes with your IDE.

**Table 17-11**    Interfaces defined in the java.sql package

| Interface | Description |
|---|---|
| Array | Defines the Java mapping for the SQL type **ARRAY**. |
| Blob | Defines the Java mapping for binary large objects or an SQL **BLOBs**. |
| CallableStatement | Provides the methods you call to execute stored procedures. |
| Clob | Defines the Java mapping for character large objects or SQL **CLOBs**. |
| Connection | Encapsulates a connection to the database or a database session. |
| DataBaseMetaData | Describes the database as a whole. |
| Driver | Defines the methods all database vendors must implement in their JDBC drivers. |
| PreparedStatement | Represents precompiled SQL statements. |
| Ref | Used to reference SQL structured types stored in the database. |
| ResultSet | A collection containing the results of a database query. |
| ResultSetMetaData | Provides information about the types and properties of fields in a **ResultSet**. |
| SQLData | Allows custom mappings from SQL user-defined types to Java types. |
| SQLInput | An input stream containing values for an instance of an SQL structured or distinct type. |
| SQLOutput | An output stream for writing attributes of a user-defined type to the database. |
| Statement | Provides the methods you call to execute SQL statements. |
| Struct | Defines the standard mapping of an SQL structured type. |

**Table 17-12**  Classes defined in the java.sql package

| Class | Description |
|-------|-------------|
| Date | Wraps a millisecond value so that SQL can use an instance as an SQL **DATE** value. |
| DriverManager | Gives you access to database drivers. |
| DriverPropertyInfo | Contains the property information drivers need to make a connection. |
| Time | Wraps a **java.util.Date** object so that SQL can use it as an SQL **TIME** value. |
| Timestamp | Wraps a **java.util.Date** object so that SQL can use it as an SQL **TIMESTAMP** value. |
| Types | Defines constants used to identify generic SQL types. |

The SQL package also defined exception types **BatchUpdateException**, **DataTruncation**, **SQLException**, and **SQLWarning**. JDBC methods can throw these exceptions, and most can throw **SQLException** and **SQLWarning** exceptions. You should always provide a handler for these exceptions and provide some feedback to your users to say the operation could not be completed.

The JDBC API have been available since the original Java platform but were enhanced considerably in the Java 2 platform. The following types and methods are new to Java 2: **Array**, **Blob**, **Clob**, **Ref**, **SQLData**, **SQLInput**, **SQLOutput**, **Struct**, and **BatchUpdateException**. The enhanced JDBC is known as JDBC 2. It provides support for additional data types and more flexibility than was available in JDBC 1. For example, you can navigate freely, both forward and backward, through a JDBC 2 **ResultSet** object, but a JDBC 1 **ResultSet** class provided only a forward-moving cursor.

## Loading DataBase Drivers

To access a database, you need a suitable driver. Usually, drivers are supplied by the database vendor. Drivers that consist of classes that the JDBC API can call are JDBC drivers. Some databases do not supply JDBC drivers but do have ODBC drivers. Microsoft Access is in this category.

You can access databases that have only ODBC drivers using the ODBC–JDBC bridge. The ODBC-JDBC bridge is a database driver provided by Sun Microsystems in the package **sun.jdbc.objc.JdbcOdbcDriver**. It consists of a mixture of Java code and native code connected through the **Java Native Interface (JNI)**. For an introduction to JNI, see Appendix B. Until more JDBC drivers become available, using the JDBC-ODBC bridge is considered preferable to programming directly to an ODBC driver.

**17**

There are four recognized types of drivers: 1, 2, 3, and 4. They are described in Table 17-13. Usually, you choose the driver for your RDBMS that is likely to give the best performance. Use a type 2 if possible and then try types 3 or 4 before resorting to type 1.

**Table 17-13**    Four types of database drivers

| Type of Driver | Description |
| --- | --- |
| 1 | Uses the JDBC-ODBC bridge. |
| 2 | Uses a direct connection to the database. The RDBMS or client-access support provided by the database vendor must reside on the same host as the client program. This is the most efficient driver. However, you cannot use it in a distributed environment unless all classes that operate on the database reside on the database host. The ski club example uses DB2's type 2 driver because the servlets and the RDBMS reside on the same host. |
| 3 | The client is connected to the database over a TCP/IP connection. Applets must use a type 3 or 4 driver, as must any program that does not reside on the same host as the database. Use a type 3 or 4 driver is the database client and server are on different hosts. |
| 4 | A type 4 driver is like a type 3 driver but contains only Java code. Therefore, a type 4 driver is as portable as any Java program. Only type 4 drivers are guaranteed to be pure Java. |

Usually, the database driver takes the form of classes packaged into a JAR or ZIP file. Add this file to your CLASSPATH environment variable so the JVM can find the classes when you need them.

Before you can connect to a database from a Java program, you must load the database driver into your JVM. Instead of instantiating an object of a class, use the class loader to load the driver classes. Usually, you do this with by calling the **Class.forName** method. For example, the following line loads the DB2 type 2 driver supplied by IBM with the DB2 product:

```
Class.forName( "COM.ibm.db2.jdbc.app.DB2Driver" )
```

## Establishing a Database Connection

After the driver is loaded and before you can issue SQL statements, you must connect to the database. For this, you need an object of type **Connection**.

*Interface*

**java.sql.Connection**

## Purpose

The **Connection** interface defines the behavior of the context within which you issue SQL statements and receive results.

## Methods

➤ **void close( )**
The **close** method releases the JDBC resources used by the connection. If you do not call this method explicitly, the resources are released by the JVM and the **Connection** object goes out of scope.

➤ **boolean isClosed( )**
The **isClosed** method returns **true** if this connection is closed and **false** if it is open.

➤ **void commit ( )**
**void rollback ( )**
The **commit** method makes any changes made since the last call to **commit** or rollback **permanent**. Call the **rollback** method to undo all changes since the last call to **commit** or **rollback**. These methods also release database locks held by the connection.

➤ **boolean getAutoCommit( )**
**void setAutoCommit( boolean** *autoCommit* **)**
Call the **setAutoCommit** method passing a value of **false** if you do not want changes to be committed to the database until you call the **commit** method. This gives you the opportunity to back out changes with the **rollback** method and is a good idea if a single transaction requires more than one database query. Call **setAutoCommit** passing **true** to turn autocommit on. To find out the current setting, call **getAutoCommit**.

➤ **void createStatement( )**
**void createStatement( int** *resultsetType*, **int** *resultSetConcurrency* **)**
The **createStatement** method instantiates a **Statement** object to contain the SQL statement. Java 2 adds an overloaded version with arguments you can set to override the default type and concurrency of the result set.

➤ **void prepareCall( String** *sql* **)**
**void prepareCall( String** *sql*, **int** *resultsetType*, **int** *resultSetConcurrency* **)**
The **prepareCall** method creates a **CallableStatement** object that you can use to call stored procedures. Java 2 adds an overloaded version with arguments you can set to override the default type and concurrency of the result set.

➤ **void prepareStatement( String** *sql* **)**
**void prepareStatement( String** *sql*, **int** *resultsetType*,
       **int** *resultSetConcurrency* **)**

**17**

The **prepareCall** method creates a **PreparedStatement** object for sending parameterized SQL queries. Java 2 adds an overloaded version with arguments you can set to override the default type and concurrency of the result set.

To get a **Connection** object, call the **DriverManager.getConnection** method. By default, a **Connection** automatically commits changes when each statement is complete.

*Class*

**java.sql.DriverManager**

*Purpose*

The **DriverManager** class is a service class that manages JDBC drivers. It also can explicitly load drivers on demand.

*Methods*

➤ **Connection getConnection(String** *url* **)**
**Connection getConnection(String** *url***, Properties** *info* **)**
**Connection getConnection(String** *url***, String** *user***, String** *password* **)**
The **getConnection** method establishes a connection to the database at the given URL. The URL has the form "*protocol:subprotocol:subname*". The protocol is "jdbc". Possible subprotocols include db2, oracle, and odbc. You can specify the user id and password in a separate **Properties** object or as **String** arguments in overloaded versions of this method. If the connection fails, the method throws an **SQLException**.

The `skiclub.SkiClubDB` class has a method `getConnection` to open a database connection for the web. Because building connections and then tearing them down takes time, the sample web uses only one connection and stores it in a class variable of the `SkiClubDB` class. The methods in the `SkiClubDB` class are declared synchronized so that only one servlet thread uses the connection at a time. This approach is acceptable for demonstration purposes, but a real web is likely to use more sophisticated techniques such as connection pooling. Here is a listing of the part of the `SkiClubDB` class:

```
package skiclub;
import java.sql.*;
import java.util.*;
public class SkiClubDB {
static Connection connection = null;
    static final String dbDriver =
        "COM.ibm.db2.jdbc.app.DB2Driver";
```

```
static final String dbUrl= "jdbc:DB2:SKICLUB";
static final String dbName = "SKICLUB";
//  set dbOwer to id of user who created the database
static final String dbOwner = "USERID";
// set dbUser to any user on your Windows
static final String dbUser = "USERID";
// set dbPassword to the windows password for dbUser
static final String dbPassword = "PASSWORD";
static final String memberTable = "MEMBERS";
static final String tripTable = "SKITRIPS"
static final String bookTable = "BOOKINGS";

synchronized static Connection getConnection()
    throws DBopException {

    if ( connection == null ) {
        try {
           Class.forName( dbDriver );
         connection = DriverManager.getConnection(
             dbUrl, dbUser, dbPassword);
        } catch ( ClassNotFoundException e ) {
            throw new DBopException (
            "Cannot load database driver: for DB2, " +
            "your classpath must include " +
            "SQLLIB\\JAVA\\DB2JAVA.ZIP." );
        } catch ( SQLException e ) {
            throw new DBopException (
            "Cannot connect to database: for DB2, " +
            "check that DB2 is running and the SKICLUB "
            + "database exists." );
        }
    }
    return connection;
}
// lines omitted
}
```

The `skiclub` class stores information such as the database URL and driver, table names, and the user id and password in class variables. As a result, the various methods in the `SkiClubDB` class can refer to the class variables instead of hardcoding literal strings. For demonstration purposes, this approach is simple and adequate, but a better place to store this data is in a properties file. See the **ReadMe.html file** on the CD-ROM for instructions on modifying the fields `dbOwner`, `dbUser`, and `dbPassword` for your workstation.

The `skiclub.SkiClubDB.getConnection` method catches exceptions that may occur while the connection is being built and throws an exception of a type `skiclub.DBopException`. This type is defined in the skiclub package. The catch clauses set the message property of the `DBopException` to be

more helpful to the user than the messages in the **SQLException** or
**ClassNotFoundException** objects.

## Issuing Dynamic SQL Statements

Java code that issues any dynamic SQL statement must work through the following standard steps:

1. Get a connection to the database by calling the
   **DriverManager.getConnection** method.

2. Get a Statement object from the **Connection** object acquired in Step 1.
   Call the **Connection.createStatement** method to get an object in
   which you can execute a **SELECT**, **UPDATE**, **INSERT**, or **DELETE**
   statement.

3. Build the SQL statement in a **String**. The **String** contains the exact SQL
   you would type to a database command-line processor.

4. Call a method for the **Statement** object created in Step 2, passing the
   SQL command as its argument. The **Statement** interface provides different methods for different SQL statements.

5. Receive results as the return value of the method of the **Statement** interface.

6. Process the results and then either explicitly close the result object or let it
   be implicitly closed when you close the **Statement** object.

7. Implicitly or explicitly close the **Statement** object. Usually, you create a
   new **Statement** object for each dynamic SQL statement and then close
   the **Statement** objects after you have processed the statement's results.

8. Implicitly or explicitly close the **Connection** object.

The **Statement** interface encapsulates the behavior of dynamic SQL statements.

---

*Interface*

**java.sql.Statement**

---

*Purpose*

Use **Statement** objects to execute SQL queries and obtain results. Each
**Statement** object can have one result. If a result object exists when one of the
execute methods is called, the existing result object is closed.

---

*Methods*

➤ **void close( )**
   The **close** method explicitly releases the resources taken by the
   **Statement** object. If you do not call this method, the resources are
   released when the **Statement** object is automatically closed.

➤ **ResultSet executeQuery( String** *sql* **)**
The **executeQuery** method execute statements that return a single result
set. Use this method for **SELECT** statements. The method throws an
**SQLException** if a database access error occurs.

➤ **int executeUpdate( String** *sql* **)**
Call the **executeUpdate** method to execute **INSERT**, **UPDATE**, and
**DELETE** statements. The return value is the number of rows in the database affected by the statement. The method throws an **SQLException** if a
database access error occurs.

➤ **int getQueryTimeout( )**
**void setQueryTimeout( int** *seconds* **)**
You can specify how long the driver can wait for a query to run by calling
**setQueryTimeout**. The **getQueryTimeout** method returns the number
of seconds the driver will wait for the statement to run.

➤ **ResultSet getResultSet( )**
The **getResultSet** method returns the results of the query as a **ResultSet**
object. You should call this method only once after a statement has executed.

➤ **int getUpdateCount( )**
The **getUpdateCount** method returns results of the query as an update
count. If the query returns a **ResultSet** object, **getUpdateCount** returns
−1. You should call this method only once after a statement has executed.

➤ **int getMaxRows( )**
**void setMaxRows( int** *max* **)**
Call **setMaxRows** method to specify that any **ResultSet** should be limited to the specified number of rows. Call **getMaxRows** to see what limit
has been put on the number of rows returned.

➤ **int getMaxFieldSize( )**
**void setMaxFieldSize( int** *max* **)**
Call **setMaxFieldSize** method to limit the number of bytes in any column to the specified number of bytes. Call **getMaxFieldSize** to see how
many bytes a column may hold.

**17**

The ski club web has occasion to perform all four basic operations on the
database. An example of each follows, but not every database operation done
by the web is included here. The class `SkiClubDB` has a method for every
database query. All the methods follow the eight standard steps, so only a brief
description of each method is given.

The ski club web issues many different **SELECT** statements to extract data
from the database. Therefore, the `SkiClubDB` provides the following two
helper methods to build the **SELECT** statements in a **String** and then issue

the query. The first method, getAllColumns, can be called to retrieve all the columns of a table or a join. It has two arguments. The first argument is an array of **Strings** holding the names of the tables. The second argument is a **String** containing a condition such as **WHERE** ... and **ORDER BY**... clauses. The second method, getSelectedColumns, has an additional argument: an array containing the names of the columns. Both methods return a **ResultSet** object. The next section describes how to process a **ResultSet**:

```
synchronized static ResultSet getAllColumns(
    String[] tables, String condition )
    throws DBopException {

    String[] columns = {"*"};
    return getSelectedColumns( columns, tables,
        condition );
}


synchronized static ResultSet getSelectedColumns(
    String[] columns, String[] tables,
    String condition )
    throws DBopException
{
    String select = "SELECT ";
    try {
        Statement query = getConnection().
            createStatement();
        for ( int i = 0; i < columns.length; i++ ) {
            select += columns[i];
            select += i + 1 < columns.length ? "," : " ";
        }
        select += "FROM ";
        for ( int i =0; i < tables.length; i++ ) {
            if ( dbOwner.length() > 0 ) {
                select += dbOwner + ".";
            }
            select += i + 1 < tables.length ? "," : " ";
        }
        select += condition;
        System.out.println( select );
        return query.executeQuery( select );
    } catch ( SQLException e ) {
        throw new DBopException (
            "Cannot extract data with SQL statement:\n"
            + select );
    }
}
```

The getAllColumns method sets up a **String** array containing one element, "*", to represent all columns, and then defers to the getSelectedColumns method. The bulk of the getSelectedColumns method builds a grammatically correct **SELECT** statement from the arguments of the method. The for loops set up the list of columns and tables, inserting a comma between each column or table name and space after the last name. When the statement is complete, it is written to the console output stream for debugging purposes. Then the getSelectedColumns method executes the **SELECT** statement using the **Statement.executeQuery** method.

---

**Mini Quiz 17-6**

Does the client see the output directed to **System.out**?

---

The following is the method that adds a new member to the database. The addMember issues an **INSERT** statement using the **Statement.executeUpdate** method. The method retrieves the values to insert into the columns of the new row in the table from the object of type ClubMember that it receives as an argument:

```
synchronized static public void addMember(
        ClubMember member )
        throws SQLException, DBopException {
    int rowInserted = 0;
    Statement insert = getConnection().
        createStatement();
    String addrecord = "INSERT INTO " +
        ( dbOwner.length( ) > 0 ? dbOwner + "." : "" ) +
        memberTable + " VALUES (" + member.getId() +
        ",'" + member.getFirstName() + "','" +
        member.getMiddleName() + "','" +
        member.getLastName() + "','" +
        member.getPhoneNumber() + "','" +
        member.getAbility() + "')" ;
    System.out.println( addrecord );
    rowInserted = insert.executeUpdate(addrecord);
    if ( rowInserted != 1 ) {
        throw new DBopException(
            "Unable to add new member to database" );
    }
    return;
}
```

**17**

The return value of the **executeUpdate** method is an integer that says how many rows of the table are affected by the execution of the statement. Adding a new member to the MEMBERS table should touch only the new row, so any return value other than one from this call of **executeUpdate** indicates a problem.

The following is the method that changes the record for a member after the member updates his or her registration information. The main difference between the `addMember` method and the `updateMember` method is the content of the SQL statement. The `updateMember` method issues an UPDATE statement:

```
synchronized static public void updateMember(
     ClubMember member )
     throws SQLException, DBopException {

   Statement update =
          getConnection().createStatement();
   String changeRecord = "UPDATE " +
     ( dbOwner.length( ) > 0 ? dbOwner + "." : "" ) +
     memberTable + " SET " +
     "FNAME = '" + member.getFirstName() + "'," +
     "MNAME = '" + member.getMiddleName() + "'," +
     "LNAME = '" + member.getLastName() + "'," +
     "PHONENUM = '" + member.getPhoneNumber() + "'," +
     "ABILITY = '" + member.getAbility() + "'" +
     "WHERE ID = " + member.getId();
   System.out.println( changeRecord );
   int changed = update.executeUpdate( changeRecord );

   if ( changed < 1 ) {
      throw new DBopException(
         "No changes made to database" );
   } else if ( changed > 1 ) {
      throw new DBopException(
         "More than one member's data was affected: "
         + changed + "records changed." );
   }
   return;
}
```

The last of the four basic row operations is a **DELETE**. In the ski club application, the only time a row is deleted is when a member cancels a ski trip booking. This transaction affects two tables because the number of members booked on a trip must be updated in the SKITRIPS table and the booking record must be deleted from the BOOKINGS table. Below is the method that deletes the record from the BOOKINGS table. Another method not listed here updates the SKITRIPS table:

```
synchronized public static void dropBooking(
      Booking booking )
     throws DBopException, SQLException {
   int rowDeleted = 0;
   Statement delete = getConnection().
      createStatement();
   String addrecord = "DELETE FROM " +
      ( dbOwner.length( ) > 0 ? dbOwner + "." : "" ) +
      bookTable + " WHERE MEMBERID=" +
```

```
        booking.getMemberId() +
        " AND TRIPID=" + booking.getTripId();
    System.out.println( addrecord );
    rowDeleted = delete.executeUpdate( addrecord );
    if ( rowDeleted != 1 ) {
        throw new DBopException(
            "Problem dropping booking for trip" +
            booking.getTripId( ) );
    }
    return;
}
```

## Processing a ResultSet

The **Statement.executeQuery**, **PreparedStatement.executeQuery**, and
**Statement.getResultSet** methods return a **ResultSet** object. Use
**PreparedStatement.executeQuery** for precompiled **SELECT** statements
and **Statement.getResultSet** for stored procedures called using the
**CallableStatement** class. The **ResultSet** objects encapsulate the data
retrieved from the database. The contents of a **ResultSet** is a collection of
rows. You must call methods defined in the **ResultSet** interface to move to a
particular row and then to get individual column values from the current row.
A **ResultSet** object has a cursor that is positioned at one row in the
**ResultSet** at a time. That row is the current row or, if the database is updateable, may be the insert row. The insert row is a buffer in which you can build a
row in preparation for inserting a new record in the database.

*Interface*

**java.sql.ResultSet**

*Purpose*

The methods that extract data from the database return **ResultSet** objects. The
**ResultSet** interface defines a large number of methods. Not all of the methods that navigate through the **ResultSet** or manipulate **String** and **int** column values from the current row are listed here. The interface defines methods
to **get** and **update** column values of all the types listed in Table 17-10. The
interface also defines several constants and other methods that give additional
information about the **ResultSet**.

*Methods*

> ▶ **void close( )**
> The **close** method explicitly releases the resources taken by the **ResultSet**
> object. If you do not call this method, the resources are released when the
> **ResultSet** object is closed automatically.

**17**

➤ **void deleteRow( )**

The **deleteRow** method deletes the current row from this **ResultSet** and the database. The method throws an **SQLException** if the current row is the insert row.

➤ **void insertRow( )**

The **insertRow** method inserts the contents of the insert row into this **ResultSet** and the database. The method throws an **SQLException** if the current row is not the insert row.

➤ **void updateRow( )**

The **updateRow** method updates the database to match updates made to the current row in the **ResultSet**. The method throws an **SQLException** if a database access error occurs.

➤ **void refreshRow( )**

The **refreshRow** method sets the values in the current row to the latest values set in the database. The method throws an **SQLException** if the current row is an insert row.

➤ **void moveToInsertRow( )**
**void moveToCurrentRow( )**

Use the methods **moveToInsertRow** and **moveToCurrentRow** to switch between the insert row and the current row. The **moveToInsertRow** method records the position of the current row. The **moveToCurrentRow** method has no effect unless the cursor is on the insert row. These methods throw an **SQLException** if the database is not updateable.

➤ **int findColumn( String** *columnName* **)**

The **findColumn** method returns the column index named column or throw an **SQLException**.

➤ **boolean first( )**
**boolean last( )**
**boolean next( )**
**boolean previous( )**
**boolean relative( int** *rows* **)**

You can move to any row in the result set by calling methods **first**, **last**, **next**, **previous**, or **relative**. The **relative** method moves forward or backward by the specified number of rows. Supply an argument with a negative value to move backward toward the first row in the **ResultSet**. This method throws an **SQLException** if you ask for improper move, such as moving backward when the **ResultSet** type is **TYPE_FORWARD_ONLY**.

➤ **int getInt( String** *columnName* **)**
**int getInt( int** *columnIndex* **)**

Call the **getInt** method to get the value of the specified column of the current row. The column in the database must hold a type that maps onto a Java **int**. You can specify the name or the index of the column. The method throws an **SQLException** if a database access error occurs.

➤ **String getString( String** *columnName* **)**
**String getString( int** *columnIndex* **)**
Call the **getString** method to get the value of the specified column of the current row. The column in the database must hold a type that maps onto a Java **String**. You can specify the name or the index of the column. The method throws an **SQLException** if a database access error occurs.

➤ **void updateInt( int** *columnIndex*, **int** *value* **)**
**void updateString( int** *columnIndex*, **String** *value* **)**
The **update***Xxx* methods assign values to the specified column in the current row. They do not change the database. Call **updateRow** or **insertRow** to transfer the changes to the database. The methods throw an **SQLException** if a database access error occurs.

Column numbers start at one and reflect the order of columns in the database, so that column one is the first field in a record. If you refer to columns by name, supply the column name exactly as it appears in the database, except that the name is not case-sensitive. If you do not include column names in the statement that retrieved the **ResultSet**, you should identify the columns by number only. The safest approach is to read each column once only in a left-to-right order.

Different databases may have different properties. For example, the cursor can move only in a forward direction if the type of the **ResultSet** is **TYPE_FORWARD_ONLY**.

The following is a method from the ski club application that reads all the rows from the SKITRIP table. It creates a `SkiTrip` object for each row and copies the fields from all the columns into the `SkiTrip` object:

```
synchronized static public Vector retrieveTrips( )
        throws DBopException {
    Vector trips = new Vector();
    try {
        String[] tables = { tripTable };
        ResultSet result = getAllColumns( tables,
            "ORDER BY ID" );
        while( result.next() ) {
            SkiTrip trip = new SkiTrip();
            trip.setId( result.getInt( "ID" ) );
            trip.setWeek( result.getInt( "WEEK" ) );
            trip.setDay(
                result.getString( "DAY" )trim() );
            trip.setCapacity(
                result.getInt( "CAPACITY" ) );
            trip.setBooked( result.getInt( "BOOKED" ) );
```

**17**

```
            trips.addElement(trip);
         }
      } catch ( SQLException e ) {
         throw new DBopException (
            "Error reading Table: " + tripTable);
      }
      return trips;
   }
```

# SUMMARY

The information technology industry is adopting Java as an acceptable, and even preferred, language for server-side programming. A special kind of program, the **servlet**, has been defined to support distributed applications when the delivery mechanism is HTTP protocol and HTML documents. Servlets run on Java-enabled web servers and prepare HTML documents for delivery to a web browser. Servlet classes extend **javax.servlet.http.HttpServlet**.

Servlets and **Java Server Pages (JSPs)** generate dynamic HTML pages. You can use ordinary HTML pages, JSPs, servlets, and supporting classes in one web.

To develop servlets using the tools that you can download from Sun Microsystems, you need the **Java Server Web Development Kit (JSWDK)** in addition to the Java platform. To deploy servlets, you need a Java-enabled web server.

By default, only one instance of a servlet runs in the server's JVM. The servlet creates a new thread for every HTTP request, so servlets should be designed for multithreading.

The web server passes the HTTP request and the HTTP response to the servlet wrapped in Java objects of type **HttpServletRequest** and **HttpServletResponse**. The server can call the servlet's **service** or **doGet** methods when the client issues an HTTP **GET** method to request a page or the servlet's **doPost** method when the client issues an HTTP **POST** method by submitting an HTML form.

A **doPost** method can call the methods **HttpServletRequest.getParameterNames**, **getParameterValues**, and **getParameter** on the request object to read data submitted on an HTML form.

Http requests and responses are stateless. The best way to provide continuity from servlet to servlet as the client moves about a web is to create an **HttpSession** object to store state information. **Session** objects are stored on the server, and the server uses cookies or URL rewriting to send the session id to the client. Subsequent servlets can then get the session from the HTTP request.

Coding servlets can be clumsy because you must write HTML in print method calls. A more elegant solution that encourages good MVC separation is to use JSPs, which are written in HTML but have snippets of Java embedded in them:

In JSPs:

> Java directives are enclosed in <%@ ... %> tags.
> Java declarations are enclosed in <%! ... %> tags.
> Java expressions are enclosed in <%= ... %> tags.
> Java statements are enclosed in <% ... %> tags.

For greatest flexibility and separation of HTML from Java source, use **<jsp:useBean .. />** tags to use JavaBeans in JSPs. You can get and set properties with **<jsp:getProperty.../>** tags and **<jsp:setProperty ... />** tags. You can call methods on Java beans.

Java code in JSPs can use implicitly defined variables: **session, in, out, request**, and **response**.

Any Java program can access relational databases using the **Java DataBase Connectivity (JDBC)** package **java.sql**. Usually database access happens on the server side of a distributed application.

The JDBC classes are part of the Java platform. Before you can use them, you need a relational database management system (RDBMS) and a driver that usually comes with the RDBMS. The JDBC classes communicate with the database through the driver.

JDBC maps SQL data types onto Java types and provides API to support:

> Drivers: Usually, you load the driver with the following statement:

```
Class.forName( driver );
```

> Connections: You can connect to the database and commit or rollback transactions under program control. Call **DriverManager.getConnection** to open a connection and get a **Connection** object.

> Statements: You can build an SQL statement as a **String** and execute it by calling a method of the **Statement** interface. Call **executeQuery** for **SELECT** statements, and call **executeUpdate** for **UPDATE, INSERT**, and **DELETE** statements.

The **ResultSet** class encapsulates the rows returned from a **SELECT** statement. It is a collection and provides methods to move from row to row and to operate on the values stored in the columns.

JDBC also support precompiled SQL and stored procedures.

**17**

## QUESTIONS

1. Which of the following statements are accurate? Select all that apply.
    a. All web servers support servlets.
    b. With servlets, you can generate web pages that have dynamic content—even for web browsers that do not support Java.
    c. The Java 2 platform provides two packages that you use to build servlets: **javax.servlet** and **javax.servlet.http**.

    d. One way for a user to run a servlet is to direct the web browser to a URL of the form:

      **http://***domain***:***port***/servlets/***ServletClassName*

    e. A web page created by a servlet can contain an applet or Javascript.

2. A class that extends **HttpServlet** can override which of the following methods? Select all that apply.

    a. **doGet**

    b. **doPost**

    c. **getSession**

    d. **doPut**

    e. **service**

3. Which of the following insert the value of the Java expression represented by *expression* in an enclosing JSP? Select all that apply.

    a. `<%!` *expression* `%>`

    b. `<%=` *expression* `%>`

    c. `<%@` *expression* `%>`

    d. `<jsp:expr>`*expression*`</jsp:expr>`

    e. `<% out.println(` *expression* `); %>`

4. Which of the following variables can you use in expressions and scriptlets in a JSP without explicitly declaring them? Select all that apply.

    a. **session**

    b. **sessionId**

    c. **context**

    d. **request**

    e. **response**

5. How can you make sure only one client at a time runs a method in your servlet? Select all the following solutions that apply.

    a. Ask your server administrator to register your servlet as single threaded.

    b. Declare the servlet class to implement **SingleThreadModel**.

    c. Begin the servlet class definition with the keyword **synchronized**.

    d. Begin the method definition with the keyword word **synchronized**.

    e. Do nothing; the server lets only one client at a time run a servlet.

6. When may Java classes generated by the page-compile process be loaded into the server's JVM? Select all that apply.

    a. When the server process starts, depending on the options the server administrator sets.

    b. When a JSP is first used after the server process starts.

    c. Every time the JSP is used.

    d. The first time the JSP is used after the source was changed.

    e. Never; classes generated by JSPs are downloaded to and run on the browser's JVM.

7. Which of the following are true statements? Select all that apply.
   - a. A servlet can forward an HTTP request and response to another servlet or JSP.
   - b. A JSP can forward an HTTP request and response to another JSP or servlet.
   - c. A servlet can output HTML with print statements and embed HTML produced by a JSP.
   - d. A JSP outputs HTML and can insert HTML generated by embedded Java scriplets.
   - e. The servlet produced by the page-compile process has a **service** method, and you cannot add a **doGet** or **doPost**.

8. Which of the following are reasons for using JSPs rather than servlets to output HTML? Select all that apply.
   - a. You can better implement a MVC design pattern by using JSPs with JavaBeans than with servlets because servlets must also act as controllers.
   - b. JSPs are given access to the HTTP request and response and session object through intrinsically defined object references.
   - c. HTML authors with minimal Java programming skills can produce JSPs.
   - d. The JSP page-compile process generally gives better performance than creating a thread to run a servlet.
   - e. Servlets run in the server's JVM, but JSPs are compiled and then downloaded to the client.

9. Which one of the following is *not* true of JDBC and RDBMS drivers?
   - a. Applets access RDBMS using a type 3 or 4 driver.
   - b. If the database has an ODBC driver but no JDBC driver, you can use the JDBC-ODBC bridge or type 1 driver.
   - c. A standalone application can use any of the four types of drivers to access a local RDBMS.
   - d. Servlets can use any of the four types of drivers to access a database on a different host from the web server.
   - e. Type 2, 3, or 4 drivers are usually provided by the RDBMS software vendor.

10. Which one of the following methods of the **java.sql.Statement** class do you call to execute an SQL **DELETE** statement?
    - a. **executeQuery**
    - b. **executeDelete**
    - c. **executeModify**
    - d. **executeUpdate**
    - e. **execute**

**17**

11. What usually happens when the database cannot complete the operation that you request by calling a JDBC API? Select the best answer.
    a. The return value is **null** or **0**, depending on the method you called.
    b. A **JDBCException** is thrown.
    c. An **SQLException** is thrown.
    d. An **Exception** is thrown. The type of the **Exception** object is defined by the database driver.
    e. Your program is terminated.

12. What type do you use to call a stored procedure for a database?
    a. **java.sql.Statement**
    b. **java.sql.PreparedStatement**
    c. **java.sql.CallableStatement**
    d. **java.sql.StoredStatement**
    e. **java.sql.StoredProcedure**

# EXERCISES

## Debugging

1. This is the first part of a three-part debugging exercise. The answers to debugging Exercises 1, 2, and 3 together make a very small complete web that is a Celsius to Fahrenheit or Fahrenheit to Celsius temperature converter. Correct all errors in the following HTML page so that it calls the servlet class **questions.c17.Debug_2** when the user presses the **Do Conversion** button.

```
<HTML>
<HEAD>
<TITLE>Temperature Conversion Web Debuq_1 page</TITLE>
</HEAD>
<BODY>
<H3>Temperature Conversion Exercise </H3>
<P>This mini-web is an example of MVC.
<UL COMPACT>
<LI>The model is the class
    <b>questions.c17.TempConvert</b>.</LI>
<LI>The controller is the servlet class
    <b>questions.c17.TConvert1</b>.</LI>
<LI>The view is this page,
    <b>questions.c17.TConvert1.html</b> on input
    and<br>
    <b>questions.c17.TConvert1.jsp</b> or
    <b>questions.c17.ErrorPage.jsp</b> on output.</LI>
</UL>
<FORM ACTION=
"http://localhost:8080/servlet/questions.c17.Debug_2">
<TABLE>
<TR>
```

```
<TD>1. Enter a number of degrees</TD>
<TD><INPUT TYPE=TEXT NAME=DEGREES VALUE=0></TD>
</TR><TR>
<TD>2. Select a conversion</TD>
<TD><SELECT NAME=CONVERT >
  <OPTION VALUE=CTOF SELECTED>
     Celsius to Fahrenheit</OPTION>
  <OPTION VALUE=FTOC>Fahrenheit to Celsius</OPTION>
</SELECT></TD>
</TR><TR>
<TD>3. Press when ready:</TD>
<TD><INPUT TYPE="text" VALUE="Do Conversion"></TD>
</TR>
</TABLE>
</FORM>
</BODY>
</HTML>
```

To deploy your answer for testing, save the HTML document in the file X:\jswdk\webpages\questions\c17\Debug_1.html and direct your web browser to URL http://localhost:8080/questions/c17/Debug_1.html. At this stage, expect to receive a browser error when you press the **Do Conversion** button because the called servlet is not yet available.

2. This is the second part of the three-part debugging exercise begun in debugging Exercise 1. Correct all errors in the following servlet so that it processes the parameters from the form in **Debug_1.html**. Then, the servlet must call either **questions.c17.Debug_3.jsp** or **questions.c17.ErrorPage.jsp** to generate a response:

```
package questions.c17;
import javax.servlet.*;
import javax.servlet.http.*;
public class Debug_2 extends HttpServlet {
   public void doPost(HttpServletRequest request,
                      HttpServletResponse response)
      throws ServletException
   { try {
        String input = response.getParameter(
          "DEGREES" );
        double degrees =
          ( new Double (input ) ).doubleValue();
        String convert =
          request.getParameter( "CONVERT" );
        HttpSession session = request.getSession(
          null);
        TempConvert tc = new TempConvert();
        if ( convert.equals( "CTOF" ) ) {
          tc.setDegrees( degrees );
        } else {
          tc.setDegreesF( degrees );
```

**17**

```
      }
      session.addValue( "tc", tc );
      RequestDispatcher rd = getRequestDispatcher(
            "/questions/c17/Debug_3.jsp");
      rd.forward( request, response);
   } catch ( Exception e ) {
      e.printStackTrace( System.out );
      RequestDispatcher rd = getServletContext().
         getRequestDispatcher(
            "/questions/c17/ErrorPage.jsp" );
      rd.forward( request, response );
   }
  }
}
```

This exercise and Exercise 3 use the following JavaBean. This class contains no errors:

```
package questions.c17;
public class TempConvert {
   double degrees;
   public TempConvert( ) {
      degrees = 0D;
   }
   public void setDegrees( double degrees ) {
      this.degrees = degrees;
   }
   public void setDegreesF( double degrees ) {
      this.degrees = ( degrees -32 ) / 9 * 5;
   }
   public double getDegrees( ) {
      return Math.round( degrees * 10 ) / 10D;
   }
   public double getDegreesF( ) {
      double temp = degrees / 5 * 9 + 32;
      return Math.round( temp * 10 ) / 10D;
   }
}
```

To deploy your answer for testing, save and compile both classes in the folder X:\jswdk\classes\questions\c17\. Copy or move the compiled servlet file, **Debug_2.class**, into the folder **X:**\*jswdk*\webpages\web-inf\servlets\questions\c17\. At this stage, expect to receive a browser error because the JSPs are not yet available.

3. This is the third part of a three-part debugging exercise. Correct all errors in the following JSP so that it generates the correct HTML page when called from the servlet Debug_2:

```
<HTML>
<HEAD>
<TITLE>Temperature Conversion Debug_3 JSP</TITLE>
</HEAD>
```

```
<BODY>
<h3> Temperature Conversion Example</h3>
<jsp:useBean name="tc" class="questions\c17\TempConvert
"
     scope="session" />
<p>
<%= request.getParameterName("DEGREES" ) %>
degrees
<%= ( request.getParameter( "CONVERT" ).equals( "CTOF"
) )
    ? "Celsius" : "Fahrenehit"; %>
is approximately equal to
<%= ( request.getParameter( "CONVERT" ).equals( "CTOF"
) )
    ? tc.getDegreesF( ) + " Fahrenheit."
    : tc.getDegrees( ) + " Celsius.";
%>
</p>
<p><a href=/questions/c17/Debug_1.html>
Try another?</a></p>
</HTML>
</BODY>
```

The following JSP is called by the **Debug_2** servlet when the user does not supply valid input. This JSP contains no errors:

```
<HTML>
<HEAD>
<TITLE>Temperature Conversion ErrorPage JSP</TITLE>
</HEAD>
<BODY>
<h3>JSP error page</h3>
<p>Cannot process input, check type and values
of data you entered.</p>
<p>Go <b>Back</b> to try another conversion.</p>
</HTML>
</BODY>
```

To deploy your answer for testing, save both JPSs, Debug_3.jsp and ErrorPage.jsp in the folder *X:\jswdk*\webpages\questions\c17\. The web should now be complete.

4. The version of DB2 that comes with this book includes a sample database called SAMPLE. If have not yet built the sample database, do so now. Log in to Windows as USERID so the database SAMPLE is owned by USERID. Then select:

**Start > ProgramsDB2 for Windows > First Steps >**

**Create the Sample database.**

For more information on creating the sample database, refer to the **Readme.html** file on the CD-ROM. The SAMPLE database contains several tables, including the EMPLOYEE table.

**17**

Correct the following program so that it uses JDBC and the DB2 type 2 driver to list the first name and last name of all the designers working in the company. Literal names of tables, columns, and data values quoted in this problem are correct:

```
package questions.c17;
import java.sql.*;
import java.util.*;
public class Debug_4 {
    public static void main( String [] args ) {
        try {
        Connection con = DriverManager.getConnection(
            "jdbc:DB2:SAMPLE" );
        String sql = "SELECT FIRSTNME,LASTNAME FROM "
        +"USERID.EMPLOYEE WHERE JOB = DESIGNER";
        Statement s = con.createStatement();
        ResultSet rs = s.executeQuery( sql );
        System.out.println( " The designers are: " );
        do {
            String output = rs.getString( 0 ).trim();
            output += ", " + rs.getString( "LAST-
NAME" );
            System.out.println( output );
        } while ( rs.next() )
        rs.close();
        s.close();
        con.close();
    } catch( Exception e ) {
        System.out.println( e.getMessage() );
        e.printStackTrace();
    } finally {
        System.out.println(
            "There should be no exceptions." );
    }
  }
}
```

You can test and run this program from the command line or using the VisualAge for Java IDE.

## Complete the Solution

1. Extract the file **questions\c17\Complete_1.java** from the **question.jar** file on the CD-ROM that accompanies this book. Complete the definition of the **Complete_1** servlet class by inserting code as indicated by comments. The **doGet** method outputs a change-password form. For test purposes, an initial password is set to "password". The **doPost** method must check the three input fields. Did the user enter in the correct old password, supply a new password that contains five to eight characters, and type the new password identically twice? The **doPost** method then either changes the password and outputs a confirmation page or outputs a page giving the reason for not changing the password.

To deploy your answer for testing, copy or move the compiled files, **Complete_1.class** and **PasswordException.class**, into the folder *X:\jswdk* \webpages\web-inf\servlets\questions\c17\. Direct your browser to URL: http://localhost:8080/servlet/questions.c17.Complete_1.

2. This exercise uses the same sample DB2 database as debugging Exercise 4. If have not yet built the sample database, do so now. Log in to Windows as USERID so the database SAMPLE is owned by USERID. Then select:

**Start > DB2 for Windows > First Steps > Create the Sample database.**

The SAMPLE database contains several tables, including EMPLOYEE and DEPARTMENT.

Extract the file **questions\c17\Complete_2.java** from the **question.jar** file on the CD-ROM that accompanies this book. Complete the definition of the **Complete_2** class by inserting code as indicated by comments. This class is an application that outputs a line for each department showing the department's identifier, its name, and its manager's first and last names. Include only the departments that have a manager. The first two values are in fields DEPT-NO and DEPTNAME of the DEPARTMENT table. The MBRNO field identifies the employee who manages the department and matches the field EMPNO in the EMPLOYEE table. Get the manager's name from the LASTNAME and FIRSTNME fields of the EMPLOYEE table.

You can test and run this program from the command line or using the VisualAge for Java IDE.

3. Extract the file **questions\c17\Complete_3.jsp** from the **question.jar** file on the CD-ROM that accompanies this book. Complete the definition of the **Complete_3** JSP by inserting JSP tags as indicated by comments. Use the **questions.c17.Complete_2** class as a JavaBean to complete the JSP. This JSP outputs the same information as the **main** method of the **Complete_2** class, but the delivery mechanism is an HTML page and the data is formatted into a table.

To deploy your answer for testing, copy or move the compiled class from Exercise 2, **Complete_2.class**, into the folder *X:\jswdk*\classes\questions\c17\. Put the JSP file Complete_3.jsp into the folder *X:\jswdk*\webpages\questions\c17. Direct your browser to URL: http://localhost:8080/questions/c17/Complete_3.jsp.

4. Extract the file **questions\c17\Complete_4.java** from the **question.jar** file on the CD-ROM that accompanies this book. Complete the definition of the **Complete_4** servlet class by inserting code as indicated by comments. This servlet prints the names and values of all cookies supplied in the HTTP request. Then, generates a random number in the range 0 to 25 and returns the value of the number to the client as a cookie. If the number is 0 the cookie is

**17**

named "A". If the number is 1, the cookie is named "B," and so on. The page output by the servlet includes a link to itself so you can return to the same servlet to see the value of the cookie just added. Note that if the same random number is generated twice, the existing cookie with the same name is replaced. The cookies accumulate over a browser session but are not persistent.

To deploy your answer for testing, copy or move the compiled file, **Complete_4.class** into the folder *X:\swdk*\webpages\web-inf\servlets\questions\c17\. Direct your browser to URL: http://localhost:8080/servlet/questions.c17.Complete_4.

---

# DISCOVERY

1. Write a command-line application that the organizers of the SKICLUB database might use. Prompt the user for a user id and password with which to connect to the database. Then prompt them to enter a trip id in the range 1 to 24. Print a list of the members booked on that trip, in alphabetic order by last name. State each trip member's skiing ability.

2. Add a new feature to the Near Hills Ski Club web to let members withdraw from the club. Add a new option **Withdraw from the club** to the list on the bottom of the member home page shown in Figure 17-10. You will have to write a servlet to handle this option. The servlet must do the following:

   ➤ Update the BOOKINGS table to delete any bookings made by the member.

   ➤ Update the SKITRIPS table to correct the number booked on any trip the member had booked.

   ➤ Delete the member's record from the MEMBERS table.

   ➤ Invalidate the member's session.

   ➤ Respond with an HTML page that says goodbye to the former member.

   Add any methods you need to copies of existing classes such as `ski-club.ClubMember` and `skiclub.SkiClubDB` in subfolders of *X:\swdk*. Test thoroughly. What happens when the former member presses the browser's **Back** button after withdrawing from the club?

3. Write a simple chat room servlet. One servlet class can have a **doGet** and **doPost** method. The **doGet** method displays all messages entered by previous clients, followed by a form for the user to enter, sign, and submit a new message. The **doPost** method adds the new message and client's signature to the list of messages and then redirects the server to the **doGet** method of this servlet. When you test, use some imagination and pretend other clients are adding messages and reading yours. There is no need to make the messages persistent. The chat room can start with an empty list of messages every time the servlet is loaded into the server.

# PROGRAMMER AND DEVELOPER CERTIFICATION

After completing this book, you may be ready to join the ranks of professionals pursuing rewarding and challenging careers using Java and related technologies. Many studies show that Java and Internet-related technologies are among the fastest-growing sectors of an ever-expanding industry. Moreover, the demand for skilled and qualified application developers at all levels, from entry-level programmers to software architects, exceeds the supply.

Finding the right position, however, is still a challenge, and filling positions with capable developers is a concern for employers. Companies need assurance that candidates have the required expertise and are proven performers. Furthermore, they need proof that candidates have the required skills and can keep up with rapidly evolving technology. Candidates need some way to demonstrate their level of competence and professionalism. The industry as a whole benefits from standards for knowledge and skills assessment.

Sun, IBM, and other companies offer certification certificates in Java and related technologies. This book is designed to prepare you for the exam that at the time of this writing is accepted throughout the industry as the competency test for Java programming. In 1999, a number of leading companies started to collaborate in a certification initiative. Their goals encourage the growth of the pool of professionals with proven competency levels to meet future demands. New certification exams based on the existing exams and objectives defined by the collaborating companies may become available in the near future. The existing certifications will be recognized as long as the technologies on which they are based remains current.

# CERTIFICATION PROGRAMS AS OF SUMMER 1999

Two companies have taken the lead in creating certification programs for Java technologies: Sun Microsystems and IBM. The Sun exams are the de facto standards used by the industry. IBM certification is recognized within IBM and by companies that use IBM technology. The existing certification programs also serve as a model for the new Java certification initiative.

## Sun Certification Programs

Sun Microsystems offers a suite of certification exams in Java Programming. There are exams for the different versions of the Java platform, and this book is based on the exam you take to become a **Sun Certified Programmer for the Java 2 Platform**.

The first page of each chapter in this book lists chapter objectives, or skills taught. Objectives are divided into two categories, distinguished by the symbols ☕ and ➤. The former are identified by Sun as requirements for the certified programmer exam. There are questions relating to these topics on the exam. The latter are covered in the chapter because they are important to all Java programmers; they are not on the exam for a variety of reasons. For example, the exam has no questions about applets because programming an applet requires no different skills than programming an application does, except perhaps HTML tagging and some knowledge of web browsers. The goal of this book is to cover topics that all professional programmers should be familiar with, at least to the level of detail presented in this book. Therefore, much of the material later chapters in later chapters of this book fall into this category.

The Java 2 programmer exam is multiple choice or short answer. It is identified by the exam number 310-025. There are 59 questions to be answered in 120 minutes, and the pass mark is 71% correct. You must take the test online at a testing center, and there are centers in most large or medium-sized North American cities. For details on how to take the take the exam, see the URL:

http://suned.sun.com/use/cert_progs.html.

An excellent way to prepare for the exam is to try the quiz questions and work through the exercises at the end of each chapter. The chapters you should concentrate on for the exam are 2, 3, 4, 5, 6, 8, 9, 10, 11, and 13. The quiz questions are similar in style and difficulty to what you will encounter on the exam. You also can try the sample questions posted on the Sun certification web site. You will see that the exam focuses more detailed knowledge of syntax and sound understanding of concepts, such as encapsulation, than on the broad scope of the API. The exam has a reputation for being tricky, so learn the rules of Java grammar well.

Generally, the programmer exam concentrates on the Java language and some of the key core classes. Some topics, such as Remote Method Invocation (RMI) and Java Database Connectivity (JDBC), are not tested by this exam but are required at higher levels of certification. Sun currently offers a number of higher-level exams, including:

➤ **Sun Certified Developer for the Java 2 Platform:** The testing process consists of a programming assignment and an essay exam. You do the programming assignment on your own time, remotely, after downloading instructions. When you upload the solution, you become eligible to complete this level of certification by passing the written exam.

➤ **Sun Certified Architect for Java Technologies:** The objectives test your ability to apply Java technologies in a way that maximizes the business advantages of using Java. For example, questions test whether you can evaluate different distributed object architectures, your understanding of security and performance issues, and whether you can deploy Java solutions in production environments.

Sun continues to offer certification exams based on version 1.1 and 1.0 of the Java platform. The Java 2 exams became available in 1999.

## IBM Certification Programs

IBM offers a certification program that builds on the Sun Java Programmer certification and knowledge of the VisualAge for Java development environment. IBM is a major player in the new certification initiative. As of this writing, the exams in the IBM VisualAge for Java certification track are the following:

➤ **IBM Certified Developer Associate (CDA):** For CDA certification, you must be a Sun Certified Java Programmer and pass a multiple-choice exam that tests your skill using the VisualAge for Java tool.

➤ **IBM Certified Solution Developer (CSD):** For CSD certification, you must have CDA and pass a multiple-choice exam on object-oriented design and analysis (OOAD) using the **Unified Modeling Language (UML)**. This exam is not based on any particular programming language and is also used by IBM certification tracks for C++ and Smalltalk.

➤ **IBM Certified Advanced Technical Expert (CATE):** For CATE certification, you must have CSD and successfully complete a week-long practicum in which you must apply your skills in Java programming, using VisualAge for Java tools, and OOAD to create a realistic business application.

For more details on the IBM certification tracks, see this URL:

http://www.software.ibm.com/ad/certify

# CERTIFICATION INITIATIVE

The formation of the certification initiative is a significant step toward creating consistency in skill assessment across the industry. The collaborating companies are leaders in Java technology:

➤ **Sun Microsystems**, the company that created Java technology, is the recognized authority on the Java programming language.

➤ **IBM** is the world's largest information technology company. It offers the widest range of applications, middleware, and operating systems for all types of computing platforms.

➤ **Novell** is the world's leading provider of directory-enabled networking software. Novell software gives companies complete control over their private networks and access to the Internet.

➤ **Oracle**, the world's leading supplier for information management, offers strong database, application, and application-development products.

➤ The **Sun-Netscape Alliance** was formed by America Online and Sun Microsystems to provide the industry's most scalable, integrated infrastructure for comprehensive enterprise and e-commerce solutions.

➤ **Sylvan Prometric** is the world's leading provider of educational services to families, schools, and industry. The certification exams are administered through Sylvan's network of authorized test centers.

The initiative will provide both common exams that will be cross-recognized by participating companies and the vendor-specific exams. Therefore, the certification initiative acknowledges the reality that tools skills are essential for productivity but are largely transferable from one tool to another. The goal of the initiative is to promote standards for validating the skills of Java professionals, from programmers using the core language to designers of enterprise applications.

Five exams spanning three levels of certification have been identified:

1. **Level I   Exam I: Java Programming Language**
   Certification at this level requires one exam. Table A-1 lists the exam objectives and the chapters in this book that cover them. As you see, these objectives map very closely onto the Sun Certified Programmer for the Java 2 Platform exam.

2. **Level II  Exam I: Application Development for the Java Platform**
   This is a tool-based exam that tests your ability to apply the features of the tool to developing a solution. Topics such as database access, applets, and source-code version control are covered. If you follow the IBM track, this exam maps closely onto IBM CDA certification. This book covers some of the Java programming topics tested at level II but not level I. However, this

book does not give adequate detail on using any proprietary IDE to prepare you for the exam.

3. **Level II  Exam II: Object Oriented Analysis and Design with UML**
This exam tests your ability to perform OOAD and knowledge of UML. Questions test your understanding of abstraction, encapsulation, inheritance, and polymorphism, iterative and incremental development, and design models. To pass, you must be able to design a system of objects for a Java-based application. If you follow the IBM track, this exam maps closely onto IBM CSD certification. This book introduces many object-oriented concepts but does not discuss or use UML.

4. **Level III Exam I: Enterprise Connectivity with Java Technology**
This exam covers topics such as security, object serialization, database connectivity using JDBC, creating distributed objects with RMI and Internet Inter-Orb Protocol (IIOP), interoperability with the Common Object Request Broker Architecture (CORBA) using Java Interface Definition Language (Java IDL), and creating Enterprise Java Beans (EJB). The book introduces some of these topics but does not attempt to prepare you for this exam.

5. **Level III Exam II: Enterprise Development with an Application Server**
This exam reflects the industry trend toward more Java implementations at the server level in distributed and heterogeneous enterprise architectures. The topics covered relate to security, servlets, transactional support for databases, EJB, performance issues such as load balancing, and accessing folders and files using Lightweight Directory Access Protocol (LDAP) or Java Naming and Directory Interface (JNDI). These are all advanced topics, but Chapters 17 and 18 of this book give you insight into some of the issues involved.

The objectives listed in Table A-1 are the objectives published by the certification innovative in July 1999. A more detailed breakdown is not yet available. As you can see, there are some broad topics that span several chapters in this book. Mostly, these objectives coincide with the objectives for the existing **Sun Certified Programmer for the Java 2 Platform** exam. However, the following are additions:

➤ Using the JFC to build visual applications.

➤ Using the internationalization APIs.

➤ Distributing programs using the **jar** command.

The new objectives are covered in this book or its supplemental materials but not marked with ☕ symbols in the list of objectives at the start of the relevant chapters.

**Table A-1** Objectives of the Certification Initiative Level 1 exam

| Java Programming Exam Objectives for Level 1 Certification | Covered in Chapter |
|---|---|
| Demonstrate knowledge of Java programming language fundamentals by writing correctly structured Java classes for applets and applications and appropriately using all data types. | 3, 4, 14 |
| Determine the result of applying every combination of operators and assignments to any combination of types. | 2 |
| Declare variables and classes with appropriate use of access control, initialization, and scope. | 2, 4, 5, 9 |
| Make correct use of all flow control constructs, including exception handling. | 2, 6 |
| Make correct use of overloading, overriding, and inheritance. | 4, 5 |
| Identify guaranteed garbage collection and finalization behavior. | 3, 4 |
| Make correct use of Threads, Runnable, wait(), notify(), synchronized. | 11 |
| Use the facility of java.lang, java.awt, java.awt.event, and java.io packages. | 2, 3, 8, 12, 13 |
| Recognize the benefits of encapsulation in the Object Oriented paradigm, and be able to implement tightly encapsulated classes in the Java programming language. | 4, 5 |
| Use the Java Foundation Classes (JFC) software to build visual applications. | 12, 13 |
| Write applications that are independent of language or location, using the internationalization APIs. | *see CD-ROM* |
| Use the jar command to package together the components of a Java technology-based application. | 1 |

# Appendix B

## Native Methods

This appendix is a high-level introduction to the **Java Native Interface (JNI)**. It explains how classes can use code that executes outside the Java Virtual Machine (JVM). The feature of the Java programming language that supports the JNI is native methods. You use native methods to access code that is written using other programming languages.

# APPENDIX C

## Notes for C++ Programmers

The Java programming language has some striking similarities with C++. Indeed the developers of Java deliberately used many C++ syntactic constructs when designing their new language. If you are a C++ programmer, you will find the similarity in grammar between the two languages to be your advantage. However, the Java language is not just a simplified version of C++. There are some additional facts that you need to know. This appendix will help you grasp those facts and point out some subtle differences.

# APPENDIX D

## Web Resources for the Java Platform

The World Wide Web offers abundant resources to help you get the most out of the Java platform. This appendix lists the URLs for a few of the sites that offer these useful resources. As you sit back with your cup of java and cruise these sites, remember that web sites are always subject to change. You may find that some of these URLs are no longer available or that they direct you to more current pages.

# APPENDIX E

## Mini Quiz Answers

What is the fun of mini quizzes if you can't check the answers? In this appendix, you will find not only answers to the mini quizzes, but discussions of why each correct answer is well, correct. We've found with our students that these mini quizzes make great study guides for tests, exams, and high-stress meetings. So, take a look at the answers and see how well you measure up on the "java-meter" of knowledge.

# INDEX

# U

## Part 1 – General Terms

PLEASE READ THIS AGREEMENT CAREFULLY BEFORE USING THE PROGRAM. IBM WILL LICENSE THE PRO-GRAM TO YOU ONLY IF YOU FIRST ACCEPT THE TERMS OF THIS AGREEMENT. BY USING THE PROGRAM YOU AGREE TO THESE TERMS. IF YOU DO NOT AGREE TO THE TERMS OF THIS AGREEMENT, PROMPTLY RETURN THE UNUSED PROGRAM TO IBM.

The Program is owned by International Business Machines Corporation or one of its subsidiaries (IBM) or an IBM supplier, and is copy-righted and licensed, not sold.

The term "Program" means the original program and all whole or partial copies of it. A Program consists of machine-readable instruc-tions, its components, data, audio-visual content (such as images, text, recordings, or pictures), and related licensed materials.

**This Agreement includes Part 1 – General Terms and Part 2 – Country-unique Terms and is the complete agreement regard-ing the use of this Program, and replaces any prior oral or written communications between you and IBM. The terms of Part 2 may replace or modify those of Part 1.**

## 1. License

### Use of the Program

IBM grants you a nonexclusive, nontransferable license to use the Program.

You may 1) use the Program only for internal evaluation, testing or demonstration purposes, on a trial or "try-and-buy" basis and 2) make and install a reasonable number of copies of the Program in support of such use, unless IBM identifies a specific number of copies in the doc-umentation accompanying the Program. The terms of this license apply to each copy you make. You will reproduce the copyright notice and any other legends of ownership on each copy, or partial copy, of the Program.

You will 1) maintain a record of all copies of the Program and 2) ensure that anyone who uses the Program does so only for your authorized use and in compliance with the terms of this Agreement.

You may not 1) use, copy, modify or distribute the Program except as provided in this Agreement; 2) reverse assemble, reverse compile, or oth-erwise translate the Program except as specifically permitted by law without the possibility of contractual waiver; or 3) sublicense, rent, or lease the Program.

This license begins with your first use of the Program and ends on the termination of this license in accordance with the terms of this Agreement. You will destroy the Program and all copies made of it within ten days of when this license ends.

## 2. No Warranty

SUBJECT TO ANY STATUTORY WARRANTIES WHICH CANNOT BE EXCLUDED, IBM MAKES NO WARRANTIES OR CONDITIONS EITHER EXPRESS OR IMPLIED, INCLUDING WITHOUT LIMITATION, THE WARRANTY OF NON-INFRINGEMENT AND THE IMPLIED WARRANTIES OF MERCHANTABILITY AND FITNESS FOR A PARTICULAR PUR-POSE, REGARDING THE PROGRAM OR TECHNICAL SUPPORT, IF ANY. IBM MAKES NO WARRANTY REGARDING THE CAPABILITY OF THE PROGRAM TO CORRECTLY PROCESS, PROVIDE AND/OR RECEIVE DATE DATA WITHIN AND BETWEEN THE 20TH AND 21ST CENTURIES.

This exclusion also applies to any of IBM's subcontractors, suppliers or program developers (collectively called "Suppliers").

Manufacturers, suppliers, or publishers of non-IBM Programs may provide their own warranties.

## 3. Limitation of Liability

NEITHER IBM NOR ITS SUPPLIERS ARE LIABLE FOR ANY DIRECT OR INDIRECT DAMAGES, INCLUDING WITHOUT LIMITATION, LOST PROFITS, LOST SAVINGS, OR ANY INCIDENTAL, SPECIAL, OR OTHER ECONOMIC CONSEQUEN-TIAL DAMAGES, EVEN IF IBM IS INFORMED OF THEIR POSSIBILITY. SOME JURISDICTIONS DO NOT ALLOW THE EXCLUSION OR LIMITATION OF INCIDENTAL OR CONSEQUENTIAL DAMAGES, SO THE ABOVE EXCLUSION OR LIMITATION MAY NOT APPLY TO YOU.

## 4. General

Nothing in this Agreement affects any statutory rights of consumers that cannot be waived or limited by contract.

IBM may terminate your license if you fail to comply with the terms of this Agreement. If IBM does so, you must immediately destroy the Program and all copies you made of it.

You may not export the Program.

Neither you nor IBM will bring a legal action under this Agreement more than two years after the cause of action arose unless otherwise provided by local law without the possibility of contractual waiver or limitation.

Neither you nor IBM is responsible for failure to fulfill any obligations due to causes beyond its control.

There is no additional charge for use of the Program for the duration of this license.

IBM does not provide program services or technical support, unless IBM specifies otherwise.

The laws of the country in which you acquire the Program govern this Agreement, except 1) in Australia, the laws of the State or Territory in which the transaction is performed govern this Agreement; 2) in Albania, Armenia, Belarus, Bosnia/Herzegovina, Bulgaria, Croatia, Czech Republic, Georgia, Hungary, Kazakhstan, Kirghizia, Former Yugoslav Republic of Macedonia (FYROM), Moldova, Poland, Romania, Russia, Slovak Republic, Slovenia, Ukraine, and Federal Republic of Yugoslavia, the laws of Austria govern this Agreement; 3) in the United Kingdom, all disputes relating to this Agreement will be governed by English Law and will be submitted to the exclusive jurisdiction of the English courts; 4) in Canada, the laws in the Province of Ontario govern this Agreement; and 5) in the United States and Puerto Rico, and People's Republic of China, the laws of the State of New York govern this Agreement.

# Part 2 – Country-unique Terms

## AUSTRALIA:

No Warranty (Section 2): The following paragraph is added to this Section: Although IBM specifies that there are no warranties, you may have certain rights under the Trade Practices Act 1974 or other legislation and are only limited to the extent permitted by the applicable legislation.

Limitation of Liability (Section 3): The following paragraph is added to this Section: Where IBM is in breach of a condition or warranty implied by the Trade Practices Act 1974, IBM's liability is limited to the repair or replacement of the goods, or the supply of equivalent goods. Where that condition or warranty relates to right to sell, quiet possession or clear title, or the goods are of a kind ordinarily acquired for personal, domestic or household use or consumption, then none of the limitations in this paragraph apply.

## GERMANY:

No Warranty (Section 2): The following paragraphs are added to this Section: The minimum warranty period for Programs is six months.

In case a Program is delivered without Specifications, we will only warrant that the Program information correctly describes the Program and that the Program can be used according to the Program information. You have to check the usability according to the Program information within the "money-back guaranty" period. Limitation of Liability (Section 3): The following paragraph is added to this Section: The limitations and exclusions specified in the Agreement will not apply to damages caused by IBM with fraud or gross negligence, and for express warranty.

## INDIA:

General (Section 4): The following replaces the fourth paragraph of this Section: If no suit or other legal action is brought, within two years after the cause of action arose, in respect of any claim that either party may have against the other, the rights of the concerned party in respect of such claim will be forfeited and the other party will stand released from its obligations in respect of such claim.

## IRELAND:

No Warranty (Section 2): The following paragraph is added to this Section: Except as expressly provided in these terms and conditions, all statutory conditions, including all warranties implied, but without prejudice to the generality of the foregoing, all warranties implied by the Sale of Goods Act 1893 or the Sale of Goods and Supply of Services Act 1980 are hereby excluded.

## ITALY:

Limitation of Liability (Section 3): This Section is replaced by the following: Unless otherwise provided by mandatory law, IBM is not liable for any damages which might arise.

## NEW ZEALAND:

No Warranty (Section 2): The following paragraph is added to this Section: Although IBM specifies that there are no warranties, you may have certain rights under the Consumer Guarantees Act 1993 or other legislation which cannot be excluded or limited. The Consumer Guarantees Act 1993 will not apply in respect of any goods or services which IBM provides, if you require the goods and services for the purposes of a business as defined in that Act. Limitation of Liability (Section 3): The following paragraph is added to this Section: Where Programs are not acquired for the purposes of a business as defined in the Consumer Guarantees Act 1993, the limitations in this Section are subject to the limitations in that Act.

## UNITED KINGDOM:

Limitation of Liability (Section 3): The following paragraph is added to this Section at the end of the first paragraph: The limitation of liability will not apply to any breach of IBM's obligations implied by Section 12 of the Sales of Goods Act 1979 or Section 2 of the Supply of Goods and Services Act 1982.